MOON

W9-BYH-594

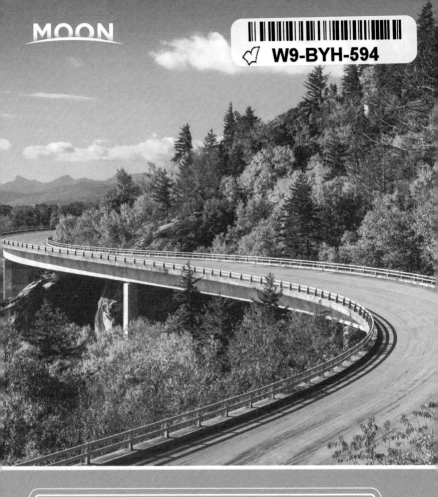

BLUE RIDGE
PARKWAY
Road Trip

JASON FRYE

CONTENTS

DISCOVER
the Blue Ridge Parkway

I n the friendly little mountain town of Floyd, Friday nights mean three generations of locals including cloggers, mountain dancers, farmers, artists, and musicians blowing off workweek steam by playing, listening to, or dancing along with live bluegrass while imbibing a little 'shine in the mountain tradition.

Floyd was my first stop on the Blue Ridge Parkway, the 469-mile ridge-riding ribbon that runs from Shenandoah National Park in Virginia to Great Smoky Mountains National Park. But it certainly wasn't my last. Every season here is gorgeous, from scarlet-leaf-filled fall to summer, when the heady scent of honeysuckle coaxes you out of your car. In winter, snow dusts the highest passes and the mountains grow a charming beard of icicles; spring is when wildflowers bloom and fawns peer out of the brush.

For these reasons, and at least 469 others—figure there's at least one for every mile marker—the Blue Ridge Parkway is known as "America's favorite scenic drive." But it's more than just a drive. It's fields and balds filled to capacity with fireflies blinking in the summer twilight, mountains aflame with fall color as far as the eye can see, more wildflowers and spring peepers croaking than you could count in a lifetime, and the stillness of snow falling from a white winter sky to cover the blacktop highway. It's cultured cities like Asheville and Roanoke, hiking trails to waterfalls, and sights that celebrate our national heritage, from Oconaluftee Indian Village to the National D-Day Memorial in small-town Bedford. It's quiet moments on a mountainside overlook, gazing out over Virginia's vast plains and the folded hills of North Carolina and realizing that the road that led you here will take you home…but you'll be different for having driven its miles and drunk in its beauty.

PLANNING YOUR TRIP

Where to Go

The Shenandoah Valley

Shenandoah National Park and **Skyline Drive** form the northern cap to this monumental mountaintop ride. Here, wide valleys and rivers give the landscape an interesting character. Hike a leg of the storied **Appalachian Trail** or discover the interesting character of the region underground at **Luray Caverns.** Nearby, the **monuments, museums,** and vibrant culture of **Washington DC** beckon.

Virginia Blue Ridge

This stretch of the Parkway is the **easiest to drive.** As the Blue Ridge Mountains give way to planes, the views are long, with many a rolling hill, pasture, and bucolic farmhouse or church in the distance. **Small towns** like Floyd and Bedford offer big attractions like Floyd's unforgettable **Friday Night Jamboree.** Orchards and **wineries** dot the hills around **Roanoke.**

North Carolina High Country

As you enter North Carolina, you begin to climb, and the mountains take center stage. The peak of **Grandfather Mountain** looms high over the Blue Ridge Parkway, and places like **Blowing Rock,** a stunning outcrop where snows falls upside down, add to the magic of the region. The spectacular **Linn Cove Viaduct,** which seems to float off the mountainside, is part of the commute, and countless **waterfalls** are just a short hike away.

Asheville and the Southern Blue Ridge

Between Asheville and Cherokee is the **highest and most crooked part of the drive.** Here, the mountains are tall and steep, making for **dramatic views** from hikes and overlooks. Many small towns remained relatively isolated until the early 20th century and are rich with

© AVALON TRAVEL

history and culture. Asheville is home to the lauded **Biltmore Estate** and some of the best **restaurants** in the South. **Cherokee,** where the Blue Ridge Parkway ends, is the ancestral home of the Eastern Band of the Cherokee Nation.

Great Smoky Mountains

Great Smoky Mountains National Park is the **most visited national park** in the country. The scenery and **wildlife**— rounded peaks and jagged mountaintops, crystal-clear trout streams and white-water rivers, elk and bear, morning mist and evening firefly shows— explains why. The tourist towns of **Gatlinburg** and **Pigeon Forge** welcome millions of visitors who flock to **Dollywood** and the park. **Knoxville,** one of the nation's top outdoor towns, is fun in any season.

When to Go

The obvious season to visit the Blue Ridge Parkway is **autumn.** The leaves blaze with color from the end of September through October. The timing for peak color varies by region, but you're just about guaranteed a great color show anywhere October 5-20. Expect mild weather, with warm days and chilly evenings (you'll be fine in long sleeves and a vest or jacket).

Winter along the Parkway is tricky as the high elevations and exposed ridgelines are especially susceptible to snow and ice. Only a few sections of the Parkway (the ones that also double as public roadways) are plowed and salted during winter, so long stretches and point-to-point segments are closed from November through spring. The Blue Ridge Parkway maintains a live link of road closures available at www.nps.gov/maps/blri/road-closures/.

Spring is lovely, though trails can be muddy. There's a great payoff to spring rains, though: widlflowers and waterfalls. It's also the time you may see young animals trailing their mothers across the road or along the wood's edge.

Summer draws big numbers of visitors taking advantage of warm weather and vacation days. The elevation keeps the Parkway cooler than the flatlands, and the overlooks are rich with the deep green of summer leaves.

Before You Go

If you're visiting from outside driving distance, you'll likely fly into one of the **airports** in Washington DC, Baltimore, or Knoxville. **Pack** your hiking boots for the miles of trails along the drive. Swimsuits are recommended for enjoying the waterfalls and mountain streams, and rain gear and binoculars are a good idea. A tripod and zoom lens are handy for landscape or wildlife photography. **Reservations** are recommended at **campgrounds** in both national parks and along the Blue Ridge Parkway, especially during the peak seasons of summer and fall. Reservations for **hotels and B&Bs** along the route are recommended during peak times as well.

The Blue Ridge Parkway and Great Smoky Mountains National Park are free to visit and use. An **entrance fee** ($25 per vehicle, $20 per motorcycle, $12 pedestrians and cyclists; admission good for one week) is required for Shenandoah National Park, payable at any of the four entrances to the park along Skyline Drive.

Weather can be a factor when visiting any spot along this route. In any season you may face thick fog and sudden storms, though most rain is of the springtime or summer thunderstorm variety. Hail is not unheard of, especially at higher elevations, which are also vulnerable to snow and ice during late fall, winter, and early spring. Sections of the Blue Ridge Parkway and Skyline Drive are apt to be **closed or restricted** due to weather in any season. Check road conditions at www.nps.gov/maps/blri/

clockwise from top left: banjo mosaic outside the City Market building in Roanoke; Chimney Rock; Arlington National Cemetery road-closures/. In North Carolina, Ray's Weather (www.raysweather.com) offers highly-localized weather reporting and forecasting, often including color reports in the autumn.

Note that **cell phone reception** can be very spotty, especially as the route ventures away from more populated areas.

Driving Tips

Both the Blue Ridge Parkway and Skyline Drive are organized by **mileposts.** Markers, signs, and pillars note each mile, and waypoints include directions like "Blue Ridge Parkway Milepost 52.6." This system makes it easy to anticipate where the next sight, visitor center, or hike may be. On Skyline Drive, you'll travel from mile 0 in Front Royal, Va., to mile 105.5 at Rockfish Gap, near Waynesboro, Va. At Rockfish Gap, the Blue Ridge Parkway begins with mile 0, then carries on down the mountain chain to Cherokee, N.C., and mile 469.

You can drive your own car the 740-mile length of the Skyline Drive-Blue Ridge Parkway-Great Smoky Mountains National Park route, or you can pick up a **rental car** at or near the airport or train station where you begin your journey. Do check that you will have a place to turn in the car at the other end if you plan on taking a one-way trip, and note that some companies levy hefty fees for this service.

Gasoline is available at only one place along Skyline Drive and nowhere on the Blue Ridge Parkway. You'll need to fuel up at the towns, cities, and waysides off the parkway. Fuel availability is noted at the beginning of relevant chapters in this guidebook, but as a rule, you'll find a gas station near any town or major route that crosses the Parkway.

The **speed limit** on the Parkway is 45 mph, though it slows to 35 or even 25 in certain areas. Along Skyline Drive, the speed limit is 35 mph. You'll encounter a great deal of wildlife along the drive. At any faster than the speed limit, you pose a threat to animals and yourself, as you may not have adequate time to stop if you encounter an animal. The National Park Service can pull you over and issue tickets, so keep your speed appropriate to the traffic and weather. Traffic slows considerably during peak seasons. During autumn, you may never reach the speed limit.

Many locals choose to travel a segment of the Parkway then **return home via Interstates** to reduce travel time. If you fly into one of the travel hubs in this guidebook, you'll likely travel one way, north or south, along the route and depart from an airport on the other end. Otherwise, you may do like the locals, traveling the Parkway one direction and a faster route on the return trip.

HIT THE ROAD

The 14-Day Blue Ridge Parkway Road Trip

Tracing the ridges and hillsides of the Blue Ridge Mountains, the Blue Ridge Parkway hosts millions of visitors every year, lured by the hum of tires on the road and the whisper of mountain winds through the trees. In just two weeks, you can drive the 716 miles from Washington DC to Knoxville, via one of the greatest scenic roads in the nation. You can also easily reverse this route by beginning in Knoxville and ending in DC.

Day 1
ARRIVE IN WASHINGTON DC

Settle in to your hotel, then spend the rest of the day at museums of your choice. The museums of the Smithsonian Institution, including the **National Air and Space Museum, National Portrait Gallery,** and **National Museum of Natural History** are fascinating, as are the **International Spy Museum** and **Phillips Collection.** Try dinner at **We the Pizza** or **Hill Country Barbecue** before taking in a concert at **9:30 Club** or the **Black Cat** or taking a **nighttime bicycle tour** of the Mall.

Day 2
EXPLORE WASHINGTON DC

Pay your respects at the **United States Holocaust Memorial Museum,** then cross the river to **Mount Vernon,** George Washington's home, or **Arlington National Cemetery,** or both. For dinner, head to **The Oceanaire Seafood Room,** which will transform the way you look at fish.

Day 3
WASHINGTON DC TO SHENANDOAH NATIONAL PARK
70 miles; 1.5 hours

Head to the **National Mall,** a grand grassy avenue lined with the museums of the Smithsonian Institution, the most iconic monuments—**Washington Monument, Lincoln Memorial, Vietnam Veterans Memorial**—and, of course, views of the **United States Capitol** and **White House.** Have lunch at **Ben's Chili Bowl,** a DC institution, or one of the many ethnic restaurants like **Rasika,** or hit the road and dine in **Front Royal,** at the entrance to **Skyline Drive** and **Shenandoah National Park.** Along Skyline, **75 overlooks** in the park give a sense of the vast wilderness that once blanketed the countryside. Hike to **Dark Hollow Falls,** and spend the night inside the park at **Skyland** or **Big Meadows Lodge.**

Day 4
SHENANDOAH NATIONAL PARK TO WAYNESBORO AND CHARLOTTESVILLE
160 miles; 4.5 hours

Head outside the park to the spectacular **Luray Caverns,** one of the best cave systems in the nation. When you're finished, drive down to **Waynesboro,** near the end of Skyline Drive and the start of the Blue Ridge Parkway, and check in at **Iris Inn.** Then take I-64 east for 24 miles to **Charlottesville.** Tour **Monticello,** Thomas Jefferson's home, only a few miles from downtown, then walk the grounds of the **University of Virginia,** which was founded by Jefferson and bears his architectural mark. If you have time, a **wine tour** will take you to some of the region's best wineries. Try dinner at **C&O Restaurant** or **Peter Chang China Grill,** or eat at **The Green Leaf Grill** in Waynesboro and prepare for the Parkway on the morrow.

Best Hikes

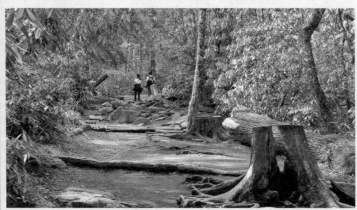

on the trail to Linville Falls

Skyline Drive

* **Mary's Rock Trail (MP 33.5):** Views from Mary's Rock are some of the best along Skyline Drive, with full panoramas of the mountain chain stretching off into the distance (page 67).

* **Dark Hollow Falls Trail (MP 50.7):** This short but taxing trail in Shenandoah National Park leads to a beautiful 70-foot waterfall (page 70).

Blue Ridge Parkway

* **Linville Falls Trail (MP 316):** Take in three views of one of the most beautiful waterfalls in what's called the "Grand Canyon of the East" (page 194).

* **Crabtree Falls Trail (MP 339.5):** This moderate hike takes you to one of the most picturesque falls in North Carolina (page 198).

Great Smoky Mountains National Park

* **Andrews Bald:** Wildflowers abound in this bald, a high meadow in Great Smoky Mountains National Park (page 285).

* **Hen Wallow Falls Trail:** A short trail leads you to a photogenic 90-foot waterfall that starts out only 2 feet wide but spreads to 20 feet at the base (page 293).

* **Rich Mountain Loop:** Climb up above Cades Cove for a big view of this onetime homestead in Tennessee's Smoky Mountains (page 305).

Day 5

WAYNESBORO TO ROANOKE

132 miles; 4 hours

Have breakfast at Iris Inn, then start your journey south along the **Blue Ridge Parkway.** Make your first stop the **Humpback Rocks** (MP 5.9) and take the one-mile trail to the namesake rocks. Stop at the **James River Visitor Center** (MP 63.6), the lowest point on the Parkway, and stretch your legs on one of the short walks that detail the history of the river or the diverse plant life here.

At Milepost 86, detour off the Parkway for lunch in **Bedford.** You can spend the afternoon in Bedford, taking a docent-led tour of the **National D-Day Memorial** followed by fruit-picking at a nearby **apple orchard,** or head to the **Peaks of Otter** (MP 85.9) for a quick but strenuous hike to the peak of **Sharp Top** (2.5-3 hours). Afterwards, continue south to **Roanoke.**

Enter the city via the Mill Mountain Parkway at Milepost 120 and pass by the famous **Roanoke Star,** then rest up at one of the **B&Bs** in town before heading to **Lucky** for dinner.

Day 6
ROANOKE TO FLOYD
56 miles; 1.5 hours

It's a short day today, so you have time to explore Roanoke. Have an egg sandwich at **Texas Tavern,** then wander over to the **Market Square,** where the farmers market will be in full swing any day of the week. Look in at the **Taubman Museum of Art** or shop at the downtown boutiques before heading for **Floyd.** Have lunch near Floyd at **Chateau Morrisette,** one of the oldest wineries in Virginia, before checking into **Ambrosia Farm Bed & Breakfast.** Time your visit to coincide with Floyd's weekly **Friday Night Jamboree,** and have dinner at quirky **Oddfellas Cantina.**

Day 7
FLOYD TO STONE MOUNTAIN
STATE PARK
85 miles; 2.5 hours

The drive from Floyd to the North Carolina state line is one of the most beautiful on the Parkway. Stop at **Mabry Mill** (MP 176.1) for legendary buckwheat pancakes and a look at a working waterwheel-powered gristmill and sawmill. At **Groundhog Mountain** (MP 188.1), enjoy spectacular views from the observation tower. Learn how country and bluegrass music originated in these very hills at the **Blue Ridge Music Center** at the state line. Camp at **Stone Mountain State Park,** and squeeze in a quick hike to the top of the namesake bald granite dome. Head into nearby **Elkin** for dinner and drinks (just be back before the park is locked for the night).

Day 8
STONE MOUNTAIN TO BLOWING ROCK
75 miles; 2.5 hours

North Carolina's High Country is no joke. The mountains are steep, and the road grows aggressively curvy, making for unworldly views as you round corners with nothing but space and the Blue Ridge Mountains in front of you. Stretch your legs on the 30 miles of trails in **Doughton Park** (MP 238.5), which also has a picnic area, or hike the **Cascade Falls Trail** at E. B. Jeffress Park (MP 272). Stop at the **Moses H. Cone Memorial Park** (MP 294.1) for a look at a turn-of-the-century manor house that's home to the gift shop of the **Southern Highland Craft Guild. Blowing Rock** is just a few miles away, and so are your accommodations as well as dinner at **Bistro Roca.**

Day 9
BLOWING ROCK TO ASHEVILLE
93 miles; 3 hours

Before heading to Asheville, check out the **Blowing Rock,** where you'll have sweeping views of peaks, including Grandfather Mountain. Back on the Parkway, prepare yourself for one of the road's most striking stretches: the **Linn Cove Viaduct** (MP 304.4). Just past the viaduct, drive to the top of **Grandfather Mountain** and take the **Mile High Swinging Bridge** to one of its lower peaks for 360-degree views of the Blue Ridge. Have lunch here, then continue down the road. Just off the Parkway at Milepost 316.3 is the entrance to **Linville Falls.** This waterfall requires a short hike to see and a slightly longer one for postcard views, but it's worth the effort. At Milepost 364.6, stop at **Craggy Gardens** to take in the summertime blooms of rhododendrons and flame azaleas, then continue to the **Folk Art Center** (MP 382), just outside Asheville.

In Asheville, spend the night in the mountains at the **Sourwood Inn** or downtown at the swank **Aloft Asheville Downtown** hotel. Dinner can be fancy or affordable; there's no shortage of places to eat in this town. Spend a late night downtown checking out the breweries and bars and listening to a little music.

clockwise from top left: downtown Asheville; the gardens at Bedford's D-Day Memorial; Sparks Lane near Cades Cove, Great Smoky Mountains National Park

Day 10
EXPLORE ASHEVILLE

Start the day in Asheville with breakfast at the **Early Girl Eatery** downtown, then head over to the **Biltmore Estate.** Tour the home, walk the gardens, take lunch in the former stable, then head to the estate's winery and wine-tasting room (it's the most visited one in the nation). Sample some wine and head back to your accommodations to freshen up before hitting town again for excellent food at **The Admiral** and interesting beers at the **Thirsty Monk.**

Day 11
ASHEVILLE TO CHEROKEE
89 miles; 3 hours

The winding section of the Parkway between Asheville and the southern terminus in Cherokee is quite beautiful. Before you hit the road, down a giant biscuit at **Biscuit Head.** Continue down the Parkway and take in the view of **Mount Pisgah** (MP 408.6) and hike to **Devil's Courthouse** (MP 422.4)—a short hike that's not as fearsome as it sounds and has a view you won't want to leave. **Richland Balsam Overlook** (MP 431.4) is the highest point on the Blue Ridge Parkway, so stop here and mark your trip with a selfie. Stop at the **Waterrock Knob Visitor Center** (MP 451.2) for a four-state view and panorama of the **Great Smoky Mountains.** At Milepost 461.9, you'll reach **Big Witch Overlook,** the last overlook before the Parkway terminates at milepost 469.1. Take one last long look before heading into **Cherokee** for the night. Spend the night at **Harrah's Cherokee Casino,** where you can gamble, visit the spa, and grab a bite in one of the casino's restaurants.

Day 12
CHEROKEE TO GREAT SMOKY MOUNTAINS NATIONAL PARK
43 miles; 1.5 hours

Today you'll drive Newfound Gap Road through Great Smoky Mountains National Park. Before you start your drive, visit the **Qualla Arts and Crafts Mutual** in Cherokee. Stop at the **Oconaluftee Visitor Center** for a park map and to check out **Mountain Farm Museum.** The twisting **Newfound Gap Road** is popular for motorcyclists and is stunning in fall; along the way you'll likely see black bears and white-tailed deer. Stop along the way at any of the overlooks—in a landscape this stunning, there are no bad views. Before you leave the park, drive out to **Cades Cove,** a one-time mountain community, where you might spy bears lounging in the remnants of an apple orchard. Check into a hotel in **Gatlinburg,** then take a walk down the main drag of this tourist haven. Grab some moonshine at **Sugarlands Distilling Company** and dinner at **Smoky Mountain Trout House.**

Day 13
GATLINBURG TO KNOXVILLE
30 miles; 45 minutes

Head straight from your Gatlinburg hotel to **Dollywood,** where mountain music, mountain crafts, mountain food, and mountain folks are interspersed with roller coasters. Spend half the day here, then head to Knoxville (45 minutes away) for lunch at **Dead End BBQ** before checking in to your downtown hotel. Walk the **World's Fair Park** and climb to the top of the **Sunsphere** for the best view in town. Then, take in a concert at the historic **Tennessee Theatre** or stop in at the **Knoxville Museum of Art** and the **East Tennessee History Center.** Dinner at **Stock & Barrel** will put you in the heart of downtown, where you can explore to your heart's content.

Day 14
KNOXVILLE BACK TO WASHINGTON DC
487 miles; 7 hours

You'll definitely want to make better travel time on the return drive to Washington DC. Take I-81 north through Tennessee and Virginia to I-66 east, which will carry you right into DC. This route is doable in a day, rather than two or three at Parkway speeds.

Four Days from Washington DC

Get a taste of Washington DC's history and culture, hit the trail in Shenandoah National Park, spend a night under the stars, and see the homes of two former presidents, all in one mini-expedition.

Day 1
WASHINGTON DC TO SHENANDOAH NATIONAL PARK
70 miles; 1.5 hours

Begin your trip in DC at one of the most recognizable structures in town: the **Lincoln Memorial.** Step out to the landing where Martin Luther King, Jr. delivered his "I Have a Dream" speech. Then, with your preordered, time-stamped tickets in hand, get in line for the elevator ride to the top of the **Washington Monument** for a view of the Mall, monuments, White House, and Capitol.

Grab an early lunch at **We the Pizza** before heading west to **Manassas Battlefield National Park,** site of the First and Second Battles of Bull Run. From Manassas, continue west to the town of **Front Royal,** where you can grab lunch if you didn't do so in DC. Downtown Front Royal is only about a mile from **Shenandoah National Park** and the start of incredibly scenic 105-mile **Skyline Drive,** which bisects the park and will be your route for the next couple days. Camp at **Matthews Arm Campground,** the first campground in the park as you travel south, or **Big Meadows Campground,** or stay at one of the park's two famous lodges, **Skyland Resort** or **Big Meadows Lodge.** Get dinner at either lodge, then sit back and watch the sunset.

Day 2
SHENANDOAH NATIONAL PARK TO WAYNESBORO
110 miles; 3 hours

Cook yourself a camp breakfast or dine at your lodge of choice, then head out on Skyline Drive. Your first stop is **Dark Hollow Falls,** a short hike to a 70-foot waterfall that spills over a ferny cliff, with a steep ascent on the way back. Afterwards, if you're hoping for a hiking reprieve, make the easy jaunt to **Blackrock Summit,** 30 miles south, for enormous views of the countryside. If you're in the mood for more trail time, hike the **South River Falls Trail,** which leads to an 83-foot waterfall, one of the largest in the park.

Continue south to **Waynesboro** and your room or cabin at the mountaintop **Iris Inn.** Have dinner in town at **The Green Leaf Grill.**

Day 3
WAYNESBORO TO CHARLOTTESVILLE
28 miles; 30 minutes

After yesterday's day on the trail, it's time for a day in the city. Just a few miles east is **Charlottesville,** home of the **University of Virginia** and site of **Monticello.** After touring Jefferson's home, stop by a few of the wineries on the **Monticello Wine Trail** to sample some of Virginia's best and a have bite to eat.

Check in at **200 South Street Inn** in the heart of town, and make reservations at **Peter Chang China Grill,** or try **C&O Restaurant** for something a little more Southern.

Day 4
CHARLOTTESVILLE TO MOUNT VERNON AND DC
131 miles; 3 hours

Don't leave Charlottesville without a bagel from **Bodo's Bagels.** On the way back to DC, avoid the congestion of the interstate and take **US-29** through the countryside until you get back to Manassas Battlefield National Park. From here, head east to **Mount Vernon,**

Best Views

Mabry Mill in fall

Along Skyline Drive and the Blue Ridge Parkway are a number of **overlooks** and **roadside attractions.** In every instance below, it's worth pulling over for an eyeful:

Skyline Drive

* **Hogback Mountain Overlook (MP 20.8):** The longest overlook on Skyline Drive gives you expansive views of mountains and valley.

* **Crimora Lake Overlook (MP 92.6):** Expect big views centered around Crimora Lake, a remnant of a manganese mining operation.

Blue Ridge Parkway

* **Peaks of Otter (MP 85.9):** Get to the summit of Sharp Top via either a strenuous hike on the Sharp Top Trail or an easy shuttle ride, then enjoy views of the parkway, the lights of Bedford, and Abbott Lake.

* **Mabry Mill (MP 176.1):** This picturesque millhouse with water wheel is one of the most photographed on the Parkway.

* **Groundhog Mountain (MP 188.1):** The view of the observation tower is lovely but nothing compared to the view from it.

* **Beacon Heights (MP 305.2):** Whether you stay at the car and admire the view of Grandfather Mountain or take the short hike to a rocky bluff with massive views, you won't be disappointed.

* **Richland Balsam Overlook (MP 431.4):** From the highest point on the Blue Ridge Parkway you'll have great views of several mountain ranges.

* **Waterrock Knob Visitor Center (MP 451.2):** This visitors center parking lot is the perfect vantage point for taking in the sunset and star-filled sky.

the riverside home of our first president, just a couple of miles south of Alexandria and only 15 miles from DC. Tour Mount Vernon and have lunch alfresco at one of the many charming restaurants and cafés in **Old Town Alexandria.** Then return to DC. For a relaxed dinner, try **Burger, Tap & Shake,** or try **DAS Ethiopian Cuisine** for something more refined.

Five Days from Knoxville

With just five days, you can explore Knoxville, traipse into Dollywood, log some quality trail time, explore Great Smoky Mountains National Park, catch an amazing firefly display, ride a steam train…and drive a short, but beautiful, section of the Blue Ridge Parkway.

Day 1
KNOXVILLE TO DOLLYWOOD
43 miles; 1 hour

Grab a tasty breakfast at **Pete's Coffee Shop** in Knoxville, then head over to the **Sunsphere** for a selfie in front of the city's golden-crowned monument. Get a feel for the people and culture of East Tennessee and the Smoky Mountains at the **East Tennessee History Center** downtown, then hit the road, following US-441 south toward the mountain towns (and tourist meccas) of **Pigeon Forge** and **Gatlinburg.** Have lunch and check into a hotel in Gatlinburg, then backtrack to Pigeon Forge and spend the rest of the day at **Dollywood.**

Day 2
DOLLYWOOD TO GREAT SMOKY
MOUNTAINS NATIONAL PARK
44 miles; 2 hours

Have breakfast at the **Pancake Pantry** in Gatlinburg, then follow US-441 south two miles into **Great Smoky Mountains National Park**, stopping at the **Sugarlands Visitor Center** to pick up maps and park tips. Set up camp in the **Elkmont Campground.** Here, for a two-week window in the summer, one of only four colonies of synchronous fireflies in the United States puts on a dazzling show, so reserve your site early. Drive a loop around **Cades Cove,** which was once home to a mountain community. At the various buildings throughout the community, you can stop and hike, so pick up a map at the visitor center, select a

couple of hikes, and hit the trail. **Wildlife viewing** is awesome here, with massive herds of deer and black bears playing in the boughs of apple trees. Good dinner options are located in Gatlinburg and Pigeon Forge.

Day 3
GREAT SMOKY MOUNTAINS
NATIONAL PARK TO CHEROKEE
47 miles; 1.5 hours

After breakfast, begin your cross-park drive via **Newfound Gap Road.** You'll find trailheads all along this twisting mountain road, but for a hike with impressive views, save yourself for **Clingmans Dome,** the highest peak in Tennessee and GSMNP. You'll see signs for Clingmans Dome as Newfound Gap Road crests the Smokies. Head down this spur road to "climb" to the top (the summit is accessible via a walkway and concrete observation platform, not much of a climb) for jaw-dropping views. From here, a 1.75-mile trail leads to **Andrews Bald,** the highest such meadow in the park. In summer, the trail is bombarded with flame azalea and rhododendron.

After hiking to Andrews Bald, get back to Newfound Gap Road and descend into North Carolina and the town of **Cherokee.** Browse the **Qualla Arts and Crafts Mutual,** then stop in at the **Museum of the Cherokee Indian** across the street or **Oconaluftee Indian Village** just up the hill. Spend the night at **Harrah's Cherokee Casino** or opt for a campground or nearby chain hotel.

Day 4
CHEROKEE TO BRYSON CITY
AND CATALOOCHEE
69 miles; 2 hours

Try your hand at the nickel slots on your way out of Harrah's (you never know) before stopping at **Granny's Kitchen** for a country breakfast buffet. Your next stop is the nearby town of Bryson City for a mountainside ride aboard the **Great Smoky Mountains Railroad.** You can pair

Where to Spot Wildlife

All along Skyline Drive and the Blue Ridge Parkway and in Great Smoky Mountains National Park, you'll have the chance for some spectacular wildlife-viewing (if you keep your eyes peeled).

a young elk grazing

- **Hawksbill Mountain:** From this peak in the Shenandoah National Park you can see a number of raptors—hawks, falcons, eagles, and the like—riding thermals and hunting the hillsides (page 69).

- **Big Meadows:** The largest meadow along Skyline Drive is visited by dozens of white-tailed deer each morning and evening (page 71).

- **Grandfather Mountain:** On Grandfather Mountain you'll find a small zoo with native animals (including a cougar and pair of bald eagles), but at the Mile High Swinging Bridge, you'll see a number of raptors and vultures riding thermals, and, if you're lucky, a raven or two playing on the wind, flying upside down or holding on to one another as they soar overhead (page 191).

- **Cataloochee:** The Blue Ridge Mountains were the home of elk until the species was hunted out. Today you can see reintroduced herds of elk at Cataloochee Valley, a lovely spot on the north end of Great Smoky Mountains National Park (page 290).

- **Elkmont:** At Elkmont you'll see one of the most rare sights in the world: synchronous fireflies. In a meadow here for approximately two weeks each summer, swarms of fireflies blink in unison at groups on the ground, who blink back (page 300).

- **Cades Cove:** Deer graze the fields and bear laze in the remnants of the apple orchards in this onetime mountain community in Tennessee's Smoky Mountains (page 301).

your train ride with a little white-water rafting or zip-lining, or you can keep it tame and simply enjoy the scenery.

Backtrack to Cherokee and hop on the **Blue Ridge Parkway.** Today, you'll traverse 25 miles of the Parkway, including some of the road's most rugged mountains and impressive overlooks. After following the Parkway for a short ways, exit onto the Great Smoky Mountains Expressway (US-441) and head north toward Waynesville, where you can grab lunch before connecting with I-40 and making your way to the beautiful **Cataloochee Campground** on the North Carolina side of GSMNP. Cataloochee is another former mountain community, but this one has a few residents: **elk.** Cataloochee is a prime spot to see them. Be sure to bring in something to cook; it's a bit of a drive back out for dinner.

Day 5
CATALOOCHEE TO KNOXVILLE
96 miles; 2 hours
If you missed the elk last night, get up early and watch the tree line at the edge of the fields. You'll see them see them eating their way around the perimeter. Take a little time this morning to check out the haunting and picturesque old church and hike among the other structures in Cataloochee.

The Shenandoah Valley

Bordered to the west by the sharp peaks of the Allegheny Mountains and to the east by the gentle crest of the Blue Ridge Mountains, the Shenandoah Valley cuts a slash along Virginia's western border.

© AVALON TRAVEL

Highlights

★ **National Air and Space Museum:** Showcasing the crowning achievements of U.S. aeronautics, this museum displays everything from the *Wright Flyer* to space suits and artifacts from the Apollo missions (page 37).

★ **United States Holocaust Memorial Museum:** This moving memorial illustrates the rise of Nazi Germany and the atrocities perpetrated upon European Jews and other ethnic and social groups during World War II (page 38).

★ **Arlington National Cemetery:** The second oldest National Cemetery contains the Tomb of the Unknown Soldier, the gravesite of JFK, and monuments, memorials, and headstones marking major events in our history (page 41).

★ **Manassas Battlefield National Park:** The site of two bloody battles during the Civil War, this battlefield is the place where General "Stonewall" Jackson earned his nickname and the Confederate army earned two early victories and opened the way for a Southern invasion of Northern territory (page 55).

★ **Hogback Mountain Overlook:** From here you can spot 11 bends of the Shenandoah River and mountains as far as you can see (page 65).

★ **Luray Caverns:** Just west of Skyline Drive, these caverns were discovered in the 1870s and found to contain human bone fragments embedded in a stalagmite. Today, more than 500,000 people tour the caves annually (page 67).

★ **Mary's Rock Trail:** A moderate trail leads to a beautiful rock outcrop with sweeping views of the countryside (page 67).

★ **Dark Hollow Falls Trail:** This short trail leads you to a beautiful 70-foot waterfall just off Skyline Drive (page 70).

★ **Monticello:** Thomas Jefferson designed his plantation and primary residence just outside Charlottesville. Today, you can visit his home and his grave (page 85).

The Great Valley, as the Shenandoah Valley is known today, wore the moniker The Great Wagon Road for nearly a century as the United States emerged from colonial rebellion and began to form a nation unto itself. Early settlers found it to be an easier route into the unknown interior of the fledgling states than direct routes west.

Hikers on the storied Appalachian Trail experience these seemingly endless ridge lines firsthand (or firstfoot, as it were), much like the early settlers. Traveling stunning Skyline Drive, which runs the length of Shenandoah National Park, gives you a taste of the mountains, and you can even follow the Appalachian Trail for a ways. Hiking in Shenandoah National Park reveals the true wild nature of this place: secluded waterfalls, overlooks with hundred-mile views, caves of unplumbed depths, black bears and white-tailed deer, the hush and hum of nature.

Just 75 miles to the east of Shenandoah National Park's entrance is Washington DC, our nation's capital. Here, museums like those of the Smithsonian Institution are repositories for much of what the United States holds dear and significant in our nation's history, and monuments honor George Washington, Abraham Lincoln, and Martin Luther King, Jr. But museums and monuments are only part of the DC experience. Thanks to the influence of diplomats, immigrants, and international visitors, Washington DC has amazing international cuisine and a vibrant culture. You can always find some sort of visual or performing arts to watch, listen to, or take part in yourself.

Washington DC is also a great place to start your 700-mile road trip south along Skyline Drive, the Blue Ridge Parkway, and on to Great Smoky Mountains National Park. On this segment of your journey, from Washington to Front Royal and on to Charlottesville near the start of the Blue Ridge Parkway, you'll pass by the homes of George Washington and Thomas Jefferson as well as Revolutionary and Civil War battlefields. As you travel Skyline Drive through Shenandoah National Park, look out over the countryside. With a little imagination, you can picture this view through the eyes of those settlers, patriots, or Civil War soldiers who marched into battle on their home soil. It's beautiful, wild, and steeped with history.

Planning Your Time

You could spend as little as two days or as much as a week on this stretch of your drive. Washington DC alone is worth a week's stay, and it would be no problem to spend two or three days exploring Shenandoah National Park and then another two or three in Charlottesville.

For the quickest route, spend a day in Washington seeing the monuments and touring your museum of choice, then jump on the road to Front Royal and drive south along Skyline Drive until you reach your campground or room at Big Meadows Lodge or Skyland Resort. The next morning, get in a quick hike and drive through to the end of Skyline Drive, then head to the busy college-town of Charlottesville (30 minutes east) or laid-back Waynesboro (5 minutes west) for dinner and to spend the night before starting the Blue Ridge Parkway on the morrow.

If you're into museums and the cultural attractions offered up by Washington DC and its suburbs, stretch out your time there and spend a couple of days (you still won't be able to tour all the museums and monuments you want to see). Hikers will want to spend more time in Shenandoah National Park, logging some trail miles and enjoying the waterfalls, peaks, and wide views. Wine lovers will want to linger around Charlottesville and tour the wineries there. Monuments, historic sites, and stories line every mile of this route. History buffs will want to slow down and soak it in.

Seasons in this region are on the whole gentle. In summer, temperatures sometimes rise into the 90s, though heat like this is uncommon in all but the densest urban areas. Thunderstorms may pop up from time to time, and higher elevations may experience hail and lightning. Watch the weather forecast and plan around oncoming storms.

Driving Considerations

In winter, the region receives snow, but blizzards are nonexistent and shutdowns of major roads or even surface streets are rare in the cities and towns of the region. The exception is Skyline Drive, which, unlike the Blue Ridge Parkway, remains open all winter, except when snow accumulation outpaces the Park's ability to maintain roadways. Along Skyline Drive, fog can pop up in any season. If it does, slow down or stop if you need to.

Getting There

Starting Points

If you're following the full 740-mile route prescribed in this guide, you'll begin in **Washington DC,** the major travel hub on the northern end of your monumental road trip. From here, you'll travel west along **I-66** to **Front Royal, Va. Skyline Drive** originates here, meaning that Front Royal is the true start of your journey through the National Parks lands. Skyline Drive heads south through **Shenandoah National Park** for **105.5 miles,** ending in **Rockfish Gap** where the **Blue Ridge Parkway** begins.

Car

Several major interstates—**I-95, I-81, I-64, I-270, I-66**—serve as vehicular arteries for the region, with most roads (excepting I-81 and I-64) leading to Washington DC.

For driving directions to Washington DC, see page 29.

Front Royal, Va., and the entrance to Shenandoah National Park, is just a few miles east of where I-66 meets I-81 (18 miles west). US-340 and US-522 also go through Front Royal. On Skyline Drive,

Best Accommodations

★ **Morrison-Clark Historic Inn & Restaurant, Washington DC:** This Civil War-era Victorian mansion is conveniently located for sightseeing (page 51).

★ **The Hamilton Crowne Plaza Hotel, Washington DC:** Convenient to transportation lines, this hotel offers comfortable and cozy accommodations (page 51).

★ **Arlington Court Suites Hotel, Arlington:** Relax in recently renovated suites that are enormous by Washington DC standards (page 52).

★ **Iris Inn, Waynesboro:** Enjoy gorgeous views from your mountaintop room, cabin, or cottage (page 81).

★ **200 South Street Inn, Charlottesville:** Sleep in an 1800s home with Jeffersonian connections, in a great location to boot (page 90).

★ **Arcady Vineyard Bed & Breakfast, Charlottesville:** Wine tour and massage packages make this a perfect home base for a wine country getaway (page 90).

★ **Keswick Hall, Keswick:** Golf or enjoy a spa treatment at this gorgeous resort on a 600-acre estate (page 91).

there are only two points where roads intersect your route. US-211 crosses Skyline Drive at Thornton Gap (MP 31.5); from here, the town of Luray is less than 10 miles west. Farther south, US-33 intersects Skyline at Swift Run Gap (MP 62.7); the town of Elkton is only seven miles west. There are entrance stations to Shenandoah National Park at both Thornton Gap and Swift Run Gap.

Charlottesville lies on I-64, only 90 minutes west of Richmond, Va. Rockfish Gap, where Skyline Drive ends and the Blue Ridge Parkway begins, is 24 miles to the west. The small city of Waynesboro is 30 minutes west of Charlottesville and only four miles from the Skyline Drive/Blue Ridge Parkway convergence. I-81, less than 20 minutes to the west of Rockfish Gap, provides easy automobile access to both the Parkway and Skyline Drive for travelers arriving via the I-81 corridor.

In both Charlottesville and Washington DC, plenty of **car rental agencies** will set you up with a nice ride.

Fueling Up
Gasoline is readily and plentifully available along this leg of the route; however, the Big Meadows Wayside (MP 51.2) is the only place to fuel up on Skyline Drive.

Air
A quartet of major airports serves the region: **Dulles International Airport** (1 Saarinen Circle, Dulles, Va., 703/572-2700, www.metwashairports.com) and **Reagan National Airport** (2401 Smith Blvd., Arlington, Va., 703/417-8000, www.metwashairports.com) in Washington DC, **Baltimore Washington International Airport** (410/859-7111, www.bwiairport.com) in Baltimore, and **Charlottesville Albemarle Airport** (100 Bowen Loop, Charlottesville, 434/973-8342, www.gocho.com). **Richmond International Airport** (1 Richard E. Byrd Terminal Dr., Richmond, 804/226-3000, www.flyrichmond.com) is another option as it's only 116 miles south of DC and is served by American Airlines, Delta, Jet Blue Airways, Southwest, United, US Airways, and Interjet.

Train and Bus
Rail and bus lines stretch into both Charlottesville and Washington DC. For information on service to Washington DC, see page 30.

Best Restaurants

★ **Ben's Chili Bowl, Washington DC:** This DC institution, open since 1958, has served the likes of President Obama (page 52).

★ **Hill Country Barbecue, Washington DC:** This is Texas barbecue at its best (page 52).

★ **Rasika, Washington DC:** Hit up this new spot to taste lesser-known Indian dishes and wine off a renowned list (page 54).

★ **We the Pizza, Washington DC:** From the Forest Shroomin' to the China Poblano Spicy Mexican Pie, this pizza is out of the ordinary (page 54).

★ **Peter Chang China Grill, Charlottesville:** Taste impeccable Szechwan cuisine prepared by the lauded "Master of Peppers" (page 91).

★ **Mas Tapas, Charlottesville:** Dip into a large menu of small plates at this Spanish- and Mediterranean-inspired restaurant, where many ingredients are locally sourced (page 92).

★ **C&O Restaurant, Charlottesville:** Savor meat-heavy, French-inspired dishes in elegant surroundings (page 92).

At **Charlottesville's Amtrak station** (CVS, 810 W Main St., 434/296-4559, www.amtrak.com, 6am-9:30pm daily), the Cardinal/Hoosier State, Crescent, and Northeast Regional lines pass through daily. The **Charlottesville Greyhound station** (310 W. Main St., 434/295-5131, www.greyhound.com, 4am-10am, 11:30am-6:30pm, and 8pm-10pm daily) is just a few blocks from the Amtrak station.

Washington DC

Despite all the partisan bickering that goes on in the capital of the United States, there's one thing every political party can agree upon: this city is one of the best in the world. There's great food from far-flung foreign cuisines to Texas barbecue, shopping both vintage and haute couture, and more museums and monuments than you can count. Washington DC is a treasure trove of culture, history, art, and architecture. From the all-business bustle on Capitol Hill to multilingual Dupont Circle to late-night rock shows at the 9:30 Club to the cool gorge that is Rock Creek Park to the quiet reverence of Arlington National Cemetery, DC offers something for everyone.

Any time of day, the city has beautiful sights to behold: rowing crews slicing down the Potomac at dawn, food vendors undertaking morning rituals at markets across the city, crowds visiting museums and coming out more enlightened for it, monuments lit at night. Casual sightseers will find most of what they came for centered around the National Mall. Explorers looking for the neighborhood treats and DC-only surprises will find what they seek on the side streets away from the busy center of town. The mix of immigrants and emissaries, Congressional staffers and corporate lobbyists, and residents and visitors is the glue that holds the city together.

Getting There and Around

Fortunately, most of the major sightseeing highlights in central DC—the National Mall, White House, a bevy of monuments and memorials, the Smithsonian museums, Holocaust Memorial Museum, and Newseum—are within walking distance of one another. Other sights, like Arlington National Cemetery and neighborhood-specific destinations, are easy to get to thanks to an easy-to-use, efficient rail and bus system. Since so much of what first time and returning visitors clamor to see is located on or within a block or so of the National Mall, many opt for bike tours or to work their way from sight to sight on foot.

You can drive yourself around the city, but if you're not familiar with the odd diagonal streets, the circles, and a secret place to park near your destination, you're better off with public transportation or a cab. Once you get your bearings and can identify a few landmarks around you, navigating the city on your own is pretty simple.

Car

To get to Washington DC from Richmond, Va., drive 108 miles (three hours with traffic) north on I-95. From New York, drive four hours south on I-95 and the New Jersey Turnpike, a toll road. Baltimore, Md., is only an hour north on MD-295 and US-50; Philadelphia, Pa., is 2.5 hours north via I-95, MD-295, and US-50. Pittsburgh is just over four hours to the west along I-70 and I-270.

You'll find the offices for most car rental agencies in any of the airports or at Union Station. Available car rental agencies include **Alamo** (800/462-5266, www.alamo.com), **Enterprise** (800/736-8222, www.enterprise.com), **Hertz** (800/654-3131, www.hertz.com), **National** (800/227-7368, www.nationalcar.com), and **Thrifty** (800/367-2277, www.thrifty.com).

Air

Three airports serve the Washington area. **Dulles International Airport** (1 Saarinen Circle, Dulles, Va., 703/572-2700, www.metwashairports.com) accommodates domestic and international travelers. Around three-dozen airlines serve Dulles, and if you're flying internationally, this airport is much closer to downtown than your other options.

Reagan National Airport (2401 Smith Blvd., Arlington, Va., 703/417-8000, www.metwashairports.com) sees primarily domestic flights and a few international flights. Airlines here include Air Canada, Delta, Frontier, Southwest, Jet Blue, United, and Virgin America.

In Baltimore, Md., 35 miles to the northeast, the **Baltimore Washington International Airport** (410/859-7111, www.bwiairport.com) sees a handful of international flights but mostly domestic airlines very similar to those serving Reagan National Airport. Depending on your departure city, flying into Baltimore may be cheaper, but know that even though it's only 35 miles away, the traffic around Washington is notorious and it could be a costly cab ride or a frustrating commute in your rental car if you land here.

Taxis are readily available at each airport. Fares vary according to traffic and time. Trips generally cost around $15 from Reagan, $70 from Dulles, and close to $100 from Baltimore. You can use **Supershuttle** (800/258-3826, www.supershuttle.com, around $15 from Reagan, $30 from Dulles, and $40 from Baltimore) to get to downtown from any airport.

Train

Amtrak (202/906-3260, www.amtrak.com) pulls into **Union Station** (50 Massachusetts Ave. NE, 24 hours daily) with trains arriving and departing from destinations all over the eastern seaboard. Amtrak services include the Acela Express, Northeast Regional, Silver Service/Palmetto, Cardinal/Hoosier State, Crescent, Vermonter, Capitol Limited, and Carolinian/Piedmont. Via Amtrak, you're 3.75 hours from New York City, 2.25 hours from Philadelphia, 1.25 hours from Baltimore, Md., and 3.25 hours from Richmond, Va.

The Amtrak line connects directly to the **Maryland Area Rail Commuter (MARC)** system (410/539-5000 or 866/743-3682, www.maryland.gov/marc-train), a Monday-Friday commuter service with dozens of trains connecting the Baltimore-Washington corridor, southern Maryland counties, and northeastern West Virginia. It also connects to **Virginia Railway Express** (703/684-1001, www.vre.org), which runs to Manassas and Fredericksburg.

Metro

The Washington Metropolitan Area Transit Authority (WMATA) operates the DC subway system called the **Metrorail** (202/673-7000, www.wmata.com, 5am-midnight Mon.-Thurs., 5am-3am Fri., 7am-3am Sat., 7am-midnight Sun.), or simply "the Metro." It covers the downtown area and the suburbs, and expansion is almost constant. Metro stations are identified by a large letter "M" atop a black pylon. For as chaotic as DC can get, the Metro system is surprisingly fast, clean, and efficient.

Fares range from $1.75 to $5.90 depending on the distance you're traveling and whether you're traveling during peak commute times. There are trains every 5-6 minutes during peak times and every 10-15 minutes at other times. One-day passes are $14.50, and seven-day passes are $36-59.25. Make sure you get on the right side of the tracks for your destination (look at the maps located by the fare machines and at the digital displays on the various platforms, showing which trains are coming and how soon).

Bus

Greyhound Bus Lines (202/289-5141

or 202/789-4318, www.greyhound. com) serves Washington DC, arriving and departing from **Union Station** (50 Massachusetts Ave. NE, 24 hours daily).

Metrobuses, run by WMATA, connect with Metrorail stations for travel to outlying areas. Fares are $1.75-4 per trip (exact change only); transfers from the Metrorail are free. One-week passes are $17.50. Buses run on roughly the same schedule as trains. Rail-to-bus and bus-to-bus transfers are possible—simply hand your bus-transfer pass, which you must purchase for each transfer, to the driver of the second bus.

The **DC Circulator** (202/962-1423, www.dccirculator.com) bus system runs five loops:

- **Dupont Circle to Georgetown to Rosslyn** (7am-midnight Sun.-Thurs., 7am-2am Fri.-Sat.)

- **Georgetown to Union Station** (7am-9pm daily)

- **Potomac Ave. Metro to Skyland** (winter 6am-7pm Mon.-Fri., summer 6am-9pm Mon.-Fri. and 7am-9pm Sat.)

- **Union Station to the Navy Yard** (winter 6am-7pm Mon.-Fri., summer 6am-9pm Mon.-Fri. and 7am-9pm Sat.)

- **Woodley Park to Adams Morgan to McPherson Square** (7am-midnight Sun.-Thurs., 7am-3:30am Fri.-Sat.)

Buses pass every 10 minutes, and tickets are $1.

Taxi

Taxicabs in DC operate on time- and distance-based meters. Fares start at $3.25 plus $0.27 for each one-eighth of a mile, with wait time costing $35/hour (counted fractionally and charged when cab is stopped or slowed less than 10 miles per hour for more than one minute). There are other fees as well: a $0.25 passenger

surcharge; $1 for each additional passenger; $2 for telephone dispatch; $15 for a declared snow emergency. It can add up, especially in the oft-heinous traffic here. Top cab companies include **Yellow Cab** (202/546-7900, www.dcyellow-cab.com) and, if you're traveling to and from Virginia, **Red Top Cab of Arlington** (703/522-3333, www.redtopcab.com). You can also try **Taxi Transportation Service** (202/398-0500, www.dctaxionline.com, or download their app for your phone or tablet), a cab service with a network of more than 16 cab companies on call in the area.

Sights
The National Mall

In the midst of the hard urban landscape of Washington DC is a green space to end all green spaces: **the National Mall** (www.nps.gov/nama). When Pierre L'Enfant began planning the future city of Washington DC, his designs included a mile-long, garden-lined boulevard stretching away from the Capitol building. He never knew that this lawn would be the gathering place for Martin Luther King, Jr.'s "I Have A Dream" speech, protests against the Vietnam War, the site where the AIDS quilt was first displayed, and many other historic events.

Activism notwithstanding, the National Mall is a popular spot for visitors and residents of the greater DC area. On sunny days, Congressional staffers, FBI types, families, college kids, young professionals, and people from all walks of DC life gather to eat lunch and take in the fresh air, peeling off shoes and socks to feel a little grass between their toes. More than 25 million people visit the National Mall each year. Considering that it's the site of some of the most iconic monuments and memorials—the Washington Monument, reflecting pool, Lincoln Memorial, and the Vietnam War Memorial—and the museums of the Smithsonian Institution, which form its outer border, it's a wonder that number isn't larger.

The National Mall stretches west nearly two miles from the Capitol to the Lincoln Memorial; the Washington Monument stands sentinel in between. At its widest, the Mall is nearly 1,600 feet side to side; at its most narrow, it's still twice the size of a football field. There are a number of free attractions on the Mall. For more information, you can stop a Ranger during your visit, or contact the Park Superintendent (900 Ohio Dr. SW, 202/426-6841 or 202/485-9880).

Lincoln Memorial

One of the most recognized structures in the United States, the **Lincoln Memorial** (2 Lincoln Memorial Circle NW, Washington DC, 202/426-6841, www.nps.gov/linc, 24 hours daily, free), stands at the west end of the National Mall. Consisting of three iconic parts—the reflecting pool between this memorial and the Washington Monument, the Colorado Yule marble exterior resembling a Greek temple, and the 19-foot tall statue of a seated Abraham Lincoln inside—the Lincoln Memorial is a presence. Part of that palpability comes from Lincoln himself (savior of the Union, breaker of the shackles of American slavery, assassinated in office) and part from the deep-seeded significance to the Civil Rights Movement. Martin Luther King, Jr. delivered his famous 1963 "I Have A Dream" speech to a crowd of 250,000 strong from these steps, and a performer on the program, contralto Marian Anderson, performed on the steps that day for the second time in her life. Her first performance marked another milestone in Civil Rights history, though one lesser known. In 1939 she was scheduled to perform for the Daughters of the American Revolution in nearby Constitution Hall. They refused to allow a woman of color to take the stage. First Lady Eleanor Roosevelt and a cadre of like-minded women resigned from the organization over the flap, but Roosevelt took it a step further and arranged an Easter Sunday performance on the steps of the Lincoln Memorial featuring none other than Marian Anderson. Anderson sang that day to a nationwide radio audience and live crowd of 70,000 gathered at the foot of the steps and around the reflecting pool.

Vietnam Veterans Memorial

The evocative **Vietnam Veterans Memorial** (5 Henry Bacon Dr. NW, 202/426-6841, www.nps.gov/vive, 24 hours daily, free) is a simple, but revolutionary, structure, described by designer Maya Lin as "a rift in the earth." Rather than trumpeting the glory of struggle or the legacy of some lauded general, the memorial lists the names of more than 58,000 servicemen and women who died in America's longest war. The names, inscribed on a 492-foot wall of polished black granite, are listed chronologically in order of death. As you read the names, you can see your face reflected back. At the foot of the wall are flowers, flags, tokens, mementos, letters, photographs, and offerings left for the dead. To witness a Vietnam Veteran visit the wall, rest his hand against a name, and bow his head in grief or prayer is crushing. It's an important reminder of the power of war, and also of the power that art and monuments can hold.

Vietnam veteran Jan Scruggs raised the funds to construct the memorial. It is America's most potent shrine, a place of grief and cleansing. Every year, tens of thousands of people bring offerings of poems and rings, harmonicas, and sardines for lost friends, sons, or parents they never knew.

Registers at either end of the wall list the names alphabetically and provide a key to their location for those who are looking for a specific name. The memorial also includes two bronze sculptures. The first depicts three weary but alert servicemen, and the other portrays three women tending an injured soldier,

One Day in Washington DC

Even if you're eager to start your drive, you need to give DC at least a day.

Morning

Start your day by visiting the **National Mall,** where the majority of the Smithsonian's museums line the perimeter. Pick a pair to speed through, or select one to savor with a longer visit. If you're visiting only one museum, make it the **National Air and Space Museum.** If you have time for two, add the **National Museum of American History,** where you can see everything from Kermit the Frog to the Ruby Slippers from *The Wizard of Oz* to gowns and artifacts worn by First Ladies over the years.

Afternoon

When it's time for lunch, walk east on the Mall toward the Capitol where you can snap a few shots of our seat of government on the way to **We the Pizza.**

After lunch, find a Metro station and take a ride to **Arlington National Cemetery,** where you can pay your respects to John F. Kennedy and countless other American heroes and heroines. While you're there, visit the **Tomb of the Unknown Soldier** to witness the ceremonial changing of the guard.

Evening

On your way back into town, stop by the **Kennedy Center** for one of their **free concerts** held nightly at 6pm on the Millennium Stage, or take a three-hour **nighttime bicycle tour** of the National Mall and monuments with **Bike and Roll.** Then hop in a cab and head to Georgetown for dinner at **DAS Ethiopian Cuisine,** or stick close to the Mall and try **Rasika,** a top-notch, award-winning Indian restaurant with a tasting menu that's out of this world.

communicating the emotional bond that formed between the male soldiers and women who served primarily as nurses and support staff.

Washington Monument

According to federal law, no structure in the capital can be built higher than the 555-foot tapered shaft of the **Washington Monument** (2 15th St. NW, 877/444-6777 or 877/559-6777 for tickets, www.nps.gov/wamo, 9am-5pm daily except Christmas and July 4, open till 10pm daily Memorial Day-Labor Day, free but tickets are required). In 1783, the Continental Congress first suggested a monument honoring the nation's inaugural president, but more than a century passed before the idea became reality; from cornerstone to completion took 40 years. During one embarrassing interlude from 1854 to 1876, the obelisk languished as an unsightly stump of 150 feet, described by Mark Twain as "a factory chimney with the top broken off."

When work began again, the marble originally drawn from a Maryland quarry had been exhausted; thus the noticeable change in shade of the remaining 400 feet. The monument finally opened in 1888 with women and children dutifully trudging up the 898 steps (the elevator was considered patently dangerous, braved only by men). Today everyone rides the elevator, ascending to 360-degree views of the capital's historic heart through narrow windows.

Tickets (877/559-6777, www.recreation.gov) to visit the Washington Monument are free, available each day from the kiosk at 15th Street and Madison Drive on a first-come, first-served basis. Since they tend to go quickly, get there early—as in 7am—or just reserve them for a small fee ($1.50) by phone or online.

Jefferson Memorial

A little ways off the Mall proper, the **Jefferson Memorial** (southern end of the Mall, next to the Tidal Basin, 202/426-6841, www.nps.gov/thje, 24 hours daily, free) has an iconic look similar to the

Lincoln Memorial, but it lacks the weight, both visually and in its impact. Though Jefferson was immeasurably important to the foundation of the nation, the interior of his memorial lacks the emotional punch you find in Lincoln's. Inscriptions on the walls are long passages from the Declaration of Independence, bills he authored, and letters he penned. They're stuffy and lackluster unless you have the proper historic context. Jefferson was a minister to France, secretary of state, vice president, president, negotiator of the Louisiana Purchase, writer, architect, inventor, and all around fascinating guy, so to get an idea of his import, try to visit the memorial when park rangers and staff are offering interpretive **tours** (every hour on the hour 10am-11pm daily). This memorial is jaw-dropping beautiful in the spring when the cherry trees that line the Tidal Basin in front of it are in full bloom.

Martin Luther King, Jr. Memorial

Not far from where he delivered his impassioned "I Have A Dream" speech, Martin Luther King, Jr. stands memorialized in stone. **The Martin Luther King, Jr. Memorial** (near intersection of West Basin Dr. SW and Independence Ave. SW, 202/426-6841, www.nps.gov/mlkm, 24 hours daily, free) opened in 2011, 48 years to the week of that famous speech. The memorial's entrance is a monstrous granite slab, cleaved in two as a symbol for the despair felt by African Americans

The National Mall

under segregation and Jim Crow laws. Inside the memorial, curved walls inscribed with quotes from King surround you and a 28-foot tall statue of King himself emerges from a rough-hewn rock known as the Stone of Hope. It's a fascinating monument.

National Gallery of Art

One of the finest collections in the world, the **National Gallery of Art** (600 Constitution Ave. NW, 202/737-4215, www.nga.gov, 10am-5pm Mon.-Sat., 11am-6pm Sun., closed Christmas Day and New Year's Day, free) is housed in two separate facilities. In the 1930s, the museum's west wing sprang full-grown from the wallet of rapacious banker Andrew Mellon, who wisely declined to append his name to the edifice. I. M. Pei designed the angular east wing, which was built in 1978 and boasts one of the sharpest corners you'll ever see on a building. Both wings are constructed of pink Tennessee marble, but there the similarity ends: the east displays 20th-century works by the likes of Miró, Magritte, and Matisse, while the homier, more crowded west wing is the domain of classic art by the likes of Raphael, Rembrandt, and Renoir.

Historians of the presidency are invariably drawn to the west wing, which sits over the bones of the old B&P Railroad Station where, in 1881, President James A. Garfield was shot twice in the back by Charles Guiteau. Across 7th Street from the west wing is a pleasant **sculpture garden** (10am-7pm Mon.-Thurs. and Sat., 10am-9:30pm Fri., 11am-7pm Sun., free) full of whimsical works.

The **Gallery Shops** at the National Gallery of Art is one of the best gallery shops of its kind. They have an extensive collection of art books that range from pricey coffee table books to nonfiction books about artists, and a great selection of children's books and art activities. Some great, affordable, takeaways are unframed prints, postcard books, calendars, magnets, stationery, and select jewelry pieces.

Smithsonian Institution

When English chemist James Smithson passed away in 1829, he willed to the United States 105 bags of gold sovereigns to found "at Washington, under the name of the Smithsonian Institution, an establishment for the increase and diffusion of knowledge." This was no small sum of money, in fact, it was his entire estate, totaling around $500,000, which, at the time was one-sixty-sixth of the total budget for the United States. After several long conversations, Congress accepted the gift in 1836, but it wasn't until 1846 that President Polk signed an act of Congress to establish the Smithsonian Institution. The resulting museums are some of the most important in the world, holding troves of artifacts and relics relevant not only to U.S. history, but to the development of human culture as a whole.

Eighteen museums, galleries, gardens, and zoos in DC operate under the **Smithsonian Institution** (administrative offices at 1000 Jefferson Dr. SW, 202/633-1000, www.si.edu) name. Most of them are on the National Mall or within a few blocks. Individual museum hours differ,

---

top to bottom: National Museum of Natural History; cherry blossoms framing the Washington Monument; the courtyard at the National Portrait Gallery but generally they're open 10am-5:30pm daily (except Dec. 25); check to be sure of museum hours. Best of all, they're free, meaning anyone can bask in the "increase and diffusion of knowledge" Smithson envisioned.

The **National Museum of Natural History** and **National Air and Space Museum** are two of the most popular Smithsonian museums. Others include the **Smithsonian Castle** (1000 Jefferson Dr. SW, 202/633-1000, www.si.edu, 8:30am-5:30pm daily, free), **National Museum of American History** (14th St. and Constitution Ave. NW, 202/633-1000, www.americanhistory.si.edu, 10am-5:30pm daily, free), **American Art Museum** (8th St. and F St. NW, 202/633-1000, www.americanart.si.edu, 11:30am-7pm daily, free), **National Museum of African Art** (950 Independence Ave. SW, 202/633-1000, www.africa.si.edu, 10am-5:30pm daily, free), the **National Museum of the American Indian** (4th St. and Independence Ave. SW, 202/633-6644, www.nmai.si.edu, 10am-5:30pm daily, free), the **National Zoo** (3001 Connecticut Ave. NW, 202/633-4888, www.national-zoo.si.edu, 10am-6pm daily Apr.-Oct., 10am-4:30pm daily Nov.-Mar., free), the **Freer Gallery of Art and the Arthur M. Sackler Gallery** (1050 Independence Ave. SW, 202/633-1000, www.asia.si.edu, 10am-5:30pm daily, free), and **The National Portrait Gallery** (8th St. and F St. NW, 202/633-8300, www.npg.si.edu, 11:30am-7pm daily, free), among others.

National Museum of Natural History

The **National Museum of Natural History** (10th St. and Constitution Ave., 202/633-1000, www.mnh.si.edu, 10am-5:30pm daily, closed Christmas Day, open late select dates, free) is just one small part of a larger set of facilities around the United States (and in a few foreign locales) that collect, analyze, and exhibit items that tell the story of our world, inside and out. The museum's holdings are impressive—126 million specimens and artifacts, including 30 million insects, 7 million fish, 4.5 million plants, and 2 million cultural artifacts from around the globe.

Only a small portion of their awesome and extensive collection is on display, but what is shown at the National Museum of Natural History is a wonder. Take a look at the Hope Diamond, a 45.52 carat diamond (it's the size of a walnut) with a long and twisting history that includes a possible curse; it's just one part of a spectacular display of gems. There are also displays on ocean life (including a living coral reef), a butterfly pavilion, mummies from ancient Egypt (including a mummified cat), and rotating displays and exhibits that often include some of the best wildlife and cultural photography from every corner of the globe.

★ National Air and Space Museum

From the moment you walk through the door of the **National Air and Space Museum** (Independence Ave. and 6th St. SW, 202/633-2214, www.airandspace.si.edu, 10am-5:30pm daily, closed Christmas Day, open late select dates, free), you're immersed in the technology and boldness that allowed human kind to take to the sky and explore outer space. Rockets, satellites, and spy planes hang from the ceiling. In each of the 20 or so exhibition halls you'll find everything from the Wright Flyer to space suits to a moon rock some four billion years old that you can touch. There's the Apollo 11 Command Module, Sputnik, Charles Lindbergh's *Spirit of St. Louis* (the first plane to complete a nonstop transatlantic flight), and a collection of WWII aircraft. This is the most popular museum in the United States, seeing more than eight million visitors a year here and at the **Steven F Udvar-Hazy Center** (14390 Air and Space Museum Parkway, Chantilly, Va., about 25 miles west, 703/572-4118, www.airandspace.si.edu, 10am-5:30pm daily, closed Christmas Day, free), so expect company no matter when you visit.

★ United States Holocaust Memorial Museum

Nothing prepares you for a visit to the **Holocaust Memorial Museum** (100 Raoul Wallenberg Pl. SW and Independence Ave., 202/488-0400, www.ushmm.org, 10am-5:20pm daily except Yom Kippur and Christmas Day, free), and in truth, there's little understanding of this historical black mark either before or after a visit. But it's a required sight if for no other reason than the adage "those who don't know history are destined to repeat it" holds more truth than we may like to admit.

The building exterior was designed to resemble the high brick ovens used to dispose of the bodies of millions of European Jews. Inside, exhibits methodically trace the rise of Nazi Germany and the systematic implementation of its policy of genocide. The displays make clear that government officials in the United States and elsewhere were well aware of Hitler's implementation of the "Final Solution" but chose not to act. Visitors witness many depictions of horrific atrocities, but perhaps the most affecting items are the heaps of personal effects the Nazis collected from those they murdered, including piles of shoes, brushes, and hair.

You'll need a timed pass to visit the permanent collection. A limited number are distributed at the museum each morning; otherwise, you can order passes and make reservations for your tour for a nominal fee (www.ushmm.extremetix.com, $1). Allow at least 4-5 hours to visit. The permanent exhibition is not recommended for children under age 11.

The White House

First occupied by John Adams, the mansion at 1600 Pennsylvania Avenue NW was known as the President's House until it was whitewashed to cover smoke damage from the 1814 British burning of the city. It's not nearly as accessible today as it was during Jefferson's time, when the president examined mastodon fossils in the East Room and enthusiastic dairymen would bustle in to deposit huge cheeses. Nevertheless, it's the only chief executive's abode in the world that is open to tourists. When visiting the **White House** (1600 Pennsylvania Ave. NW, 202/456-7041, www.whitehouse.gov, by tour only), don't step across the boundary ropes or make other foolish moves—those friendly folks patrolling the halls can turn serious quickly.

Tours (7:30am-11:30am Tues.-Thurs., 7:30am-1:30pm Fri.-Sat., free) are available, though on a very restricted schedule. For tickets to the self-guided tour, contact your Member of Congress; foreign citizens must submit tour requests through their Washington DC embassy. Requests for tickets can be submitted up to six months in advance and no less than 21 days before your visit. Submit your request early as this is a very popular tour. Also, it *is* the White House, so tours can be canceled on a moment's notice.

United States Capitol

Any first-time visitor to DC should take advantage of the opportunity to peek into the **Capitol** (east end of the National Mall, 202/226-8000, www.visitthecapitol.gov, by tour only) and see our elected congressional officials at work. The small but well-appointed Senate chamber offers each senator a private desk separate from the rest, whereas House representatives are jammed together in long, curved pews. The rest of the building presents its own peculiar charms: halls and rotundas stuffed with statues, and the frenzied frescoes of Constantino Brumidi, whose work was incisively described by Mark Twain as "the delirium tremens of art." A word of warning: Much of the Capitol is off-limits to non-officeholders, and visitors must heed the guidance of Capitol police.

Visiting the Capitol on a guided **tour** (www.tours.visitthecapitol.gov, 8:50am-3:20pm Mon.-Sat., free) is much easier than securing a ticket for a White House tour. You still need to schedule a tour in advance, through your Senator or Representative, or online. There is also a **Visitor Center** (8:30am-4:30pm Mon.-Sat. except Thanksgiving, Christmas, and New Year's Days, and also Inauguration day) at the Capitol. If you're interested in observing the Senate or House of Representatives when they're in session, you can get a pass from your Senator or Representative that will allow you access to the balcony galleries in their respective chambers.

Sightseeing Tours

One of the best ways to see the monuments and museums on the National Mall is by bicycle. Though most of DCs surface streets lack bike lanes (and what city biking novice wants to negotiate that traffic?), around the Mall, you'll find biking easy. **Bike and Roll** (955 L'Enfant Plaza SW, 202/842-2453, www.bikethesites.com, open daily for tours Mar. through the first week of Dec., bike tours $30-45 adults, $20-30 kids, Segway tours $64-74 adults only, call for age and height requirements) leads a number of guided excursions to see the sights and hear tidbits of DC trivia on the Mall via bike and Segway. One of the best tours is the Capital Sites@Nite, which leads you on a three-hour ride to the monuments, memorials, and famous buildings on the Mall. All of these places are lit up at night, so even if you toured them during the day, they change quite dramatically when lit. Other tours in the city lead you around the monuments by day and around to the various Smithsonian buildings, but you can also bike to Mount Vernon or book a personalized tour. Bike and Roll also rents a variety of adult and kids bikes.

Outside the Mall
The Newseum

It's easy to spend hours at the **Newseum** (555 Pennsylvania Ave. NW, 202/292-6100, www.newseum.org, 9am-5pm daily, closed Thanksgiving, Christmas, and New Year's Days, $23 adults, $19 seniors, $14 ages 7-18, free 6 and younger), one of the best museums in DC. Seven floors of interactive exhibits (ever wanted to be a weatherman? Now's your chance) display of some of the most famous newspaper front pages in history as well as artifacts, photographs, news reels, and firsthand accounts, helping you understand the importance of journalism (the so called "fourth estate") and our First Amendment rights.

Downstairs, there's a long section of the Berlin Wall and a guard tower that once watched over it. Upstairs, the 9/11 Gallery contains a huge piece of the spire from the World Trade Center's North Tower and a wall of front pages from every major paper around the globe as they relayed word of the attack; it's an overwhelming exhibit. On the main floor, a gallery containing all of the Pulitzer Prize-winning photographs gets to the heart of what constitutes great journalism.

Inside the excellent **gift shop,** you'll find journalism-related gifts (so, lots of coffee mugs). They also have books of award-winning photography and essays, and headline bloopers. You'll find a whole range of *Anchorman* (with Ron Burgundy, like you needed to be reminded) gifts as well.

The Phillips Collection

The Phillips Collection (1600 21st St. NW, 202/387-2151, www.phillipscollection.org, 10am-5pm Tues.-Sat., 11am-6pm Sun., open until 8:30pm on first Thurs. of the month, museum collection by donation Tues.-Fri., ticketed exhibitions and extended Thurs. hours $12 adults, $10 students and seniors, free 18 and under), America's first museum of modern art, opened in 1921. Housed in a beautiful 1897 Georgian Revival house in the Dupont Circle neighborhood, The Phillips Collection contains some remarkable pieces, with works by Van Gogh, Renoir, Matisse, Cezanne, Winslow Homer, Arthur Dove, Paul Klee, Mark Rothko, Willem de Kooning, Jackson Pollock, and many more. One spectacular painting by Marjorie Phillips, *Night Baseball*, depicts Joe DiMaggio at bat against the Washington Senators and is certainly worth contemplating.

International Spy Museum

Live out your secret agent fantasies at the **International Spy Museum** (800 F St. NW, 202/393-7798, www.spymuseum. org, 10am-6pm daily, $22 adults, $16 seniors, military, and law enforcement, $15 ages 7-11, free 6 and under), where interactive exhibits include the tools used by spies the world over, information on tradecraft, famous spy capers and incidents, and a series of stations where you, under cover as a spy with an assumed name and backstory, have to use what you've learned to evade capture by counter-intelligence agents. When I visited, there

was a display of Bond memorabilia, each of his villainous counterparts, and even one of his cars. The **Spy Museum Store** (order online at www.spymuseumstore. org, admission not required) has a ton of fun toys, games, and "spy" gadgets; clothes; books; and keepsakes. Gadgets include things like camera ties, secret message kits, and rearview glasses, the essentials for a budding spy.

National Portrait Gallery

The **National Portrait Gallery** (8th and F Sts. NW, 202/633-8300, www.npg.si.edu, 11:30am-7pm daily, closed Christmas Day, free) tells the story of America through the individuals that helped shape its history and culture. Exhibitions of portraits, sculptures, and busts include ones dedicated to key figures and events from 1600-1900, 20th-century Americans, performing artists, sports figures, pop-culture icons, and presidents. The National Portrait Gallery is connected to the **Smithsonian American**

on duty at the Tomb of the Unknown Soldier

Art Museum (8th and F Sts. NW, 202/633-7970, www.americanart.si.edu, 11:30am-7pm daily, closed Christmas Day, free), where you can see some absolutely astounding pieces of fine and folk art. Between the two buildings is the lovely and restful Kogod Courtyard (where there's free Wi-Fi and decent coffee).

Sightseeing Tours

City Segway Tours (502 23rd St. NW, 202/626-0017, www.dc.citysegwaytours.com, $65-75) zips you around to the museums, monuments, and memorials on those fun little two-wheeled vehicles. If you've never ridden one, this is a good place to try it. They're easy to get the hang of.

DC Ducks (Union Station, 50 Massachusetts Ave. NE, 855/323-8257, www.dcducks.com, $39 adults, $29 kids 12 and younger) take you on a tour of the city in these strange World War II amphibious vehicles we call "ducks." Your driver will be part historian and part comic, which makes the ride lots of fun. At the end, you'll head into the Potomac River to ride to a point near National Airport.

Old Town Trolley Tours (Union Station, 50 Massachusetts Ave. NE, 888/910-8687, www.trolleytours.com, $39-45 adults, $29 kids age 4-12, free 3 and under) offers hop-on, hop-off sightseeing that takes you all around the city, making 20 stops along the way. Stops include Arlington National Cemetery, the National Cathedral, Georgetown, the National Mall, and a ton of monuments.

The **Potomac Riverboat Company** (703/684-0580 or 877/511-2628, www.potomacriverboatco.com) has a small fleet that plies the waters around the capital. There is a 40-minute narrated sightseeing tour to Alexandria (hourly during the day Mar.-Aug. and on weekends Sept.-Oct., $12 adults, $6 children); another boat runs between the Alexandria and Georgetown docks (every 1-2 hours daily Mar.-Sept. and on weekends in Oct., $24 adults, $12 children round-trip, with half-price one-way tickets also available). You can also take a cruise to Mount Vernon and Alexandria, Va. (departing from Alexandria at 10:30am, the Gaylord National Hotel in Md. at 11am, and National Harbor, Md., at 11:10am, $14-41 adults, $7-21 ages 6-11).

★ Arlington National Cemetery

The country's second-oldest national cemetery, **Arlington National Cemetery** (across Memorial Bridge from the Lincoln Memorial, Arlington, Va., 877/907-8585, www.arlingtoncemetery.mil, 8am-7pm daily Apr.-Sept., 8am-5pm daily Oct.-Mar., free, parking $1.50 for the first three hours, $2.50/hour thereafter), spreads over 624 acres of rolling hills across the Potomac from DC. The resting place for more than 400,000 active duty service members, veterans, their families, heads of state, and others whose service to our country is unheralded, Arlington is a beautiful and somber place to visit.

The gravesite of John F. Kennedy and the elaborate Changing of the Guard at the Tomb of the Unknown Soldier attract visitors wishing to pay their respects to the sacrifices made by the individuals interred here.

History

Arlington National Cemetery began as an 1,100-acre plantation owned by George Washington Parke Custis, grandson of Martha Washington and adopted son of George Washington. The centerpiece was Arlington House, built as a memorial to our first president. In 1857, the property came into the hands of Custis' daughter, Mary, and her husband, General Robert E. Lee. When General Lee accepted command of Virginia's army at the onset of the Civil War, he resigned his commission with the U.S. Army and left, never to return to Arlington House. After a brief occupation by Virginia militiamen, the house and estate were taken and held by Union forces.

In 1864, the 1,100-acre estate was confiscated by the federal government when Mary couldn't appear in person to pay the property taxes. Quartermaster Gen. Montgomery Meigs, a Georgian who had remained loyal to the Union, considered Lee the worst kind of traitor and came up with a scathing revenge: the burial of Union dead, literally, in Lee's backyard. Meigs crossed the Potomac to personally oversee the interment of the first Union soldiers in Mary's rose garden. Eventually, 16,000 soldiers were buried in the fields around Arlington House.

After the war, Lee's grandson, George Washington Custis Lee, sued the U.S. government for possession of the estate and won after taking the case to the Supreme Court. In 1883, he sold it back to the government for $150,000 (more than $3 million in today's dollar). Two hundred surrounding acres were set aside to start the cemetery.

Visiting the Cemetery

Your first stop should be the **Welcome Center** (by the cemetery entrance, 877/907-8585, www.arlingtoncemetery. mil, 8am-7pm daily Apr.-Sept., 8am-5pm daily Oct.-Mar., closed Christmas Day), where you can view displays detailing the history of the cemetery, and, more importantly, grab a map. You'll need it, as the cemetery can be confusing, and it's a hike between commonly visited sites—namely the Kennedy graves and the Tomb of the Unknown Soldier. **ANC Tours** (202/488-1012, www.anctours.com, from 8:30am-6:30pm daily Apr.-Sept, 8:30am-4:30pm daily Oct.-Mar., $9 adults, $4.75 ages 3-11, $8 seniors), by Martz Gray Line, takes a small "bus" to the major spots in the cemetery. Tickets are available online or at the Welcome Center. If it's hot, if you're tired, or if you're traveling with little ones or seniors, the tour is a great idea.

The most visited spot in the cemetery is the Kennedy graves. Situated on a grassy knoll that has magnificent views of the National Mall across the Potomac are the graves of President **John F. Kennedy,** his wife **Jacqueline Kennedy Onassis,** and their two infant children, with an **Eternal Flame** burning at their heads. Nearby are the graves of Senators **Robert** and **Ted Kennedy.**

On the hilltop above the Kennedys sits **Arlington House** (703/235-1530, www.nps.gov/arho, 9:30am-4:30pm daily, free), the Greek Revival mansion that Robert E. Lee described as the spot "where my affection and attachments are more strongly placed than at any other place in the world." The house was transferred to the care of the National Park Service in 1933 and filled almost to its 12-foot ceilings with Lee-era antiques and reproductions. Today the Memorial Bridge heads straight from Arlington House toward the Lincoln Memorial in a symbolic link between the two former adversaries. Pierre Charles L'Enfant, Revolutionary War veteran and designer of the capital, was reburied in front of the house in 1909.

Look for the white marble **Memorial Amphitheater** and pass behind it to reach the **Tomb of the Unknown Soldier.** This tomb holds the remains of unidentified soldiers from World War I, World War II, and the Korean War. Dating back to 1926, the tomb was built from more than 50 tons of white Yule marble from Colorado. Guards from the Army's 3rd Infantry, called the Old Guard, keep a constant vigil. These tomb sentinels march 21 unerring steps back and forth, then snap their heels and recouch their rifles at every turn. Crowds gather for the **changing of the guard** (every 30 minutes Apr.-Sept., every hour throughout the night and during winter) and watch in awed silence as the on-duty officer inspects and gives orders to the sentinel going on duty and the one coming off. For a moment, they march in unison, looking like reflections of each other. You may be wondering about the Vietnam War. The tomb also held that unknown Vietnam War veteran until 1998, when DNA evidence revealed his identity as Lt. Michael Blassie, an Air Force pilot shot down in 1972. Blassie was disinterred and reburied closer to home.

Two more memorials of note are worth seeing. The **Women in Service Memorial** (www.womensmemorial.org), at the entrance to the cemetery, pays tribute to the women who have served in all five armed services as well as the affiliated women's auxiliaries like the WAVES and WACS of World War II. The **U.S. Marine Corps War Memorial** (www.nps.gov/gwmp) depicts in bronze the iconic photograph of a group of marines raising the American flag on Iwo Jima in World War II and honors all marines who've given their lives in service to the United States since the inception of the Corps.

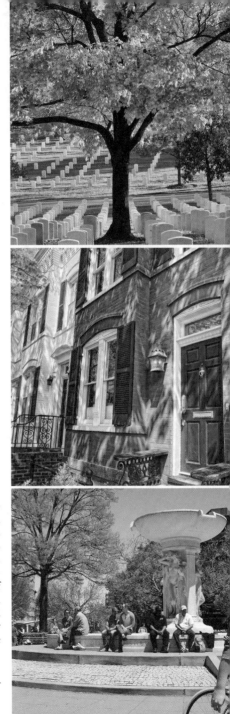

top to bottom: Arlington National Cemetery; colorful homes in Georgetown; Dupont Circle

Mount Vernon

Just 15 miles southwest of DC is **Mount Vernon** (3200 Mount Vernon Memorial Hwy., Mount Vernon, Va., 703/780-2000, www.mountvernon.org, 9am-5pm daily, $17 adults, $16 seniors, $8 ages 6-11, free under 5), the riverfront plantation of George Washington. The property includes Washington's 1735 manor; acres of manicured gardens and wooded grounds; outbuildings and working building for the plantation; and the tombs of George and Martha Washington. From the bluff nearly 200 feet above the Potomac River, the mansion overlooks the countryside of Maryland. A few miles west are Washington's distillery and gristmill. In 1799, Washington's distillery was the largest in the country, producing nearly 11,000 gallons of whiskey.

In the mansion and Donald W. Reynolds Museum and Education Center are impressive collections of furnishings and artifacts, including the key to the Bastille and even some of Washington's false teeth. You'll see for yourself (you read it here first!) that they're not made of wood.

A variety of themed tours are available, including garden tours, a tour about slave life, and a tour detailing canine life at Mount Vernon. From mid-March into fall, you can take a **Potomac River Tour** ($10 adults, $6 ages 6-11, free 5 and under) with the **Potomac Riverboat Company** (703/684-0580 or 877/511-2628, www.potomacriverboatco.com).

Guided bus tours from **Gray Line** (202/289-1995, www.grayline.com, from $55) and **On Board Tours** (301/839-5261, www.washingtondctours.onboardtours.com, Mon.-Fri. $80 adults, $70 kids; Sat.-Sun. $90 adults, $80 kids) will bring you to Mount Vernon and Alexandria. Bikers can pedal to the estate on the 18-mile long **Mount Vernon Trail,** though the 36 miles round-trip from Arlington to Mount Vernon is taxing. By car, take the George Washington Memorial Parkway, which passes right by Arlington National Cemetery and Reagan National Airport, along the Potomac, through Alexandria, and right to Mount Vernon. **Potomac Riverboat Company** (703/684-0580 or 877/511-2628, www.potomacriverboatco.com, $41 adults, $21 ages 6-11, Mount Vernon admission included) offers tours of the Potomac with a four-hour stopover at Mount Vernon.

Entertainment

Nightlife

Bars and Clubs

ChurchKey (1337 14th St. NW, 202/567-2576, www.churchkeydc.com, 4pm-1am Mon.-Thurs., 4pm-2am Fri., noon-2am Sat., 11:30am-1am Sun.), upstairs from Birch & Barley, serves a small menu of tasty snacks and small plates, but it's the beer that brought you here. They have five cask ales, 50 beers on draft, and 500 bottles at any given time, and they've designed their beer menu with headings like 'Fruit & Spice," "Roast," "Tart & Funky," so that you can easily find a beer you'll like. I prefer dark, heavy beers or sours, lambics, and wild ales, and ChurchKey has plenty to offer someone with my palate. They also have an awesome array of IPAs, lagers, and ales.

Bourbon (2321 18th St. NW, 202/332-0800, www.bourbondc.com, 5pm-11pm Tues.-Sat., 4pm-9pm Sun., brunch 11am-4pm Sat.-Sun.) is a dining saloon, so it's not open late, but it does have a damn impressive selection of bourbon. Of the hundred or so bottles they keep, you can spend anywhere from $5-50 for a one-ounce pour. My advice: either go for it and pick a bourbon or whiskey you're not likely to find again, price be damned; or tell the bartender what you like and how much you have to spend, and go on his or her recommendation. Either way, you won't be sorry.

Number Nine (1435 P St. NW, 202/986-0999, www.numberninedc.com, 5pm-late Mon.-Sat., 3pm-late Sun., happy hour 5pm-9pm daily) is a chic gay bar in the heart of Logan Circle. The second floor (cheekily called 9 1/2) is a video bar

Day Trip to Old Town Alexandria

For a great day trip from DC, visit **Mount Vernon**, the home of our first president, then stop in **Alexandria** (www.visitalexandriava.com) on the way back for dinner and shopping. In Alexandria, you'll find a charming downtown, a lovely waterfront, and an impressive collection of shops, restaurants, and sights. The center of it all is charming Old Town Alexandria, which stretches back a few blocks from the Potomac River.

Grab a bite to eat at **Gadsby's Tavern** (134 N. Royal St., 703/746-4242, www.gadsbystavernrestaurant.com, lunch 11:30am-3pm Mon.-Sat., dinner nightly 5:30pm-10pm, brunch 11am-3pm Sun., lunch $10-15, dinner $22-30), where George Washington celebrated his 66th birthday; **Taverna Cretekou** (818 King St., 703/548-8688, www.tavernacretekou.com, 11:30am-2:30pm and 5pm-10pm Tues.-Fri., noon-10:30pm Sat., 11am-3pm and 5pm-9:30pm Sun., $12-20), a Greek restaurant with lovely outdoor seating; or **Caphe Banh Mi** (407 Cameron St., 703/549-0800, www.caphebanhmi.com, 11am-3pm and 5pm-9pm Mon.-Fri., 11am-9pm Sat.-Sun., under $10), a Vietnamese restaurant with a killer banh mi.

There are a number of high-end shops and boutiques to check out. **Dash's of Old Town** (1114 King St., 703/299-4015, www.dashsofoldtown.com, 11am-6pm Wed.-Sat., noon-5pm Sun., closed Mon. and Tues.) sells fine Italian suits and men's clothing; **Bishop Boutique** (815-B King St., 571/312-0042, www.bishopboutique.com, 10am-7pm Mon.-Sat., 11am-6pm Sun.) has shoes and accessories; **An American in Paris** (1225 King St., Suite 1, 703/519-8234, www.anamericaninparisoldtown.com, 11am-8pm Mon.-Fri., 11am-7pm Sat.-Sun.) is filled with one-of-a kind, stylish pieces of clothing. Consignment shops include **Mint Condition** (103 S. Asaph St., 703/836-6468, www.shopmintcondition.com, 11am-7pm Tues.-Sat., noon-6pm Sun.) and **Current Boutique** (1009 King St., 703/549-2272, www.currentboutique.com, noon-8pm Mon.-Fri., 11am-8pm Sat., 11am-6pm Sun.).

Other spots to check out are the **Torpedo Factory Art Center** (105 N. Union St., 703/838-4565, www.torpedofactory.org, 10am-6pm Fri.-Wed., 10am-9pm Thurs., individual studio hours vary), a former torpedo factory filled with galleries, studios, and workshop spaces; and any of the dozen galleries and studios along the waterfront and a block or two back.

where they show select sports, but more often movies and music videos by the club's VJs. On the first floor you'll find a plush, well-appointed, modern bar with extensive seating options. The bartenders know their stuff, and though you can go up and order a classic cocktail, it's more fun to try a bartender's choice or one of the house specials.

Live Music
At **Columbia Station** (2325 18th St. NW, 202/462-6040, www.columbiastationdc.com, 5pm-2am Mon.-Thurs., 5pm-3am Fri., 11am-3am Sat., 11am-2am Sun.) in the Adams Morgan neighborhood, you can hear live jazz every night. It's a popular spot and known for staging some of the top regional jazz acts, so check their schedule and pick a show.

You can't write about live music in DC without including the **9:30 Club** (815 V St. NW, 202/265-0930, www.930.com, box office open noon-7pm Mon.-Fri., 6pm-11pm weekend show nights, show times vary), DC's most popular small venue for rock bands and artists from a range of genres. The stage is visible from just about everywhere in the club, and with four bars, you never have to wait long for a drink. My advice is to arrive early and find a spot up by the stage so you can check out a few songs up close. Don't be alarmed if you see kids; 9:30 is an all-ages club (except for specified shows).

Black Cat (1811 14th St. NW,

202/667-4490, www.blackcatdc.com, box office 8pm-midnight, shows vary) is a fantastic venue for live music, stand-up comics, and more. Bands tend toward the indie-rock side of things, and you'll catch both known and up-and-coming acts here. This place is cash only.

Madam's Organ (2461 18th St. NW, 202/667-5370, www.madamsorgan.com, 5pm-2am Sun.-Thurs., 5pm-3am Fri.-Sat.) features blues, R&B, rock, bluegrass, salsa, and just about every genre of music under the sun every night of the week. Four floors, five bars, and an enormous mural of the Madam herself on the outside of the building make this place hard to miss. Redheads take note: they love a redhead here, so there's always a half-price drink special just for you.

Performing Arts
The John F. Kennedy Center for the Performing Arts
The crown jewel of the DC performing arts scene is without a doubt **The John F. Kennedy Center for the Performing Arts** (2700 F St. NW, 202/467-4600 or 800/444-1324, www.kennedy-center.org). You can go on a free **tour** (10am-5pm Mon.-Fri., 10am-1pm Sat.-Sun.) of the Kennedy Center, visiting the Center's three grand performance halls, the Hall of States and Hall of Nations, and ending on the rooftop terrace. You have the option of dropping in for a walk-in tour or reserving a group tour (if you're traveling with 20 of your closest friends).

The tours are nice, but the best way to see the Kennedy Center is to take in a performance. Various theatrical performances, concerts, and events occur throughout the year, so check their calendar to see who and what will be there while you're in town.

The Kennedy Center is the home to the **National Symphony Orchestra (NSO)** (www.kennedy-center.org/nso), founded in 1931 and consistently performing 175 or so concerts a year. The **Washington National Opera** (www.kennedy-center.

org/wno) also calls the Kennedy Center home, as does **The Suzanne Farrell Ballet** (www.kennedy-center.org/programs/ballet/farrell). Ticket prices vary by performance, but it's a good idea to reserve tickets well ahead of time if you're interested in taking in a major production. If you're more inclined to a free performance, which could be anything from a concert to a comic to a dance troupe, check out the **Millennium Stage,** which hosts free events nightly at 6pm.

Other Venues
Probably the most famous of all theaters in DC, even the United States, is **Ford's Theatre** (511 10th St. NW, 202/347-4833, www.fordstheatre.org). Here, the assassin John Wilkes Booth shot president Abraham Lincoln who was sitting in his box enjoying a production of *Our American Cousin*. Take in a performance here and sit within feet of that infamous balcony box, or **tour** (9am-4:30pm daily, free) the theater with a guide, a park ranger, or on a self-directed tour. Check their calendar for exact tour times; tickets are free at the door or you can get advance tickets ($2.50) by calling the theater.

The elegant **National Theatre** (1321 Pennsylvania Ave. NW, 202/628-6161, www.thenationaldc.org) is the third oldest theater in the country, and the longest in continuous operation in DC. Just two days after opening its doors on December 7, 1835, they staged their first production, *Hamlet*. Plays like *West Side Story* and *Hello, Dolly!* premiered here, and acting greats like John Barrymore, Vivian Leigh, and Jack Lemmon have graced this stage. If you want to catch a show here, check the schedule to see what's playing, and know that the balcony seats are quite steep and narrow, so you may want to spring for floor seats.

If you're a fan of Shakespeare or just exceptional theater, then the **Folger Theatre** (201 E. Capitol St. SE, 202/544-7077, www.folger.edu) and **Shakespeare**

Theatre Company (450 7th St. NW, 202/547-1122 or 877/487-8849, www. shakespearetheatre.org) deliver exactly what you're looking for. The Folger Theatre is an extension of the Folger Shakespeare Library, and they stage several performances each year of works by the Bard and other fantastic playwrights. At the Shakespeare Theatre Company they too stage plays by Shakespeare as well as excellent contemporary playwrights.

The Capitol Steps (www.capsteps.com) comedy troupe likes to say they "put the 'mock' in Democracy," and they do. Very well. The Capitol Steps are equal-opportunity offenders, performing a 90-minute musical satire that targets the funniest situations, sound bites, and personalities from either side of the aisle. Songs have included "Obama Mia," "Ballad of the Queen Berets," and other pointed political tunes. It's all in good fun and they seek only to point out the absurdity around us. In DC, shows go on every Friday and Saturday night at the Ronald Reagan Building (1300 Pennsylvania Ave. NW, 202/312-1555; tickets: 202/397-7328, 703/573-7328, or 410/547-7328, www. ticketmaster.com, $40.50).

To see some of the best stand-up comics in the nation, head over to the **DC Improv** (1140 Connecticut Ave. NW, 202/296-7008, www.dcimprov.com). This comedy club opened in 1992 and showcased several notable newcomers (Ellen DeGeneres, Dave Chappelle, and Brian Regan, to name a few) to kick off a long and laugh-filled tenure as *the* place to see live comedy in DC. The top national comics (think Todd Glass, Bill Burr, Dave Attell) stop here and play, as do rising stars in the comedy world. Buy your tickets well ahead of time as the major comics tend to sell out fast.

Festivals and Events

In spring, DC becomes a stunning pink palate as millions of blossoms on the city's famous cherry trees open for the world to admire. The **National Cherry Blossom Festival** (877/442-5666, www. nationalcherryblossomfestival.org) commemorates the 1912 gift of 3,000 cherry trees from the Mayor of Tokyo to the city of Washington DC. The first two trees were planted by First Lady Helen Herron Taft and Viscountess Chinda, wife of the Japanese ambassador, on the north bank of the Tidal Basin in West Potomac Park. This three-week festival usually begins around the third week of March, and includes musical entertainment, fireworks, the Blossom Kite Festival, a parade, a Japanese street festival, the crowning of the Cherry Blossom Queen, and more parties than you can count. It's the biggest annual event in DC.

If you're looking for one of the premier **Independence Day** (www.nps.gov/foju, www.july4thparade.com) celebrations, you've come to the right city. Every July 4, an ocean of people flood the National Mall for a parade, food, live music, and, of course, fireworks. Events start bright and early with historical reenactors reading the Declaration of Independence at the National Archives. Then there's a parade along Constitution Avenue. Then there's *A Capital Fourth*, a huge concert on the Capitol's West Lawn. And the fireworks. If you can't get a seat on the National Mall, don't worry, there are other great spots across the river in Arlington, where you'll have a broad view of the monuments lit up and the fireworks exploding overhead. Try the hill near the Marine Corps War Memorial or the grassy slope by the Air Force Memorial; those are prime spots.

Besides the Cherry Blossom Festival and Independence Day celebrations, no DC event is as well known as the **National Christmas Tree Lighting and Pageant of Peace** (www.thenationaltree. org). Somewhere around the second week of December, the president lights the National Christmas Tree on the Ellipse in front of the White House. The first national tree was lit with some 2,500 bulbs by President Coolidge in 1923; today, the tree uses LED lights numbering in the tens of thousands. On the day of the lighting, there's a concert of both musical and choral acts. Along with the lighting of the tree is the Pageant of Peace, a four-week holiday celebration. Trees decorated by every state and territory are lit up around town, and there are a wide range of concerts, gatherings, and to-dos.

Shopping

In the heart of the Capitol Hill neighborhood is the **Eastern Market** (225 7th St. SE, 202/698-5253, www.easternmarket-dc.org, 7am-7pm Tues.-Fri., 7am-6pm Sat., 9am-5pm Sun.), where you'll find everything from flowers and fresh produce, to bakery products, butchers, cheese, pasta, and seafood. This market has been a DC fixture for more than 130 years, and on weekdays, you'll find it to be a gourmet farmers market, but on the weekends it comes alive with music, even more farmers and food purveyors, as well as artists, craftspeople, and antique sellers.

Tiny Jewel Box (1147 Connecticut Ave., 202/393-2747, www.tinyjewelbox. com, 10am-5:30pm Mon.-Sat.) has a fantastic slogan: "If it's not special, it's not here." The store started tiny, opening its 100-square-foot storefront in 1930, selling antique jewelry. Now it has four floors of outstanding jewelry and gifts. You'll still find plenty of antique and estate jewelry pieces, but now that selection is augmented by a floor of current and trend-setting designers; the third floor features watches and men's accessories; and the top floor holds all sorts of desk accessories, pens and pencils, and other corporate-type gifts.

At **Union Station** (50 Massachusetts Ave. NE, 202/289-1908, www.union-stationdc.com, 10am-9pm Mon.-Sat., noon-6pm Sun.) there are more than a few shops worth your time. Names you'll recognize—like Papyrus, H&M, and The Body Shop, to name a few—mix with

DC-only shops. **America!** (202/842-0540) sells mementos, clothing items, keepsakes, home decor, and gifts featuring all of the DC iconography you can imagine. It's the one-stop tourist gift shop for DC. **Appalachian Spring** (202/682-0505, www.appalachianspring.com) sells wonderful handmade gifts. You'll find jewelry, art glass, elegant wooden boxes, birdhouses, pottery, and scarves, all made by regional artisans and craftspeople.

While you're in **Georgetown** (www.georgetowndc.com/explore/fashion), be sure to wander a bit. You'll find more than 150 fashion stores ranging from local boutiques to well-known brands; 70 or so home decor, art, and design shops; 40 salons, spas, and beauty-related spots to visit; and countless other shops. Every Sunday, the **Georgetown Flea Market** (1819 35th St. NW, www.georgetownfleamarket.com, 8am-4pm Sun.) brings in bargain hunters, browsers, and sharp-eyed shoppers. You'll find a lot of antiques, and a few years ago, a midcentury modern furniture dealer bought a pair of matching tables for $65. The tables proved to be rare prototypes by Isamu Noguchi. He loaned one to the Noguchi Museum in New York and sold the other for $132,000. Keep your eyes peeled: you may find the next $100,000 table with a $20 price tag.

Chocolate Moose (1743 L St. NW, 202/463-0992, www.chocolatemoosedc. com, 10am-6pm Mon.-Fri.) claims they've been "serving weirdly sophisticated Washingtonians since 1978." Think gag gifts and potty humor, like Spencer's Gifts, but classy. They've got oddball toys (solar-powered, waving, Queen Elizabeth figurines); interesting jewelry and accessories (think winged pig on a tote bag); kid toys; books from The Oatmeal (if you don't know him, you should); rejected New Yorker cartoons (they're funnier than the ones that made it); and candy, including Belgian chocolates and truffles.

If you're into vintage boutiques, you must stop at **Junction** (1510 U St. NW,

202/483-0261, www.junctionwdc.com, 3pm-7pm Wed., noon-7pm Thurs.-Sat., noon-5pm Sun.). This store is packed with vintage clothing for men and women, though you will find a few contemporary pieces thrown in for good measure. Jewelry, housewares, shoes, and accessories round out the shop's offerings. The buyers here are quite selective, so you'll find a lot of great vintage pieces, with new ones arriving every day or two.

Every museum in DC has a gift shop. Most of them are good, but a few are exceptional, especially those at the **International Spy Museum** (admission not required) and **Newseum** (admission not required, tell the front desk you're there for the gift shop), as well as the **Gallery Shops** at the **National Gallery of Art** (free).

Recreation
Biking
One of the more popular bike trails is the **Capital Crescent Trail** (202/234-4874, www.cctrail.org), a former railroad bed that leads from the western end of Water Street NW in Georgetown, DC, (right underneath the Whitehurst Freeway and Key Bridge) to Silver Spring, Md. The trail is mostly paved, though there is a crushed stone section, but it's nothing to worry about. For the first few miles, it follows the Potomac on a beautiful little northwestern course before it moves northeast toward Silver Spring. Be aware, the trail is mixed use, so you'll see runners here; be sure to use proper etiquette. Other popular bike trails are found within **Rock Creek Park** (3435 Williamsburg Lane NW, park headquarters 202/895-6000, visitor information 202/895-6070, www.nps.gov/rocr, dawn to dusk daily, free).

Capital Bikeshare (877/430-2453, www.capitalbikeshare.com) has more than 2,500 bikes at unstaffed stations around the city. The bikes are anything but sexy—they're not ugly, but they're built for function. It's an interesting concept and one that's gaining traction here and in other cities. To ride, you have to become a member (sign up online) and select your plan. Visitors will want a 24-hour ($7) or three-day ($15) pass, then you'll have to pay the rental fee on bikes (first 30 minutes free, $1.50 each additional 30 minutes). **Bike Washington** (www.bikewashington.org) has some great maps, routes, and tips for bicycling the city, so if you're doing a freestyle tour, you may want to get some ideas here before starting out. In addition to leading guided bike tours, **Bike and Roll** (955 L'Enfant Plaza SW, 202/842-2453, www.bikethesites.com, bike rental: adults $16-30/two hours, kids $10/two hours) rents a variety of adult and kids bikes.

Parks
Washington DC is one of the fittest cities in the nation, thanks to a top-notch series of parks, trails, and activities in and around downtown. One of the most recognizable is **Rock Creek Park** (3435 Williamsburg Lane NW, park headquarters 202/895-6000, visitor information 202/895-6070, www.nps.gov/rocr, dawn to dusk daily, free), one of the largest forested urban parks in the nation. You'll see a bevy of animals—white-tailed deer, foxes, rabbits, squirrels, raccoons, hundreds of bird species, and even coyotes—living in the remarkably thick forest that covers the park's 2,700-acres. Rock Creek Park sits on the fall line between Virginia's piedmont and the Atlantic coastal plain, and the park shows the dramatic changes in geology as a result. In the rocky northern end you'll find steep little canyons, hillsides, and gullies. The southern end, closer to the city, eases into a broad, flat plane as Rock Creek empties into the Potomac River. There are many miles of **hiking** and **biking** trails, and it's quite popular for these activities. There's also a **Nature Center** (9am-5pm Wed.-Sun., closed Thanksgiving, Christmas, and New Year's Day, and July 4), where many ranger-led activities begin; an equestrian

program through **Rock Creek Park Horse Center** (5100 Glover Rd., 202/362-0117, www.rockcreekhorsecenter.com, $40); **tennis** (16th St. and Kennedy St. NW, $12-20/hour); **golf** (202/882-7332, www.golfdc.com, par 72, $25-30 with pull cart, rental clubs available); and plenty of space to just relax in nature.

Theodore Roosevelt Island (George Washington Pkwy. between Key and Roosevelt Bridges, 703/289-2500, www.nps.gov/this, dawn to dusk daily, free) is an even bigger break from the noise and modernity of DC than Rock Creek Park. This thickly forested island has beautiful city views, but turn your back and you're in the woods. Three short trails lead around the park, giving you the chance to walk on something other than concrete. Though the island is heavily forested and looks very natural, you may be surprised to learn that it was once home to a mansion where one of Virginia's oldest families lived, then a Union field hospital during the Civil War, at which time the whole of the forest was felled. Thanks to Frederick Law Olmstead, who planted close to 30,000 trees here and removed all nonnative flora, the island looks like virgin forest.

Spectator Sports

Located in the heart of Chinatown, the **Verizon Center** (601 F St. NW, 202/628-3200, www.verizoncenter.com) is not your typical sports venue. Home to the **NHL's Washington Capitals** (www.capitals.nhl.com), the **NBA's Wizards** (www.nba.com/wizards), and the **WNBA's Mystics** (www.wnba.com/mystics), the center features a video center showcasing historic moments in athletics, a sportscasters' hall of fame, and a gift shop; they also hold a variety of concerts and other performances here.

Washington's NFL franchise (301/276-6800, www.redskins.com)—officially called the Washington Redskins, a name that many find offensive and that some publications refuse to use—moved out of DC in 1996 and now play their games at **FedEx Field** (1600 Fedex Way 13, Kent, MD). Washington fans are rabid and loyal, hoping every year for a winning season. For some reason, this team gets it together for a season, then falls apart for the next few seasons; even so, the 79,000-seat FedEx Field is packed on game day.

The **Washington Nationals** (202/675-6287, www.washington.nationals.mlb.com), known locally as the "Nats," are the city's Major League Baseball franchise. The team plays at **Nationals Park** (1500 South Capitol St. SE, 202/675-6287, www.washington.nationals.mlb.com/was/ballpark) in southeastern DC, a great stadium that shows off the personality of the city in both its architecture and its attitude.

Robert F. Kennedy Memorial Stadium (2400 E. Capitol St. SE, 202/249-3000, www.eventsdc.com/venues/RFKstadium.aspx), known locally as "RFK," was once home to Washington's NFL franchise, but it now hosts the city's pro soccer team, **DC United** (202/587-5465, www.dcunited.com), as well as rock concerts and the occasional outdoor convention. DC United is the most successful sports franchise in town, having won two U.S. Open World Cups and four Major League Soccer Cups since the team's founding in 1995.

Accommodations

Finding a place to stay in or around DC is not hard: There are hundreds of hotels, inns, and bed-and-breakfasts. The problem is price. This is an expensive city, and the hotels here are especially expensive. Lucky for you, the city has a great public transportation system and is easy to navigate with the most rudimentary of maps. With that in mind, and thinking of the road trip ahead, I looked at lodging on the more affordable end of the spectrum.

Outside the Mall
$100-150
The Taft Bridge Inn (20070 Wyoming Ave. NW, 202/687-2007, www.taftbridgeinn.

com, $99-189) is a restored turn-of-the-century Georgian mansion within walking distance of the National Zoo, Adams Morgan neighborhood, and Dupont Circle Metro Station. They offer free Wi-Fi; parking is an additional $18 a day. The Inn is in need of a facelift, but at this price in this location, it's hard to go wrong. For rooms on the lower end of the price range, you do have to share a bathroom with other guests.

In what used to be an apartment building overlooking Rock Creek Park, the **Windsor Park Hotel** (2116 Kalorama Rd. NW, 202/483-7700, $100-153) offers guests beautiful city or park views. More than that, the Windsor Park offers convenience, as Dupont Circle and the shops, restaurants, and bars there are within easy walking distance.

Adam's Inn (1746 Lanier Pl. NW, 202/745-3600 or 800/578-6807, www.adamsinn.com, $109-179) consists of three brick townhouses and a carriage house hidden away on a leafy residential street two blocks from the heart of Adams Morgan. Built around 1913, the inn has a definite Victorian feel, with some modern touches. The common rooms are equipped with TV and computers for Internet access. A lavish continental breakfast is included in the price of your stay. A total of 26 rooms are available. As elsewhere in Adams Morgan, parking is limited, though there are four spots available at the Inn for $25 a night.

Staying at the **Hotel Harrington** (436 11th St. NW, 800/424-8532 or 202/628-8140, www.hotel-harrington.com, $135-199), you may think you're Batman (their logo is more than a little caped crusaderish), but don't expect the lavish digs Bruce Wayne would stay in. Here, the rooms are much smaller and not nearly so elegant. What makes this place special, though, is the location. It's just a couple of blocks from the Smithsonian museums and the National Mall, and that plus the price, makes it a popular spot for budget-conscious international travelers. Parking is $16 per day at a garage four blocks away.

$150-200

Downtown DC's ★ **Morrison-Clark Historic Inn & Restaurant** (1015 L St. NW, 202/898-1200 or 800/332-7898, www.morrisonclark.com, $179-224) is only a block from the convention center and close to a host of restaurants and sights. This Victorian mansion was built during the Civil War and is something of an anomaly in a neighborhood busy with office buildings. Rooms here are elegant—tall ceilings, ornate crown moldings, antique bedding and furniture, much of it true to the period of the Inn—but not ostentatious. As of late 2014, the hotel is expanding, pushing out into a neighboring space and growing by more than 43,000 square feet, an exciting development for a lovely and affordable inn.

Over $200

★ **The Hamilton Crowne Plaza Hotel** (1001 14th St. NW, 202/682-0111 or 877/227-6963, www.hamiltonhoteldc.com, $235-315) has more than 300 guest rooms that are cozy, both in size and appointments, but they're so comfortable that you won't mind the diminutive size. Larger rooms are available in the Guest Suites and on the Concierge Level if you'd like to spread out a little. One interesting offering of The Hamilton is a women's only floor catering to female business travelers. The Hamilton's Concierge is excellent and quick with suggestions for how to make the most of your visit to DC. Additionally, the hotel is convenient to the Metro train and bus lines and adjacent to a park that's lined with food trucks each day for lunch.

At the **Embassy Circle Guest House** (2224 R St. NW, 202/232-7744 or 877/232-7744, www.dcinns.com, $240-325), you'll stay in 1 of 11 rooms in a stunning house that's been restored to its original beauty. This B&B goes out of its way to deliver a high-end hospitality experience. The

B&B is staffed all day every day, and your hosts are quick with suggestions that will give you a DC local's experience. Georgetown and its abundance of shops and restaurants is only a short walk away, and Embassy Row is nearby.

Arlington
$150-200
The ★ **Arlington Court Suites Hotel** (1200 North Courthouse Rd., Arlington, Va., 703/524-4000, www.arlingtoncourthotel.com, $169-189) has comfortable, monstrously spacious suites in a location that's convenient to the Metro and just a few minutes ride to the heart of DC. The smallest suites are ample and the largest more than double the biggest rooms in DC (excepting, of course, those coveted Presidential Suites). In early 2014, they underwent a little freshen-up project in the hotel, changing small things for the sake of aesthetics and comfort, though they didn't undertake any major structural projects. It's common to see groups of business travelers here, some wearing military uniforms.

Food
Washington DC is a foodie town. Between the unbelievable array of international cuisine and ethnic restaurants, there are spots catering to vegetarians and vegans, burger fiends, those searching for the best pizza (outside of New York), farm-to-fork fanatics, and barbecue aficionados.

Outside the Mall
Burgers
I don't think you can write about DC area burgers without mentioning **Five Guys Burgers and Fries** (1100 New Jersey Ave. SE, 202/863-5070, www.fiveguys.com, 11am-10pm daily, under $10). It's burgers and fries (and hot dogs), but their cheeseburgers are truly great, the kind you wish everyone served. With several locations in and around DC and all across the country, Five Guys has garnered rave

reviews and high ratings at every turn, but you might as well visit the location where Obama famously chowed down on a burger.

Burger, Tap & Shake (2200 Pennsylvania Ave. NW, 202/587-6258, www.burgertapshake.com, 10am-11pm Mon.-Thurs., 10am-1am Fri., 11am-1am Sat., 11am-9pm Sun., $6-9) grinds their meat on-site throughout the day to get the freshest, most flavorful burger possible. They serve beef, turkey, chicken, and salmon burgers, but also a crispy falafel patty topped with pickled veggies and feta if you're not in a meaty mood. Staying true to their name, they have around two-dozen beers on draft and serve shakes. If you wish to combine your milkshake with something a little stronger, try one of their Shaketails.

Contemporary American
The sign behind the counter at ★ **Ben's Chili Bowl** (1213 U St. NW, 202/667-0909, www.benschilibowl.com, 6am-2am Mon.-Thurs., 6am-4am Fri.-Sat., 11am-midnight Sun., $4-9) reads, "The only people who eat free at Ben's are the Obamas and Bill Cosby. Everyone else pays." A meal never sets you back more than $10 here, so the sign shouldn't cause you any consternation. Ben's has been around since 1958 and is a legend in DC. Hang out here long enough and you'll see just about every city politician, Capitol Hill VIP, and celebrity in town come in for a half-smoke (a delicious, spicy sausage) or a burger. And Bill Cosby and the Obamas? Well, Cosby courted his wife here and held a press conference to announce his show was the top sitcom in the nation here (in addition to not paying, he has a menu item named for him) and President-elect Barack Obama dined at Ben's as part of his welcome to the city.

★ **Hill Country Barbecue** (410 7th St. NW, 202/556-2050, www.hillcountrywdc.com, 11am-2am daily, $15-24) is Texas barbecue at its finest. You'll find the full cadre of Texas barbecue delights: brisket, beef shoulder, beef ribs, pork spare ribs, sausages, smoked turkey, beer can chicken, and more sides than you could imagine. The brisket is an absolute knockout, and you have to try the Kreuz sausages. The kitchen closes at 10pm Sunday-Thursday, 11pm Friday-Saturday and a late-night menu (until 11pm Sun.-Tues. and Thurs., until midnight Wed. and Fri.-Sat., $6.50-20) offers the hungry a bite to eat. They sell more Shiner here than anywhere outside of Texas, and you can get $20 pitchers every day, but the real treat is a Shiner Float—your choice of Shiner's beer and a couple of scoops of Blue Bell ice cream. Needless to say, this place is packed any time a Texas sports team is on television.

Birch & Barley (1337 14th St. NW, 202/567-2576, www.birchandbarley. com, 5:30pm-10pm Tues.-Thurs., 5:30pm-11pm Fri.-Sat., 11am-3pm and 5pm-8pm Sun., dinner $16-30, brunch $13-16) has incredible food and an unreal collection of 555 craft and artisanal beers. The ever-changing menu is filled with items like lamb loin from the Shenandoah Valley; grouper caught off the coast of Maryland and Virginia; and vegetables from local suppliers. If you can't decide, get the tasting menu ($60 pp, another $25 for beer pairings). At those prices, you're getting some great beer and excellent food for less than you'd spend on yourself at many other DC eateries.

At **The Oceanaire Seafood Room** (1201 F St. NW, 202/347-2277, www.theoceanaire.com, lunch 11:30-5pm Mon.-Fri., dinner 5pm-10pm Mon.-Thurs., 5pm-11pm Fri.-Sat., and 5pm-9pm Sun., lunch $14-54, dinner $30-55) you can rack up quite the bill as you dine on the best seafood in the city. Try the Chilled Shellfish Platter, a mountain of shrimp, King Crab legs, lobster, and oysters; or go simple and order any of the dozen or so oysters on the menu. Entrées (and their prices) give off the feeling that Oceanaire is a high-end steakhouse, but instead of dry-aged Kobe, they serve fish. It's a special-event sort of place, or a spot you visit with a friend who has an expense account, but you won't regret it, the food is unbelievable.

Some locals claim **Boqueria** (1837 M St. NW, 202/558-9545, www.boquerianyc.com, 11:30am-10:30pm Mon.-Thurs., 11:30am-11:30pm Fri., 10:30am-11:30pm Sat., 10:30am-9:30pm Sun., lunch $5-16, dinner $5-39, brunch $5-39) is the best brunch spot in DC. This Spanish restaurant serves up a bevy of classic and reinterpreted tapas dishes as well as an impressive cheese and charcuterie selection. If you love tapas, the prix fixe brunch ($39) is for you. Unlimited tapas, drinks, and sweets are right there at your fingertips, so long as everyone at the table orders them, otherwise, you're going à la carte.

Ethiopian

DC is the home of an Ethiopian community, and a number of fantastic Ethiopian restaurants line U Street.

Consistently named on the list of DC's top ethnic restaurants, **Etete** (1942 9th St. NW, 202/232-7600, www.eteterestaurant.com, 11am-1am daily, $25) serves up spicy "stews" (they're more than a curry, less than a proper stew, but all delicious) that diners scoop up with the spongy injera bread. Dishes include a good number of vegetarian options alongside beef, lamb, chicken, and fish.

Where Etete, in the midst of little Ethiopia, is a little more laid-back, **DAS Ethiopian Cuisine** (1201 28th St. NW, 202/333-4710, www.dasethiopian.com, 11am-11pm daily, $15-18) is white-tablecloth, elegant dining in Georgetown. A beautiful dining room and a handful of alfresco tables start to set this restaurant apart, but it's the food that does the rest of the job. The well-curated menu has a great mix of vegetarian and meat entrées, from flax seed wat (pureed or roasted flax seed in spicy sauce) to beef awaze fitfit (injera bread soaked in a peppery sauce with beef).

Indian

★ **Rasika** (633 D St. NW, 202/637-1222, www.rasikarestaurant.com, 11:30am-11pm Mon.-Thurs., 11:30am-midnight Fri., 5pm-midnight Sat., $10-36) is Sanskrit for "flavors," and there are plenty of them here. This restaurant has been garnering some fantastic accolades since it opened, and in 2014, Chef Vikram Sunderam was awarded the 2014 James Beard Award for Best Chef in the Mid-Atlantic. Sunderam serves up *twa* (griddle), *sigri* (open barbecue), and the familiar tandoori dishes as well as a number of regional delicacies, exposing diners to much more than the expected Indian cuisine. As tempting as the menu may be, I recommend the tasting menu. Offering both vegetarian and non-vegetarian menus, you can choose from the four-course Grand Menu ($50 vegetarian, $58 non-vegetarian, $35 wine pairings) or the six-course Chef's Table Menu ($60 vegetarian, $75 non-vegetarian, $45 wine pairings). Oenophiles take note: Rasika is renowned for its wine list.

Italian and Pizza

Ristorante Tosca (1112 F St. NW, 202/367-1990, www.toscadc.com, lunch 11:30am-2:30pm Mon.-Fri., dinner 5:30pm-10:30pm Mon.-Thurs., 5:30pm-11pm Fri.-Sat., lunch $12-19, dinner $12-48) serves contemporary northern Italian food that highlights the best of seasonal ingredients. The food here is creative, but within a range that respects Italian food traditions, so don't expect anything too wild. With lobster ravioli, free-range veal chops, and branzino, it's hard to choose what to order. There are two tasting menus ($75/four courses, $95/six courses) with wine pairings ($50 and $70, respectively) that give the kitchen a chance to show off a little.

★ **We the Pizza** (305 Pennsylvania Ave. SE, 202/544-4008, www.wethepizza.com, 11am-11pm Mon.-Sat., $3-20), by Top Chef-contestant Spike Mendelsohn, turns up the volume on traditional pizza to elevate it to something more akin to Mendelsohn's fine dining establishments. Their Forest Shroomin' Pie, with wild forest mushrooms, truffles, fresh mozzarella, thyme, and Parmesan, is something you'll return for. Mendelsohn and his chefs are creating new pies that reflect different food traditions. The China Poblano Spicy Mexican Pie is laced with chipotle and cilantro; the Cajun Chicken & Andouille is a taste of New Orleans; and the Regal Pepper Farm is a peppery blast inspired by some choice Florida cuisine. They also have wings, salads, and a very interesting selection of sodas.

Vegetarian

Woodlands Vegan Bistro (2928 Georgia Ave. NW, 202/232-1700, www.woodlandsveganbistro.net, 11am-9pm Mon.-Thurs., 11am-10pm Fri.-Sat., 10am-7pm Sun., $5-12) is a longtime favorite for vegetarians, vegans, and the veg-curious. They create some very interesting vegetable-only food, drawing inspiration from the South (collards, okra and tomatoes, fried "fish"), the Caribbean (chick peas with a great Caribbean curry), and a host of Asian countries (sesame seaweed, more curries than I can list, Thai noodles). They also have a juice bar and a food truck: Woodlands Vegan Bistro...To Go!

Founding Farmers (1924 Pennsylvania Ave. NW, 202/822-8783, www.wearefoundingfarmers.com, 7am-10pm Mon., 7am-11pm Tues.-Thurs., 7am-midnight Fri., 9am-midnight Sat., 9am-10pm Sun., breakfast and brunch $7-14, lunch and dinner $11-32) is known for eclectic, Southern-inspired food created with seasonal products acquired as locally as possible. They serve steaks, chops, and seafood, but their vegetarian and vegan dishes are top notch. Try the trumpet mushroom "scallops" or the grilled cauliflower steak to see what they're capable of. Of course, you can also fill up on their fantastic salads and a number of excellent small plates.

Arlington

German

I'm not sure if **Lyon Hall** (3100 N. Washington Blvd., 703/741-7636, www.lyonhallarlington.com, lunch 11:30am-3pm Mon.-Fri., dinner 5pm-10pm Sun.-Thurs. and 5pm-11pm Fri.-Sat., brunch 9:30am-3pm Sat.-Sun., lunch $9-17, dinner $15-29, brunch $14-19) is German or German-ish, but it does serve schnitzel and features a two-page beer menu. In all seriousness, the food here is excellent. The Bohemian sausage platter gives you a trio of sausages, along with pork belly, herb spätzel, kraut, and house-made condiments. Their mussels are exceptional, and their cheese and charcuterie selection is as interesting as it is delicious.

Mediterranean

Yala Bistro (2201 N. Westmorland St., 703/533-5600, www.yalabistro.com, 11am-10pm daily, brunch served 11am-3pm Sat.-Sun., $8-19) incorporates Turkish and Greek food traditions. Flatbreads with Turkish sausage and cured beef, falafel and moussaka, and baklava and the Turkish rice pudding known as *sutlac* grace the small menu. But don't let the size of the menu fool you, the food is outstanding.

Information and Services

For a comprehensive list of restaurants, attractions, activities, and accommodations, let **Destination DC** (www.washington.org) be your guide. The site is filled with links, itineraries, and trip ideas. Nearby Arlington, Va., has a similar site (www.experiencearlington.org). The excellent team in the **Arlington Convention and Visitors Service** (www.stayarlington.com) has put together a great site that will lead you around Arlington and DC (but only to the major attractions).

On the radio, tune in to **WTOP** (103.5 FM) for traffic reports, **WAMU** (105.5) for public radio (from American University), **WASH** (97.1 FM) for adult contemporary, and **WMMJ** (102.3 FM) for urban contemporary.

George Washington University Hospital (900 23rd St. NW, 202/711-4000, www.gwhospital.com) is one of several hospitals and clinics providing emergency care and other medical services.

★ Manassas Battlefield National Park

The gently rippled hills north of Manassas—still almost as rural as they were 150 years ago—saw two major Civil War battles. The first opened the war with a horrific bang, and the second set the stage for Lee's abortive invasion of the North three years later. Any visit to the **Manassas Battlefield** (703/361-1339, www.nps.gov/mana, dawn-dusk daily, $3 adults, free ages 15 and younger) should start at the **Henry Hill Visitors Center** (6511 Sudley Rd., 8:30am-5pm daily), on Route 234 south of its intersection with Route 29. The park movie, *Manassas: End of Innocence,* which runs about 45 minutes, is free. You can pick up tour maps of the battlefields and check the daily schedule for ranger-led programs. Walk the loop trail of First Manassas in about 45 minutes, passing reconstructed houses and a muscular statue of Jackson commemorating his bold stand. During the First Battle of Bull Run (as the First Manassas is more commonly known), General "Stonewall" Jackson earned his nickname when he inspired Confederate troops to stand tall against Union attacks, earning a victory for the Confederacy. Nine sites of Second Manassas are linked by a driving tour. The Second Battle of Bull Run took place a year later, when Confederate troops again routed Union forces.

To get to Manassas Battlefield National Park, head west from DC on I-66; the park is 35 miles (about 45 minutes) outside the city. From Front Royal, the park is 37 miles (about 38 minutes) east on I-66.

Front Royal

The northern gateway to Skyline Drive and the Shenandoah National Park, as well as the Blue Ridge Parkway, is Front Royal, in Warren County. The sleepy little burgh was known as Hell Town during its frontier days, and many think it was unintentionally renamed by an exasperated colonial drill sergeant, who repeated orders for his troops to "Front the royal oak!" in the center of town (oaks were considered the royal tree of England).

The Shenandoah River runs through town, offering opportunities for fishing, tubing, and canoeing. Downtown is very attractive, with a town hall that looks like part of a movie set, many boutiques, and several restaurants.

A long bridge over the Shenandoah leads to tree-lined Royal Avenue (US-340). Turn left onto East Main Street at the Warren County Courthouse to reach the Village Commons with its gazebo, big red caboose, and the town visitors center.

Getting There

I-66 runs by Font Royal just outside of town limits; Washington DC is 70 miles to the east, and I-81 is 15 miles to the west. Winchester, Va., is only 30 minutes north via I-66 and I-81 or by taking US-340 north. The town of Luray, Va., is 24 miles to the southwest on US-340. There is no train service or bus service to Front Royal, nor is there an airport of any consequence.

Sights

The **Warren Rifles Confederate Museum** (95 Chester St., 540/636-6982, www. vaudc.org, 9am-4pm Mon.-Sat., noon-4pm Sun. Apr. 15-Nov. 1, $4) contains a large collection of arms, uniforms, flags, pictures, and personal items that evoke the Civil War exploits of Stonewall Jackson, Mosby's Rangers, J. E. B. Stuart, and Robert E. Lee. There are also artifacts from the famous Civil War player Belle Boyd.

Practically across the street from the Warren Rifles Confederate Museum is the **Belle Boyd Cottage** (101 Chester St., 540/636-1446, www.warrenheritagesociety.org, 10am-4pm Mon.-Fri., 11am-4pm Sat.-Sun. June-Oct., $3). Boyd was a charming spy who helped Stonewall Jackson capture Front Royal in 1862. She was well known among Union forces, reported for suspicious activity more than 30 times, arrested a half dozen times, and even spent a little while behind bars. For a while, Front Royal was her base of operations and you can learn more about her spy exploits here.

Opened to the public in 1939, **Skyline Caverns** (10344 Stonewall Jackson Hwy./US-340, 800/296-4545, www.skyline-caverns.com, 9am-5pm Mon.-Fri. and 9am-6pm Sat. and Sun. Mar. 15-June 14; 9am-6pm daily June 15-Labor Day; 9am-5pm Mon.-Fri. and 9am-6pm Sat.-Sun. Labor Day-Halloween; 9am-4pm Nov.1-Mar. 14; $18 adults, $9 ages 7-13, free 6 and under) were discovered a few years earlier by means of a giant sinkhole where the parking lot now sits. The highlights of these caves, otherwise overshadowed by their southern neighbors, are glittering calcite formations called anthodites. These delicate spikes are found in only one other cave in the United States (and there in much smaller quantities). They grow one inch every 7,000 years, either pure white or stained brown by iron oxide. Skyline Caverns' crop sprouted in a vacuum left by a receding underground pool. Throughout the rest of the cave, high, smooth passages evoke the slot canyons of the American southwest. Kids love the Skyline Arrow ($4 ages 3 and up, free 2 and under), an outdoor miniature train that crawls near the entrance. There's also a Mirror Maze ($6 ages 5 and up, free 4 and under). The caverns are on US-340, about one mile south of Route 55.

Entertainment

There's very little nightlife to speak of in Front Royal. Most of the bars are attached to restaurants, so don't expect any out-till-dawn evenings. There are, however, four fun festivals in town. In May, the one-day **Virginia Wine and Craft Festival** (historic downtown Front Royal, 540/635-3185, www.wineandcraftfestival.com, admission is free, tasting tickets are $25 in advance, $30 day of) draws 20 or so Virginia wineries to dole out samples; more than 100 vendors, artists, and crafters; and tons of fair food.

The **Warren County Fair** (Fairgrounds Rd., 540/635-5827, www.warrencounty-fair.com, $30 weekly tickets) comes to town for a week in early August, bringing with it concerts, 4-H events, a demolition derby, a tractor pull, ATV drag racing, and everything you'd expect to find at a county fair.

In late September, the **Brew & Blues Festival** (historic downtown Front Royal, 540/635-3185, www.brewandblues.com, tasting tickets $15 in advance, $20 day of) brings blues music and beer tastings from three-dozen or so microbreweries to downtown Front Royal. Area restaurants and food purveyors will be on hand to serve up munchies and plates of food that should make all that beer tasting go a little easier.

The Warren Heritage Society holds their annual fundraiser, the **Festival of Leaves** (historic downtown Front Royal, 540/636-1446, www.warrenheritagesociety.org) in mid-October. Bluegrass, blues, rock, and country acts perform throughout the day; there's a parade and vendors selling food and crafts, and a kids area.

Shopping

On summer weekends and holidays, the **Front Royal Antique and Flea Market** (S. Commerce Ave. between Stonewall Dr. and South St., 540/636-9729) is *the* place for assorted treasures, junk, and crafts spread among 100 booths. Alternately, you can shop for antiques of all sorts at **Arleen Brown Antiques** (301 E. Main St., 703/789-1245, 11am-5pm Mon.-Sat., noon-5pm Sun.) and see what sort of eclectic home goods they have at **Valley Finds** (505 South Royal Ave., 540/622-6200, www.valleyfinds.com, noon-6pm Mon.-Tues. and Thurs.-Fri.).

The **Royal Oak Bookshop** (207 S. Royal Ave., 540/635-7070, www.royaloakbook-shop.com, 10am-6pm Mon.-Sat., noon-5pm Sun.) stocks thousands of rare, used, out-of-print, and new books. Visit with Willa Catter, the bookshop cat, while you're there.

Recreation

Several local outfitters take advantage of the fact that one of Virginia's favorite rafting rivers flows practically through their backyard. Most operate campsites down the South Fork of the Shenandoah for overnight visitors during the floating season of March-November. Prices should include equipment, brief instruction, maps, and shuttle service.

The **Front Royal Canoe Company** (8567 Stonewall Jackson Hwy., 540/635-5440 or 800/270-8808, www.frontroyalcanoe.com, 9am-6pm Mon.-Fri., 7am-7pm Sat.-Sun., starting at $33) runs canoe, raft, and kayak trips, with longer excursions of 2-3 days also available. Tubing ($25) is also popular. You can also rent canoes ($50/day), kayaks ($30/solo, $50/tandem per day), and stand-up paddleboards ($40/day) to explore the river on your own.

Take a guided horseback ride with **Royal Horeshoe Farm** (509 Morgan Ford Rd., 540/636-6375, www.royalhorse-shoe.com, starting at $35). They lead trail rides year-round and can tailor an excursion to fit your skill level and desire for adventure.

Mountain bikers will find several challenging trails nearby. At the **Elizabeth Furnace Trail,** experts will find quite the adventurous track to ride. Located 11 miles west of Front Royal in the George Washington National Forest (www.slingletracks.com), the 15-mile trail starts with an easy uphill climb on a fire road before a long, rough downhill with a dozen or so water crossings, rock outcrops, technical trail sections, and rock gardens. At the **Shenandoah River State Park** (350 Daughter of Stars Dr., Bentonville, 540/622-6840, park at www.dcr.virginia.gov, trail maps at www.virginiaoutdoors.com, 8am-dusk daily, parking $4), 9 miles southwest of Front Royal, there is a 13-mile network of trails better suited to less-experienced mountain bikers. Most of these trails are wide and smooth, though there are a few challenging climbs. Plus, there are great views of the river from many trails.

Accommodations

The **Holiday Inn Hotel & Suites Front Royal Blue Ridge Shadows** (111 Hospitality Dr., 540/631-3050, www. ihg.com, $152-185) is adjacent to the Blue Ridge Shadows Golf Club. There are 124 rooms in this seven-story hotel where you'll have free Wi-Fi, a 24-hour fitness center, and a heated indoor pool.

There's a **Hampton Inn** (9800 Winchester Rd., 540/635-1882, www. hamptoninn3.hilton.com, $149-182) in Front Royal. On weekday mornings, you'll have a free hot breakfast or to-go breakfast bags, and every day you'll have free Wi-Fi, acces to a pool and sun deck, and a fitness center. The hotel is located about four miles out of town.

Tom and Kathy Conkey operate the impressive Edwardian mansion known as **Killahevlin** (1401 North Royal Ave., 540/636-7335 or 800/847-6132, www. killahevlin.com, $155-285), built by a local limestone baron on one of the highest hilltops in town. A strong Irish influence pervades, from the reproduction wallpaper to the private pub with its oak bar and Irish beer on tap.

the Shenandoah mountains

Woodward House on Manor Grade (413 S. Royal Ave., 540/635-7010 or 800/635-7011, www.acountryhome.com, $110-225) has seven guest rooms (each with a private bath) and a private cottage. Every day there's a homey breakfast ranging from hot or cold cereals to omelets to French toast. Guests can also enjoy complimentary beer or wine at the on-site pub. The view from here is lovely as the house sits on top of a hill overlooking the valley.

Campers should head to **Shenandoah River State Park** (350 Daughter of Stars Dr., Bentonville, 540/622-6840, www.dcr.virginia.gov, campsites $20-35, cabins $83-147, lodge $369), nine miles southwest of Front Royal. They have a number of tent sites, cabins, and a lodge.

Food

L Dee's Pancake House (522 E. Main St., 540/635-3791, www.LDeespancakehouse.com, 6am-2pm Mon. and Wed.-Sat., 7am-1pm Sun., closed Tues., under $8) offers breakfast all day, with fantastic French toast and great omelets. Their lunch menu is of the burger and sandwich variety that you'd expect at a little diner-like restaurant such as this.

Set in the old Proctor Biggs feed mill building next to the town park, the **Main Street Mill Restaurant & Lounge** (500 E. Main St., 540/636-3123, 10:30am-9pm Sun.-Thurs., 10:30am-10pm Fri.-Sat., $8-22) serves up familiar American cuisine. For lunch, they have burgers, sandwiches, and salads, with a few plated entrées; and for dinner, it's steak, ribs, pasta, and the like.

The **Stonewall Jackson Restaurant** (915 N. Royal Ave., 540/635-1862, restaurant 11am-10pm daily, bar 4pm-1am Sun.-Thurs. and 4pm-2am Fri.-Sat., lunch $5-12, dinner $9-22) is another American-cuisine restaurant serving a selection of steaks, pasta, chicken, seafood, and a bevy of fried appetizers. The prices are low and portions very generous, and while nothing is overwhelmingly great, nothing is mind-bogglingly bad either.

Information and Services

The **Front Royal/Warren County Visitor Center** (414 E. Main St., 540/635-5788 or 800/338-2576, www.discoverfrontroyal.com, 9am-5pm daily, closed Thanksgiving, Christmas, and New Year's Days) is located in the restored train station in the town park.

For emergencies, go to **Warren Memorial Hospital** (1000 Shenandoah Ave., Front Royal, 540/536-8000, www.valleyhealthlink.com).

Shenandoah National Park

Well over one million people visit **Shenandoah National Park** (540/999-3500, www.nps.gov/shen) each year. This 200,000-acre park is only 75 miles west of Washington DC and is a popular escape *pass* ↓

for those living in the DC metro area and the densely populated areas of Virginia, Maryland, and Pennsylvania.

This is a prime park for hiking. More than 500 miles of trails, many of which are accessible from Skyline Drive, wind through lush forests and across long ridgelines. On these hikes you'll find more than a dozen waterfalls and wildflowers, and be granted the opportunity to take a look at some of the parks wildlife. It's common to see white-tailed deer and black bears, but also bald eagles, coyotes, and even the timber rattlesnakes are spotted throughout the park with regularity. Remnants of former home sites are visible in crumbling walls and chimneys and mossy cemeteries hidden in the underbrush. A 101-mile segment of the **Appalachian Trail** (AT) threads its way down Skyline Drive, making it ideal for short hikes as it crosses and re-crosses the road. Many loop trails include part of the AT.

Visiting the Park
Getting There and Around
Washington DC is 75 miles to the east; I-66 carries you right to Front Royal, where you'll find the northern entrance to Shenandoah National Park. Only 10 miles to the west, I-81 cuts a northward diagonal path along the Blue Ridge Mountains towards Pennsylvania to the north.

The 105-mile vista-to-vista ridgetop **Skyline Drive** carries you through Shenandoah National Park from Front Royal to Rockfish Gap, just outside of Waynesboro, where the drive continues via the Blue Ridge Parkway. Along the route, 75 overlooks offer views of the Shenandoah Valley to the west and the piedmont of Virginia to the east. The drive is lovely in any season but most colorful in the fall. Spring buds and wildflowers and jewel-green summer mountains are other seasonal attractions.

The park itself is divided into three sections, designated by roads bisecting Skyline Drive. The **Northern District** stretches from Front Royal (US-340, MP 0) to Thornton Gap (US-211, MP 31.5). The **Central District** continues south to Swift Run Gap (US-33, MP 62.7). Rockfish Gap (I-64, US-250, MP 104.6) marks the southern boundary of the **Southern District.**

Along the length of Skyline Drive, everything is referred to by milepost. The milepost markers make it easy to orient yourself in the park and give you an easy measure from place to place. Milepost 0 is at Front Royal, at the northern end of Skyline Drive. Milepost 104.6 is at Rockfish Gap at the southern end. It takes around three hours to drive from end to end.

3 hrs

Entrances
There are entrance stations at four points along Skyline Drive:

- **Front Royal** (MP 0)

- **Thornton Gap** (MP 31.5)

- **Swift Run Gap** (MP 62.7)

- **Rockfish Gap** (MP 104.6)

At each of these entrances you can pay your fees and pick up a short informational guide to the park. Rangers stationed at the entrances are happy to answer questions and give directions or suggestions, but be aware of the traffic behind you and try to be courteous to your fellow park visitors.

Park Passes, Permits, and Regulations
Shenandoah National Park's early years—when it cost a quarter to enter and a buck for an annual pass—are long gone. Today, a **pass** (good for 7 consecutive days) costs $25 per vehicle, $20 per motorcycle, or $12 per pedestrian or bicyclist.

trail maps

Pets are allowed on most trails, but only on leashes; ask at the visitor centers about which trails are off-limits. **Bicycles** are only allowed on Skyline Drive and other paved areas.

Backcountry camping permits are required, but are free and are available from entrance stations, park headquarters, and visitor centers. You may also download a backcountry camping permit application from www.nps.gov/shen and send it to Shenandoah National Park for advanced trip planning. **Appalachian Trail permits** (for long-distance AT hikers) are available by self-registration on the Trail near Shenandoah National Park entry points.

Anglers will want to familiarize themselves with Shenandoah National Park **fishing regulations** (available at www.nps.gov/shen), and obtain a **fishing license** from the state of Virginia. Licenses are available at sporting goods retailers across the state and online through the Virginia Department of Game and Inland Fisheries (www.dgif.virginia.gov, $8-47).

Visitors Centers

Shenandoah National Park has two visitor centers: the **Dickey Ridge Visitor Center** (MP 4.6; 8:30am-5pm daily early Apr.-mid-Nov., closed Tues. and Wed. around the middle of Nov.) and the **Harry F. Byrd, Sr. Visitor Center** (MP 51; 9am-5pm daily late Mar.-Nov.; 9:30am-4pm Sat.-Sun. Dec.-early Jan.; open Sat. only early Jan.-end of Mar.). Each visitor center has trail maps, along with topographical maps and detailed maps of the entire park. Various trail guides are available at the bookstore in the park visitor centers.

The **Park Headquarters** (540/999-3500, www.nps.gov/shen, 9am-5pm Mon.-Fri.) is four miles east of Luray on US-211.

Seasons

The most popular time to visit Shenandoah National Park and cruise along Skyline Drive is autumn, when the leaves turn and the broad, green valley views of summer turn to a riot of color. This can mean long lines at entrance stations and slow traffic along Skyline, so expect a lot of leaf-peeping companions, especially on weekends. Inclement weather can close the road any time of year, and spring and summer storms can bring heavy rain, lightning, fog, and hail to the area. During deer-hunting season (mid-Nov.-early Jan.), Skyline is closed at night to give the deer a little break.

The park is open year-round, though in winter, many sections of Skyline Drive, and most of the amenities are closed (check the website or call for closures). During winter, many people hike in or drive a short way up Skyline to take in the snowy views.

Accommodations
Camping

Backcountry camping is free, though you do need a permit (available online, by mail, or at visitor centers and entrance stations). In addition to backcountry campsites, there are four campgrounds in Shenandoah National Park:

- **Matthews Arm Campground** (MP 22.1, 540/999-3132, reservations at 877/444-6777 or www.recreation.gov, $15, groups $50)

- **Big Meadows Campground** (MP 51.2, 540/999-3500 x3231, $20, groups $45)

- **Lewis Mountain Campground** (MP 57.5, $15)

- **Loft Mountain Campground** (MP 79.5, $15, groups $35-50)

These are open spring, summer, and fall, but are closed in winter. All of the campgrounds have showers and potable water. Each of the campgrounds has tent sites, and all but Lewis Mountain

Food.

Campground have space for RVs (note, though, there are no water hookups, although there are dump stations and potable water available). You can make reservations (877/444-6777, www.recreation.gov) at three of the campsites; Lewis Mountain Campground is first-come first served.

Lodges and Cabins

There are two lodges and a set of cabins in Shenandoah National Park:

- **Skyland Resort** (MP 41.7 and 42.5, $128-295)

- **Big Meadows Lodge** (MP 51.2, $130-203)

- **Lewis Mountain Cabins** (MP 57.5, $133)

These are all operated by DNC Parks & Resorts; reservations (877/847-1919, www.goshenandoah.com) can be made for all lodges and cabins. None of these accommodations are luxurious by any stretch. They are built instead to facilitate the enjoyment of the park, so the beds will be passable and the shower hot, but don't expect plush robes and after-dinner cordials.

Food and Supplies

Unlike many national parks, Shenandoah offers two full-service dining rooms: one inside Skyland Resort, and one inside Big Meadows Lodge.

If a full-service, sit-down meal isn't what you had in mind, you can stop by one of three Wayside Food Stops: the Elkwallow Wayside, Big Meadows Wayside, and Loft Mountain Wayside.

Camping supplies are available at four places in the park: the Elkwallow Wayside, Big Meadows Wayside, Lewis Mountain Cabins and Campstore, and Loft Mountain Wayside.

Inside the park, gasoline is only available at the Big Meadows Wayside (MP 51.2).

Information and Services

In addition to the visitor centers, you can also ask the helpful folks at any of the accommodations for information, or visit the official site for the park (www.nps.gov/shen) or the official site for the lodging and food vendor for the park (www.goshenandoah.com). The **Shenandoah Valley Travel Association** (www.visitskylinedrive.org) has more information on Skyline and the park.

If you need medical assistance, there are a few hospitals nearby. **Warren Memorial Hospital** (1000 Shenandoah Ave., Front Royal, 540/536-8000, www.valleyhealthlink.com) serves Front Royal and is convenient to the northern section of the park. In Luray, **Page Memorial Hospital** (200 Memorial Dr., Luray, 540/743-4561, www.valleyhealthlink.com), a 25-bed hospital, can provide emergency care if you need it. At the southern end of Skyline Drive, **Augusta Health** (78 Medical Center Dr., Fisherville, 800/932-0262, www.augustahealth.com) can treat most any problem that may arise. In a true emergency, dial 911 and report your situation and location along Skyline Drive.

Northern District
Dickey Ridge Visitor Center (MP 4.6)

This is the first stop for most as they travel south along Skyline Drive. There's a very nice view, as well as the usual accouterments of a visitor center: restrooms, racks full of informational brochures, and a gift shop. What sets it apart are the pleasant park rangers. It's evident that they love Shenandoah National Park and are excited to help you have a great visit. Take 10 minutes to watch the video (it starts on request rather than on a timer).

Fox Hollow Trail

Distance: 1.2-mile loop
Duration: 0.5-1 hour
Elevation gain: 300 feet

Difficulty: easy
Trailhead: across Skyline Drive from the Dickey Ridge Visitor Center, MP 4.6

Park at the Dickey Ridge Visitor Center and cross Skyline Drive to the trailhead. Turn left and begin to descend slightly. You'll pass a cement post at 0.15 miles, turn left and follow the blue-blazed trail for 0.2 miles along a pleasant forest walk. At 0.3 miles you'll reach a second concrete post and you'll turn right here to join Fox Hollow Trail and continue on past piles of rocks left over from clearing the forest and preparing agricultural fields.

A 0.5 miles in, you'll pass the Fox Farm Cemetery; take a few minutes to check it out. As you continue along, you'll pass a spring and an ornamental mill wheel. The trail crosses old farmland here, so keep an eye out for deer. The trail begins to rise after you pass the cemetery, but it's a gradual climb. Continue on, noting the rock piles and rock fences to either side. If you notice the path, it's wide, well graded, and relatively smooth. That's because it's an old road that once connected the farms here with Front Royal, a few miles north.

Gooney Run Overlook (MP 6)

Looking out from the Gooney Run Overlook you can see Gooney Run, the stream that drains Browntown Valley. Several turns of the Shenandoah River are visible here as well, as is Signal Knob and Dickey Ridge. The original name of Gooney Run was Sugar Tree Creek, but Lord Fairfax was hunting here with his favorite dog, Gooney, and the dog had the misfortune to drown. Farifax honored the hound by renaming the creek.

Lands Run (MP 9.2)

A short wooded stroll on the Lands Run Falls Trail is perfect for those pressed for time who want to see one of the park's waterfalls.

Lands Run Falls Trail
Distance: 1.2 miles out and back
Duration: 0.5-1 hour
Elevation gain: 300 feet
Difficulty: easy
Trailhead: Lands Run parking area, MP 9.2

This short, pleasant hike leads down an old road to views of a small, but pretty waterfall. Follow the fire road from Lands Run parking area as it descends immediately. At 0.6 miles in, you'll see a stream coming down the mountain from your left before passing through a culvert under the road. Look to the right and you'll see the falls. If you take a short spur trail, you can get some very good views. Retrace your steps back up the fire road to the parking area.

Fort Windham Rocks and Compton Gap (MP 10.4)

Carson Mountain (2,580 ft.) is unremarkable except for the summit, Fort Windham Rocks. Geologists say the rocks are 600-800 million years old and are examples of the Catoctin lava formations. Rock climbers will tell you that they're great for easy to moderate top rope climbs if you feel like packing gear in, or perfect for bouldering if you're going in a little lighter.

Fort Windham Rocks Trail
Distance: 0.8 miles out and back
Duration: 30-45 minutes
Elevation gain: negligible
Difficulty: easy
Trailhead: Fire road at Compton Gap, MP 10.4

From the parking area, follow the fire road (which is also part of the Appalachian Trail) to a four-way intersection. Turn left onto Dickey Ridge Trail (which will lead you to the Dickey Ridge Visitor Center). The path ascends quite gently, then, as it levels, you'll see the Fort Windham Rocks to your right. There's a short spur that leads into the rocks, where you should linger a bit, scramble around on the outcrop, and check out the rocks before retracing your steps back to the parking lot.

★ Hogback Mountain Overlook (MP 20.8)

Truly one of the top views in the park, the Hogback Mountain Overlook provides a great look at Hogback Mountain, but the best part is the shimmering shape of the Shenandoah River as it snakes through the landscape. The largest overlook area in Shenandoah National Park, this is a popular stop.

Matthews Arm Campground (MP 22.1)

One of the largest campgrounds in the park, **Matthews Arm Campground** (540/999-3132, reservations at 877/444-6777 or www.recreation.gov, $15, groups $50) has nearly 200 tent and RV sites. This campground is wooded and shady, making for a nice break from summer heat and a great view right outside your door in autumn. Matthews Arm is near **Overall Run Falls** (a taxing hike), which has the highest drop of all the falls in the park.

Elkwallow Wayside (MP 24.1)

At **Elkwallow Wayside** (9am-6pm daily mid-Apr.-early Nov.), you can pick up something to snack on or cook from a limited grocery store, or order carry-out from a small menu.

◈ US-211: Whiteoak Canyon, Old Rag, and Luray Caverns (MP 31.5)

From Skyline Drive, take **US-211 East** to Whiteoak Canyon and Old Rag, or **US-211 West** to Luray Caverns.

Whiteoak Canyon Trail

Distance: 5.8 miles out and back
Duration: 3-4 hours
Elevation gain: 1,700 feet
Difficulty: moderate to strenuous

---

top to bottom: Old Rag Mountain Trail; motorcyclists on Skyline Drive; Dark Hollow Falls

Trailhead: parking area near Cedar Run

Directions: At MP 31.5, take US-211 east to Sperryville; turn south on US-522 for 0.8 miles; turn right onto VA-231 and go 9.5 miles to Route 643; follow Route 643 south for 10 miles; turn right onto Route 600 for 3.6 miles to the place where the road fords Cedar Run. The trailhead is in the parking area.

Finding the trailhead is the most daunting part of this hike, aside from its distance, but the reward is worth the effort as it takes you to a secluded canyon where you can get up close and personal with a half-dozen waterfalls. Going in, this hike is all uphill, so keep that in mind as you get on the trail. It means that coming back you just have to coast downhill.

Starting from that near-secret trailhead, cross Cedar Run via a footbridge. Immediately you'll see a cement post marking the junction with Cedar Run Trail. Stay on Whiteoak Canyon Trail. At 0.7 miles, continue on, bearing right. The ascent can be steep and could require you to scramble around a few large rocks. At 1.5 miles, a cement post marks the first of the falls. Continue along for the next 1.4 miles to see the rest of the falls here. Take your time, dip your feet in the pool beneath at least one waterfall, take some pictures, and maybe eat a little lunch. It's a pleasant spot to linger. When it's time to go back, follow the trail back out by retracing your steps.

Old Rag Mountain Trail

Distance: 8.8-mile loop
Duration: 7-8 hours
Elevation gain: 2,380 feet
Difficulty: strenuous
Trailhead: Nethers, Va., at the Shenandoah National Park border along Route 600

Directions: Though the peak lies inside the park, the trailhead is outside the park, near the community of Nethers. Exit Skyline Drive at Thornton Gap (MP 31.5) and follow US-211 east to US-522 south in Sperryville. Follow the signs to VA-231/F. T. Valley Road south and stay on this road for 7.8 miles. Turn right onto State Route 601/Peola Mills Road and continue along 601 until it turns into State Route 707/Nethers Road. Just over a mile from Nethers you'll reach the

trailhead to Old Rag Mountain. An entrance permit to Shenandoah National Park is required; if you didn't pay at the entrance station, there's a self-serve station here.

Hiking Old Rag Mountain is a rite of passage for many visitors to Shenandoah National Park and offers some great views. It's harsh and rocky, and exposure near the summit is total, so if there's the chance of bad weather (especially lightning), keep an eye on the sky. Before you go, visit www.nps.gov/shen and watch the video about safety on Old Rag Mountain.

Prepare for a full, strenuous day by bringing a map, good shoes, at least two liters of water per person, an emergency kit, food, and your trekking poles. Park near the trailhead and walk up Nethers Road about 0.8 miles to the proper trailhead. The blue-blazed trail climbs steadily for 0.75 miles, growing much steeper as you climb the ridge. In another 0.5 miles, you'll reach the top of the ridge and emerge onto the rocks. This is where the scramble begins. As you climb over granite boulders you'll have some wide Piedmont views or closer views of Weakley Hollow and the Blue Ridge Mountains.

As you climb, you'll be convinced, several times, that you've reached the summit. There are a number of false summits along the trail; you'll know you've reached one when you see a higher peak ahead. The real summit is marked with a concrete post. Check out the view from here, walk over to the second summit on a 200-yard or so side trail, and get a look at the true peak. While you're there, look for "buzzard baths," potholes in the rock where water gathers.

You can return the way you came, a trip of 2.8 miles (making 5.6 miles total), but you'll have to climb through that boulder field again. The **Saddle Trail** is a longer route—4.4 miles—that's all downhill with nothing to climb over; it's the preferred option if you have the time. For the Saddle Trail, turn right when you reach Ridge Trail from the summit. Descend along the ridge for 0.4 miles to a marker post at Old Rag Saddle. Ahead Byrds Nest Shelter No. 1 (day use only) is in sight. Turn right and descend for 1.1 miles to the Old Rag Shelter and spring. Continue along the fire road. At 0.4 miles beyond the shelter, you'll reach a double junction. Turn right onto Weakley Hollow fire road, which goes 2.6 miles back to your starting point.

★ Luray Caverns

Along the northern reaches of the Blue Ridge Mountains, the hills are full of holes, and caverns abound. **Luray Caverns** (MP 31.5 to US-211 west, 101 Cave Hill Rd., Luray, 540/743-6551, www.luraycaverns.com, open 9am daily with tours departing every 20 minutes, final tour times vary by season: Apr. 1-June 14 6pm, June 15-Labor Day 7pm, day after Labor Day-Oct. 31 6pm, Nov. 1-Mar. 31 4pm and 5pm on weekends, $24 adults, $22 seniors, $12 ages 6-12, free ages 5 and under) are the cream of the crop. This awe-inspiring cavern system has been wowing visitors since it was first discovered in 1878, though as their tourist literature likes to say, the spectacle was four million centuries in the making. Paved walkways lead through massive cavern "rooms" filled with stalagmites, stalagtites, and columns of pillars where they sometimes join. Along the way you'll see chambers as tall as 10-story buildings and tiny stalagmites, no bigger than a nipple on a baby's bottle, which formed before the founding of our nation.

There's too much to see on the tour to describe here, but the **Stalacpipe Organ** is definitely worth mentioning. It's considered the largest musical instrument in the world, and seeing as it's made of stalactites covering some 3.5 acres, who's to argue? The organ produces symphonic sounds when the stalactites are tapped by rubber-tipped mallets. It took 36 years to perfect the organ, but visitors can hear it played on every tour. It sounds like something straight out of *Chiller Theatre*. If that's not creepy enough, how about this: shortly after the caves were discovered, human bone fragments were found embedded in a stalagmite. That story's both creepy and amazing when you consider how slowly stalagmites grow.

Your general admission ticket covers the cavern tour and admission to the **Car and Carriage Caravan Museum** (which has restored modes of transportation from 1725 to 1941) and the **Luray Valley Museum** (interpreting Shenandoah Valley culture as far back as pre-contact Native Americans). The **Garden Maze** and the **Rope Adventure Park** are extra ($7 adults, $5 ages 6-12 per attraction).

Central District
Mary's Rock Tunnel and Trail (MP 32)

Mary's Rock is solid granite and sits astride the Skyline Drive route, making a tunnel the easiest way over, around, or through. At only 12.66 feet, Mary's Rock Tunnel is a little tight, so be aware if you're driving an RV, camping trailer, or horse trailer. The 670-foot long tunnel was cut through Mary's Rock in 1932. No one is quite sure how Mary's Rock got its name, though it's thought to have originated with Francis Thornton who, according to one story, married a woman named Mary and brought her to this rock to show her the lands they'd own together; according to another story, Thornton's daughter Mary paid a visit to the rock and returned home with a black bear cub.

★ Mary's Rock Trail
Distance: 2.6 miles out and back
Duration: 2-3 hours
Elevation gain: 820 feet
Difficulty: moderate
Trailhead: Meadow Spring Trailhead, MP 33.5
Directions: Park at the Meadow Spring parking area

and walk 50 feet or so along Skyline Drive to access Meadow Spring Trailhead.

The hike to the top of Mary's Rock is well worth it for the 360-degree views of Shenandoah National Park. There are a couple of ways to reach Mary's Rock; this route has less elevation gain by around 400 feet and is nearly a mile shorter than the alternative. Immediately the trail ascends, then levels and ascends again. You'll pass the remains of a huge stone chimney, all that remains of a Potomac Appalachian Trail Club built in the 1930s (it burned down in 1946), at 0.4 miles in. Keep climbing through this typical hardwood forest. You'll reach the Appalachian Trail and a cement signpost at 0.6 miles in. Turn right here and follow the Appalachian Trail as it ascends, then descends. You'll reach a second post in another 0.6 miles. Turn left onto the spur trail that will lead you to the summit of Mary's Rock.

Pinnacles Overlook (MP 35.5)
From Pinnacles Overlook you have a great view of Old Rag Mountain. In fall, when the colors sweep down either side of the valley and end with the bulk of Old Rag, it's quite a sight, but it's a nice spot in any season.

Highest Point on Skyline Drive and Skyland Resort (MP 41.7)
The highest point along Skyline Drive is at the northern entrance to Skyland Resort where the road reaches 3,680 feet in elevation. Though the highest point of Skyline Drive is here at the resort, the highest point in the park is nearby Hawksbill Mountain. Less than a mile away by trail is the second highest peak in the park, Stony Man Mountain.

Skyland Resort
Skyland Resort (MP 41.7 and 42.5, 540/999-2212, $128-295) has been around since 1888, when George Freeman Pollock, Jr. found a 16-acre tract in the mountains high above the Shenandoah

Valley with views he called "beauty beyond description." Today, his retreat is Skyland Resort, and it does have some unreal views in any season. There are traditional rooms as well as cabins here. Know that eight of the cabins have multiple rooms, each sold individually, so if you're not traveling with a group large enough to rent the whole thing or you're no good with sharing a cabin with strangers, you may want to stick to a room or one of the four private cabins.

The **Pollock Dining Room** (open daily, breakfast 7:30am-10:30am, lunch noon-2:30pm, dinner 5:30pm-9pm; breakfast $2-9, lunch $7-14, dinner $11-25) at Skyland Resort serves three meals a day of seasonal, regional cuisine. Meals are simple, but hearty. The **Mountain Taproom** (2pm-11pm daily, $7-14) has a few items on the menu and a number of specialty cocktails and a decent selection of domestic, import, and micro-brew beers. Skyland Resort also has grab-and-go options.

Stony Man Summit Trail
Distance: 1.4 miles out and back
Duration: 1-2 hours
Elevation gain: 350 feet
Difficulty: easy
Trailhead: Stony Man parking area at Skyland Resort
Hop onto the Appalachian Trail at the Stony Man parking area in Skyland and follow it to the right. At 0.4 miles, the Appalachian Trail crests the highest point in the park. The Stony Man Horse Trail branches off left, but you should stick to the blue-blazed Stony Man Trail. At 0.5 miles in, the trail splits, with both sides leading to the summit, forming a loop. Either fork works. You'll be at the summit in less than a quarter mile from here.

Hawksbill Mountain (MP 45.6)
The **highest peak in the park,** 4,050-foot Hawksbill Mountain, is accessible only by a moderate hike. As you'd guess, the mountain drew its name from the great

number of hawks that can be seen here circling on the thermals. While you climb, and once you summit, keep your eyes open for raptors on the wing.

Hawksbill Summit Trail
Distance: 2.8-mile loop
Duration: 2-3 hours
Elevation gain: 800 feet
Difficulty: moderate to strenuous (because of elevation gain)
Trailhead: Hawksbill Gap parking lot, MP 45.6

At the north end of the parking lot is the trailhead to the summit of Hawksbill Mountain. A spur trail about 100 yards long leads to the Appalachian Trail, which you'll follow to your left, and begin to climb. The trail is rocky for the first 0.4 miles, then you reach a slope of scatter rock (called talus), then a short clear section and a second talus slope. Along here you have great views of the valleys and mountains around.

One mile in you'll reach a cement signpost noting the Appalachian Trail mileage and arrows pointing to Hawksbill and to Fishers Gap. Make a hard left onto the Salamander Trail and keep climbing. In a quarter mile, you'll come to a very rocky point, so be careful of your steps. As you approach the top, you'll join a fire road, making the rest of the route very easy. The summit is at 1.9 miles, so you're close.

On the summit you'll find the Byrds Nest, a shelter built for former U.S. Senator and Virginia Governor Harry F. Byrd, Sr. There's no water and no camping here. The summit is a few yards away.

The summit view is commanding. In every direction, mountains fade into the distance. To your north is Stony Man, Brown Mountain is to the west, Graves Mountain to the south, and Skyline Drive just below you. If you're lucky, you'll see the endangered peregrine falcon, the fastest bird in the nation, which can dive at speeds up to 120 miles per hour.

To return, retrace your steps to the shelter and turn left on the fire road to a cement post directing you to the Lower Hawksbill Trail. Turn left and head back to the parking area. Be careful going down, it's rocky, steep in places, and taxing.

Dark Hollow Falls (MP 50.7)
★ **Dark Hollow Falls Trail**
Distance: 1.4 miles out and back
Duration: 1.5-2 hours
Elevation gain: 440 feet
Difficulty: moderate to strenuous
Trailhead: Dark Hollow Falls Trailhead at MP 50.7

Dark Hollow Falls is one of the most popular waterfall hikes in Shenandoah National Park, and for good reason: the short hike and excellent view. Moss and ferns cling to the cliff around the falls, and at the base, there are several great opportunities for photographers to shoot leaf-littered rocks and small cascades, especially in autumn.

This short hike takes you to one of the most popular and easily accessible waterfalls. Take "easily accessible" with a grain of salt, though, as the trail is all downhill on the way to the 70-foot Dark Hollow Falls and a 440-foot elevation gain on the way back up. It's a thigh-burner for sure.

From the parking area, the trail descends and follows Hog-camp Branch. You'll reach your first overlook of Dark Hollow Falls at 0.6 miles. Continue on the trail to the base of the falls at 0.7 miles. Climb back up to get to your car.

Along the way, you'll notice a rail to help you with your footing and keep you on the path. Don't be foolish and go past the rail and fences, not only do they prevent trail erosion, they also keep you safe.

Byrd Visitor Center (MP 51)
The **Harry F. Byrd, Sr. Visitor Center** (9am-5pm daily late Mar.-Nov.; 9:30am-4pm Sat.-Sun. Dec.-early Jan.; open Sat. only early Jan.-end of Mar.) has the usual visitor center facilities—restrooms, information desk, videos—as well as a great exhibit telling the story

of the establishment and development of Shenandoah National Park.

Story of the Forest Trail

Distance: 1.8-mile loop
Duration: 1-1.5 hours
Elevation gain: 300 feet
Difficulty: easy
Trailhead: across from the north entrance to the Byrd Visitor Center at MP 51

The Story of the Forest Trail is an easy loop and generally a good place to see wildlife, so it's good for children or to use as a leg-stretching break from a day in the car. The trail is wide and transitions from gravel to forest floor to paved. You pass over Ho Branch at 0.2 miles in, then meet up with a horse trail at 0.4 miles. At 0.8 miles you'll reach the Big Meadows Campground. Turn left here and follow the paved bike/walking path back to the visitor center.

Big Meadows (MP 51)

Big Meadows is home to the largest open meadow in Shenandoah National Park, a lodge, a campground, and a full-service dining room. There's also a long, but fairly leisurely (save a few spots), hike leading to one of the highest waterfalls in the park. For excellent wildlife viewing, observe the fields shortly after dawn and before dusk when the deer herds appear to graze. If you choose to hike at these times, be quiet and go slow. You'll be surprised at how much wildlife you can see.

Big Meadows Campground (MP 51.2, 540/999-3500 x3231, $20, groups $45) has more than 220 tent and RV sites. At **Big Meadows Wayside** (MP 51.2, 9am-5:30pm Sun.-Thurs. and 8am-7pm Fri.-Sat. Apr.-Nov.) you can get groceries, a meal, camping supplies, and gasoline.

Big Meadows Lodge

Big Meadows Lodge (MP 51.2, 540/999-2222, $130-203) was built in 1939 of native stone and chestnut wood paneling. It's a beautiful property and listed on the National Resister of Historic Places. Accommodations here range from lodge rooms to small, rustic cabins. The lodge is near the really large meadow that lends Big Meadows its name.

At Big Meadows Lodge, you can dine in the **Spottswood Dining Room** (MP 51.2, open daily, breakfast 7:30am-10am, lunch noon-2pm, dinner 5:30pm-9pm; breakfast $2-9, lunch $8-11, dinner $7-28) or get a picnic-to-go box lunch to take with you (place your order at the front desk or at the hostess stand). Entrées here include smoked pork ribs, prime rib, roast turkey, and pan seared trout. At the **New Market Taproom** (4pm-11pm Mon.-Fri., 2pm-11pm Sat.-Sun.) you can get a little food and a number of cocktails, wines by the glass, and beer.

Lewis Spring Trail

Distance: 3.3-mile loop
Duration: 3-3.5 hours
Elevation gain: 1,000 feet
Difficulty: moderate
Trailhead: Big Meadows Campground, MP 51.2

Starting from the amphitheater behind the picnic area, take the Appalachian Trail to the left. At 0.1 miles, follow the blue-blazed Lewis Spring Falls Trail to the right. The trail is very well maintained, though it's rocky, requiring caution and some good boots. For about a mile, you'll descend into a hollow. When the trail levels out, you'll hear the waterfalls. At one mile, a short ascent delivers you to a nice open view of the mountains to the west. To your left is an observation point just down the trail. Cross a stream and continue along until you reach Lewis Spring Falls. The fourth-highest in the park at 81 feet, the falls are more a cascade than a proper waterfall, but they're beautiful nonetheless.

From the overlook, backtrack to the blue-blazed trail and head uphill. You'll parallel a creek on your left and ascend via a set of switchbacks. At 1.9 miles you'll reach a cement marker. Follow Lewis Spring Fire Road for 70 or 80 yards, then turn left onto the Appalachian Trail. Follow the path uphill to the lodge and campground.

Rapidan Camp (MP 52.8)

A moderate to difficult hike from Milam Gap will take you to a waterfall and the retreat of President Hoover; this is the only way to get to this perfect presidential mountain getaway. Hoover had three requirements for his retreat: It had to be within 100 miles of Washington DC; it had to be located on a trout stream; and it had to be at least 2,500 feet above sea level. This spot met all three criteria and at one time there were 13 cabins and structures that served him and his guests during these working getaways. Today only 3 of the original 13 remain.

Rapidan Camp Trail

Distance: 4 miles out and back
Duration: 2.5-3 hours
Elevation gain: 850 feet
Difficulty: moderate to strenuous

Trailhead: Milam Gap parking lot, MP 52.8

Cross Skyline Drive to the trailhead. You'll follow the Appalachian Trail a short ways until it joins Mill Prong Trail. Turn left onto Mill Prong Trail, descending as you parallel the stream (where fishing is allowed, provided you catch and release, using only single-hook, artificial lures). At 1.5 miles, you pass Big Rock Falls and continue downhill where you'll cross Mill Prong. Two miles in, cross the bridge and climb up to Rapidan Camp. The camp's namesake river is just a few paces away. Retrace your steps back uphill to the parking area.

Bearfence Mountain (MP 56.4)

From the top of 3,640-foot Bearfence Mountain, you'll get a commanding, 360-degree view of Shenandoah National Park. The view takes in several notable peaks—Massanutten Mountain to the west, and Bluff Mountain and Fork Mountain to the east, to name a

approaching Big Meadows on Skyline Drive

few—and is from one of the best park mountaintops.

Bearfence Mountain Trail

Distance: 1.2-mile loop
Duration: 1-1.5 hours
Elevation gain: 380 feet
Difficulty: moderate to strenuous
Trailhead: across Skyline Drive from the Bearfence Mountain parking area, MP 56.4

This hike requires some real rock scrambling, but no technical gear or real technical experience, just common sense, a little upper-body strength, and the ability to determine when it's time to pack it in and turn back for the trailhead. Cross Skyline Drive from the parking area and set foot on the trail. It climbs uphill quickly and then at 0.1 miles, the blue-blazed trail crosses the Appalachian Trail. Bearfence Mountain Trail immediately gets rocky and you'll begin to make your way through huge boulders only a few hundred yards from the parking area. Look closely and you'll notice

that many of the boulders have a greenish hue. They're called greenstone, and it's taken millions of years for their color to show thanks to fractures and fissures in the rocks.

The boulder field is only a couple hundred yards long, though it feels longer. At 0.4 miles you'll reach the summit, as evidenced by the view: You can see everything from here.

There are two ways back, though one is a little shorter. You can return to the parking lot by the way you arrived, a shorter route of only 0.8 miles; or you can continue toward the Appalachian Trail by turning right from the summit. From here you'll intersect with the Appalachian Trail 0.5 miles farther on, then follow the trail north to the parking lot.

Lewis Mountain (MP 57.5)

At Lewis Mountain, you'll find some first-come, first-served camping; some cute, rustic cabins; and a camp store to serve your minor grocery needs. **Lewis Mountain Campground** (540/999-2255, $15) is the smallest campground in the park, with only 31 sites. You won't find any RVs or reservations here, so if you want to camp at Lewis Mountain, show up early. **Lewis Mountain Cabins** (540/999-2255, $133) are cozy and quaint. How quaint? There's no phone signal to be had or wireless Internet access to speak of, but each cabin does have electricity, a private bathroom, linens, and an outdoor grill. To top all this off, the **Lewis Mountain Campstore** (540/999-2255, 9am-6pm Sun.-Thurs., 9am-7pm Fri.-Sat.) carries a limited selection of groceries, a few retail gift items, and a small selection of alcohol, so everything you need for a night or two at the campground or cabins.

◆ US-340 West: Grand Caverns (MP 62.7)

Grand Caverns (5 Grand Caverns Dr., Grottoes, Va., 540/249-5705 or

888/430-2283, www.grandcaverns.com, 9am-5pm daily Apr.-Oct., 10am-4pm daily Nov.-Mar., closed Thanksgiving Day, Dec. 24-25, and Jan. 1, $18 adults, $11 children, $16 seniors, $15.50 adults and $9 children of military, AAA, and AARP) is the oldest continually-operating show cave in the nation, seeing its first paying visitors in 1806. It was discovered in 1804 by Bernard Weyer as he sought to retrieve one of his traps. Weyer spent the next two years exploring and mapping the cave before opening it to the public. During the Civil War, Union and Confederate soldiers visited the cave (though on separate occasions) and some 230 of the visiting soldiers signed their names on the cave walls.

On a guided tour of the cave, you'll pass through nine "rooms," each with distinct characteristics and structures. The largest chamber is Cathedral Hall, which is 50 feet tall at its highest and 280 feet long. Other rooms of note include the Grand Ball Room, where many candlelit balls and dances were held; the Lily Room, which has a huge formation that resembles a calla lily; and the Chapel, which has formations resembling a pulpit, organ, and chandelier, and was the site of many church services and still hosts weddings.

Tours take about 70 minutes. Wear comfortable, closed-toe shoes and a jacket as it's a constant 54°F in the caverns.

To reach Grand Caverns, you have a couple of options. From Skyline Drive, exit onto US-340/US-33 (also called the Spotswood Trail) at Swift Run Gap (MP 62.7) and travel west to Elkton, Va., then turn south on US-340 to Grottoes. This route is 23 miles long and takes approximately 30 minutes. Another option is to follow US-340 north from Waynesboro to Grottoes, a trip of 15 miles, taking approximately 25 minutes.

Southern District
South River Falls (MP 62.8)
These 83-foot waterfalls are the third

largest in Shenandoah National Park, and you can only see them on a hike along the South River.

South River Falls Trail
Distance: 4.4 miles out and back
Duration: 2-3 hours
Elevation gain: 800 feet
Difficulty: moderate to strenuous
Trailhead: South River Picnic Area, MP 62.8

To the right of the drinking fountain at the South River Picnic Area, you'll find the trailhead to South River Falls. The trail descends 0.1 miles until it meets with the Appalachian Trail, marked by a cement post. Follow the blue blazes and descend a series of gradual switchbacks. At times the trail here is rocky, but generally it's wide and smooth.

You'll pass by several creeks as they flow out of the mountain to join with South River. At 0.75 miles, you'll encounter a creek to your left that's almost entirely hidden by the rocks, although you can hear it. The South River begins to parallel the trail around here.

Another stream joins the South River, then, suddenly, the river plunges into a deep grotto. There's no real view of the falls from here, but there's a good overlook at 1.3 miles. Some may choose to return to the trailhead from here (making a 2.6-mile hike), and to do so, simply go back the way you came. I recommend continuing on the longer 4.4-mile hike.

To make the 4.4-mile trail, continue along and join up with an old road at 1.5 miles. Stay on the South River Falls Trail, which descends then turns back toward the falls and a cement post at 2.1 miles. According to the post, the park's boundary is nearby and there's a short spur trail to the base of the falls 0.1 miles away. Take the spur trail to the large pool at the base of South River Falls. Take off your shoes and socks and go for a wade; it's refreshing and you'll find that it will help with the climb back to the top.

Shenandoah National Park, Southern District

SWIFT RUN GAP ENTRANCE STATION

SWIFT RUN OVERLOOK

Hightop 3,587ft

BACON HOLLOW OVERLOOK

EATON HOLLOW OVERLOOK

MP-70

Flattop Mtn 3320ft

McGaheysville

Rocky Mount 2,740ft

Brokenback Mountain 1,750ft

LOFT MTN OVERLOOK

MP-75

TWO MILE RUN OVERLOOK

Ivy Creek

BROWN MTN OVERLOOK

IVY CREEK OVERLOOK

County Line Mountain 1,980ft

LOFT MOUNTAIN WAYSIDE/BIG FLAT MOUNTAIN

MP-80

BIG RUN OVERLOOK

LOFT MOUNTAIN

Shenandoah National Park

DOYLES RIVER OVERLOOK

DUNDO GROUP CAMP

810

Grottoes

GRAND CAVERNS

BLACKROCK SUMMIT

Blackrock

MP-85

BLACKROCK GAP

TRAYFOOT MTN OVERLOOK

Pasture Fence Mountain 2,880ft

614

MP-90

RIPRAP OVERLOOK

MOORMANS RIVER OVERLOOK

810

CRIMORA LAKE OVERLOOK

Bucks Elbow Mountain 2,787ft

Crozet

MP-95

SAWMILL RUN OVERLOOK

250

Turk Mountain 2,960ft

64

CALF MTN OVERLOOK

MP-100

MCCORMICK GAP OVERLOOK

254 250

Waynesboro

250

MP-105

ROCKFISH GAP (SOUTH) ENTRANCE STATION

64

N

0   2 mi

0   2 km

© AVALON TRAVEL

Brown Mountain Overlook (MP 76.9)

Traveling the Skyline Drive to Blue Ridge Parkway route from the north, this is the first Brown Mountain you'll encounter, but not the last. At least two more (including the North Carolina iteration where many have seen the strange Brown Mountain Lights appear in the dark of night) await on your journey south. Shenandoah National Park's Brown Mountain Overlook is excellent. The ridges descend to the valley floor in stacked waves, and at their head, a mountain, which in autumn is ablaze with color, save the spots where rocky protrusions show through the trees.

Loft Mountain (MP 79.5)

At the **Loft Mountain Wayside** (MP 79.5, 540/999-2255, 9am-6pm daily mid-Apr.-early Nov.), you can grab a bite to eat from a snack counter, pick up some grocery-type supplies, and add to your arsenal of camping and hiking equipment. You can also take a nearly three-mile trail to the summit of Loft Mountain and take in some remarkable views of the valleys and mountains surrounding the peak.

Loft Mountain Loop Trail

Distance: 2.7-mile loop
Duration: 2 hours
Elevation gain: 600 feet
Difficulty: easy
Trailhead: Loft Mountain Wayside parking lot, MP 79.5

This easy trail is family-friendly and canine-compatible, making it a popular leg-stretching hike. Walk north on Skyline Drive 150 or so yards from the wayside parking lot. You'll pass the Patterson Ridge Trail trailhead on the left, but continue on to the first dirt road and head to the Ivy Creek Hut. At 0.6 miles, a cement post marks the junction with the Appalachian Trail. Turn right and follow the white blazes through the forest.

Approaching the summit of Loft Mountain, you'll notice the trees grow thinner and the undergrowth, particularly the blackberry bushes, grow thicker. The trail will level off as it follows the ridgetop around one mile in. At 1.1 miles you'll reach an overlook on the left side that gives you a nice panoramic view of the Piedmont to the east. Continue along the trail until you reach the next cement post at 1.4 miles. Turn right on Frazier Discover Trail (note: dogs are not allowed on Frazier, so if you brought the pooch, simply turn around and head back to the car) and make your way back to the Loft Mountain Wayside and your car. Prepare yourself for some monster views along Frazier Discovery Trail as a number of rock outcroppings afford you awesome vantage points.

Big Flat Mountain (MP 79.5)

The second highest peak in the Southern District of Shenandoah National Park, Big Flat Mountain is just that: big and flat. Strange that on top of Big Flat Mountain, at the largest, most level spot, is **Loft Mountain Campground** (MP 79.5, 540/999-2255, $15, groups $35-50), with more than 200 campsites for tents and RVs. The campground took its name from nearby Loft Mountain as the Park Service felt "Big Flat" Campground was not nearly so flattering as "Loft Mountain" Campground. Having logged my share of nights sleeping in a tent on an uneven or rocky slope, a big, flat campground sounds pretty good to me.

Blackrock Summit (MP 84.8)

Not only is this a beautiful spot to stop and take in the scenery, it's also got an interesting history. During the Revolutionary War, Virginia Governor Thomas Jefferson was concerned about the state archives and the Great Seal of Virginia. He gave them to a friend for safekeeping. That friend hid them in a cave at Blackrock Mountain until the end of the war.

Blackrock Summit Trail

Distance: 1-mile loop
Duration: 30-45 minutes
Elevation gain: 180 feet
Difficulty: easy
Trailhead: Blackrock parking lot, MP 84.8

This is an easy hike for families as it is just over 0.5 miles to the summit, and reaching the summit involves a short, rocky scramble through a boulder field, making hikers with less experience feel like they've accomplished a minor feat of mountaineering prowess.

Near the sign that describes the mountain's geography, step onto Trayfoot Mountain Trail and ascend rather steeply for 0.1 miles until you reach the Appalachian Trail. Turn left on the Appalachian Trail and follow the white-blazed, nearly-level path 0.4 miles to where the trail ends just before the summit. To reach the summit, there's a short scramble through a boulder field to a great panoramic view of the valley below. Be careful on the boulders, they can be tricky as far as footing is concerned. Also, hikers have reported seeing rattlesnakes sunning themselves here, so keep an eye and an ear open for them.

Riprap Overlook (MP 90)
Riprap Hollow Trail

Distance: 9.8-mile loop
Duration: 6-7 hours
Elevation gain: 2,300 feet
Difficulty: strenuous
Trailhead: Riprap Overlook, MP 90

One of the best loop hikes in the Southern District of Shenandoah National Park, Riprap Hollow Trail will lead you to some great views and awesome swimming holes in a spring-fed stream. Walk 50 yards along the blue-blazed trail from the Riprap parking area to where it intersects with the white-blazed Appalachian Trail. Turn right and head uphill 0.4 miles to the intersection with Riprap Hollow Trail.

Turn left at Riprap Hollow Trail and descend into a hollow on the ridge before a short climb leading you to the first vista at 0.7 miles. In another 0.3 miles you'll reach Chimney Rock and a fantastic view. Linger here a moment before descending into Cold Springs Hollow. In 1.7 miles you'll reach a stream that cuts through a small gorge and leads to a 20-foot waterfall.

Continue past the waterfall another quarter mile to a large swimming hole. Just past this is a trail across the stream leading to an old shelter. After a side trip to the shelter, continue along the blue-blazed Riprap Hollow Trail next to the stream for 0.7 miles until it intersects with Wildcat Ridge Trail.

At Wildcat Ridge, turn left, cross the stream, and make your way through a small gorge. In 0.6 miles you'll reach a steep section and a set of switchbacks. Follow the trail for two miles to a four-way intersection with the Appalachian Trail. Turn left on the Appalachian Trail and hike back the final 2.8 miles to the Riprap parking area.

Crimora Lake Overlook (MP 92.6)

This is one of the top views along Skyline Drive primarily because of the beautiful Crimora Lake forming the centerpiece of the view. Framed by Turk Mountain and Rocks Mountain, the lake is an absolute jewel. Crimora Lake is not a natural one, it's a relic of the valley's mining days. The mines here extracted more manganese than anywhere in the United States and at one time were among the largest manganese mines in the world.

Calf Mountain Overlook (MP 96.9)

From an elevation of 2,485 feet, the Calf Mountain Overlook provides some dizzying views. As you round the bend here, the road seems to continue right out into the air, but it really just makes a tight turn. The overlook is a long one, with near-360-degree views. To the south you can see Bear Den Mountain, while to the north you can see the Shenandoah Valley, the course of Sawmill Run, and a handful of named peaks. Calf Mountain is right behind you, and if you want to hike to the summit, the trailhead is just three miles down Skyline Drive.

Calf Mountain Trail
Distance: 2 miles out and back
Duration: 1-1.5 hours
Elevation gain: 525 feet
Difficulty: moderate
Trailhead: Beagle Gap parking area, MP 99.5 (3 miles south of Calf Mountain Overlook, MP 96.9)

Don't expect a view from the summit as it is treed in, but it's a pleasing, easy hike with chances to see wildflowers and berry bushes along the way. From the parking area, pass through the wire fence and begin to ascend through a broad meadow. As you enter the woods, the trail will become steeper, though it levels out again quite quickly and takes you through the remnants of an apple orchard (some of the trees still bear fruit).

At one mile in, you'll find a cairn (stack of stones) on the trail. Nearby, embedded in some rock, is a USGS marker noting the summit of Calf Mountain. If you choose to continue on to the Calf Mountain Shelter, a spur trail (blue-blazed) nearby leads down a 0.2-mile path to the shelter.

Waynesboro

Known early on as Teasville, Waynesboro sits at the point where the Appalachian Trail, Skyline Drive, and Blue Ridge Parkway meet. This town of 22,000 takes advantage of this confluence and welcomes guests in, offering up a number of surprisingly good local restaurants and even more national chains. Outfitters for outdoor adventure, from fly-fishing to river tubing, call Waynesboro home and cater to Appalachian Trail hikers. In the hills above town you'll find some lovely inns and grand vistas of the Shenandoah River Valley.

countryside near Waynesboro

Getting There

If time is of the essence, you can reach Waynesboro from DC in just three hours; this 164-mile route follows I-66 west to I-81 south to I-64 east. If you prefer to take Skyline Drive through Shenandoah National Park, it's a five-hour drive of 179 miles following I-66 west from DC to Front Royal, Va., then south along Skyline Drive to its southern end, where you're just five minutes west of Waynesboro.

Sights *look up*

The **Waynesboro Heritage Museum** (420 W. Main St., 540/943-3943, www.waynesboroheritagefoundation.com, 9am-5pm Tues.-Sat., free) shows the history of this town from its 1797 inception to the present day. Permanent and rotating exhibit galleries allow conservators to highlight both major historical events and focus on the families, people, and smaller events that shaped this town.

There are 32 (and counting) wineries, breweries, and ciderworks within 30 miles of Waynesboro, making for a tasty day trip. Some of the nearest are **Barren Ridge Vineyards** (984 Barren Ridge Rd., Fisherville, 540/248-3300, www.barrenridgevineyards.com, 11am-6pm Mon.-Wed., 11am-sunset Thurs.-Sat., 1pm-6pm Sun.), six miles away in Fisherville; **Afton Mountain Vineyards** (234 Vineyard Lane, Afton, 540/456-8667, www.aftonmountainvineyards.com, 11am-5:30pm Thurs.-Mon.), eight miles away in Afton; and **Blue Mountain Brewery** (9519 Critzers Shop Rd., Afton, 540/456-8020, www.bluemountainbrewery.com, 11am-10pm Mon.-Sat., 11am-9pm Sun.), nine miles away in Afton. Tastings are $5-10 at each of these three vineyards.

Entertainment
Nightlife

The Hot Spot (901 W. Broad St., 540/949-5216, www.hotspotentertainment.org, 7pm-1am Tues.-Sat.) is a live music venue in Waynesboro. Acts here range from smaller nationally known acts to regional/college circuit performers to local musicians gathering for the weekly blues jam. They do host the Comedy Square Table, a group of enthusiastic area comedians.

Heritage on Main Street (309 W. Main St., 540/946-6166, www.heritageonmainstreet.com, 11am-midnight Sun.-Thurs., 11am-1am Fri.-Sat., live music 7pm Wed., 9pm Sat., music is free) is open late every night of the week. This downtown sports bar serves a full menu of bar food. The wings are especially good, as is the burger (they have 22 types of burgers). And there are 22 taps pouring some of the best beer and cider around; they carry both local and national craft beer and cider, and a handful of domestics. This is the spot to stop in to catch a fight, be it boxing or the UFC; a ballgame; or to see a band.

Chauncey's Smokehouse & Bar (2323 W. Main St., 540/221-2048, 11am-11pm Tues.-Wed., 11am-midnight Thurs., 11am-1am Fri.-Sat., noon-5pm Sun.)

serves up some excellent barbecue all while keeping you entertained with both live music and cold beer. They have a full bar, and musical entertainment tends toward the bluesy side.

Festivals and Events

In April, the **Virginia Fly Fishing & Wine Festival** (on the banks of the South River, 540/241-5054, www.vaflyfishingfestival. com, tickets $20 single day, $35 weekend pass) draws anglers from across the mid-Atlantic for lectures, tips on fly-fishing in Virginia, and the chance to catch a fish or two on the South River. It's the largest outdoor fly-fishing event on the East Coast, and with events and activities for veteran and novice anglers, there's a little something for everyone. Several area and regional microbreweries and wineries are on hand as well, bringing with them some fine beer and wine to help everyone celebrate spring's arrival.

Shopping

Rockfish Gap Outfitters (1461 W. Main St., 540/943-1416, www.rockfishgapoutfitters.com, 10am-6pm Mon.-Sat., noon-5pm Sun., closed Thanksgiving, Christmas, New Year's Day, Easter, and July 4) has everything you'll need to mount a successful expedition along the Blue Ridge Parkway or Skyline Drive, including all of the hikes, picnics, waterfalls, and roadside stops you'll include on your journey. You'll find clothing and gear from Patagonia, Exofficio, Merrell, Outdoor Research, and a host of other top-rated outdoor brands. The shop is a popular stop for Appalachian Trail thru-hikers and segment hikers. At Rockfish Gap, you can get the skinny on the best hikes, river floats, and mountain biking trails (as well as those great local fishing holes) from outdoor enthusiasts who call the area home and know the top spots.

Market On Main (407 W. Main St., 540/943-6418, www.marketonmain-street.com, 9am-6pm Mon.-Wed., 9am-9pm Thurs.-Sat.) advertises itself as the

"Biggest Little Specialty Shop and Bistro in Waynesboro," and I have no reason to doubt them. They serve breakfast, lunch, and dinner ($3.50-8) off a tiny menu, but the real draw is their selection of microbrews and wine. More than 200 wineries and 30 or so microbreweries are represented on their shelves, so they have a little bit of everything.

Mariah Amine Couture (112 S. Wayne Ave., 540/942-9022, www.mariahamine. com, 11am-5pm Tues.-Wed., 11am-6pm Fri., 10am-4pm Sat., closed Sun.-Mon. and Thurs.) is filled with objects created by local artisans. Jewelry, hats, scarves, blankets, handbags, yarn, canine accessories, and other finds pack the shelves here, making for an interesting mix of items. If you're in town on Friday from 3pm-6pm and have your knitting needles (or crochet hooks, needlepoint project, or cross stitch gear), head over for a little sewing-circle meet-up with the locals.

At the **Shenandoah Valley Art Center** (SVAC; 126 S. Wayne Dr., 540/949-7662, www.svacart.com, 10am-4pm Tues.-Sat., 2pm-4pm Sun.), you'll find a collection of galleries where art from SVAC members is displayed alongside high-quality shows by individual artists, group exhibits, and juried exhibitions. They have a gift shop where you'll find the typical art gallery gifts: jewelry, glass art, and pottery. The gift shop also showcases a selection of one SVAC artist's work.

Recreation

Shenandoah River Adventures (415 Long Ave., Shenandoah, 38 miles north of Waynesboro, 888/309-7222, www. shenandoahriveradventures.com, tubes $17-20, canoes and kayaks $35-55) has kayaks, canoes, and tubes you can rent and take out onto the Shenandoah River. If you feel more adventurous, they offer full-day canoe and kayak trips ($40-65) and multi-day trips ($55/kayak first two days, $15/day thereafter; $85/canoe first two days, $25/day thereafter). You'll find a number of Appalachian Trail hikers giving their feet a little break and "Aquablazing" part of the monumental trail. Aquablazing is when they come off the trail and canoe or kayak from one spot to another; here it's generally done along the Shenandoah River since it runs parallel to the Appalachian Trail as it passes through Shenandoah National Park.

In addition to selling outdoors gear, **Rockfish Gap Outfitters** (1461 W. Main St., 540/943-1416, www.rockfishgapoutfitters.com, $35 single kayaks and paddleboards, $60 double kayaks) rents kayaks and stand-up paddleboards by the day. They also provide tips on the best places to get on the water.

South River Fly Shop (317 W. Main St., 540/942-5566, www.southriverflyshop.com, 9am-6pm Mon.-Fri., 9am-5pm Sat., noon-4pm Sun.) is run by two young men who have been fishing in mountain waters their entire lives. They know their flies, they know what gear is built to last, and they know where to go to put you on the fish. In their shop they carry a selection of fly-tying materials and tools, rods and reels, clothing, boots and waders, and just about anything else you could need to spend a day on the water. They also offer a **guide service** that takes you out on the South River to fish for trout ($175 for 1-2 people, half day; $275 full day); a full-day float trip for smallmouth bass and trout along the Shenandoah River ($395), the James River ($425), and the Jackson River ($450); and full-day trips into Shenandoah National Park ($325).

Fly-fishing enthusiasts shouldn't miss the **Virginia Fly Fishing & Wine Festival** (on the banks of the South River, 540/241-5054, www.vaflyfishingfestival.com, tickets $20 single day, $35 weekend pass) in April.

Accommodations

At the **Belle Hearth Bed & Breakfast** (320 S. Wayne Ave., 540/943-1910, www.belle-hearth.com, $105-160) expect a candlelit breakfast at a table set with china and actual silver silverware. They've won a number of awards and accolades for their breakfast, which always includes some outstanding biscuits, fresh seasonal fruits and herbs, and a rotating array of quiches and breakfast casseroles. The house is Victorian in style, which sometimes means over-decorated, but not so at Belle Hearth; it's Victorian for certain, but tastefully so.

Tree Streets Inn (421 Walnut Ave., 540/949-4484 or 877/378-0456, www.treestreetsinn.com, $110-135) is a 1914 Colonial Revival home just three miles from Skyline Drive and the Blue Ridge Parkway. Each morning they serve a full breakfast in the dining room, but are happy to deliver a continental breakfast to your door if you so choose, and they can accommodate vegetarian, gluten free, and diabetic diets with ease. In the midst of the beautiful landscaping around Tree Streets Inn is a private pool that's open in every season.

The ★ **Iris Inn** (191 Chinquapin Dr., 540/943-1991, www.irisinn.com, $209-319) looks out over the valley from a 12-acre Blue Ridge mountaintop. Built in 1991 to be an inn, the property includes the six-room inn, a half-dozen cabins, and three cottages. Every room has fabulous views and is decorated in a contemporary style that combines the mountaintop/cabin/nature feel of the Inn with tasteful design. The common areas are beautiful: high ceilings, wood and stone accents, and abundant natural light.

There are also several chain hotels in Waynesboro. The **Best Western Waynesboro Inn & Suites Conference Center** (109 Apple Tree Ln., 540/942-100, www.bwwaynesboro.com, $135-200) is a 75-room, 19-suite, pet-friendly hotel with free continental breakfast and a heated indoor saltwater pool, and it's right off I-64, making it easy to spot and even easier to get to. The **Residence Inn Waynesboro** (44 Windigrove Rd., 540/943-7426, www.residenceinn.mariott.com, $139-229) has 90 suites, free

Internet, and spacious suites in addition to a continental breakfast.

Food

Stella, Bella, & Lucy's (327 W. Main St., 540/949-5111, www.stellabellalucy.com, breakfast 9am-10:30am Mon.-Sat., lunch 11am-2:30pm Mon.-Sat., breakfast $450-7.50, lunch $7.50-8.50) was named for a trio of dogs beloved by the restaurant's proprietors, but the food is anything but table scraps. Serving both breakfast and lunch, they keep it simple with smaller menus of very well executed food. For lunch, try the pineapple boat (chicken or turkey salad on a wedge of fresh pineapple and a bed of lettuce) or the stuffed tomato; need something more filling, then try The Granny, a corned beef sandwich with homemade pimento cheese.

You don't expect to find a good meal in a bookstore, but at **Stone Soup Books** (908 W. Main St., 540/943-0084, www.stonesoupbooks.net, 10am-6pm Mon.-Thurs. and Sat., 10am-9pm Fri., around $7), you will be pleasantly surprised. The menu is made up of soups and sandwiches, and both are outstanding. Soups rotate daily but the tomato-garlic soup and African chicken stew with beans are favorites. For sandwiches, the goat cheese and spiced walnut is an odd, but delicious, option, or you could stick with the smoked turkey and cranberry chutney sandwich for something more familiar. While you're there, be sure to peruse the bookshelves.

Scotto's Italian Restaurant and Pizzeria (1412 W. Broad St., 540/942-8715, www.scottos.net, 11am-9:30pm Mon.-Thurs., 11am-10:30pm Fri.-Sat., 11:30am-9:30pm Sun., $7-24) is a local favorite for all things pasta and pizza. Pies come in both deep-dish Sicilian style and hand tossed, and you can build your own or let them guide you with one of their specialty pies. The Pizza à la Scotto's (white sauce, ham, spinach, and mozzarella) is quite good.

The Green Leaf Grill (415 W. Main St., 540/949-4416, www.thegreenleafgrill.com, 11am-9pm Tues.-Thurs. and Sun., 11am-10pm Fri.-Sat., $10-20) has a very good beer selection, stone-oven pizzas, and a menu filled with dishes that reflect a variety of influences. There's lasagna, crawfish etouffée, coconut curry, steaks, burgers, and fish tacos. Impressively, they do a good job with all of it.

Information and Services

Visitors to Waynesboro will find information and tools to help them plan a trip through the **Waynesboro Department of Tourism** (301 W. Main St., 540/942-6512, www.visitwaynesboro.net). There's more information available through **Waynesboro Downtown Development, Inc.** (301 W. Main St., 540/942-6705, www.waynesborodowntown.org).

Radio stations include **WWWV** (96.5 FM) for rock and **WKCI** (970 AM) for sports and talk.

For police assistance, contact the **Waynesboro Police Department** (250 S. Wayne Ave., 540/942-6675, www.waynesboro.va.us), the **Waynesboro City Sheriff** (250 S. Wayne Ave., 540/942-6639, www.waynesboro.va.us), or the **Augusta County Sheriff's Department** (127 Lee Hwy., Verona, 540/942-5113, www.co.augusta.va.us). **Augusta Health** (78 Medical Center Dr., Fisherville, 800/932-0262, www.augustahealth.com) is the nearest local hospital.

Charlottesville

Established in 1762 along an important trade route, Charlottesville is a beautiful town of 45,000. It's home to the University of Virginia, an interesting array of restaurants and shops, and a deep field of historic and artistic figures, most notably, a pair of U.S. presidents, Thomas Jefferson and James Monroe. (James Madison, another U.S. president, lived one county over.) Jefferson's home, Monticello, draws nearly 500,000 visitors

a year and is the most popular tourist destination in the area. Other recognizable Charlottesville figures include Edgar Allan Poe, who went to UVA for a semester; John Grisham; Dave Matthews and several bandmates; Corey Harris; NFL veteran Howie Long and son Chris Long; and actor Rob Lowe.

One of the most charming parts of the city is the Downtown Mall on West Main Street. This long, tree-shaded, statue-adorned pedestrian area is lined with shops, restaurants, and vendors, and capped by a movie theater and ice rink at one end, and the Charlottesville Pavilion at the other. The grounds of the University of Virginia are the very picture of a university campus, and the student population helps keep the town fresh and on trend.

Getting There

Both Skyline Drive and the Blue Ridge Parkway are only 24 miles west of Charlottesville, and I-81 is only 12 miles farther.

I-64 runs right by downtown Charlottesville. Richmond is 70 miles to the east along I-64; I-95 passes through Richmond, connecting that city and the I-64 corridor to a larger range of big cities on the East Coast. To the west, Beckley, W.Va., is 186 miles away; there, I-77 and I-79 connect to a number of other destinations along the mid-Atlantic.

Charlottesville is served by **Charlottesville Albemarle Airport** (100 Bowen Loop, Charlottesville, 434/973-8342, www.gocho.com). Airlines flying to and from here include Delta, American Airlines, United Airlines, and US Airways. At the **Charlottesville Amtrak station** (CVS, 810 W. Main St., 434/296-4559, www.amtrak.com, 6am-9:30pm daily), the Cardinal/Hoosier State, Crescent, and Northeast Regional Lines pass through daily. The **Charlottesville Greyhound station** (310 W. Main St., 434/295-5131, www.greyhound.com, 4am-10am, 11:30am-6:30pm, and

8pm-10pm daily) is just a few blocks from the Amtrak station.

The **Charlottesville Area Transit** (615 E. Water St., 434/970-3649, www.charlottesville.org, schedules vary, rates are from $0.75 for a one-way fare up to $1.50 daily, $20 unlimited monthly pass), or CAT, has 11 routes and a free trolley serving the University of Virginia and downtown.

Sights
University of Virginia

The **University of Virginia** (434/924-0311, www.virginia.edu) is consistently among the top-rated state universities in the nation. Thomas Jefferson founded the university, which opened in March 1825 with a mere 123 students. For the first year of operations, Jefferson was heavily involved in the university, but he died on July 4, 1826. Today, UVA adds more than 20,000 students to the population of Charlottesville during the school year.

The main grounds (you never call UVA's campus a campus, it's uncouth) are on the west side of Charlottesville. A focal point on UVA's grounds is Thomas Jefferson's Academical Village. Rather than use that clumsy and odd-sounding name, most just call it "the Lawn." The Lawn reflects Jefferson's idea that at university, daily life should be infused with learning. To further that end, he designed 10 pavilions, each focused on a different subject. These pavilions had faculty living quarters upstairs, classrooms downstairs, and were attached to several rows of student housing. Today, only a select group of students and faculty live on the Lawn and in the Pavilions.

At one end of the Lawn, Jefferson had constructed a Rotunda to serve as a library, rather than building a chapel, as you'd find on most university campuses in that day. The Rotunda is a replica of the Pantheon and is quite picturesque, though it is currently closed for extensive renovations until 2016. **Tours** (10am, 11am, and 2pm daily, free) of the Rotunda and Lawn typically meet at the Rotunda, but for the duration of the renovation, they will meet in the Harrison Institute/Small Special Collections Library instead.

Fralin Museum of Art

The University of Virginia's **Fralin Museum of Art** (155 Rugby Rd. in the Thomas H. Bayly Building, 434/924-3592, www.virginia.edu, noon-5pm Tues.-Sun., free) has a collection of more than 13,000 artifacts including 15th- to 20th-century European and American paintings and sculpture, Asian art, photography, and American figurative art. They continually bring in temporary exhibits and have an interesting collection of Greek and Roman coinage.

Kluge-Ruhe Aboriginal Art Collection

The **Kluge-Ruhe Aboriginal Art Collection** (400 Worrell Dr., 434/244-0234, www.kluge-ruhe.org, 10am-4pm Tues.-Sat., 1pm-5pm Sun., closed Mon., free) is the only museum in the United States fully dedicated to the artwork of Australian Aboriginal peoples. Their collection is a fascinating array of sculptures; paintings and drawings on canvas, paper, and eucalyptus bark; carvings; musical instruments; and more. The museum is located three miles east of UVA.

Virginia Discovery Museum

The **Virginia Discovery Museum** (524 E. Main St., 434/977-1025, www.vadm.org, 10am-5pm Mon.-Sat., $6 all ages, discounts of $0.50 for seniors, AAA members, and military; free to members) is a kid-oriented museum at the east end of the Downtown Mall. Small by comparison to other children's museums, this is still a great resource for travelers with little ones in tow, especially on rainy days. Exhibits are of the bright, hands-on variety that you'd expect, and they have a beehive you can peek in on and an exhibit called A-Mazing Airways, in which puffs of air push balls and scarves through a complicated and twisted series of clear pipes.

★ Monticello

Thomas Jefferson's stunning mountaintop home, **Monticello** (931 Thomas Jefferson Pkwy., 434/984-9800, www.monticello.org, 8:30am-6pm daily, $25 adults, $8 ages 5-11, free 4 and under), is just four miles southeast of Charlottesville. This is one of the most beautiful and historic sites in the region. This 5,000-acre plantation was the home of Jefferson, the third president, author of the Declaration of Independence, and founder of the University of Virginia. Oh, and as if that wasn't enough, he designed his home.

Jefferson began building Monticello when he was just 26, shortly after inheriting the land from his father. For the rest of his life, he lived here, expanding his home and experimenting with different crops and agricultural methods. Though it doesn't look the part, the Italian Renaissance architecture-inspired home was intended to be a functioning plantation house.

Touring the home takes a little more than 30 minutes. The home itself is notable for its interesting design choices, including the columns ringing the house and the octagonal dome that tops it. Inside, two large rooms, the entrance hall and a parlor/music room, anchor the interior, which measures some 11,000 square feet. Jefferson used the entrance hall to display items of scientific import or curiosity and the parlor/music room for spending what little idle time he had. The dome room is, unfortunately, off limits (thanks to fire regulations), but the floors are painted grass green and the octagonal walls "Mars yellow."

Be sure to spend time exploring the picturesque gardens and outbuildings, which include slave quarters and structures typical for a plantation home in those days. Mulberry Row, a mulberry tree-lined road, is quite nice.

There are several tour options available in addition to the standard house tour. Options include a Behind the Scenes Tour ($45) that takes you upstairs; the Revolutionary Garden Tour ($45), which allows guests to participate in seasonal gardening activities; and private tours (starting at $600 for four guests). Other tours, like the Slavery at Monticello and Garden and Grounds Tours, are free and don't require reservations.

There were two vineyards at Monticello, which Jefferson and his workers struggled to keep growing as a result of pests and disease that ravaged European root stock (a problem not solved until much later with the invention of modern pesticides and grafting and hybridizing techniques). Jefferson experimented with many other grapes, and did make wine using native grapes, though the poor quality of the fruit made for a poor-quality wine; nonetheless, Jefferson was committed to the idea of American-grown grapes and American-produced wines. Because of this, he's often called America's "first distinguished viticulturist."

Indeed he was important to the industry, important enough for the **Monticello Wine Trail** (434/566-0747, www.monticellowinetrail.org) and the wineries on the trail to draw inspiration for his vision of American winemaking. There are more than 30 wineries on the Monticello Wine Trail, including **Jefferson Vineyards** (1353 Thomas Jefferson Pkwy., 434/977-3042, www.jeffersonvineyards.com, tours: 1pm and 2pm daily, tasting room: 10am-6pm daily, tastings $10-20), on a site adjacent to Monticello where Thomas Jefferson and Italian Filippo Mazzei decided to first establish a vineyard. Tastings include a souvenir glass.

Carter Mountain Apple Orchard
You can pick your own apples and peaches (depending on the season, of course) at **Carter Mountain Apple Orchard** (1435 Carters Mountain Trail, 434/977-1833, www.cartermountainorchard.com, hours vary by season and day, daily mid-Apr.-Nov., weekends Dec. 5-21). This is apple country, and toward the end of August, the trees are heavy with ripening apples, which you can pick yourself or buy a bag or basket of apples. The orchard is beautiful, ripe apples or no, and they kick off spring with an East Egg Hunt, celebrate the arrival of apple blossoms with a Spring Fling Festival in May, and host the Ol' Fashioned Peach Festival in July.

Wineries and Vineyards
Established by Dave Matthews in 2000, **Blenheim Vineyards** (31 Blenheim Farm, 434/293-5366, www.blenheimvineyards.com, tastings 11am-5:30pm daily, $5) is just a short drive southeast of the city. Between their two vineyards, they grow chardonnay, cabernet franc, cabernet sauvignon, petit verdot, and viognier. The tasting room features a long section of glass flooring that looks down into the barrel and tank room below; it's pretty cool.

First Colony Winery (1650 Harris Creek Rd., 434/979-7105, www.firstcolonywinery.com, tastings 10am-6pm Mon.-Fri. and 11am-6pm Sat.-Sun., tours 1pm and 3pm Sat.-Sun.) started small, with only 4.5 acres of merlot and cabernet sauvignon planted, then expanded to a 6.5-acre vineyard growing chardonnay, petit verdot, cabernet franc, and vidal blanc. There are plans to keep expanding until they have 20 or more acres "under vine." As it stands now, though, the grounds are beautiful and ripe with picnic spots, and the tasting room is quite lovely.

At **Keswick Vineyards** (1575 Keswick Winery Dr., 434/244-3341, www.keswickvineyards.com, 9am-5pm daily, closed Thanksgiving, Christmas, and New Year's Day, tastings $6-10), they produce small lots of wine, employing a minimalist approach to growing their grapes that comes down to this: the focus is on growing the best fruit possible. They have a number of international award winners, with more than 60 silver medals and nearly 50 gold medals to their credit. Keswick is proud of the fact that they don't import any grapes into their vineyard, using only estate-grown fruit to make their wine.

Pippin Hill Farm and Vineyard (5022 Plank Rd., North Garden, Va., 20 minutes from Charlottesville, 434/202-8063, www.pippinhillfarm.com, tastings 11am-5pm Tues.-Sun., $6) is among the area's primo wedding locations, and one look at the facilities and vineyards and it's easy to see why. The kitchen here puts out fabulous food you can pair with wine for a tasting or a full meal. One notable thing about Pippin Hill is that they employ a sustainable viticulture program to produce their high-quality grapes.

If you want a day of touring vineyards, check out **Blue Ridge Wine Excursions** (434/531-5802, www.blueridgewineexcursions.com); they know the wines and vineyards and will put together a tour that you'll love.

Entertainment
Nightlife
Beer and Breweries
Beer Run (156 Carlton Rd., 434/984-2337, www.beerrun.com, 8am-11pm Mon.-Thurs., 8am-midnight Fri.-Sat., 11am-10pm Sun.) is one of the best beer bars in town and *Draft Magazine* named Beer Run one of "America's 100 Best Beer Bars 2014." They have an extensive draft and bottle list, and a crazy good bottle shop on premises. If you get hungry, they have a pretty big menu too.

In Crozet, **Fardowners** (5773 County Rd. 1217, Crozet, 434/823-1300, www.fardowners.com, 11am-midnight Mon.-Thurs., 11am-1:30am Fri.-Sat., 10am-midnight Sun.) has a great neighborhood feel and a tight little beer list and set of cocktails like you'd expect at the bar around the corner. They emphasize the local breweries, so it's a good spot to stop and sample some of the area suds. They also serve a pub-grub menu, and their burgers, especially the Fardowners Burger (on a pretzel bun) is very good.

You can tour six area breweries that are on the **Brew Ridge Trail** (434/263-7015, www.brewridgetrail.com). The trail leads through Nelson and Albemarle counties on a pleasant and scenic drive, then into Charlottesville. Stops along the Brew Ridge Trail include:

- **Blue Mountain Barrel House** (495 Cooperative Way, Arrington, 434/263-4002, www.bluemountainbarrel.com, 11am-6pm Mon.-Thurs., 11am-8pm Fri.-Sun., open later in summer)

- **Blue Mountain Brewery** (9519 Critzers Shop Rd., Afton, 540/456-8020, www.bluemountainbrewery.com, 11am-10pm Mon.-Sat., 11am-9pm Sun.)

- **Devils Backbone Brewing Company** (200 Mosbys Run, Roseland, 434/361-1001, www.dbbrewingcompany.com, 11:30am-last call daily)

- **South Street Brewery** (106 W. South St., Charlottesville, 434/293-6550, www.southstreetbrewery.com, 11am-1am daily)

- **Starr Hill Brewing Company** (5391 Three Notched Rd., Crozet, 434/823-5671, www.starrhill.com, 1pm-8pm Wed.-Thurs., noon-8pm Fri., 11am-8pm Sat., noon-6pm. Sun., closed Mon.-Tues.)

- **Wild Wolf Brewing Company** (2461 Rockfish Valley Hwy., Nellysford, 434/361-0088, www.wildwolfbeer.com, 11:30am-last call Mon.-Fri., 11am-last call Sat.-Sun.)

Live Music
Charlottesville's music scene is very vibrant, as you'd expect in a town with a

college that numbers more than 20,000 students. The most well known of the local talent is Dave Matthews. He and several of his bandmates attended UVA. While they were here, Dave was a bartender at **Miller's Downtown** (109 W. Main St., 434/971-8511, www.millers-downtown.com, 11:30am-2am daily). This restaurant and bar is on the Downtown Mall and it stays open late, serves a full menu until closing time, and always has a full schedule of bands from jazz to rock.

Many believe the **Jefferson Theatre** (101 E. Main St., 434/425-4980 or 800/594-8499, www.jeffersontheatre.com) to be the best theater in town, though much of that debate is colored by music preference. Superlatives aside, the Jefferson Theatre was opened in 1912, showing silent movies and vaudeville acts, and seeing performers like Houdini and The Three Stooges grace the stage. Today, it has a state-of-the-art sound and light system and hosts bluegrass, heavy metal, hip hop, electronic, jam, and rock acts.

Performing Arts

The **Paramount Theatre** (215 E. Main St., 434/979-1333, www.theparamount.net, box office 10am-2pm Mon.-Fri.) opened in 1931 and quickly became a landmark, flourishing during the Great Depression. It closed in 1974 and sat empty for more than three decades before reopening in 2004. Now restored to its former glory, the Paramount shows classic movies, hosts plays and opera performances, brings in lecturers and comics, and even airs cult classics like *The Rocky Horror Picture Show*.

Festivals and Events

In mid-April, the city holds its largest festival, the **Dogwood Festival** (434/961-9824, www.charlottesvilledogwoodfestival.org). It lasts two weeks, includes a carnival, fireworks, that indulgent festival food, and a parade, and is the perfect way to welcome spring. The carnival is held in McIntire Park (off US-250 between US-29 and McIntire Rd.). Other events take place across the city.

October is officially **Virginia Wine Month** (www.virginiawine.org), and all month, visitors pack the wineries in Charlottesville and other spots across the state to take in the fall leaves and find a new favorite vintage. Around Charlottesville, there are around 30 vineyards you can visit for Wine Month festivities or check out any other day of the year.

In November, the **Virginia Film Festival** (multiple venues, 434/924-3376, www.virginiafilmfestival.org) brings in close to 100 films and the same number of guest artists during this three-day film bonanza. In addition to nearly around-the-clock screenings, there are lectures and panel discussions covering all aspects of the film process or examining topics pertinent to film history.

Shopping

On the **Downtown Mall** (www.downtowncharlottesville.net), you'll find more than 120 shops (and 30 restaurants, many of them with outdoor seating) in the historic buildings on and around Old Main Street. Now a pedestrian area, the Mall is the perfect stop for those looking to shop, browse, or simply people-watch.

Those of you into vinyl will want to browse a bit at **Melody Supreme** (115 4th St. SE, 434/760-3618, www.melodysupreme.org, 11am-6pm Mon.-Thurs., 11am-7pm Fri.-Sat., 1pm-5pm Sun.). This independent record store specializes in limited editions, deluxe editions, and a staff who knows their stuff.

Bittersweet Clothing and Accessories (106 E. Main St., 434/977-5977, www.shopbittersweet.com, 10am-7pm Mon.-Thurs., 10am-8pm Fri.-Sat., noon-5pm Sun.) is a boutique catering to women who want to wear something a little different. It's not avant-garde fashion or haute couture at its hautest, but it is very fashionable and thoughtfully stocked.

The owner makes it a point to work with small designers and buy in smaller quantities as a way to ensure both quality and the true one-of-a-kind sense of the clothing and accessories here.

At **Alakazam Toys & Gifts** (100 E. Main St., 434/971-1717, www.alakazamtoys. com, 10am-6pm Mon.-Thurs., 10am-7pm Fri.-Sat., noon-5pm Sun.) you'll find gifts, toys, and games for kids. They have a ton of stuff: scooters and balance bikes, costumes for boys and girls, juggling kits and hula hoops, art kits, plush animals, and wooden toys, to name just part of their selection. If you have any kids in tow, this is a good place to stop and get them a little something special for the trip.

If you find yourself ill prepared for some of the hikes coming up in your journey, visit **Great Outdoor Provision Company** (1125 Emmet St. N., 434/995-5669, www.greatoutdoorprovision.com, 10am-9pm Mon.-Fri., 9am-6pm Sat., noon-6pm Sun.). Great Outdoor carries a full line of hiking, camping, fishing, snow sports, and adventure travel gear, including brands like Patagonia, Mountain Hardwear, Columbia, The North Face, Prana, and Smartwool.

In Charlottesville, you'll find used bookshops everywhere you turn. Two of the best are **Oakley's Gently Used Books** (112 W. Main St. #9, 434/977-3313, www. oakleysusedbooks.com, 10am-6pm Mon. and Wed.-Sat., closed Tues. and Sun.) and **Dadedalus Used Bookshop** (121 4th St. NE, 434/293-7595, 10am-5pm Mon.-Thurs., 10am-6pm Fri.-Sun.). Oakley's has more than 15,000 books on their shelves, with a big selection of science fiction and fantasy. At Daedalus Used Bookshop you'll find a curious cat and even more curious staff, who are funny, witty, and quick with suggestions for authors and titles that may surprise you.

Though it's not a used bookshop, **New Dominion Bookshop** (404 E. Main St., 434/295-2552, www.newdominionbook-shop.com, 9:30am-5:30pm Mon.-Wed. and Sat., 9:30am-8pm Thurs.-Fri., 1pm-5pm Sun.) is a great one. The oldest independent bookseller in Virginia, New Dominion hosts readings and literary events, and has a broad selection of genres on their shelves. Browse a bit; if you don't see what you like, ask one of the staff, they're fellow bibliophiles and will be happy to help.

Recreation

Mountain bikers of a certain skill level should ride the five-mile single-track trail at **Walnut Creek Park** (4250 Walnut Creek Park Rd., North Garden, 434/296-5844, 7am-dark daily, $3 adults, $2 children). The loop is challenging, so beginner bikers beware, but intermediate and experienced bikers, strap on those helmets. The trail flows through a hardwood forest around a 23-acre lake on a twisty, tight, and sometimes technical route. For those beginner to intermediate bikers who don't want to challenge this ride, there are 15 miles of trails in this 480-acre park, which gives you plenty of space to sharpen your skills. There's also an 18-hole **disc golf** course here.

The 104-acre **Beaver Creek Lake** (4365 Beaver Creek Rd., 434/296-5844, 7am-sunset daily) is well stocked with large-mouth bass, sunfish, and channel catfish. If you have your Virginia fishing license, see what you can catch.

Try something a little different with **Blue Ridge Ballooning** (434/589-6213, www.blueridgeballoon.com, from $225). You'll have a view of the countryside that you can get no other way than by hot air balloon. Packages include sunrise and sunset flights, picnic flights, hot air balloon weddings, and private flights. In late September and through October, it's best to make reservations well in advance so you'll have a spot and the best leaf-peeping vantage of your life.

Spectator Sports

There are no professional sports teams in Charlottesville, so the focus falls to the **Virginia Cavaliers** (434/924-8821 or 800/542-8821, www.virginiasports.com) and the 23 varsity sports at University of Virginia. Football is played at **Scott Stadium,** basketball at the **John Paul Jones Arena,** soccer and lacrosse at **Klöckner Stadium,** and other sports at various on- and off-campus venues.

The **Charlottesville Derby Dames** (www.charlottesvillederbydames.com) are a roller derby team and member of the Women's Flat Track Derby Association. If you've never seen roller derby, do yourself a favor and take in a bout (yes, it's a bout, like boxing or MMA, not a game like football or golf). Watch these athletes as they speed around the track and clobber each other at every turn. Yes, it's violent, but in a fun way; every derby contestant demonstrates good sportsmanship.

Accommodations
$100-200

The **English Inn of Charlottesville** (2000 Morton Dr., 434/971-9900, www.englishinncharlottesville.com, $100-280) is a 106-room independent hotel. The rooms and suites are comfortable, and the staff quite friendly. This Tudor-style hotel is a few miles from downtown.

At ★ **200 South Street Inn** (200 W. South St., 434/979-0200, www.southstreetinn.com, $130-285) you'll find 24 guest rooms and suites in an unbeatable location: two blocks from the Downtown Mall, one mile from the University of Virginia, and a four-mile drive to Monticello. The Inn combines two houses. The larger of the two was built in 1856 for Thomas Jefferson Werenbaker, son of a close friend to Thomas Jefferson, and transformed from home to girls' finishing school to boarding house to its current role as Inn. The smaller house was built in 1890 and became part of the Inn during the 1980s. Each room has a private bath, and many rooms have whirlpool tubs. Though the rooms may lack some conveniences found in chain hotels, they aren't missed; the attentiveness

of the innkeepers makes sure of that. There's a continental breakfast in the morning and cookies, wine, and cheese in the afternoon.

Rooms at the **Hilton Garden Inn Charlottesville** (1793 Richmond Rd., 434/979-4442, www.hiltongardeninn3.hilton.com, $139-259) are what you'd expect from this well-known chain: comfortable, clean, and reasonably priced. Located on the east side of town, the hotel is about four miles from UVA and three miles from the downtown historic area and downtown shopping and dining.

The **Hampton Inn Charlottesville** (2035 India Rd., 434/978-7888, www.hamptoninn3.hilton.com, $159-219) is also a few miles from downtown, within an easy drive. There is free breakfast every morning and a number of restaurants and shops within walking distance.

$200-300

Consistently rated as the top B&B in Charlottesville, the **Foxfield Inn** (2280 Garth Rd., 434/923-8892 or 866/369-3536, www.foxfield-inn.com, $185-310) is known to pamper guests and provide a place to escape the rush of daily life. There are five rooms here, so it's small, but each room offers you enough space to feel at home. Breakfast is of the three-course gourmet variety, and the four deluxe rooms have fireplaces, two-person whirlpool tubs, and large, walk-in showers.

★ **Arcady Vineyard Bed & Breakfast** (1376 Sutlers Rd., 434/960-0820 or 434/872-9475, www.innarcadyvineyard.com, $250-275) was started by a couple with decades of experience in the hotel, restaurant, and wine industries. Each room is large and comfortable, and several packages compliment the excellent accommodations. Packages include wine tours ($492-855), massages ($100), and "Sweetheart Celebration" ($302-915, weekend package includes wine tour), perfect for that romantic getaway in Virginia's wine region.

The **Clifton Inn** (1296 Clifton Inn Dr., 434/981-1800, www.clifton-inn.com, $269-419) was built and used by Thomas Jefferson's son-in-law, Thomas Mann Randolph (who was also the governor of Virginia). The Inn sits on 100 quiet acres, and has 17 rooms and suites, each spacious, comfortable, and decorated with its own personality. They have an infinity pool, clay tennis court, croquet greensward, and several hiking trails to keep you active.

At the **Boar's Head Inn** (200 Ednam Dr., 434/296-2181, www.boarsheadinn. com, $175-735), the official hotel of the University of Virginia, expect nothing but the best. The 175 guest rooms and suites are furnished and decorated with antique pieces but still outfitted with all the modern conveniences you would require for your stay. You'll find the luxury experience in the private balcony and spa-like bathroom in your room, and if that's not enough, their restaurants (there are four) will treat you to a fabulous dining experience.

Award-winning ★ **Keswick Hall** (701 Club Dr., Keswick, 434/979-3440, www. keswick.com, $250-700) was transformed from beautiful 1912 Italianate villa into stunning grand resort by the widower of designer Laura Ashley. Sitting on a 600-acre estate in Keswick (about 15 minutes from Charlottesville), the resort offers guests access to the Keswick Club, where you can play golf, tennis, visit the spa, or swim in the saltwater pool. There are only 48 rooms, and each one is impeccable. For those who can spring for the princely price tag, it's worth every penny.

Food

C'Ville Food Tour (tickets 800/979-3370, email for information, www.cville-foodtour.com, 10am, 1pm, 3:30pm, and 6:30pm Sat., $39-59) offers two tours that give you a fun opportunity to sample the flavors (in food and culture) of Charlottesville. The tours are roughly three hours long, and take you into 6-8 restaurants and food purveyors for samples of food and drink (yes, some drinks are alcoholic). Many of the top restaurants on the Downtown Mall are stops on the tour, so this is a great way to pick a place for dinner reservations.

Asian

★ **Peter Chang China Grill** (2162 Barracks Rd., 434/244-9818, www.peter-chang-charlottesville.com, 11am-10pm daily, lunch $8-12, dinner $8-20) is an unbelievable Szechwan Chinese restaurant headed up by Chef Peter Chang. Chef Chang moved to the United States to work as the chef in the Chinese Embassy and has since worked in a number of kitchens before opening his own place. Rightfully nicknamed the "Master of Peppers," Chang cooked this fiery regional cuisine for the embassy and now for us civilian diners. In April 2014, the *New York Times* published an article about him called "Where Peter Chang Cooks, They Will Follow," and it's true, he has a loyal and legion fan base. One bite and you'll join the converted.

Himalayan Fusion (520 E. Main St., 434/293-3120, www.himalayanfusion. com, lunch 11:30am-2:30pm Mon.-Fri. and noon-3pm Sat.-Sun., dinner 5:30pm-10pm Wed.-Sun., lunch $8-9, dinner $10-18) serves up Himalayan food, a cuisine not often seen outside big cities, but one that's quite tasty. Calling on Indian and Chinese influences, Himalayan dishes are rich and delicious, with a number of options for vegetarians. Not sure about it? Try them for lunch, when they serve a buffet of 20 or so items that will give you a taste of what you'll find at dinner.

TEN (120-B E. Main St., 434/295-6691, www.ten-sushi.com, 5:30pm-10pm Mon.-Thurs., 5:30pm-11pm Fri.-Sat., bar opens at 5pm, $7-39) serves outstanding sushi rolls and some very creative Japanese cuisine. Their fish selection is always driven by the freshest, most flavorful fish available; and the Japanese dishes vary from Wagyu beef tenderloin to simple Yakatori skewers.

Fine Dining

★ **Mas Tapas** (904 Monticello Rd., 434/979-0990, www.mastapas.com, 5:30pm-2am Mon.-Sat., $4-30) creates beautiful tapas dishes using ingredients sourced from local and regional farms and has become known as one of the best restaurants in town. Their menu of Spanish and Mediterranean small plates is enormous, with over 100 items. Dishes range from a simple plate of Padron peppers and olive oil to stone crab claws in an orange, garlic, and smoked paprika sauce. Reservations are recommended.

Expect a menu full of creative, French-influenced, American dishes at ★ **C&O Restaurant** (515 E. Water St., 434/971-7044, www.candorestaurant.com, dinner 5pm-10pm Sun.-Thurs. and 5pm-11pm Fri.-Sat., late night 10pm-1am Sun.-Thurs. and 11pm-1am Fri.-Sat., dinner $25-35, late night $6-15). The restaurant has six distinct dining areas, from a barnwood-paneled bar to a cozy brick patio to a mezzanine warmed on cool nights by a wood-burning stove. In each of these spaces, the elegant dishes are equally at home. The menu is meat heavy with limited choices for vegetarians. The roast chicken with black truffle butter, local mushrooms, and potato gnocchi; and the steak chinoise—beef tenderloin with gruyere-thyme potatoes and a tamari-ginger pan sauce—are some dishes you'll talk about for a long time.

The Whiskey Jar (227 W. Main St., 434/202-1549, www.thewhiskeyjar-cville.com, 11am-midnight Mon.-Wed., 11am-2am Thurs.-Sat., 10am-2:30pm Sun., lunch $8-15, dinner $10-30) has a broad selection of Scotch, rye, Irish whiskey, and bourbon, but also be prepared for a meal that's Southern to the core but with a fine-dining twist. Their fried organic chicken with collards and chicken gravy (which goes well with a Bowman Brothers bourbon and ginger ale) is a great example: succulent chicken from a local Mennonite farmer, collards like the chef's grandmothers made, and the perfect chicken gravy. The chef owns a farm himself and uses his own fresh produce.

Italian and Pizza

Sal's Caffe Italia (221 E. Main St., 434/295-8484, www.salscaffeitalia.com, 11am-10pm Mon.-Sat., 11am-8pm Sun., lunch $7-13, dinner $9-18) is one of the many restaurants on Charlottesville's Downtown Mall. Their full-blown Italian menu is complimented by a wine list featuring bottles and house pours from across Italy and more than a few bottles from nearby wineries. But the draw is their fantastic outdoor seating, with more seats outside than in. Grab a table out here and do a little people-watching while you eat your linguini with white clam sauce.

Dr. Ho's Humble Pie (4916 Plank Rd., North Garden, 434/245-0000, www.drhoshumblepie.com, 11:30am-9pm daily, $9-22) is a short drive from downtown, and totally worth it. The pizza here is killer with creative toppings (eggs? arugula? crayfish tails?) and creative names (Jack London? Buddha? Buff Orpington?). You'll also find burgers, Philly cheesesteaks, lasagna, and other hearty items.

Not to be confused with downtown's Sal's Caffe Italia is **Sal's Pizza** (5752 Three Notch'd Rd., Crozet, 434/823-1611, www.salspizzacrozet.com, 11am-10pm Tues.-Sat., 4pm-8pm Sun., $7-20, pizza slice $2) in nearby Crozet, just west of Charlottesville. They sell their awesome pizza by the slice and serve a full menu of Italian dishes from baked ziti to eggplant parmesan to chicken picatta; you can also get subs on housebaked bread if you're not in a pasta or pizza mood.

Local Favorites

Bodo's Bagels (1418 Emmet St., 434/977-9598, 6:30am-8pm Mon.-Fri., 7am-8pm Sat., 7:30am-4pm Sun.; 505 Preston Ave., 434/293-5224, 6:30am-8pm Mon.-Fri., 7am-8pm Sat., 8am-3pm Sun.; and

1609 University Ave., 434/293-6021, 7am-8pm Mon.-Fri., 8am-8pm Sat., 8am-4pm Sun.; www.bodosbagels.com, $1-5) has three locations around town serving the best bagels you'll find in Charlottesville. These New York-style "water bagels" are quite popular, so expect a line if you get there at a busy time.

Every self-respecting Southern city has at least one legendary fried chicken joint: **Wayside Ole' Virginia Fried Chicken** (2203 Jefferson Park Ave., 434/977-5000, www.waysidechicken.com, 9am-9pm Mon.-Thurs., 9am-9:30pm Fri.-Sat., closed Sun., breakfast $1.50-4.25, dinner $1.50-9) is Charlottesville's. *Southern Living Magazine* listed Wayside, which has been frying chicken for more than 50 years, in their "Best in the South." The food here is dirt cheap and you can get chicken by the piece, meal, or bucket. They also serve burgers and sandwiches, but why bother when there's delicious fried chicken to be had?

Tip Top Restaurant (1420 Richmond Rd., 434/244-3424, www.tiptoprestaurant.com, 6am-10pm Mon.-Sat., 7am-3pm Sun., breakfast $3-14, lunch and dinner $5-20) does breakfast all day and serves a robust menu with pizza, steaks, salads, burgers, sandwiches, and salads. It's a cute little spot, and if the weather is cooperating, grab one of their outdoor tables; if not, sit at the counter.

Information and Services
Charlottesville and Albemarle County Tourism (610 E. Main St., 434/293-6789, www.visitcharlottesville.org, 9am-5pm daily, closed Christmas Eve, Christmas Day, and New Year's Day) has a rich online listing of activities, accommodations, restaurants, and resources to help you plan a trip; you can also call or stop in at the Visitors Center for in-person help with questions. The **Downtown Business Association of Charlottesville** (434/295-9073, www.downtowncharlottesville.net) also maintains a robust listing of downtown businesses and services, as well as information on parking and other logistics.

Tune in to public radio at **WTJU** (91.1 FM) or urban contemporary music at **WUVA** (92.7 FM) or **WNRN** (91.9 FM).

If you need police assistance, there are several agencies that can help. The **Charlottesville Police Department** (606 E. Market St., 434/970-3280, www.charlottesville.org), the **Virginia State Police** (900 Natural Resources Dr., 434/293-3223, www.vsp.state.va.us), **Albemarle County Police Department** (1600 5th St. Suite D, 434/296-5807, www.albemarle.org), and **Albemarle County Sheriff's Office** (411 E. High St., 434/972-4001, www.albemarleso.org) are all here to serve.

Charlottesville's **Martha Jefferson Hospital** (500 Martha Jefferson Dr., 800/633-6353 or 434/654-7000, www.marthajefferson.org) and the University of Virginia's **University Hospital** (1215 Lee St., 434/924-3627, www.uvahealth.com) have ample facilities and access to specialists.

Virginia Blue Ridge

Rockfish Gap marks Mile 0 of the Blue Ridge Parkway. For the next 217 miles, the road follows the gentle swales and curves of Virginia's Blue Ridge Mountains.

200 mi / 322 km
4 hrs

© AVALON TRAVEL

Virginia Blue Ridge – North

Shenandoah National Park
Charlottesville
256
250
64
29
SKYLINE DR
ROCKFISH GAP
254
Waynesboro
250
340
64
6
HUMPBACK ROCKS
151
6
664
MP-10
WINTERGREEN RESORT
SHERANDO LAKE
664
MP-20
151
CRABTREE FALLS
Steeles Tavern
WHETSTONE RIDGE
11
MP-30
56
56
YANKEE HORSE RIDGE
29
Amherst
George Washington National Forest
81
MP-40
Blue Ridge Parkway
60
Buena Vista
MP-50
60
Lexington
501
Bluff Mountain
OTTER CREEK
130
MP-60
Glasgow
JAMES RIVER OVERLOOK
130
501
MP-70
Big Island
Natural Bridge
Apple Orchard Mountain
George Washington National Forest
122
221
MP-80
81
Buchanan
43
PEAKS OF OTTER
11
MP-90
PURGATORY OVERLOOK
43
Bedford
43
Jefferson National Forest
460
221
460
N
GREAT VALLEY OVERLOOK
MP-100
N&W RAILROAD OVERLOOK
Chamblissburg
24
122
0   5 mi
0 5 km
© AVALON TRAVEL
Stewartsville
MP-110
Roanoke

Virginia Blue Ridge – South

Jefferson National Forest
Chamblissburg
24
MP-110
Stewartsville
VIRGINA'S EXPLORE PARK
★
581
Roanoke
MILL MOUNTAIN AND THE ROANOKE STAR
★
Salem
MP-120
Roanoke Mtn
220
Boones Mill
ROANOKE VALLEY OVERLOOK
MP-130
Cahas Mtn 3,571ft
81
Poor Mtn 3,760ft
460
11
MP-140
Blue Ridge Parkway
DEVILS BACKBONE OVERLOOK
MP-150
Christiansburg
221
SMART VIEW
MP-160
Floyd
Sugarloaf Mtn 2,961ft
Woolwine
ROCKY KNOB RECREATION AREA
CHATEAU MORRISETTE WINERY
★
MP-170
Blue Ridge National Park
Buffalo Mtn 3,971ft
PRIMLAND
58
MABRY MILL
Meadows of Dan
MP-180
58
GROUNDHOG MOUNTAIN
MP-190
Hillsville
Fancy Gap
VIRGINIA
MP-200
77
221
52
Mount Airy
NORTH CAROLINA
74
MP-210
BLUE RIDGE MUSIC CENTER
601
MP-220
N
0   5 mi
0 5 km
77
© AVALON TRAVEL

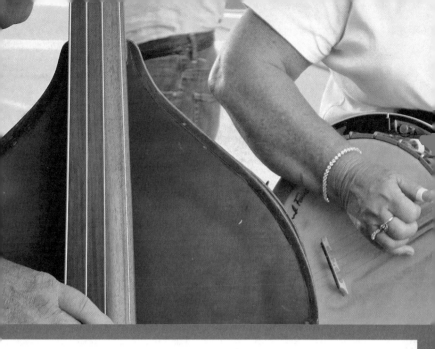

Highlights

★ **Natural Bridge:** This 215-foot tall natural limestone span is one of the oldest tourist destinations in the United States (page 107).

★ **National D-Day Memorial:** The young men of Bedford paid a grave price when Allied Troops invaded Nazi-controlled France in a bid to turn the tide of WWII. This hilltop memorial tells the story of D-Day and ultimately the Allied victory (page 113).

★ **O. Winston Link Museum:** Famous for his photography of the final days of Norfolk & Western's steam trains, Link is memorialized here in a former N&W rail station where many of his best photos are on display (page 123).

★ **McAfee Knob:** One of the most photographed spots on the Appalachian Trail is a short drive and pleasant hike from Roanoke. From this stone outcropping, the Blue Ridge Mountains look like they go on forever (page 127).

★ **Roanoke Star:** This 88.5-foot-tall neon star started as a Christmas tradition and is now Roanoke's most famous landmark. The views from its observation platform are unrivaled (page 134).

★ **Friday Night Jamboree:** In the eclectic mountain town of Floyd, seventh generation farmers and new-age artists meet every week for bluegrass music and mountain dancing (page 138).

★ **Chateau Morrisette Winery:** Virginia has many mountaintop wineries, but no other has the stunning Blue Ridge views you'll find here (page 143).

★ **Andy Griffith Sights:** In Andy Griffith's hometown of Mount Airy (his inspiration for Mayberry), visit sights that will make you feel like you're on the set of *The Andy Griffith Show* (page 146).

★ **Blue Ridge Music Center:** Catch a free concert and learn about musicians who hail from the mountains of North Carolina and Virginia at a museum that straddles the state line (page 152).

The first stretch of the Parkway is characterized by a pleasant patchwork of pastures, meadows, and hayfields, river crossings, more than a few lakes, and overlooks that take in wide valleys. Thick, mid-elevation hardwood forests grow all along the mountainsides, creating a lush green blanket in spring and summer and a bright patchwork in fall. A huge variety of wildflowers grows alongside the road.

For some ways, the Appalachian Trail (AT) parallels the Blue Ridge Parkway, either closely or on the next ridgeline over. For AT hikers, the long, nearly flat ridges of Virginia's mountains provide a well-earned break on their trek along the crest of the mountain chain. You'll find similar features on your drive. There are curves—what mountain road is missing curves?—and you will climb a mountain or two, but this part of the Parkway is the easiest to drive.

Blue Ridge Parkway planners elected to chase the wandering ridgelines of the mountains along the Virginia stretch of the route, often giving travelers spectacular views to the east and west without having to rely on so many overlooks. There are overlooks, though, and when you stop at one, the sight is often breathtaking. Many look across wide, flat-bottomed river valleys that were the interstate highways of their day, carrying settlers from New York to Alabama. Looking out from the highest vantage, Sharp Top in the Peaks of Otter, you'll gaze across valleys and up the slopes of the mountains some miles distant, the heads of their brothers peeking over their shoulders. Gaps—passes through the mountains, connecting east with west—appear periodically. These spots, used by Native Americans and European settlers alike to cross these hills more easily, are blessed with the most panoramic of views.

Planning Your Time

You could use anywhere from two days to a week to explore this region. If hikes aren't your thing, then the trip is shorter (2-4 days), as the easiest hikes don't take long to get you to some outstanding spots, and the sights, cities, and towns here will draw you in for a night or at least a day-long side trip. Hikers and thorough sightseers will want closer to a week, as some of the best hikes are half-day treks (or more), cities like Roanoke deserve at least two days to explore, and Floyd has a Friday-night-only happening that you simply must experience.

Planning ahead is key on this leg of the journey. The Parkway is open year-round, although few facilities outside Peaks of Otter are open beyond May-October. There are few restaurants along the Parkway and only a handful of places to rest your head, and if you're traveling during peak times (read: an autumn trip to take in some incredible fall colors), you may be in for a wait or be left with no place to stay. Make hotel or campground reservations sooner rather than later. Many of the best places can book up for late September and all of October—peak color months—nearly a year out. Roanoke, the largest city in the region, has the widest selection of accommodations.

Driving Considerations

The Blue Ridge Parkway through Virginia is the easiest stretch along the route. Along this part of the Parkway, the weather is generally mild, though winter ice and snow can (and often does) close the Parkway. Perhaps the largest travel factor to take into account is traffic. During peak color season—anytime from late September through October—the

Parkway gets crowded, things slow down, roadways are lined with leaf peepers and prime color photographers, and the overlooks are filled to capacity. That said, it's a marvelous time to visit, you just have to be alert to traffic and pedestrians and patient with your travels.

Getting There

Starting Points

If you're following the route prescribed in this guide, you'll join the Blue Ridge Parkway at **Rockfish Gap**, near Waynesboro and Charlottesville, as soon as you leave Skyline Drive and Shenandoah National Park. Following the Parkway south from here, you'll cover **217 miles,** a little less than half the distance of the whole route. At Milepost 216.9, the Parkway crosses the **North Carolina state line,** but not before passing close by the town of Galax, Va., and Mount Airy, N.C.

Car

Getting on and off the Blue Ridge Parkway isn't difficult on this segment. Two major interstates—**I-64** and **I-77**—intersect the Parkway at the northern

and southern ends of the route. I-64 is a major east-west route. Richmond, Va., is 90 minutes east of the parkway entrance on I-64. Beckley, W.Va., is 2.5 hours west. I-77 is a major north-south route. Charlotte, N.C., is 110 miles south on I-77. Beckley, W.Va., is the same distance to the north.

Both I-77 and I-64 intersect I-81, which travels along the western flank of Virginia, parallel to the Parkway. Along I-81, major cities include Knoxville, Tenn., 342 miles to the south of Waynesboro, Va., and the Parkway's start; Hagerstown, Md., 146 miles north of Waynesboro; and Harrisburg, Pa., 218 miles north of Waynesboro.

Roanoke, the largest city in the region, is a good starting point for trips north or south along the Parkway, and with I-81 running right by the city, it's easy to reach. Knoxville, Tenn., is 259 miles to the south; Harrisburg, Pa., 295 miles north; Beckley, W. Va., 125 miles west (along either I-77 or I-64); and Lynchburg, Va., only 56 miles east of Roanoke. Two major North Carolina cities are within striking distance to Roanoke. From Raleigh and the RDU International Airport, it's a trip of 159 miles to the north to reach Roanoke.

Best Accommodations

★ **Sherando Lake Recreation Area campground, Lyndhurst:** Kick back in a campsite with easy access to miles of hiking trails and a swimming beach (page 103).

★ **Peaks of Otter Lodge, Bedford:** Bed down in an excellent location right on the Parkway (page 112).

★ **Dovetail, Bedford:** Drink in views of the Peaks of Otter from the wraparound porch of this four-bedroom cabin (page 117).

★ **Hotel Roanoke, Roanoke:** View historic murals painted by the Civilian

Conservation Corps in the lobby of this luxe, yet affordable, hotel (page 129).

★ **Black Lantern Inn, Roanoke:** This green-certified inn offers jetted massage tubs as well as complimentary golf clubs and bicycles (page 130).

★ **Ambrosia Farm Bed & Breakfast, Floyd:** Unwind at this farmhouse retreat, nestled into hills and pastures (page 140).

★ **Primland, Meadows of Dan:** Enjoy incredible views and activities galore, from horseback riding to stargazing (page 145).

T-U2L

Charlotte and Charlotte Douglas International Airport lie only 200 miles south along I-77.

There are a number of other points you can use to enter the Blue Ridge Parkway, as many highways intersect with this part of the route.

Fueling Up
These are the most convenient spots to fuel up along this route:

- **MP 0,** US-250 less than one mile west

- **MP 45.6,** US-60 less than five miles west

- **MP 63.7,** US-501 less than two miles south

- **MP 90.9,** VA-43 less than five miles north

- **MP 106,** US-460 less than four miles west

- **MP 112.2,** VA-24 less than two miles east or west

- **MP 121.4,** US-220 less than five miles north

- **MP 177.7,** US-58 less than one mile east

- **MP 199.4,** US-52 less than one mile north

- **MP 215.8,** VA-89 less than eight miles north

Air
The two major airports in the region are in Charlottesville and Roanoke. **Charlottesville Albemarle Airport** (100 Bowen Loop, Charlottesville, 434/973-8342, www.gocho.com) is served by Delta, American Airlines, United Airlines, and US Airways, with flights arriving daily from cities all across the Eastern seaboard and Midwest. Airlines flying out of the **Roanoke-Blacksburg Regional Airport** (5202 Aviation Dr., NW, Roanoke, 540/362-1999, www.fly-roa.com) include Allegiant Air, American Airlines, Delta Airlines, United Airlines, and US Airways.

The **Richmond International Airport** (1 Richard E. Byrd Terminal Dr., Richmond, 804/226-3000, www.flyrichmond.com) is

Best Restaurants

★ **Town Kitchen Provisions, Bedford:** Nosh on classic, casual American fare on the ground floor of a historic home (page 117).

★ **Texas Tavern, Roanoke:** Belly up to one of this tavern's 10 counter seats for the Cheesy Western, a fried-egg-topped cheeseburger (page 131).

★ **Lucky, Roanoke:** Pair your duck leg confit with a cocktail here. The drinks are the best in Roanoke (page 131).

★ **The Blue Apron Restaurant and Red Rooster Bar, Salem:** The small plates here are a clever fusion of South American and Southern American cuisine (page 132).

★ **Oddfellas Cantina, Floyd:** You can't go wrong with this eclectic restaurant's philosophy—"whole food for whole people." Frequent live music is an added bonus (page 140).

★ **Mabry Mill Restaurant, Meadows of Dan:** There's a good reason the pancakes here are famous (page 145).

★ **The Snappy Lunch, Mount Airy:** Feel like you've stepped into Mayberry at this cafe in Andy Griffith's hometown. It was even mentioned on *The Andy Griffith Show* (page 151).

only about 90 minutes east of Rockfish Gap and Milepost 0 of the Blue Ridge Parkway along I-64, and may be a viable option.

Train and Bus

At the **Charlottesville Amtrak station** (CVS, 810 W Main St., 434/296-4559, www.amtrak.com, 6am-9:30pm daily), the Cardinal/Hoosier State, Crescent, and Northeast Regional Lines pass through daily.

The **Lynchburg Amtrak station** (LYH, 825 Kemper St., Lynchburg, 800/872-7245, www.amtrak.com, 5am-12:45pm and 4pm-11:45pm daily), about an hour east of Roanoke, is served by Amtrak's Crescent and Northeast regional lines. Currently, Roanoke does not have rail service, though in 2014, Virginia and Norfolk Southern Railroad signed an agreement to improve tracks and build a station in Roanoke, extending Amtrak passenger service from Lynchburg to Roanoke. Service is expected to begin no later than fall 2017.

Both Charlottesville and Roanoke have Greyhound stations near downtown where it is easy to get to accommodations or a car rental agency. The **Charlottesville Greyhound station** (310 W. Main St., 434/295-5131, www.greyhound.com, 4am-10am, 11:30am-6:30pm, and 8pm-10pm daily) is just a few blocks from the Amtrak station. The **Roanoke Greyhound station** (26 Salem Ave. SW, 540/343-5436, www.greyhound.com, midnight-2am, 9am-5pm daily) is very convenient to downtown.

Rockfish Gap (MP 0.0)

At only 1,909 feet high, Rockfish Gap offered wildlife, then Native Americans, then colonists and settlers, and now endless interstate traffic—including you—an easy place to pass through these mountains. It's a rather ho-hum start to the epic Blue Ridge Parkway; there's little more than a sign here announcing the Parkway and another sign with the speed limit.

Humpback Rocks (MP 5.9)

The first visitor center you come to on the Blue Ridge Parkway is at Milepost 5.9, the **Humpback Rocks Visitor Center** (MP 5.9, 540/377-2377, 10am-5pm daily May-Nov.). At the visitor center, you'll find maps and pamphlets about many of the on- and off-Parkway attractions nearby, as well as restrooms. There are two short hikes here: one to a farm and homestead made up of relocated buildings and structures on Parkway land, which have been assembled here as a whole farm; the other to the namesake Humpback Rocks.

The self-guided Mountain Farm Trail leads through a reconstructed 19th-century farmstead, with exhibits on life in the rural Blue Ridge. Across the road, a steep, two-mile trail climbs to the jagged top of Humpback Rocks (3,080 ft.) for a 360-degree view of the mountains. Past Devil's Knob (3,851 ft.) is a turnoff to VA-664 east toward Wintergreen Resort.

Mountain Farm Trail

Distance: 0.5 miles out and back
Duration: 20 minutes
Elevation gain: negligible
Difficulty: easy
Trailhead: Humpback Rocks Visitor Center parking area at MP 5.9

Less of a hike and more of a stroll, this trail takes you through an 1890s mountain farm. Grab a brochure about the trail at the visitor center and follow the paved trail to a gravel path that leads through the farm. Along the way, you'll pass a cabin, a weasel-proof chicken house, a collection of farm tools, a garden, a barn and a pigpen, and the springhouse. All along the way you'll have a view of Humpback Rocks.

Winter green resort condo

Humpback Rocks Trail

Distance: 2 miles out and back
Duration: 90 minutes
Elevation gain: 750 feet
Difficulty: moderate to strenuous
Trailhead: Humpback Gap parking area at MP 6 (or cross the Parkway from the end of the Mountain Farm Trail)

A short hike, but one that is at times steep and rocky, this is more than a leg-stretching hike but less than a monumental undertaking. The sight of Humpback Rocks and the views from the pinnacle make the effort worth it.

Starting from the Humpback Gap parking area, follow the blue-blazed trail to the left of the kiosk. The trail ascends steeply, but it's in good condition. At the trail intersection at 0.5 miles, stay straight on the blue-blazed trail. The next 0.4 miles are tough—rocky with a few sets of wooden and rock steps in the hardest parts—but you're almost there. At the next intersection, bear left on a spur trail to the Rocks (it's obvious). From your perch on the rocks, the view is simply spectacular. This is an especially good spot for a sunrise expedition as the sight of the countryside coming alive is quite remarkable.

Wintergreen Resort (MP 13.7)

look up

Just off the Parkway at Reed's Gap, **Wintergreen Resort** (39 Mountain Inn Loop, Roseland, 434/325-2200, www.wintergreenresort.com, open year-round) has plenty of accommodations, ranging from two-person studios, lodges, and condos ($155-265) to two-to six-bedroom homes (requiring a two-night stay, $289-880) and lodges ideal for very large groups ($799-1590). To get here, leave the Parkway at Milepost 13.7, then take VA-664 one mile to the resort entrance (on your left). Many environmentalists, Parkway advocates, and supporters of the Appalachian Trail weren't too happy when private land adjacent to the Parkway was turned into Wintergreen Resort; the construction rerouted the Appalachian Trail and cluttered up the ridgeline opposite the Parkway with condos. Though it gets a bad rap with some land-use advocates, the resort is known for its preservation program and on-property trail system. The whole resort is 11,000 acres, with more than 6,000 acres permanently dedicated to forest preservation and over 30 miles of trails lacing the mountainsides.

Activities include that extensive network of hiking trails that includes part of the old Appalachian Trail (hiking guides $3), fly-fishing guide services, archery, zip-lining, a mini golf course, mountain biking, and too many more activities to list. They also have a huge snow-tubing park and the odd thrill of summer tubing (it's down a track, not on snow), and 26 ski and snowboard trails, including a terrain park. There are two golf courses at Wintergreen: **Devil's Knob Golf Course** (par 70, 6,712 yards, $49-109 depending on season), the highest course in Virginia; and **Stoney Creek Golf Course** (par 72, 7,158 yards, $39-75, depending on season).

There are several dining options available at Wintergreen, though they are for resort guests and members. If you're staying here, try **The Edge** (434/325-8080, 11am-10pm Sun.-Thurs., 11am-midnight Fri.-Sat., entrées $10-19, late night $6-15), serving pub food and a fun late night menu; **The Copper Mine Bistro** (434/325-8090, breakfast 7am-11am daily, dinner 5:30pm-9pm Mon.-Sat., breakfast $6-11, dinner $13-35), where you can grab breakfast and a fun Mediterranean-inspired dinner menu; and **Devils Grill** (434/325-8100, lunch 11:30am-4pm daily, dinner 5:30pm-9:30pm Mon.-Sat. and 5pm-9pm Sun., lunch around $10, dinner $17-36), serving lunch and a hearty dinner with dishes like pasta Bolognese, steaks, and fish.

Sherando Lake (MP 13.7)

Just off the Parkway is **Sherando Lake Recreation Area** (96 Sherando Lake Rd., Lyndhurst, 540/291-2188, www.fs.usda. gov, Apr.-Oct., $8/vehicle day-use fee). To get here, turn west on VA-664 at Reed's Gap (MP 13.7). Follow VA-664 for 2.6 miles, then take your first left; 2 miles in, turn right and you'll be at the recreation area.

Built by the Civilian Conservation Corps in the 1930s as a recreation area and flood control measure, the distinctive features of the area are the lakes. The 25-acre lower lake has a sandy swimming beach and is open for boating; the 7-acre upper lake is known for trout, bass, and bluegill fishing. A 37-site campground, ★ **Sherando Lake Recreation Area campground** (96 Sherando Lake Rd., Lyndhurst, 877/444-6777, www.recreation.gov, $20), rings the lakes, and there are miles of hiking trails in the surrounding George Washington and Thomas Jefferson National Forests. It's picturesque, well appointed, and rich with activities perfect for kids and Parkway explorers; combine this with its location and you have the makings of a great campground.

Recreation

Hiking

Pick up a trail map at the campground and take a look at what hikes might appeal to you. Most everyone will at least want to take the mile-long **Lakeside Trail,** which circles Sherando Lake. You can add to that the short, but steep, 0.75-mile **Cliff Trail.** Both of these hikes will put you in prime position for some great photos of the lake, especially when fall colors are in full blush.

Most of the longer hikes here are full-day affairs. This shorter one gives you a view of the lake and a taste of ridgetop hiking:

Blue Loop Trail

Distance: 3-mile loop
Duration: 2 hours
Elevation gain: 950 feet
Difficulty: moderate with strenuous sections
Trailhead: Sherando Lake Recreation Area campground

Begin climbing out of the campground on a moderate incline as you follow one arm of the mountain up to the ridgetop proper. Sections of the trail are rocky, so watch your footing. Also keep an eye out for poison ivy, which you can see in a few places. For the most part, the trail is narrow, but there is no exposure to heights or steep drop-offs to speak of. At just over 0.5 miles into the hike, you'll come to a rocky overlook (possibly the site of a small landslide) where there's a great view of the larger of the two lakes.

Continue on the trail another quarter mile to the ridge, where Blue Loop Trail meets Torry Ridge Trail. Turn right and follow the ridgeline about a mile before turning right again down Blue Loop Trail. Along the ridge, it's very flat and easy to make good time, but pace yourself as the water you brought is all the water you'll have on the hike. Once you turn right back onto Blue Loop, it's about 0.5 miles to a Forest Service Road (FDR 91). From the road, it's another 0.5 miles back to the campground.

Mountain Biking

Mountain biking enthusiasts know Sherando as the home of one of the burliest trails in this part of the state. Head up the steep, rocky **Blue Loop Trail** past the lake toward the park entrance—you'll end up carrying your bike, trust me—to the yellow-blazed **Torrey Ridge** trail, 1,000 feet above. Go down the ridgeline, carrying your bike yet again through a nasty rock garden, then head down the blue-blazed **Slacks Trail** to the orange-blazed **White Rock Trail** back to the lake. The whole thing is an 11-mile loop, and all the carrying makes the ride down that much sweeter. **Odyssey Adventure**

Racing (www.oarevents.com) holds races here that combine trail running, mountain biking, and swimming, including the borderline-insane Off-Road Iron Triathlon, which involves swimming 2.4 miles, biking 112 miles, and running 26.2 miles.

Crabtree Falls (MP 27.2)

Where North Carolina and Great Smoky Mountain National Park to the south are rife with waterfalls, there are few that impress in Virginia, but when you find one like Crabtree Falls, it really impresses. Crabtree Falls descends down a set of five cascades, the first of which you can see after an easy, 10-minute hike from the trailhead. Called the highest waterfall "in Eastern America," the "highest in Virginia," and the "highest in the Virginia Blue Ridge," it's a tough call to say which is true, though through some crafty manipulation of the numbers, they all could be. At the very least, it's the highest waterfall in the Virginia Blue Ridge. This isn't the only Crabtree Falls you'll encounter on the Blue Ridge Parkway, the other is in North Carolina (at MP 339.5).

Crabtree Falls Trail

Distance: 3.4 miles out and back
Duration: 2-2.5 hours
Elevation gain: 1,500 feet
Difficulty: strenuous
Trailhead: To reach the trailhead of Virginia's Crabtree Falls, exit the Parkway at MP 27.2 and head east on VA-56 for 6.6 miles. The parking area is on the right side of the road.

You're in for a climb as the trail gains 1,500 feet in only 1.7 miles. Start your climb by crossing the Tye River, then follow the trail a quarter mile to the first overlook. At 0.4 miles, you'll come to another platform and a great view of a 70-foot cascade. The next good view is at 0.7 miles, where you'll be able to look back

downstream and get a feel for the elevation here. From this point, the falls become steeper and more impressive.

At 0.9 miles, the creek falls over a smooth, nearly vertical rock face, but as impressive as it is, it's not the best. At 1.5 miles, you'll come to the base of the upper and most impressive falls. As it falls, it splits, taking multiple paths down the face, making for some very interesting photos. The trail continues beside the falls for another 0.2 miles, taking you to the top. The view from here is bad, you're too close to the action to gain any real perspective. Take the footbridge across the creek and follow a short side trail to another observation platform. Though the view of the falls from here is scant at best, you will be able to get a great look at the valley and gorge you just ascended.

The trail continues on another 1.2 miles to VA-826 (a four-wheel-drive-only road) and a second trailhead there. You're more than welcome to explore the forest here, but to get back to the trailhead, go back down the path and take a second look at Crabtree Falls on the way down.

Whetstone Ridge (MP 29)

Whetstone Ridge was so named because early settlers found the fine-grained stone along this ridge ideal for sharpening stones. You'll find flush toilets and little else here aside from a trailhead to the long Whetstone Ridge Trail.

Whetstone Ridge Trail

Distance: 23.6 miles out and back
Duration: 2 days, 8-9 hours total
Elevation gain: 1,700 feet
Difficulty: strenuous
Trailhead: MP 29 at the end of the parking area

This hike is quite pleasant other than the distance. Much of the trail follows the original route of the Appalachian Trail (dating back to the 1930s). In summer, there are no views to speak of as the greenery completely hems you in. In fall and winter, the views are expansive in every direction. Bring plenty of water (especially if you plan to camp), as there are no reliable water sources along the trail.

The hike is straightforward—ascend the ridgeline via a few switchbacks and follow the combination forest service road and trail. At four miles in, you'll reach a small **campsite.** At 5.7 miles you'll begin a rocky descent that's steep at times. Ascend at six miles, just as steeply. At 7.3 miles you'll come to one of the only summertime views of the distant countryside. When you reach the knob at 8.2 miles, you'll have a good view of the Parkway as it winds along the crest of the Blue Ridge Mountains. At 9.2 miles, a side road cuts away, down the mountain: stay on the ridge. You'll leave the road at 9.5 miles and begin a long descent along a pretty narrow path. Continue on this route until you reach VA-603 in 2.3 miles.

The trail is open to hikers, **bicyclists,** and **horseback riders.** Trail etiquette goes like this: horses have the right of way; hikers yield to horses; bicyclists yield to horses and hikers. This trail is maintained by the U.S. Forest Service, but Park Service regulations prohibit bikes on their trails (unless marked otherwise), so please walk your bike in the first 0.25 miles to the clearly marked boundary with Forest Service land. Horse folks and bicyclists can do this trail in one day pretty easily. The same is not so true for hikers. Camping is permitted, making this near-marathon-length hike doable in two long segments or three shorter ones. It is best to either camp or arrange for another car to pick you up at the VA-603 trailhead.

Yankee Horse Ridge (MP 34.4)

I love an odd place name, and Yankee Horse Ridge fits the bill. The story goes that during the Civil War, a hard-riding Union soldier drove his horse to exhaustion here. When the horse fell and couldn't get up, he did the only humane thing: put it down. The story is likely true as these mountains, ridges, and passes saw considerable activity during the Civil War. This stop is notable for two reasons: a pleasant little hike and waterfall, and a chance to see the remnants of a century-old logging operation.

Yankee Horse Overlook Trail

Distance: 0.2-mile loop
Duration: 20 minutes
Elevation gain: negligible
Difficulty: easy
Trailhead: MP 34.4 at the end of the parking area

Many like to think that the Blue Ridge Parkway passes through virgin forest and untouched lands, but the reality is that Native Americans and European settlers built homes and raised families here for hundreds of years before industrialists found the mineral- and timber-rich mountains and used them to their ends. This path follows a section of the Irish Creek Railway, a narrow-gauge railroad that carried more than 100-million board feet of lumber off the mountain and to mills below.

The trail starts with a short set of steps that lead to a reconstructed portion of the railroad laid on its original bed. Turn right onto the tracks and cross a bridge over Wigwam Creek. In a moment, the trail will turn left, up the hill, but you should continue along the tracks and railroad bed for a little ways more. It's interesting to see how the forest reclaims the railroad, yet the railroad stays clearly visible once you know what to look for. Retrace your steps to the turn and head uphill. You'll find a pair of bridges across Wigwam Creek where you can take a gander at the 30-foot Wigwam Falls before continuing around this little loop and back to the parking area.

Bluff Mountain (MP 53.1)

If you needed evidence of the gentleness of Virginia's Blue Ridge Mountains, your evidence can be found here, at Bluff Mountain. Engineers only built 1 tunnel on the whole 217 miles of Virginia's Blue Ridge Parkway and 25 tunnels in North Carolina. The Bluff Mountain Tunnel is that lone Virginia subterranean crossing. It's 630 feet long and 13 feet tall (some sources claim 13 feet, seven inches, but if you're concerned about tunnel height, it's best to err on the side of caution).

Otter Creek (MP 60.8)

There are several overlooks providing glimpses of Otter Creek as it makes its way to a parallel track with the Parkway. Otter Creek descends from 1,100 feet down to 650 feet, the lowest point on the Parkway, at the James River a few miles distant. Starting at Milepost 57.6, then again at Mileposts 58.2, 59.7, 60.4, 60.8, 61.4, 62.5, 63.1, and finally 63.2, you can catch glimpses of Otter Creek. One of the best views is at Milepost 60.4 at The Riffles Overlook, where Otter Creek drops over a 20-foot cascade.

At Milepost 60.8, you'll find the **Otter Creek Campground** (877/444-6777, www. recreation.gov, open May-Oct., $16), with 42 tent sites and 26 RV sites, and Otter Creek Trail.

Otter Creek Trail

Distance: 6.8 miles out and back
Duration: 3-3.5 hours
Elevation gain: 200 feet
Difficulty: easy to moderate
Trailhead: Otter Creek Campground

Aside from one steep ascent/descent, this is a languid walk beside a very pleasant creek. Cross Otter Creek via a set of concrete stepping stones immediately after starting the trail. You'll reach a Parkway overpass at 0.3 miles and a nice look at the creek at 0.4 miles (in the creek are some inviting large, flat rocks, perfect for sunbathing and navel gazing). At 0.6 miles, you'll reach some steps to Terrapin Hill Overlook, a short trail with an elevation gain of nearly 800 feet. A stone culvert and concrete tunnel take you under the Parkway and VA-130 just before you cross Otter Creek and pass beneath a fern-laden cliff. The trail begins to ascend a little more steeply at 1 mile, becoming a little tougher at 1.2 miles.

When you reach the 1.4-mile mark, take a moment to check out the small cave just off the trail. Then begin the short, steep descent and return to Otter Creek. You'll soon pass the Lower Otter Creek Overlook (MP 62.5) and continue downstream. Cross Otter Creek again by boulder hopping at 2 miles in, and continue until you meet with Otter Lake Loop Trail, 2.4 miles into your trip.

Walk the banks of the lake, then cross over Otter Creek at the dam and turn right (turn left and you'll loop the lake, which you can do on the return trip or as a separate hike). At 3 miles into the hike, you'll have excellent views of the creek and see some deep pools that you may want to dip your feet into. At 3.4 miles, you'll arrive at the **James River Visitor Center** (no phone, 10am-5pm Wed.-Sun.), where you can rest, check out the displays, ride back to the campground (if you are traveling with companions and you've arranged your own shuttle ahead of time) or retrace your steps back to base camp.

Otter Lake Loop Trail

Distance: 1-mile loop
Duration: 20 minutes
Elevation gain: 100 feet
Difficulty: easy to moderate
Trailhead: Otter Lake Overlook at MP 63.1

The trail starts at the dam where you'll cross the stream via a set of concrete stepping stones, then ascend some stone steps. Follow the trail 0.3 miles to a bench where a short trail leads down to another lake view. On the main trail, you'll ascend gradually to the high point above the lake. At 0.4 miles, there's another bench and the trail descends. Cross a little creek and pass through a small wetland where the creek feeds the lake, then cross over Little Otter Creek at 0.5 miles. After you cross Little Otter, you'll come to the ruins of an old cabin. Take a moment to check it out and see how early settlers here built their homes to last quite some time.

Soon after the cabin, you'll come to a marked junction with Otter Creek Trail. Cross the bridges and head back to the parking area along the edge of the Parkway.

James River Overlook (MP 63.2)

The Parkway hits its lowest point—649.4 feet—where it crosses the James River at Milepost 63.2. Just beyond, at Milepost 63.6, there's a **Visitor Center** (10am-5pm Wed.-Sun.), a picnic area, and a couple of trails: the **Trail of Trees Self-Guiding Trail** and **James River Self-Guiding Trail,** both of which are 0.4 miles long and pretty easy. The Trail of Trees is a loop that details the relationships between 40 or so plants and trees common to the region. The James River Trail is quite interesting as it leads to a system of canals and locks built to use the James River for shipping. It's a nice walk beside the river.

⊙ ★US-501 West: Natural Bridge
(MP 63.7)

One of Virginia's most impressive sights stands tall just 16 miles from the Blue Ridge Parkway. Exiting the Parkway at

top to bottom: a rocky trail near Wintergreen Resort; Otter Creek Trail; overlook sign directing sightseers to stunning views

Milepost 63.7 and following US-501 west will take you right to **Natural Bridge** (15 Appledore Lane, 800/533-1410, www.naturalbridgeva.com, 8am-8pm daily, $18 adults, $10 children ages 7-17, 6 and under free, 10 percent discount for seniors and military), a jaw-dropping 215-foot tall limestone span. Thomas Jefferson, one-time owner of Natural Bridge, said it was "so beautiful in archeology, so elevated, so light, and springing as it were up to Heaven, [that] the rapture of the spectator is really indescribable." Which is to say a visit to this natural wonder will leave you speechless.

According to native legend, the "Bridge of God" materialized to help a band of Monocan Indians who were fleeing from raiding Shawnee and Powhatans. In 1749, British Lord Fairfax hired Col. Peter Jefferson (father of six-year-old Thomas, a son destined to become president) to survey the land around today's US-11. One young assistant carved his initials on the stone wall; the faint "GW" is still visible, making George Washington the only president to have officially defaced a Virginia landmark. In 1773, Thomas Jefferson gained title to the bridge and 157 surrounding acres from King George III for 20 shillings (that's about $140 in today's money). Near the base he built a two-room log cabin (one for him, one for guests) and installed a "sentiment" book in which prominent visitors could record their impressions. During the Revolutionary War, soldiers made bullets by pouring molten lead from the bridge into the creek below and mined saltpeter from nearby caves for gunpowder.

Today, all visits to Natural Bridge start at the main ticket building, which encloses a gargantuan gift shop, an indoor pool, a miniature golf course, an ATM, and a post office. Walk downhill or take a shuttle bus to the beginning of the trail, where the **Summerhouse Cafe** (540/291-2121 x7836, 11:30am-dusk daily Apr.-Nov., around $10) offers light fare in an open patio alongside the creek. Children's voices echo up the deep, wooded gorge, where you'll get your first glimpse of the sheer size of the thing. At 50-150 feet wide and 90 feet long, it's massive, but surprisingly graceful for 36,000 tons of stone. The trail continues along the creek. It's a pleasant walk when it's not too crowded. You'll encounter an old saltpeter mine, picnic areas, and the Lace Waterfalls past an open space where Easter sunrise services have been held since 1947.

By night, the bridge becomes an intriguing interplay of light and sound as the **"Drama of Creation"** (8:30pm daily, $9), a narrated, music-backed light show, tells the biblical story of the seven days of creation. It's a moving display, no matter your faith or background, and a popular evening activity. If you have the time and money, it's worth seeing at least once.

In 2014, the Virginia Conservation Legacy Fund (VCLF) purchased Natural Bridge and immediately began working to improve the site, adding new walking and horseback trails, improving educational offerings, hiring naturalists, and remodeling the on-site hotel to bring it up to date in terms of decor and sustainability. They're also improving the recreational offerings in terms of festivals and gatherings. VCLF intends to eventually fold the property into the Virginia State Parks system, but as of this writing, the conservation group still owns and manages Natural Bridge.

Other Sights

It's said that the ghost of a woman haunts the **Natural Bridge Caverns** (15 Appledore Lane, 540/291-2121, www.naturalbridgeva.com, 10am-5pm daily Mar.-Nov., $16 adults, $10 children ages 7-17, free 6 and under), the deepest cave on the East Coast. How deep? Thirty-seven stories, that's how deep. Guided tours to spots including the Wishing Well Room, Colossal Dome Room, and Mirror Lake leave every half hour. Be aware, it's a hike to the bottom—a series of staircases, actually, and you have to take them back up.

Natural Bridge Zoo (5784 S. Lee Hwy., 540/291-2420, www.naturalbridgezoo.com, 9am-6pm daily Mar.-late May, 9am-6pm Mon.-Fri. and 9am-7pm Sat.-Sun late May-Sept. 1, 9am-5pm Mon.-Fri. and 9am-6pm Sat.-Sun. Sept. 2-late Oct., 9am-5pm daily late Oct.-late Nov., 9am-4pm daily late Nov.-early Dec., $12 adults, $10 seniors 65 and older, $8 children ages 3-12, free 2 and under), on US-11 south, harbors the usual: giraffes, camels, bears, and monkeys, along with rare and endangered species such as a white tiger born in 1997. It also boasts the largest petting zoo in the state.

If you haven't had your critter fix by now, stop by the **Virginia Safari Park** (229 Safari Lane, 540/291-3205, www.virginiasafaripark.com, 9am-5:30pm daily Mar.-May and Sept.-Nov., until 6:30pm weekends Apr.-May, and late May-Aug., 9am-5pm daily Nov., $17 adults, $16 65 and up, $11 children ages 2-12, free 1 and under), a 180-acre drive-through zoo. A three-mile road takes you past bison, zebra, antelope, and ostriches roaming free (more or less). There's also a petting zoo, an aviary, and a primate house. Kids love the giraffe feeding station. Buy four buckets of feed for $12 and giraffe grain for $0.50/serving and take a peek at these exotic animals up close.

Accommodations

The **Natural Bridge Hotel** (15 Appledore Lane, 540/291-2121, www.naturalbridgeva.com, $89-109) underwent extensive remodeling in 2014-15. The redesigned rooms are comfortable and environmentally responsible, and the facility as a whole has a new life. Along with the remodel, the hotel began using a number of green products, and sustainable practices are going into practice across the entire property. Those who believe green cannot equal comfortable or luxurious are wrong in this case. There are around 115 rooms total, including hotel rooms and cottages. Four restaurants serve cuisine from fine dining to pub standards.

Apple Orchard Mountain (MP 76.5)

Looking at these mountainsides, it's easy to imagine that the sparse trees and lower understory were either groomed to look this way or were planted, as the name suggests, as an apple orchard. After all, there are plenty of orchards in this part of Virginia. In fact, weather conditions have pruned the trees over time, peeling them back again and again, giving the mountainside the appearance of a cultivated orchard. Considering that Apple Orchard Mountain, at 3,950 feet, is the highest peak along Virginia's stretch of the Blue Ridge Parkway, it makes sense that it's a prime target for the wind, ice, and snow that gave the mountain its peculiar appearance and name. The "orchard" isn't the only odd sight here: the thing that looks like a giant golf ball on top of the mountain is a huge radar array that was used during the Cold War for defense purposes. Today, the FAA uses it to monitor air traffic.

Apple Orchard Falls Trail

Distance: 2.4 miles out and back
Duration: 1.5-2 hours
Elevation gain: 1,000 feet
Difficulty: moderate to strenuous
Trailhead: Sunset Field Overlook at MP 78.4
Directions: To reach the trailhead, drive south along the Parkway to MP 78.4.

This hike drops off the Parkway for a very pleasant 1.2-mile hike to Apple Orchard Falls and a return trip that will have your thighs burning as you gain 1,000 feet in elevation.

Head past the trail sign and cross the Appalachian Trail to enter the Jefferson National Forest (camping is allowed within the National Forest) just 0.2 miles into the hike. There's a series of switchbacks that will be a mild nuisance on the way down, but you'll love them on the return trip. At 0.6 miles, you'll come upon a roadway, then at 0.8 miles a wider roadway and Cornelius Creek Trail to the left. Continue straight for Apple Orchard Falls.

At one mile, the path begins to parallel the creek. Soon after, the trail descends steeply beneath a large rock outcropping and a rhododendron thicket. Once you cross the creek via a footbridge, the trail will ascend just as quickly, leading you immediately to Apple Orchard Falls.

Apple Orchard Falls drops some 150 feet over a rock face. The stone is lichen covered, fern riddled, and looks like the sort of place fairies would live. Walk around a bit and take in the waterfall, which looks quite different from different perspectives. When you've looked to your heart's content, reverse your path and head down from the falls, then immediately (and steadily) head back up the mountain to the parking area at Sunset Field Overlook.

Peaks of Otter (MP 85.9)

After dipping to its lowest point and climbing to the highest peak in Virginia, the Blue Ridge Parkway winds its way to the **Peaks of Otter Recreation Area** (MPs 83.1-85.9). Indeed there are two peaks: Flat Top, a lumpy mountain nearly indistinguishable from the others around it, and the conical Sharp Top, the shorter, more iconic, and more easily identifiable of the two. Sharp Top was believed by many to be the highest peak in Virginia for a long time (but it's actually Mount Rogers in the southwestern corner of the state), and in 1852, believing this was the case, state officials offered a chunk of stone from Sharp Top for inclusion in the Washington Monument. It was embedded into the obelisk with the inscription: "From Otter's summit, Virginia's Loftiest peak, To crown a monument, To Virginia's noblest son."

Archaeological evidence suggests that Native Americans hunted elk in these valleys and on these mountainsides at least 8,000 years ago, and it's no doubt Sharp Top cut quite the sight then as now. In more recent history, the valley was visited by Algonquian, Cherokee, Iroquois, and Sioux tribes hunting buffalo, elk, deer, and bear. European settlers knew of the area long before beginning to clear land here in 1766, and the first permanent settlers began to arrive soon after the end of the Revolutionary War. In the late 1830s or early 1840s, an ordinary (another name for tavern) opened, and by 1860, it was a popular spot for wealthy vacationers from flatter regions of the state. Polly Wood's Ordinary still stands today between the Peaks of Otter Picnic Area and Abbott Lake. When the Park Service acquired land for the Blue Ridge Parkway in the 1930s, a community of 20 families lived here, including the Johnson family, for whom the Johnson Farm Trail is named. A church and school stood where the Peaks of Otter Lodge stands today.

Just down the Parkway from the Peaks of Otter Lodge is the **Peaks of Otter Visitor Center** (MP 86 at the junction with VA-43, 85919 Blue Ridge Pkwy., Bedford, 540/586-4496, 10am-5pm daily). In addition to restrooms, there are a few displays on the history, flora, and fauna of the region. Three trails—**Harkening Hill Trail, Johnson Farm Trail,** and **Elk Run Trail**—make loops from here and range from easy to strenuous.

You can climb the marvelous peaks of both Sharp Top and Flat Top. There is also a **shuttle** (hourly 10am-4pm Wed.-Sun. late-May-Oct., Fri.-Sun. in May and Nov., one-way: $5 adults, $4 children ages 12 and under; round-trip: $8 adults, $6 children ages 12 and under) to a point near the summit of Sharp Top, and you can get a one-way or round-trip ticket from the Country Store in the lodge. The shuttle departs from the trailhead. There's no bus to the top of the longer, but easier, Flat Top.

Flat Top Trail

Distance: 9 miles out and back
Duration: 6-6.5 hours
Elevation gain: 1,400 feet
Difficulty: moderate to strenuous
Trailhead: Flat Top Mountain Overlook parking area at MP 83.5

This hike goes from the Flat Top Mountain Overlook at Milepost 83.5 to the Peaks of Otter Picnic Area. If you have two cars, it's a great shuttle hike of 4.5 miles. Otherwise, you can hike to the picnic area and return, making a nine-mile trip; or turn back at the summit for a hike just under six miles.

The first 0.3 miles is a steady ascent along a ridgeline, but once you cross through the small gap, the trail gradually becomes steeper until, at 0.6 miles, you begin a set of switchbacks that carry you to mile 1.3. Along the way, you'll pass through mountain laurel and rhododendron and enter a small, rocky field.

At mile 1.5, you'll reach a bench and a new series of switchbacks. This is even

Sharp Top, one of the Peaks of Otter

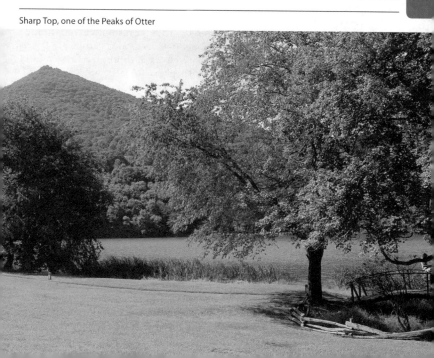

steeper and rockier than the last section. At two miles in, you'll reach a second bench and a quarter mile on, an intersection with Cross Rock Trail. Drop briefly into a small gap at mile 2.7, then begin climbing through some impressive boulders. You'll reach the 4,001-foot summit at mile 2.8. From here, you'll have spectacular views of the Piedmont to the east, Sharp Top to the south, and Harkening Hill to the west.

Here you have two choices: press on to the picnic area or reverse course back to the trailhead. If you reverse course, take your time picking through the boulder field. If you press on, at mile 3, the view opens and you have a nice look at Sharp Top. At 3.4 miles, you'll cross a ridgeline, then a second one at mile 3.6. At mile 4, you'll swing around onto the southeast face of the mountain and descend a series of laurel-lined switchbacks. The trail eases as you near the Peaks of Otter Picnic Area at mile 4.5.

Sharp Top Trail

Distance: 3 miles out and back
Duration: 2.5-3 hours
Elevation gain: 1,500 feet
Difficulty: strenuous
Trailhead: near MP 86, across the road from the Peaks of Otter Visitor Center

This hike is a lung-busting, thigh-burning workout, so take your time. In many places the trail is rocky, and you could twist an ankle if you misstep or are wearing improper footwear. But at the top, your effort pays off with unheralded views. You can hike pre-dawn to the summit in time for sunrise (be sure you have a strong headlamp with fresh batteries). It's windy and a good six degrees cooler on the summit, so you may want to pack an extra layer.

From the trailhead, begin your ascent and cross the bus road at 0.2 miles (no pedestrians on the bus road, so don't think of hiking it up or back). The trail is steep in places and very rocky in others, but it's pretty straightforward. When you reach

the 1.2-mile mark, a spur trail to your right will take you to Buzzards Roost, a lesser peak on the mountain, but one with good views. Immediately after passing the spur to Buzzards Roost, the trail turns much steeper and there are handrails bolted into the rock in places. As you approach the summit, which is made of giant, house-sized boulders, you'll meet one more path, which branches off to the left to the shuttle stop. Just below the summit is a stone shelter that exists in case of inclement weather (which can come up fast, so keep your eyes peeled). Head up another set of stone stairs to the summit, where you'll be treated to 360-degree views. You can see the lodge, Abbott Lake, the Parkway snaking off to the north and south, the lights of Bedford, and the bulk of Flat Top. To go back, simply reverse course, or head to the bus stop to catch a ride, provided you bought a ticket.

Accommodations

The ★ **Peaks of Otter Lodge** (85554 Blue Ridge Pkwy., Bedford, 866/387-9905, www.peaksofotter.com, limited openings Dec.-Mar., from $154) celebrated its 50th anniversary in 2014 with plans for a complete overhaul. Given the promising remodeling plans and the lodge's prime location on the Parkway, it's a must-stay, especially during leaf season. The food at the lodge's **restaurant** (540/586-1081, breakfast 7:30am-10:30am, lunch 11:30am-4pm, dinner 4pm-9pm daily, breakfast $4-10, lunch and dinner $9-22) is all right, but the view of Abbott Lake and Sharp Top rising above as it's reflected in the lake's waters is quite striking. Get to your meal a little early to grab a window seat for an unobstructed view. On Friday nights, a seafood buffet and carving station ($28 adults, $15 children) is pretty popular. In addition to the restaurant, there's a grab-and-go case and coffee shop (8am-4:30pm Mon.-Fri., 7am-4:30pm Sat.-Sun., around $8), a gift shop (9am-8pm daily), and lounge (4pm-9pm Mon.-Fri., 2pm-9pm Sat.-Sun.).

The **Peaks of Otter Campground** (10454 Peaks Rd., Bedford, 540/586-7321, reservations at 877/444-6777, www.recreation.gov, open May-late-Oct., $16-19) has 140 sites for tents and RVs (there are no electric hookups). Campsites are shady and generally cool, and the Peaks of Otter Lodge is a short walk away.

◆ VA-43 South: Bedford (MP 86)

The first time I saw Bedford, established as the Town of Liberty in 1782, I was hooked. The people are welcoming, the town center is a throwback to that idealized Main Street of old, and the mountain setting is beautiful. It's small, but Bedford lacks that cloistered feel that some small towns exude. Locals are open and kind, and most visitors leave with fond memories and a desire to return. Given its proximity to the Peaks of Otter and the Blue Ridge Parkway, it's a fantastic waypoint if you'd rather stay in a B&B than a lodge or campground on the Parkway, and there are enough good restaurants in town to make any meal one to remember. While in town, take a little time to learn some of the history and culture of Bedford by paying a visit to the Bedford Museum, the National D-Day Memorial, or Thomas Jefferson's other Virginia home—Poplar Forest.

VA-43 meets the Parkway at the Peaks of Otter, and Bedford is 11 miles to the southeast. At Milepost 106, US-460 will also take you to Bedford (21 miles east).

Sights
★ National D-Day Memorial
Bedford's **National D-Day Memorial** (3 Overlord Circle, 866/935-0700, 10am-5pm daily, closed Christmas Day, New Year's Day, Thanksgiving Day and Mondays Dec.-Feb., $8 adults, $5 ages 6-18 and with college ID) honors the men who fought and lost their lives in the Normandy Invasion of World War II. The memorial stands on an 88-acre hilltop overlooking Bedford and is designed to be toured in chronological order, first telling of the planning and preparation for Operation Overlord (commonly known as D-Day), then leading through the storming of the beachheads at Normandy, and the eventual victory of Allied Forces. Informational placards and sculptures represent the generals, admirals, and commanders that made victory possible. The most moving element is the quartet of sculptures on the pool and simulated Normandy beach. *Through the Surf, Death on Shore, Across the Beach,* and *Scaling the Wall* show soldiers in various poses—rushing through the water onto the shore with rifle held high overhead; fallen on the sand; rushing across the beach; scaling the cliffs above—and tell the story of that day's events. A large stone arch at the top of the memorial signifies the end of the war in Europe.

As you enter the memorial from the Gift Shop, you'll find *Homage,* a statue honoring the Bedford Boys, a group of young men from Bedford. The Bedford Boys were part of the 29th Infantry Division, 116th Infantry Regiment, Company A, which assaulted Omaha Beach on D-Day. That morning, 31 men from Bedford loaded into landing craft to be part of the first wave of attackers. One landing craft struck an obstacle, keeping five of the Bedford Boys out of immediate action. Of the 26 who reached the beach, 16 were killed and 4 were wounded within minutes. Three were unaccounted for and later presumed killed in action. On D-Day, Bedford suffered the worst loss, per capita, of any community in the United States. When Congress approved plans for the National D-Day Memorial, Bedford was the natural choice.

Touring the Memorial on your own is fine, but the **guided tours** ($2, free for veterans, tours often led by veterans, blue grass

Poplar

though seldom WWII veterans) offer a glimpse into the stories and symbolism that went into the overall design of the memorial and its individual elements, including those life-size statues on the "beach."

Bedford Museum

In the heart of Bedford is the **Bedford Museum and Genealogical Library** (201 E. Main St., 540/586-4520, www.bedfordvamuseum.org, 10am-5pm Mon.-Fri., call for Sat. hours, $3 suggested donation), where you can walk through the history of Bedford and Bedford County. Rooms dedicated to telling the stories of Native Americans and African Americans, daily life in the 19th century, the town's involvement in conflicts from the Civil War to the Bedford Boys of World War II are filled with artifacts and antiques that bring these stories to life. On the first, third, and fourth Fridays of the month, the third floor of the Bedford Museum turns into a stage for bluegrass musicians as the museum hosts a jam session. On the second Friday, a local or regional bluegrass band performs, and there's a small cover charge (they typically ask for a $10 donation).

Thomas Jefferson's Poplar Forest

In 1773 Thomas Jefferson inherited a 4,812-acre working tobacco farm from his father-in-law, providing the future president with a welcome source of income. In 1806 he laid the foundation there for a house he would come to cherish. "When finished," he said, "it will be the best dwelling house in the state, except that of Monticello; perhaps preferable to that, as more proportioned to the faculties of a private citizen." **Poplar Forest** (1542 Bateman Bridge Rd., Forest, 434/525-1806, www.poplarforest.org, 10am-4pm daily Mar. 15-Dec. 30, $15 adults, $13 seniors and military, $7 students and youth 12-18, $3 children ages 6-11, free under 6) served as a year-round retreat from that other "curiosity of the

neighborhood," which had already become a magnet for visitors. Eventually Jefferson was making the three-day ride from his official residence three or four times a year and staying at Poplar Forest up to two months at a time.

Poplar Forest was sold in 1828, two years after Jefferson's death. A nonprofit organization began restoration in the early 1990s. The exterior has been completely restored, but work continues inside and on the wing of service rooms. The sparsely furnished interior emphasizes the structure's simple, classical lines. Guided tours are included with admission. In the Hands-On History pavilion (open in mid-summer), kids can learn colonial-era skills, like writing with a copy of Jefferson's polygraph and using a drop spindle.

A winding gravel drive leads to the north portico. The entire house forms a perfect octagon, reflected in the shape of two brick privies on the opposite side. Similarities to Monticello appear in the three-piece windows that fill the parlor with light, and alcove beds, one of which has been reproduced here. Twin earth mounds on either side of the house were formed from soil excavated from the wine cellar and sunken lawn and were once planted with aspens and weeping willows.

To reach Poplar Forest, take VA-811 from US-221 or US-460, then turn onto VA-661 (Bateman Bridge Rd.) and follow the signs.

Apple Orchards

This is apple country, and there are plenty of orchards to visit around Bedford. **Gross' Orchard** (6817 Wheats Valley Rd., 540/586-2436, www.grossorchards.com, 8am-7pm Mon.-Sat. year-round, free) has been family owned and operated since the late 1800s, so these folks know their apples. Located at the foot of the Peaks of Otter, they grow peaches and several types of apples. Peaches are available in summer, from mid-June to mid-Sept., and the first of the fall apples come in around the first of September, with different types ripening throughout the season. In the store, you can buy an assortment of jams, jellies, butters, and other homemade treats.

Johnson's Orchards (2122 Sheep Creek Rd., 540/586-3707, www.johnsonsorchards.com, noon-5pm Sat.-Sun. Jan.-Mar., noon-5pm daily Apr.-Dec., free) is another longtime family-owned orchard, dating back to the late 1800s as well, but the family's farming life in these mountains predate the farm by another century. On the 200 or so acres of the orchard, they have close to 200 varieties of apples on 7,500 trees, including the Gold Nugget, an apple they developed on site. Grab a basket and go pick your own or simply buy some from the store, but do take a few minutes to wander out into the beautiful orchard for views of the neat rows of trees and the surrounding mountains.

Bedford Wine Trail

There are six wineries within a short drive of Bedford, and the **Bedford Wine Trail** (www.bedfordwinetrail.com) leads across some beautiful countryside as you learn a bit about Virginia's wine. Pick up a trail map at the **Bedford Welcome Center** (816 Burks Hill Rd., 540/587-5681 or 877/447-3257, www.visitbedford.com, 9am-5pm daily, closed Thanksgiving, Christmas, and New Year's Days) and have it stamped at all six wineries, then return it to the welcome center for a free gift.

Stops on the trail include: **Hickory Hill Vineyards** (1722 Hickory Cove Lane, Moneta, 540/296-1393, www.hickoryhillvineyards.com, 11am-5pm Fri.-Mon.), **LeoGrande Vineyards and Winery** (1343 Wingfield Dr., Goode, 540/586-4066, www.leograndewinery.com, 11am-6pm daily), **Ramulose Ridge Vineyards** (3061

top to bottom: Bedford's D-Day Memorial; a fun photo op at an apple orchard; eclectic Town Kitchen Provisions in Bedford

Hendricks Store Rd., Moneta, 540/309-6375, noon-5pm Thurs.-Mon.), **Savoy-Lee Winery** (5800 Johnson Mountain Rd., Huddleston, 540/297-9275, www.savoy-lee.com, noon-6pm Sat., noon-5pm Sun.), **White Rock Vineyards** (2117 Bruno Dr., Goodview, 540/890-3359 or 540/798-0323, www.whiterockwines.com, noon-5pm Thurs.-Mon.), and **Peaks of Otter Winery** (2122 Sheep Creek Rd., Bedford, 540/586-3707, www.peaksofotterwinery.com, noon-5pm Sat.-Sun. Jan.-Mar., noon-5pm daily Apr.-Dec.). Tasting fees range from complimentary to $10.

Entertainment
Nightlife
Bedford is a small town, so if you want to watch a sporting event or have a late-night beer, your choices are severely limited. One of the only spots to head to is **Clam Diggers** (109 S. Bridge St., 540/587-6727, 5pm-9:30pm or later Wed.-Sat., $6-25). They serve an assortment of seafood dishes, including steamed shrimp, crab, and clams, but the real attraction is their full bar and small but decent selection of draft beer.

Festivals and Events
Bedford has received several iterations of the "Main Street U.S.A." designations, and **Centerfest** (540/586-2148, www.centertownbedford.com, typically the fourth Saturday in Sept., free) is certainly one of the reasons why. This one-day gathering has been occurring every year for more than three decades and regularly draws crowds in excess of 10,000 to Bedford's Main Street. Among the things you'll find at Centerfest are arts and crafts booths, pony rides and similar activities for kids, and, of course, fair food.

Shopping
The **Bedford Country Store** (115 N. Bridge St., 540/586-2222) sells a little bit of everything: antiques; garage-sale-worthy junk; a few antiques; handcrafted pieces of art and crafts; and a selection of local meat, produce, and dairy. It also has a deli and ice cream counter. It's an interesting little spot, though it's less country store than the name leads you to believe.

In the nearby town of Moneta, the **Diamond Hill General Store** (1017 Diamond Hill Rd., Moneta, 540/297-9309, www.diamondhillgeneralstore.net, 7am-9pm Mon.-Thurs., 7am-9pm Fri., 8am-9pm Sat., 9am-8pm Sun.) sells gifts, wine, gas, bait and fishing tackle, groceries, and has a deli, ice cream counter, and garden center. It's the oldest operating business around Smith Mountain Lake, and the original part of the store dates back to 1857.

Peddler Antiques (1165 Burnbridge Rd., Forest, 434/525-6030, 11am-4pm Mon. and Wed.-Sat., 1pm-5pm Sun., closed Tues.) is located near Thomas Jefferson's Poplar Forest and is one of the oldest antique shops in the region. Located in a brick schoolhouse, it has a nice assortment of furniture, jewelry, vintage accessories, fine china, and books. If you're in the area, it's worth the stop.

Recreation
Golf
The rolling hills around the lower elevations here are ideal for mountain golf. At **Ivy Hill Golf Club** (1148 Ivy Hill Dr., Forest, 434/525-2680, www.ivyhillgc.com, 18 holes, par 72, 4,811-7,107 yards, $39-44, rates vary by season) in Forest, 14 miles east from Bedford on US-221, is a course that's both fun and challenging. Water in play on four holes offers an additional challenge as you account for the slight grade and elevation changes.

Also in Forest is **London Downs Golf Club** (1400 New London Rd., Forest, 434/525-4653, www.londondowns.com, 18 holes, par 72, 4,965-6,938 yards, $20-49, rates vary by season), another nice club where you'll find wide, forgiving fairways that often favor long hitters.

Smith Mountain Lake State Park
The 20,600-acre, 40-mile long Smith

Mountain Lake has more than 500 miles of shoreline and more opportunities to fish, camp, swim, canoe, and kayak than you have time for in one visit. A great way to get a feel for the second largest freshwater lake in Virginia is by visiting **Smith Mountain Lake State Park** (1235 State Park Rd., Huddleston, 540/297-6066, www.dcr.virginia.gov/state-parks, 8:15am-dusk daily). **Cabins** as well as tent and RV **camping** are available (800/933-7275, www.reserveamerica.com, $20-125). Two public **beaches** on the lake are open from Memorial Day through Labor Day and are guarded during operating hours.

If you're interested in **fishing,** many charters are available and the Smith Mountain Lake website (www.visitsmith-mountainlake.com) has a comprehensive list and detailed information on acquiring a Virginia fishing license (if your guide doesn't take care of that for you). One of the more intriguing guides is Captain Bert with **Captain Bert's Fishing Charters and Waterfront Lodging** (540/721-5788, www.captainbert.com, $325 two people half day, $500 two people full day, add $25 per person for additional anglers). Captain Bert is none other than Daniel Berthiaume, former NHL Goalie, and today he searches Smith Mountain Lake for another record fish. The lake already holds the record for a lake-caught striped bass at 49.4 pounds.

Boat rentals are available at several places. One of the easiest to get to is **Bridgewater Marina's State Park Rentals** (1235 State Park Rd., Huddleston, 540/297-3642, www.bwmarina.com, 10am-6pm daily Memorial Day-Labor Day) at the park marina. You can rent a pontoon ($95/three hours, $170/day), a ski boat ($175/three hours, $255/day), a Wave Runner ($180/three hours, $270/day), kayaks and canoes ($10/hour or $60/24 hour rental), hydro bikes ($12/hour, $60/24 hour rental), and tandem kayaks and paddle boats ($15/hour, $80/24 hour rental).

Accommodations

While you're in Bedford, you might as well go for the whole country experience. **Reba Farm Inn** (1099 Reba Farm Lane, 540/583-1906, www.rebafarminn.com, $105-115) is located on an amazing piece of country property that you can explore on foot or horseback. Trail rides are available through Saddle Soar Equitainment (see what they did there?), owned by the inn's proprietors. Amenities include a pool, outdoor whirlpool tub, game room, and a range of trail rides.

If you're traveling with a group, it's hard to beat ★ **Dovetail** (1047 Dovetail Lane, 757/603-0273, www.dovetailonsuckmountain.com, $170-335/night), a four-bedroom cabin on 20 acres just a few minutes from Bedford and the Parkway. The property is stunning in any season with huge views taking in the Peaks of Otter and the undulating mountains. The cabin has a first-floor master bedroom with attached bath, an upstairs master bedroom, two bedrooms with twin beds, and a large, open floor plan. A full kitchen lets you spend an evening in, cooking up your own locally-sourced meal, and the wraparound porch gives you the ideal spot for after-dinner drinks.

Vanquility Acres Inn (105 Angus Terrace, 540/587-9113 or 540/761-3652, www.vanquilityacresinn.com, $75-225/night) has both B&B style rooms and cabins on their 10-acre farm. The rooms are large, and the cabins perfect for groups. Every morning they serve a full country breakfast on the back deck or in the dining room. Amenities include an outdoor fireplace, hot tub, massive deck, and a covered patio. Unlike many B&Bs of the "country" ilk, this one is very tastefully decorated, with enough flourishes to get the "country" across without drowning you in it.

Food

★ **Town Kitchen Provisions** (309 N. Bridge St., 540/586-0321, www. townkitchenprovisions.com, 11am-7pm

Tues.-Fri., 10am-3pm Sat.-Sun., under $10) serves a small but creative menu of sandwiches (including an excellent bahn mi and the Woody, their spin on a Reuben), salads, and frittatas; has an excellent little bottle shop with carefully curated wine and beer sections; and a nice assortment of local cheeses and other foodstuffs. Everything from the rotating selection of daily soups to the sides and mountainous sandwiches is top notch. The restaurant is on the first floor of a historic home, so interior seating is limited to a series of tables for two in the wide hallway and in the back, but there's seating outside that's perfect for groups. I recommend eating outside, weather permitting.

Folks Country Restaurant (1619 Forest Rd., 540/589-9041, 6am-2pm Mon.-Sat., 7am-2pm Sun. and daily in winter, under $5) serves homestyle grub—biscuits, hotcakes, burgers, and sandwiches—every day of the week. You can get breakfast all day, and, if you're daring or just interested in trying some authentic country food, order the pork brains and eggs. Pork brains are something like soft tofu: they scramble up nicely and take on the flavors of whatever is around. The hardest thing about eating them is wrapping your head around what's on your fork, but they are tasty.

Joppy's Deli and Bakery (405 Crenshaw St., 540/587-8777, 8am-6pm Sun.-Wed., 8am-9pm Thurs.-Sat., breakfast around $5, lunch $7-16, dinner $15-18) is a full bakery with a nice little dinner menu served Thursday-Saturday. They're one of the few places in town to get a good cup of coffee, especially if you want any sort of cappuccino or latte. Breakfast is good, but lunch and dinner are where it's at—great burgers and sandwiches, and the entrées (largely Italian) are tasty as well.

For the best cup of coffee in town, try **Parallel Café** (612 N. Bridge St., 719/371-3364, 9am-6pm Tues.-Fri., 5pm-late Sat., $1-8.50). This eclectic little café makes

great coffee and is kid-friendly. The menu is short, and aside from six breakfast items, everything else can be made into panini or crepes. Try the Tomato or Tomoto, or The Club; they're both tasty.

Located in a historic railroad station, **Liberty Station** (515 Bedford Ave., 540/587-9377, www.oldelibertystation. com, 11am-10pm Mon.-Thurs., 11am-11pm Fri., noon-10pm Sat., closed Sun., lunch $7-9, dinner $7.50-20) features a menu full of familiar all-American restaurant dishes: steak, chicken, ribs, burgers, a little seafood, and salads. Don't leave without trying the cheesecake; it's really quite good, especially after a day of playing outside.

Information and Services

The **Bedford Welcome Center** (816 Burks Hill Rd., 540/587-5681 or 877/447-3257, www.visitbedford.com, 9am-5pm daily, closed Thanksgiving, Christmas, and New Year's Days) contains the typical racks of brochures advertising area attractions, restaurants, and accommodations, but this welcome center also contains a number of display cases representing the local cultural attractions. An architectural model of the National D-Day Memorial and two cases of memorabilia from WWII give you a taste of what the memorial has to offer, and from the back deck, you can see the victory arch and memorial on top of the hill; artifacts on loan from the Bedford Museum tease the stories they have to tell there; and other cases are filled with local art, crafts, and artisanal items, many of which are available in the small gift shop or area stores. The most helpful thing here are the staff, most of whom are lifelong residents with a deep and abiding love for this small town and what it has to offer. You can also purchase tickets to the D-Day Memorial here. The welcome center's website (www.visitbedford.com) provides plenty of information on the town of Bedford, the National D-Day Memorial, the Peaks of Otter, and the countryside around this part of the Parkway.

Centra Bedford Memorial Hospital (1613 Oakwood St., 540/586-2441, www.bedfordmemorial.org) offers 24-hour emergency services at their 50-bed facility in town.

If you need police services, look to the **Bedford Police Department** (215 E. Main St., 540/587-6011, www.bedfordva.gov) or **Bedford County Sheriff** (1345 Falling Creek Rd., 540/586-7827, www.bedfordva.gov).

Purgatory Overlook (MP 92.1)

Near Purgatory Overlook, a carriage road once wound though the mountains and valleys on a track so rough, passengers felt they'd been sentenced to Purgatory. Fortunately, the Blue Ridge Parkway is more like a bit of heaven than that. Less than 0.5 miles down the road, at the Sharp Top Parking Area (MP 92.5), you'll have a fantastic view of Sharp Top. This is a great spot to photograph the iconic mountain, so have your camera ready.

Great Valley Overlook (MP 99.6)

Looking west from the Blue Ridge Parkway, you'll notice that the valley is wide, flat-bottomed, and nearly arrow-straight. Today, I-81 travels this route from Pennsylvania down to Tennessee, but for hundreds of years it's been a highway of sorts. Called the Great Valley, this essentially unbroken path runs from New York to Alabama, bordered by the Blue Ridge on the east and the Allegheny Mountains on the west. There's evidence of it being used as a war path, a trading route, and a hunting path for Native Americans. German and Scots-Irish pioneers from Pennsylvania followed this route as they migrated into the wilds of the new continent and settled here and there along the way. Plus, it's a pretty great valley to look at.

N&W Railroad Overlook (MP 106.9)

The Norfolk and Western Railroad played a very significant role in the development of the city of Roanoke, just a few miles from here. In 1852, the first rails were laid on a track running from Lynchburg (near Bedford) to Bristol, Tenn. The view here is among the best on the Parkway. Green pastures on rolling hills dotted with farmhouses, the easy slope of the Blue Ridge Mountains, and that incredible expanse of sky overhead make this a place to linger.

Roanoke

Roanoke, the largest city in southwestern Virginia, sits in the Roanoke River valley beneath the peaks of the Blue Ridge, and adjacent to the Great Valley. The metro area—which includes Roanoke and the nearby cities of Salem and Vinton—has a population of more than 300,000. Aided by accolades like Top 50 Cities for Expansion and Relocation, a Five Star Community (for quality of life), and being named one of the 100 Best Places for Business Development, as well as the city's proximity to the major corridor that is I-81, Roanoke is on a track for continual growth.

As the cultural, medical, and transportation center for the region, Roanoke can rightfully be called the "Capital of the Blue Ridge." Vibrant neighborhoods throughout the city each have their own flair, and you'll find that residents of these neighborhoods, in particular the hip Grandin Village, are especially proud of where they live. This lends the whole city a pride in the place, a pride that is well deserved. Downtown, the City Market Building, a historic market dating back to the city's earliest days, and Market Square Plaza, with its long row of permanent farmers market stalls, provide a focal point for visitors and residents alike, as a number of the top restaurants and shops are within shouting distance of one another.

Roanoke is known by two other names, Magic City and The Star City. Magic City came about due to its unprecedented growth following the arrival of the N&W. The Star City was earned in 1949, when downtown merchants installed a giant star on nearby Mill Mountain as a "Christmas decoration."

Getting There and Around
Car
At Milepost 106, US-460 will take you to Roanoke (nine miles southwest). From Milepost 112.2, you're only five miles from Roanoke, and from Milepost 121.4, the Parkway meets US-220, putting Roanoke only five miles north. Salem, a suburb of Roanoke, is only 12 miles west and accessible easily from any of these points as well.

With I-81 running right by the city, Roanoke is easy to reach. Knoxville, Tenn., is 259 miles to the south; Harrisburg, Pa., 295 miles north; Beckley, W.Va., 125 miles west (along either I-77 or I-64); and Lynchburg, Va., only 56 miles east. Two major North Carolina cities are within striking distance to Roanoke. From Raleigh and the RDU International Airport, it's a trip of 159 miles to the north to reach Roanoke. Charlotte and Charlotte Douglas International Airport lie only 200 miles south along I-77.

Air
The largest airport in southwest Virginia is the **Roanoke-Blacksburg Regional Airport** (5202 Aviation Dr., NW, Roanoke, 540/362-1999, www.flyroa. com). Airlines serving this airport include Allegiant Air, American Airlines, Delta Airlines, United Airlines, and US Airways.

It's just a short cab ride to downtown; **Yellow Cab** (540/345-7710) is one option. There are several car rental agencies with locations in the airport, including **Avis** (540/366-2436, www.avis.com), **Budget** (540/265-7328, www.budget.com), **Enterprise** (540/563-8055, www.enterprise.com), and **Hertz** (540/366-3421, www.hertz.com).

Train and Bus
In 2014, Virginia and Norfolk Southern Railroad signed an agreement to improve tracks and build a station in Roanoke, extending Amtrak passenger from Lynchburg to Roanoke. As of the writing of this book, planning for the station was nearing completion, and Amtrak and Norfolk Southern said that service will begin no later than fall 2017. Until then, travelers can make use of the **Lynchburg Amtrak station** (LYH, 825 Kemper St., Lynchburg, 800/872-7245, www.amtrak. com, 5am-12:45pm and 4pm-11:45pm daily), which is served by the Crescent and Northeast regional lines. If you take a train into Lynchburg, you'll be hopping on a bus to complete the journey to Roanoke. The **Greyhound Bus terminal** (26 Salem Ave. SW, 540/343-5436, www. greyhound.com, midnight-2am and 9am-5pm daily) is convenient to downtown, just a couple of blocks away from the City Market Building and Market Square.

Valley Metro (1108 Campbell Ave., SE, 540/982-0305 or 800/388-7005, www. valleymetro.com, $1.50 one way, weekly unlimited pass $14) provides bus service across Roanoke and to nearby Salem. The Star Line, a free trolley, will take you on a downtown route that's convenient to many shops and restaurants.

Sights
Market Square
In 1882, 25 area "Hucksters" (that's an antiquated term for vendors) received licenses to open for business in stalls,

Downtown Roanoke

To McAfee Knob

HOLIDAY INN EXPRESS

ROANOKE CIVIC CENTER ★

HOTEL ROANOKE ●

O. WINSTON LINK MUSEUM ★

VIRGINIA MUSEUM ★ OF TRANSPORTATION

THE INN ON CAMPBELL ●

SEE DETAIL

BLUE 5 ▼ RESTAURANT

TEXAS ▼ TAVERN

Elmwood Park

To Walnut Ave, Mill Mountain and Blue Ridge Pkwy

WALKWAY

TAUBMAN MUSEUM OF ART ★

ALEXANDER'S

MARKET SQUARE

ROANOKE SYMPHONY ■

CENTER IN ★ THE SQUARE

CLUB 202 ▼

© AVALON TRAVEL

0   0.25 mi

0   0.25 km

booths, and in the open air in the **Historic Roanoke City Market** (market: always open; vendors: 8am-5pm Mon.-Sat., 10am-4pm Sun.) in the heart of downtown Roanoke. Today, it's the oldest continuously-operating open-air market in Virginia and one of the oldest such markets in the nation. And judging by weekend crowds and the bustling street and stalls any time, any day of the week, it's only grown in popularity. As Roanoke has evolved into its current personality—a friendly, surprisingly cosmopolitan city—Market Square, as it's often called, served as a sort of anchor to the downtown renaissance.

As the city saw the value in the market, they installed permanent awnings to shade vendors and sidewalk shoppers, and tables to hold the produce and wares for sale every day of the week. In 2014, they took another step and closed two small parking lots in the square and bricked them in, installing more awnings and tables and creating a wide, pedestrian-friendly area. You can find the usual locally-grown fruits and vegetables here, as well as eggs, flowers, cheese and other dairy products, and live plants. In fact, the market's oldest continuous vendor—Martin's Plant Farm—has been selling here since 1904. The market stalls only close two days a year: Christmas and New Year's Days. The market is always open (it's a public square and street); during growing season many farmers are planting, picking, and preparing for the market on Sunday-Monday, so selection may be limited. On Saturdays in April-September you'll find live music and a few activities for kids in the market from 11am-2:30pm.

City Market Building

Across Campbell Avenue from Market Square is the **City Market Building**

(32 Market Sq. SE, 540/986-5992, www.citymarketbuilding.com, 11am-7pm Mon.-Thurs., 11am-9pm Fri.-Sat., 11am-3pm Sun.). It's been quite some time since the City Market Building has been the sight of livestock auctions or the home to butcher shops, fishmongers, and wholesale produce, but the sprit of the place survives on. After an $8 million renovation in 2011, the City Market Building now houses a half-dozen restaurants, an interior food court, public restrooms, and ample outdoor seating.

Across the street, on the corner of Salem Avenue and Market Street, is an interesting cast-iron fountain. Since 1898, the **Dog Mouth Fountain** (so named because of the dog head on the fountain) has offered cool, clean drinking water to human and beast alike. As with all good things, there's a legend that goes with it. It is said that if you drink from this fountain, you'll always feel the need to return.

Center in the Square

Center in the Square (1 Market Sq. SE, 540/342-5700, www.centerinthesquare.org, building open 10am-5pm Mon.-Fri., 10am-6pm Sat., 1pm-6pm Sun., check hours for individual museums) opened in 1982 as a central place for Roanoke's arts and museum scene. In the late 1970s, Roanoke was planning for a revitalization. On the wish list composed by community leaders and members was a focal point for the city's cultural offerings, a place where various arts groups and museums could have permanent homes in a central location. Center in the Square is that vision realized. After a $7.5-million renovation of the building once home to the W.E. McGuire's Farmers' Supply Co., five arts and science organizations moved in and began final touches on establishing their spaces. On opening weekend, 40,000 visitors flooded through the doors and it's been a success ever since.

In the lobby, there's a trio of aquariums,

Roanoke is a charming blend of old and new.

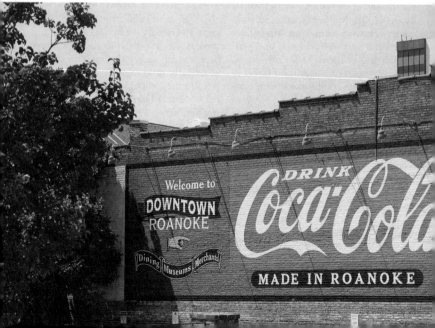

one showing Roanoke River aquatic life, one with area turtles, and another that's a living coral reef. The **Mill Mountain Theatre** (540/342-5749, www.millmountain.org, performance times and prices vary), which puts on plays, concerts, and dance recitals throughout the year is also in the lobby. You can find out a little more about what each museum offers and purchase tickets at the box office before taking the stairs or elevator to your museum of choice. Before you leave, be sure to head up to the sixth floor and go out onto the roof; the views are quite nice.

On the second floor, the **Harrison Museum of African American Culture** (540/857-4395, www.harrisonmuseum.com, 10am-5pm Mon.-Sat., 1pm-5pm Sun., $7 adults, $4.75 ages 5-17, free 4 and under) celebrates the art, history, and culture of African Americans in the Roanoke River Valley. The **History Museum of Western Virginia** (540/342-5770, www.vahistorymuseum.org, 10am-5pm Mon.-Sat., 1pm-5pm Sun., $8.75 adults, $7.75 military, students, and seniors, $5.75 ages 4-12, free 3 and under) is located on the second and third floors of Center in the Square. Permanent exhibits tell the story of the Roanoke River Valley dating back thousands of years and coming up to the present; special exhibits include pieces of historic Roanoke memorabilia, Appalachian musical instruments, and other subjects on a rotating basis.

The fourth and fifth floors are taken up by the **Science Museum of Western Virginia** (540/342-5710, www.smwv.org, 10am-5pm Mon.-Sat., 1pm-5pm Sun., $11.50 adults, $11 seniors and military, $10.50 ages 6-17 and students with ID, $5 ages 2-5, free under 2, butterfly garden add $4 to each ticket, butterfly exhibit alone $7). This is a great museum for kids, with tons of interactive exhibits (like a living river touch tank and the butterfly garden).

★ O. Winston Link Museum

The **O. Winston Link Museum** (101 Shenandoah Ave., 540/982-5465, www.linkmuseum.org, 10am-5pm daily, $5 adults, $4.50 seniors, military, and students, $4 ages 3-11, free 2 and under) displays the work of Brooklyn photographer Winston Link, who captured the end of the steam locomotive era. Depicting exclusively the N&W Railroad (the last major rail line to operate exclusively on steam engines) in Virginia, West Virginia, Maryland, and North Carolina in the 1950s, the dramatic photographs, almost all of which are black and white, bring the beauty and power of steam engines to life. Contrast the photographs of steam trains roaring past drive-in theaters with ones where they make their way around long, gentle curves in the mountains. In the latter photos, the landscape is as much the focus as the trains. It's a small museum, but it contains hundreds of photos as well as a few films.

BEST BET ARTS

Other Museums

From the O. Winston Link Museum, a pedestrian bridge leads across the tracks to the Market Square and the Center in the Square areas. On the opposite side, a path leads to the **Virginia Museum of Transportation** (303 Norfolk Ave. SW, 540/342-5670, www.vmt.org, 10am-5pm Mon.-Sat., 1pm-5pm Sun., $8 adults, $7 seniors, $6 ages 3-11, joint tickets with the O. Winston Link Museum available for $12 adults, $10 seniors, and $8 ages 3-11), which serves as a monument to the many methods of simply getting from one place to another. Inside the restored freight station three blocks west of Market Square are an O-scale model railroad, a gift shop, and a gorgeous collection of antique autos, including a 1934 Ford V-8 Model A Sedan and a 1950 Studebaker Landcruiser, more spaceship than car. Dozens of train engines and cars, a few of which are open to visitors, fill the lot out back. Steam engines, diesel locomotives, post office cars, and a classic caboose cover virtually the entire history of rail travel.

The **Taubman Museum of Art** (110 Salem Ave. SE, 540/342-5760, www.taubmanmuseum.org, 10am-5pm Tues.-Sat., open until 9pm Thurs. and first Fri., closed Sun.-Mon., free, guided tours $8) is in a beautiful contemporary building that was and sometimes still is the subject of some ire from community members who do not like the design. Permanent exhibits include fine examples of folk art, as well as galleries of works by contemporary artists and American art from 1820 through the recent past. They have a small restaurant here, **Norah's Café** (11am-2:30pm Tues.-Sat., 5pm-8pm Thurs. and first Fri., around $8), serving sandwiches, panini, and salads.

Entertainment
Nightlife
Bars and Nightclubs

Most of the better restaurants in town have bars, with a couple of exceptional spots downtown (Lucky and Metro! come to mind). But if you're just looking for a place to have a drink, listen to some music, and hang out for as long as you like, there are a few spots to check out.

The Coffee Pot (2902 Brambleton Ave. SW, 540/774-8256) is a historic landmark (really, it's on the National Register of Historic Places) and the oldest roadhouse in the state. They hold concerts here on occasion; you'll have to call ahead to find out who's playing what when. After you settle on a show and head to The Coffee Pot, don't worry about driving past it, there's a giant coffee pot sticking out of the roof. It's hard to miss.

The **Community Inn** (1304 Grandin Rd. SW, 540/342-2351, www.community-inn.com, 10:30am-1am Mon.-Fri., noon-1am Sat., noon-midnight Sun.) serves the best bar food in Roanoke at one of the best throwback bars in town. It's not fancy, it's not flashy, it's just some booths and a bar and they serve burgers with tater tots and that square pizza like you'd get in the school cafeteria (but way better). They have a full bar, friendly bartenders, and a vibe that's friendly and welcoming whether it's your first time or 50th time coming in.

Club 202 (202 Market St. SE, 540/343-6644, www.stefanosonthemarket.com, 11:30am-2am Mon.-Sat., 11:30am-9pm Sun.) is part of Stefano's On The Market, an Italian restaurant, cigar lounge, and club. At Club 202, DJs come in on Friday and Saturday nights.

Breweries

Roanoke is catching on to the craft beer scene at an incredible pace. New breweries and craft-beer-centered bars seem to open monthly. The following are three of the best breweries you can visit:

Parkway Brewing Company (739 Kesler Mill Rd., Salem, 540/314-8234, www.parkwaybrewing.com, 4pm-8pm Thurs.-Fri., 3pm-8pm Sat.) is my favorite. Their Raven's Roost Baltic Porter is on its way to becoming my favorite porter.

Parkway always has something going on, like live music, food trucks, Lego building contests, and tarot readings. You may catch a belly dancer or a burlesque show (though Parkway is kid-friendly, I'd leave Junior at home for this one), or get sucked into a one-night cornhole tournament.

One wall of **Soaring Ridge Craft Brewery** (523 Shenandoah Ave., 540/529-2140, www.soaringridge.com, 4pm-8pm Thurs., 4pm-9pm Fri., 2pm-9pm Sat.) is practically all windowed garage doors. The brewery rolls them up in good weather to extend the party outside. They have live music, food trucks, and more.

Roanoke Railhouse Brewery (3106 Franklin Rd. SW, 540/293-2423, www.roanokerailhouse.com, 5pm-8pm Fri., 1pm-4pm Sat.) produces beer with fun railroad names. Their Track1 lager, Switch monkey Belgian pale ale, Broken Knuckle IPA, and Conductor's Choice seasonal beer (of which the chocolate stout is a fine brew) have developed a cult following in and around Roanoke.

Performing Arts

Fans of opera, ballet, and symphony productions will be happy to know that Roanoke has all three. **Opera Roanoke** (540/982-2742, www.operaroanoke.org) puts on nearly a dozen performances a year, from full operas to Opera 101 lectures to short concerts, at venues across the region. **Roanoke City Ballet** (540/345-6099, www.roanokeballet.org) puts on performances at a number of venues throughout Roanoke. You can hear the **Roanoke Symphony** (128 E. Campbell Ave., 540/343-0065, www.rso.com) at a number of performances during the year at venues large and small. Past performances include works by major classical composers and themed holiday performances, as well as interesting arrangements of contemporary musicians

top to bottom: Roanoke's Center in the Square; the Taubman Museum of Art; farmers market bounty like Billy Joel and Procol Harum. If you want to attend a concert by major touring acts, the **Roanoke Civic Center** (710 Williamson Rd., 540/853-2241, www.roanokeciviccenter.com) hosts dozens of concerts every year.

An outstanding example of the possibilities of regional theater, the **Mill Mountain Theatre** (540/342-5740 or 800/317-6455, www.millmountain.org) shows original works, classics, and children's plays at Center in the Square.

Cinema

There are a couple of multiplex theaters in and around Roanoke, but why not see a movie in the only locally-owned theater? The **Grandin Theatre** (1310 Grandin Rd. SW, 540/345-6177, www.grandin-theatre.com) opened in 1932 and was the city's first theater to show "talkies." Through the years it's gone through ups and downs, opening, then closing three times. In 1990, Bill Murray hosted a benefit there to help raise money for the theater. Murray's efforts worked, for a time, but this gem of a theater closed a third time in 2001. Then the Grandin Theatre Foundation was established and a new campaign undertaken to revive and renovate the theater. It worked and now it's a popular spot in a cool neighborhood. They show current releases as well as special screenings.

Festivals and Events

Roanoke has street fairs, free concerts, festivals, and to-dos all year-round. To see what's going on when you plan to be in town, go to www.visitroanokeva.com/things-to-do/calendar/.

- **Blue Ridge Kite Festival:** April (www.srcchamber.org)

- **Roanoke Mountain Campground Music Series:** May-October (Sunday evenings, Parkway MP 120.4)

- **Strawberry Festival:** May (www.strawberryfestivalroanoke.com)

- **Virginia Mountain Peach Festival:** August (540/342-0233, www.nwchilddevelopmentcenter.org)

- **Green Hill Highland Games:** September (540/777-6326, www.roanokecountyva.gov)

- **Virginia Science Festival:** October (540/342-5718, www.virginiasciencefestival.org)

Shopping

One definite stop in Roanoke, whether you're a shopper or not, is **Black Dog Salvage** (902 13th St. SW, 540/343-6200, www.blackdogsalvage.com, 9am-5pm Mon.-Sat.). This shop is an emporium, no, a wonderland of reclaimed and salvaged architectural pieces, antiques, and decor items. There are some crazy treasures to be found here, like a bin of mannequin parts, numbered nails used by railroad workers, old signs, and a dynamite plunger more at home in a cartoon than in real life. There are also all sorts of things in their expansive yard, and if you're looking for something specific, ask, they may just be able to find it for you.

Sumdat Farm Market & Wine Shop (209 Market St. SE, 540/982-2164, www.gottrust.org/sumdat, 10am-6pm Tues.-Sun.) carries an extensive selection of Virginia-made goods. Cheese, beer, wine, ham, candy, peanuts, preserves, honey, you name it, they probably have it. Stores like this are fun because they introduce you to the local and regional tastes and food traditions.

Since you're traveling along the Blue Ridge Parkway, it's safe to assume you'll be doing a hike or two. If you find that you need something—new socks, a water bottle, a daypack, a quick-dry shirt—**Walkabout Outfitter** (301 Market St. SE, 540/777-2727, www.walkaboutoutfitter.

com, 10am-5pm Mon.-Sat., 11:30am-3:30pm Sun.) carries a small selection of camping and hiking goods as well as clothing and accessories you can use on the trail.

Roanoke Natural Foods Co-Op (1 Market Sq., 540/904-2733, www.roanokenaturalfoods.com, 10am-7pm Sun.-Mon., 9am-7pm Tues.-Sat.) is the largest cooperatively owned natural foods grocery in Virginia. The store carries a well-curated selection of organic, natural, and good-for-you items in their location on Market Square. At their second location in Grandin Village (1319 Grandin Rd., 540/343-5652, www.roanokenaturalfoods.com, 8am-9pm daily), they have a full grocery store stocked with the highest quality products they can find.

Also in Grandin Village is **Too Many Books** (1504 Grandin Rd. SW, 540/985-6469, www.toomanybooksroanoke.com, 10am-5:30pm Mon.-Sat., 1pm-5pm Sun.), a used, rare, and out-of-print books shop. For book nerds and the other folks who love the smell of those old pages, this is an awesome bookstore where you can plunder for hours. They have two stories (pun intended) of books, from the strange to the top sellers.

Appalachia Press (108 Salem Ave. SE, www.appalachiapress.com, 9am-5pm Sat., Mon.-Fri. by appointment only, closed Sun.) produces beautiful letterpressed cards, invitations, and other paper goods. They offer custom design services if you are in need of stationery or cards, but even if you're not, it's a cool shop to check out when they're open.

In downtown, **310 Rosemont** (312 Market St., 540/345-5326, www.310rosemont.com, 10am-6pm Mon.-Fri., 10am-5pm Sat., 11:30am-3:30pm Sun.) carries a chic collection of contemporary fashion for men and women. Inside, you'll find premium denim, help in pulling together an outfit or two from what they have, and fashion advice.

The Market Gallery (23 Salem Ave., 540/342-1177, www.marketgalleryroanoke.com, 10am-5:30pm Tues.-Sat.) is an artist member cooperative gallery. Close to 30 regional artists exhibit their work here. Paintings, drawings, prints, photographs, sculpture, and other diverse art forms are represented, and everything (well, just about everything) is for sale, so when you see something you like, take it home with you.

Recreation

From urban greenways to the Appalachian Trail to watersports to caves, there's an awful lot to do outdoors in and around Roanoke. For trip ideas, outfitter details, and a crazy comprehensive catalog of things to do and see, go to www.roanokeoutside.com.

★ McAfee Knob

The Appalachian Trail extends nearly 2,200 miles on its way from Georgia to Maine. In Virginia, it passes near Roanoke and Salem. Just a few miles from a trailhead in the mountains above Salem, you'll find one of the most iconic overlook spots on the trail: **McAfee Knob.** Even if you don't know the name, you've seen the pictures: a hiker, maybe two, standing on a rock ledge seemingly suspended in mid air, the valley below and mountains behind.

McAfee Knob Trail

Distance: 7 miles out and back
Duration: 3.5-4 hours
Elevation gain: 1,750 feet
Difficulty: moderate
Trailhead: 6 miles from I-81 exit 141 on VA-311 North
Directions: Finding the trailhead can be tricky. From Roanoke, get on I-81 South and take exit 141 for Salem. Turn left onto VA-419/Electric Road and go 0.4 miles to the next traffic light and turn right onto VA-311 North. Take VA-311 5.6 miles to the top of the mountain. The trailhead is on the left. Be careful as you park and pull out; it's nearly a blind curve.

This is a great hike for novices, and the views at the end are incredible. The distance is the toughest thing as the trail is easy and the ascent pretty gradual. In all, it's a good way to get a feel for hiking on a well-made, well-maintained trail. You don't need high-end hiking boots; boots are best, but comfy shoes with a beefy sole will suffice.

The trail to McAfee Knob begins across VA-311. An informational kiosk awaits around a quarter mile into the hike; here you can get a little more info on the trail ahead. Moving on, you'll cross a series of wooden walkways before you reach the John Springs Shelter about 0.8 miles in. Take a break, drink some water and continue on. There are another five walkways between John Springs Shelter and the Catawba Mountain Shelter, which you'll come to in 1.4 miles. Just before you reach the shelter, you'll pass a spring where you can refill water bottles (provided that you have something to use to treat the water).

The Appalachian Trail crosses a fire road, then goes through a right of way for a high-tension power line. About 0.3 miles beyond the power line is one of the first good overlooks, giving you a view of the Catawba Valley. A half-mile on, you'll come to the short spur trail leading to McAfee Knob.

The view from McAfee Knob is about 270 degrees. To the west, you're looking at Catawba Valley and North Mountain; this is a spectacular view as the Allegheny Mountains ripple away into the distance. To the east is the Roanoke Valley. To the north you can see Tinker Cliffs, and to the northeast, you can see Sharp Top poking into the sky.

To return, retrace your steps.

Greenways and Blueways

Roanoke has an outstanding set of **urban trails** and **greenways** spread throughout the city. In fact, there are greenway trails in Salem and in Vinton, and plans to eventually connect the three towns via a contiguous multi-use trail. As it stands, though, the greenway system (several of which are former railroad beds) currently takes you on pleasant paths between equally pleasant neighborhoods, from downtown to the Star on Mill Mountain, along the Roanoke River, and into parts of the city you don't see or pay attention to when zipping past in a car. Walk, jog, run, rent a bike (or bring your own) and explore the city a bit using one of the amenities that helps make the quality of life here so high. Maps are available in the visitor center (101 Shenandoah Ave. NE, 9am-5pm daily) and at www.roanokevalley.org. **UnderDog Bikes** (1113 Piedmont St. SE, Roanoke, 540/204-4276, www.underdogbikesva.com, 10am-7pm Mon., Thurs.-Fri., 10am-6pm Sat.-Sun.) is right on the greenway, making picking up or dropping off a bike easy as can be. They have rental bikes ($12/hour or $30/24 hours); tandem bikes ($20/hour or $50/24 hours), kids trailers ($9/hour or $20/24 hours), and trail-a-bikes ($9/hour or $20/24 hours).

What the greenway is to terrestrial travel, the blueway is to aquatic travel. The **Roanoke River Blueway** (540/343-4417, www.rvarc/blueway) is a 45-mile water trail that runs from East Montgomery County Park, through Roanoke, Salem, and Vinton, and on to Smith Mountain Lake. The Roanoke River is a great spot for sports like waterskiing and wakeboarding, as well as calmer endeavors like fishing, tubing, and wading. You can canoe, kayak, stand-up paddleboard, and generally splash around all along the river.

On the Greenway (129 Mill Lane, Salem, 540/761-6360, www.onthegreenway.com, 11am-6pm Fri.-Sun., Mon.-Thurs. by appointment for two or more rentals only, Apr.-Oct.), an outfitter in Salem, rents bikes ($10/two hours adults, $7/two hours kids, $5/two hours pull along) and tubes (per trip: $10 adults, $8 kids, $5 cooler tube).

Unfortunately, canoes, kayaks, and stand-up paddleboards are difficult to come by in Roanoke, with the nearest outfitter a 20-minute drive away.

Geocaching

Geocaching is a game you play using a GPS (Global Positioning System) to help you find a set of coordinates and then, usually, a hidden box where you can sign a log of cache-finders, take or leave a prize (if there's one in the cache), and go find another. It's one part hide-and-seek, one part scavenger hunt, and one part Sherlock Holmes, which all adds up to fun. Worldwide, there are around a million geocaches in 100 countries registered on www.geocaching.com (where you'll find caches in an around Roanoke and all along the Blue Ridge Parkway). Roanoke has its fair share, and the Roanoke Valley Convention and Visitors Bureau has placed three downtown to welcome you to Roanoke and to geocaching.

Caves

If you can't find enough to do outside exploring the mountains, how about going inside? There are caves all up and down the Blue Ridge Mountains, and near Roanoke, you have a couple of easy options. At **Dixie Caverns** (5753 W. Main St., Salem, 540/380-2085, www.dixiecaverns. com, 9:30am-5pm Mon.-Fri., 9:30am-6pm Sat.-Sun., $12 adults, $6 ages 5-12, free under 5), take a 45-minute guided tour of this cave system, discovered by a dog (and then two farm boys) in 1920. They also have a **rock shop** (9am-6pm Mon.-Fri., 9am-7pm Sat.-Sun.), where you can buy all sorts of minerals, gems, and semi-precious stones and stone art pieces, as well as a **campground** ($8/person for tents, $30 RV camping).

Guided tours of a cave that's well lit, packed with handholds, and filled with visitors is one thing, donning some coveralls, a helmet, and a headlamp is another type of cave exploration entirely. **Wilderness Adventure at Eagle Landing** (11176 Peaceful Valley Rd., New Castle, 540/864-6792, www. wilderness-adventure.com) is a teen adventure camp, but they periodically run caving trips for small groups and families. Call for a schedule.

Spectator Sports

Salem is home to the **Salem Red Sox** (540/389-3333, www.salemsox.com, tickets: $13 for behind home plate, $11 box seats, $9 general admission), a Class A farm team for the Boston Red Sox. They play home games at LewisGale Field (1004 Texas St., Salem) and tickets are dirt cheap. With full concessions—that means hot dogs, those wonderfully salty soft pretzels, beer, and wine—and an enthusiastic home crowd, taking in a game here is just about the perfect way to spend a summer evening.

Accommodations
Under $100

In Salem, **Baymont Inn and Suites** (179 Sheraton Dr., Salem, 540/342-2048, www. baymontinns.com, $95-160) is convenient to I-81, only a 15-minute drive into downtown Roanoke, and budget friendly. Remodeled in 2014, the property underwent major changes, like the creation of several two-room suites and improvements to the hotel pool. Other changes were more subtle—paint and carpet, fixtures, mechanical upgrades—and others, like new beds, linens, and televisions, improved the guest experience in noticeable ways. Given that you can get into a room for right at $100 with tax, it's hard to pass up.

$100-200

Holiday Inn Express (815 Gainsboro Rd., 540/982-0100, www.ihg.com, $116-130) is convenient to the Roanoke-Blacksburg Regional Airport, downtown, and the Civic Center. It's a Holiday Inn Express, so you know what you're getting yourself into here, but this one has a superior location to its brother hotels around Roanoke and Salem.

One of the most luxurious accommodations in town, ★ **Hotel Roanoke**

(110 Shenandoah Ave., 540/985-5900, www.hotelroanoke.com, $169-344) is surprisingly affordable, and rooms at the upper end are multi-room suites. Part hotel, part conference center, Hotel Roanoke has one of the most beautiful lobbies you'll find. The fine woodworking, half-dozen murals painted by Civilian Conservation Corps artists during the Great Depression, and stunning chandeliers set you up to expect greatness, and they deliver. The hotel, which originally contained fewer than three-dozen rooms, was built in 1882 by the Norfolk and Western Railroad to accommodate visitors and executives carried here by the new railroad. It eventually expanded, even through the Great Depression, when the N&W spent $225,000 upgrading the hotel with modern luxuries like electric fans. By 1989, the N&W was folding up shop and donated the property to the Virginia Tech Real Estate Foundation. In 1993, Virginia Tech and the City of Roanoke began a multi-million dollar renovation project; two years later, the Hotel Roanoke reopened. Two dining rooms— **The Regency Room** (breakfast $6-12, lunch $12-18, dinner $21-43, brunch $24 adults, $12 age 4-12) and **The Pine Room** (around $12)—serve guests and visitors. You must try the peanut soup at The Regency Room (the recipe is about as old as the hotel), and don't even think of skipping dessert.

★ **Black Lantern Inn** (1226 Franklin Rd. SW, 540/206-3441, $149-189) has three rooms, each one well appointed with a private bath with jetted thermal massage tub, complimentary bicycles and golf clubs, king-size bed with super-soft linens, and "pillows galore." A variety of drinks and refreshments are available. Breakfast offerings accommodate anyone from gourmet to vegan. The Inn is Virginia Green certified and there's a nice view of the Roanoke Star on Mill Mountain.

Rooms at **Burgh's Inn of Salem** (1226 Lynchburg Turnpike, Salem, 540/312-9138, www.brughsinn.com, $99-135) all have gas log fireplaces, queen-size beds, and free Wi-Fi. If you're cost-conscious, you can skip the full breakfast for a pretty nice continental spread and save a few dollars (but spring for the breakfast, you're on vacation). The rooms are nicely decorated and spacious enough to spread out in for a few days. There is a screened porch, which is a great spot to start the day with a cup of coffee or tea, and a great place to end it with a glass of wine.

The **King George Inn** (315 King George Ave., 575/675-4034, www.kinggeorgeinnbandb.com, $135-155) is walkable to downtown Roanoke, but that's not the only reason to stay here. Four large, TV-free rooms with private baths, a gourmet breakfast every morning, and a gift basket with soaps made especially for the inn should help persuade you. It's a beautiful home and it's beautifully cared for. Decorations are tasteful and appropriate, the colors throughout are calming, and the overall decor is quite relaxing.

Over $200

Perhaps the most decadent accommodation in Roanoke, **The Inn on Campbell** (118 Campbell Ave. SW, 540/400-0183, www.theinnoncampbell.com, $250-375) is so elegant, comfortable, and romantic, you won't want to leave. Each of the four rooms (two single rooms, two suites) is sumptuously appointed with down bedding and silky-soft sheets. The innkeepers are a friendly, interesting (she was the first female pro boxing judge and first female boxing announcer for HBO sports), entertaining pair who know how to treat their guests. Staying here is truly an elite experience.

Camping

It's a city, but, surprisingly, there is one campground nearby. **Dixie Caverns** (5753 W. Main St., Salem, 540/380-2085, www.dixiecaverns.com, $8/person for tents, $30/RV) in Salem has around 60 campsites for tents and RVs, plus there's a cool cave to check out.

Food

Part recreation, part meal on the run, **Discover Roanoke Food Tours** (800/656-0713, www.roanokefoodtours.com, tours from $42/adults, $30 ages 8-12, $18 ages 7 and under) is a great way to get a look at the city, learn a little of its more interesting stories, and find some great places to eat. They hit 5-6 restaurants for a bite and often a sip of something good. Tours include the Downtown Food and Cultural Tour, the Sunday Brunch Food Tour, and the Roanoke Craft Beer Tour. Your guides know their city and know a thing or two about food, so don't be shy about asking what you're seeing, smelling, or tasting, they'll have the answer (or they'll make something up, they're a fun-loving bunch too).

Bakeries and Cafés

Mill Mountain Coffee & Tea (117 Campbell Ave. SE, 540/342-9404, www.millmountaincoffee.com, 6:30am-11pm Mon.-Thurs., 6:30am-midnight Fri., 7am-midnight Sat., 8am-9pm Sun., $4-8) is your typical coffee shop serving a variety of drinks and baked goods alongside a small selection of sandwiches and salads. What makes this place notable is this: the coffee is really good, like *really* good, and it's a late-night hangout. With hours until 11pm through the week and midnight on Friday and Saturday, it's the place to get your late night cup of coffee or just unwind for a few minutes before heading home.

Bread Craft (106 S. Jefferson St., 540/562-4112, www.breadcraftbakery.com, 7am-2pm Mon.-Sat., breakfast $4-7, lunch $7-9) is a bakery, sandwich shop, and breakfast spot, just a couple of blocks away from the City Market. Pastries and cookies ($2-3) are all made here, and when you taste them, you'll wonder why they're so cheap. Breakfast includes dishes like the chorizo and eggs cocotte, which are flavor-packed and filling. Lunch consists of sandwiches and panini.

American

★ **Texas Tavern** (114 W. Church Ave., 540/342-4825, www.texastavern-inc.com, 24 hours daily, under $4), also known as "Roanoke's Millionaires Club," was established in 1930 and has been serving up burgers, breakfast, and their famous chile (yup, that's how they've spelled it for more than 20 million bowls) in the heart of downtown ever since. It's an out of place building—squat white brick with one door and a window that looks in over the tiny cooktop—with only 10 seats, all at the counter. Specialties include that chile, as well as the Cheesy Western, a cheeseburger topped with a fried egg, relish, pickles, and onions.

Don't skip **The Roanoker** (2522 Colonial Ave. SW, 540/344-7746, www.theroanokerrestaurant.com, 7am-9pm Tues.-Sat., 8am-9pm Sun., breakfast $3-8, lunch $6-8, dinner $8-17), a local favorite since 1941. If you love biscuits, theirs are among the best you'll ever eat.

Italian and Pizza

In the Grandin Village neighborhood, **Grace's Place** (1316 Grandin Rd., 540/981-1340, www.gracesplacepizzeria.com, 11am-9pm Sun. and Tues.-Thurs., 11am-10pm Fri.-Sat., closed Mon., $8-18) serves pizzas, pasta, and sandwiches you can eat in their dining room or at a sidewalk table, or take them to go. The pizza is consistently named the best in Roanoke and Grace's deserves every compliment. The toppings are very fresh and the selection of specialty pies creative and fun.

Fine Dining

A meal at downtown's cool and fun ★ **Lucky** (18 Kirk Ave. SW, 540/982-1249, www.eatatlucky.com, 5pm-9pm Mon.-Wed., 5pm-10pm Thurs.-Sat., bar open until late, small dishes $7-13, entrées $16-40) is one you'll tell your friends about. Just about everything is sourced from Virginia or neighboring states. Start with a salad, Octopus and Shoshito Peppers, or marrow bones, then move on to fried chicken, duck leg confit, or an amazing seafood dish. Vegetarians: there is always at least one vegetarian entrée available, and a few of the salads and small plates will fit the bill. Or you can always ask and they're happy to whip something up for you. Now let's talk cocktails. These are, hands down, the best cocktails in Roanoke. The bartender considers the flavors, aromas, and textures of the ingredients in each glass the same way a chef looks at ingredients before creating a new dish. They've been known to smoke glasses and liquors, freeze freshly juiced fruits and vegetables into giant ice cubs, and put new twists on classic drinks. And if that's not enough, they have Prosecco on draft.

The menu at ★ **The Blue Apron Restaurant and Red Rooster Bar** (210 E. Main St., Salem, 540/375-0055, www.blueapronredrooster.com, lunch 11:30am-2:30pm Tues.-Sat., dinner

served at 5pm Tues.-Sat., $8-28) in Salem is built around small, sharable plates. Most everything can be sized up to become an individual entrée, but the only way to eat here is to order at least two small plates per person and share them. Chef Scott Switzer changes the menu seasonally, so there's always something new to try. The Spanish white gazpacho was an interesting take on the classic cold soup, and the Mahi Escabeche (mahi mahi with Chimichurri and fried green tomatoes) was an eye-opening twist on South American and Southern American flavors. The wine list and cocktail menu pair well with the food, rounding out the whole experience. Reservations are recommended; this is a hot spot.

When local dining publications name their best anything, downtown Roanoke's **Metro!** (14 Campbell Ave. SE, 540/345-6645, www.metroroanoke.com, lunch 11:30am-3pm Fri.-Sat.; dinner 5pm-10pm Mon.-Thurs., 4pm-11pm Fri.-Sat., 4pm-10pm Sun; brunch 11am-3pm Sun.; bar

Fences like this one are built using traditional designs and methods.

4pm-last call Mon.-Thurs., 11:30am-2am Fri.-Sat., 11:30am-last call Sun., $12-40) makes the list. Best Chef, Best Brunch, Best Martini, and Most Romantic are just a few of their accolades. Their wide-ranging menu includes sushi, sashimi, tacos de lengua, fried green tomato BLTs, and main courses like shrimp and grits, rack of lamb, and lobster bouillabaisse. Their Bloody Marys are just about a meal in and of themselves.

City Market

The City Market Building (32 Market Sq. SE, 540/986-5992, www.citymarketbuilding.com) has around a half dozen restaurants in it. Among the best are **Marco & Luca** (434/295-3855, 10:30am-8:30pm Sat.-Thurs., 10:30am-10pm Fri.), a dumpling and noodle shop where items range $1-4 and you can order (and eat) every single item on the tiny menu for around $15; **Firefly Fare** (540/206-2630, www. fireflyfare.com, lunch 11am-3:30pm Mon.-Sat. and 11am-3pm Sun., dinner

5pm-9pm Wed.-Sat., $10-15), a "farm to table on the go" place with a fresh juice bar and very tasty (and healthy) dishes, including a number of vegetarian-friendly items; and **Fork in the Market** (540/400-0644, www.marketfork.com, 11am-10pm Mon.-Wed., 11am-11pm Thurs.-Sat., 11am-9pm Sun., $5-18), serving giant burgers, a crazy array of hot dogs and sausages, and pizzas topped with everything from the expected to mac-n-cheese. (Fork in the Market has two sister restaurants: Fork in the Alley and Fork in the City, and a food truck, you guessed it, Fork in the Road).

Information and Services

Your first stop for travel information should be this guide, but your second stop should be the **Roanoke Valley Convention and Visitors Bureau** (540/342-6025, www.visitroanokeva. com); their website is chock full of information and itineraries. The staff at the **Roanoke Valley Visitor Information Center** (101 Shenandoah Ave. NE, 9am-5pm daily) will give you those locals-only tips that put you at the best restaurants, in the best shops, and out experiencing the city the way locals do.

On the radio, **WUVT** (90.7 FM) is the Virginia Tech College Station. Top 40 hits are played on **WXLK** (92.3 FM).

Police can be contacted at the **Roanoke City Police Department** (348 Campbell Ave. SW, 540/853-2212, www.roanokeva. gov) and the **Roanoke County Police Department** (5925 Cove Rd., 540/777-8601, www.roanokecountyva.gov).

Carilion Roanoke Memorial Hospital (1906 Bellview Ave. SE, Roanoke, 540/981-7000, www.carilionclinic.org) is one of the biggest in Virginia.

Virginia's Explore Park (MP 115)

At Blue Ridge Parkway Milepost 115, you'll find **Virginia's Explore Park** (MP 115, 540/427-1800, www.explorepark. org, dawn-dusk daily year-round, free), an 1,100-acre park with 14 miles of walking and mountain biking trails, a picnic area, and plenty to explore, all open to the public at no charge. There's a **Blue Ridge Parkway Visitor Center** (9am-6pm daily May-Oct.) here with a gift shop; two exhibit galleries detailing the history of the Parkway and the settling of the region around Roanoke, the highlight of which is a giant relief map/model of the Parkway; and a short film about the Parkway, which is worth the watch if you haven't seen it at any of the other visitor centers.

You'll also find two other buildings, the Arthur Taubman Center and Mountain Union Church, beside the visitor center, but these are generally only open for recreational programs and activities, or for private events. There are a few other reconstructed buildings throughout the park, each of which tells some part of the story of settling here. Among these structures are a grist mill, Kemp's Ford School House, and a frontier fort.

If you're interested in hiking, pick up a trail map at the visitor center and go for a stroll in the woods. The trails are generally in good condition, though some of the mountain biking trails can get sketchy in spots. Speaking of mountain biking, nine miles of the trails here are International Mountain Biking Association sanctioned.

Old Salem Turnpike Trail

Distance: 1.36-mile loop, with options to extend the hike
Duration: 1 hour
Elevation gain: 300 feet
Difficulty: easy to moderate
Trailhead: beside the Blue Ridge Parkway Visitor Center

This easy hike takes you around the central point of Explore Park and down to the banks of the Roanoke River. Departing from the trailhead behind the Parkway Visitor Center and Taubman Center, the path wanders a relatively flat track for a little more than a quarter-mile before a side trail leads to Palmer's Pond, a small forest pond that can be quite pretty. If you decide to head out to the pond, the trip is 0.8 miles out and back.

Continuing on, the trail reaches the River Walk and Roanoke River about a half-mile in. Follow the banks and you'll find a trio of spur trails leading to a small network that weaves its way through the historic area. If you choose to explore here, you can add a half-mile (and a half-hour) or more to the walk. Around a mile in, you'll reach a second connector with the River Walk, and the Old Salem Turnpike Trail will turn right and lead you back up to the trailhead.

Mill Mountain and the Roanoke Star (MP 120)

Standing between Roanoke and the Blue Ridge Parkway is a single peak: Mill Mountain. The Roanoke Star, the city's most famous landmark, stands just below its summit.

Sights
★ Roanoke Star

In 1949, the Roanoke Merchants Association decided to announce the start of the Christmas season with a fantastically big decoration: a giant star to crown Mill Mountain and shine over downtown. They raised $28,000 for the construction and installation, and throughout the summer, Roanoke Iron & Bridge Works built the structure for the star and its supports. Once satisfied with the design, they drove it to the chosen site just below the summit of Mill Mountain. The 88.5-foot tall **Roanoke Star** was set in place, outlined with more than 2,000-feet of neon tubing, and wired for electricity. On November 23, 1949, Thanksgiving Eve, the switch was thrown and the star blazed with light. Visible from 60 miles away, it was quite the sight then as now. Though the Merchants Association intended it as a holiday decoration, it was so popular that the city left it on year-round. The star was lit white for a long time, then, in 1976, to celebrate the Bicentennial, the design was changed to include a red and blue star.

The views of the city and valley from the observation platform at the Roanoke Star are unrivaled. A trolley ran up here around 1910, but it was soon shut down as folks preferred the drive up winding Walnut Avenue. Today, most visit the star from the Blue Ridge Parkway (MP 120) or via the system of greenways throughout Roanoke. To drive to the star, simply follow Walnut Avenue up the mountain and follow the signs. You can also walk or bike there by taking the Mill Mountain Greenway to the Discovery Center and parking area, where two hiking trails—the long and the short versions of the **Star Trail**—lead to the star and a tremendous overlook.

Mill Mountain Zoo

The **Mill Mountain Zoo** (Mill Mountain Park, 540/343-3241, www.exemplum.com/mmzoo, 10am-4:30pm daily, $7.50 adults, $5 ages 3-11, free age 2 and under) has 175 animals representing 90 species, and among those numbers, 21 are listed as vulnerable species. You can see a red wolf, snow leopard, and red panda here. There's a ZooChoo Train ($2) that circles the zoo; zookeeper talks; and fun activities like Breakfast With The Animals (every third Saturday, $15 adults, $11 children, reservations required) and Zoo Boo (regular admission costs only), a day-long, trick-or-treating, costume-contest Halloween-themed zoo bonanza.

Hiking

There are several walking and hiking trails on Mill Mountain. The **Star Trail** leads to the Roanoke Star, but others connect to neighborhoods in Roanoke. Parents with little hikers in tow may want to pay a visit to **Crystal Spring Trail** (trailhead at the end of Ivy St., get there from the Parkway by turning onto Mill Mountain Parkway at MP 120.5, continuing along the J P Fishburn Pkwy. and Walnut Ave. SE, then turning left on Ivy St.), a 1.2-mile out-and-back hike that's about as easy as it gets. The good thing about this trail is that it's an easy way to get kids excited to hike. Surrounded as you are by the forest here, there's the sense that you're somewhere wild, not three blocks from civilization.

Star Trail (Long)

Distance: 2.8 miles out and back
Duration: 1.5-2 hours
Elevation gain: 900 feet
Difficulty: moderate
Trailhead: on Walnut Avenue about 1 mile from Ivy Street
Directions: To reach the trailhead, exit the Blue Ridge Parkway at the Mill Mountain Parkway (MP 120.5); continue along to the J P Fishburn Parkway and then Walnut Avenue SE; turn left onto Ivy Street and the trailhead is at the end of the street.

There's an easier way to reach the Roanoke Star, but this route lets you earn the view and takes you through a dense forest filled with woodpeckers.

From the parking area, cross the street and head up a short set of stone steps. Immediately you'll be faced with six or eight fairly long switchbacks as you ascend. The switchbacks keep the trail at a nice, accessible grade and provide plenty of spots for benches where you can sit and soak up the noise of the forest. Continue along the trail until you reach the top, just under 1.5 miles into the hike. There, you'll find a junction with a gravel road and some brochures with trail maps. Turn left and you'll be in a paved parking area; turn right, you'll meet up with a paved path at the Roanoke Star and the overlook.

Star Trail (Short)

Distance: 0.4 miles out and back
Duration: 15 minutes
Elevation gain: 50 feet
Difficulty: moderate
Trailhead: parking area at the summit of Mill Mountain

Park in the paved parking area at the summit of Mill Mountain, then follow the gravel path and you'll be at the Roanoke Star in no time flat.

Roanoke Mountain
(MP 120.4)

The scenic four-mile, one-way Roanoke Mountain Loop Road makes its way around Roanoke Mountain. Along the way there are seven overlooks, which provide really good views of Roanoke, the Roanoke Valley, and Mill Mountain. At the top, there's a short spur road to a parking area where you'll find a trail that takes you to the summit.

Roanoke Mountain Summit Trail

Distance: 0.3-mile loop
Duration: 10 minutes
Elevation gain: 60 feet
Difficulty: easy to moderate
Trailhead: parking area on Roanoke Mountain Loop Road

This pretty little hike affords you a few good landscape shots and gives you a good place to watch the sun set. Begin at the set of stone steps at the far end of the parking lot and descend. You'll immediately ascend up a second set of stone steps and come to the summit. Wintertime is when the views are best, though it's quite pretty in summer when the mountain laurel is blooming. Continue on the trail and ascend again to the parking lot.

Roanoke Valley Overlook (MP 129.6)

Take one last look at Roanoke and the Roanoke Valley from this overlook, perched at 2,100 feet.

Devils Backbone Overlook (MP 143.9)

You'll find a lot of references to the Devil, Hell, and Purgatory in exceptionally rocky spots like Devils Backbone. I guess if I had to pick my way through rocky fields and outcroppings while on a wagon loaded with all my earthly possessions, I'd come up with a similar name for these places. As you look out here, Devils Backbone is the steep point jutting out between the overlook and Pine Spur.

Smart View (MP 154.1)

The **Smart View Overlook** (MP 154.1) gives you a great look at a beautiful valley. The **Smart View Recreation Area** (MP 154.4), a 500-acre recreation area at 2,503 feet, has 42 or so picnic tables, a restroom, and drinking water. A loop trail at the recreation area wanders the ridge and can be broken down into a couple of shorter hikes, though the longer one is recommended. Some of you may be wondering about the name. Well, it's an antiquated way of saying "good view." In the case of Smart View, the smart part applies to the pastoral beauty of the long view here.

Smart View Loop Trail

Distance: 3-mile loop
Duration: 1.5-2 hours
Elevation gain: 150 feet
Difficulty: easy to moderate
Trailhead: parking area at Smart View, across from the picnic area

Squeeze through the fence and cross an

Virginia's Heritage Music Trail

In the hills and hollers of the Blue Ridge are stories that beg to be told. Thanks to **The Crooked Road** (276/492-2409, www.myswva.org/tcr), we're learning the stories of the people whose musical talent created bluegrass and country music, two genres that have influenced musicians for nearly a century.

The Crooked Road is a 333-mile-long driving trail stretching from Rocky Mount to Breaks Interstate Park at the Virginia-Kentucky border, connecting visitors with southwestern Virginia's incredibly rich musical history. The road connects nine major music venues and 60 or so affiliated venues and festivals, crossing 19 counties, four cities, 50 towns, and one state line. Along the way, you can stop for a concert or impromptu jam session, learn some of the history here at any of 26 waysides, where you can also hear recordings of musicians and songs important to the area, or attend one of the many music festivals and gatherings that celebrate these deep musical roots.

All along The Crooked Road, you'll hear names like the Carter Family (June Carter Cash, wife of Johnny Cash, was a second-generation Carter Family singer), "Tennessee" Ernie Ford, Dr. Ralph Stanley, the Mullins Family Singers, and the Stoneman Family. Each of these individuals or family troupes plucked their guitar, bass, and banjo strings and sent out musical vibrations that touched future musicians like Hank Williams, Bob Dylan, The Rolling Stones, Ray Charles, Nirvana, Grateful Dead, Willie Nelson, Steve Earle, and Ryan Adams.

The Floyd Country Store is one of the stops on The Crooked Road Music Trail, so it's easy to begin exploring some musical history from here. The Crooked Road is not an official byway in the manner of the Blue Ridge Parkway or Skyline Drive, but rather a recommended route along country roads. You can easily hit three highlights of The Crooked Road along the Parkway by visiting **Floyd, Galax,** and the **Blue Ridge Music Center,** each of which lies along or near the Parkway.

open meadow to enter the woods. At 0.2 miles you'll meet a side trail to the picnic area, ignore it (unless you're hungry) and continue on. At 0.4 miles you'll reach another trail, this leads to the Smart View Overlook (MP 154.1); bear right. Here the trail descends through ferns and switchbacks until it crosses the creek. After crossing, you'll ascend through a rhododendron thicket. From this point south, the rhododendron thickets are a constant companion as the Parkway continues to gain elevation.

At 0.7 miles in, you'll reach a set of steep rock steps, then at 1 mile you'll find that the restrooms are just to your right; keep going. In a few hundred yards, there's a second trail to the picnic area; rather than go that way, descend on the path to the left. The Trails family cabin at mile 1.2 was built in the 1890s. It's an attractive structure (if you're into the whole rustic thing), and between it and

the views of Virginia's Piedmont to the east, you can spend a few minutes taking photos here. Cross a small creek via a stone bridge, then ascend a small knob. A path to the right will lead back to the parking lot where the hike began if you need to shorten it.

Continuing down the trail from the knob, you'll have more great Piedmont views, then descend into a little pine grove. From here, the trail carries you right back to the parking area.

⏀VA-8 North: Floyd (MP 165.2)

Floyd is a rare place where you'll find hippie holdouts, fifth-generation Floyd County families, retired college professors, and yurt-dwelling, alpaca-owning neo-hippies living side by side, and they all get along. Somehow the mix of old and

Floyd

PENN RD NW
TISE ST NE
NEWTON RD
N LOCUST ST
E OXFORD ST
E MAIN ST
HOWARD ST

ODDFELLAS
CANTINA ▼

NEW MOUNTAIN
MERCANTILE

REPUBLIC OF
FLOYD EMPORIUM

FLOYD COUNTRY STORE/
FRIDAY NIGHT JAMBOREE

0   350 yds
0   350 m

© AVALON TRAVEL

8
To
Jacksonville
▼ Center for the Arts

new, mainstay and counterculture, contemporary art and long-held traditions works. It must be the music.

On Friday nights (well, on most nights, really, but especially on Friday nights), the streets of this small town echo with the high lonesome sound of bluegrass and old-time bands. In the Floyd Country Store, a hundred feet slap out a rhythm to the music as cloggers, flatfooters, and mountain dancers keep time. On the dance floor are homemakers and teachers, farmers and preachers, children and grandparents, newcomers and old-timers, all in this place to hear the music and share in a moment. This encapsulates the town. It's a place that people want to share and keep visiting every chance they get.

The town of Floyd is accessible via VA-8 at Milepost 165.2. Floyd is six miles north.

★ Friday Night Jamboree

There's only one stoplight in downtown Floyd, so it's easy to find the **Floyd Country Store** (206 S. Locust St., 540/745-4563, www.floydcountrystore.com, 10am-5pm Mon.-Thurs., 10am-10:30pm Fri., 10am-6pm Sat, noon-5:30 Sun.), the psychic center of this town. In 1910, a business called Farmer's Supply opened here, and the building has been in continuous use ever since. It changed hands more than a few times, and in the 1990s, the decision was made to close the store, except for one evening a week, for the now legendary **Friday Night Jamboree** (206 S. Locust St., 540/745-4563, www.

floydcountrystore.com, begins 6:30pm Fri., $5). The store underwent a revitalization in 2007, and the Floyd Country Store is now back in full swing, with a retail business, a **café** (11am-3pm Mon.-Sat., noon-3pm Sun., under $7), and a lauded music series.

Through the week you can get everything from overalls to penny candy to books on home remedies to a pair of hand-knit alpaca socks at the Floyd Country Store, but all that changes for the Friday Night Jamboree. Racks and shelves are cleared out, pushed to the side to make room for a dozen rows of folding chairs and a good-sized dance floor. The crowds build on the street. Musicians tune banjos and mandolins, and play runs on their fiddles and guitars on sidewalks, in parking lots, and doorways. Spontaneous songs build as one musician joins another. Then, promptly at 6:30pm, the music starts inside and the Jamboree is on.

The Jamboree celebrates the best of traditional Appalachian music, with acts ranging from country (real country, not the pop, Top-40 radio country) to bluegrass to old time. "Granny's Rules" apply here, and that means "no smoking, no drinking alcohol, no bad language, and no conduct unbecoming to a lady or gentleman." Don't be shy, work your way up front and get a seat where you can see the dancers, and, if the spirit so moves you, join in. Local bands, as well as regional and national touring acts perform here, so you'll hear top talent every week.

There are two other musical programs at the Floyd Country Store, both also aimed at preserving the music of these hills. On Saturdays, they have **American Afternoon** (noon-1:30pm Sat.), followed by an Americana-themed open mic. On Sundays, there's an **open jam** (2pm-4pm Sun.) led by local old-time and bluegrass bands (old-time bands get the first and third Sundays, bluegrass the second and fourth).

FloydFest

For five days in July **FloydFest** (894 Rock Castle Gorge Rd., 888/823-3787, www.floydfest.com, tickets $100-300) descends on the town, bringing with it an eclectic crowd hungry to hear music from a wide range of musical acts. Past performers include David Grisman, Los Lobos, Lauryn Hill, Lettuce, Thievery Corporation, and other acts from bluegrass to jam bands and everything in between. It's kid-friendly (but no dogs), you can camp (and even glamp), and with certain tickets, you can come and go as you please (and as traffic allows you). If you're a music fan and are looking for an excuse to tour the Parkway, here's your reason.

Shopping

The **Jacksonville Center for the Arts** (220 Parkway Lane S., 540/745-2784, www.jacksonvillecenter.org, 10am-5pm Mon.-Sat., noon-5pm Sun.) is an old farm complex that has been transformed into a center for art, mountain music, theater, dance, crafts, and rural heritage. It's half a mile south of town on VA-8, with a gallery and gift shop on the premises.

New Mountain Mercantile (114 S. Locust St., 540/745-4278, www.newmountainmercantile.com, 11am-5pm Mon.-Thurs., 11am-6pm Fri., 10am-6pm Sat., 11am-4pm Sun.) sells locally made art, jewelry, clothing, and home and garden accessories. You can pick up handmade aromatherapy products as well as soaps, candles, and crystals in this funky little shop. Next door is the **Republic of Floyd Emporium** (114-B S. Locust St., 540/745-2898, www.republicoffloyd.com, 11am-6pm Mon., Wed.-Thurs., and Sat., 11am-8pm Fri., 11am-4pm Sun.), a store featuring micro-brews and imported beer; snack foods; a good wine selection;

top to bottom: the sound of the fiddle at the Floyd's Friday Night Jamboree; flume supplying water to the wheel at Mabry Mill; curved road near Chateau Morrisette Winery and all sorts of hats, shirts, prints, and collectibles designed by Floyd artists.

Accommodations

Two cabins built from hand-hewn logs and a 200-year-old log farmhouse make up ★ **Ambrosia Farm Bed & Breakfast** (271 Cox Store Rd., 540/745-6363, www. ambrosiafarm.net, $90-135). The innkeepers—she has her MFA in ceramic sculpture and he's an engineer focused on energy efficiency—have done a lot to make the accommodations feel like escapes. And their work pays off. Surrounded by pastures and hills, the farm is truly a retreat. Each of the rooms is comfortable, and breakfast focuses on the farm philosophy of using what's in season, easily available, and of the highest quality.

I wasn't kidding about the yurts. Stay in one of these great, round, tent-like structures with **Floyd Yurt Lodging** (540/505-4586). Yurts are portable, circular tents built on collapsible frames traditionally used by nomads in far-flung places like Siberia and Mongolia. So, why a yurt in Floyd? Why not? It's spacious and comfortable and quite the different place to stay, but it's fun and unusual.

Food

★ **Oddfellas Cantina** (110 N. Locust St., 540/745-3463, www.oddfellascantina. com, lunch 11am-2:30pm Tues.-Sat. and 10am-3pm Sun., dinner 5pm-9pm Wed., 4pm-9pm Thurs., 4pm-9:30pm Fri.-Sat., and 5pm-9pm Sun., $12-22) offers "whole food for whole people" and more live music. The menu here is quite eclectic. You can order a perfectly cooked rib eye, duck glazed with pomegranate, tempeh, and even house-made soy proteins. Their wine and beer selection is very good. From time to time there's live music in the dining room.

Two miles north of town, **The Historic Pine Tavern Restaurant** (585 Floyd Hwy. N, 540/745-4482, www.thepinetavern. com, 4:30pm-9pm Fri., noon-9:30pm Sat.,

11am-8pm Sun., $14) offers family-style meals on shared platters. Meals include heaping platters of fried chicken, roast beef, and country ham; and bowls overflowing with mashed potatoes, dumplings, green beans, pinto beans, cole slaw, and buttermilk biscuits. Oh, and you get dessert too. Come hungry.

Dogtown Roadhouse (302 S. Locust St., 540/745-6836, www.dogtownroadhouse.com, 5pm-10pm Thurs., 5pm-midnight Fri., noon-midnight Sat., noon-10pm Sun., $5-15) offers up some fabulous wood-fired pizzas as well as a great beer selection. There are only six pizzas on the menu; fortunately, they're all delicious.

Information and Services

The **Floyd County Chamber of Commerce** (202 S. Locust St., 540/745-4407, www. visitfloyd.org, 9am-4pm Mon.-Wed., 10am-2pm Thurs.-Sat.) happily supplies information on the area. The website has a few good details for visitors.

◆VA-8 South: Fairy Stone State Park (MP 165.2)

At Milepost 165.2, the Parkway crosses over VA-8. From here it's only 23 miles southeast to **Fairy Stone State Park** (967 Fairystone Lake Dr., Stuart, 276/930-2424, www.dcr.virginia.gov, 8am-10pm daily). From VA-8, turn onto VA-57 to get into the park. This is one of the six original state parks in Virginia, and the largest one to boot. At 4,639 acres, there is plenty to explore at Fairy Stone, from more than 15 miles of hiking trails to a 168-acre lake, where you can fish, swim, or go boating, to seeking out some of the namesake fairy stones for yourself.

There's also a **campground** (800/933-7275, www.reserveamerica.com, $20 group camping, $30 RVs) and **cabins** ($102). With 25 one- and two-bedroom

Searching for Fairy Stones

Fairy stones are small, red-brown cruciform stones found in and around Fairy Stone State Park. People collect them, make jewelry out of them, and generally wonder at these strange little stones, which, according to mountain lore, ward off illness, accidents, and haints (that's mountain talk for witches).

The legend behind the stones goes like this: Hundreds of years before Pocahontas' father, Chief Powhatan, reined the tribes of Virginia, fairies lived near the springs in the mountains, spending their days with naiads and nymphs. One day an elfin messenger from far away arrived bearing the news of the death of Jesus Christ. Upon hearing of his good works, suffering, and crucifixion, the fairies wept. Being magical creatures, their tears were imbued with this same magic. When they struck the ground, their tears crystallized into crosses. Today, we find the remnants of their tears—fairy stones.

The scientific truth is that these stones, called staurolite, are composed of silica, iron, and aluminum, which together crystallize at 60- or 90-degree angles to form crosses both perfect and imperfect. To find out where to locate them, talk to park rangers; at different times they've held fairy stone hunts and necklace making workshops. Or just ask the next fairy you see.

cabins, one lodge, 50 tent and RV sites, and six group campsites, it's not difficult to find a place to spend the night, though reservations are recommended.

Rocky Knob Recreation Area (MP 167)

The **Rocky Knob Recreation Area** consists of more than 4,000 acres of backcountry that bulges out from the Blue Ridge Parkway, encompassing Rock Castle Gorge. This narrow, deep, impressive valley is breathtakingly beautiful, and the hikes will have you panting, too. The high-elevation meadows, deep coves, and craggy peaks, combined with the drastic elevation changes and abundant streams, create an area where the plant life is among the most diverse along the Parkway.

As inhospitable as these mountains may seem, at one time around 70 families lived in the immediate area. They scratched family farms out of the mountainsides, built sawmills and gristmills, and raised kids and livestock in this beautiful and rugged place.

The **Rocky Knob Campground** (MP 167, 877/444-6777, www.recreation.gov,

May-Oct., $19) has more than 80 tent sites and close to 30 RV sites. It's a popular stop, especially during summer and fall, so call ahead for reservations.

While you're at Rocky Knob, whether you're staying here or not, it's worthwhile to get out on the trails and take a look at the mountains up close and personal.

Rock Castle Gorge Trail

Distance: 10.6-mile circuit
Duration: 7-8 hours
Elevation gain: 1,050 feet
Difficulty: strenuous
Trailhead: Rocky Knob Campground

With steep, narrow descents and grueling ascents, this is not a trail to be taken lightly. From the Rocky Knob Campground, cross the Parkway and pass through the fence. Turn left and head into the woods. Switchbacks start at 0.3 miles in, and here you'll cross Little Rock Castle Creek, thick with rhododendrons. Keep descending until you reach an old road at 0.5 miles. Follow the road another half mile to where a bench lets you rest before descending to an area that looks as if it were settled long ago.

At 1.5 miles, you'll reach another ridge. Descend again. The trail is steep here, and will stay this way until you reach a draw at 2.3 miles in, where it still descends, but a bit more easily. You'll reach some pools in Little Rock Castle Creek at 2.5 miles in. Here the valley opens up a good bit. Continue on the trail until you reach a fire road at 3 miles. Turn right. In a quarter mile you'll reach a **backcountry camping** area, the site of a Civilian Conservation Corps work camp from the late 1930s. Stay on the road until it begins to swing away from the creek and skirt the lower part of the mountain. Cross a bridge at 4.25 miles in and make your way to the White House, once the home of a wealthy community member, at the 4.5-mile mark. The property is still privately owned, so take nothing but photos.

After you leave the White House, cross the creek a couple of times and begin ascending through more rhododendron thickets. Five miles in, you'll see a few small waterfalls, cascades, and rills. A tall rock face that's dry except during spring rains, at which time it turns into a lovely waterfall, will greet you at 5.4 miles. In a quarter mile, the trail will leave the road and you'll turn right. The road continues on to some now-defunct cabins a little over a mile distant.

There's a mess of boulders called Bare Rocks at mile 5.8. Though it may be tempting to stick your head into the small caves and clefts found here, don't. They are perfect spots for copperheads, rattlesnakes, and other woodland creatures. The ascent turns steep at mile 6.2, then lessens a bit once you reach a set of switchbacks after a dense rhododendron and mountain laurel thicket. At mile 7.1, you'll arrive at Grassy Knoll. For the next quarter mile or so, you'll be on lovely pasture land, then, at mile 7.5, a cell phone tower will give you a jarring reminder of our intrusion into nature.

Keep on the trail and emerge from the woods into an absolutely stunning meadow around mile 7.6. The 360-degree views here are exactly what you've been working toward all day. After half a mile, you'll reenter the woods and come out again into another beautiful meadow.

At mile 9, you'll pass Rock Castle Gorge Overlook at Milepost 168.7, then begin to ascend Rocky Knob. Take the right-hand trail at 9.4 miles in, then make your way to the ridgeline leading to Rocky Knob. There's a shelter where Earl Shaffer, the first Appalachian Trail thru-hiker stayed when this was part of the Appalachian Trail. At the 10-mile mark, you'll reach a trail leading to the picnic area in just over 0.5 miles; you can go this way and cut the trail short if you like. If not, keep climbing, cross another knob, then through a fence and into a final pasture. You'll go through a small orchard, then parallel the Parkway before arriving back where you started.

Shorter hikes are also possible here. From the picnic area at Rocky Knob, it's possible to do 1.1-, 2.3-, and 2.6-mile hikes that provide some of the same views as the 10.6-mile Rock Castle

Gorge Trail, taking you through some of those meadows described at the end of the gorge trail.

★ Chateau Morrisette Winery (MP 171.5)

At Milepost 171.5, head west on Black Ridge Road to Winery Road, where you'll find **Chateau Morrisette Winery** (287 Winery Rd. SW, Floyd, 540/593-2865, www.thedogs.com, winery 10am-5pm Mon.-Thurs., 10am-6pm Fri.-Sat., 11am-5pm Sun.), a popular spot for locals and visitors, especially for their Sunday Brunch. The winery is composed of 13 acres of vines, an amazing 32,365-square-foot timber-frame tasting room made from salvaged timbers, and a great set of outdoor spaces for parties big and small.

Chateau Morrisette is one of six Virginia wineries started prior to 1980, making it one of the oldest wineries in the state. Though grape production began on the property in the early 1970s, it wasn't until 1978 that Chateau Morrisette Winery came about. Then, winemaker and owner David Morrisette, a graduate of Mississippi State University's inaugural Viticulture and Enology program, ripped out the vines his father had planted, planted his own, and became the first official winemaker for Chateau Morrisette Winery. A mere 2,000 gallons of wine were produced in their first vintage in 1982; today, the winery produces well over 60,000 cases annually.

Visitors to the winery can take part in **tastings and tours** (tours begin 11am, 1pm, and 3pm Mon.-Thurs.; 11am, 1pm, 3pm, and 5pm Fri. and Sat.; noon, 2pm, and 4pm Sun.). Tastings come in two flavors: the standard, 10-wine tasting and a winery tour ($8), or the Elite Wine Tasting ($30) with 10 bottles of the current vintage and possibly barrel tastings or the pouring of a reserve wine. The Elite Tasting includes an in-depth talk about terroir, grape varieties, and

view from Chateau Morrisette Winery

Virginia wine as a whole. You'll also discuss pairing ideas and leave with a keepsake glass. Reservations are required for the Elite Wine Tasting but not for the standard tasting or for tours.

Speaking of pairings, you can sample some of their fine wine with their fine food at the on-site **restaurant** (11am-2pm Wed.-Thurs., 11am-9pm Fri.-Sat., 11am-3pm Sun., closed Mon.-Tues. Apr.-Nov.; 11am-4pm Thurs. and Sun., 11am-8pm Fri.-Sat. Jan.-Mar.; $13-30 dinner, $25 adults and $12.99 children for brunch). Lunch and dinner are good with internationally-influenced Southern fare, but the brunch is legendary in these parts, consisting of around 40 items from prime rib to quiche to Virginia ham to pancakes to salads. Reservations are highly recommended. The **HUT** (noon-4pm Sun. June-Oct., $3-8) serves picnic fare and welcomes a variety of musicians to perform in their Sunday Sounds concert series.

Chateau Morrisette hosts events throughout the year. **The Black Dog Music Festivals** take place July-October, starting off with the Rhythm and Vine Festival, then the Summer Music Festival, followed by September's Music and BBQ Festival (a popular one, plan for it well ahead of time), and the finale, a Beach Music Festival. Tickets are $25 in advance, slightly higher at the gate if there are any left.

You may notice that Chateau Morrisette seems to have a dog theme. Most of their labels feature a handsome black lab, and more than a few of their wines—The Black Dog, Our Dog Blue, Frosty Dog, Star Dog, Liberty Service Dog Red, Blushing Dog—include dogs in the name. The dogs go back to the early days of the winery, or before that, in fact, back to David Morrisette's college days when Hans, a black Labrador Retriever, stuck by his side. Hans helped David with studies, with planting and pruning and harvesting, and with the winemaking for many years. One thing Hans exceled at was lapping up spilled wine. David's love

for Hans, and all dogs, really, inspired the label and names, and is the reason Chateau Morrisette is dog-friendly.

Mabry Mill (MP 176.1)

Called by many "the most picturesque spot on the Blue Ridge Parkway," Mabry Mill is among the top five places to photograph in any season, making it a sure-stop on your journey. The Mill sits just off the road, fed by a series of flumes and chutes that channel the water from a nearby stream to the water wheel, which turns the grist mill and sawmill inside, and empties into a little pond in front of the building. The pond is almost always still, though sometimes the surface is rippled by wind or the ducks that live here, so it reflects the sky, mill, and trees, making for a perfect postcard shot. In the fall, when the trees are lit with color, it's quite striking.

The Mabry family settled in the area around 1782 when they received a land grant one county over. Ed Mabry was born here in 1867, spent a little time away, then moved back with his wife Lizzy. He built the mill in 1903 to provide blacksmithing and wheelwright services to the community. Soon he was operating a sawmill here, then a gristmill.

A half-mile trail takes you through the grounds, where you'll learn about mountain industries, starting with the water-powered sawmill and **gristmill** (where you can buy cornmeal, buckwheat, and other meals ground on-site, demonstrations 9am-4pm daily May-Nov.), passing by a lumber-drying rack and log cart, the family cabin, then a moonshine still (not exactly industrious work, but work that was appreciated on many a farm nonetheless) before seeing the sorghum mill and blacksmith shop. By the blacksmith, you can take the path back to your car or wander back to where one of the flumes directing water to the mill start, either way, you'll be off the trail in no time.

The ★ **Mabry Mill Restaurant** (266 Mabry Mill Rd. SE, 276/952-2947, www.mabrymillrestaurant.com, 7:30am-6pm daily May-Oct., $4-10) is famous for their pancakes, which come in buckwheat, cornmeal, sweet potato, and plain old pancake. You must order a stack. Breakfast is served all day, and it's the good, hearty country fare you'd expect. Lunch and dinner include meatloaf, pulled pork, chicken potpie, roast turkey, a burger, and a half-dozen sandwiches.

Primland (MP 177.7)

Perched on 12,000 acres in the Blue Ridge Mountains not far from the Parkway, ★ **Primland** (2000 Busted Rock Rd., Meadows of Dan, 866/953-8058, www.primland.com, $207-1,200/night) is more than a resort: it's an escape into luxury that most of us will only know a few times in our lives. The main lodge has rooms and suites, cottages line the fairways of the resort's golf course, and there are mountain homes suitable for large gatherings. Most fantastic of all are the tree houses, which sit high on the ridge overlooking the Dan River Gorge, the Roaring Creek Gorge, or the confluence of Roaring Creek and the Dan. From their decks, the view is stupendous. The interior of the tree houses (and all the rooms, cottages, and houses, for that matter) is sheer elegance. Everything is comfortable and plush, designed to help you forget the outside world for a while.

You can do just about anything you want at Primland. There's an ATV trail riding program, birding outings, fly-fishing, horseback riding, mountain biking, sporting clays and other sports, a spa, and an acclaimed stargazing program. There's one of the prettiest disc golf courses you could ever play and a real golf course that's the height of mountain course design.

Dining is exceptional. The dining room, **elements,** serves breakfast (7am-11am daily, $6-16), afternoon tea (4pm-5pm daily, free), and dinner (6:30pm-9:30pm daily, $30-45), as well as a seven-course tasting menu ($80) and Chef's Table nine-course tasting menu ($150). The **19th Pub** (11am-11pm daily, lunch $12-22, dinner $12-29) serves lunch and dinner in a less-formal atmosphere. There's also **Stables Saloon,** open seasonally for breakfast and periodically for events.

Groundhog Mountain (MP 188.1)

The tower (which looks like a tall tobacco barn) atop Groundhog Mountain is one of the loveliest sights on the Parkway. The grassy knob; the hand-hewn, primitively constructed fence; and the breadth of the sky above all add up to beautiful. There is a picnic area here and a comfort station with restrooms, so you can linger here if you want to watch the sun go down (or come up, if you're an early riser). Views from here are sweeping, to say the least. You can see the Dan River Valley and the mountains easing into Piedmont as well as Pilot Mountain's odd, quartzite peak jutting upwards.

Down the road at Orchard Gap (MP 194), you'll see a series of cabins on the top of a bald ridge just off the parkway. These are the **Loneseome Pine Cabins** (64 Lonesome Cabin Lane, Fancy Gap, 888/799-9214, www.lonesomepinecabins.net, $95-135), and it's quiet and starry here, making for a nice one-nighter in this area.

Fancy Gap (MP 199.5)

The Blue Ridge Parkway skirts the southern edge of Fancy Gap, and US-52 crosses its path here. Just a couple of minutes off the Parkway you'll find pretty much all Fancy Gap has to offer—a handful of shops, restaurants, hotels, and gas stations. US-52 will take you south to Mount Airy, N.C., and I-77 is just four minutes from the Parkway, making access easy from the north or south.

Fancy Gap was originally known as Foggy Camp, but the name changed sometime in the 1800s. Rumor has it that young Ira Blair Coltrane, who would become a self-taught engineer and a colonel in the Confederate Army, was helping his grandfather drive a wagon up a steep and rutted road. He looked around, saw a better route up the mountain across the valley and said that it would make a "Fancy Road."

There are a trio of eateries in Fancy Gap. **The Gap Deli at the Parkway** (7975 Fancy Gap Hwy., 276/728-3881, 11am-7pm daily, around $8) serves sandwiches, salads, soups, and some killer peanut butter pie. **Lakeview Restaurant** (7830 Fancy Gap Hwy., 276/728-7841, 7am-9pm Mon.-Sat., 7am-2:30pm Sun., around $8) has a really good breakfast (it's where the locals go) and the fried chicken is spot on. **Rap's Orchard Gap** (1113 Dusty Ridge Rd., 276/398-2204, www.rapsva.com, 11am-9pm Thurs.-Fri., 9am-9pm Sat., 9am-2pm Sun., breakfast around $6, lunch under $10, dinner $11-25) has hours that change with the wind (so call ahead), but their food is simple, comfort food. It's relatively inexpensive for breakfast and lunch, and it's filling.

US-52 South: Mount Airy, NC (MP 199.5)

In downtown Mount Airy you'll notice 1960s police squad cars, business names that may seem oddly familiar, and cardboard cutouts of Barney Fife peering out from shop windows. Mount Airy is the hometown of Andy Griffith and a mecca for fans of *The Andy Griffith Show*. People who grew up in small towns in the Carolinas (and probably elsewhere, too)

recognize their families and neighbors in the fictional residents of Mayberry. The show's inspired writing and acting are a deep well of nostalgia, and its fans are legion.

Getting There and Around
You can reach Mount Airy from the Blue Ridge Parkway by turning south on US-52 at Fancy Gap (MP 199.5), a 14-mile journey; by taking I-77/74 south to NC-89 west, a trip of 24 mostly-interstate miles; or by taking a curvy backroad that will let you catch a glimpse of life on the slopes of the Blue Ridge Mountains. To take the backroad, VA-679/NC-1717, turn onto Orchard Gap Road at Milepost 194, then stay straight on Wards Gap Road, which will lead you into town over the course of a 14-mile, 30-minute journey.

Sights
★ Andy Griffith Sights
You can't leave Mount Airy without paying a visit to the sites that honor favorite son Andy Griffith. It isn't open for tours, but you can rent **Andy's boyhood home** (711 E. Haymore St., 336/789-5999, $175/night) on Haymore Street if you care to spend the night. The **Andy Griffith Museum** (218 Rockford St., 336/786-7998, www.andygriffithmuseum.com, 9am-5pm Mon.-Fri., 11am-4pm Sat., 1:30pm-4:30pm Sun., $3, $5 with audio guide) features hundreds of pieces of memorabilia from Griffith's long career in television, movies, and music, including scripts and props from his still-running eponymous TV show. Outside the museum and the attached **Andy Griffith Playhouse** (www.surryarts.org, show times and ticket prices vary) stands a lifelike statue of Andy and Opie with fishing poles in tow that looks like it was grabbed right out of *The Andy Griffith Show* opening credits.

If you can't get enough of Andy and Barney, hop into a Mayberry squad car to tour all the major sights in town. **Mayberry Squad Car Tours** (625 S. Main

Mount Airy

To Giant Milk Carton and Great Big Man

■ BRIGHT LEAF DRIVE-IN

■ THE OLD CITY JAIL

MOUNT AIRY MUSEUM OF REGIONAL HISTORY

■ THE MERRY-GO-ROUND

OPIE'S CANDY STORE

■ THE SNAPPY LUNCH

FLOYD'S CITY BARBER SHOP

THE ANDY GRIFFITH PLAYHOUSE/ ANDY GRIFFITH MUSEM

MAYBERRY COURTHOUSE AND WALLY'S SERVICE STATION

ANDY'S BOYHOOD HOME

0   400 yds
0   400 m

© AVALON TRAVEL

St., 336/789-6743, www.tourmayberry.com) leave from "Wally's Service Station" and cost "$35 for a carload." And if that's not enough, stop by **Floyd's City Barber Shop** (129 N. Main St., 336/786-2346, 7am-5pm Mon.-Wed. and Fri., 7am-3pm Sat.) for a haircut. You won't find Floyd the barber in there, but you will find some friendly folks in an old-fashioned barbershop. If you're in the mood for a trim, you may just sit in the same seat as Andy Griffith, who received many a haircut here during his Mount Airy days.

The Merry-Go-Round Show

Teamed up with WPAQ 740 AM, the Surry Arts Council hosts *The Merry-Go-Round* (Earle Theater, 142 N. Main St., Mount Airy, 336/786-2222, www.surryarts.org, show: 11am-1:30pm Sat., $5), the country's third-longest-running live bluegrass and old-time music radio show. Come to the Earle Theater for the show, or show up as early as 9am toting an instrument if you'd like to join in the pre-show jam session. It's one of the state's great small-town treats.

Other Sights

Two roadside oddities in Mount Airy make for other interesting sights. It now advertises Pet Milk, but the **Giant Milk**

radio

Carton (594 North Andy Griffith Pkwy./ US-52), a 12-foot-tall metal sculpture, has advertised for Coble Dairy and Flavo-Rich Milk since its creation in the 1940s. Out-of-towners who come to Mount Airy for the annual fiddlers convention remember to turn off the highway to get to Veterans Park when they see the **Great Big Man** (at the intersection of US-52 and Starlite Dr.), a very tall metal service station attendant.

Entertainment
WPAQ Radio
When you're in the area, tune in to **WPAQ** (AM 740, www.wpaq740.com), which has provided a venue for live local talent to perform old-time, bluegrass, and gospel music for over 60 years. To get a really good idea of this community's life, tune in for the live Saturday-morning *The Merry-Go-Round* show (11am-1:30pm Sat.), or any other day of the week when you'll hear local call-in shows, old-style country preaching, and more music.

Festivals and Events
A local institution that has a great deal to do with the vitality of Mount Airy's musical traditions is the **Bluegrass and Old-Time Fiddlers Convention** (631 W. Lebanon St., 336/345-7388, www. mtairyfiddlersconvention.com), held for almost 40 years during the first full weekend in June at Veterans Memorial Park. Thousands of people come to the festival from around the world to play old-time and bluegrass music with their friends and compete in what is a very prestigious competition in this genre. The heart of the action takes place at the hundreds of individual campsites that spring up all over the park in informal jam sessions among old and new friends. It's some of the best old-time music to be heard anywhere.

top to bottom: the lookout tower on Groundhog Mountain; the Snappy Lunch in Mount Airy; storefronts in Mount Airy

Welcome to Mayberry R.F.D.

"People started saying that Mayberry was based on Mount Airy. It sure sounds like it, doesn't it?"

Andy Griffith

Surely the bucolic town of Mount Airy was the inspiration for Mayberry. Comedian and actor Andy Griffith grew up here, drawing inspiration for his stand-up comedy, hit television show, and just about every character he ever played during his long career from its landscape and people. Like its fictional counterpart, Mount Airy is filled with friendly folks, and something in the air here just feels like yesteryear. It's calmer, easier, slower.

Griffith got his break in 1953 when a recording of one of his stand-up routines, a story called "What it was, was Football," sold more than 800,000 copies and landed him a spot on *The Ed Sullivan Show* the next year. The premise is pretty simple: a country preacher, naïve to all but his little world, happens upon a college football game. Having never heard of nor seen football, he's a bit confused. Griffith describes the game and field ("a purty little green cow pasture") like this: "somebody had took and drawed white lines all over it and drove postes in it and I don't know what all. And I looked down there and I seen five or six convicts a-runnin up and down and a-blowing whistles...I looked down and I seen 30 or 40 men come a-running out of one end of a great big outhouse down there. And everybody where I was a-sittin got up and hollered." The quote only does it so much justice and you owe it to yourself to hear Griffith deliver it in his charming drawl.

The Surry Arts Council is a hub of artistic activity in the Mount Airy-Surry County area. They sponsor and host many events throughout the year that showcase local talent in drama, visual arts, and especially music. Local and regional old-time and bluegrass bands perform in the **Voice of the Blue Ridge Series** (7:30pm on the third Sat. of the month, $10 adults, free under age 6) at the Earle Theater (142 N. Main St., Mount Airy, 336/786-2222).

The Surry Arts Council also hosts the citywide **Mayberry Days,** an annual fall festival entering its second decade. During Mayberry Days, members of TAGSRWC (www.imayberry.com), an intentionally obtuse acronym for *The Andy Griffith Show* Rerun Watchers Club, gather with other fans, some of the remaining cast members, and impersonators of Mayberry characters, who come to town and have a big-eyed time getting haircuts at Floyd's City Barber Shop, riding in squad cars, and arresting each other. TAGSRWC boasts hundreds of chapters whose names reference the series, such as "Her First Husband Got Runned Over by a Team of Hogs" (Texas) and "Anxiety Magnifies Fearsome Objects" (Alabama).

Recreation
Golf

A rare golf course among the pastures and hay fields is the beautiful **Cross Creek Country Club** (1129 Greenhill Rd., 336/789-5131, www.crosscreekcc.com, 18 holes, par 72, greens fees $41 Mon.-Fri., $46 Sat.-Sun. and holidays, 9 holes $23 Mon.-Fri., $25 Sat.-Sun. and holidays, includes cart) in Mount Airy. Course conditions are always fantastic, and the course presents quandaries to golfers of all levels.

If you want a fun little par-3 course, head to **Hardy's Custom Golf** (2003 W. Pine St., 336/789-7888, www.hardrockgolf.net, 18 holes, par 54, greens fees $8, with cart $10, 9 holes $5, with cart $8). The course is lighted for play day or night. If the weather isn't cooperating, try the golf simulator (18 holes $25, 9 holes $15), where you can play 40 different world-famous courses, including St. Andrews and Pinehurst.

Hot Air Ballooning

It's an 18-mile trip south from Mount Airy, but sometimes you have to take a little drive if you want to ride in a hot air balloon. Balloon pilots Tony and Claire Colburn lead tours of the Yadkin Valley by hot air balloon any time of year, weather permitting. **Yadkin Valley Hot Air Balloon Adventures** (Rockford Rd., Booneville, 336/922-7207, www.balloonadventure.net) requires advance reservations—contact the Colburns for rates and availability; it's an amazing way to see the Carolina foothills. While you're near Rockford, you might as well make a day of it by renting a kayak from Yadkin River Adventures.

Kayaking and Canoeing

Yadkin River Adventures (104 Old Rockford Rd., Rockford, 336/374-5318, www.yadkinriveradventures.com, canoe trips $50/2 hours, $60/4 hours, and $70/6 hours; kayak trips $30/2 hours, $40/4 hours, $50/6 hours) in Rockford offers rentals of canoes, kayaks, and sit-on-tops, along with shuttle service for full- and half-day paddling adventures. The Class I Yadkin River is great for paddlers of all ages and experience levels, and it has beautiful views of Pilot Mountain.

Parks

Pilot Mountain State Park (1792 Pilot Knob Park Rd., Pinnacle, 336/325-2355, http://ncparks.gov) is a beautiful place for **hiking, swimming, rock climbing, rappelling** (in designated areas), **canoeing** on the Yadkin River, and **camping** (Mar. 15-Nov. 30, $20, $15 over age 61) at one of the 49 designated tent and trailer sites. Each site has a tent pad, a picnic table, and a grill, as well as access to drinking water and hot showers. There are a dozen trails here, ranging in length from 0.1 miles (from parking lot to overlook) to 4.3 miles (circling the mountain) to 6.6 miles (connecting the two sections of the park). Pilot Mountain, the park's namesake 1,400-foot tall rocky

The sun burns off the morning mist near Fancy Gap.

protrusion, is a startling sight that reminds some of a UHF knob on an old television set, the kind you may have used to watch *The Andy Griffith Show*. Pilot Mountain is so named because it's a prominent and obvious landmark; it appears in *The Andy Griffith Show* as Mount Pilot.

The 400-foot rock faces that extend for two miles are the most striking feature of **Hanging Rock State Park** (1790 Hanging Rock Park Rd., Danbury, 336/593-8480, http://ncparks.gov, 8am-6pm daily Nov.-Feb., 8am-8pm daily Mar.-Apr. and Sept.-Oct., 8am-9pm daily May-Aug.), about 40 minutes outside Mount Airy. If you've exhausted the routes on Pilot Mountain (doubtful), this is a great place for **rock climbing** and **rappelling** (a permit and registration with park staff are required; climbers must also finish and exit the park by closing time). You can also **hike** to waterfalls and beautiful overlooks, and **swim** in a nearby lake. Hanging Rock State Park has 73 tent and trailer **campsites** ($13-20), one of which is **wheelchair-accessible.** Each site has a tent pad, a picnic table, a grill, access to drinking water, and access to a washhouse (mid-Mar.-Nov.) with hot showers and laundry sinks. There are also two-bedroom, four-bed vacation **cabins** (around $450 weekly in summer, $88 daily off-season) for rent. Reserve camping or cabins at least a month in advance with the park office.

Accommodations

In Mount Airy, **Quality Inn** (2136 Rockford St., 336/789-2000, www.qualityinn.com, from $70), **Holiday Inn Express** (1320 Ems Dr., 336/719-1731, www.hiexpress.com, from $80, pets allowed), and **Hampton Inn** (2029 Rockford St., 336/789-5999, www.hamptoninn.com, from $100) are good options.

Pilot Knob Inn Bed and Breakfast (361 New Pilot Knob Lane, Pinnacle, 336/325-2502, www.pilotknobinn.com, $129-249) in Pinnacle is an unusual B&B in that guests can stay in suites in the main lodge or in one of several restored century-old tobacco barns on the property. Each one-bedroom barn-turned-cabin is well equipped with modern conveniences, including two-person hot tubs and stone wood-burning fireplaces. Children and pets are not allowed, but horses can occupy a stall on the property for an additional $50 per night.

Food

While you're in Mount Airy, you have to eat at ★ **The Snappy Lunch** (125 N. Main St., 336/786-4931, www.thesnappylunch.com, 5:45am-1:45pm Mon., Wed., and Fri., 5:45am Tues., Thurs., and Sat., $1-5), a diner whose claims to fame include mentions on *The Andy Griffith Show* and a "World Famous Pork Chop Sandwich," which is notoriously sloppy, delicious, and cheap. Eating here is like stepping back in time.

The Snappy Lunch has been in the community since 1923.

There's only one source for good strong coffee in Mount Airy, the **Good Life Café** (Main-Oak Emporium, 248 N Main St., 336/789-2404, www.mainoakemporium.com, 10am-6pm Mon.-Sat., 1pm-5pm Sun. Jan.-Aug., 10am-6pm Mon.-Thurs. and Sat., 10am-8pm Fri., 1pm-5pm Sun. Sept.-Dec.), which makes a surprisingly good cappuccino. **The Copper Pot Restaurant** (123 Scenic Outlet Lane, Suite 4, 336/352-4108, www.copperpotrestaurant.com, 6am-8pm Mon.-Thurs., 6am-9pm Fri.-Sat., around $10) is a down-home restaurant specializing in dishes of the "meat and two" or "meat and three" variety. It's country cooking all the way, so prepare for fried okra, pinto beans, and inexpensive food.

Information and Services

Find out more of what Mount Airy has to offer by stopping by the **Mount Airy Visitors Center** (200 N. Main St., 800/948-0949 or 336/786-6116, www.visitmayberry.com, 8:30am-5:30pm Mon.-Fri., 10am-5pm Sat., 1pm-4pm Sun.).

There is a hospital in town, **Northern Hospital of Surry County** (830 Rockford St., 336/719-7000, www.northernhospital.com). If you require the police, contact the **Mount Airy Police Department** (150 Rockford St., 336/786-3535, www.mountairy.org).

Sugarloaf Mountain

(MP 203.9)

From the Piedmont Overlook at Milepost 203.9, you have a grand view of the piedmont of Virginia and North Carolina rolling away from you. To the southwest, beside I-77, is Sugarloaf Mountain, which gets its name from the distinctively loafy roundness to its peak.

★ Blue Ridge Music Center (MP 213)

The **Blue Ridge Music Center** (700 Foothills Rd., Galax, 276/236-5309, www.blueridgemusiccenter.org, museum: 10am-5pm daily May-Oct., free, concerts $10) is a museum dedicated to the roots music of the hills in this part of North Carolina and Virginia. Video and audio displays help tell the story of the development of old-time and bluegrass music and show how this distinct sound has influenced other genres throughout the years. As you tour the Music Center, you'll see fantastic antique and contemporary examples of banjos, fiddles, guitars, and dobros. **Midday Mountain Music concerts** (noon-4pm daily, free) give area musicians opportunities to play for a crowd, and regular evening concerts by more established acts draw crowds from all over.

High Meadow Trail

Distance: 2.8 miles out and back
Duration: 1.5 hours
Elevation gain: 100 feet
Difficulty: moderate
Trailhead: Blue Ridge Music Center parking area

From the handicapped parking area of the Music Center parking lot, descend along a service road. Very soon you'll go down some steps and cross a stream via a footbridge. You'll cross another bridge at 0.25 miles, but in the meantime enjoy the walk in these piney woods.

The Fisher Peak Trail joins our trail at 0.35 miles. Keep to the right to stay on the High Meadow Trail. A half mile in, there's a little rock face and a bench where you can rest. From here, you can hear concerts from the Music Center if someone's playing. Enter the meadow at 0.6 miles, then weave in and out of the woods and meadow for the next 0.4 miles. At 1 mile, the Fisher Peak Trail goes off to the left. Bear right and begin a gradual descent until you reach Foothills Road at 1.4 miles.

To return, you can retrace your steps, or go along the Fisher Peak Loop Trail, a trek that's just a little longer than your return trip. If you want to go this way, there's a short spur trail to the peak, but besides that, Fisher Peak Trail joins the High Meadow Trail 0.35 miles from the parking lot, at which point you'll turn right and return to your car.

◆ VA-89 North: Galax (MP 215)

Music has played an important part in most cultures' development, and the Scots-Irish settlers who established communities in these mountains were no different. They brought with them fiddles, mandolins, and bagpipes, and they would

have been happy to learn that today, music from these instruments (from fiddles and mandolins mostly) echoes off the hillsides around Galax. Galax calls itself "The World Capital of Old Time Mountain Music." The number of people who play an instrument, sing, square dance, clog, flatfoot, or mountain dance is astonishing. That's one of the reasons Galax has hosted the Old Fiddler's Convention every August for the last 80 years.

Galax is just seven miles north of the Parkway at Milepost 215 via VA-89.

Music and Events

The quiet village is brought to raucous life during the annual **Old Fiddler's Convention** (276/236-8541, www.old-fiddlersconvention.com, $40 full convention, or $6-12/day, camping on site $80 for the convention), the oldest and

Old Fiddler's Convention

The annual six-day **Old Fiddler's Convention** (276/236-8541, www.old-fiddlersconvention.com, early Aug., $40 full convention, or $6-12/day, camping on site $80 for the convention) defines the character of Galax. Tens of thousands of musicians, mountain dancers, and music lovers descend on this town to play in impromptu groups in the campground and on the streets, meet up with seldom-seen friends, trade instruments, and swap stories of conventions past. Don't be surprised to see multiple generations of a family who've been coming every year since the convention was started in 1935.

The Fiddler's Convention is about getting together and playing, but it's also about friendly competition and a little showing off. Every day of the festival, musicians, bands, and dancers compete on-stage. Young musicians can compete to see who is the best fiddler (old-time and bluegrass), mandolin player, clawhammer and bluegrass banjo picker, guitar player, and band. The competition is stiff, but it gets stiffer in other divisions. Old-time and bluegrass bands compete for a $775 top prize. Small cash prizes also go out to fiddlers, autoharp, guitar, mandolin, dulcimer, dobro, and both clawhammer and bluegrass banjo styles. The best folk song, the best flatfoot dance, and the best all around performer also go home with a little folding money in their pockets.

They're strict about their music here, and competition rules say things like: "to qualify, a band must consist of at least a banjo, a fiddle, and a guitar," "no bluegrass banjo style picking to be in old-time band. No old-time banjo style picking to be in bluegrass band," and "dulcimer competition is for lap dulcimer only." If you're not attuned to the differences between bluegrass and old-time music, clawhammer versus bluegrass banjo styles, or exactly what a lap dulcimer may be, don't worry, you'll be surrounded by folks who will be more than happy to get into deep discussions explaining the finer points of these two genres.

---

largest mountain music convention in the country. It was begun in 1935 with the stated purpose of "Keeping alive the memories and sentiments of days gone by and mak[ing] it possible for people of today to hear and enjoy the tunes of yesterday," and that still holds true. Every year, top competitors go home with a little spending money and a lot of pride as they compete to be the best in several divisions. The clack of clogs and the slap of flatfoot combine with arts, crafts, and food booths the second week of August. Tickets and camping at the convention are on a first-come, first-served basis.

No music-loving mountain town is complete without a jam session or two. In Galax, you can come together with other fans and bluegrass, country, and old-time musicians at **Stringbean Coffee Shop** (215 S. Main St., 276/236-0567) for a musical gathering starting at 6:30pm on Tuesday nights. In nearby Independence, there's a **jam session** (6:30pm-9pm Wed.) at the **Historic 1908 Courthouse** (107 E. Main St., Independence). And on Saturdays, the **Blue Ridge Music Center** has a **concert series** (from 4pm-6pm Sat., free).

Every Friday, WBRF 98.1 FM and the Galax Downtown Association sponsor **Blue Ridge Backroads** (8pm-10pm Fri.), one of the few remaining live bluegrass radio shows in the country. It's held at the historic **Rex Theater** (111 E. Grayson St., 276/236-0329, www.rextheatergalax.com), which also hosts live bluegrass and country bands. Ticket prices vary for concerts, but to attend a recording of Blue Ridge Backroads, tickets are $5 and available at the door only.

In mid-July, Galax hosts hordes of barbecue lovers during the two-day **Virginia State Barbecue Championship** (276/236-2184, www.smokeonthemountainva.com). There's a $10,000 purse for the event, which is sanctioned by the Memphis Barbecue Network and the Kansas City BBQ Society, and is a qualifying event for the World Food Championships. This is no backyard barbecue; pro teams come from all over the nation to compete for big money and the chance to qualify for more contests.

Accommodations

The Doctor's Inn (406 W. Stuart Dr., 276/238-9998, www.thedoctorsinnvirginia.com, $149) was built in 1913 and is listed on both the Virginia Landmark Register and the National Register of Historic Places. The six rooms here can accommodate just about any party, from a couple on a romantic getaway to a girls' weekend in the mountains to someone passing through solo. Breakfast ranges from lighter fare like oatmeal or yogurt with granola to more filling meals like biscuits, sausage casseroles, and country ham.

Fiddler's Roost Bed & Breakfast Cabins (485 Fishers Peak Rd., 276/236-1212, www.fiddlersroostcabins.com, $120-350) consists of six private log cabins. Cabins include a three-bed, two-bath unit with a wraparound porch and hot tub, ideal for groups of six; other cabins are perfect for a pair of travelers. You may think that with separate accommodations you won't be getting breakfast, but you're wrong; the innkeepers deliver a full gourmet breakfast right to your door every morning of your stay.

Old Cranks (407 Railroad Ave., 276/236-5114, www.oldcranks.com, $30/night, 450/night during the Old Fiddler's Convention) offers RV and tent camping near the site of the Old Fiddler's Convention and less than a mile from downtown Galax. There's also an ice cream shop and motorcar museum

here. And the name doesn't come from a cranky owner, it refers back to the old cranks you had to use to start your car on the earliest models.

Food

Bogey's (103 Country Club Lane, 276/601-2536, www.bogeysgalax.com, 4pm-9pm Wed.-Thurs., 4pm-10pm Fri.-Sat., 11am-2:30pm Sun., dinner $10-20, brunch $6-12) serves a menu chock full of American classics: steaks and chops, prime rib sandwiches, cheeseburgers, and a bevy of fried appetizers. They have a view of the Country Club's golf course and the food is quite good, so heading here for dinner or drinks is an easy choice.

The Galax Smokehouse (101 N. Main St., 276/236-1000, www.thegalaxsmokehouse.com, 11am-9pm Mon.-Sat., 11am-3pm Sun., lunch around $10, dinner $9-20) is, according to locals, one of the best restaurants in Galax. Specializing in barbecue, they serve pork spare ribs, boneless rib tips, pulled pork barbecue, Texas-style beef brisket, smoked chicken, burgers, and all the barbecue sides you'd expect. Their sauce comes in seven varieties ranging from hot and spicy Texas style to sweet Tennessee sauce to the vinegar-based eastern North Carolina style.

It's worth eating at **Scoots** (104 N. Main St., 276/236-2006, www.scootsofgalax.com, 11am-8pm Mon.-Thurs., 11am-9pm Fri.-Sat., under $9) if for no other reason than the name. The sandwich-heavy menu includes a monster burger (topped with onion rings, among other things) and a double hamburger, grilled pimento cheese, a flounder sandwich, and corn dogs. There are also a few plates, like the seafood trio, a flounder diner, and something called the Pig Wing Dinner (I'm still not sure what that one is).

North Carolina High Country

The Blue Ridge Mountains grow rugged here. The landscape visitors encountered through much of Virginia is paltry in comparison to the grade, elevation, and vistas of North Carolina's High Country.

Bristol

Cherokee National Forest

Galax

Pisgah National Forest

BOONE

LINN COVE VIADUCT

GRANDFATHER MOUNTAIN

Blowing Rock

Pisgah National Forest

LINVILLE FALLS

Little Switzerland

CRABTREE FALLS TRAIL

220 mil / 350 km
4.5 hrs

Asheville

Hickory

© AVALON TRAVEL

North Carolina
High Country

TENNESSEE

NORTH CAROLINA

Appalachian Trail

Roan Mtn

To
Little Switzerland,
Crabtree Falls,
Mount Mitchell,
and Asheville.

Roan Mtn
Park

Elk
Park

BLUE

MP-320

LINVILLE FALLS
Recreation Area

LINVILLE CAVERNS

BEECH
MOUNTAIN

Banner Elk

HAWK'S NEST
SNOW TUBING

SUGAR
MOUNTAIN

Grandfather
Mountain

Linville

LINN COVE
VIADUCT

MP-310

FLAT ROCK

BEACON
HEIGHTS

MP-300

Valle
Crucis

Foscoe

Julian Price
Memorial Park

RIDGE

BOONE

Moses H. Cone
Memorial Park

MP-290

Blowing Rock

To
Hickory

Happy
Valley

Fort
Defiance

LENOIR

Elk Knob
State Park

West Jefferson

Mt Jefferson
State Park

Jefferson

Glendale
Springs

MP-280

E. B. Jeffress
Park

MP-270

THE LUMP

MP-260

New River

PARKWAY

New River
State Natural
Area

NEW RIVER
OUTFITTERS

River

Laurel
Springs

MP-250

Blue Ridge
Parkway

MP-240

Doughton
Park

Stone Mountain
State Park

MP-230

To
Cumberland Knob
and Roanoke.

To
Elkin

North
Wilkesboro

Wilkesboro

To
Winston-Salem

To
Statesville

Fork

S Fork

New River

N

0   10 km
0   10 mi

© AVALON TRAVEL

Highlights

★ **Art Galleries in Blowing Rock:** Galleries celebrating the region's beauty and inspiration line Main Street in this small town (page 184).

★ **Linn Cove Viaduct:** One of the most iconic spots on the Parkway, this curved, elevated roadway is as beautiful as it is fun to drive (page 190).

★ **Grandfather Mountain:** Walk across the Mile High Swinging Bridge and take in views that are spectacular any time of year (page 191).

★ **Linville Falls:** One of the most photographed places in North Carolina, these falls tumble 90 feet over steep cliffs into Linville Gorge. Five trails lead to overlooks for spectacular views of the falls (page 194).

★ **Emerald Village:** Mine for gems and pan for gold at this group of once-active mines nestled in the mountains (page 197).

★ **Grassy Creek Waterfall:** It's a quick and easy hike to this mossy waterfall and cascade just off the Parkway (page 198).

★ **Crabtree Falls Trail:** Hike to this 70-foot cascade that spills delicately down a rock face. In spring, it's surrounded by wildflowers (page 198).

In 1752, a settler crested a ridge in North Carolina's High Country and remarked, "We saw mountains to the right, to the left, before and behind us, rising like great waves in a storm." He wouldn't be surprised to learn that this section of North Carolina remained untamed for another century and a half.

Eventually, wagons gave way to automobiles and improved roads. Then the Blue Ridge Parkway opened, and the area opened to travelers. Though access improved and visitors have flocked here since the day the Parkway opened, the Blue Ridge Parkway was far from complete until the 1980s. Then, the final piece of the roadway, the Linn Cove Viaduct, was finished, tying together Great Smoky Mountains and Shenandoah National Parks.

This is a land of stories, and a good portion of the folklore to come out of Appalachia in the last century or so was collected and recorded here. It stretches back further, however. Here, a young Confederate veteran called Tom Dooley was memorialized in song after committing a gristly crime. Here too is where moonshiners plied their trade from colonial days to the present.

Stands of virgin forest blanket a few mountainsides here, though most have been logged, but not in some time, and to the untrained eye there is little difference. It's not all backwoods and backroads, though. Villages and towns like Blowing Rock, Elkin, West Jefferson, and Little Switzerland are charming, hospitable, and surprisingly artistic. Those interested in folk arts and crafts will find the Penland School of Crafts as well as Blowing Rock and its galleries of particular interest. Getting into certain corners of the region can still be challenging, but that just adds to the beauty.

Planning Your Time

Plan for at least three days here for a good overview, but five days to thoroughly experience the hikes, historic sites, waterfalls, peaks, and parks. This area offers several levels of accommodations, so you can rough it in beautiful campgrounds, stay in luxury lodges and inns, or somewhere in between. Your best bet for chain hotels is Boone, but if you're looking for a more rural, B&B experience, a handful of places in and around West Jefferson have

Best Accommodations

★ **River House Country Inn and Restaurant, Grassy Creek:** Relax in luxurious digs on the banks of the North Fork of the New River (page 173).

★ **New River State Park, West Jefferson:** You'll appreciate amenities like showers and grills at these campsites, some of which can be accessed only by canoe (page 173).

★ **Blowing Rock Inn, Blowing Rock:** This quiet inn has a fun retro vibe (page 185).

★ **Westglow Resort and Spa, Blowing Rock:** Taking in views of Grandfather Mountain from your private deck is the definition of luxury (page 186).

★ **Switzerland Inn, Little Switzerland:** Stunning views await at themed accommodations like the Heidi or Alpine Suites (page 198).

beautiful countryside and river views, and Blowing Rock is filled with inns and B&Bs. Further down the Parkway, in the town of Little Switzerland, you'll find some lovely places to stay as well. These cities are also the best (and the only) places to get a bite to eat along this leg of the trip.

Most visitors come in October for fall foliage, or mid-summer for the cooler temperatures found at these high elevations. At these times, reservations for B&Bs and inns go fast, and it can be tough to come by a table at prime dining hours in the best restaurants. There are many seasonal businesses, so in winter and early spring, your selection of places to eat and shop may be limited. That said, business is booming at several ski resorts around Boone.

Driving Considerations

Traveling via the Parkway presents difficulties in the deepest part of winter, when ice, snow, and unpredictable weather cause periodic road closures. It's advisable to check real-time closures and road advisories on the National Parks Service website (http://maps.nps.gov/blri/road-closures/). In early spring, the Parkway should be open in this region, though as you get into the highest elevations of this leg—around Grandfather Mountain and Linn Cove Viaduct—and approach Asheville, you'll find more closures.

Getting There

There are no train or bus services along this leg of the Parkway.

Starting Points

This drive begins near where the Blue Ridge Parkway crosses from Virginia into North Carolina, at **Cumberland Knob** (MP 217.5), and ends **147 miles** later at **Craggy Gardens** (MP 364.6). It's possible to drive from one end of this segment to another in about four hours. The nearest major travel hubs to this region are Raleigh and Charlotte, N.C.

Car

I-77 crosses the Blue Ridge Parkway in Virginia, just over the Virginia-North Carolina state line. **I-40** intersects the Parkway just outside of Asheville, to the southwest. The two main routes used to access this region of North Carolina are Highways 321 and 421. **US-321** begins to the southeast in Gastonia (just outside of Charlotte), passes through Hickory, and leads into Blowing Rock. **US-421** comes in from the east, picking up Winston-Salem and I-77 in quick succession, then tracing an east-northeast path through North Wilkesboro to Boone.

From Raleigh, it's a three-hour, 188-mile drive to Boone along I-40 West and US-421 North. Charlotte is closer, and it's only a shade over two hours on the 117-mile drive via I-77 North and US-421

Best Restaurants

★ **Sunrise Grill, Boone:** Friendly service makes the best breakfast in Boone that much better (page 180).

★ **Joy Bistro, Boone:** Fusing Southern cooking with French techniques delivers unforgettable flavor (page 181).

★ **The Chestnut Grille, Blowing Rock:** Globally-inspired cuisine from an award-winning chef graces this menu (page 186).

★ **Bistro Roca and Antlers Bar, Blowing Rock:** Chow down on filling dishes like lobster mac-and-cheese at the oldest operating bar in North Carolina (page 186).

North, and slightly shorter—only 102 miles—if you take US-321 North.

Fueling Up

Take note of the following places where you can fuel up and grab a snack. Not only are they the most convenient, they're the only reliable places to gas up:

- **MP 229.7,** US-21 less than eight miles west

- **MP 248.1,** NC-18 less than three miles west

- **MP 261.2,** NC-16 less than 12 miles west

- **MP 291.8,** US-321 less than two miles north or south

- **MP 312,** NC-181 less than three miles north

- **MP 330.9,** NC-226 less than three miles north

Air

From Boone, **Charlotte Douglass International Airport** (5501 R C Josh Birmingham Pkwy., Charlotte, 704/359-4013, www.charlotteairport.com) is two hours south, and **Raleigh-Durham International Airport** (2400 John Brantley Blvd., Morrisville, 919/840-2123, www.rdu.com) is three hours east.

Cumberland Knob (MP 217.5)

The Blue Ridge Parkway crosses into North Carolina at Milepost 216.9, and less than a mile away is Cumberland Knob, the place where construction began on this jewel of a roadway on September 11, 1935. At the Cumberland Knob Recreation Area, you'll find a comfort and information station with restrooms, and 1,000 acres to explore via a pair of hikes, one very easy, one more strenuous.

Cumberland Knob Trail

Distance: 0.6 miles out and back
Duration: 30 minutes
Elevation gain: 100 feet
Difficulty: easy
Trailhead: the Woodland Trail sign to the right of the information station at Cumberland Knob, far right trail

This easy hike leads to a fabulous stone picnic shelter at the top of Cumberland Knob. As you approach the Woodland Trail sign, you'll see two paved trails that go to the right. Take the furthest one to the right, which passes right by a small cemetery. The path leads right to the stone shelter and a view that's unremarkable. Once you're there, simply reverse course and head back to the trailhead. Due to the length of the trail and the lack of a memorable vista, you'll get the most out of this "hike" if you go at a brisk pace and use it to stretch out.

Gully Creek Trail

Distance: 2.5-mile loop
Duration: 1.5-2 hours
Elevation gain: 830 feet
Difficulty: strenuous
Trailhead: the Woodland Trail sign behind the information station at Cumberland Knob, trail to the left

The Gully Creek Trail begins on the ridge, then dips into Gully Creek before making a short but strenuous climb back to the parking area, with an option for an additional climb to the peak of the unremarkable Cumberland Knob.

Soon after setting foot on the trail, you'll begin to descend through thickets of mountain laurel and rhododendron via a series of switchbacks. After a short ways, you'll follow Gully Creek, which you'll cross several times in the next half mile. There are a few nice small waterfalls and cascades here. At 1.2 miles in, you'll begin to ascend on switchbacks that are blanketed in ferns. After a quarter-mile of ferns, you'll reenter the rhododendron and mountain laurel thickets, which you'll be with for much of the trail back.

At 2.2 miles, you'll reach an intersection. To the left, a 0.2-mile trail leads to Cumberland Knob and the picnic shelter there. If you go that way, you can return to the parking area via a 0.4-mile Cumberland Knob Trail or you can double back to Gully Creek. As Cumberland Knob doesn't offer much by way of views, bear right and stick to Gully Creek Trail. At 2.4 miles, the summit trail joins yours for the final 0.1 miles to the parking area.

⚑ US-21 South: Roaring Gap to Elkin (MP 229)

At Milepost 229, the Blue Ridge Parkway crosses over US-21. Following US-21 South, you'll reach the unincorporated village of Roaring Gap in 4 miles, and the town of Elkin 22 miles off the Parkway. There is beautiful country in Roaring Gap, but not much else. Elkin, however, sits on the northwestern edge of North Carolina's Yadkin Valley Wine Country, a 1.4-million-acre wine region. As a town that calls itself "The Best Small Town in America" (and it is a good one), it's friendly and hospitable, so you can find a great meal or a comfy bed, though the selections may be limited.

Wineries

There are eight wineries within easy driving distance of Elkin, though the Yadkin Valley as a whole has more than three-dozen wineries spread across North Carolina's first designated American Viticultural Area. My favorite is **McRitchie Winery & Ciderworks** (315 Thurmond P.O. Rd., Thurmond, NC, 336/874-3003, www.mcritchiewine.com, noon-5pm Thurs.-Sun.), which makes a pair of great red blends—Arcturus and Ring of Fire—as well as a sweet and dry hard sparkling cider.

Grassy Creek Vineyard and Winery
(235 Chatham Cottage Circle, State Road, 336/835-2458, www.grassycreekvineyard. com, 11am-6pm Thurs.-Sat., 1pm-5pm Sun., tasting $5) produces wine in a variety of French styles with grapes grown here and at their sister vineyard in a town nearby. **Jones von Drehle Vineyards & Winery** (964 Old Railroad Grade Rd., Thurmond, 336/874-2800, www.jonesvondrehle.com, 11am-6pm Wed.-Sat., noon-5pm Sun., tasting $8) is one of the newest wineries in the region, but one that's gaining new fans daily with their rose and their better red and white vintages. **Elkin Creek Vineyards** (318 Elkin Creek Mill Rd., Elkin, 336/526-5119, www.elkincreekvineyard.com, 11am-5pm Thurs.-Sun., tasting $6-7) planted their first vines in 2001 and bottled their first vintage just four years later, and today they're one of the more popular stops in the area. In downtown Elkin, **Brushy Mountain Winery** (125 W. Main St., Elkin, 336/835-1313, www.brushymountainwine.com, 1pm-5pm Thurs. and Sun., noon-8pm Fri.-Sat., tasting $6-12) uses grapes from around the Yadkin Valley to make a number of notable blends; combine tasty wine with a downtown tasting room, and you have a must-stop, must-sip winery.

Carolina Heritage Vineyard and Winery (170 Heritage Vines Way, Elkin, 336/366-3301, www.carolinaheritagevineyards.com, 1pm-6pm Sat.-Sun.) is North Carolina's first solar-powered winery and first USDA Certified Organic Vineyard. They have 35 acres, just three miles east of Elkin, where you can stop in for a tour, a talk on organic farming techniques, and, of course, a glass of wine. Most of their wines are blends, though their Chambourcin and Traminette are solid, single-grape bottles. They also have a wine made from the native muscadine grape, a grape that is often too sweet for my taste, but one they handle well.

Accommodations and Food
Roaring Gap

In Roaring Gap, you can stay at **High**

Meadows Inn (10498 US-21, 336/363-2221, www.nikolas-highmeadowsinn.com, $75-120) and dine at the attached restaurant, **Nikola's** (336/363-6060, $11-26), serving a variety of pasta dishes and steaks as well as a small seafood selection.

Elkin

Just south of the Blue Ridge Parkway at Milepost 227 is the **Glade Valley Bed and Breakfast** (330 Shaw Lane, Glade Valley, 336/657-8811 or 800/538-3508, www.gladevalley.com, $120-170). Glade Valley B&B has six bedrooms and a private cabin built to look like a classic frontier cabin. This bed-and-breakfast sits on 29 acres of mountainside with miles of walking trails and tremendous views, making it a relaxing place to rest for a night or two. In addition to breakfast, they provide guests with complimentary bottled water.

If you want to make an event of the region's wineries, you'll need a place to sleep off the day's adventures. At **Frog Holler Cabins** (564 E. Walker Rd., 336/526-2661, www.froghollercabins.com, $95-145) you can stay in a well-appointed cabin with a fireplace and a hot tub overlooking Big Elkin Creek. Three cabins, The Cottage, Hawks Nest, and Mill House, are around 400 square feet and suitable for a couple; Deer Run is a bit bigger and sleeps four. There's plenty of peace and quiet, and they're within 30 minutes of more than two-dozen vineyards and wineries. On the property are miles of hiking trails and a fishing pond, but one of the big draws is the fact that you can park and take a guided tour ($60) of wineries. With their driver, everyone in your party can enjoy the wine tasting.

You can also stay at two vineyards: **Elkin Creek Vineyards** (318 Elkin Creek Mill Rd., Elkin, 336/526-5119, www.el-kincreekvineyard.com, $120-150/night) and **Grassy Creek Vineyard and Winery** (235 Chatham Cottage Circle, State Road, 336/835-2458, www.grassycreekvineyard.com, $150-700/night).

In downtown Elkin, **Twenty One & Main Restaurant and Wine Bar** (102 E. Main St., 336/835-6246, www.twentyoneandmain.com, dinner from 5:30pm Tues.-Sat., $10-27, 3-course tasting menu $36, 5-course $60, wine pairings $4 per course) serves an eclectic menu that changes biweekly. Dishes are meat-heavy, with steaks, lamb, pork, and seafood often taking center stage. Twenty One & Main is an upscale restaurant but unpretentious and quite comfortable. The staff is quick with reliable food recommendations and drink pairings.

222 Public House (222 E. Main St., 336/526-0067, www.222publichouse.com, 5pm-midnight Thurs., 11:30am-midnight Fri.-Mon., closed Tues.-Wed., $7-15) serves wood-fired pizzas, wings, salads, and chicken sandwiches, and a very good selection of microbrews in a sports-bar atmosphere.

Stone Mountain State Park (MP 229)

You can't see the namesake Stone Mountain upon entering **Stone Mountain State Park** (3042 Frank Pkwy., Roaring Gap, 336/957-8185, www.ncparks.gov, 7am-6pm daily Nov.-Feb., 7am-8pm daily Mar.-Apr. and Sept.-Oct., 7am-9pm May-Aug., closed Christmas Day), but when you do, you'll remember it. Just a few miles south of the Parkway along US-21, this 14,000-acre park's most prominent feature is the 600-foot granite dome that is Stone Mountain. The 25-square-mile pluton (an upthrust of igneous rock) is fun to hike, but difficult to see from the park. For the best views, get back on the Blue Ridge Parkway and head to the **Stone Mountain Overlook** (MP 232.5).

Sights

Stone Mountain State Park was established in 1969 and named a National Natural Landmark in 1975. In the years before it was a park, the lands around were settled by the typical mix of Europeans who make up much of the Appalachian ancestry—English, Irish, Scots-Irish, and German, with a few French families thrown in for good measure. They shaped churches, farms, log homes, and all they needed to create a community out of these woods, and three sites around the park show different aspects of life for the early European inhabitants here. The **Mountain Culture Exhibit** in the park office provides some historical context to these bold families who settled here. The **Hutchison Homestead** was built in the mid-1800s and is representative of a typical homestead for the region; it includes a log cabin, barn, outbuildings, and even a blacksmith shop. Finally, the **Garden Creek Baptist Church,** built in 1897, is one of the few original churches in the county that stand in nearly original form, having undergone no remodeling or major repairs during its long life.

Local stone was used to make the bridges on the Blue Ridge Parkway.

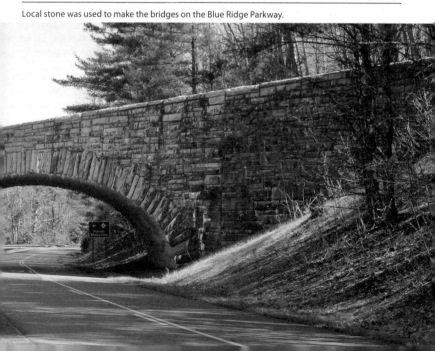

Hiking

There are a number of hiking trails in the park, ranging from easy forest strolls to the challenging Stone Mountain Loop Trail that takes you to the top of the impressive granite dome.

Stone Mountain Loop Trail

Distance: 4.5-mile loop
Duration: 3-3.5 hours
Elevation gain: 500 feet
Difficulty: strenuous
Trailhead: Upper Trailhead parking lot
Directions: Exit the Parkway at MP 229 and follow US-21 south and turn onto Oklahoma Road/Old Gap Road/Stone Mountain Road. Once in the park, follow the road to the trailhead across from the Stone Mountain State Park campground.

This hike is a killer, especially during late summer when the granite gets so hot that you feel like you're baking as you cross the wide stone face. Fall (specifically, mid-Oct.) is when the views are best and the weather is ideal for this hike.

Start on a short spur trail that leads to a sign marking the trail. Follow the trail to the left and head to Stone Mountain Falls, a 200-foot waterfall. A set of nearly 300 very steep stairs leads to the bottom of the falls.

Continue on the trail to a pair of side trails leading to Lower and Middle Falls Trails. Unless you are a big waterfall fan, you can skip these (save your energy for the uphill portion of the hike as the spur trail is about 0.5 miles). About 1.7 miles into the hike, you'll notice the trees beginning to thin and Stone Mountain begins to show a little granite. Just down the trail from here is the Hutchison Homestead, which is a good spot to catch your breath. The parking area for the lower trailhead is nearby. That trail is a more direct approach to the summit, but you should go for the loop because the whole hike is worthwhile, not just the main attraction.

Soon after you leave the Homestead, the trail gets steep enough that there are a few cables along the way to help you climb. Don't stray far from the trail—it's marked with orange dots—as the granite can be slick. From the summit you'll have a good view of the mountains. Look to the northwest and west: you may see the Blue Ridge Parkway cutting across the opposite hills. To complete the trail, simply follow the markings off the summit, back into the trees, and back to the spur trail that leads to the trailhead.

Cedar Rock Trail

Distance: 1 mile out and back
Duration: 30 minutes
Elevation gain: 250 feet
Difficulty: moderate
Trailhead: Lower Trailhead parking lot near the Hutchison Homestead

Some say this hike is easy, others say moderate, but it's relatively easy except for a couple of short, steep spots that may make you winded on the way up and give your quads a workout on the way back. Depart from the Lower Trailhead parking area where you'll also find the Wolf Rock and Black Jack Ridge Trailheads. Follow the sign and the round red blazes. From the trailhead, you'll take the Stone Mountain Loop past the Homestead, then turn right. When the trail forks, Cedar Rock stays to the right and you'll ascend to the small summit. Along the way, and especially at the top, you'll have some good views of Stone Mountain.

Camping

There are several camping options in **Stone Mountain State Park** (reservations: www.northcarolnastateparks.reserveamerica.com or www.ncparks.gov). The Family Campground A and C Loops ($20/day, $15/day for those 62 and older) consist of 47 non-electric campsites, while the B Loop ($25/day, $19/day for 62 and older) has 41 sites with both electrical and water hookups; both of these sites are close to a washhouse with hot showers and drinking water, and there is an RV dump station available. There cabin

are four group campsites ($48/day), each suitable for up to 25 people; these sites are also convenient to the washhouse and water facilities. For those interested in a little backcountry camping, there are six primitive sites ($10/day).

Doughton Park (MP 238.5)

The open bluegrass meadows of Doughton Park are some of the best places for wildlife viewing in North Carolina's High Country. At just over 7,000 acres, Doughton Park is simply crawling with white-tailed deer, who forage the fields by the dozens in the early morning and shortly before sunset. Keen-eyed observers may catch a glimpse of a bobcat, red fox, bear, or even coyote at the edge of the woods or crossing a path ahead in the distance.

One of the more interesting points of Doughton Park is the fact that it looks much like these meadows and balds would have looked in the early 1900s when mountain farmers carved pastures and gardens out of the forest. Of course, today the Parks Service periodically mows the fields, doing the job of livestock with modern machinery, but it paints an interesting picture of how life here got along in the early 20th century.

Views here are huge. To the south and east, the Parks Service owns much of the land, so it remains lovely and uninhabited. To the northwest, there are clusters of houses that some feel detract from the scenery, but they only serve to provide some much-needed scale on these ridgelines, and reaffirm why people have felt drawn to these mountains for hundreds of years. If you look east, you'll see the granite face of Stone Mountain not too far away.

Sights
Just off the Parkway at Milepost 238.5 stands the **Brinegar Cabin,** one of

the relics showing human habitation along the ridgetops of the Blue Ridge Mountains. Originally part of a 125-acre farm purchased in 1876 (for the princely sum of $200), this cabin was the home of the bachelor Martin Brinegar for two years until he took for his wife the 16-year-old Carolina. On this farm, they raised four children as well as crops of food to sustain them through the year. Martin made shoes, and acted as a Justice of the Peace and a Notary Public. When he died in 1925, Carolina became sole owner of the farm. In 1935, when the Blue Ridge Parkway made plans to come through their farm, she sold it to the state of North Carolina for inclusion in Parkway lands. As was common at the time, the Parks Service granted her lifetime rights to the cabin, which would have allowed her to live on the property for as long as she wanted (with a few restrictions on hunting, wood gathering, and the like). Shortly after the park was established, she left the farm, saying the traffic had made her mountaintop home too "noisy" a place to live.

Today, you can peek in the windows of the small cabin, learn about farming techniques that the Brinegars would've used at the garden maintained by the Parks Service, and check out their spring house (where the spring still flows). On weekends in peak seasons, a park ranger gives presentations about the garden and about other aspects of daily life here.

Recreation
There are **Ranger-led programs** on the flora, fauna, and folkways of the mountains and farms nearby (check the schedule at the Doughton Park office at MP 241.1, 336/372-1947) and also **fishing** for rainbow and brook trout in the Basin Cove Creek complex (MPs 238-244). You'll need a valid North Carolina or Virginia fishing permit as of the time of this writing, but check with the folks at the visitors center for current regulations.

Hiking

Thirty miles of trails crisscross Doughton Park, and hiking is what lures many visitors out of their cars here. A number of trails lead through the park, the shortest of which is **Wildcat Rocks Overlook,** a five-minute, 0.1-mile, leg-stretching loop that will take you from the defunct Bluffs Lodge to an overlook where you can see the miniscule **Caudill Cabin** and the expanse of Basin Creek Cove. In this tiny, one-room cabin, Martin and Jamie Caudill raised 14 children, a tremendous family until you consider that Martin's father, who lived just down the hill (his cabin is no longer standing), had 22 children.

Of the other hikes in Doughton Park, Fodder Stack Trail is short and sweet, and the others grow longer and more strenuous as you climb the peaks and explore waterfalls.

Fodder Stack Trail

Distance: 1 mile out and back
Duration: 45 minutes
Elevation gain: 40 feet
Difficulty: easy to moderate
Trailhead: far end of the Bluffs Lodge upper parking area (MP 241.1) on the southeast side of the Parkway

Unobstructed views to the east make this hike popular for early risers staying at the campgrounds in Doughton Park. From the Bluffs Lodge upper parking area, follow the marked trail down a short steep section, then along an easy path to the end, where the stone outcropping known as Fodder Stack stands. Along the way, you'll see a range of wildflowers depending on the time of year.

Bluff Mountain Trail

Distance: 15 miles out and back
Duration: 8-9 hours
Elevation gain: 400 feet
Difficulty: moderate

top to bottom: the Brinegar Cabin in Doughton Park; grapes growing in the Yadkin Valley; informative sign about Tom Dula, of the folk song "Tom Dooley," who hailed from these parts

Trailhead: Brinegar Cabin Overlook parking area, MP 238.9

The toughest thing about this hike is the distance, which is especially tough to handle when it's hot. Most of the trail is pretty easy, and some folks call this "the best walking" on the Parkway.

Start at the trail sign at the end of the Brinegar Cabin parking area and ascend. A quarter-mile in, you'll reach an intersection with the Cedar Ridge Trail (to the left); keep to the right and continue on Bluff Mountain Trail. The path widens and you'll enter a field shortly after the trail intersection, then, a mile in, you'll walk through the RV portion of the campground. At 1.3 miles, you'll cross the Parkway and come to the main part of the campground and a trail-map poster. Keep going and head into the hardwood forest and rhododendron tunnels.

Two miles into the hike, you'll come to another field, followed by another crossing of the Parkway. At 2.7 miles, you'll reach the (unfortunately) closed Doughton Park Coffee Shop at Milepost 241.1. Keep going up the steps at the far end of the parking lot to cross the Parkway again and head into the woods.

A little over four miles in, you'll intersect with Bluff Ridge Trail (to the left), stay right to reach Bluff Mountain. Immediately after the intersection are a cliff and a set of switchbacks. Here is one of the best views of the Parkway.

For the next mile or so, you'll parallel the Blue Ridge Parkway. At mile 4.7, you'll reach the Alligator Back Overlook (MP 242.4), then the Bluff Mountain Overlook (MP 243.4) at 5.8 miles. There's an old road at mile 6.3; don't follow it. Stay left for the pathway below the roadbed. Soon, you'll cross Grassy Gap Fire Road and another large meadow. From here, it's an easy walk to the end of the trail. Flat Rock Ridge Trail intersects your trail at mile 7.4. At mile 7.5, you're at the end.

Cedar Ridge Trail

Distance: 9 miles out and back
Duration: 5-6 hours
Elevation gain: 2,100 feet
Difficulty: moderate to strenuous
Trailhead: Brinegar Cabin Overlook parking area, MP 238.9

Starting from the Brinegar Cabin Overlook parking lot, you'll ascend the Bluff Mountain Trail for a quarter mile, then turn left through the fence stile to continue along Cedar Ridge Trail. Soon after you split off from the Bluff Mountain Trail, you'll enter a rhododendron tunnel and a series of switchbacks. The trail will narrow and ascend a little over the next mile, until you begin to walk along a ridgeline. A set of switchbacks at 1.8 miles will take you up, then down a steeper section. At 2.3 miles, you'll be descending again.

The mountain laurel becomes abundant at 3.5 miles. Continue along this trail until you reach Grassy Gap Fire Road. From here, you can turn around or head up Basin Creek Trail to see a few waterfalls and Caudill Cabin.

Basin Creek Trail

Distance: 5.6 miles out and back
Duration: 3-3.5 hours
Elevation gain: 1,200 feet
Difficulty: moderate to strenuous
Trailhead: Cedar Ridge Trail and Grassy Gap Fire Road
Directions: From the Brinegar Cabin Overlook parking area, hike the 4.5-mile Cedar Ridge Trail to the Basin Creek Trailhead.

As you ascend alongside Basin Creek, keep in mind that the prolific Caudill family called this cove home. Along the way, you'll spy a few signs of their existence, but you'll end the hike at Caudill Cabin (which you can see from Wildcat Rocks Overlook).

Begin the trail at the intersection of Cedar Ridge Trail and Grassy Gap Fire Road. Walk a quarter mile up the fire road to Basin Creek Trail to your right. The trail is lined with rhododendron, and there are a number of deep pools in the creek. Anglers love to visit this area as the streams are rife with trout. As you continue up the trail, you'll pass several more pools, some of which may just be the perfect place to cool off in warmer weather.

At 0.6 miles and 1.9 miles, you'll pass the remnants of old chimneys. You'll find some pretty cascades and small waterfalls around a mile in. At 1.3 miles, though, there's one of two 30-foot waterfalls that's quite nice to admire. Cross the stream several times as you climb on through pastures and then through steeper grazing lands. At 2.4 miles, you'll cross Basin Creek and see the second 30-foot falls. Soon you'll arrive at the Caudill Cabin, where you'll take a breather and retrace your steps back to Grassy Gap Fire Road, then back along Cedar Ridge Trail to the trailhead at Brinegar Cabin.

Accommodations

Accommodations are limited to tent and RV camping. Bluffs Lodge, one of three lodges along the Parkway, has unfortunately been unused for some time.

Camping

At Milepost 241 there is a **campground** (336/372-8877, www.recreation.gov for reservations, all sites $19/night) with 110 campsites, 25 trailer/RV sites, four restrooms, and a fire circle where many folks like to gather. In 2014, the C Loop section of the campground was closed for renovations, as is the case with the campgrounds along the Parkway from time to time. Note that maps on the National Park Service website incorrectly show a coffee shop (it closed, following the same fate at Bluffs Lodge) and small gas station here. Campsites are well maintained and pleasant.

Sally Mae's on the Parkway (MP 259)

Formerly Northwest Trading Post, **Sally Mae's on the Parkway** (414 Trading Post Rd., Glendale Springs, N.C., 336/982-2543, 9:30am-5:30pm daily Apr. 15-Nov. 15) is a great version of the "old country store" right on the parkway. It's worth a stop to stretch your legs and grab a sandwich (around $7); it's one of the few places to get something more than a snack along the whole Parkway. Take a long look at the handcrafted art, jewelry, and food items they carry.

There is a great little hike just down the road from here. At Milepost 260.3, you'll find the Jumpinoff Rocks parking area and small picnic area. From there, you have a pretty flat, one-mile hike to a rock observation deck with expansive views. Given that most folks will drive right by, it's a great place to take some fall foliage shots.

NC-163 West: West Jefferson (MP 261)

Just 11 miles from Milepost 261 on NC-163 West is the charming small town of West Jefferson, a good launching off point to explore this corner of the North Carolina High Country. From here, New River State Park is only 12 miles away, and the quaint little community of Todd is only 16 miles to the southwest.

West Jefferson, Jefferson, and Todd are in Ashe County, which is where the North and South Forks of the New River join to create the second oldest river in the world, the New. The New flows through North Carolina, Virginia, then West Virginia, where it joins other rivers on the way to the Ohio. In West Virginia, the New River is known for whitewater rafting and an impressive single-span arch bridge. Here, though, the river is wide, gentle, and slow, and you're more likely to wade it while casting a fly rod or float it in an inner tube than brave rapids in a raft or kayak.

Ashe County is also the center of two of North Carolina's more interesting industries: Christmas trees (Fraser firs, mostly) and cheese. North Carolina is the second-largest producer of Christmas trees in the United States; the industry brings in more than $100 million annually. The cheese here is also quite good.

West Jefferson is a surprisingly artsy town. There are 15 (at my last count) murals adorning buildings downtown, creating a lovely walking tour that gives you a look at how local artists have interpreted their history and surroundings. You'll also spot these strange concrete squares, once utilitarian (they were the bases of long-gone streetlights), now painted in whimsical forest scenes.

NC-194, which runs through West Jefferson and is connected to Jefferson by US-221, roughly parallels the Parkway. It's a beautiful drive in and of itself, leading by red barns and countless tree farms with orderly rows of Fraser firs. Many of these barns are decorated with vivid color-block paintings that resemble old fashioned quilts. They're part of the **Quilt Trails of Western North Carolina** (www. quilttrailswnc.org), an ongoing art project. There are two dozen in the vicinity of West Jefferson, and even more in other parts of North Carolina.

Entertainment
Festivals and Events
The center of the arts community is the **Ashe County Arts Council** (303 School Ave., 336/846-2787, www.ashecountyarts. org, 9am-5pm Mon.-Fri., 10am-4pm Sat. Apr.-Dec.). They have a gallery showing a rotating series of exhibitions by local artists and art collectives working in any medium imaginable, and they help put on musical events and plays in the community. The Arts Council is also heavily involved in the **West Jefferson Arts District Gallery Crawl** (second Fri. of the month

in June-Oct.), with a final **Christmas Crawl** taking place in early December.

There are plenty of goings on in West Jefferson. On Friday nights in May-August, the **Backstreet Park Concert Series** (5:30pm-7pm on the third, fourth and fifth Fri., free) brings in family-friendly musical entertainment in the form of traditional, old-time, and bluegrass musicians. Every July 3 and 4 they have the **Christmas in July Festival** (www. christmasinjuly.info), with music, a street fair, a farmers market, Civil War reenactors, activities for kids, and a pretty sizable crowd. September brings the **On The Same Page Literary Festival** (www. onthesamepagefestival.org), the **Old Time Antiques Fair** (336-846-1231), and **Art on the Mountain** (www.ashecountyarts.org).

Shopping
Broomfields Gallery (414 E. 2nd St., 336/846-4141, www.broomfieldsgallery. com, 11am-5pm Mon. and Wed.-Sat.) is chock full of a diverse selection of fine art, crafts, and antiques. The proprietors have been collecting for more than half a century, and they're selective in what they bring in to the store. **Originals Only Gallery** (3-B N. Jefferson Ave., 336/846-1636, www.originalsonlygallery.com, 10am-5pm Tues.-Sat.) has works by only a few Ashe County artists, but the works they carry—paintings, pottery, and furniture—are excellent.

Recreation
There are two undeniable natural features in West Jefferson that beg to be explored: Mount Jefferson (visible from the Mount Jefferson Overlook at Parkway MP 267) and the New River.

Mount Jefferson State Natural Area
Just outside of town is the **Mount Jefferson State Natural Area** (1481 Mt. Jefferson State Park Rd., 336/246-9653, www.ncparks.gov, 8am-6pm daily Dec.-Feb., 8am-8pm daily Mar.-Apr. and Oct., 8am-9pm daily May-Sept., 8am-7pm

daily Nov., closed Christmas Day). The two main activities here are **picnicking** and **hiking.** A winding road dotted with scenic overlooks takes you close to the summit of the 4,683-foot Mt. Jefferson, and from there you can reach the summit after a short 0.3-mile hike. From the **Summit Trail,** you can join up with the strenuous **Rhododendron Trail** (1.1 miles), which circles the summit ridge and passes through innumerable rhododendron thickets. From Rhododendron Trail you can hike out to Luther Rock, an odd exposed piece of the black volcanic rock that makes up this massif. There's also **Lost Province Trail,** a 0.75-mile loop off Rhododendron Trail that passes through a lovely hardwood forest. Each of these trails are accessible from the Summit Trail trailhead in the parking lot and are well marked, making it quite easy to doing a little hiking. If you do anything, though, be sure to hit the summit; from here you can see a number of the Christmas tree farms in the county, the New River (on a clear day), and the interesting shape of the mountains and river valley.

New River State Park

New River State Park (358 New River State Park Rd., Laurel Springs, 12 miles from West Jefferson, 336/982-2587, www. ncparks.gov, 7am-7pm daily Dec.-Feb., 7am-9pm daily Mar.-Apr. and Oct., 7am-10pm daily May-Sept., 7am-8pm daily Nov., closed Christmas Day) is 2,200 acres of hills, meadows, and river just northeast of West Jefferson. This is a great park for **canoeing** and **kayaking** (there are no rentals available in the park, so bring your own or contact the park office for a current list of outfitters). Bass **fishing** is quite good on the North and South Forks of the New River, while trout fishing is best along the feeder streams and smaller, faster tributaries. You'll need a North Carolina fishing license (available at the WalMart in West Jefferson or online at www.ncwildlife.

org/licensing, $20-36) and heed fishing regulations as established by the NC Wildlife Resources Commission (www. ncwildlife.org/fishing). In addition to fishing, there are six miles of trails spread throughout the park. The best hikes are canoe-access only, so be sure to hop in a boat and head to the Alleghany Access for the **Farm House Loop Trail** and **Riverview Trail;** they're both filled with beautiful views of the river and park environs.

Outfitters

In Todd, 13 miles to the southwest, **RiverGirl Outfitters** (4041 Todd Railroad Grade Rd., Todd, 336/877-3099, www.rivergirlfishing.com, 9am-5pm daily, closed seasonally, call for availability, $35 and up) offers fishing lessons, fly-fishing guided trips, kayak and canoe rentals, and tubing trips on the New River. Kelly, the RiverGirl herself, changed careers from being a fisheries biologist to a river guide and angler, and has ingrained herself into the community of Todd, drawing in thousands of visitors every year for fishing, tubing, and other river activities. Before you leave, take your picture with Petunia, a huge potbellied pig.

New River Outfitters (10725 US-221 N., Jefferson, 800/982-9109, www.canoethenew.com, 8:30am-6pm daily, call for off season availability, from $15) gets you on the water for a short, 3.5-mile paddle or an overnight adventure. They also have tubing trips, which is a popular way to pass an afternoon here. Located just nine miles north of Jefferson, they're close enough to the Parkway for an impulse tubing session.

Accommodations

There are a few B&Bs and cabin rentals in and around West Jefferson, as well as options for camping.

Buffalo Tavern Bed and Breakfast (958 W. Buffalo Rd., 877/615-9678, www.buffalotavern.com, $80-160) is a four-bedroom B&B built in 1872. This beautiful home is situated just outside of West Jefferson, surrounded by Bluff, Buck, and Three Top Mountains. Though it was a tavern in its early days, now it's a tastefully-decorated, comfortable spot to rest your head for a night or two.

★ **River House Country Inn and Restaurant** (1896 Old Field Creek Rd., Grassy Creek, 336/982-2109, www.riverhousenc.com, $99-225) has close to a dozen rooms and cabins spread out across a farm along the banks of the North Fork of the New River. The property and rooms are stunning. Whether you go for a cozy room in The Caretaker's Cottage, The Chicken House (which is much more romantic than it sounds), or the Carriage House, your accommodations will be outstanding. They also have a great restaurant on site, serving prix-fixe ($45) and à la carte menus ($20-36) filled with fine dining delights. If you're looking for a luxurious stopover in this area, River House is it.

In Deep Creek, south of West Jefferson, is **Fall Creek Cabins** (176 Surber Rd., Fleetwood, 336/877-3131, www.fallcreekcabins.com, $200-225), a 78-acre private retreat with eight, two-story cabins and a trout stream running right through the property. It's beautiful and private, and close to the Parkway. Exit at Milepost 276 and you're just a few minutes away.

Camping

The best camping in the area is at ★ **New River State Park** (358 New River State Park Rd., Laurel Springs, 12 miles from West Jefferson, 336/982-2587, www.ncparks.gov), where you'll find canoe-access only campsites ($13/day), two-dozen canoe-in/walk-in sites ($20/day, $15/day 62 and up), a pair of improved group campsites ($48/day, maximum of 35 people), a primitive group site ($2/person per day, $13 minimum), and 20 drive-to campsites for tents and RVs ($25/day, $19/day 62 and older). The improved campsites, especially the tent/RV sites, are very nice, with water, restroom, and shower facilities available and picnic tables and grills at each site.

Food
Restaurants

Breakfast at **Hillbilly Grill** (601 S. Jefferson Ave., 336/846-4745, 7am-2pm daily, around $6) is of the down-home variety, and you can get full on a stack of pancakes for just a few bucks. They have fun with those pancakes too, offering up bunny, snowman, and heart-shaped flapjacks on the appropriate holiday, and even writing your name (ok, your kid's name, but if you ask nicely, you never know) in pancake batter for a birthday treat. Their burgers are hand-pattied and dripping with cheese and greasy-spoon goodness.

Over the last few years, North Carolina has experienced a brewery boom, but West Jefferson only has one brewpub—**Boondocks Brewing Tap Room & Restaurant** (108 S. Jefferson Ave., 336/246-5222, www.boondocks-brewing.com, 11am-9pm Sun.-Thurs., 11am-11:30pm Fri.-Sat., $6-32). Boondocks serves their own beer—they have a Kolsch, IPAs, a stout, a saison, and other seasonal creations—and a number of North Carolina brews, in addition to a handful of domestics and imports. On their menu, you'll find steaks, quiche, flat bread pizza, burgers, and other expected pub fare.

Black Jack's Pub & Grill (18 N. Jefferson Ave., 336/246-3295, www.blackjackspubandgrill.com, 11am-late daily, $6-10) is known for two things: fantastic burgers and wings galore (seriously, you can get an order of 30). If you're not in the mood for either of those, try the Philly Jack, a tasty take on the Philly cheesesteak. But if you are in the mood, especially for a burger, try the Black Jack's Hamburger Challenge, a timed race to eat a three-pound burger and giant order of fries. This is a sports bar, so expect larger crowds on game days and fight nights.

For a sit-down meal, try **The Hotel Tavern** (6 W. Main St., 336/846-2121, www.thehoteltavern.com, 11:30am-9pm Tues.-Thurs., 11:30am-10pm Fri.-Sat., 11:30am-2:30pm Sun., closed Mon., $9-24), where you'll find a mix of higher-end entrées like short ribs, steaks, and seafood, as well as pizza, burgers, and bar nosh. When the weather is good, you'll often find a band playing on the outdoor patio. Of late, Sunday brunch has been popular here.

Cheese

Though it's not a restaurant, **Ashe County Cheese** (106 E. Main St., 800/445-1378, www.ashecountycheese.com, 8:30am-5pm Mon.-Sat.) is worth a visit. They've been making cheese here since 1930, and you can watch the process or just pick up some cheese, butter, fudge, or other homespun food goods in their store. You can pick up any number of styles of cheese, all made here in North Carolina's Blue Ridge Mountains, at specialty shops and grocers at stops all along the Parkway.

Delis, Baked Goods, and Snacks

If you find yourself spending the day on the river, you may wind up in Todd, 13 miles to the southwest. The **Todd General Store** (3866 Todd Railroad Grade Rd., Todd, 336/877-1067, www.toddgeneralstore.com, 10am-5pm Mon.-Thurs., 10am-4:30pm Sat., 11:30pm-4pm Sun., closed Jan.-mid-Mar.) has a deli and ice cream counter in addition to assorted snacks, homemade foodstuffs, collectibles, and gift items. Every Tuesday evening they have storytelling, a mountain tradition, and live bluegrass music on Friday nights 6:30pm-9:15pm.

You have one more option in Todd, the **Todd Mercantile** (3899 Todd Railroad Grade Rd., Todd, 336/877-5401, www.toddmercantile.com, 10am-4pm Mon., 9:30am-5pm Wed.-Sat., 9:30am-4pm Sun., closed Tues.). They have a bakery here, so don't come looking for

Christmas trees line the hills in neat rows near West Jefferson.

a full meal. The cinnamon rolls are legendary, however, so grab a couple for the road.

Information and Services

Find information on cheese and more at www.ashechamber.com.

The Lump (MP 264.4)

The Lump, despite its lackluster name, is a must stop. The name is well earned as a tall grassy knoll rises oddly from the hillside around forming a sort of lump of earth that you can wander at your leisure. A sign telling an abbreviated version of the story of Tom Dula (pronounced Dooley, yes, the Tom Dooley of folk-song infamy) stands at the foot of the Lump. A short trail up the side of the small, round, treeless Lump leads to some spectacular views of the Yadkin Valley and the transition from Blue Ridge Mountains to North Carolina's Piedmont region.

E. B. Jeffress Park (MP 272)

When the creators of the Blue Ridge Parkway were first discussing the project, the idea of it being a toll road came up. One of the men who led the fight for keeping it free of charge was E. B. Jeffress, onetime chairman of the North Carolina State Highway and Public Works Commission. At this park named in his honor, you'll find some picnic tables, restrooms, and a great little hike to Cascade Falls.

Cascade Falls Trail

Distance: 1-mile loop
Duration: 30 minutes
Elevation gain: 175 feet
Difficulty: moderate
Trailhead: E. B. Jeffress Park, opposite the picnic area

Thanks to some signage from the Park Service, this trail gives you a good idea of the ecological diversity you'll find all along the Parkway. Twenty plaques tell about the environment here, and on a trail this short, they pack in a lot of information.

Keep right where the trail splits, just a few dozen paces into the hike, and begin to descend through some lovely wildflowers. At 0.1 miles in, there's a bench. Then at 0.3 miles you'll cross Falls Creek. Bear right here and you'll quickly find yourself at the upper viewing platform at the cascades' top. The lower viewing platform is nearby and gives you a closer look at the falls. Once you've seen your fill, retrace your steps to the trail junction and bear right again. Ascend up the trail and take one more right turn and you're back at the start of the trail. The falls are best in the spring, after a rain, or in the late fall and early winter, when they're bearded with ice.

MerleFest

It began as a small folk festival more than 20 years ago, but **MerleFest** (www.merlefest.org, late Apr., $40 per day, multiday packages $135-260), held annually in North Wilkesboro, 22 miles southeast of the Parkway, has grown into one of the premier roots-music events in the country. It was founded in honor of Merle Watson, the son of legendary guitarist Doc Watson. Merle, also a guitarist, died unexpectedly in 1985 in a tractor accident, cutting short an influential career. Doc Watson, who grew up in the nearby community of Deep Gap (MP 276.4), was the festival's ceremonial host until his death in 2012, and though his absence is deeply felt by musicians and fans alike, MerleFest is as strong and successful as ever, speaking to his lasting legacy in bluegrass, roots, and Appalachian music. MerleFest draws thousands of visitors every year for many of the top-name performers in folk, country, and bluegrass music. Recent headliners have included Steep Canyon Rangers, Chatham County Line, Sam Bush, Jim Avett, The Avett Brothers (Jim's sons), and Tift Merritt. With multiple stages and dozens of artists, there's a great deal of musical variety to sample.

Tomkins Knob Trail

Distance: 1.2 miles out and back
Duration: 1 hour
Elevation gain: negligible
Difficulty: easy
Trailhead: E. B. Jeffress Park, at the back of the picnic area

Starting from picnic area at E. B. Jeffress Park, follow the trailhead into the woods, where you'll soon enter a stand of pine trees. You'll climb a little through sassafras trees and wildflowers until you reach the Cool Spring Baptist Church. It's not what you'd expect—steeple and white clapboard—but a rather rustic structure. This is because the congregation usually met inside during inclement weather, the rest of the time they met outside, surrounded by the glory of nature. Soon after the church, you'll find Jesse Brown's Cabin, and almost immediately the Tomkins Knob parking lot at Milepost 272.5. Reverse course and head back to the start.

US-321 North: Boone (MP 291.9)

Boone is the quintessential western North Carolina city, a blend of old and new, where proponents of homesteading and holistic living find a congenial habitat in the culture of rural Appalachia. It's also a college town, home to Appalachian State University and some 18,000 students, lending the city an invigorating youthful verve. Boone continues to grow as more people discover how amenable this part of the state is for year-round living. In recent years, the town has received a number of accolades, including being named one of the 10 Best Places to Retire by *U.S. News.*

Daniel Boone and his family inspired the name for the town. Local legend, and historical evidence, says Boone camped here several times on trips to explore the region and blaze his trail west into Tennessee and Kentucky. His nephews, Jesse and Jonathan Boone, were founders of the first church in town, Three Forks Baptist, which still stands today. *Horn in the West*, an outdoor drama running since 1952, tells the story of Daniel Boone and an interesting slice of the region's history.

Getting There and Around

Boone is easily accessible from the Blue Ridge Parkway. At Milepost 276.4, the Blue Ridge Parkway crosses over US-421, which you can take 11 miles west to Boone. At Milepost 291.9, you can access

Boone

- APPALACHIAN ANTIQUE MALL
- FOOTSLOGGERS
- ROCK DIMENSIONS
- MELANIE'S FOOD FANTASY
- OUR DAILY BREAD
- CAPONE'S PIZZA
- MAST GENERAL STORE
- JONES HOUSE COMMUNITY AND CULTURAL CENTER
- TURCHIN CENTER FOR THE VISUAL ARTS
- DAN'L BOONE INN
- JOY BISTRO
- BEST WESTERN BLUE RIDGE PLAZA
- HORN IN THE WEST
- COMFORT SUITES
- HIGH MOUNTAIN EXPEDITIONS
- APPALACHIAN MOUNTAIN BREWERY/ FARM TO FLAME
- SUNRISE GRILL
- RIVER AND EARTH ADVENTURES
- HOLIDAY INN EXPRESS
- FAIRFIELD INN AND SUITES

LL INN

WEST QUEEN ST

Boone Creek

IN DEPOT RD

194

Appalachian State University

RIVERS ST

STADIUM DR

321

OAK ST

TRACY CIRCLE

105

NEW MARKET BLVD

PERKINSVILLE DR

EAST KING ST

221

DANIEL BOONE RD

South Fork New River

STATE FARM RD

DR

SHADOWLINE

Winkler Creek

321

DEERFIELD RD

GREENWAY RD

MEADOWVIEW DR

Middle Fork New River

Boone Golf Club

POPLAR HILL DR

Hodges Creek

105

JORDAN V COOK RD

WINKLERS CREEK RD

Winkler Creek

Flannery Fork

To Foggy Mountain Gem Mine, The Greater Foscoe Gem Mining Co., Smoketree Lodge

0   500 yds

0   500 m

© AVALON TRAVEL

Boone via US-321. Both of these highways connect Boone to the larger world. Along US-321, Hickory and I-40 are just over an hour south, and along US-421, Boone is 52 miles west of I-77. Winston-Salem is 90 minutes east (along US-421), Charlotte two hours south (via US-321 and US-74), and Asheville two hours southwest (via US-221 and I-40).

Sights

The mountains of North Carolina are loaded with artists and art lovers. At Appalachian State University, the **Turchin Center for the Visual Arts** (432 W. King St., 828/262-3017, www.tcva. org, 10am-6pm Tues.-Thurs. and Sat., noon-8pm Fri., closed Sun.-Mon., free) provides access to the arts to the community and visitors in Boone. The Kay Borowski Sculpture Garden displays contemporary sculpture outdoors, while six indoor galleries exhibit the Turchin's permanent collection as well as traveling exhibitions. Throughout the year, photography and drawing competitions grace gallery walls.

In the heart of downtown Boone, the **Jones House Community and Cultural Center** (604 W. King St., 828/268-6280, www.joneshousecommunitycenter.org, noon-5pm Tues.-Fri., concert and event prices vary), a beautiful home built in 1908, serves as a gallery for community artists, a meeting place for area groups, and a center for Independence Day and Christmas celebrations. Outdoor summer concerts and indoor fall concerts bring in string bands, bluegrass and roots country musicians, and other mountain music acts.

Entertainment
Nightlife

Appalachian Mountain Brewery (163 Boone Creek Dr., 828/26-1111, www.appalachianmountainbrewery.com, 4pm-10pm Mon., 4pm-11pm Tues.-Thurs., 3pm-11pm Fri., 1pm-11pm Sat., 1pm-10pm Sun.) is a new microbrewery that's become popular with beer connoisseurs (and the college crowd). They brew about three dozen beers (and a cider), some of which are seasonals. Though many love their IPAs, their dark beers—Belgian Dark Strong, Oatmeal Stout, Porter, Imperial Stout, Schwartz Bier, and the like—are quite good. On any given night, some college band will set up in the corner of the main room and play for the evening. Outside there's a giant set of Jenga blocks to play with. And if you're hungry, the Brewery also owns **Farm to Flame** (www.f2flame.com, at the Brewery 5pm-10pm Mon.-Fri., 3pm-10pm Sat., $8-12), a pizza food truck. There's a sizable wood-fired pizza oven onboard, and it takes about 90 seconds for them to cook a pie.

Theater

One thing worth checking out in the summer is *Horn in the West* (828/264-2120, www.horninthewest.com, 8pm Tues.-Sun. late-June-mid-Aug., adults $20-35, children 12 and under $10-24), the outdoor drama telling part of Daniel Boone's story. *Horn* is part of a long history of outdoor dramas in North Carolina, its most notable sister productions being *Unto these Hills* (written by the same playwright) in Cherokee and *The Lost Colony* in the Outer Banks.

Shopping

Several antique shops in Boone make the downtown a great place for browsing. **Appalachian Antique Mall** (631 W. King St., 828/268-9988, www.appalachianantiquemall.com, 10am-6pm Mon.-Sat., 11am-6pm Sun. summer; 10am-5pm Mon.-Sat., noon-5pm Sun. winter) is one of the best and biggest in the area. You'll find everything from farm implements to paintings and furniture from far and wide. **Footsloggers** (139 S. Depot St., 828/262-5111, www.footsloggers.com, 9:30am-5:30pm Mon.-Thurs., 9:30am-6pm Fri.-Sat., noon-5pm Sun.) has been selling gear for climbing, hiking, and camping for 40 years. They have a 40-foot climbing tower that simulates many conditions you might find climbing the real rock faces that attract so many climbers and outdoor enthusiasts to this area.

There are several branches of the **Mast General Store** (630 W. King St., 828/262-0000, www.mastgeneralstore.com, 10am-6pm Mon.-Sat., noon-6pm Sun.) in the North Carolina High Country, but the original is in Valle Crucis (Hwy. 194, 828/963-6511, www.mastgeneralstore.com, 7am-6:30pm Mon.-Sat., noon-6pm Sun. summer, hours vary in winter), about 20 minutes west of Boone. It has been a visitor attraction for about 30 years, but its history as a community institution goes back before the 1880s. When the Mast family owned it the store had the reputation of carrying everything "from cradles to caskets," and today it still has a varied inventory, with specialties in outdoor wear (Carhartt, Columbia, Mountain Hardware, Patagonia, Teva), camping gear, and more penny candy than a modern-day store should have.

Recreation

There's plenty to do in Boone. If Appalachian State University has a sporting event, you can catch a home game and root for the Mountaineers; if not, it's not difficult to find something to do.

Gem Mining

Many people don't know that North Carolina is rich in gems and gold. Around Boone and the more heavily visited places in the mountains you'll find businesses that offer gem "mining." You don't need a pick and a shovel, just a keen eye and a few bucks. To "mine," you buy a bucket of material, graded and priced according to the likelihood of it having a valuable gem in it, and then sort, sift, and pan it yourself. You get to keep what you find, and you really can come across some beautiful specimens, some even worthy of jewelry. **River and Earth Adventures** (1655 Hwy. 105, 866/411-7238, www.raftcavehike.com, $15-100) offers gem mining, as does **Foggy Mountain Gem Mine** (4416 Hwy. 105, 828/263-4367, www.foggymountaingems.com, $17-120), where you can get gemstones cut and polished in-house, and **The Greater Foscoe Gem Mining Co.** (8998 Hwy. 105, 828/963-5928, www.foscoeminingco.com, $16-212), where 24 kinds of gemstones can be found and the owner, a master goldsmith and stone cutter, will cut and polish the larger gems you find.

Golf

Around Boone are a number of private golf courses. Among the few public courses is **Boone Golf Club** (433 Fairway Dr., 828/264-8760, www.boonegolfclub.com, 18 holes, par 71, Apr.-Nov., greens fees $41-57), which has wide, forgiving fairways that are playable for all skill levels and from any tee set. Designed by Ellis Maples in the late 1950s, the course is picturesque and enjoyable to play.

Hiking, Rafting, and Cave Trips

Down the road from the Mast General Store in Valle Crucis, **River and Earth Adventures** (1655 Hwy. 105, 866/411-7238, www.raftcavehike.com) leads all sorts of exciting trips on the water, in the woods, and in the area's deep caves. Rafting expeditions ($45-85 adults, $35-75 children) ride the French Broad River (Class III-IV) and Watauga River (Class II-III), or, for big white water, try the Watauga Gorge Ex-Stream Whitewater trip ($125, 4-person minimum), which gives you more than five miles of Class III, IV, and V rapids. This trip runs spring through fall, using rafts during high water and inflatable kayaks during low water. Participants must be at least 18 years old. Cave trips (daily year-round, $45-75 pp) meet at their Elizabethton, Tennessee, outpost, about an hour away, for a day's spelunking in Worley's Cave. Guided hiking trips are available that include all-day kids-only hikes with adult guides to free up parents who'd like a day on their own. If you're looking to hike or go rock climbing or bouldering, they offer guide services; inquire about routes and rates.

High Mountain Expeditions (1380 Hwy. 105 S., Banner Elk, 800/262-9036, www.highmountainexpeditions.com), which also has a Boone location, leads rafting trips on the Watauga River (Class I-III) and the much more challenging Nolichucky River (Class III-IV). They also lead caving expeditions for adults and children, for which no experience is necessary.

Rock Climbing

Rock Dimensions (139 Depot St., 828/265-3544, www.rockdimensions.com, from $65) is a guide service that leads rock climbs at gorgeous locations throughout western North Carolina and parts of Tennessee and Virginia. Guides teach proper multi-pitch, top-rope anchoring, and rappelling techniques, and they lead caving expeditions ($330 for 4 people).

If you're an experienced climber, take a look at the **Boone Adventure Guide** (http://advguides.com/boone), a website that will lead you to some nice pitches and help you find places for other outdoor activities such as fly-fishing, hiking, and dog-friendly adventures.

Winter Sports

The Banner Elk area has some of the state's best ski slopes. **Sugar Mountain** (1009 Sugar Mountain Dr., 828/898-4521, www.skisugar.com, lift tickets $41-68 adults, $32-45 children, rentals $21-36 adults, $15-28 children) is North Carolina's largest winter resort, with 115 acres of ski slopes and 20 trails. In addition to skiing, activities on the 5,300-foot-high mountain include snow-tubing, skating, snowshoeing, and in summer, the Showdown at Sugar National Mountain Bike Series. They offer lessons in skiing and snowboarding for adults and children.

Ski Beech Mountain Resort (1007 Beech Mountain Pkwy., Beech Mountain, 800/438-2093, www.skibeech.com, lift tickets $30, rentals $9-26) peaks 300 feet higher than Sugar Mountain and has 15 slopes and 10 lifts, as well as skating and snowboarding areas. In summer they shift focus to mountain bikes and disc golf, with a beautiful disc course as well as challenging downhill biking trails that range from beginner-friendly to expert.

Hawksnest Snow Tubing (2058 Skyland Dr., Seven Devils, 828/963-6561, www.hawksnesttubing.com, 1.5 hours $25-30, zip-lining $75-85) is on a 4,800-foot mountain in Seven Devils. It has 12 slopes all dedicated to the family-friendly art of tubing, making it one of the largest snow-tubing parks on the East Coast. Throughout the year you can experience the thrill of zip-lining on more than four miles of zip-lines, including two longer than 2,000 feet, at speeds up to 50 mph.

Accommodations

The **Lovill House Inn** (404 Old Bristol Rd., 800/849-9466, www.lovillhouseinn.com, $129-219) is close to the Appalachian State University campus, and it was in the parlor of this 1875 farmhouse that

the papers were drawn up that led to the founding of the university. The inn sits on 11 evergreen-shaded acres and is a lovely place to relax and read.

The **Smoketree Lodge** (11914 Hwy. 105 S., 800/422-1880, www.smoketree-lodge.com, from $75 summer, from $55 off-season) is another good choice; it's a large hotel with basic but comfortable guest rooms and efficiencies, a large rustic lobby, a nice indoor pool, and saunas.

The **Yonahlossee Resort** (Shulls Mill Rd., 800/962-1986, www.yonahlossee. com, from $129), between Boone and Blowing Rock, is a former girls camp built in the 1920s. The resort has a big stone inn and studio cottages, a fitness center and sauna, tennis courts with a pro shop, and a 75-foot indoor heated pool.

Parkway Cabins (599 Bamboo Heights, 828/262-3560 or 866/679-3002, www. parkwaycabins.com, $150-350) is just 5 minutes from downtown Boone and 10 minutes from Blowing Rock; it sits at 4,000 feet in elevation, providing a panoramic view of Grandfather Mountain, Beech Mountain, Seven Devils, and other peaks. Most of the cabins sleep four or more, making them perfect for mountain excursions with a group.

Among area chain motels, some good bets are **Fairfield Inn and Suites** (2060 Blowing Rock Rd., 828/268-0677, www. marriott.com, from $79), **Comfort Suites** (1184 Hwy. 105, 828/268-0099, www. choicehotels.com, from $55), **Holiday Inn Express** (1943 Blowing Rock Rd./US-321 S., 828/264-2451, www.hiexpress.com, from $90), and **Best Western Blue Ridge Plaza** (840 E. King St., 828/266-1100, www.bestwestern.com, from $65).

Food

Boone is a college town with dining that suits both students and their visiting parents. That means three things must be done well: pizza, breakfast, and moderately priced bistro or steakhouse fare. This town delivers on all counts.

★ **Sunrise Grill** (1675 Hwy. 105,

828/262-5400, 6:30am-2pm Mon.-Fri., 7am-3pm Sat.-Sun., around $8) is widely considered the best breakfast place in Boone. It's a regular bacon-and-eggs sort of place with some interesting omelets, tasty grits, and hot coffee, but everything is done well and the staff are friendly.

Melanie's Food Fantasy (664 W. King St., 828/263-0300, www.melanies-foodfantasy.com, 8am-2pm Mon.-Sat., 8:30am-2:30pm Sun., $6-9) is worth a special trip to Boone. The breakfast menu is nothing short of spectacular, with a variety of whole-grain waffles, pancakes, and French toast, all sorts of fancy omelets (try the spinach, garlic, provolone, and swiss), and enough options to keep both carnivores and vegetarians full. Lunch at Melanie's is every bit as good.

★ **Joy Bistro** (115 New Market Centre, 828/265-0500, www.joybistroboone.com, dinner from 5:30pm Tues.-Sun., $12-35) is Southern-French cuisine—not from the south of France but rather a fusion of French techniques and Southern flavors. You'll find a lot of ingredients from local and regional food producers; the baby beet salad, for instance, uses beets from a local farmer, and the ravioli is made fresh by a local pasta maker. Standards like the filet mignon (served with Boursin cheese mashed potatoes and finished with a roasted garlic and chive compound butter) are fantastic, and dishes like the scallops au poivre or lamb loin chop deliver big flavor.

The **Gamekeeper Restaurant and Bar** (3005 Shull's Mill Rd., 828/963-7400, www.gamekeeper-nc.com, bar from 5pm daily, dinner from 5pm Wed.-Sun., $24-41) is tucked away between Boone and Blowing Rock at the Yonahlossee Resort. Since opening, this restaurant has built and maintained a reputation for high-quality meals using exotic meats. It's common to see ostrich, venison, bison, boar, and the like on the frequently changing menu. Don't miss the bourbon bread pudding and white Russian cheesecake—or the seemingly endless wine list ($20-215 per bottle).

The menu at **Our Daily Bread** (627 W. King St., 828/264-0173, www.ourdailybreadboone.com, 11am-8pm Mon.-Thurs., 11am-10pm Fri.-Sat., noon-6pm Sun., about $10) includes no fewer than 30 specialty sandwiches, from their best-selling Jamaican Turkey Sub to the Fruity Chicken Sammy—chicken salad with shredded apples, red grapes, and walnuts on a fresh croissant. Try their tempeh Reuben, a daring mixture of flavors that features marinated tempeh, sauerkraut, swiss cheese, and mustard on rye. It sounds outrageous but it works. Our Daily Bread also makes a variety of fresh soups and meat and veggie chilies every day.

The **Dan'l Boone Inn** (130 Hardin St., 828/264-8657, http://danlbooneinn.com, hours vary, dinner $17 adults, $10 ages 9-11, $8 ages 6-8, $6 ages 4-5, free under age 4; breakfast $10 adults, $7 ages 9-11, $6 ages 6-8, $5 ages 4-5, free under age 4) serves old-time country food family style. Despite the complicated pricing system, the food is straightforward good. At breakfast, feast on country ham and red-eye gravy, stewed apples, and grits; at dinner, there's fried chicken, country-style steak, ham biscuits, and lots of vegetable sides.

For good college-town pizza, **Capone's Pizza** (454 W. King St., 828/265-1886, http://caponesboone.com, 11am-10:30pm Mon.-Thurs., 11am-11pm Fri.-Sat., noon-10:30pm Sun., $8-22) hits the spot. The staff are funny and friendly and make a good pie. You can go with the standard pepperoni and cheese or go off the rails with some odd pizza topping combinations. Try Big Joe's Buffalo Pizza, with spicy sauce, blue cheese, buffalo chicken, crumbled bacon, and red onion; it's different and delicious.

Information and Services

You can find all sorts of visitor information at the official site of the **Watauga County Tourism Development Authority** (www.ExploreBooneArea.com). You can also stop by the **High Country Host**

The Legend of Blowing Rock

Adding to its otherworldly draw, there's a Native American legend associated with Blowing Rock. The story goes that a Chickasaw chieftain, fearful of the admiration his beautiful daughter was receiving, journeyed far to Blowing Rock, where he hoped to hide her away in the woods and keep her safe and pure. One day, the maiden spied a Cherokee warrior wandering in the valley below. Smitten by his looks, she shot an arrow in his direction, hoping he would seek her out. It worked. He found her arrow, tracked her down, and soon appeared at her home, courting her with songs of his land. They became lovers, and one day, a strange reddening sky brought the pair to the Blowing Rock. He took it as a sign that he was to return to his people in their coming time of trouble; to her it spelled the end of their love. She begged him not to go, but he was torn between staying loyal to his duties and following his heart; in his desperation he leapt from their perch into the gorge below. The young maiden prayed for him to be spared death, but it didn't work. Still, she remained at the site, praying for his return, and one day the sky reddened and the now-famous winds of the John's River Gorge shifted, blowing her lover back into her world and her arms. Since that day, a perpetual wind has blown up onto the Rock from the valley below.

Visitor Center (1700 Blowing Rock Rd./US-321, 828/264-1299, 9am-5pm Mon.-Sat., 9am-3pm Sun.). The **Blue Ridge National Heritage Area** (www.blueridge-heritage.com) has a great deal of traveler resources available online, covering not just Boone and the High Country, but the extent of North Carolina's Blue Ridge Mountains.

Radio stations include **WASU** (90.5 FM) and **WQUT** (101.5 FM).

Watauga Medical Center (336 Deerfield Rd., 828/262-4100, www.apprhs.org) is a 117-bed complex with primary and specialty care.

Blowing Rock (MP 291.9)

Blowing Rock, named for a nearby geological oddity, is an old resort town filled with beautiful homes that once belonged to wealthy early-20th-century industrialists. It's a small town, but the surprising array of restaurants, cafés, and galleries make it pleasant to stroll, window-shop, and sit to enjoy an ice cream. Boone also provides easy access to Moses Cone Manor and other notable landmarks.

Aside from the Blowing Rock itself, the best thing to see in Blowing Rock is downtown. Main Street is lined with shops, galleries, and restaurants, and it's a good spot for people-watching most of the year (winter excluded). The vibe here is very relaxed, so you won't find much by way of active entertainment, for that you'll need to venture out onto the Parkway or into nearby Boone.

Blowing Rock is 15 minutes away from Boone, south along US-321. You can also access Blowing Rock from US-221 and the Blue Ridge Parkway at Milepost 291.9.

Sights

The **Blowing Rock** (US-321 S., 828/295-7111, www.theblowingrock.com, hours vary, $6 adults, $1 ages 4-11, free under age 4) is a strange rock outcropping purported by *Ripley's Believe It or Not* to be the only place in the world where snow falls upward. Indeed, light objects (think handkerchiefs, leaves, hats) thrown off Blowing Rock—not allowed, by the way, to prevent the valley from filling up with litter—do tend to come floating back up.

The **Blowing Rock Art and History Museum** (159 Chestnut St., 828/295-9099, www.blowingrockmuseum.org, 10am-5pm Tues.-Wed., 10am-7pm Thurs., 10am-5pm Fri.-Sat., 1pm-5pm Sun., $8 adults, $5 over age 5, students, and military) opened in October 2011 after more than a decade of work. In addition to rotating exhibits of fine art from private collections, gallery shows by local and regional artists, and traveling exhibitions, BRAHM also has galleries with rotating exhibits displaying artifacts of historical value to the area. It's small, but the art displayed is carefully curated and excellent. It's easy to spend a couple of hours admiring the collections.

Between Blowing Rock and Boone, **Tweetsie Railroad** (300 Tweetsie Railroad Rd., 828/264-9061, http://tweetsie.com, 9am-6pm Fri.-Sun. mid-Apr.-late May, 9am-6pm daily late May-mid-Aug., 9am-6pm Fri.-Sun. late Aug.-Nov., Ghost Train 7:30pm Fri. late Sept.-early Nov., $37 over age 12, $23 ages 3-12, free under age 3) is a veritable gold mine for kids who are into trains. There are opportunities to pan for gold and gems in one section of the park, a Country Fair-themed area, a Western store and Cowboy Cantina in another, the Tweetsie Junction area where you'll find a saloon, a blacksmith, and an antique photo parlor. And, of course, the train: The Tweetsie Railroad's steam engines, number 12 or *Tweetsie,* and number 190, *Yukon Queen,* encircle the amusement park on a narrow-gauge track as part of a Wild West show featuring a frontier outpost and Indian attacks. The railroad isn't all fun and games; it's also partly a history lesson, as the *Tweetsie* was an actual working train in the early part of the 20th century, until washed-out tracks and the advent of reliable automobiles and roads rendered it obsolete.

One little oddity in Blowing Rock is **Mystery Hill** (129 Mystery Hill Lane, 828/264-2794, www.mysteryhill-nc.com, 9am-8pm daily June-Aug., 9am-5pm daily Sept.-May, adults $9, seniors $8, children 5-12 $7, 4 and under free.). Like Mystery Hills in other states featuring some gravitational anomaly, this one is fun, but only to a point for grown-ups. It's best for kids, which is fine, because

it's fun to watch them try to figure out the mystery of Mystery Hill.

Adjacent to Mystery Hill is **Doc's Rocks Gem Mines** (129 Mystery Hill Lane, 828/264-4499, www.docksrocks.net, 9:30am-5pm Mon.-Thurs., 9:30am-6pm Fri.-Sun.). Like other gem mines, here you'll buy a bucket of ore that they source from a variety of mines across the Blue Ridge, and then you pan and sift through it for gems and fossils. As you make your way through your bucket (buckets are $12-55), they will help you identify the stones you find. You can find all sorts of things, from a variety of fossils to gems like rubies and emeralds.

Entertainment
Festivals and Events
Blowing Rock may be a small town, but you won't want for things to do. You won't find a free concert or wine tasting every night of the week, but the events and activities that go on here are put on well and are well attended.

The biggest event to hit Blowing Rock kicks off in spring and brings thousands of foodies into town. The **Blue Ridge Wine & Food Festival** (various locations, 828/295-7851, www.blueridgewinefestival.com) takes place during the second week of April. The tastings, classes, dinners, and events take place at hotels, inns, bars, and restaurants all around town. The Grand Tasting Tent is home to Taste!, a tasting event with some of the top restaurants and wineries in the area, and the Grand Wine Tasting. Generally running from Thursday through Sunday, it's four days of great food and drink, and many of the locals and visitors at the festival are ready to cut loose and celebrate the passing of winter and arrival of spring.

From May through mid-October, the **Blowing Rock Farmers Market** (4pm-6pm Thurs.) takes over Park Avenue, brining all sorts of baked goods, artisanal cheeses, and the usual bounty of fruits and veggies. The **Music on the Lawn**

(5:30pm-8:30pm Fri. May-Oct.) series has made **The Inn at Ragged Gardens** (203 Sunset Dr., 828/295-9703, www. ragged-gardens.com) a hot spot every Friday night. They have a cash bar and serve a limited menu, so get there early, find a place for your blanket, and order a bite to eat.

Shopping
★ Art Galleries
Along Blowing Rock's Main Street, you'll have your pick of galleries. Park at the **Blowing Rock Art and History Museum** (159 Chestnut St.), which also happens to be the location of the visitor center, and gallery hop your way down Main Street.

Morning Star Gallery (1151 S. Main St., 828/295-6991, www.morningstar-galleryusa.com, 10am-5pm Mon.,Wed., and Fri., 11am-5pm Tues., Thurs., and Sat., closed Sun.) showcases fine arts and crafts by contemporary American artists, including a good number of local and regional artists. Works include blown glass, pottery and ceramics, paintings, prints, photography, and fiber arts.

At **Traditions Pottery** (1155 Main St., 828/295-6128, www.traditionspottery. com, 10am-6pm Sun.-Thurs., 9am-7pm Fri.-Sat.) fifth and sixth generation potters have their own works and wares on display alongside pottery and ceramics from other local artists.

Other Shops
There's more than a fair share of antique stores, boutiques, and gift shops on Main Street. If you're in the market for antiques, it's hard to beat **Windwood Antiques** (1157 Main St., 828/295-9260) and **Carriage Trade Antiques** (1079 Main St., 828/295-3110), both on Main Street. **Blowing Rock Estate Jewelry & Antiques** (167 Sunset Dr., 828/295-4500) has a large and constantly changing selection of fine estate jewelry; with an eye for precious gems and heirloom pieces, this is the spot to look for a piece of stunning jewelry from past ages. **Possum Hollow Antiques**

From the Blowing Rock you can feel the enormity of the Blue Ridge.

(247 Possum Hollow Rd., 828/295-3502, www.possumhollowantiques.com), just a few minutes out of downtown, specializes in antique furniture, and you can find some truly marvelous specimens.

At **Gaines Kiker Silversmith** (132 Morris St., 828/295-3992, www. gaineskikersilversmith.com, 11am-5pm Tues.-Sat.) the silver jewelry is exquisite. Gaines Kiker finds inspiration for the shapes and curves of his jewelry in the mountains around him, and his work displays a simplicity and elegance that's difficult to master.

Celeste's (1132 Main St. #1, 828/295-3481, www.celestesinteriors.com, 10am-5pm Sun.-Thurs., 10am-6pm Fri.-Sat.), a boutique offering a range of lifestyle, fashion, and home goods, was chosen as *Southern Living Magazine*'s "Favorite Stores," and for good reason. Their selections range from whimsical to funky, but all with a touch of Southern class.

If it's a souvenir T-shirt you're looking for, try **Sunset Tee's & Hattery** (1117 Main St., 828/295-9326). They have loads of gift items from tacky to 'fridge-worthy, and the selection of hats is huge. In the back of the store, everything from poker visors to baseball caps to leather stovepipe hats to bowlers and derbys are for purchase.

Barking Rock (131-1 Morris St., 828/295-8883, www.thebarkingrock.com, 11am-5pm Mon.-Fri., 10:30am-5pm Sat., 1pm-5pm Sun.) has what you need for the canine member of your family. Inside, you'll find dog treats, cool collars and leashes, toys galore, and even sweaters. They also carry a few equestrian items as well.

Recreation

Sky Valley Zip Tours (634 Sky Ranch Rd., Blowing Rock, 855/475-9947, www.sky-valleyziptours.com, $79) operates one of the best zip lines I've been on. Their signature zip, Big Mamma, is massive—more than 1,600 feet long and nearly 300 feet high—but one of the wildest parts of this zip-line tour is the Leap of Faith between lines five and six, where you hook into a self-belay device and step off the edge of a 40-foot cliff. It's fun and the staff knows how to make zipping comfortable for novices and exciting for veterans.

VX3 Trail Rides (828/963-0260, www. vx3trailrides.com, rides departing at 10am and 2pm daily, $100) offers horseback riding outings with Tim Vines, a trail guide with decades in the saddle. Groups are small, typically a maximum of four riders, unless it's one family or group, and you need reservations at least a day in advance.

Accommodations
$50-100
★ **Blowing Rock Inn** (788 US-321 Business, 828/295-7921, www.blowingrockinn.com, open seasonally Apr.-early Dec., rooms $80-130, villas $129-169) has the feel of an old motor court, with rooms wrapped around a lawn and parking area, but it's been upgraded to modern standards. Just a short walk or even shorter

drive to downtown, Blowing Rock Inn is both quiet and conveniently located. The inn provides free Wi-Fi, and you can add all sorts of packages to your room or villa, including a wine basket, cake, and flowers.

Alpine Village Inn (297 Sunset Dr., 828/295-7206, www.alpine-village-inn. com, from $60), in downtown Blowing Rock, has comfortable accommodations at good rates. The guest rooms are located in the main inn and in a motel-style wing. It's a convenient location for checking out the shops and restaurants in town. Another good value is the **Cliff Dwellers Inn** (116 Lakeview Trail, 828/295-3098, www.cliffdwellers.com, from $90), with clean, simple guest rooms and a beautiful lakefront view.

$100-150

The Inn at Ragged Gardens (203 Sunset Dr., 828/295-9703, www.ragged-gardens. com, from $145) is a stone-walled and chestnut-paneled manor, a handsome and stylish turn-of-the-20th-century vacation home. The plush guest rooms feature goose-down bedding, fireplaces, and in most rooms, balconies and whirlpool tubs. A sister property to the Inn at Ragged Gardens, the **Blowing Rock Ale House and Inn** (152 Sunset Dr., 828/414-9254, www.blowingrockalehouseandinn. com, $125-160) is an eight-room bed-and-breakfast and full pub. It has been in operation as a B&B since the late 1940s, once heralded as a fancy place to stay because most guest rooms had private baths. Today, the addition of the **Blowing Rock Brewing Co. restaurant and tavern** (828/414-9600, http://blowingrockbrew-ing.com, 11am-6pm daily, around $14) has helped keep this long-running institution going in a new era.

Over $300

The lavish 1916 Greek revival mansion of painter Elliot Daingerfield is now home to the ★ **Westglow Resort and Spa** (224 Westglow Crescent, 828/295-4463 or 800/562-0807, www.westglow.com, from $325, spa packages from $425). In addition to the cushy guest rooms, many of which have whirlpool tubs, private decks, and views of Grandfather Mountain, the menu of spa treatments and health services befits the elegance of the surroundings. All kinds of massage and body therapy are available, as well as fitness classes, cooking and makeup lessons, and a variety of seminars in emotional well-being. Taking advantage of the spa's wonderful location, visitors can also sign up for hiking, cycling, snowshoeing, and camping trips.

Food

★ **The Chestnut Grille** (9239 Valley Blvd., 828/414-9230, www.greenparkinn.com, from 6pm Tues.-Sun., $17-25) is in the Green Park Inn on the edge of town. Chef James Welch, a James Beard Award nominee and winner of a number of state food awards, directs the kitchen. The food draws inspiration from across the globe; Cuban spice-rubbed scallops, seared tuna with wasabi and soy-ginger sauce, rigatoni with chicken, lamb, steaks, pulled pork, and even tempeh grace the menu. The **Divide Tavern** (9239 Valley Blvd., 828/414-9230, www.greenparkinn.com, from 5pm daily, $8-11), also in the Green Park Inn, serves a smaller menu of pub food such as wings and other handhelds.

Storie Street Grille (1167 Main St., 828/295-7075, www.storiestreetgrille. com, 11am-3pm and 5pm-9pm Mon.-Sat., lunch $5-13, dinner $10-30) has a long lunch menu of sandwiches and main-course salads. Try the ever-elusive Monte Cristo, the salmon cake, or the bacon, Brie, and apple panini. For dinner they serve a few Italian choices, grilled steak, and seafood. The vegetarian sauté, a mix of mushrooms, spinach, roasted garlic, almonds, and shallots served with smoky adobo sauce and fingerling potatoes, will satisfy even a hungry carnivore.

★ **Bistro Roca and Antlers Bar** (143 Wonderland Trail, 828/295-4008, http://

bistroroca.com, 11:30am-3pm and 5pm-10pm Wed.-Mon., bar 11am-midnight Wed.-Mon., $10-30) serves hearty and creative dishes like lobster mac-and-cheese, their take on coq au vin (made with riesling instead of red wine), and a pork rib eye with goat cheese "butter" and a peach *gastrique*. An interesting note is that the Antlers Bar has been open since 1932, making it the oldest continuously serving bar in the state.

Twigs (7956 Valley Blvd., 828/295-5050, http://twigsbr.com, 5:30pm-9:30pm Tues.-Thurs. and Sun., 5:30pm-10pm Fri.-Sat., bar until 11pm Sun. and Tues.-Thurs., until 1:30am Fri.-Sat., $10-35) is popular with locals and visitors alike. It has both a casual bar and a fancier dining room, and serves popular regional dishes like shrimp and grits and mountain trout alongside more unusual fare like venison. They have about 18 wines available by the glass and another 200 by the bottle, featuring a wide selection of California wines as well as Australian, European, and Argentine choices.

Blowing Rock Grille and Bert's Bar (349 Sunset Dr., 828/295-9474, www.theblowingrockgrille.com, 5pm-late daily, $15-34) turns out some fine food. Their Kobe Beef Burger will make you rethink your top five burgers, and their seafood—which runs the gamut from mountain trout to salmon and grouper to shrimp and grits—is always on point. Most of the wine on their menu is available by the glass, with the exception of the excellent reserve list.

Foggy Rock Eatery & Pub (8180 Valley Blvd., 828/295-7262, www.bobcatalley.com/foggyrock, 11:30am-9:30pm daily, around $15) is a sports bar with up-graded food. Seafood graces their menu, with dishes like Appalachian Fish 'n' Chips (fried catfish and waffle fries) and Trout Trout Trout (a trio of trout), and they have a good selection of sandwiches, burgers, and Philly cheesesteaks. The Notorious P.I.G.—with house-smoked pork, pulled ham, diced bacon, pepper jack cheese, and Sriracha aioli—is a fine and filling sandwich.

Roots Restaurant (7179 Valley Blvd., 828/414-9508, www.roots-restaurant.com, 5:30pm-9pm Mon.-Sat., 11am-2pm Sun., $13-35) has a great menu filled with rich and creative takes on some classic dishes. Their chicken and dumplings are made in the traditional Southern-style, but drizzled with truffle oil. The rib eye is rubbed with a hops-infused seasoning. The meatloaf is stuffed with blue cheese. Everything they serve has some sort of tie back to simple country food, but it's all prepared with a bent toward fine dining.

In downtown Blowing Rock, there's not much going on after 10pm, so if you're looking to grab a beer and a bite to eat a little later in the evening, your options are limited. At the north end of Main Street you'll find **The Town Tavern** (1182 Main St., 828/295-7500, www.towntavernbr.com, 11am-2am Mon.-Sat., 11am-midnight Sun., around $10). This is a sports bar, with all the wings, fried ap-petizers, burgers, and nachos you'd ex-pect to find. With more than 30 bottled beers and about a dozen local brews on draft, they have a good beer selection too.

Information and Services

You'll find all the information you need about Blowing Rock at the **Visitor Center** inside of the Blowing Rock Art and History Museum (159 Chestnut St., 828/295-4636, www.blowingrock.com).

The nearest hospital is the **Watauga Medical Center** (336 Deerfield Rd., Boone, 828/262-4100, www.apprhs.org).

Moses H. Cone Memorial Park (MP 294)

The **Moses Cone Manor** (MP 294, 828/295-7938, 9am-5pm daily Mar. 15-Nov., free), more commonly called Flat Top Manor, is a wonderfully crafted house, a huge white and ornate moun-tain palace built in 1901 that was the country home of North Carolina textile baron Moses Cone. He became a leading philanthropist, and as you drive around the state, especially in the northern Piedmont, you'll notice his name on quite a few institutions. Today, the manor is the centerpiece of the Moses H. Cone Memorial Park. Appropriately, it is home to one of the **Southern Highland Craft Guild** (828/295-7938, www.southernhighlandguild.org, 9am-5pm daily mid-Mar.-Nov.) stores, a place to buy beautiful textiles, pottery, jewelry, furniture, and dolls handmade by some of the best craftspeople of the Appalachian Mountains. There are also extensive hiking and riding trails on the estate.

Hiking

The 3,500-acre Moses H. Cone Memorial Park is one of the Parkway's largest developed areas set up for public recreation. There are 25 miles of trails for hiking and horseback riding, a 16-acre trout lake, and a 22-acre bass lake on the property. You can pick up a map of the trails at the Manor house and Bass Lake Entrance (on US-221). The trails here are largely old carriage roads, so they're wide, well maintained, and pretty gentle.

Flat Top Road Trail

Distance: 5.6 miles out and back
Duration: 3-3.5 hours
Elevation gain: 600 feet
Difficulty: moderate
Trailhead: Moses Cone Manor parking area at the far end (away from the house)

This out-and-back hike will take you to the summit of Flat Top, where you'll have an unobstructed view of mountains in every direction. From the top of this 4,558-foot peak, you'll understand what drew the Cone family here.

As soon as you start the trail, which is really a carriage road, you'll cross under the Parkway via a tunnel, and emerge onto the north side. Follow the trail into the meadow until you reach a fork; the left trail leads to Rich Mountain Road, so

bear right and leave the meadow behind. Just under a mile in, you'll see a spur trail on your left leading to the Cone family graves.

The trail will cross another meadow, then turn back into the woods. At two miles in, the trail takes a couple of tight turns, then makes its way to the summit. On the summit there's a tower you can climb if it's open. The climb up is breezy and can be a little disconcerting, but the views pay off. To get back, simply retrace your steps.

Rich Mountain Trail

Distance: 5.2 miles out and back
Duration: 3-3.5 hours
Elevation gain: 510 feet
Difficulty: moderate
Trailhead: Moses Cone Manor parking area at the far end (away from the house)

Rich Mountain is known by another name by some in these parts: Nowhere Mountain. While it is in the middle of nowhere (at least it was ages ago), it's definitely somewhere to be. In the winter, you'll find many people cross-country skiing or snowshoeing to the summit.

The trail begins by crossing under the Parkway into the meadow on the north side. Here the trail splits, with Rich Mountain going to the left and Flat Top bearing right. Follow the trail to the left and cross the wide meadow before entering the forest. Before you reach the notable corkscrew path to the summit, there's little of note save the scenery, though you do pass through several rhododendron tunnels and thickets, and at the right times of year, this path can be packed with wildflowers.

Rich Mountain Trail's most notable feature is the corkscrew path (a double corkscrew, actually) to the top of the 4,370-foot peak. As the path begins the ever-tightening turns, you'll see the view from all possible angles. Take a break at the top before returning to the trailhead. Before you go, take a look at the trees here. Many are stunted, windblown, and damaged by ice and snow. Many of the mountains around here are high enough to get frequent snow and ice throughout the year, so be aware of weather reports if you're hiking late in the season, during winter, or early spring.

Bass Lake Trail

Distance: 0.8-mile loop
Duration: 30 minutes
Elevation gain: none
Difficulty: easy
Trailhead: Bass Lake entrance on US-221, one mile south of Parkway MP 294.6

This easy loop hike around Bass Lake gives you some absolutely stunning views of Moses Cone Manor in any season, but it's especially beautiful when autumn leaves are in full blaze or winter's snow blankets everything around. From the parking area, take either trail; they both circle the lake and will both take you right back here.

Julian Price Memorial Park (MP 297.1)

Julian Price Memorial Park (828/936-5911, www.recreation.gov) abuts Moses H. Cone Memorial Park, but unlike Cone, which was a family home and estate, Price was set aside as a retreat for the employees of Julian Price's insurance company. Price's death in 1946 put those plans on hold and the land was deeded to his company. His company, with the approval of his family, turned the land over to the National Park Service for inclusion in the Blue Ridge Parkway, so, in a roundabout way, Price's wish that this beautiful mountain land be used and enjoyed by his employees came to be. Today, there's a 47-acre pond, created by the damming of Boone Fork; as well as a large amphitheater; more than 100 picnic sites; camping; and the 13.5-mile Tanawha Trail, which parallels the Parkway and skirts the lower edges of Grandfather Mountain.

There are 197 **campsites** (828/936-5911,

www.recreation.gov, mid-May-late Oct., $16-19/night) at Julian Price Memorial Park, with spaces for tents and RVs. Canoeing on the lake is also a possible activity here.

Price Lake Trail

Distance: 2.5-mile loop
Duration: 2-2.5 hours
Elevation gain: none
Difficulty: easy to moderate
Trailhead: Price Lake Overlook at MP 296.7 or Boone Fork Overlook at MP 297.2

If you want to get a great look at Price Lake and check out the campground (if you're not already staying there), this loop hike will give you what you're looking for.

Since this trail is a loop, you can start from either trailhead and go in either direction. Much of what you'll see on the hike will be dominated by the lake. Along the west side of the lake, near the Price Lake Overlook, you'll have fantastic views of Grandfather Mountain, no matter the season. There are plenty of benches along the trail, so taking a moment to rest or soak in the view is no problem. As you circle the lake, you'll see the typical wildflowers, rhododendron, and mountain laurel that blanket the mountainsides here.

If you depart from the Boone Fork Overlook, the first half-mile or so of the hike is a good one for those in **wheelchairs** as part of the trail crosses over a marshy area on a long boardwalk.

Green Knob Trail

Distance: 2.1-mile loop
Duration: 2-2.5 hours
Elevation gain: 460 feet
Difficulty: easy to moderate
Trailhead: Sims Pond Overlook at MP 295.7

Immediately after you leave the trailhead, you'll cross the bridge across the spillway and the dam forming the small, but picturesque Sims Pond. The path turns left along the shore, then climbs gradually through a stand of hemlock trees. For a long while, you'll hike beside Sims Creek, but about a half-mile in, the sound of the stream will periodically be drowned out by the sound of cars passing over on the Viaduct above. As you continue on the trail, the gorge around you will narrow and climb and you will make several crossings of the stream. At 0.6 miles in, you'll be in for some great scenery along the trail at the Sims Creek Viaduct Overlook (MP 295.3).

After the overlook, the trail steepens and crosses a number of side streams. At the 1-mile mark you'll enter a meadow. There are a dozen or so concrete pillars guiding you across the grassy expanse and pointing you to the trail as it reenters the woods a quarter mile on.

The trail doesn't touch the summit of Green Knob, but rather stays below it a couple hundred feet. At 1.4 miles, you're as close to the summit as you'll ever be, so if you want to climb up to check it off your list, now's the time. Otherwise, take in the view of Grandfather Mountain and continue on. From here, the trail descends through the woods back to the trailhead.

Tanawha Trail to Rough Ridge

Distance: 1.6 miles out and back
Duration: 1-1.5 hours
Elevation gain: 550 feet
Difficulty: moderate to strenuous
Trailhead: Wilson Creek Overlook at MP 303.6

The Tanawha Trail is a trail-building masterpiece that cost $750,000 and required helicopters to place bridges during construction. The whole trail is 13.5 miles and stretches from Price Lake to Beacon Heights, just below Grandfather Mountain. One of the best sections of the Tanawha Trail is to Rough Ridge from the Wilson Creek Overlook.

Starting at Wilson Creek, pass under the Parkway and meet with the Tanawha Trail; here you'll turn right and cross Little Wilson Creek. The trail descends for the next 0.1 miles, then reaches a long, gradual climb through a boulder field

interspersed with tall trees and beautiful wildflowers.

Shortly after climbing through a small pine grove, you'll reach stone steps that will carry you to the top of Rough Ridge, where the views, especially in fall, are smashing. From here, retrace your steps to the trailhead.

If you'd like to extend the hike, push on through to the Rough Ridge parking area and walk back along the side of the Parkway (about 0.8 miles), making this a 2.4-mile hike.

★ Linn Cove Viaduct
(MP 304.4)

One of the most iconic spots along the Blue Ridge Parkway, the Linn Cove Viaduct is a bridge-like structure hanging from the side of the mountain in a dizzying S-curve. At nearly 1,300 feet long, this amazing feat of engineering makes you feel like you might just fly off into space if you lose focus. A pair of viewing areas about 0.25 miles from either end of the viaduct give you the chance to stretch your legs and snap a few pictures of this amazing part of the road.

Grandfather Mountain looming above offers great photo opportunities, as does the road itself when it ducks back into one deep cove and emerges on the side of the mountain opposite, snaking away into the trees. The sight of this lifelike concrete and asphalt peeking out from the trees and following the contours of the mountains is enough to take your breath away.

The story of the viaduct is a long one, but one well told at the **Linn Cove Viaduct Visitors Center** (828/298-0398, 10am-5pm daily) at Milepost 304.4. It was the last piece of the Parkway to be completed, and upon its completion on September 11, 1987, 52 years after construction began on this jewel of a road, the route from the Shenandoah Valley to the Great Smoky Mountains was whole.

What caused the delay? One reason was the route. Hugh Morton, the owner of Grandfather Mountain, wasn't fond of the proposed site of the Parkway, which would have climbed much higher up the side of Grandfather Mountain. After the Parkway route was settled at a lower elevation, Morton donated land to the National Park Service, and all that was left was the engineering.

Linn Cove Viaduct Trail

Distance: 1 mile out and back
Duration: 30 minutes
Elevation gain: 60 feet
Difficulty: easy to moderate
Trailhead: Linn Cove parking area at the Visitors Center

The first 0.15 miles of the trail is paved, making it ideal for **wheelchairs.** At the turnaround, you'll have great views of the underside of the viaduct.

Pushing farther along the trail, in 0.5 miles, you'll reach a postcard view of the viaduct, which you can achieve by taking a short spur trail to the top of a rocky outcrop. It really is a phenomenal view and worth taking a few minutes to climb onto this rocky perch for the shot.

★ Grandfather Mountain (MP 305)

Grandfather Mountain (US-221, 2 miles north of Linville, 828/733-4337, www.grandfather.com, 8am-7pm daily summer, 9am-6pm daily spring and fall, 9am-5pm daily winter, weather permitting, $20 adults, $18 over age 60, $9 ages 4-12, free under age 5), at a lofty 5,964 feet, is not the highest mountain in North Carolina, but it is one of the most beautiful. The highest peak in the Blue Ridge Mountains (the only peak higher, Mount Mitchell, is in the Black Mountains), Grandfather is a United Nations-designated biosphere reserve. Privately owned for decades though open to the public, Grandfather Mountain has remained a great expanse of deep forests and wildlife with many hiking trails. The main attraction is the summit and the **Mile High Swinging Bridge.** It is indeed a mile high, and it swings a little in the breeze, but it should be called the "Singing Bridge" because of the somewhat unnerving sound of the constant wind through the steel cables holding it in place. The view from Grandfather Mountain is stunning, and the peak is easily accessible via the scenic road that traces the skyward mile. From the parking lot just below the summit, you can access a number of trails (open during park hours only) that lead to nearby peaks, under the crest of Grandfather, and along nearby ridgelines.

Though the Mile High Swinging Bridge is a mile above sea level, it's not that far above the gap it crosses from the gift shop to a sub-peak of Grandfather Mountain. Even so, with the giant views all around and the dizzying distance to the valley floor below, some visitors find themselves more than a little nervous when it comes time to cross the bridge. If you find that the bridge is a little much for you, don't sweat it, just take in the impressive view from the parking lot and spend some time at the other attractions on Grandfather Mountain. The **Wildlife Habitats** are always popular. Here, large enclosures provide a place for white-tailed deer, eagles, river otters, black bear, and cougars to live. Daily feedings draw the animals out of their secret places in each enclosure and bring them into view.

Hiking

Aside from the view, many come to Grandfather Mountain for the hiking. There are a few short hikes along the drive to the top, and more hikes that will test your stamina and mettle as your climb to the true summit of Grandfather Mountain. At the Grandfather Mountain Picnic Area, the 0.4-mile **Woods Walk** trail leads you on an easy walk through the forest on the lower flanks of the mountain; it's gentle on the youngest and oldest visitors. Near the Swinging Bridge, park in the Trails parking area and hike the **Bridge Trail,** another 0.4-mile winding trail that takes you under the Swinging Bridge. There's one more, easier hike of note, but the rest are significantly tougher.

Black Rock Nature Trail

Distance: 2 miles out and back
Duration: 1.5-2 hours
Elevation gain: 400 feet
Difficulty: moderate
Trailhead: Trails parking area
Directions: Exit the Parkway at MP 305 and follow US-221 north one mile to the entrance to Grandfather Mountain. Follow the road up Grandfather Mountain to the Hikers parking area three turns below the summit.

This is a straightforward hike that leads through a forest of rhododendron, galax, Fraser fir, and red spruce, down a gentle grade to a short loop where you'll have views of Grandmother Mountain, Beacon Heights, and, of course, the Blue Ridge Parkway. Along the way, a number of interpretive signs provide information on the route and environment. The trail is rocky, but not too bad, but that gentle grade that led you to the end of the trail will seem a little steeper on the way back up.

Grandfather Trail

Distance: 4.8 miles out and back
Duration: 6-7 hours
Elevation gain: 1,800 feet (with several 700-800 foot ascents and descents)
Difficulty: strenuous
Trailhead: Parking area at the top of Grandfather Mountain

This unusual hike traverses the finest sub-alpine/alpine environments in the South. Though many believe the promontory at the end of the Swinging Bridge is the peak of Grandfather Mountain, it's not, but this trail will take you to the next three highest points on the mountain: MacRae Peak (5,845 ft.), Attic Window

The Mile High Swinging Bridge on Grandfather Mountain is thrilling to cross.

Peak (5,949 ft.), and Calloway Peak (5,964 ft.). This trail is marked with blue diamonds (it was blue blazes and in places the ghosts of these marks may be visible).

The trail is relentless, beginning with a short, steep switchback ascent. This section is a good taste of the rest of the hike and may help you decide whether to continue. At a quarter-mile in, you'll reach a spot called The Patio that has great views of MacRae Peak ahead. Shortly after passing the 0.5-mile mark, you'll come to the first of several cables that have been bolted into the rock faces to provide safety handholds. You don't need any special gear, just hang on. Continuing on the trail, you'll climb a half-dozen ladders (which can make you feel a bit exposed at times). After climbing the final ladder, you'll be on a narrow ledge that leads to the summit ridge. Wind through the forest to a 20-foot ladder that takes you to the top.

When you've had your fill of the view, climb back down and head to Attic Window Peak. You'll encounter a pair of interesting spots before reaching Attic Window: The Subway and The Chute. The Subway is a jumbled stretch of massive boulders. The Chute is a steep, narrow climb up the side of Attic Window Peak. Be sure of your hand and foot placement as you climb The Chute. From here, the trail continues along the edge of the cliff until you pass over a significant rock outcropping and descend back into the woods.

Soon after descending into the woods, Profile Trail meets Grandfather Trail at Calloway Gap. As you climb to Calloway Peak, there are several steep sections, but nothing too bad considering what you've done so far. The view from the top isn't much, but you've made it to the highest point on Grandfather Mountain. To get back, retrace your steps and be careful on those ascents and descents.

Beacon Heights (MP 305.2)

Beacon Heights sits on the edge of Grandfather Mountain, affording you a fabulous view of the slope and one of the peaks of Grandfather as the Parkway sweeps around the massif. The Grandfather Mountain view is from the parking area, but a spectacular, sweeping view of the lands south of the Parkway can be had at the actual Beacon Heights—a rocky escarpment up a short trail.

Beacon Heights Trail

Distance: 0.2 miles out and back
Duration: 30 minutes
Elevation gain: 300 feet
Difficulty: moderate
Trailhead: Beacon Heights parking area a MP 305.2

This trail is short and often in a state of disrepair, making for some rocky footing nearly the whole way. The reward, though, are the excellent views sweeping from the southeast to the northeast as the trail emerges onto a rocky bluff.

Flat Rock (MP 308.3)

A short walk from the Parkway is a rather large, flat slab of stone aptly named Flat Rock. From here, you have a great view of Grandfather Mountain and the Linville Valley.

Flat Rock Loop Trail

Distance: 0.7-mile loop
Duration: 30 minutes
Elevation gain: 100 feet
Difficulty: easy
Trailhead: Flat Rock parking area at MP 308.3

Somehow trail designers managed to build one here that appeals to both experience hikers and Parkway drivers. If you want, this trail can be either a quick walk to a nice view or a longer woodland stroll if you take your time to read the interpretive signage along the way, then stop for a picnic. Either way, this path through a rhododendron-filled hardwood forest is a pleasant one.

From the parking area, a short trail connects you to the loop. At the loop, turn left and take the trail around to a pair of viewpoints, the first being Flat Rock, a massive slab of quartzite, and the second providing a great vantage of Grandfather Mountain. Continue along the trail until you descend and return to the trail from the parking lot.

Linville Gorge (MP 316.3)

The deepest gorge in the United States, **Linville Gorge** is located near Blue Ridge Parkway Milepost 316.3 in a 12,000-acre federally-designated wilderness area. It's genuine wilderness, and some of the hollers in this preserve are so remote that they still shelter virgin forests—a rarity even in these wild mountains. The National Park Service operates the **Linville Falls Campground** (MP 316.3, 828/765-2681, www.linevillefalls.com, $20) near the spectacular Linville Falls.

Tent and RV sites are interspersed, and water and flush toilets are available May-October.

★ Linville Falls

Linville Falls (MP 316.3) is one of the most photographed places in North Carolina, a spectacular series of cataracts that fall crashing into Linville Gorge. It can be seen from several short trails that depart from the **Linville Falls Visitors Center** (MP 316.3, 828/765-1045, 10am-5pm daily Apr. 25-Nov. 2), including the recommended **Linville Falls Trail.**

Recreation
Linville Falls Trail

Distance: 2 miles out and back
Duration: 1-1.5 hours
Elevation gain: 300 feet
Difficulty: easy to moderate
Trailhead: Linville Falls Visitors Center

There are three overlooks providing the best views of Linville Falls and the Linville Gorge from the west side. This trail will lead you to all three. For the most part, this trail is easy, though if you're speed hiking it, the steep parts can be a little challenging, and there is a section of the trail that's often wet; for those reasons, it's a moderate rather than easy hike.

From the Visitors Center, cross the bridge over the Linville River and along a parallel path. A little less than 0.5 miles in, you'll come to an intersection with a sign directing you to turn left for Upper Falls and right for the other views. Turn left and take the short spur trail to an overlook at the falls. Here, the drop is small—only 15 feet—but the pool below is huge, and you can feel the power of the water rushing toward the bigger drop just downstream.

Rejoin the main trail and follow it for another 0.1 miles, then turn left again to descend some steep, often wet, steps to Chimney View, where you'll have a great look at the whole falls. Many people find this to be their "picture postcard" view, and it's good, but I prefer the vista at Erwin's View. To get there, head back up the steps and climb into the piney woods. The trail dead ends at Erwin's View, where a set of steps and platforms leads to views of the gorge from several spots and then a massive view of the gorge, river, and falls that truly shows the size of this place. When you're done, head back.

Rock Climbing

Linville Gorge has some great climbing spots, including Table Rock, parts of which are popular with beginning climbers and other parts of which should only be attempted by experts. Other extremely strenuous options are the Hawksbill cliff face and Sitting Bear rock pillar. Speak to the folks at the visitors center or at **Fox Mountain Guides** (3228 Asheville Hwy., Pisgah Forest, 888/284-8433, www.foxmountainguides), a Hendersonville-area service that leads climbs in the gorge, to determine which of Linville Gorge's many climbing faces would be best suited to your skill level.

US-221 South: Linville Caverns
(MP 317.4)

A complete visit to the Blue Ridge Mountains includes more than looking at their outsides: **Linville Caverns** (US-221, between Linville and Marion, south of MP 317, 800/419-0540, www.linvillecaverns.com, 9am-4:30pm daily Mar. and Nov., 9am-5pm daily Apr.-May and Sept.-Oct., 9am-6pm daily June-Aug., 9am-4:30pm Sat.-Sun. Dec.-Feb., $7.50 adults, $6.50 over age 61, $5.50 ages 5-12) is one of the venerable underground attractions of the Southern mountains. The natural limestone caverns feature all sorts of strange rock formations, underground

top to bottom: the entrance to Linville Caverns; Linville Falls; on the trail to Linville Falls trout streams, and, of course, a gift shop. Don't worry if you're mildly claustrophobic; the caverns are much bigger than you might think.

McKinney Gap (MP 327.5)

McKinney Gap is the lowest pass through the Blue Ridge Mountains for a hundred miles. Long before European settlers pushed this far west, Cherokee Indians used this gap as a hunting and trading route. The first permanent European settler here was Charlie "Cove" McKinney, who settled down in the 1790s with his family. And what a family it was; he had four wives and 48 children. Many of the McKinneys are buried on the mountain.

In the late 1800s, McKinney Gap caught the eye of the railroads who sought easy passage across the mountains. By 1908, the Clinchfield Railroad opened. Four thousand workers built 18 tunnels and 13 miles of track on, through, and around the hills nearby. The railroads renamed McKinney Altapass. A resort sprang up, as did two hotels and a golf course adjacent to the railroad station. In a few years, Clinchfield ceased passenger service and the resort began to fail. The end came finally when a highway was built through a nearby pass.

During the building of the railroad, Clinchfield planted hundreds of acres with apple trees. The geography here—hills facing southeast, the land largely free of frost, cold air at night but warm in the day, good sun exposure—made it perfect for apples. **The Orchard at Altapass** (MP 328, 1025 Orchard Rd., Spruce Pine, 888/765-9531, www.altapassorchard. org, 10am-6pm Wed.-Mon. Nov.-Sept., 10am-6pm daily Oct.) was born. In its best years it produced 125,000 bushels of apples (to get a sense of how many apples that would have been, consider that today's standard for a bushel of apples is 48 pounds). Today, though, apples are just part of the concern of the orchard. From May to October, they have all sorts of programs—from dancing to music to educational opportunities—all centered around the nature, history, and culture of this part of the Appalachian Mountains.

Museum of North Carolina Minerals (MP 331)

The mountains around here are absolutely packed with minerals and gems; in fact, they're some of the richest in the nation. The **Museum of North Carolina Minerals** (214 Parkway Maintenance Rd., Spruce Pine, at MP 331 and NC-226, 828/765-2761, 9am-5pm daily year round, free) displays more than 300 types of minerals and gems found in the vicinity. You can also view interactive displays on mining and exhibits outlining the geological processes that put rubies, emeralds, and other precious and semiprecious gems in the ground here.

❖ NC-226 West: Penland School of Crafts (MP 331)

In the 1920s, Lucy Morgan, a teacher at a local Episcopal school, and her brother embarked on a mission to help the women of the North Carolina mountains gain some hand in their own economic well-being. Equipping several households in the Penland area with looms, they touched off a local cottage industry in weaving, which quickly centralized and grew into the Penland School, a center for craft instruction and production. Several "folk schools" sprouted in the southern Appalachians in that era, most of them the projects of idealistic Northerners wanting to aid benighted mountaineers. The Penland School, however, is one of the few such institutions that was truly home-grown, as Miss Lucy was herself a child of the rural Carolina highlands. Today, the **Penland School of Crafts** (off Penland Rd., Penland, 828/765-2359, www.penland.org) is an arts instruction center of international renown. More than 1,000 people, from beginners to professionals, enroll in Penland's one-, two-, and eight-week courses every year to learn about crafts in many different media. Tours of the workshops (Tues. and Thurs. Apr.-Dec., reservations required) are available, and the school operates a beautiful shop, the **Penland Gallery** (Conley Ridge Rd., 828/765-6211, www. penland.org, 10am-5pm Tues.-Sat., noon-5pm Sun.), where visitors can purchase works by many of the school's instructors and students.

Little Switzerland

(MP 334)

Little Switzerland earned its name thanks to the views of the surrounding mountains and deep valleys, which are reminiscent, many say, of the foothills of the Swiss Alps. The mountains around here have been mined for years— millennia, if some archaeological findings are correct. Mica, that shiny stone, is found here in abundance, and there's evidence to suggest that Native Americans mined for it here some 2,000 years ago. Desoto is thought to have visited the area around 1540, searching for gold and silver but finding mica instead. Mica was mined here during the Civil War and Reconstruction. In 1895, emerald mining began. Soon Tiffany's and the American Gem & Pear Company had a large mine here. That mine is abandoned today, but gem hunters and rock hounds still find their way inside to see what they can find. And for good reason: In addition to mica and emeralds, mines nearby have produced aquamarine, beryl, garnet, kyanite, and smoky quartz.

History

Little Switzerland was founded in 1910 by Heriot Clarkson, a North Carolina Supreme Court member and powerful member of the state's Democratic Party. Clarkson held some despicable beliefs that informed the creation of this town, which he saw as a "whites only" village. To this day, there are (thankfully unenforceable) laws on the town's books stating that African Americans cannot own property here.

Clarkson's influence also affected Blue Ridge Parkway construction. Proposed routes had the Parkway detouring to Tennessee near Linville, though some continued along the present-day route. After the route through North Carolina was settled, Clarkson, one of the largest landholders in town, was appalled at the acreage that the National Park Service was seeking. He hired several lawyers and fought for a higher price for his land, getting $575 per acre, nearly 10 times the average paid for land elsewhere. His demands also included an interchange at the Switzerland Inn and a very narrow right of way. Luckily, Little Switzerland has shaken off the avarice and ill-informed biases of its founders and embraces both the Blue Ridge Parkway and anyone who chooses to travel any part of its length.

Sights
★ Emerald Village

Emerald Village (331 McKinney Mine Rd., Spruce Pine, 800/765-6463, www. emeraldvillage.com, 9am-5pm daily Apr.-Oct., 9am-6pm daily Memorial Day-Labor Day, free), a can't-miss collection of gem mines and historical attractions, shows the story of Little Switzerland's long mining history. Emerald Village has seven mines to explore, the **North Carolina Mining Museum** (a self-guided underground mine tour, $7 adults, $6 seniors, $5 students), and gem mining, gold panning, and dig-your-own emeralds. The very unusual Black Light Mine

Tour is held on select Saturdays. This tour is wild, as the minerals shine with other-worldly light under the black light.

★ Grassy Creek Waterfall

An easy hike leads to the pretty **Grassy Creek Waterfall** (trailhead on Grassy Creek Falls road, off Chestnut Grove Church Rd. after it passes under the Parkway). Park before the "No Parking Beyond This Point" sign and follow the road about 0.6 miles, then turn at the sign another 0.3 miles to the 30-foot falls. It's mossy and lush, and when there's been rain, the thin sheets of water flowing over the falls are quite lovely.

Accommodations and Food

The ★ **Switzerland Inn** (86 High Ridge Rd., 800/654-4026, www.switzerlandinn.com, $69-230) opened in 1910 and still serves travelers today with accommodations ranging from The Diamondback Motorcycle Lodge (a collection of eight rooms and a central living area catering to motorcyclists) to the luxurious Heidi and Alpine Suites. There are two restaurants on site, the **Fowl Play Pub** (hours vary by season, entrées around $12) and the **Chalet Restaurant** (serving breakfast, lunch, and dinner year-round, hours vary by season, breakfast and lunch under $15, dinner around $18), that dish up some tasty food from pub grub to more refined fine dining dishes. This inn is simply stunning, so if you want to stay at a place with fabulous views, make reservations early.

Big Lynn Lodge (10860 NC-226A, 828/654-5232, www.biglynnlodge.com, $105-169) is another fixture in the Little Switzerland lodging community. It started 75 years ago with a collection of cabins on a dahlia farm and has grown into a 42-room lodge. Rooms include breakfast and dinner, and it really is a charming little spot to stay.

You can stay and eat at the **Skyline Village Inn & Cavern Tavern** (12233 NC-226A, 828/765-9394, www.

skylinevillageinn.com, $80-125). They have 16 rooms and each one is extremely affordable, though in need of some updating. One of the coolest things about this spot is the Cavern Tavern. It seems that in the 1940s, a cave under the parking lot was the perfect place for a moonshine still. Today there's no illegal moonshine, though there is a good selection of craft beer. They serve breakfast ($6.50) and dinner (under $12), and both menus are what you'd expect from a mom-and-pop place like this: easy to prepare comfort food.

The **Switzerland Café** (9440 NC-226A, 828/765-5289, www.switzerlandcafe.com, 9am-6pm daily mid-Apr.-Oct., under $12) is a combination restaurant and general store, so you can pick up everything from a barbecue sandwich to a souvenir T-shirt. Most of their food is smokehouse inspired, and their trout is surprisingly good.

Crabtree Falls (MP 339.5)

Crabtree Meadows Recreation Area is a small recreation area—only 253 acres—but it's quite scenic. One of the best waterfalls on the Parkway is here, as is a great **camping** area (877/444-6777, www.recreation.gov, $19/night). The camping area has close to 100 total tent and RV sites. The highlight, though, is the 70-foot Crabtree Falls, easily accessible via a 2.5-mile trail.

★ Crabtree Falls Trail

Distance: 2.5-mile loop
Duration: 1.5-2 hours
Elevation gain: 480 feet
Difficulty: moderate
Trailhead: Crabtree Meadows Campground at MP 339.5

At the parking area you'll find a trailhead sign and a short spur trail leading to the loop. Once at the loop, turn right and wind your way into a shady cove, down some steep stone steps. You'll cross a bridge that's dry most of the time, but can be wet and slick if the falls are raging or if it's rained recently. When you cross the bridge, you'll find that the trail has become a bit rougher and you can hear the falls not far off.

The trail goes through several switchbacks, rock steps, and damp areas before you reach the falls. At the base of the 70-foot falls there's a bridge with benches, a great spot to sit and look. These falls are particularly photogenic, thanks in no small part to the strange little "island" below the falls. Take shots from the left or right for foolproof angles.

Continuing on the loop, just beyond the falls is the hardest part of the hike—a 200-foot elevation gain in less than a quarter mile. Climb up and catch your breath at the bench on top before heading out. The next section is a long set of stairs that lead to the ridge above.

Follow the ridge for a little ways until you arrive at a rocky outcrop with a handrail. You can see the falls from here, barely, but to do so, you have to lean out past the rail, so don't bother. Continue along the trail and begin to descend, crossing a couple of streams as you do. Soon you'll see a trail and sign at an intersection. This leads to the campground, so continue on down the trail and you'll soon find the place where the trail from the parking area met the loop.

Mount Mitchell State Park (MP 355.3)

At 6,684 feet, **Mount Mitchell** (accessible from MP 355.3, near Burnsville, 828/675-4611, http://ncparks.gov) is the highest mountain east of South Dakota. It is the pinnacle of the Black Mountain range, a 15-mile-long J-shaped ridge that was formerly considered one mountain. Now that the various peaks are designated as separate mountains, 6 of them are among the 10 highest in the eastern United States. Elisha Mitchell, for whom the mountain is named, is buried at the summit. He was one of North Carolina's first great scholars, a geologist and botanist who taught at the University of North Carolina in Chapel Hill. His skill as a scientist is demonstrated by his 1830s calculation of the height of the peak that now bears his name; using the technology of the day, the height that he estimated was within 12 feet of today's measurement. In the 1850s, he became embroiled in a controversy when Senator Thomas Clingman, one of his former students, disputed the calculation. On a return trip to re-measure Mount Mitchell, Elisha Mitchell fell from the top of a waterfall (now Mitchell Falls) and drowned in the water below. The rivalry recalls the climactic moment when Sherlock Holmes and his nemesis, Dr. Moriarty, fall to their deaths from the top of a waterfall—although in this case, Senator Clingman went on to live another 40 years. He also has a mountain named for him, Clingmans Dome, a mere 41 feet shorter, which glares up at Mount Mitchell from the Tennessee state line.

The best view of the mountain is at milepost 350. **Mount Mitchell State Park** (MP 355.3, 2388 NC-128, 828/675-4611, http://ncparks.gov) is not only a place to get an amazing panoramic view—up to 85 miles in clear weather—it also has an education center, a gift shop, and nine **campsites** (877/722-6762, late Apr.-late Oct., $20, $15 seniors, off-season $12). There is also a **restaurant** (828/675-1024, 10am-8pm daily May-Aug., 10am-7pm daily Sept.-Oct., around $15), which is unremarkable to all but hungry hikers.

Mt. Mitchell Summit Trail

Distance: 0.3 miles out and back
Duration: 20 minutes
Elevation gain: 40 feet
Difficulty: easy
Trailhead: upper parking lot just below the summit

You can take NC-128 right to the top of Mt. Mitchell, some 6,684-feet above sea level, and this hike puts you in the parking lot and leaves you with a very short hike to the observation tower. Park in the parking lot, then walk up the ramp. It's that easy. If you're able, the better option is to spend the day hiking all the way to the top on the Mt. Mitchell Trail. Whichever way you decide to get here, the views are fantastic from the highest peak east of the Mississippi.

Mt. Mitchell Trail

Distance: 12 miles out and back
Duration: 6-7 hours
Elevation gain: 3,700 feet
Difficulty: strenuous
Trailhead: Black Mountain Campground off Forest Road 472
Directions: Finding the trailhead is the trickiest part of the hike. Turn off the Parkway at MP 344 and head west on NC-80. Go 2.2 miles and turn left onto Forest Road 472. In 3 miles you'll reach the Black Mountain Campground and the trailhead.

The trail, which is blazed with blue marks, skirts a small nature trail (a loop, if you're interested) and crosses a few streams as it climbs. At 1.5 miles, you'll come to a junction with Higgins Bald Trail; stay right on the Mt. Mitchell Trail. You'll cross Setrock Creek at 2.5 miles, then meet up with the Higgins Bald Trail again at 2.7 miles. Continue along the trail and meet up with the Buncombe Horse Range Trail, where you'll turn left up a rocky climb. Near the summit, you'll join with Balsam Nature Trail. Keep climbing until you reach the top of the observation tower.

On the return trip, take a right on the white-blazed Higgins Bald Trail. The detour is short—only 0.3 miles—and the bald is beautiful, as is the waterfall you'll find there. Continue down Mt. Mitchell Trail until you arrive back at your car.

Craggy Gardens (MP 364)

Craggy Gardens is one of the most appropriately named spots on all of the Parkway. The principal features here are the rocky crags studded with rhododendrons, mountain ash, wildflowers, and other rare plants. As with much of Appalachia, this area was settled by Scots and Scots-Irish, and the rugged rocks along the peak reminded them of the craggy mountains back home.

The **Craggy Gardens Visitor Center** (MP 364.6, 10am-5pm daily Memorial Day-Oct.) has information on the flora and fauna of this part of the park, and the folks there can answer just about any question you throw at them. There's a picnic area here, as well as a pair of worthwhile hikes.

Craggy Pinnacle Trail

Distance: 1.4 miles out and back
Duration: 0.75-1 hours
Elevation gain: 250 feet
Difficulty: moderate
Trailhead: Craggy Dome parking area at MP 364, north of the visitor center

This is *the view* you're looking for. The whole of the Parkway is filled with great views, but this is one of the best. As you climb up, the view opens up to give you a 360-degree look at the country around. On a clear day, you can see a dozen notable peaks, maybe more. This trail is easy enough for young hikers, just watch them when you get to the top, which is somewhat exposed and could be dangerous.

Follow the trail to a junction at 0.3 miles. To the left is a vista that looks over the visitor center, but if you stay straight on the trail, you'll go right to the top for that stunning view you were hiking to see. To return, simply turn around and head back to the car.

Craggy Gardens Trail

Distance: 1.6 miles out and back
Duration: 1 hour
Elevation gain: 150 feet
Difficulty: moderate
Trailhead: Craggy Gardens Visitor Center

The trail begins on the south side of the Craggy Gardens Visitor Center, climbing through one of the most perfectly shaped rhododendron tunnels you'll ever see. Benches and signs naming the plants line the trail. As you leave the woods, you'll reach Craggy Flats and a picnic shelter built in the 1930s by Civilian Conservation Corps workers. From here, there's a short side trail that leads to a stone observation platform. If you continue on this trail, you'll reach the Craggy Gardens Picnic Area in about a half mile. To get back to the car, simply reverse your path and head back down that marvelous rhododendron tunnel.

Asheville and the Southern Blue Ridge

The final leg of the Blue Ridge Parkway is its most rugged and twisty section, but all those curves are worth it. Time and again you're rewarded with stunning vistas—some of which are all the more breathtaking due to the lack of guardrails.

TENNESSEE

Pisgah National Forest

NORTH CAROLINA

Great Smoky Mountains National Park

Boone

85 mi / 140 km
2.5 hrs

ASHEVILLE

CHIMNEY ROCK

Cherokee

Bryson City

137 mi / 220 km
4 hrs

Nantahala National Forest

© AVALON TRAVEL

Asheville and the Southern Blue Ridge

Great Smoky Mountains National Park

Bryson City

Cherokee

Cherokee Indian Reservation

SOUTHERN END

BIG WITCH GAP OVERLOOK

HEINTOOGA OVERLOOK

MP-460

WATERROCK KNOB VISITOR CENTER

MP-450

Maggie Valley

Dellwood

MP-440

RICHLAND BALSAM

MP-430

Waynesville

Canton

Cherokee National Forest

DEVIL'S COURTHOUSE TRAIL

GRAVEYARD FIELDS OVERLOOK

MP-420

Blue Ridge Parkway

LOOKING GLASS ROCK OVERLOOK

Cold Mountain 6,030ft

CRADLE OF FORESTRY OVERLOOK

COLD MOUNTAIN OVERLOOK

MP-410

Mt. Pisgah 5,721ft

Pisgah National Forest

Nantahala National Forest

Brevard

LAKE POWHATAN

MP-400

NORTH CAROLINA ARBORETUM

Asheville

MP-390

To Chimney Rock

Pisgah National Forest

© AVALON TRAVEL

0 25 km
0 25 mi

Highlights

★ **Folk Art Center:** Part gallery, part store, the Folk Art Center displays works like woven baskets and wood-carvings by master crafts-people from the southern Appalachians (page 209).

★ **Asheville's Downtown Architecture:** Asheville's downtown district is packed with art deco and Beaux-Arts masterpieces (page 212).

★ **Biltmore Estate:** Asheville's most popular attraction is not only an awe-inspiring palace and symbol of the Gilded Age, it's also a collection of great little res-taurants, shops, and a popu-lar winery, all in a beautiful riverside setting (page 213).

★ **Chimney Rock:** A natu-ral tower of stone growing out of a mountainside like a rhino's horn, Chimney Rock is the centerpiece of a large park with amazing hiking trails and rock-climbing routes (page 234).

★ **Qualla Arts and Crafts Mutual:** Ancient craft traditions thrive among Cherokee artists in western North Carolina. At the Qualla Mutual, visitors can learn about and purchase the work of today's masters (page 261).

★ **Oconaluftee Indian Village:** This living history site leads visitors through a recreated Cherokee Indian village where you can see traditional dances, arts, and crafts performed and made by tribe members (page 261).

★ **Great Smoky Mountains Railroad:** See the Blue Ridge in its deepest summer green or a blaze of autumn color on a rail tour departing from the historic depot in Bryson City (page 266).

★ **Fly-Fishing the Tuckasegee River:** Several outfitters can hook anglers up for a great day on the Tuckasegee River, which con-veniently flows right through Bryson City (page 266).

Asheville, the largest city in this region but small by many standards, may surprise you with its cosmopolitan flair. Having recently garnered international attention for its award-winning restaurants and breweries, Asheville's food scene has bolstered the city's reputation as an artistic, musical town. The Biltmore Estate, a palatial home built by George Vanderbilt, shows how the wealthy lived in the late 19th and early 20th centuries. The Folk Art Center just outside Asheville showcases traditional Southern Appalachian folk art alongside contemporary works.

As the Blue Ridge Parkway wriggles toward Cherokee, you'll pass trailheads and wildflower-filled meadows. Go ahead and stop: President Obama and the First Lady couldn't resist the lure of a hike on their vacation here, and neither should you. While you're exploring towns like Brevard in Transylvania County, detour into waterfall country, where more than 250 cascades lie within a few miles of

each other, just a few minutes from the Parkway.

At the southern end of the Parkway in the town of Cherokee, the ancestral home of the Eastern Band of the Cherokee Nation, you'll encounter a mix of tribal traditions, yesteryear kitsch, and modern luxury. Signs are in English as well as Tsalagi, the Cherokee language, and you're likely to hear Cherokee greetings like *Osiyo* (OH-si-yo) on the street.

Here too are elk, a species recently reintroduced to the region, and the unimaginable biodiversity of the deep mountains. Trout-filled streams run out of the hills and form rivers where whitewater rafters and kayakers challenge nature, and the Great Smoky Mountains Railroad provides unforgettable tours of the landscape. All across this region, you'll find folks who are proud of their heritage and their land. And with this beautiful bounty right outside their doors, how can you help but join them?

Planning Your Time

Plan to spend at least four days in this region. Asheville is a food mecca and

Best Accommodations

★ **Sourwood Inn, Asheville:** Tucked high in the hills just outside Asheville, this picturesque inn offers exquisite views and comfy beds (page 225).

★ **Grove Park Inn Resort & Spa, Asheville:** Relax in a renowned spa and some truly amazing guest rooms (page 226).

★ **Sunset Motel, Brevard:** This affordable and classic motel is just kitschy enough, and the owners and staff are a fun bunch (page 247).

★ **Balsam Mountain Campground, Maggie Valley:** This isolated campground is the highest one in Great Smoky Mountains National Park (page 258).

★ **Harrah's Cherokee Casino and Hotel, Cherokee:** A fabulous spa, several quality restaurants, comfortable rooms, and a casino set Harrah's apart (page 263).

★ **Panther Creek Cabins, outside Cherokee:** These rustic, comfortable cabins are nestled in the hills away from the bright strip of downtown (page 264).

Cherokee is so rich in history and culture that you should spend at least a day in each. Both make good overnight stops. Add another day for hiking, camping, or checking out the waterfalls just off the Parkway, and one last day to do what you love. Get a taste for the nightlife in or visit Harrah's casino or some Cherokee cultural activities before exploring Great Smoky Mountains National Park.

Summer is always a popular time to hit mountain towns on this end of the Blue Ridge Parkway. The elevation and breezes that cross the mountaintops and sweep down coves bring cooler temperatures than you'll find in flatter, lower climes. Pack a light jacket or a long-sleeved shirt, as nighttime temperatures can be a bit too cool for summer garb.

The southern end of the Blue Ridge Parkway is beautiful year-round, but many restaurants, attractions, and accommodations (particularly B&Bs) are seasonal. Check ahead if you're traveling in early spring, late fall, or winter. Of the places that remain open during these times, many operate with limited hours. That said, larger towns like Asheville, and to some extent, Cherokee can see an increase in the number of

visitors as weather turns colder. Smaller towns feel the effects of the seasons more strongly.

Driving Considerations

Traveling this stretch of the Parkway can be difficult at certain times of year as weather conditions—snow, ice, extreme fog—can cause road closures. During winter and the earliest and latest parts of spring and fall, it's advisable to check real-time maps of road closures and advisories on the National Parks Service website (http://maps.nps.gov/blri/road-closures/).

Getting There

Starting Points

This drive begins northeast of **Asheville** and ends **120 miles** southwest in **Bryson City,** a quaint town on a beautiful river in the Smoky Mountains. You can pick up the drive at either end and easily drive it in an afternoon. Another convenient starting point is **Cherokee,** site of the southern terminus of the Blue Ridge Parkway, only 10 miles from Bryson City.

Best Restaurants

★ **Luella's Bar-B-Que, Asheville:** This smokehouse serves up traditional North Carolina 'cue, house-made sauces, and even vegetarian options (page 228).

★ **Biscuit Head, Asheville:** Tear into awesome biscuits topped with crazy delicious items like fried green tomatoes, Sriracha honey, bacon jam, and house-made marmalade (page 228).

★ **The Admiral, Asheville:** Inside this low-slung cinderblock building are adventurous chefs who aren't afraid to try something new (page 229).

★ **Chai Pani, Asheville:** Chai Pani's

street-food inspired dishes are hands-down the best Indian fare in Asheville (page 229).

★ **All Souls Pizza, Asheville:** House-milled grains plus locally sourced ingredients equals awesome pie (page 230).

★ **Hobnob Restaurant, Brevard:** This eatery is earning a reputation as one of the best restaurants in Brevard (page 248).

★ **Joey's Pancake House, Maggie Valley:** Who doesn't love a roadside pancake house? On weekends, come early or expect a wait (page 258).

Seasons of Color

As you plan your trip, think of the seasons. **Spring wildflowers** begin to appear in late March, peaking in mid- to late-April. Azalea, mountain laurel, and rhododendron put on the best show during summer, blooming first in lower elevations, then creeping up the mountains. Flame azalea is a funny plant, peaking in different areas as the microclimates here dictate; they're ablaze with color between April and July. Mountain laurel overlaps some with blooms in May and June, and rhododendron shows its color in June and July.

Fall colors appear in the opposite order, with the mountaintops the first to show autumn's arrival in early October, then the colors bleed down until mid- to late-October and early November, when trees from the foot to the crest of the mountains are alight with color. Summer heat can throw the schedule for springtime blooms and fall colors off a bit, as can rainfall levels. Call the Great Smoky Mountains National Park or check with regional websites to find out how the leaf season is progressing.

Car

Asheville lies at the crossroads of **I-40**, North Carolina's primary east-west highway, and **I-26**, a roughly north-south artery through the Southern Highlands. Splitting the difference, **US-19** runs at a diagonal, deep into the Smokies in one direction and into the northern Blue Ridge in the other. The Blue Ridge Parkway passes by just a few miles from downtown as it moves west-southwest toward Cherokee.

To get to Asheville from Charlotte, the closest major travel center in North Carolina, take I-85 South and I-26 West, or take slightly more picturesque US-74 West to I-26 West. Either way, the trip is about 125 miles (2 hours, 10 minutes). From Charlotte, you can also take NC-16 North to I-40 West, a trip of just over two hours. From Knoxville, Asheville is 115 miles (about 2 hours) east on the quickest route (I-40); or you can take the scenic route through the national park and Cherokee, adding a few more miles and an hour of drive time.

Cherokee is located on a particularly pretty, windy section of US-19, between Maggie Valley and Bryson City. From Knoxville, you can take US-441 south to Cherokee. It's only 70 miles but is a two-hour drive through Great Smoky Mountains National Park and the towns of Gatlinburg and Pigeon Forge, Tenn.

Fueling Up

These are the most convenient spots to fuel up along this route:

- **MP 382.5,** US-70 less than two miles east or west

- **MP 384.7,** US-74A less than three miles south

- **MP 388.8,** US-25 less than one mile south, less than three miles north

- **MP 393.6,** NC-191 less than three miles north

- **MP 411.8,** US-276 less than 10 miles north

- **MP 443.1,** US-74/23 less than three miles east

- **MP 455.7,** US-19 less than three miles east

- **MP 469.1,** US-441 less than one mile south

Air

Asheville is served by **Asheville Regional Airport** (61 Terminal Dr., 828/684-2226, www.flyavl.com). The next-closest airport in North Carolina is the **Charlotte-Douglas International Airport** (5501 Josh Birmingham Pkwy., 704/359-4910, www.charmeck.org), two hours away. Charlotte-Douglas is the 10th-largest hub in the United States, with nonstop flights to and from more than 125 destinations worldwide.

In South Carolina, only 80 minutes south of Asheville, is the **Greenville-Spartanburg International Airport** (2000 GSP Dr., Greer, South Carolina, 864/848-6254, www.gspairport.com). Airlines serving Greenville-Spartanburg include Allegiant (702/505-8888, www.allegiant-air.com), American Airlines (800/433-7300, www.aa.com), Delta (800/221-1212, www.delta.com), Southwest (www.southwest.com), and United (800/525-0208, www.ual.com).

The closest airports to Cherokee are the Asheville Regional Airport and the **McGhee Tyson Airport** (2055 Alcoa Hwy., Alcoa, Tenn., 865/342-3000, www.tys.org) in Alcoa, Tenn., just south of Knoxville, about two hours northwest of Cherokee. Airlines serving McGhee Tyson include Allegiant, American Airlines American Eagle, Delta, Frontier (800/432-1359, www.flyfrontier.com), United, and US Airways (800/428-4322, www.usairways.com).

Bus and Train

There is a **Greyhound station** (2 Tunnel Rd., 828/253-8451, www.greyhound.com) in Asheville. There is no direct bus or rail service to Cherokee.

★ Folk Art Center

(MP 382)

The **Folk Art Center** (828/298-7928, 9am-5pm daily Jan.-Mar., 9am-6pm daily Apr.-Dec., free) is home to the Southern Highland Craft Guild and is one of the most popular stops on this part of the Blue Ridge Parkway. The Guild was established in 1930 to preserve the traditional crafts and techniques found in nine states that comprise the southern Appalachians.

There are around 30,000 feet of space at the Folk Art Center, including three galleries, an auditorium, a research craft library, a small Blue Ridge Parkway information booth, and the Allanstand Craft Shop, the oldest continuously operating craft shop in the United States. Started in 1897 by a Presbyterian missionary, Allanstand is your chance to take home a beautiful piece from some talented Appalachian craftsperson. Though the galleries only take up a portion of the building's footprint, they're exceptional. For more than 20 years, the Folk Art Center has displayed and sold fine folk art. Their eye has become quite discerning, so only the best pieces are on display or for sale.

There is a permanent collection of some 2,400 pieces of art and assorted artifacts, mainly focused on the decorative arts of the southern Appalachians, on display year round. Pieces include hand-stitched quilts in traditional patterns like double wedding ring and log cabin; delicate lace; intricate needlework tapestries; pine needle, river rush, and willow baskets; musical instruments; clay pots and vessels; and even toys, every one made from natural materials. If you find yourself wondering, "How'd they make that?" stick around and ask an artist. Every day, one or more members of the Southern Highlands Craft Guild is on hand to demonstrate their craft at the entrance to the Folk Art Center. They may be whittling away at a chunk of wood with their pocket knife, spinning wool into yarn or weaving, or tying brooms. No matter what they're doing, they're happy to talk to you and explain their process and the history of their craft.

FOLK ART CENTER

Folk Art Center ADA Trail

Distance: 0.4-mile loop
Duration: 10-15 minutes
Elevation gain: 50 feet
Difficulty: easy
Trailhead: Folk Art Center parking area, MP 382

This fully **wheelchair-accessible** pathway starts at the front of the Folk Art Center parking lot, follows the **Mountains-to-Sea Trail** for a short bit, and loops around to put you back where you started. Along the way, interpretive signs note a number of trees, particularly those trees used in making traditional crafts like the ones inside the Folk Art Center.

As you leave the parking lot, join with the Mountains-to-Sea Trail until you come to an intersection; keep to the right. Follow the trail another 0.1 miles where the Mountains-to-Sea Trail separates. You'll stay on the main trail, which narrows a bit not far from here. A quarter-mile in, you'll get to another trail intersection; this leads to another area of the parking lot, but to get back to the starting point, stay left and continue on another 0.2 miles.

Asheville (MP 382.5)

Asheville is filled with a lively assortment of chefs, artists, musicians, dancers, and other creative sorts whose collective efforts have earned the city the moniker "Paris of the South." Though it sounds trite, it's true; this progressive city has made itself open to change and outside influence while retaining a strong grasp on its roots.

In its early days, Asheville served as a trading post and regional center. Situated around the confluences of the Swannanoa ("swan-uh-NO-uh") and French Broad Rivers and a mountain stagecoach road, commerce found its way here throughout the 18th and 19th centuries. When rail lines began to bring vacationers to Asheville in the late 1800s, the town was discovered by the rich. The mild summer climate and fresh mountain air helped turn Asheville into a summer retreat for wealthy industrialists, among them George Vanderbilt, who built his mountain home, the Biltmore, just south of downtown.

The mountains around Asheville are thick with centuries-old folk art and music. Events like the thoroughly modern Moog Fest, which pays homage to the godfather of electronic music, Robert Moog, are part of the reason Asheville's music scene is so lively, but much of the credit goes to the tireless buskers you'll see around town, picking banjos and playing spoons, washtub basses, and even theremins. Galleries and studios around town display folk carving and weavings as well as contemporary works. A number of entrenched arts organizations like the **Southern Highland Craft Guild** (www.southernhighlandguild.org) help preserve traditional arts, while places like the River Arts District and a number of small guilds, groups, and galleries support contemporary artists.

All of this makes Asheville feel like a counterculture center. Elements of Haight-Ashbury circa-1968 mix with Woodstock, the Grand Ole Opry, Andy Warhol's Factory, and a beatnik vibe, but with better food, to create an electric atmosphere.

Getting There and Around

Car

From Charlotte, take I-85 South and I-26 West, or take slightly more picturesque US-74 West. Either way, the trip is about 125 miles (two hours, 10 minutes). From Knoxville, Asheville is 115 miles (about two hours) east on the quickest route (I-40); or you can take the scenic route through the national park and Cherokee, adding a few more miles and an hour of drive time.

Air

Asheville Regional Airport (61 Terminal Dr., 828/684-2226, www.flyavl.com) is

One Day in Asheville

Only have one day to devote to Asheville? Here are the city's must-see, must-do, and must-eat attractions:

Morning

Start the day with some great breakfast grub from **Early Girl Eatery** on Wall Street in the heart of downtown. Spend the morning **exploring boutiques and galleries** like those in the **Grove Arcade** and **Woolworth Walk,** taking time to stroll by examples of Asheville's notable **downtown architecture,** including the First Baptist Church and the Jackson Building.

Afternoon

At lunchtime, linger downtown for the **Eating Asheville** food tour, which begins at the Grove Arcade. **Luella's Bar-B-Que,** a five-minute drive north on Merrimon Avenue from downtown, and **All Souls Pizza,** a six-minute drive from downtown in the River Arts District, are other good lunch options. After lunch, get a new perspective on the city by boarding the **LaZoom Comedy Tour** bus, floating down the French Broad River with **Zen Tubing,** or zip-lining over the forests north of Asheville with **Navitat.**

Alternatively, spend the afternoon at the **Biltmore Estate,** a three-mile drive from downtown. Enjoy lunch at the **Stable Café,** but make sure to leave at least three hours to tour the house and gardens before they close at 4:30pm (3:30pm in winter).

Evening

Head back downtown for the evening, kicking the night off with beer flights at **Wicked Weed Brewing** or Belgian brews at **The Thirsty Monk.** When you're ready for dinner, try **Table** for inventive American cuisine or **Chai Pani** for Indian. Walk dinner off with a stroll—a number of buskers will entertain you. Grab a nightcap at **The Imperial Life** or a chocolate at **French Broad Chocolates.** If you're in town on a Friday, check out the drum circle at **Pritchard Park.**

---

20 minutes south of the city on I-26. **ART** (www.ashevillenc.gov, $1), Asheville's public bus system, connects the airport with downtown Asheville. A taxi from the airport to downtown will run around $45.

Bus

There is a **Greyhound station** (2 Tunnel Rd., 828/253-8451, www.greyhound.com) in Asheville. Asheville's extensive public bus system, **ART** (www.ashevillenc. gov, 6am-11:30pm Mon.-Sat., $1, $0.50 seniors), connects most major points in the metropolitan area, including the airport, with downtown. See the website for routes and schedules.

Sights

★ Downtown Architecture

As beautiful as Asheville's natural environment may be, the striking architecture is just as attractive. The Montford neighborhood, a contemporary of the Biltmore, is a mixture of ornate Queen Anne houses and craftsman-style bungalows. The Grove Park Inn, a huge luxury hotel, was built in 1913 and is decked out with rustic architectural devices intended to make vacationing New Yorkers and wealthy people feel like they were roughing it. In downtown Asheville is a large concentration of art deco buildings on the scale of Miami Beach. Significant structures dating to the boom before the Great Depression include the **Buncombe County Courthouse** (60 Court Plaza, built in 1927-1929); the **First Baptist Church** (Oak St. and Woodfin St., dating to 1925); the **S&W Cafeteria** (56 Patton Ave., 1929); the **Public Service Building** (89-93 Patton Ave., 1929); and the **Grove Arcade** (37 Battery Park Ave., 1926-1929).

The **Jackson Building** (22 S. Pack Sq., built in 1923-1924) is a fine example of neo-Gothic architecture with a disturbing backstory. According to legend, on

Downtown Asheville

© AVALON TRAVEL

the day of the stock market crash in 1929 that started the Great Depression, one of the wealthiest men in Asheville lost it all and leaped to his death from the building. Three or four (depending on who's telling the story) more of Asheville's wealthiest followed suit. What is known to be true is that there's a bull's-eye built into the sidewalk in front of the building as a morbid monument to the story.

★ Biltmore Estate

Much of downtown Asheville dates to the 1920s, but the architectural crown jewel is the **Biltmore Estate** (1 Approach Rd., 800/411-3812, www.biltmore.com, 9:30am-3:30pm daily Jan.-mid-Mar.,

9am-4:30pm daily mid-Mar.-Dec., $44-69 adults, $22-34 ages 10-16, free under age 10, additional fees for activities), built in the late 1800s for owner George Vanderbilt, grandson of Gilded Age robber baron Cornelius Vanderbilt. Like many of his wealthy Northern contemporaries, George Vanderbilt was first introduced to North Carolina when he traveled to Asheville for the mountain air and nearby hot springs. He was so awestruck by the land that he amassed a 125,000-acre tract south of Asheville where he would build his "country home" and enjoy the area's restive and healthful benefits. He engaged celebrity architect Richard Morris Hunt to build the home, and because the land and the views reminded them of the Loire Valley, they planned to build the home in the style of a 16th-century French château. The Biltmore Estate was once the largest privately owned home in the country. Vanderbilt also hired the esteemed Fredrick Law Olmstead, creator of New York City's Central Park, to design the landscape for the grounds, gardens, and surrounding forest, a project nine times the size of the New York project for which he is famous.

A three-mile-long approach road leads through manicured forests, revealing bits of the landscape and hiding the house until you are upon it, creating a sense of drama and wonder for arriving visitors. While the Biltmore Estate's original 125,000 acres are now greatly diminished—the estate comprises a little more than 8,000 acres today—it's easy to see just how big it was. Standing on the South Terrace and looking south and west, everything in view was once part of the estate. A large tract of the land was donated to the federal government and has become part of the Pisgah National Forest; what remains is immaculately manicured.

Primary construction of the home was done between 1888 and 1895, although construction continued through World War II, when part of the home was used as a bunker to store treasures from the National Gallery of Art. More than 250 rooms were built, and there are more than three acres of open floor space here, most of which is open to visitors on a self-guided tour or a behind-the-scenes tour into seldom-seen corners of the home, even onto the roof. The art and decoration are as grand as the architecture, with paintings by Renoir, James Abbott Whistler, and John Singer Sargent; a stunning collection of European antiques, among them Napoleon's chess set; and room upon room of masterwork in tiling, woodworking and carving, masonry, and stone carving. For its time,

the Biltmore was a technological marvel, with electricity, elevators, central heat, and hot water. In the basement, an indoor pool that could be filled with heated water, a gymnasium, and a bowling alley seem over-the-top by today's standards, which may be one reason the 1994 film *Richie Rich* was filmed here.

George Vanderbilt found the concept of a self-sustaining estate appealing, and he included a working farm with crops, herds of cattle, a dairy, and all the farmers and workers required for such an operation. The Asheville neighborhood known as **Biltmore Village** was part of this mountain empire.

If he could see it today, George Vanderbilt might be happy to find that the estate is ogled by 500,000 people every year and that his vision of a self-sustaining estate endures. A vineyard (not open to the public) produces grapes that are processed at the estate's winery; a livestock breeding program produces fine stock; and a farm supplies more than 70 percent of seasonal and specialty vegetables to the estate's restaurants. Visitors can eat, shop, tour, explore, relax, and unwind without leaving the grounds, and there's easily enough here to fill a weekend.

The **Biltmore Winery** in **Antler Hill Village,** which is part of the estate, operates in what was formerly the estate's dairy; check out the industrial-farm rafters in the tasting room. Daily tours and tastings allow visitors to sample some award-winning wines and see how they're made. More than 500,000 people visit the tasting room annually, so expect a wait if you're here in high season.

Antler Hill Village is also home to **Cedric's,** a brewery named after a beloved family dog, as well as a small museum, a souvenir shop, and a green to relax on. **River Bend Farm** is a beautiful compound that was once the hub of the estate's farming operation but now stands as a showpiece for traditional period crafts like woodworking and blacksmithing. Be sure to stop by the blacksmith's shop and watch master blacksmith Doc Cudd speak with considerable eloquence about the art of smithing as he hammers out everything from common nails to decorative leaves, flowers, and other pieces. Ask him to make the anvil sing and he'll happily oblige; he's one of a handful of smiths who know how to play the anvil as a musical instrument in the 18th- and 19th-century fashion. It's a beautiful, almost haunting sound you won't soon forget.

The **Equestrian Center** gives lessons and the opportunity to ride more than 80 miles of equestrian trails, many with sweeping views of the estate and glimpses of the main house that will take your breath away. Other ways to tour the estate include carriage rides, paved bike trails and mountain bike trails, canoes, kayaks, and rafts (the French Broad River bisects the estate), Segways, and, of course, on foot. You can even challenge your driving skills at the **Land Rover Experience Driving School.**

Admission cost for the Biltmore Estate varies by season and includes the house, gardens, and winery; activities such as horseback riding, rafting, and behind-the-scenes tours cost extra. Special events, like the Christmas Candlelight Tour (Nov.-Dec.) also have additional fees. Parking is free, and a complimentary shuttle takes you from parking lots to the house.

Botanical Gardens
The **Botanical Gardens** (151 W. T. Weaver Blvd., adjacent to UNC-Asheville campus, 828/252-5190, www.ashevillebotanicalgardens.org, dawn-dusk daily year-round, donations accepted) is a 10-acre preserve for the region's increasingly threatened native plant species. Laid out in 1960 by landscape architect Doan Ogden, the gardens are an ecological

top to bottom: the Flatiron Building in downtown Asheville; the Biltmore Estate; a pre-'cue pint at Luella's Bar-B-Que haven. The many "rooms" are planted to reflect different environments of the mountains, including the Wildflower Trail, the Heath Cove, and the Fern and Moss Trail. Spring blooms peak in mid-April, but the Gardens are an absolutely lovely and visually rich place to visit any time of year. Because of its serious mission of plant preservation, neither pets nor bicycles are allowed. Admission is free, but as the Gardens are entirely supported by donations, your contribution will have a real impact. On the first Saturday in May, the **Day in the Gardens** brings food and music to this normally placid park, and garden and nature enthusiasts from all around come to tour and to buy native plants for their home gardens. There is also a **gift shop** (10am-4pm Mon.-Sat., 1pm-4pm Sun. Apr.-Oct., noon-4pm daily Nov.-Dec.).

Western North Carolina Nature Center

Asheville, and western North Carolina in general, tend to be very ecologically conscious, as reflected in the **Western North Carolina Nature Center** (75 Gashes Creek Rd., 828/259-8080, www.wildwnc.org, 10am-5pm daily, $8 adults, $7 seniors, $4 ages 3-15, free under age 3, under age 16 must be accompanied by an adult). On the grounds of an old zoo—don't worry, it's not depressing—wild animals that are unable to survive in the wild due to injury or having been raised as pets live in wooded habitats on public display. This is the place to see some of the mountains' rarest species—those that even most lifelong mountain residents have never seen: cougars, wolves, coyotes, bobcats, and even the elusive hellbender. What's a hellbender, you ask? Come to the Nature Center to find out.

Black Mountain College

Considering the history of Black Mountain College from a purely numerical standpoint, one might get the false impression that this institution's brief, odd life was a flash in the pan. In its 23 years of operation, Black Mountain College had only 1,200 students, 55 of whom actually completed their degrees. But in fact, between 1933 and 1956, the unconventional school fired a shot heard round the world as an innovative model of education and community life.

The educational program was almost devoid of structure. Students had no set course schedule or requirements. They lived and farmed with the faculty, and no sense of hierarchy was permitted to separate students and teachers. Most distinguished as a school of arts, Black Mountain College hired Josef Albers as its first art director, when the Bauhaus icon fled Nazi Germany. Willem de Kooning taught here for a time, as did Buckminster Fuller, who began his design of the spacecraft-like geodesic dome while he was in residence.

Black Mountain College closed in 1956, due in part to the prevailing anti-leftist climate of that decade. The **Black Mountain College Museum and Arts Center** (56 Broadway, 828/350-8484, www.blackmountaincollege.org, noon-4pm Tues.-Wed., 11am-5pm Thurs.-Sat., free) is located not in the town of Black Mountain, but in downtown Asheville. It's both an exhibition space and a resource center dedicated to the history and spirit of the college.

Entertainment
Nightlife
Bars and Nightclubs

Asheville is growing a reputation as a craft-cocktail destination to match its food renown, and one big contributor to that movement is **The Imperial Life** (48 College St., 828/254-8980, http://imperialbarasheville.com, 4:30pm-late Wed.-Mon.), specializing in pre-Prohibition cocktails, a wine list that showcases lesser-known varietals, and small batch spirits. They serve a limited menu of small plates made downstairs at Table (http://tableasheville.com), a much-lauded restaurant under the same ownership.

W Xyz bar (Aloft Asheville Downtown, 2nd Fl., 51 Biltmore Ave., 828/232-2838, www.aloftashevilledowntown.com, 5pm-midnight Sun.-Thurs., 3pm-2am Fri.-Sat.) is a trendy bar that feels like Asheville five years in the future. The bartenders are some of the most innovative in the city. They specialize in cocktails that use North Carolina-distilled spirits in flavorful drinks that let the spirits shine without becoming overpowering. Weekends feature music, ranging from DJs to small local live acts, all in keeping with the bar's hip vibe.

Nightbell (32 South Lexington Ave., 828/575-0375, www.thenightbell.com, 6pm-12:30am Sun. and Wed.-Thurs., 6pm-2am Fri-Sat., closed Mon. and Tues.) is the latest from James Beard Rising Star Chef of the Year Nominee 2014, Katie Button, whose eatery, Cúrate, is one of the finest in Asheville. This speakeasy-esque bar serves sophisticated, imaginative cocktails and some mighty fine nosh.

A new favorite in Asheville is **MG Road** (19 Wall St., 828/254-4363, www.mgroad-lounge.com, 5:30pm-12:30am Wed.-Thurs., 5:30pm-1:30am Fri-Sat., closed Sun.; open as Punk Wok 6pm-10pm Mon. and Tues.), the bar and lounge tied to top-notch Indian Restaurant Chai Pani. MG Road prides itself on a selection of cocktails, local beers, and eclectic wines that are hard to match, all in an atmosphere that is simultaneously neighborhood bar and haute hangout. On Monday and Tuesday nights, MG Road is taken over by **Punk Wok**, a pop up restaurant that calls itself "vietnamese-chinese-japanese-thai-southern-fusion-punk-rock'n'roll-cooking." Whether you're there for food or drink, MG Road does not disappoint.

Brewpubs and Taprooms

Asheville's reign as Beer City USA and subsequent years as a contender for the title demands discussion of the city's finest tap rooms, breweries, and specialty beer bars. Beer is serious business here, but don't be intimidated; whether you're a beer novice or suds expert who can tell the hop varietal at a sniff, there's a pint waiting to meet you.

My go-to specialty beer bar in Asheville is the **Thirsty Monk** (92 Patton Ave., 828/254-5470, http://monkpub.com, 4pm-midnight Mon.-Thurs., noon-2am Fri.-Sat., noon-10pm Sun.). This unique bar in a purple building serves American craft beer upstairs, and unusual and awesome Belgian brews downstairs in a cozy basement. If you find the menu overwhelming, the knowledgeable barkeeps can point you to a beer you'll like. Ask for a tasting pour of their drafts, or just order a flight of beer and sample a range; it's a great way to find your favorite.

If you prefer hoppy beers or sours (sometimes called "wild ales"), **Wicked Weed Brewing** (91 Biltmore Ave., 828/575-9599, www.wickedweedbrew-ing.com, tasting room 3pm-11pm Mon.-Tues., 3pm-midnight Wed.-Thurs., 3pm-2am Fri.-Sat., 3pm-11pm Sun., restaurant 11am-11pm Mon.-Tues., 11am-midnight Wed.-Thurs., 11am-2am Fri.-Sat., noon-11pm Sun.), which opened in 2011, is a good place to visit. Wicked Weed is gaining fans across the state for their hops-forward brews. They feature some two-dozen beers in their tasting room, with Belgian red ales, fruit-forward sours, IPAs, and even a handful of porters and stouts. Wicked Weed's new bar, the **Funkatorium** (147 Coxe Ave., 828/552-3203, 4pm-10pm Mon.-Thurs., 4pm-midnight Fri., 1pm-midnight Sat., 1pm-10pm Sun.) focuses on those funky sour beers and wild ales that are becoming prominent in the U.S. beer scene.

Lexington Avenue Brewery (39 N. Lexington Ave., 828/252-0212, www.lexavebrew.com, 11:30am-midnight Mon.-Tues., 11:30am-2am Wed.-Sat., noon-midnight Sun.), or LAB, is a brewery and pub in the heart of downtown. With seating areas that open to the street and a 92-foot-long custom-built curved bar to sit at, it's a great place to spend an afternoon people-watching and enjoying a pint of Belgian White Ale or Nitro Chocolate Stout.

How can you go wrong with pizza and beer? **Barley's Taproom and Pizzeria** (42 Biltmore Ave., 828/255-0504, http://barleystaproom.com, 11:30am-2am Mon.-Fri., 11:30am-midnight Sat., noon-1am Sun., $2-21) serves piping hot pies and a plethora of pints. Barley's has 29 beers on draft downstairs and a full suite of 29 different beers on tap upstairs. They also have around 40 brews available in bottles. They pour everything from local brews to the top craft beers from across the nation. You'll need some pizza, a calzone, a burger, or even a tofu sandwich to go with your beer, and they serve a small but tight menu that satisfies your hunger for some first-stop or last-stop grub.

To sample a variety of Asheville's great microbreweries, join a tour from **Asheville Brews Cruise** (828/545-5181, www.brewscruise.com, from $50). The enthusiastic beer experts will shuttle you from brewery to brewery in the Brews Cruise van to sample some beer, learn about the growth of Asheville's beer scene, and gain some insight in the art and craft of brewing. On the tour, you'll visit **Asheville Pizza and Brewing Company** (675 Merrimon Ave., 828/254-1281, http://ashevillebrewing.com, 11am-midnight or later daily), where you can start off the evening with this pizzeria, microbrewery, and movie house's tasty beers and fortify yourself for the evening by filling up on good pizza. The **French Broad Brewing Company** (101 Fairview Rd., 828/277-0222, www.frenchbroadbrewery.com, 1pm-8pm daily) is another popular local nightspot that's grown up around a first-rate beer-making operation, where you can choose from a varied menu that includes signature pilsners, lagers, and ales while listening to some good live music. The third destination on the cruise is the **Highland Brewing Company** (12 Old Charlotte Hwy., Suite H, 828/299-3370, www.highlandbrewing.com, tasting room 2pm-8pm Mon.-Sat., tours 4pm and 4:45pm Mon.-Fri., 2:45pm, 3:30pm, 4pm, and 4:45pm Sat.), Asheville's first microbrewery. They've been making beer and raking in awards for well over a decade, and on first sip you'll understand why they're one of the Southeast's favorite breweries.

Live Music

Great live music is the rule in Asheville, and not just national touring acts, also regional and local bands that give the national acts stiff competition for audiences on any given night. Everywhere you turn in this town, you'll find musicians—buskers on street corners, solo guitarists in cafés, a bluegrass trio set up on a restaurant's deck, and especially in **Pritchard Park** (where Patton Ave., Haywood, and College Streets join, or just follow the sound) where a huge drum circle forms every Friday night. There are also formal music venues where you can hear rock, jam bands, bluegrass, funk, blues, country, rockabilly, alt-country, mountain swing, old-time music, electronica, and too many other genres to name.

A favorite spot for live music is the **Orange Peel Social Aid and Pleasure Club** (101 Biltmore Ave., 828/398-1837, www.theorangepeel.net, noon-midnight or later daily). They're billed as "the nation's premier live music hall and concert venue," and they can back that up with some powerful acts taking the stage, including Bob Dylan, Smashing Pumpkins, Bruce Hornsby, Mickey Hart of Grateful Dead fame, Mike Gordon from Phish, Chvrches, Beastie Boys, Flaming Lips, and My Morning Jacket. The Orange Peel is a cool concert hall with a big dance floor, great sound, and great history.

One of the best venues in town for roots music and eclectic small bands is the **Grey Eagle Tavern and Music Hall** (185 Clingman Ave., 828/232-5800, www.thegreyeagle.com). It's a small space set up more like a listening-room than a bar or club, meaning folks come to listen to the music and interact with the performer rather than grab a beer and hop to the next bar. Don't underestimate their local beer selection, though.

Ballet

Asheville's noteworthy ballet company, **Terpsicorps** (2 South Pack Sq., 828/252-4530, http://terpsicorps.org) performs for two brief but brilliant runs in the summer. Under the direction of North Carolinian dancer and choreographer Heather Malloy, Terpsicorps takes advantage of what is normally a slow season for other companies and hires some of the country's best dancers for a brief stint in Asheville. Summer productions usually have three-night runs, so tickets sell out fast.

Comedy

Around Asheville you may have noticed a giant purple bus zipping through the streets, laughter and bubbles (yes, bubbles) emanating from the windows. That's the **LaZoom Comedy Tour** (1½ Battery Park Ave., departing from 90 Biltmore Ave., 828/225-6932, www.lazoomtours.com, $24 adults, $18 ages 13-18, $22 seniors), delivering tours big in history and hilarity. The tour guides are outrageous—they're some of Asheville's weirdest (in a good way) people. They also offer the Haunted Comedy Tour (departing from 92 Patton Ave., $21), which adds in a supernatural note and includes tales of some of Asheville's spectral denizens.

Festivals and Events

Twice yearly, in late July and late October, the Southern Highland Craft Guild hosts the **Craft Fair of the Southern Highlands** (U.S. Cellular Center, 87 Haywood St., 828/298-7928, www.southernhighlandguild.org, 10am-6pm Thurs.-Sat., 10am-5pm Sun., $8 adults, under age 12 free). Since 1948 this event has brought much-deserved attention to the Guild's more than 900 members, who live and work throughout the Appalachian Mountains. Hundreds of craftspeople participate in the event, selling all sorts of handmade items.

Foodies looking for a festival should attend the **Asheville Wine and Food Festival** (U.S. Cellular Center, 87 Haywood St., and venues around town, www.exploreasheville.com), an annual event held over three days each August. Palate-pleasing events include competitive dining, dessert-centric parties, mixology demonstrations, and the Grand Tasting.

Moog Fest (various venues, www.moogfest.com) is an annual electronic music festival that honors the legacy of Robert Arthur "Bob" Moog, godfather of electronic music and inventor of the iconic Moog synthesizer. Huge national and international acts and influential DJs descend on Asheville in late April for a two- or three-day party at music venues across the city.

Shopping
Antiques

For lovers of vintage, retro, and aged things, the **Antique Tobacco Barn** (75 Swannanoa River Rd., 828/252-7291, www.atbarn.com, 10am-6pm Mon.-Thurs., 9am-6pm Fri.-Sat., 1pm-6pm Sun.) has more than 77,000 square feet of goodies to plunder through. This perpetual winner of the *Mountain XPress* "Best Antiques Store in Western North Carolina" has toys, art, tools, furniture, radios, sporting equipment, folk art, farm relics, oddball bric-a-brac, mid-century furniture, and all those great weird things you can only find in a collection this large.

One of the best stores in Asheville is the tiny curiosity shop **Not Your Average Antiques** (21 Page Ave., across from the Grove Arcade, 828/252-1333, www.notyouraverageantiques.com, hours vary). This folk art and antiques shop is like some madcap fantasyland of vintage toys. Trading almost exclusively in toys coveted between 1900 and 1960, the cases are packed with tin robots, spacefarers, ray guns, flying saucers, posters for magicians and circuses, and some fantastic folk art. It's quite the shop and quite the find in Asheville.

Books, Toys, and Crafts

One of Asheville's social hubs is the fun and progressive **Malaprop's Bookstore and Café** (55 Haywood St., 828/254-6734, www.malaprops.com, 9am-9pm Mon.-Sat., 9am-7pm Sun.), which carries a deep selection of books that includes tomes by North Carolina authors and a particularly fine collection of regional authors. You'll find the requisite coffee bar and café with wireless Internet access, making it a good spot to hang out. It's bright, comfortable, and the staff are well versed in all sorts of literature, so they can help you find a local author you'll enjoy reading. People in all walks of Asheville life come to Malaprop's, so expect to see creative dressers, the tattooed, business types, artists, students, and grandparents.

Dancing Bear Toys (518 Kenilworth Rd., 800/659-8697, www.dancingbeartoys.com, 10am-7pm Mon.-Sat., noon-5pm Sun.) is located among the motels and chain restaurants out on US-70 (Tunnel Rd.), but inside it has the ambience of a cozy village toy shop. Dancing Bear has toys for everyone from babies to silly grown-ups: a fabulous selection of Playmobil figures and accessories, Lego, Brio, and other favorite lines of European toys; beautiful stuffed animals of all sizes; all sorts of educational kits and games; and comical doodads.

There are a lot of jewelry makers in North Carolina, and in Asheville they come to **Chevron Trading Post & Bead Company** (40 N. Lexington Ave.,

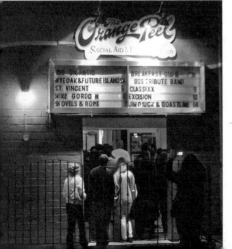

top to bottom: a quirky shop along the Parkway; smoky ribs prepared in the Western North Carolina barbecue style at Luella's; concert at the Orange Peel

828/236-2323, www.chevronbeads.com, 10am-6pm Mon.-Sat., noon-5pm Sun.). Millions of beads in bowls and tubes and strands on every surface in the shop are so irresistibly twinkly and colorful that even if you're not crafty, you'll want to buy them by the basket just to hoard. Best of all, there's Rosie, a rotund orange-and-white cat known to help shoppers with their selection.

The **Mast General Store** (15 Biltmore Ave., 828/232-1883, www.mastgeneralstore.com, 10am-6pm Mon.-Thurs., 10am-9pm Fri.-Sat., noon-6pm Sun.) is an institution in western North Carolina and beyond. They call themselves a general store, but they mean it in a very contemporary way. Cast-iron cookware, penny candies, and Mast logo shirts and jackets sit alongside baskets and handmade crafts. A good selection of top-shelf outdoor clothing and equipment can get you outfitted for some time in the woods.

Galleries

Downtown Asheville has a number of galleries, and while most exhibit works from multiple artists, none can match the size of the **Woolworth Walk** (25 Haywood St., 828/254-9235, www.woolworthwalk.com, 11am-6pm Mon.-Thurs., 11am-7pm Fri., 10am-7pm Sat., 11am-5pm Sun., soda fountain closes 1 hour before the gallery), a two-story, 20,000-square-foot gallery featuring more than 160 local artists. Nearly every conceivable medium is represented, including digitally designed graphic prints, oil paintings, watercolors, jewelry, and woodworking. This gallery is a favorite not just because it has a soda fountain but because the work on display is affordable as well as stunning.

American Folk Art and Framing (64 Biltmore Ave., 828/281-2134, www.amerifolk.com, 10am-6pm Mon.-Sat., noon-5pm Sun.) does a wonderful job of displaying contemporary Southern folk artists, including potters, painters, and woodcarvers, as well as helping the art-appreciating public learn more about local folk-art traditions and styles. They host six openings a year in the gallery, so work changes frequently, keeping the place bubbling with energy.

More great galleries and studios are located within **Grove Arcade** (1 Page Ave., 828/252-7799, www.grovearcade.com) and the **River Arts District** (www.riverartsdistrict.com).

Outdoors Gear

As Asheville is surrounded by the great outdoors, it's no surprise that there's a busy market for secondhand outdoor goods. **Second Gear** (415-A Haywood Rd., 828/258-0757, www.secondgearwnc.com, 10am-6pm Mon.-Sat., 11am-5pm Sun.; 15 W. Walnut St., downtown, 828/505-8160, 11am-7pm Mon.-Thurs., 10am-8pm Fri.-Sat., 11am-7pm Sun.), with two locations, carries just about everything the outdoor adventurer needs: mountain bikes, kayaks, canoes, clothing, guidebooks, boots, backpacks, tents, and climbing gear.

Shopping Centers and Districts
Grove Arcade

One of Asheville's shopping highlights is the 1929 **Grove Arcade** (1 Page Ave., 828/252-7799, www.grovearcade.com), a beautiful and storied piece of architecture that is now a chic shopping and dining destination in the heart of downtown. The expansive Tudor revival building, ornately filigreed inside and out in ivory-glazed terra-cotta, was initially planned as the base of a 14-story building, a skyscraper by that day's standard. There are some fantastic galleries and boutiques, including **Mountain Made** (828/350-0307, www.mtnmade.com, 10am-6pm Mon.-Sat., noon-5pm Sun.), a gallery celebrating contemporary art created in and inspired by the mountains around Asheville. Another favorite is **Alexander & Lehnert** (828/254-2010, www.alexanderandlehnert.com, 10am-6pm Mon.-Sat.), a gallery showcasing the work of two talented jewelers with different styles—Lehnert takes an architectural approach to designs, and Alexander chooses organic forms as inspiration. Not all stores in the Grove Arcade sell fine art and jewelry; at **Asheville Home Crafts** (828/350-7556, www.asheville-homecrafts.com, 10am-6pm Mon.-Sat., noon-6pm Sun.), you can buy specialty yarn, patterns, hooks, and needles for all sorts of knitting, weaving, and crocheting projects. Or you can buy a piece made by local artists. At the Grove Arcade you'll also find a number of restaurants, a wine bar, home-goods shops, and places to relax and primp.

River Arts District

Along the Swannanoa River, a number of Asheville's old warehouses and industrial buildings are being transformed into studio spaces, galleries, restaurants, and breweries in an area known as the **River Arts District** (828/552-4723, www.river-artsdistrict.com). More than 160 artists have working studios here, and twice a year, during the first weekends of June and November, nearly every artist in the district opens their studios to the public for a two-day **Studio Stroll.** On the second Saturday of each month some of the studios (they rotate based on medium, so one month may be photography, the next clay, the next painting and drawing) are open for **A Closer Look,** a day of artist demonstrations, classes, workshops, and creative activities.

Some studios are open daily, among them **Jonas Gerald Fine Art** (240 Clingman Ave., 828/350-7711, 10am-6pm daily), where the namesake artist specializes in abstract art that uses vivid colors and unusual composition to draw the viewer in. He works across many media, so there's a lot to see. **Odyssee Center for Ceramic Arts** (236-238 Clingman Ave., 828/285-0210, www.odysseyceramicarts. com, 9am-5pm Mon.-Sat., 1pm-5pm Sun.) is full of sculptors and teachers. Part of their mission is to promote artistic appreciation and advancement of ceramic arts; they hold regular classes, workshops, and talks led by master ceramic artists.

At the 1910 **Cotton Mill Studios** (122 Riverside Dr., at W. Haywood St., 828/252-9122, www.cottonmillstudiosnc. com, hours vary), several painters work alongside potters and jewelers. **Riverview Station** (191 Lyman St., 828/231-7120, http://riverviewartists.com, hours vary) is a circa-1896 building that houses the studios of a wonderful array of jewelers, ceramicists, furniture designers, painters, and photographers. Another favorite gallery is **CURVE Studios & Garden** (6, 9, and 12 Riverside Dr., 828/388-3526, www. curvestudiosnc.com, 11am-4pm daily). A fun, funky studio that has been around since before the River Arts District was a thing; it was once a punk-rock club called Squashpile. CURVE is home to encaustic painters, ceramic workers, jewelry designers, glass artists, and fiber artists. This is just a sampling of what's happening in the River Arts District; visit the website for detailed listings of the artists and their studios.

Recreation

Asheville is a "go out and do it" kind of town. It's not unusual to see mountain bikers, road riders, runners, hikers, flat-water kayakers, and their daredevil white water-loving cousins all on the streets in town. A number of gear shops call Asheville home, and access to trails, rivers, and mountain roads are all right here.

Biking

In town, take a tour by bicycle. **Electro Bike Tours** (departing from Weaver Park's Merrimon Ave. entrance, 828/513-3960, http://electrobiketours.com, tours 10am daily, $45 with two-hour rental) provides pedal-assisted bikes that make the hills easier and the flats seem like nothing at all. To show off how well the pedal-assist system works, your first shot is straight up the hill to the Grove Park

Inn, the first stop on a two-hour tour around Asheville's historic and cultural sites. The bikes really are ingenious because rather than rely on a throttle like a moped or electric scooter, they use their power to make pedaling easier, meaning you still have to work, just not as hard, to get where you're going.

Golf

Golf in the mountains can be a challenge, with course layouts big on blind approaches and hard doglegs, but it pays off with beautiful views and long downhill shots that can make you feel like you hit it like a pro.

The **Asheville Municipal Golf Course** (226 Fairway Dr., 828/298-1867, www.ashevillenc.gov, 18 holes, par 72, greens fees $31-36, includes cart, tee-time reservation required) opened in 1927 and is one of the oldest in the western part of the state. This Donald Ross-designed course is nearly 6,500 yards long from the championship tees and features a good mix of forgiving and narrow fairways, par-5 fairways begging for a birdie, and par-3 fairways that will challenge your ball placement.

Play a round at the **Grove Park Inn Golf Club** (290 Macon Ave., 828/252-2711, ext. 1012, www.groveparkinn.com, 18 holes, par 70, greens fees 9 holes $50-85, 18 holes $85-149, includes cart, discounts for juniors, late play, and off-season), where President Obama played a round during his 2010 stay. *Golf Digest* named this course one of the top 10 courses that are at least 100 years old, and it plays beautifully. This is a must-play course for serious golfers, and not just because the views are spectacular but also because the course contains so much history.

Hiking

Ready for mountain air? Join **Blue Ridge Hiking Co.** (15 Hildebrand St., 828/713-5451, http://blueridgehikingco.com, half-day and full-day hikes $35-185) on a half-day, full-day, or overnight hike in the Pisgah National Forest. Founder Jennifer Pharr Davis has hiked more than 11,000 miles of long-distance trails and became the first woman to be the overall record holder for fastest thru-hike of the Appalachian Trail: She hiked its 2,181 miles in 46.5 days. Don't worry, she and her guides don't go that fast on the trail; they like to slow down, enjoy the moment, and make sure everyone gets a look and feel for what they love about hiking.

Water Sports

Asheville Adventure Rentals (704 Riverside Dr., 828/505-7371, http://ashevilleadventurerentals.com, 10am-6pm Mon.-Thurs., 10am-6:30pm Fri.-Sun., rentals from $30 per day) specializes in sports that get you wet, namely stand-up paddleboards, kayaks, and bellyaks—a cross between a kayak and an ergonomically designed surfboard. You lie down on a bellyak and paddle like you're swimming, and take the river's rapids head on. It's a fun ride on the small but exciting rapids of the French Broad River when it's at normal levels, and it's a thrilling ride when the river is running a little high. If you've come to Asheville equipped with your own paddleboard or kayak, Adventure Rentals rents helmets, dry suits, PFDs, kayak skirts, and more.

The French Broad and Swannanoa Rivers offer a lot of opportunities to try your hand at stand-up paddleboarding on the river. It's much different than on a lake, marsh creek, or even the ocean, and you have to know how to read the river for underwater hazards and how to fall off correctly. **Asheville Outdoor Center** (521 Amboy Rd., 828/232-1970, www.paddlewithus.com, introductory lessons $65 for 1.5 hours, tours $40-65) provides lessons to make sure you're safe, and rentals to make sure you keep having fun. They offer tours ranging from a few to many miles, and all are scenic and mostly downstream.

Zip-Lining

For a different perspective on the Asheville area, head north for 30 minutes along I-26 West and spend the day at **Navitat** (242 Poverty Branch Rd., Barnardsville, 855/628-4828 or 828/626-3700, www.navitat.com, 8am-5pm daily, Mon.-Fri. $89, Sat.-Sun. $99). You can streak through the forest canopy on a pair of zip line courses like an overgrown flying squirrel. The tallest zip line here is an incredible 350 feet high—they say "don't look down," but do, it's amazing. The longest is more than 3,600 feet; that's a long ride. Two rappels, a pair of sky bridges, and three short hikes provide interludes from all the zipping and flying, and there are plenty of opportunities for photos and action-camera videos.

On the Biltmore Estate

The Biltmore Estate (1 Approach Rd., 800/411-3812, www.biltmore.com, 9:30am-3:30pm daily Jan.-mid-Mar., 9am-4:30pm daily mid-Mar.-Dec., $44-69 adults, $22-34 ages 10-16, free under age 10, additional fees for activities) really is an all-in-one vacation compound. You can spend a few days here and not exhaust the activities, and I'm not even talking about touring the house or visiting the winery; there are a variety of outdoor recreational opportunities offered in this 8,000-acre backyard. For starters, there are countless miles of **bicycle trails** on the estate, and you can bring your bike or rent one in Antler Hill Village from the **Bike Barn** (800/411-3812, single-speed beach cruiser $15 per hour; mountain and hybrid bikes half-day and full-day $30-60 adults, $20-40 children, $50 tandem bikes; estate admission not included). Riding on paved roads is not allowed (they're too narrow to share with cars), so stick to the marked paths, which will take you past prime photo-taking spots and some of the most beautiful land on the estate.

The Biltmore is an Orvis-endorsed **fly-fishing school,** and it's an excellent place to learn or hone your technique. Outings include two-hour introductory lessons ($125), half-day lessons ($225), kids' fishing outings ($125), full-day guided fishing float trips on the French Broad River, and wading trips on a private trout stream ($350-450 for 1-2 people). A fishing license is not required.

Hiking on the Biltmore Estate can mean anything from walking the 2.5 miles of mulched paths in the manicured gardens to exploring the hills, meadows, streams, and riverbank on more than 22 miles of trails. None are rugged, so you don't need any special equipment, just water, your camera, and maybe a walking stick. The **Outdoor Adventure Center** (800/411-3812) in Antler Hill Village has maps and can help you identify the right hike. For a more placid outing, try a **river float trip** (800/411-3812, raft trips $35 adults, $25 under age 13, kayaks $25 pp) on a raft or kayak down the French Broad River. Raft trips feature a guide who knows the land and its history and will regale you with stories; kayak trips are more private, self-guided affairs, but either way it makes for a relaxing afternoon.

Finally, for a loud, blood-pumping good time, try **clay target shooting** ($100-450). If you've never handled a shotgun before or have never shot clay targets, the introductory sporting clays lesson will have you on target in no time. For more experienced shooters, two-hour advanced lessons, a sporting clay course, and even full-day shotgun sports clinics will challenge your skills and help you refine them. All equipment is provided for activities on the Biltmore Estate (except your hiking shoes). The **Outdoor Adventure Center** (800/411-3812) in Antler Hill Village has full information on these activities and can make reservations and recommendations.

Accommodations

Under $100

With so many neo-hippie types, college

kids, dirt bags (it's not an insult, it's what rock climbers often call themselves), kayakers, hikers, and bikers coming through, it's no surprise to find a nice hostel nestled in among the hotels and bed-and-breakfasts. At the **Asheville ArtHaus Hostel** (16 Ravenscroft Dr., 828/423-0256, http://aahostel.com, $60, bungalow with private bath $88) you'll find only private guest rooms and even a private bungalow. Reservations are available up to five months in advance, so it's easy to get a room if you know when you're traveling. At the hostel you'll find free waffles, coffee, and tea at make-your-own stations; free Wi-Fi; free parking; and downtown is within walking distance.

Bon Paul and Sharky's Hostel of Asheville (816 Haywood Rd., 828/350-9929, www.bonpaulandsharkys.com, cash only) is a pleasant, old, white house with a porch and a porch swing, high-speed Internet access, and dorm-style bunks in women-only or coed shared rooms ($25) as well as camping ($18) in the yard. If you want a little more of a retreat, a private room with a TV and a queen bed ($68) and a cottage are available. Dogs must stay in the outdoor kennels. And, Bon Paul and Sharky, because I know you were wondering, were goldfish.

An artsy little inn just 10 miles west of Asheville is the **Fox & Fiddle** (31 Toms Rd., Candler, 828/665-9830, www.foxandfiddle.net, $45-60, seventh night free), where breakfast is only available on weekends ($15 per room). Guest rooms here are simply appointed but comfortable, and in addition to free Wi-Fi, there are also stupendous mountain views, seven acres to explore, an organic farm, and a fire pit. They roast their own coffee in-house and give a portion of their sales toward programs that support human rights.

● **$100-200**

One of the most charming and hospitable bed-and-breakfasts in Asheville is **Asheville Green Cottage** (25 St. Dunstans Circle, 828/707-6563 or 828/707-2919, www.ashevillegreencottage.com, $125-165 peak season, $95-135 off-season). This 1920s arts and crafts-style home is built of huge granite blocks and is cozy and simply decorated. Guest rooms are big enough, breakfast is outstanding, and they can cater to special dietary needs. Asheville Green Cottage is a "healthy and green" bed-and-breakfast, meaning they're smoke-free, fragrance-free, and use natural products for cleaning. It's a great place to come home to after a day of exploring Asheville.

Just off the Blue Ridge Parkway north of Asheville is an inn that's a true retreat. ● The ★ **Sourwood Inn** (810 Elk Mountain Scenic Hwy., Asheville, 828/255-0690, www.sourwoodinn.com, $155-200 for rooms in the inn, $200 for a separate cabin) charmed me so much the first time I saw it, I made reservations for an anniversary weekend. Situated on the end of a ridgeline, the view is nearly 270 degrees from every bedroom window and balcony. Your cell phone won't work here, and there's no Wi-Fi (by design), so you can truly unplug. There are a couple of miles of easy hiking trails, a pond, a bamboo grove, and some sculptures tucked in the woods nearby, but if you're feeling adventurous, they have a couple of options. The innkeeper's son-in-law happens to be a fly-fishing guide and an active hawker—that means he hunts with a hawk (not to be confused with falconry, which uses a falcon to hunt small game), named Rocket Girl; packages are available that will put you on the fish or put Rocket Girl on your arm. Other specials include a Blue Ridge Parkway package that includes fly-fishing, a massage, as well as horseback riding, Biltmore Estate passes, and Wild Food Foraging. Call for directions—it's tricky.

Ten miles south of Asheville and only a couple of miles off the Parkway sits **Bent Creek Lodge** (10 Parkway Crescent, Arden, 877/231-6574, 828/654-9040, $105-200 for lodge rooms, $350 for the stand-alone cabin). Each of the 10 guest rooms and three-bedroom cabin have balconies or porch access and overlook beautiful mountains. The innkeepers are friendly and their passion for the area shows in their avid mountain biking, hiking, and overall enjoyment of the outdoors. One thing that sets them apart from other accommodations is the fact that their kitchen is open, so you can sit at the bar, have some coffee, and chat them up while they make your breakfast. If you're handy in the kitchen, they may even let you lend a hand.

Over $200

Hotel Indigo (151 Haywood St., 828/239-0239, www.boutiquehotel-asheville.com, $217-399 peak season, $152-315 off-season) is shiny, modern, and steps away from downtown. The staff are attentive and courteous, and the concierges know the ins, outs, shortcuts, best restaurants and bars, and top townie things to see and do. As one of the tallest buildings in Asheville, the mountain views are spectacular from the upper floors; keep that in mind when making a reservation.

If you've spent the day touring Biltmore House, viewing the incredible splendor in which a robber baron of the Gilded Age basked, it may be jarring to return to real life, unless you're Richard Branson or European royalty. You can soften the transition with a stay at the luxurious **Inn on Biltmore Estate** (1 Approach Rd., 866/336-1245, www.biltmore.com, $499-599 peak season, $259-399 off-season, suites up to $2,000). It's everything you'd wish for from a hotel in this location. The suites are beautifully furnished and luxurious, the views are magnificent, and the lobby, dining room, and library have the deluxe coziness of a turn-of-the-20th-century lodge. On the other hand, if you do happen to be Richard Branson or Queen Elizabeth and simply need a mountain getaway, consider the Inn's **Cottage on Biltmore Estate.** This historic two-room cottage

was designed by Richard Howland Hunt, son of the mansion's designer, Richard Morris Hunt. Your own personal butler and chef come with the digs; call for rates.

In the heart of downtown, **Aloft Asheville Downtown** (51 Biltmore Ave., 828/232-2838 or 866/716-8143, www.aloftashevilledowntown.com, $290-459 peak season, $169-459 off-season) offers a hip spot to rest your head. There is a trendy bar serving rock-star cocktails, plush modern guest rooms, and fantastic city and mountain views from most rooms (others are poolside). Some of the best restaurants in Asheville are a few minutes' walk away, and the best live music in town is just a couple of blocks south.

The ★ **Grove Park Inn Resort & Spa** (290 Macon Ave., 800/438-5800, www.groveparkinn.com, $349-942 peak season, $177-755 off-season, spa and golf packages available) is the sort of place Asheville residents bring their out-of-town houseguests when giving them a grand tour of the city, simply to walk into the lobby to ooh and aah. The massive stone building—constructed by a crew of 400, who had only mule teams and a single steam shovel to aid them—was erected in 1912 and 1913, the project of St. Louis millionaire E. W. Grove, the name behind Grove's Tasteless Chill Tonic, a medicinal syrup that outsold Coca-Cola in the 1890s. You may have seen it in antiques shops; on the label was a picture of a wincing baby who looks more like he's just been given a dose of the stuff than that he needs one.

The opening of the Grove Park Inn was cause for such fanfare that William Jennings Bryan addressed the celebratory dinner party. In the coming years, at least eight U.S. presidents would stay here, as would a glittering parade of early 20th-century big shots, among them Henry Ford, Thomas Edison, Eleanor Roosevelt, Harry Houdini, F. Scott Fitzgerald, Will Rogers, and George Gershwin. Even if you don't stay

Motor Courts

In the days of yore, before budget hotels became the norm, the motor court or cottage court was the stay-over of choice for middle-class travelers. In one of the greatest road-trip movies ever, *It Happened One Night*, unmarried and feuding Clark Gable and Claudette Colbert build a "Wall of Jericho" between their beds with a rope and a blanket as a means to keep themselves in check while staying in a cottage court somewhere between Miami and New York. I like to think it was Asheville.

Today, these motor courts and cottage courts are relics of the past and few remain, but the mountains of North Carolina still contain a handful of fine examples; in the Asheville area at least two are still operating today, providing travelers with retro accommodations. **Asheville Log Cabin Motor Court** (330 Weaverville Hwy., 828/645-6546, www. cabinlodging.com, 2-night minimum stay weekends, $75-250, pets allowed for a fee), 6.2 miles north of downtown Asheville, has cable TV and wireless Internet access but no phones. Some rooms are air-conditioned, but that's not usually a necessity at this elevation. Another great cabin court is the **Pines Cottages** (346 Weaverville Hwy., 828/645-9661, http:// ashevillepines.com, $115-175, $15 per pet, up to 2 pets allowed), only 6.3 miles north of Asheville. Billed as "A nice place for nice people," how could you resist staying here?

at the Grove Park while you are visiting Asheville, swing by just to see it. You can drive right up to the front door, and if you tell the valets that you just want to go in and see the lobby, they'll probably be willing to watch your car for five minutes (don't forget to tip them). The lobby is quite amazing, a cross between a Gilded Age hunting lodge and the great hall of a medieval castle. There are 14-foot fireplaces at each end, and the elevators, believe it or not, are inside the chimneys. It's easy to imagine flappers, foreign dignitaries, mobsters, and literati milling about the lobby with their martinis when this hotel was young.

Being a guest at the Grove Park is quite an experience. In addition to the spectacle of the lodge and its multiple restaurants, cafés, bars, and shops, for an additional charge guests have access to its world-famous **spa** ($65 Mon.-Fri., $90 Sat.-Sun.). Nonguests can purchase day passes Monday-Thursday ($90). The pass gives access to the lounges, pools, waterfall, steam room, inhalation room, and outdoor whirlpool tub. The indoor pool is a fantastic place, a subterranean stone room with vaulted skylights and tropical plants. For extra fees ($109-500, mostly $200-300), guests can choose from a long menu of spa treatments: massages, facials, manicures, aromatherapy, and body wraps. For $70 you can have your aura photographed before and after the treatment to gauge the depth of your relaxation.

Food

No matter what you're craving, from Mediterranean to vegetarian, four-star to down-home, Asheville has the eateries that both embrace the Southern traditions of its mountain home and explore well beyond its borders. This is a town that clearly loves its food, with 13 active farmers markets, more than 250 independent restaurants, and 12 microbreweries in a city of fewer than 100,000 residents. Farmers work with restaurants to provide the highest-quality produce and meats, and artisanal bakers and cheese makers supply their tasty foodstuffs to restaurants.

With such a robust food scene, it can be hard to pick out where you want to go. For a sampling of the best of what Asheville has to offer the gastronome, take a walking tour with **Eating Asheville** (tours begin at the Grove Arcade, 1 Page

Ave., Suite 101, 828/489-3266, http://eatingasheville.com, daily tour $47, high-roller tour $54). Tours stop at six of Asheville's best farm-to-table restaurants for a taste of what they're cooking and provide two or three drink pairings as well as a talk about their food philosophy; sometimes tours meet the chef. Held on Saturday only, the deluxe high-roller tour visits six of the top restaurants and includes four or five beverage pairings (wine, beer, and craft cocktails); for just a few bucks more, it's the way to go.

Barbecue

What's a trip to North Carolina without barbecue? At ★ **Luella's Bar-B-Que** (501 Merrimon Ave., 828/606-9024, www.luellasbbq.com, 11am-9pm Mon.-Thurs., 11am-10pm Fri.-Sat., noon-8:30pm Sun., $6.50-15) you can try the range of styles and sauces that make North Carolina 'cue distinct. Ribs, chopped pork, brisket, smoked wings, and sides like mac and cheese, fried okra, collard greens, and hush puppies are staples here, but there's a surprising item on the menu: barbecued tempeh. (Tempeh is a soy product, a cousin of tofu.) I'm a barbecue judge (really, I'm certified), so trust me when I say it's good. Damn good. As is everything here, from the grub to the vibe to the impressive array of local beer on draft.

Breakfast and Brunch

A new arrival on Asheville's culinary scene is ★ **Biscuit Head** (733 Haywood Rd., 828/333-5154, www.biscuitheads.com, 7am-2pm Tues.-Fri., 8am-3pm Sat.-Sun., around $8) in West Asheville. They serve up an Appalachian specialty, cathead biscuits, so named because they're huge, the size of a cat's head. These biscuits are dynamite. Order the fried green tomato biscuit and you'll get more than you can eat: a cat-head biscuit, split and topped with a fried green tomato, Brie, sliced tomato, poached eggs, and smoked tomato hollandaise. Or just get the "Biscuit And," which comes with a biscuit and your choice of crazy butters, jams, hot sauces, infused honeys, and toppings from the biscuit bar, featuring all housemade spreadables. Or make a go of breakfast sans biscuit and order a number of side dishes, including Sriracha maple sausage, seitan vegetarian "sausage," smoked chèvre grits, fried chicken, and flavored bacon. The chef, his wife, and their crew did all of the work to make the restaurant interior reflect their funky outlook on food, and it does that quite well; it's a little weird, a little bit like home, and a cool spot for breakfast. If you eat outside, check out the wild terrarium tables made from salvaged windows.

West Asheville's **Sunny Point Café** (626 Haywood Rd., 828/252-0055, www.sunnypointcafe.com, 8:30am-9pm Tues.-Sat., 8:30am-2:30pm Sun.-Mon., $10-17) serves three meals most days, but it's so famous for its brunch that a line sometimes forms out the door. The breakfast menu is popular and served any time of day, even though the lunch and dinner menus are also well worth a trip. This is a great bet for vegetarians—the meatless options are imaginative and beautifully created.

Chocolate

French Broad Chocolates (10 S. Lexington Ave., 828/252-4181, http://frenchbroadchocolates.com, 11am-11pm Sun.-Thurs., 11am-midnight Fri.-Sat.) describes itself as "a sacred space for chocophiles." This mellow café serves a menu that celebrates chocolate, featuring French Broad Chocolates' own artisanal truffles, brownies, and pastries, as well as sipping chocolates and floats. If, by some freakish chance, you don't care for chocolate, you can sample Pisgah Brewing Company beers and non-chocolate desserts like pecan tart and butter cake. This is a true "bean to bar" chocolatier, as they roast their own cacao in a rooftop solar roaster at their nearby factory and **tasting room** (21 Buxton Ave.,

828/504-4996, noon-6pm Mon.-Sat., tours 2pm Sat.).

Eclectic American

Early Girl Eatery (8 Wall St., 828/259-9292, www.earlygirleatery.com, 7:30am-3pm Mon., 7:30am-9pm Tues.-Fri., 9am-9pm Sat.-Sun., $10-15) has caused a stir among area locavores and is gaining a following among visitors. More than half of the vegetables, meat, and fish used at Early Girl was raised or caught within 20 miles of the restaurant. The menu accommodates Asheville's large vegetarian and vegan contingent, but non-veg diners can feast on pan-fried trout with pecan butter, free-range chicken, or cheeseburgers made from hormone-free beef and topped with farmstead cheese, basil mayo, and all the fixings. Their breakfast, served all day, is among the best in Asheville. Their multigrain pancakes are out of this world.

Lot long after **Table** (48 College St., 828/254-8980, http://tableasheville. com, lunch 11am-2:30pm Mon. and Wed.-Sat., dinner 5:30pm-10pm Mon. and Wed.-Sat., brunch 10:30am-2pm Sun., $19-34) opened in 2005, the critical acclaim, including becoming a James Beard Award semifinalist, began to roll in. Founded by husband and wife Jacob and Alicia Sessoms and their friend Matthew Dawes, Table uses ingredients like locally caught bass and mountain-raised pork and lamb, creating a menu that takes full advantage of the culinary riches of western North Carolina. You can find some unusual items, like sweetbreads and quail, and they're renowned for their charcuterie, much of which is made in-house. The chef takes a minimalist approach, doing as little as possible to coax out maximum flavor. This tiny restaurant is always packed. Call for reservations, and if you're feeling bold, go with the chef's tasting menu, a selection of dishes that showcase the best this miniscule kitchen (you'll see it on your way in) has to offer.

★ **The Admiral** (400 Haywood Rd., 828/252-2541, www.theadmiralnc. com, 5pm-10pm nightly, small plates around $10, entrées around $28) in West Asheville has been a food destination since it opened in a humble cinderblock building in what they call "the wage earning side of town." Blue-collar roots or no, they serve some distinguished, and much-lauded, New Southern food that keeps the kitchen on its toes with interesting techniques and seasonal ingredients. It's small, but cozy and chic while somehow retaining a sort of dive-bar vibe, but in the best way. The cocktails aren't half bad either.

French

Chef Michael Baudouin grew up in France's Rhône Valley, the son of a winemaker and an excellent cook. He brings his culinary heritage to Asheville at his restaurant **Bouchon** (62 N. Lexington Ave., 828/350-1140, http://asheville-bouchon.com, from 5pm daily, small plates $6-16, entrées $12-25). Bouchon's "French comfort food" includes classics such as mussels frites, French-style trout, and roasted half-duck rubbed with cocoa nibs, sea salt, coriander, and black pepper. Delicious vegetarian options are available.

Fusion

Zambra (85 Walnut St., 828/232-1060, www.zambratapas.com, dinner from 5pm daily, $10-20) combines cuisines of the western Mediterranean—Spanish and North African—with fresh North Carolina ingredients. Specials change nightly and often feature North Carolina seafood. The long tapas menu has many choices for vegetarians.

Indian

Local favorite ★ **Chai Pani** (22 Battery Park Ave., 828/254-4003, www.chai-pani.net, lunch 11:30am-4pm Mon.-Sat, noon-4pm Sun., dinner 5pm-9:30pm Sun.-Thurs., 5:30pm-10:pm Fri. and Sat.,

ASHEVILLE

under $10) continues to win fans because of its cool atmosphere and great food. The restaurant's name means "tea and water," a phrase that refers to a snack or a small gift. This restaurant is inspired by Indian street-food vendors and serves casual and affordable specialties from all over India.

Mela (70 Lexington Ave., 828/225-8880, www.melaasheville.com, lunch 11:30am-2:30pm daily, dinner 5:30pm-9:30pm Sun.-Thurs., 5:30pm-10:pm Fri.-Sat., $10-15) is one of the best Indian restaurants in North Carolina. The elaborate menu offers dozens of choices, combining cuisines of both northern and southern India with great meat, seafood, and vegetable dishes. The restaurant is dark and elegant, but the prices are surprisingly low; you can put together a great patchwork meal of appetizers, which start at $2, along with soup and roti. Don't miss the samosas.

Italian and Pizza

Cucina 24 (24 Wall St., 828/254-6170, http://cucina24restaurant.com, dinner from 5:30pm Tues.-Fri., from 5pm Sat.-Sun., $10-26) is, as executive chef Brian Canipelli says, "not a fettuccine alfredo and lasagna kind of place; we do cooking like it's done in Italy, but with North Carolina ingredients." That's a strong statement, but his food backs it up. The menu changes completely just about weekly, and dishes are often inspired by farmers Canipelli meets in the morning while out buying for the day. A recent example is rabbit meatballs with dandelion greens, stinging nettles, and house-made gnocchi with a spicy red sauce, using foraged greens and house-made pasta.

★ **All Souls Pizza** (175 Clingman Ave., 828/254-0169, www.allsoulspizza.com, lunch 11:30am-5pm Tues.-Sat., dinner 5pm-10pm daily, lunch $7-14, dinner $7-18) in the River Arts District has gotten creative with pizza in a typical Asheville fashion. They mill their own flours and polenta from organic grains; they source meat, produce, and cheese from as close to Asheville as they can; and everything else they can get locally, they get locally. It pays off in your first bite. You'll be hooked whether you go with a plain cheese pie; smoked shrimp, chilies, and mozzarella; country ham, egg, and mozzarella; or watercress, leeks, goat cheese, and mozzarella.

Latin American

Ask an Asheville resident for restaurant recommendations, and chances are **Salsa's** (6 Patton Ave., 828/252-9805, www.salsas-asheville.com, 11:30am-4pm and 5pm-9:30pm Mon.-Fri., noon-4pm and 5pm-10pm Sat., noon-4pm and 5pm-9:30pm Sun., $10-20) will be one of the first names mentioned. Salsa's pan-Latin concoctions, from their famous fish burritos to exquisite cocktails, keep this tiny café jam-packed with locals and visitors. When the weather's good, it's fun to eat on their little street-side patio and watch the people go by.

Also delicious is **Limones** (13 Eagle St., 828/252-2327, http://limonesrestaurant.com, dinner 5pm-10pm daily, brunch 10:30am-2:30pm Sat.-Sun., $10-14). Chef Hugo Ramírez, a native of Mexico City, combines his backgrounds in Mexican and French-inspired California cuisine to create a menu unlike any other in Asheville.

Spanish

Cúrate (11 Biltmore Ave., 828/239-2946, www.curatetapasbar.com, 11:30am-10:30pm Tues.-Thurs., 11:30am-11pm Fri.-Sat., 11:30am-10pm Sun., small plates from $5-20) features the food of chef Katie Button, a James Beard Award semifinalist who cooked at the world's best restaurant, elBulli, in Spain. She serves a Spanish tapas-style menu, so you'll be making a meal of a bunch of small plates and will get to try a variety of flavors and textures. The *table de jamón* (a selection of three delicious and very different Spanish hams) and the *pulpo a'la gallega* (octopus and paprika with potatoes) are good dishes to share. There are also a number of vegan and gluten-free selections. The can't-miss street dish that people rave about is the *berenjenas la taberna*—fried eggplant drizzled in wild mountain honey and garnished with rosemary. This incredible dish can even serve as a component to a dessert course if you like a savory-sweet dessert. There's a lot of energy in this restaurant, partially because a long bar faces the kitchen, putting everyone from chef Button to her expert kitchen brigade on display.

Vegetarian

Whether you've been at the Grey Eagle or the Orange Peel, the show has just let out, it's the middle of the night, and you need to refuel with some good food, the lights are on at **Rosetta's Kitchen** (111 Broadway Ave., 828/232-0738, www.rosettaskitchen.com, 11am-11pm Mon.-Thurs., 11am-3am Fri.-Sat., brunch 11am-3pm Sun., around $10). The food is

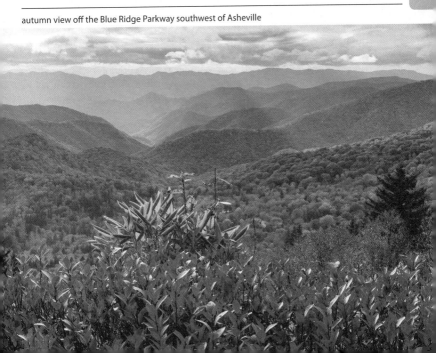

autumn view off the Blue Ridge Parkway southwest of Asheville good, it's all vegetarian and mostly vegan, and it's made with local produce in season. Best of all, it's open late on weekends. They compost everything that makes its way back to the kitchen, recycle all their trash, and make sure their used vegetable oil goes to power biodiesel cars—it's Asheville's signature countercultural reinterpretation of the South.

In Biltmore Village

In one of the historic cottages of Biltmore Village is the **Corner Kitchen** (3 Boston Way, 828/274-2439, www.the-cornerkitchen.com, breakfast 7:30am-11am Mon.-Fri., brunch 9am-3pm Sat.-Sun., lunch 11:30am-3pm Mon.-Fri., dinner 5pm daily, entrées $18-28). Head chef Joe Scully once worked at New York's Waldorf Astoria and served as executive chef at the United Nations. He is joined by Carolina-born Josh Weeks, an expert in Southern, French, and Pacific cuisines. Chefs Joe and Josh combine home-style and haute cuisines quite harmoniously. The Obamas ate at Corner Kitchen in Asheville in 2010 (but you're out of luck if you want to recreate their meal—the menu changes frequently). They had corn and crab chowder, mahi-mahi (there's always a fresh North Carolina fish on the menu), baby arugula salad, corn-fried oysters, lobster tacos, pork chops, and soufflé. A long wine list (by the bottle $20-275, by the glass $6-12) features many Napa Valley, French, and Italian wines, including several fine champagnes and sparkling whites and rosés. The cozy, cheerful dining room opens into the kitchen, where guests can see every step of their meal's preparation while chatting with the staff.

On the Biltmore Estate

There are no fewer than nine places to eat (plus snacks, ice cream, and coffee) on the **Biltmore Estate** (1 Approach Rd., 800/411-3812, www.biltmore.com, estate admission required to visit restaurants). The **Dining Room** (5:30pm-9:30pm daily, reservations required, $9-24, 5-course tasting menu $80) is an elegant restaurant, led by chef David Ryba, featuring estate-raised Angus beef, mountain trout, Biltmore wines, and vegetables grown on estate gardens. The food is spectacular, and tables with a mountain view make the meal all that much better. Evening dress and reservations are recommended.

The **Biltmore Bistro** (11am-9pm daily, lunch $15-21, dinner $19-45) in Antler Hill Village, adjacent to the winery, has a well-rounded gourmet menu sourced from the Biltmore's own kitchen garden, locally raised heirloom crops, meat and seafood delicacies, and artisanal cheeses and breads. Lunch and dinner are dramatically different (wood-fired pizza at lunch, braised veal cheeks at dinner), but each menu features something from the wood-fired oven.

The dining room of the **Deerpark Restaurant** (11am-3pm Sat., 10am-2pm Sun., Sat. buffet $18, Sun. buffet $28) is a former barn designed by architect Richard Morris Hunt, now renovated to airy splendor with walls of windows. Expect hearty and homey meals based on Appalachian cuisine. Like the Deerpark, the **Stable Café** (lunch 11am-4pm daily, dinner from 5pm daily) was once livestock housing, and guests can sit in booths that were once horse stalls. This is a meat eater's paradise, where you can order estate-raised Angus beef, and pork barbecue with the house special sauce, among others.

In the stable area near the house, both the **Bake Shop** (8:30am-5:30pm daily) and the **Ice Cream Café** (noon-5pm daily) serve fresh treats. The **Creamery** (11am-7pm Sun.-Thurs., 10am-8pm Fri.-Sat.) is the place for sandwiches and hand-dipped ice cream in Antler Hill Village. If you have a hankering for barbecue, a quick sandwich, some snacks, or a cold drink, the **Smokehouse** (noon-5pm daily) in Antler Hill Village serves just what you need.

While you're in Antler Hill Village,

check out the newest addition to the Biltmore's food offerings, **Cedric's Tavern** (11am-9pm daily, lunch $15-21, dinner $17-30). Named for George Vanderbilt's beloved Saint Bernard (you can see his huge collar on display at the entrance), Cedric's pays homage to pubs and taverns found in Britain, with a Southern twist. The fish-and-chips and scotch egg are both delicious. You can also grab a pint of Cedric's Pale or Brown Ale, both brewed by the Biltmore Brewing Company.

Information and Services

The **Asheville Visitors Center** (36 Montford Ave., near I-240 exit 4C, 828/258-6129, www.exploreasheville. com, 8:30am-5:30pm Mon.-Fri., 9am-5pm Sat.-Sun.) can set you up with all the maps, brochures, and recommendations you could need. In the same building, the **Asheville Area Chamber of Commerce** (36 Montford Ave., 828/258-6101, www. ashevillechamber.org, 8:30am-5pm Mon.-Fri.) is another source.

Listen to public radio at **WCQS** (88.1 FM) and **WNCW** (88.7 FM). **WTMT** (105.9 FM) and **WOXL** (98.1 FM) are music stations.

Mission Hospital (509 Biltmore Ave.; 428 Biltmore Ave., 828/213-1111, www. missionhospitals.org) in Asheville has two campuses and two emergency departments.

Blue Ridge Parkway Visitor Center (MP 384)

The **Blue Ridge Parkway Headquarters** (MP 384, 828/271-4779, www.nps.gov/ blri) are working park offices and offer very little to visitors. For an overview of the Blue Ridge Parkway, a gift shop, and as much information as you can handle regarding what to do, where to go, and how to get there on the Blue Ridge Parkway, try the **Blue Ridge Parkway Visitor Center** (828/298-5330, 9am-5pm daily, free). Here, a 22-foot long interactive map, displays on the history and heritage of the Parkway, and a great video (it runs about 25 minutes and is worth the wait and the watch) give you a better idea about the Parkway, but the real help comes from the desk operated by the Blue Ridge National Heritage Area (www.blueridgeheritage.com). They have information on the numerous cultural sites and happenings along the Parkway, and can provide you with directions and ideas for stops and side trips.

This building is notable for being certified Leadership in Energy Efficient Design (LEED) Gold by the U.S. Green Building Council. Energy-saving features include active/passive heating and cooling, a living roof planted with sedum, and other features designed to reduce everything from water use to nighttime lighting. All of this is in keeping with the founding principles that guided the construction of the Blue Ridge Parkway, the principles that said that the structures and buildings found in the park would have a natural look, blend in with their environments, and be generally kind to the earth nearby.

Visitor Center Loop Trail

Distance: 1.5-mile loop
Duration: 45 minutes
Elevation gain: 50 feet
Difficulty: easy to moderate
Trailhead: near the far end of the Visitor Center parking lot, near the bus and RV parking area

This popular trail was built by volunteers from the Carolina Mountain Club and Friends of the Blue Ridge Parkway to create a loop that incorporates part of the Mountains-to-Sea Trail. Not far in, you'll enter a bit of a clearing and begin to descend into the woods. Here, you'll find a rhododendron thicket and see that the ground is covered in English ivy. If you look close (and you should), you'll see poison ivy leaves here and there. Be wary, poison ivy is everywhere on this hike. But the trail is well traveled, so if you stick to the path, you should be rash free.

As you near the half-mile mark, you'll need to cross the Blue Ridge Parkway. Be quick and be safe when you do. After crossing, you have a clear hike until you reach the 0.75-mile mark when you reach the top of a small rise. Take a drink and a picture, and head on down the trail until you reach the fork where the Mountains-to-Sea Trail breaks off. This is 1.1 miles in, so you're close to the end. (If you continued on the Mountains-to-Sea Trail, in 2.5 miles you'd reach the Folk Art Center.) Continue on, pass under the parkway via a stone culvert, and stroll back to the starting point.

★ US-Alt 74 East: Chimney Rock (MP 384.7)

Chimney Rock State Park (US-64/74A, Chimney Rock, N.C., about 45 from Asheville at MP 384.7 via US-Alt 74 East,

800/277-9611, www.chimneyrockpark.com, ticket plaza open 8:30am-5:30pm daily Mar.-Oct., 8:30am-4:30pm daily Nov., 10am-4:30pm Fri.-Tues. early-Dec.-Christmas Eve, 10am-4:30pm Christmas-New Year's Eve, 10am-4:30pm Fri.-Tues. Jan.-late Mar., $15 adults, $7 ages 5-15, 4 and under free) is just one of the many geological beauties you'll find along the Blue Ridge Parkway corridor. The 315-foot tower of stone that is Chimney Rock stands on the side of the mountain. To get to the top of the chimney, you can take a 26-story elevator ride, or hike the **Outcroppings Trail,** a 0.25-mile trail nicknamed "The Ultimate Stairmaster." No matter how you get there, the view is spectacular.

There are number of additional dizzying views to take in and mountain hugging trails to hike in Chimney Rock State Park. The **"Needle's Eye"** and **"Opera Box"** are two such formations. The **Hickory Nut Falls Trail** takes you to the top of the 400-foot Hickory Nut Falls

the Blue Ridge Parkway Visitor Center and Headquarters at Milepost 384 via a moderately difficult 0.75-mile trail. One of the most recognizable views is on the **Skyline-Cliff Trail** loop, a strenuous two-hour hike that will take you to some places you may recognize from the 1992 film *The Last of the Mohicans*. There are also kid-friendly trails. Bring your little ones along on the 0.6-mile **Woodland Walk,** where animal sculptures and "journal entries" from Grady the Groundhog wait to be discovered. A trail map covering the entire park is available at the park's website (www.chimneyrockpark.com).

Chimney Rock is more than just hiking trails. In November, Santa rappels down the tower in a pre-Christmas display of his chimney-navigating prowess, but year-round you'll find rock climbers in the park for bouldering, top-rope, and multi-pitch climbs. Want to try but don't know the terms? **Fox Mountain Guides** (888/284-8433, www.foxmountainguides.com, lessons from $45 for two hours, $160-195 for half- and full-day novice climbs) will gear you up and show you the ropes.

Nearby **Rumbling Bald Mountain** (Boys Camp Rd., Lake Lure) was recently made part of Chimney Rock State Park, and climbers couldn't be happier. Here you'll find more than 1,500 bouldering "problems" (a form of low-altitude, ropeless climb that often traverses a rock face) to solve (solving it means traversing it successfully). Currently, only the south face is open to climb and no commercial climbing guides are allowed to operate there.

Rumbling Bald and Chimney Rock are the sites of some strange phenomenon over the centuries. In January 1947, Bald Mountain began giving off low rumbles that grew louder and louder as spring wore on. Then, just as the crocuses were showing their heads, the mountain gave a tremendous shake that shattered windows and knocked crockery off shelves all along the valley. A smoking, hissing crack opened in the side of the mountain, causing many to move away or find religion.

In the early 1800s, locals and visitors reported spectral sights on and above Chimney Rock. There they saw groups of people gathered on the rock pinnacle rise into the heavens and disappear. They also saw, on several occasions, two cavalry armies battling on winged horses in the air over the summit.

At least that's how the stories go.

North Carolina Arboretum (MP 393)

The enormous **North Carolina Arboretum** (100 Frederick Law Olmstead Way, Asheville, 828/665-2492, www.ncarboretum.org, 8am-9pm daily Apr.-Oct., 8am-7pm daily Nov.-Mar., greenhouse 8am-2pm Mon.-Fri., free, parking $12) is considered by many to be one of the most beautiful arboretums in the country. The

Day Trip to Carl Sandburg's Home

In 1945, American poet Carl Sandburg moved his family to the picturesque mountains of North Carolina. He wasn't seeking inspiration for his writing, he was simply seeking the best place for his wife to raise her herd of prize-winning Chikaming goats. At the 264-acre Connemara Farm, he found both.

This is where Sandburg wrote around one-third of his body of work; received his second Pulitzer Prize, the International United Poets Laureate award, and the Presidential Medal of Freedom; and passed away at the age of 89. Today you can experience the solitude and muse this poet, journalist, storyteller, folk singer, and goat raiser found at the **Carl Sandburg Home National Historic Site** (81 Carl Sandburg Ln., Flat Rock, NC, parking area at 1800 Little River Rd. across from the Flat Rock Playhouse, 828/693-4178, www.nps.gov/carl, 9am-5pm daily, closed Thanksgiving, Christmas, and New Year's Day, house tour $5 adults, $3 seniors ages 62 and over, free for 15 and under).

Tour the house and see more than 65,000 artifacts, including more than 12,000 books and the desk and office where Sandburg worked. The farm still operates a small dairy and the National Parks Service raises goats like the ones Mrs. Sandburg raised; you can find their milk in specialty stores in Flat Rock.

Connemara and the Carl Sandburg Site are crowded in fall, as the more than five miles of hiking trails that crisscross the farm come alive with leaf peepers. It's worth the stop in any season, however, as spring and summer wildflowers and winter's snow compliment Sandburg's literary legacy.

Reaching Connemara and the Carl Sandburg Site is easy from both Asheville and the Blue Ridge Parkway. From Asheville, head south out of town on McDowell Street/US-25; at Biltmore Forest, merge onto Hendersonville Street/US-25 and continue along this road. Merge on US-74/I-26 East and follow the signs to Flat Rock and the Historic Site. From the Blue Ridge Parkway, exit at Milepost 388.8 and turn south on Hendersonville Road and follow the same route. Expect a drive of around 45 minutes and 27 miles from downtown Asheville; 30 minutes and 22 miles from the Blue Ridge Parkway.

---

434 natural and landscaped acres back into the Pisgah National Forest, just off Blue Ridge Parkway. Major collections include the National Native Azalea Repository and the very special Bonsai Collection, where staff horticulturists care for over 200 bonsais, many of their own creation.

Bicycles and leashed dogs are permitted on many of the trails. Walking areas range from easy to fairly rugged, but with 10 miles of trail to choose from, it's no problem finding one that suits your skill level. **Guided tours** (1pm Tues. and Sat.) give you more on the history of the arboretum and its plants, as well as the natural history of the region. These two-mile walk and talk tours go on rain or shine, so dress to the weather. The arboretum also has a very nice café, the **Savory Thyme Café** (11am-4pm Tues.-Sat., noon-4pm Sun., $6-10) and gift shop, **Connections Gallery** (11am-4pm daily).

Lake Powhatan (MP 393)

At Milemarker 393, the Blue Ridge Parkway crosses over the French Broad River. Exit here, at Brevard Road/NC-191, and you're not far from the **Lake Powhatan Recreation Area and Campground**, the **Bent Creek Experimental Forest**, the **Shut-in Trail,** and **Zen Tubing.** Stop and hike or bike the day away, then go for a relaxing float on the river before retiring to your campsite.

Lake Powhatan Recreational Area

Lake Powhatan Recreational Area and Campground (375 Wesley Branch Rd., Asheville, 877/444-6777 for reservations, 828/670-5627 for local information, www.recreation.gov, open Apr.-Nov., campsites $22/single campsite, $44/double, RV hookups campsite fee plus $3/water and sewer, $6/electric, $9 combined; dump station $10-50, day use $2/person) is surrounded by the 6,000-acre Bent Creek Experimental Forest and miles of **mountain biking** and **hiking** trails. There are 97 **campsites** here, each with a picnic table, tent pad, and fire ring; a bathhouse outfitted with hot showers and flush toilets; and a lifeguard-protected beach and swimming lake. Downtown Asheville is just 10 minutes away, so if you're hungry for something you didn't cook yourself, if you're here for a concert, or if you just want to go out on the town, it's not far. Quiet hours begin at 10pm nightly, at which time the gates are closed and locked. If you plan on being out after the gates are closed, be sure to let someone know and you can make accommodations to get back in.

Bent Creek Experimental Forest

Surrounding Lake Powhatan is the **Bent Creek Experimental Forest** (1577 Brevard Rd., Asheville, 828/667-5261, www.srs.fs.usda.gov/bentcreek/). You may be wondering what exactly is an experimental forest. Well, it's a designated forest that's part of ongoing research on silvicultural practices that help in the development of new forest management practices. Bent Creek is the oldest federal experimental forest east of the Mississippi, and the research done here has helped sustain or rehabilitate hundreds of thousands of acres of forest in the United States alone.

top to bottom: Chimney Rock; Hickory Nut Falls in Chimney Rock State Park; covered bridge near Chimney Rock

As cool as an experimental forest is, the thing that draws most visitors here are the **hiking** and **mountain biking** trails, many of which allow **horseback riders** as well. Before you set off on any trail, note if it allows your chosen mode of exploration. And remember to bring water, your camera, and bug spray, and, if you can, a bag for any litter you find on the trail.

Hiking
Homestead Trail

Distance: 1 mile one-way
Duration: 30 minutes
Elevation gain: 30 feet
Difficulty: easy
Trailhead: near the campsites on the shore of Lake Powhatan

The Homestead Trail takes you along the shores of Lake Powhatan, past the dam, and then downstream beside Bent Creek. It's a flat, easy hike, despite a couple of footbridges and wet patches, and offers several opportunities for great photos of the lake, especially in the fall.

Small Creek Trail

Distance: 0.5 miles one-way
Duration: 15 minutes
Elevation gain: 150 feet
Difficulty: easy to moderate
Trailhead: on the Homestead Trail

On the Homestead Trail, when you pass the beach and cross Small Creek, the trail splits. Stay left for Homestead, but go right to explore the Small Creek Trail and connect to Deerfield Loop. Though Small Creek is short, it does gain a little elevation as it rises through rhododendron and mountain laurel thickets.

Deerfield Loop Trail

Distance: 0.8-mile loop
Duration: 25 minutes
Elevation gain: 250 feet
Difficulty: easy to moderate
Trailhead: off Small Creek Trail or near the start of Homestead Trail

This short loop can be made longer by combining parts of Homestead and Small Creek Trails, but on its own, it's a quick workout with a couple of steep spots (not too steep, they'll just slow you down). There is a portion where the trail ducks into a mountain cove, traversing a steep slope and a slippery spring or seep as it does so. Just use a little caution in spots where it's wet or steep and you'll do just fine.

Pine Tree Loop Trail

Distance: 2-mile loop
Duration: 1 hour
Elevation gain: 200 feet
Difficulty: easy to moderate
Trailhead: near Wesley Branch Road after it crosses Bent Creek but before it reaches Lake Powhatan

This two-mile loop takes you up the hill above Bent Creek through a mixed forest of hardwoods and the rhododendron that grows everywhere here. As you climb, you'll cross one of Bent Creek's feeder streams before gaining a little more elevation and then passing by the origins of this stream about halfway up the mountain. As you return, you'll find a couple of places where the trees open up, especially in spring and fall, to reveal the valley you're in. For the last leg of this trail, you join with Deerfield Loop until you get back to Lake Powhatan.

Lower Sidehill Trail

Distance: 3.5 miles one-way
Duration: 1.5-2 hours
Elevation gain: 400 feet
Difficulty: moderate
Trailhead: near Boyd Branch Trailhead parking area on Bent Creek Gap Road
Directions: Bent Creek Gap Road is the continuation of Wesley Branch Road. As you leave the campground at Lake Powhatan, turn left after you cross Ledford Branch at the place where you meet Wesley Branch Road, this will put you on Bent Creek Gap Road; the trailhead is just over one mile away.

The Lower Sidehill Trail is hilly, but not too difficult. It follows a number of old roads—logging and forestry roads, most likely—as it climbs smaller hills on the north end before hitting a steeper section on the south end. Along the way it passes through a range of forest types, from hardwoods to dry oak and pine to moist hemlock and other cove-found hardwoods like sycamore. Of course you'll see more of the mountain laurel and rhododendron that loves this area. This trail feels pretty remote, even though you're never far from a road or either end of the trail.

Once you reach the south end of the trail, you can reverse direction or walk back along Bent Creek Gap Road, a pleasant, flat stroll through the woods alongside the namesake creek.

Shut-In Trail

Shut-In Trail is an old one, dating back to around 1890 when George Vanderbilt, of the Biltmore Estate, established this trail to link his hunting lodge at Buck Springs, just below the summit of Mount Pisgah, to his estate. When the Blue Ridge Parkway came through, parts of the trail were lost, but the pieces that remain follow the original track. The trail earns its name from the "tunnels" the path forms through the dense rhododendron and mountain laurel thickets, giving it a close, "shut-in" feeling.

You can use this trail as a long-distance hike, but considering there's no overnight camping along the Parkway, it would be brutal. At 16.3 miles with around 3,000 feet of elevation gain, to tackle the whole trail in one go is a feat best left to ultra-hikers and long-distance trail-runners. Here, the trail is broken down into hikeable sections, using the access points to Shut-In Trail along the Blue Ridge Parkway as convenient shuttle points and starting areas:

French Broad River to Walnut Cove Overlook

Distance: 3.1 miles one-way
Duration: 2-2.5 hours
Elevation gain: 800 feet
Difficulty: moderate to strenuous
Trailhead: just off the exit at MP 393.6

Directions: There is a very small parking area on the exit ramp, but you may want to park at the Bent Creek River and Picnic Park, a few hundred yards south on NC-191 from the Parkway ramp. There, a short trail (only a few hundred feet long) takes you to the Shut-In Trail.

This first segment of the Shut-In Trail isn't as shut in by the rhododendron thickets like the rest of the trail, and, in fact, the forest here is quite open. The Mountains-to-Sea Trail follows the Shut-In Trail all the way to Mount Pisgah, so you may encounter some thru-hikers.

About a quarter mile into the Shut-In Trail, you'll find your first "tunnel" through the mountain laurel. When you emerge, it's time to ascend, and quick. The trail is steep here, but manageable as it climbs to an old road. In the late fall, winter, and early spring, you can see the river from here. The road continues to climb, then gradually descends into a hardwood forest. At just over a mile in, you'll encounter a second road; bear left and follow this road up to another road (at 1.6 miles in) and descend to mile 1.8, where you'll turn onto yet another road that parallels the Blue Ridge Parkway.

Two miles in, you'll encounter your last left turn and immediately the road will begin a series of switchbacks as it climbs the mountain. Be wary of poison ivy here as it tends to be prolific. As you descend from these heights, you'll find the road and trail are broad and tree-lined, giving the sense of a lush, manicured forest. Continue through these woods until you reach the Blue Ridge Parkway at 3.1 miles in. A right turn on the Parkway takes you to Milepost 396.4 and the Walnut Cove Overlook.

Walnut Cove Overlook to Sleepy Gap Overlook

Distance: 1.8 miles one-way
Duration: 1.25-1.5 hours
Elevation gain: 200 feet
Difficulty: moderate
Trailhead: MP 396.4 at the Walnut Cove Overlook

You're past the roads on this part of the

Shut-In Trail. Here, the trail is, well, more trail like, so take a little more care with how and where you step. For the first 0.75 miles, be wary of the poison ivy, which grows quite heartily here. At 1.25 miles in, you'll come to an intersection. This is the Grassy Knob Trail, connecting the Shut-In Trail to part of the Bent Creek trail system. Keep to the left and continue on to cross a small creek—it may be dry in summer months—then another even smaller water feature before you enter the final tunnel of mountain laurel. On the other side, you're not far from the Sleepy Gap Overlook at Milepost 397.3.

Sleepy Gap Overlook to Chestnut Cove Overlook

Distance: 0.9 miles one-way
Duration: 45-60 minutes
Elevation gain: 600 feet
Difficulty: moderate to strenuous
Trailhead: MP 397.3 at the Sleepy Gap Overlook

Here, you'll find that the hardwoods are enormous, taking on proportions that may surprise you. They remind me of the Forest Moon of Endor from *Return of the Jedi*. This short trail has a steep ascent and descent around 0.6 miles in, but the end point—Chestnut Cove Overlook at Milepost 398.3—isn't far.

Chestnut Cove Overlook to Bent Creek Gap

Distance: 2.8 miles one-way
Duration: 1.5-1.75 hours
Elevation gain: 200 feet
Difficulty: strenuous
Trailhead: MP 398.3 at the Chestnut Cove Overlook

Starting from Chestnut Cove Overlook you may be wondering which are the chestnut trees. You'll be hard pressed to find one as a blight that was accidentally introduced here from Asia destroyed the trees by the end of the 1930s. Chestnuts made up around 25 percent of the trees in many areas and it's hard to imagine the richness of these woods if they'd lived.

Here, the Shut-In Trail earns its name. The thickets of mountain laurel and rhododendron form tunnels and passageways for much of the trail as it descends into Chestnut Cove. The effect is one of isolation. Though you're close to the Parkway and not far from civilization, the sounds of the forest overtake the intermittent road sounds and you feel very remote.

For the first 1.5 miles, give or take, you'll find yourself on a slow, gradual descent that takes you in and out of the "tunnels" and patches of hardwood forest. At 1.1 miles in, you'll encounter a woods road; stay to the left and cross a creek at 1.4 miles, then it's back into the "tunnels" for the long ascent out. You'll cross two more streams, at 2 and 2.4 miles, and continue on through the rhododendron tunnels. As you near the 2.8-mile mark, you'll find Forest Service Road 479 and Bent Tree Gap. Blue Ridge Parkway Milepost 400.3 is just to the left.

Bent Creek Gap to Big Ridge Overlook

Distance: 4 miles one-way
Duration: 2.5-2.75 hours
Elevation gain: 700 feet
Difficulty: strenuous
Trailhead: MP 400.3 Bent Creek Gap

This section combines three smaller, more strenuous sections of the Shut-In Trail. The first takes us from Bent Creek Gap to the Beaver Dam Gap Overlook at Milepost 401.7, and it gives us a truly wide view of the countryside.

The trail ascends from Forest Service Road 479 near the Bent Creek Experimental Forest Sign; a short way in—about 250 feet—you'll turn onto an old road. A half mile in, you'll pass a spring with some cold and tasty water, but if you're there at the end of an especially dry or hot summer, you'll be out of luck. Continue climbing until you summit Ferrin Knob, where you have a great view to the northeast. At 1.5 miles in, you'll find yourself in the midst of a wildflower-choked gab. Enjoy it for a moment before descending to the Beaver Dam Gap Overlook at Milepost 401.7.

From here to the Stoney Bald Overlook is only 0.9 miles, but it's a tough stretch. The trail sticks close to the Parkway, but rises and falls quite steeply. Expect about 300 feet of elevation gain and loss as you crest knobs and ridges. A quarter mile in, be mindful of the poison ivy, but pay some attention to the exquisite craftsmanship that went into the rock cribbing stabilizing the hillside along the trail as you crest a high point. Descend to a low point where you'll find violets and other wildflowers and ascend again. Once you reach the ridgeline at 0.7 miles in, you'll descend the final 0.2 miles through switchbacks lined with buttercups and orchids to the Stoney Bald Overlook at Milepost 402.6.

On the final leg of this segment, the trail is more of the same: a couple of steepish sections and some wildflowers. You'll ascend immediately on this trail, and continue to climb for 0.4 miles until you reach the top of a knoll and descend. At 0.7 miles, you'll cross the Blue Ridge Parkway (be careful) and continue through until you reach the Big Ridge Overlook at Milepost 403.6.

Big Ridge Overlook to the Mount Pisgah Trailhead

Distance: 4.2 miles one-way
Duration: 2.75-3 hours
Elevation gain: 1,100 feet
Difficulty: moderate to strenuous
Trailhead: Big Ridge Overlook at MP 403.6

The final leg of the Shut-In Trail is made up of three segments. The first two are easier than the last, but the payoff is worth the effort. Keep in mind, though, that you can stop at any of the overlooks to shorten your hike if you're running low on daylight.

From the Big Ridge Overlook to Mills River Valley-Elk Pasture Gap is a pretty easy 1.1 miles. The first half of the trail is mostly flat, but 0.5 miles in you begin a steady, and increasing, ascent. Along the way, you'll pass assorted wildflowers and even blueberries (if they're in season, try

a few). A narrow ridgeline awaits at 0.8 miles in.

Like the last segment, this one features one short but steep ascent, the rest of the elevation gain is hardly noticeable. A little more than a quarter mile in, you'll pass a spring where you can refill your water bottle. Closer to the end of the section, you'll find some great trail-building work in the rock walls supporting the trail. Imagine hauling the stone to build that wall on your back. The trail just got a little easier, didn't it? Take a break at Mills River Valley-Elk Pasture Gap at Milepost 404.5; the toughest section is ahead.

If you're itching to get to Mount Pisgah, skip a couple of sections and jump right to Elk Pasture Gap. Here, at the Mills River Valley-Elk Pasture Gap (MP 404.5), you're at an elevation of about 4,200 feet. You'll climb to around 5,000 in under two miles, so get ready. Is it worth it? You bet. The views of Mount Pisgah and other peaks and valleys are worth framing (especially in fall), and there are a couple of berry patches along the way.

You'll start climbing immediately once you leave Mills River Valley-Elk Pasture Gap. Climb steadily for 0.35 miles where you reach the top of a knob. Then descend to a wide, flat gap. Then, another steep ascent at 0.7 miles with a break at 0.8 miles for a photo op of Mills River Valley to the east. Continue climbing until you begin to level out near the large patch of wild berries. The next 0.2 miles are relatively level, but then you climb again, and hard. As the elevation changes, so does the vegetation. The plants are smaller and scrubbier here than they were just a few hundred feet below. When you reach the ridgeline at 1.5 miles, you'll be rewarded with a view to the east and Mount Pisgah above and to your right. Climb a small knob (with the scantest of views from the top) and descend into a thicket of mountain laurel and hike on another 0.3 miles to the Mount Pisgah Trailhead parking area at Milepost 407.6. This is the proverbial end of the Shut-In Trail.

Water Sports

How about floating down the French Broad River, feet in the water, relaxing on an inner tube? **Zen Tubing** (1648 Brevard Rd., Asheville, 855/936-8823, mid-May-early Sept., 9:30am-7:30pm daily, trips run between 10am and 4pm, $20 adults, $15 12 and under, minimum age 4, $5 cooler carrier, $5 for same-day second trip) does just that. With single and double inner tubes and even cooler-carrier inner tubes available, it's BYOB if you choose to imbibe (no glass and be responsible with your empties). It's easy to get a group out on the water for a 1.5-2.5-hour float. Once you pay and go over some safety basics, Zen Tubing shuttles you to their put-in a few miles away. There, you back down some steps into the river and flop onto your tube. The river around here is rapid-less, so there's little to worry about other than sunburn.

Mount Pisgah (MP 408.6)

At one time, Mount Pisgah was owned by the Vanderbilts, and their estate stretched from the Biltmore Estate, some 16 miles distant in Asheville to this 5,721-foot summit. The mountain and the land between here and the Biltmore were used as a private hunting retreat. Accessing Mount Pisgah is easy from the Blue Ridge Parkway. At Milepost 408.6, you'll find the **Mount Pisgah Campground** and, across the Parkway, the **Pisgah Inn.**

Hiking

A network of trails and connectors circle Mount Pisgah. The two below are highly recommended.

Mount Pisgah Summit Trail

Distance: 2.6 miles round-trip
Duration: 2-2.5 hours

Elevation gain: 750 feet
Difficulty: moderate to strenuous
Trailhead: Mount Pisgah Trailhead (MP 407.7)

The view from the summit of Mount Pisgah is well worth the effort you'll put into getting up here. It can be strenuous, especially if you're not in the best shape, but it's hikeable if you take your time. Note that the elevation gain is about 200 feet in the first half of the hike and a little more than 500 in the second half. At times, this trail is steep.

You'll start the hike on Little Pisgah Mountain, where you'll eventually crest a ridge between Little Pisgah and Mount Pisgah. This is where it gets more difficult and many people turn back. Ahead, the trail follows the ridgeline and becomes a bit steeper before it cuts away from the ridge onto a very steep section with several difficult step-ups and rocky sections that are a little nerve wracking if you're not an experienced hiker. This is the steepest section, so if you can do this, you've pretty much summited.

After this steep section, you'll enter a mountain laurel tunnel that's long and rocky. The trail turns, switches back, and follows a new ridge to the summit as it passes through an impressive stand of beech trees.

Once on top, you'll see the transmission tower for WLOS-TV and an observation deck. Though the deck is nice, it and the giant metal tower pull you out of the nature moment and into the modern world, but the view from here is spectacular. To the west, you'll see the Shining Rock Wilderness and Cold Mountain (at the northern end) and, on clear days, the Smoky Mountains in the distance. To the north is Asheville, Craggy Mountains, Mount Mitchell, and if you're keen-eyed, the Biltmore Estate.

Buck Spring Trail

Distance: 6 miles one-way
Duration: 4 hours
Elevation gain: 500 feet
Difficulty: easy to moderate

Trailhead: behind the Pisgah Inn

This trail runs from the Pisgah Inn down the mountain to US-276, making for a long 12-mile out-and-back, and the back part, that's all uphill, so keep that in mind as you're planning how far to go and how much water to bring with you.

Some folks have called this an ideal walking path or the perfect hike. After a short section of moderately steep trail, things even out and the grade becomes so gradual, you won't notice that you're descending. Don't expect mountain vistas on this hike, it's all downhill and never really pops out to a bald or clearing with any kind of view. It does, however, have more than a dozen stream crossings, meaning the little waterfalls, pools, and cascades you'll see, many ringed with rich beds of ferns, moss, and wildflowers, which more than make up for the lost view.

Hike the trail as far as you want, but remember that it is all uphill on the way back, so it will take a little longer and tax you a little more, but most everyone should be able to enjoy a nice long, peaceful hike in the woods on this trail.

Accommodations

Up on the Blue Ridge Parkway above Waynesville and quite close to Asheville is the fantastic **Pisgah Inn** (MP 408.6, 828/235-8228, www.pisgahinn.com, Apr.-Oct., from $128), which is much like Skyland and Big Meadows on Virginia's Skyline Drive, with motel-style accommodations surrounding an old lodge with a large family-style dining room and a Parkway gift shop. The inn is on a nearly 5,000-foot-high mountaintop, so the view is sensational. Trails lead from the inn to short pretty strolls and challenging daylong hikes. The restaurant (7:30am-10:30am, 11:30am-4pm, and 5pm-9pm daily, $3-27) has a mesmerizing view and an appetizing and varied menu of both country cooking and upscale meals. The guest rooms are simple but comfortable, each with their own balcony and rocking chairs overlooking the valley, and with a TV but no telephone. The Pisgah is a perfect spot for resting, reading, and porchsitting, but it's quite kitchy, and I hope someone helps restore it to its potential.

Camping

The **Mount Pisgah Campground** (MP 408, Canton, N.C., reservations 877/444-6777, local information 828/648-2644, www.recreation.gov, early May-late Oct., campsites $16-19) has more than 60 tent-only and RV campsites. Note that although there are some modern amenities like flush toilets and drinking water, there is no electricity, water, or sewer hookups for RVs. Also, take caution with food storage and disposal as black bears frequent the area.

Food

Despite the shortcomings of the accommodations, the **Pisgah Inn Restaurant** (MP 408.6, 828/235-8228, www.pisgahinn.com, 7:30am-10:30am, 11:30am-4pm, and 5pm-9pm daily Apr.-Oct., $3-27) dishes up some tasty grub. Breakfast ranges from light to hearty, depending on what you want and what you're up to that day; lunch ranges from salads to barbecue to burgers; and dinner runs the gamut from steaks and mountain trout to chicken pot pie and the Pisgah Pasta—garlic and white wine cream sauce, fresh tomatoes, mushrooms, and spinach over pasta, served plain or with chicken or shrimp.

Cold Mountain Overlook (MP 412)

Cold Mountain is a massif everyone in these parts has known about for years, but one that was popularized in the outside world by Charles Frazier's 1997 novel and the 2003 Academy Award-winning film, *Cold Mountain*. Frazier set his historical novel in the land of his kin, and based characters on his ancestors, but one of the largest, most looming characters is certainly the mountain and the land around it. View the famed mountain from the Cold Mountain Overlook at Milepost 411.8, or, even better, from Milepost 412.2. Pull off at the Wagon Gap Road parking area (you may recognize Wagon Gap from the book) and walk north along the Parkway a short distance for a fantastic view of the mountain. When you look at it, you may say, "It didn't look like this in the movie." That's because the film was shot in Romania, not western North Carolina.

The 6,030-foot Cold Mountain has a well-earned name. This section of the Parkway is closed for much of the winter and often well into spring. According to Blue Ridge Parkway sources, most closures are from November through March and sometimes well into April. Be sure to check the closure map (www.nps.gov/blri/; click the Road Closures link).

For another great look at Cold Mountain, you can hike to the top of Mount Pisgah via the Mount Pisgah Summit Trail. And you can do more than just admire Cold Mountain from a distance—you can climb it. There's no direct access to the trail from the Parkway, but you can reach it from the Art Loeb Trail.

US-276 South: Pisgah Ranger District and Brevard (MP 412)

Wending through the mountain roads between Waynesville and Brevard, and easily accessible from the Blue Ridge Parkway at Milepost 412, US-276 carries you right into the **Shining Rock Wilderness**, a part of the larger **Pisgah National Forest**. Is it worth the drive? You bet. As part of the 79-mile **Forest Heritage Scenic Byway** (a loop that twice crosses the Parkway as it circles the Pisgah National Forest), it's simply

mountain mists near Brevard

spectacular. Continue down the Scenic Byway to reach the town of Brevard, just 18.5 miles off the Parkway. From the Parkway, it will take you around 30 minutes of driving along this beautiful, waterfall-laced road to reach downtown Brevard. Simply follow US-276 South to US-64 West and you're there.

Before you turn off the Blue Ridge Parkway and onto the Forest Heritage Scenic Byway, stop at Milepost 411 at the **Cradle of Forestry Overlook.** Here you can see **Looking Glass Rock,** a smooth, bald bit of near-white rock that's quite distinct as it shines through the surrounding green. In the fall, it's a sight, especially when the trees are in their full blaze of color.

Pisgah Ranger District
Sights
Pisgah Ranger Station
Just south of the Parkway in the town of Pisgah Forest is the **Pisgah Ranger Station** (off US-276, 828/877-3265, www.

cfaia.org/nc-pisgah-visitor-center.php, 9am-5pm daily mid-Apr.-mid-Nov., 8:30am-4:30pm daily mid-Nov.-mid-Apr.). The ranger station is the main entrance to the **Pisgah Ranger District,** which is part the Pisgah National Forest. The forest covers half a million acres, a large swath of western North Carolina, but the 157,000-acre ranger district encompasses many of the forest's favorite attractions. A good topographical map of the ranger district is available from National Geographic (www.natgeo-maps.com/ti_780). The ranger district has more than 275 miles of hiking trails.

Cradle of Forestry
If you have kids with you, make your first stop off the Parkway the **Cradle of Forestry** (US-276, Pisgah Forest, 828/877-3130, www.cradleofforestry. com, 9am-5pm daily mid-Apr.-early Nov., $5 adults, free for 15 and under), a museum and activity complex commemorating the rise of the forestry profession in the United States, which originated here at a turn-of-the-20th-century training school in the forests once owned by George Washington Vanderbilt, master of Biltmore. Plow days and living history days throughout the year give an interesting glimpse into this region's old-time methods of farming and frontier living. Self-guided trails lead through the woods to many interesting locations of this campus of America's first school of forestry. Most of what's here is geared toward little ones.

Sliding Rock
Not to be confused with Shining Rock, **Sliding Rock** (off US-276, 7.2 miles from the Parkway) is an easily accessible waterfall and swimming spot with a parking lot ($1 fee), bathhouse, and lifeguards (10:30am-6pm daily Memorial Day-Labor Day). You can actually ride down the 60-foot waterfall, a smooth rock face (not so smooth that you shouldn't wear sturdy britches) over which 11,000 gallons

of water rush every minute into the chilly swimming hole below. How chilly? It's a breathtaking 55°F in the summer. Given its proximity to the Cradle of Forestry— it's just four miles south—it's worth a stop with a car full of kids, especially if they are adventurous, even daredevilish, and outdoorsy.

Looking Glass Falls

This is the land of waterfalls, and here's a chance to see a beaut. The 60-foot **Looking Glass Falls** (off US-276, 9.3 miles from the Parkway) plunges over a granite face into a deep, and cold, swimming hole. Looking Glass Falls is both kid-friendly and **wheelchair accessible** (at least to the upper overlook); that and its proximity to the Blue Ridge Parkway make it the perfect quickie waterfall. There are a number of beautiful waterfalls in North Carolina and this is one the best. The proportions of the falls and the lush vegetation around it are reminiscent of Oahu's Waimea Falls.

Hiking
Looking Glass Rock Trail
Distance: 6.2 miles round-trip
Duration: 4 hours
Elevation gain: 1,650 feet
Effort: moderate to strenuous
Trailhead: on Forest Road 475, just south of Looking Glass Falls
Directions: Just down the road from Looking Glass Falls, heading toward Brevard, you'll pass National Forest Road 475 on your right. Turn here. In less than a half mile you'll find the Looking Glass Rock trailhead.

This is a great out-and-back hike. There's only one trail at the trailhead, and it goes straight to the top, making this a fairly easy trail to follow. The elevation gain will test your legs as you ascend and as you descend. Bring plenty of water and a snack, and dress appropriately for the weather.

The trail opens beside a small stream. Cross it and ascend through a hemlock forest. After crossing the creek, you'll top a small ridge and head into a cove on the other side. Here you'll find a larger stream with a few pretty, but small, cascades. Continue climbing.

Soon after you find the second stream, you'll encounter the first of many switchbacks. Notice that the forest has grown sparser and the view has opened up. As you climb higher, the trees will get shorter, with one notable exception that we'll get to in a moment. Soon the switchbacks will shorten, becoming tighter and more frequent as you climb up a small ridge.

When you're about a mile in, you'll reach a left-hand switchback with a large, magnificent Carolina hemlock at the tip. Behind the tree, the view opens up a bit more, revealing cliffs on the north face of the mountain. Be extremely careful if you go around the hemlock to ogle the cliffs; there's a sheer, very dangerous, 30-foot drop right behind the tree.

As you start to ascend again, you'll find that the cliffs you saw from the hemlock switchback form a sort of ring around the mountain. The trail gets steeper and rockier. This route is just about the only way up this mountain, save scaling the near vertical cliffs. The next set of switchbacks leads through this steep slope covered with Carolina hemlocks. These are different from the hemlock at the start of the trail. In fact, the Carolina Hemlock is only found in a small area around the Blue Ridge and Smoky Mountains in five states. Soon, though, these trees will all be dead due to an insect infestation.

After passing a campsite at the midway point of the hike, you'll enter an area where rhododendron and mountain laurel are more dominant. As the trail moves off the edge of the ridge you're following, you'll find a helipad painted with a large "H." It seems out of place, but even stranger is the carved signature Max Wilson left on the rock here, accompanied by the two dates he climbed to this rock in the 1930s and 1950s. The final push to the top of the mountain is steep and rocky, so watch your footing.

The round, flat summit is rather anti-climactic. For the real reason you came up here, walk a few more yards and pop out of the oak and rhododendron forest onto the top of the cliffs. The view is among the best in the area, but be careful—the surface can be slick.

Brevard

Brevard is the pleasant seat of the improbably named Transylvania County (it's not creepy, but beautiful in a very gothic forest sort of way). As you might expect, Halloween is a big deal in this town. Brevard is also known for sheltering a population of rather startling and odd-looking white squirrels. The local legend about their origin goes that their ancestors escaped from an overturned circus truck in Florida in 1940 and made their way to Brevard as pets. More likely, say researchers, is that they came from an exotic pet breeder in Florida, and were acquired by a Brevard area family. In any case, the white squirrels escaped into the wild of Transylvania County, and you'll probably see their descendants in the area when you visit.

Entertainment and Events

The **Brevard Music Center** (349 Andante Ln., 828/862-2100, www.brevardmusic.org) has attracted the highest-caliber young musicians for more than 70 years for intensive summer-long classical music instruction. Throughout the summer, Brevard Music Center students, as well as visiting soloists of international fame, put on a world-class concert series, performing works from Tchaikovsky to Gilbert and Sullivan.

Shopping

A center for a very different sort of music is **Celestial Mountain Music** (16 W. Main St., 828/884-3575, www.celestialmtnmusic.com, 10am-5:30pm Mon.-Fri., 10am-4pm Sat.). This nice little shop carries, among the usual wares of a good music store, two lines of very

special locally-made instruments. Cedar Mountain banjos, of the open-backed, old-time variety, are beautifully crafted and ring clear and pretty. The work of local fiddle builder Lyle Reedy is also sold at Celestial Mountain Music. His fiddles are handmade of a variety of fine woods and have a deep, biting sound loved by fiddlers. Musicians and woodworkers alike will enjoy a stop at this Main Street shop.

Brevard is also home to a number of artists, and if you're here for a quick bite and then it's back to the Parkway, take the time to stick your head in **Number 7 Fine Arts and Crafts Cooperative** (12 E. Main St., 828/883-2294, www.number-7arts.com, 10am-5pm Mon.-Sat., 1pm-4pm Sun.). This gallery has featured works by a diverse group of around 25 Transylvania County artists for more than 15 years. Many of the works are inspired by and created in the midst of the phenomenal nature here.

Accommodations

Slip back in time at the ★ **Sunset Motel** (523 S. Broad St., 828/884-9106, www.thesunsetmotel.com, $75-90). This kitschy motel is a throwback to the days of the classic roadside motel experience: it's cheap, comfortable, and has chairs right outside your door so you can visit with your neighbors (and they have the best modern convenience—free Wi-Fi). The staff is super friendly and ready to help with suggestions for places to eat and things to do. You can add on tickets to the Brevard Music Center, waterfall tours, and more when you book your room, so it's super convenient. And for film buffs, Robert Mitchum stayed here when he was filming *Thunder Road*.

The **Campbell House Bed and Breakfast** (243 W. Main St., 800/553-2853, www.campbellhousebrevard.com, from $159) was renovated in 2014 after a few years of neglect. The new owners didn't just return it to its former beauty, they surpassed it. The five rooms feature queen beds and private baths and, though none are suites, all are spacious. One of the innkeepers is an avid bicyclist, and uses Brevard as a base from which to ride. Though other accommodations in town are bicycle-friendly, Campbell House is the home of bicycle enthusiasts.

The Inn at Brevard (315 E. Main St., 828/884-2105, www.theinnatbrevard. com, $150-225) is spacious, beautiful, and kid-friendly. Their 14 rooms are well appointed and they serve a full breakfast.

Camping

Davidson River Campground (Davidson River Circle, reservations 800/444-6777, local information 828/862-5960, www. recreation.gov, open year-round, sites $22-44) is just outside of Brevard in the Shining Rock Wilderness Area. There are around 160 sites here, some with river access, but all have access to hot showers and flush toilets; each site comes equipped with a picnic table, fire ring, and grill. It's the most convenient campground for exploring the hiking and fishing in the area, as well as checking out the waterfalls here.

Just 10 minutes outside of Brevard, on 14 mountaintop acres is **Ash Grove Mountain Cabins and Camping** (749 East Fork Rd., Brevard, 828/885-7216, www.ash-grove.com, tents and RVs $27-44, cabins $115-165). This retreat is open year round, unlike others in the area, so you can experience all four seasons in this lovely spot. The cabins are quaint and cozy and the tent and RV sites are well maintained. Common areas include a bonfire pit, a few lawn games, and a tiny waterfall.

Just 12.5 miles south of downtown Brevard, **Black Forest Family Camping Resort** (280 Summer Rd., Cedar Mountain, 828/884-2267, www.blackforestcampground.com, Mar. 15-Nov. 15, limited facilities in winter, tent sites $31, RV sites $36, RV with full hookup $38-42, cabin $54) has 100 campsites that are level and, more importantly, shaded.

Nearby you'll find hiking, fishing, rock climbing, and mountain biking; but onsite, you'll find a playground complete with horseshoe pits, a large heated swimming pool, and a video arcade. There's also free Wi-Fi (a must these days, even if you're car camping).

Food

The Falls Landing Eatery (23 E. Main St., 828/884-2835, www.thefallslanding.com, lunch daily 11:30am-3pm, dinner daily 5pm-9pm, lunch $7-12, dinner $13-27) is a spot popular among locals. They specialize in seafood (foreshadowed by the rainbow trout on their sign), and their North Carolina trout sautéed in lemon butter and bourbon is particularly good. Don't discount their burgers, steaks, or lamb chops, though, because they deliver on flavor and value.

★ **Hobnob Restaurant** (192 W. Main St., 828/966-4662, www.hobnobrestaurant.com, lunch 11:30am-2:30pm daily, dinner 5pm-9pm daily, brunch 11am-2:30pm Sun., lunch $7-17, dinner $7-32, brunch $9-18) is one of the best places to eat in Brevard, and not just because the food is good, but because it's interesting. The sweet chili beurre blanc served with pan-seared salmon, or the seafood lasagna, and their fried green tomato caprese salad keep the menu accessible and fun.

One of the top restaurants in Brevard is **The Square Root** (33 Times Arcade Alley, 828/884-6171, www.squarerootrestaurant.com, lunch 11am-4pm Mon.-Sat., dinner 5pm-9pm Sun.-Thurs., 5pm-10pm Fri.-Sat., brunch 11am-3pm Sun., lunch around $10, dinner around $20, brunch around $10). Inside, the exposed brick walls create a warm room where the food is more like delicious art. Something as simple as a burger and onion rings comes out as a tower of food, and fine dinner entrées, like the five spice tuna or the filet mignon, are almost too pretty to eat. Almost.

For a quick bite or a shake, malt, or

ice cream soda, check out **Rocky's Grill and Soda Shop** (50 S. Broad St., 828/877-5375, 10am-5pm Mon.-Sat., 11:30am-6pm Sun.). This place has been around since 1942, and the nostalgic counter with its line of chrome stools takes you back to the heyday of this soda fountain. You can grab lunch for around $8, and for $5 or less you can get a malt, milkshake, ice cream soda, root beer float, and even egg creams (try one if you've never had one). It's a must stop, especially as a reward after a morning hike or bike ride.

Dupont State Forest

Transylvania County is known as the Land of Waterfalls, and with more than 250 in the area, it's a well-earned name. About 10 miles south of Brevard, **Dupont State Forest** (US-276, 828/877-6527, www.dupontforest.com) has more than 90 miles of hiking trails covering 10,000 acres. Some of Transylvania County's beautiful waterfalls are located within the forest and accessible by foot (most trails in the forest are moderate or strenuous) or, with special permits and advance reservation for people with disabilities only, by vehicle. Visitors should use caution, wear brightly-colored clothing, and leave their bearskin capes at home from September through the end of the year, when hikers share the woods with hunters.

Looking Glass Rock Overlook (MP 417)

Here, you'll have an impressive view of Looking Glass Rock, a mountain that's mostly bare rock that shines in the sun kind of like a looking glass.

Skinny Dip Falls Trail

Distance: 0.8 miles round-trip
Duration: 45 minutes
Elevation gain: 210 feet
Effort: moderate to strenuous

Trailhead: MP 417, across the Parkway from the Looking Glass Rock Overlook

This is a short hike with a tantalizing name, and if you're here during the right time of year and there's no one around, you can make sure that name was well earned with your own au natural swimming session at the base of the falls. If you do decide to dip more than a toe in the water, know that it's cold.

Start the hike by crossing the Parkway and ascending through a forest of oak, maple, and birch trees. Climb a set of steps and cross the Mountains-to-Sea Trail onto an old roadbed. Take this all the way to the falls. There are only a few spots where the trail gets rough with wet areas, eroded bits, and the typical rocks and roots, but other than that, the trail's about as easy as you'll find around here.

Cross a couple of bridges and go down another steep set of steps and you're here. The Yellowstone Prong runs right by and the three-tiered falls, each around 10 feet high, plunges down the cliffs. This is your chance to strip, dip, then drip dry on one of the small beaches or flat rocks.

Graveyard Fields Overlook (MP 418.8)

The East Fork Overlook at Milepost 418.3 gives you a great look back over the Shining Rock Wilderness. Look until you've had your fill and head down the road a half mile to Milepost 418.8 at the Graveyard Fields Loop Trail.

Graveyard Fields takes its name not from a literal graveyard, though if you've been vigilant, at several places along the Parkway you'll have seen little country churches and fence-ringed graveyards alongside them, but rather from the stumps left standing after decades of logging and a couple of raging forest fires. After the last, name-giving fire in 1942, the charred stumps looked like tombstones, hence the name.

Graveyard Fields Loop Trail

Distance: 2.2 miles round-trip
Duration: 1.5 hours
Elevation gain: 300 feet
Effort: easy to moderate
Trailhead: MP 418.8

The Graveyard Fields Loop Trail is easy and picturesque, and spur trails lead to two waterfalls, so during peak times (read: wildflower season and autumn), you may find parking at the trailhead difficult.

The trail begins on a paved trail through a thicket of mountain laurel and rhododendron. Soon the paving ends and the trail begins in earnest, crossing a small creek and then a rock outcropping with a small cave. This part of the trail is prone to eroding, so watch your step. Cross the river on the footbridge ahead and turn right on a short spur trail to the first waterfall, Yellowstone Falls, also called Lower Falls. Notice that the rock behind the falls is golden in the right light, giving the falls their name. As

you retrace your steps back to the footbridge, grab a handful of wild blueberries if they're in season.

Don't cross the bridge or your hike will be far too short. Instead, continue following the river upstream. Here, you're in the area known as Graveyard Fields. It's a wide expanse, dotted with wildflowers and berry bushes (wild blueberries, gooseberries, and blackberries), and is very pretty when the light is right.

Stay on this trail until you reach an intersection about 1.4 miles in. If you follow the trail to the right, you'll be on a path that's about 0.75 miles long, unmaintained, and steep. What's at the end? Upper Falls, an impressive sight and one worth seeing, but only if you're up to the task of following a potentially difficult trail. If you do head to Upper Falls it will add a little time to your hike as you must go up and then back down this steep section of trail.

The left-hand path at this intersection

Summers on the Parkway are spectacularly green.

loops back to the trailhead, crossing the river, part of which you'll need to boulder-hop or wade. Continue on the trail. When you reach a long log bridge over a marshy area, you're almost back to the start.

Devil's Courthouse
(MP 422.4)

According to Cherokee legend, this spot was the home of a giant, slope-eyed spirit named Judaculla. He's something like the Cherokee version of Sasquatch, so I'd worry more about snapping a picture if you find him holding court on this distinct rocky outcropping. Whether he's here or not, this little hike is well worth the effort.

Devil's Courthouse Trail
Distance: 0.9 miles round-trip
Duration: 45 minutes
Elevation gain: 150 feet

Effort: moderate to strenuous
Trailhead: MP 422.4

About half of this trail is paved, the other half is steep. After you pass through the spruce-fir forest, you'll pop out onto the gnarly rock outcropping that is Devil's Courthouse. It's a great place to watch for hawks and eagles riding the thermals in the valley below. It's also a great vantage point in general, providing a 360-degree view of the land around. Markers in the rock help you identify landmarks. Stay inside the designated area, though; if you don't, you risk a 200-foot sheer drop off the Courthouse.

US-215 North: Cold Mountain (MP 423.2)

Cold Mountain may not be the tallest (though it is more than 6,000 feet high) in the Blue Ridge, but its name is the most recognizable, thanks to Charles Frazier, novelist and native to western North Carolina. His novel, *Cold Mountain,* and the subsequent film adaptation, takes place here during the Civil War (and is based somewhat on his family history) and made the mountain known to those outside the region. You can view Cold Mountain from the Parkway (back at MP 411, 412, and many others) and from the summit of Mount Pisgah, but you can't drive to it. To reach the summit, or even its lower slopes, you'll have to hike in. It's tough, but beautiful, and as one of the highest peaks in the area, the views are well worth the effort.

Cold Mountain Summit Hike via the Art Loeb Trail
Distance: 10.6 miles round-trip
Duration: 6-7 hours
Elevation gain: 2,800 feet
Difficulty: strenuous
Trailhead: Daniel Boone Scout Camp
Directions: Take the exit at Parkway MP 423.2 and

follow NC-215 North for 13 miles. Turn right onto Little East Fork Road. Go 3.8 miles to the Daniel Boone Scout Camp. After you pass the last building, the trailhead is on the left.

Getting to the trailhead for the Cold Mountain Summit Hike seems like a hike in and of itself, but once you set foot on the trail, all of that disappears. Bring plenty of water, weather appropriate clothing (including something a little warmer for near the summit), something to eat (you'll be out here all day), a light, and a map.

Leaving the trailhead behind, you'll ascend via a series of switchbacks 1.1 miles to a ridgeline (and the first campsite if you're overnighting it). Two miles in, you'll cross Sorrell Creek (and see another campsite). As the trail continues to rise, you'll pass through some rich land. Keep your eyes out for wildflowers, especially the Trillium. At 3.8 miles in, turn left at Deep Gap, where you'll find another campsite. From here, you're only 1.5 miles from the summit. The primo **campsite** is near the summit, but be aware it's chilly up here, even in the summer when temperatures can dip into the 50s at night.

The summit of Cold Mountain is tree-covered and viewless, but make a stop there anyway so you can say you summited. If you backtrack 10 or 12 yards down the trail, you'll see a small spur trail that leads to a rock ledge. Here's where you'll find your million-dollar view: a 180-degree panorama to the south.

The summit trail is not marked, but it is well traveled and pretty obvious. But any time you go into the woods for a hike, especially an unmarked one, bring a detailed topographic map with you. You'll be able to find maps at any of the outdoor outfitters in Asheville and at many of the gift shops you spot along the Blue Ridge Parkway.

Richland Balsam Overlook (MP 431.4)

The last dozen miles of the Parkway have been the highest on the route, and you're about to reach the apex. At 6,047 feet, Richland Balsam is the **highest point on the Parkway.** At the Haywood-Jackson Overlook at Milepost 431 (6,020 feet), you get long views to the south and west where long lines of mountains march off into the blue distance, and, on the closer hills, spruce-fir dominated mountainsides are so thick with the dark green conifers that they seem black.

Richland Balsam Self-Guiding Trail

Distance: 1.4-mile loop
Duration: 1.25 hours
Elevation gain: 270 feet
Effort: moderate
Trailhead: MP 431

The summit to Richland Balsam is at 6,292 feet, so you have a little climb ahead of you. Begin your hike on a short section of paced trail at the end of the parking area. Continue along until you reach the loop trail intersection. Stay right and begin a steeper ascent. Along the way, you'll pass several benches where you can rest or snap a picture or two, but the best opportunities for photos are near the summit.

A little over a half mile in, you'll reach the summit. Stop, look around, take a deep breath of fir-scented air, and begin your descent. A mile in, you'll reach a break in the trees that gives you a glimpse of the land to the east. Push on through the tunnel formed by evergreen boughs, and when you reach the bench, take a long look at the excellent view here. Follow the trail back to the intersection, bear right, and you're back at the parking lot.

US-74 East: Waynesville (MP 443.1)

Waynesville, just west of Asheville and east of Cherokee, is the very definition of the word quaint. Writers have compared it to a Norman Rockwell painting with its storybook Main Street, busy with shops and lined with brick sidewalks and iron lampposts. This is an artistic little community where the art and craft galleries and studios are seemingly endless. In nearby Cullowhee, Western Carolina University is one of the mountain region's leading academic institutions, as well as the location of the Mountain Heritage Center museum and Mountain Heritage Day festival.

Waynesville is easy to reach from the Blue Ridge Parkway. From Milepost 423.4, follow US-276 north for 30 minutes right into town. From Milepost 443.1, turn onto US-74 E/US-23 N and zoom into Waynesville from the west in about 10 minutes.

Sights

One interesting stop in Waynesville is the **Museum of North Carolina Handicrafts** (49 Shelton St., 828/452-1551, www.sheltonhouse.org, 10am-4pm Tues.-Sat. May-Oct., $6 adults, $5 students, free ages 5 and under). Consisting of a farmhouse, barn, and gardens, the museum opened in 1980 and shows off the work of Native American and North Carolina heritage artists. This means mountain musical instruments, ceremonial items and crafts from Native American tribes, basketry, woodcarvings, quilts, and even antique farm tools. Tours of the museum are guided, so you'll hear plenty of stories to go with the items you see.

Shopping

Books and Specialty Items

Blue Ridge Books & News (152 S. Main St., 828/456-6000, www.blueridge-booksnc.com, 8am-7pm Mon.-Thurs., 8am-8pm Fri.-Sat., 8am-6pm Sun.) is a nice bookstore with specialties of regional interest and good coffee.

Good Ol' Days Cigars (46 N. Main St./145 Wall St., 828-456-2898, www.goodoldayscigars.com, 11am-6pm Mon.-Sat.) offers a large selection of fine tobacco and smoking products—cigars as well as pipes, loose tobacco, and rolling papers—and a lounge to enjoy them.

One of the several locations of **Mast General Store** (63 N. Main St., 828-452-2101, www.mastgeneralstore.com, 10am-6pm Mon.-Sat., noon-6pm Sun. spring-fall, hours vary in winter) is here in Waynesville. While the stores are perhaps best known among vacationers for making children clamor for the candy kept in big wooden barrels, old-time dry-goods-store style, they have an even larger selection of merchandise for adults, including camping gear, such as top-brand tents, cookware, and maps and outdoors-oriented upscale clothing and shoes by Columbia, Teva, Patagonia, and Mountain Hardwear.

Galleries

Waynesville's galleries are many and varied, although the overarching aesthetic is one of studio art with inspiration in the environment and folk arts. **Twigs and Leaves** (98 N. Main St., 828/456-1940, www.twigsandleaves.com, 10am-5:30pm Mon.-Sat., 1pm-4pm Sun.) carries splendid art furniture that is both fanciful and functional, pottery of many hand-thrown and hand-built varieties, jewelry, paintings, fabric hangings, mobiles, and many other beautiful and unusual items inspired by nature.

Studio Thirty Three (822 Balsam Ridge Rd., 828/452-4264, www.studio33jewelry.com, by appointment) carries the work of a very small and select group of fine jewelers from western North Carolina. Their retail and custom inventory consists of spectacular handcrafted pieces in a variety of styles and an array of precious stones and metals. This is a

must-see gallery if you have a special occasion coming up. The gallery describes its stock as ranging in price from "$65 to $16,000," and most items cost upward of $2,000. Even if you're not about to mark a major life event or spend that kind of money just for fun, it's worth stopping in to gaze at all that sparkle.

Art on Depot (250 Depot St., 828/246-0218, www.artondepot.com, 10am-5pm Mon.-Sat.) is a working pottery studio and gallery where local and regional artists exhibit and sell their work. Artistic creations for sale include decorative and functional pottery by the resident potter and many of her contemporaries as well as paintings, jewelry, sculpture, and a few pieces by area fiber artists.

Accommodations

Waynesville has quite a selection of luxury inns. The **Andon-Reid Inn** (92 Daisy Ave., 800/293-6190, www.andonreidinn.com, $149-239, no pets or children) is a handsome turn-of-the-20th-century house close to downtown with five tranquil guest rooms, each with its own fireplace, and a sumptuous breakfast menu that might include sweet-potato pecan pancakes and pork tenderloin, homemade cornbread with honey butter, or the intriguing baked lemon eggs. With advance notice they can cater to special dietary needs.

The **Inn at Iris Meadows** (304 Love Lane, 888/466-4747, www.irismeadows.com, from $225, dogs permitted with advance notice, no children) is another splendid house on a hillside surrounded by lush trees and gardens. Shepherd-mix Scratch and gray tabby cat Zephyrus help run the place.

In the community of Balsam, seven miles southwest from Waynesville, the **Balsam Mountain Inn** (68 Seven Springs Dr., Balsam, 800/224-9498, www.balsaminn.com, $145-225, no pets) has stood watch for a century in a haunting location—an imposing old wooden hotel with huge double porches overlooking a rather spooky little railroad platform and the beautiful ridges of Jackson and Haywood Counties beyond. The interior has barely changed since its earliest days, paneled in white horizontal bead board throughout with 10-foot-wide hallways said to have been designed to accommodate steamer trunks. The one telephone is at the front desk, and there are no TVs, so plan to go hiking or to sit on the porch before dining in the downstairs restaurant, and then curl up and read in the library. There is, incongruously, fast Wi-Fi. Among the inn's reported ghosts is a woman in a blue dress, said to originate in room 205 but to come and go elsewhere on the second floor. This inn has a few rough edges, but the atmosphere can be found nowhere else.

For absolute tip-top luxury, try **The Swag** (2300 Swag Rd., 800/789-7672, www.theswag.com, $495-800). Superb guest rooms and cabins of rustic wood and stone each have a steam shower, and several have saunas, wet bars, and cathedral ceilings. The menu is decidedly country and upscale, two things you wouldn't think go together, but they do, and quite nicely. The inn is at 5,000 feet elevation in a stunning location at the very edge of the Great Smoky Mountains National Park.

Food

Frogs Leap Public House (44 Church St., 828/456-1930, http://frogsleappublichouse.com, 4pm-9pm Tues.-Thurs., 4pm-10pm Fri.-Sat., $8-26) serves an interesting menu that's quite sophisticated but not afraid of its Southern roots. The fried green tomato and pimento cheese napoleon combines two Southern favorites with a treasured French technique, and the foie gras torchon glazed with local peaches and served with Amish butter again brings these two disparate elements together.

The ever-popular **Bogart's** (303 S. Main St., 828/452-1313, www.bogartswaynesville.com, 11am-9pm Sun.-Thurs.,

11am-10pm Fri.-Sat., $7-20) is locally famous for its filet mignon, though their local trout also has a good reputation. The menu is huge but very steakhouse-y; vegetarians will have a tough time, although a few dishes, like the chipotle black bean burger and the grilled portobello salad, are options.

If you're just passing through town and need a jolt of good strong coffee, visit **Panacea** (66 Commerce St., 303 S. Main St., 828/452-6200, http://panaceacoffee. com, 7am-5pm Mon.-Fri., 8am-5pm Sat., under $5) in the funky Frog Level neighborhood downhill from downtown. The proprietors give back to their community, and trade fairly with the communities that supply their coffee. They stock beans, blends, and brews from all around the world.

Information and Services

The **Haywood County Tourism Development Authority** (44 N. Main St., 800/334-9036, http://visitncsmokies. com/) has a wealth of information about visiting Waynesville and surrounding towns. **MedWest Haywood** (262 Leroy George Dr., Clyde, NC, 828/456-7311, www.medwesthealth.org), accessible from the Lake Junaluska exit off US-23/ US-74, is the region's hospital.

Waterrock Knob Visitor Center (MP 451.2)

The **Waterrock Knob Visitor Center** (828/775-0975, 10am-5pm daily May-Sept.) is a small affair. A tiny gift shop, restrooms with pit toilets but no running water, and a parking area with a fabulous view of the sunset of the Smokies round out what you'll find here. There is a trail that takes you out to Waterrock Knob, a picturesque spot drawing its name from a cool stream where hunters would come to fill waterskins or canteens. It's a beautiful hike that I highly recommend.

Waterrock Knob Trail

Distance: 1.2 miles round-trip
Duration: 1 hour
Elevation gain: 600 feet
Effort: strenuous
Trailhead: MP 451.2 at the Waterrock Knob Visitor Center

This trail is short but surprisingly strenuous as it's all uphill (until you come back, then it's all downhill, which is even worse). While many visitors will take the quarter-mile paved trail to a platform with a great view of its own, for the best vista, keep climbing.

As you follow the trail beyond the platform, the paving falls away and it turns into a typical dirt trail. The view keeps opening up the farther you go. You'll pass through huckleberry brambles, as well as blackberries and blueberries (ripe in late summer), and picture-perfect rock outcroppings.

In a few spots, you may have to scramble over some rocks for the best views or pictures, and so long as you're careful, it's worth it. At the summit, you'll find a bench where you can rest your legs and soak in the scenery.

Follow the trail a few steps more and you'll come to another rock outcropping where you'll have views of Climgmans Dome (6,643 ft.), Mount LeConte (6,593 ft.), and Mount Guyot (6,621 ft.), the highest peaks in Great Smoky Mountain National Park to your west.

◆ US-19 North: Maggie Valley (MP 455.7)

Maggie Valley is a vacation town from the bygone era of long family road trips in wood-paneled station wagons. Coming down the mountain toward Maggie Valley you'll pass an overlook that, on a morning when the mountains around Soco Gap are looped with fog, is surely one of the most beautiful

Maggie Valley

(Map labels:) FIE TOP RD, Maggie Valley, EVANS COVE RD, Evans Branch, Mitchell Cove Branch, VALLEY INN, GHOST TOWN IN THE SKY, JONATHAN CREEK INN AND VILLAS, MOODY FARM RD, Jonathans Creek, JOEY'S PANCAKE HOUSE, MAGGIE VALLEY OPRY HOUSE, WHEELS THROUGH TIME MUSEUM, MAGGIE VALLEY RESTAURANT, SOCO RD, Gaddis Branch, CAMPBELL CREEK RD, Campbell Creek, J. ARTHURS RESTAURANT, Pine Tree Cove Br, DOGWOOD DR, Mine Branch, SUMMIT DR, 0 500 yds, 0 500 m, © AVALON TRAVEL

vistas in the state. Only four miles east of the Blue Ridge Parkway at Milepost 455.7 via US-19 North, it's an easy spot to reach for a refuel for you or your vehicle.

Sights and Entertainment

Maggie Valley's best-known attraction is the **Ghost Town in the Sky** (16 Fie Top Rd., 828/926-1130, www.ghosttowninthesky.com, 10am-6pm daily June-Oct., weather permitting, $25 adults, $16 ages 3-12), an Old West theme park where the good guys and bad guys shoot it out daily for your viewing pleasure. There are rides—zip lines, carousels, roller coasters, a free-fall tower—as well as regular bluegrass and gospel concerts.

Bluegrass music and clogging are a big deal in this town. The great bluegrass banjo player Raymond Fairchild is a Maggie native, and after his 50-year touring and recording career, he and his wife, Shirley, are now the hosts of the **Maggie Valley Opry House** (3605 Soco Rd., 828/648-7941, www.raymondfairchild.com, 8pm daily June-Oct.). In season, you can find bluegrass and country music concerts and clogging exhibitions most every night.

In a state with countless attractions for automotive enthusiasts, Maggie Valley's **Wheels Through Time Museum** (62 Vintage Lane, 828/926-6266, www.wheelsthroughtime.com, 9am-5pm

Thurs.-Mon. late Mar.-late Nov., $12 adults, $10 over age 65, $6 ages 5-12, free under age 4) stands out as one of the most fun. A dazzling collection of nearly 300 vintage motorcycles and a fair number of cars are on display, including rarities like a 1908 Indian, a 1914 Harley-Davidson, military motorcycles from both World Wars, and some gorgeous postwar bikes. This collection, which dates mostly to before 1950, is maintained in working order—almost every one of the bikes is revved up from time to time, and the museum's founder has been known to take a spin on one of the treasures.

Recreation
Hiking

Near Maggie Valley, the mountains become rough. Located on the valley floor, Maggie Valley is surprisingly short on trails, and what trails there are are quite strenuous. There's the 2.6-mile stroll around **Lake Junaluska,** but other than that, the majority of the trails are found at the crest of the mountains, along the Blue Ridge Parkway. To the east of Maggie Valley, the mountains are a little more forgiving and there are many trails of various intensities and lengths, but in the immediate area, you'll have to take the Heintooga Spur Road, a connector road between the Parkway and Great Smoky Mountains National Park, to a mile-high campground, picnic area with unparalleled views, and the **Flat Creek Trail.** On Heintooga Spur Road, you'll pass into Great Smoky Mountains National Park proper and be treated to no fewer than five stunning overlooks, the best of which is the Mile High Overlook, offering a glimpse of Clingmans Dome, Mount LeConte, Mount Kephart, and Mount Guyot.

Flat Creek Trail

Distance: 5 miles round-trip
Duration: 3 hours
Elevation gain: 250 feet
Effort: moderate
Trailhead: Heintooga Ridge picnic area off Heintooga Spur Road, accessible at MP 458.2

Though named the Flat Creek Trail, you will find a waterfall—the 200-foot Flat Creek Falls, a beautiful but difficult-to-see waterfall—along the path. The main trail is easy, with little elevation gain or loss until you turn off onto the short spur trail that takes you to the falls. The falls trail is steep and slick, so be careful if you decide to explore in this area.

Heavy logging at the turn of the 20th century opened the forest up and allowed a thick swath of grass to grow here. Today, much of the grass remains and the forest seems to rise from it like an island in a sea of green. It's a strange sight.

Skiing and Winter Sports

Maggie Valley's **Cataloochee Ski Area** (1080 Ski Lodge Rd., off US-19, 800/768-0285, snow conditions 800/768-3588, www.cataloochee.com, lift tickets $20-60, rentals $21-30) has slopes geared to every level of skier and snowboarder. Classes and private lessons are taught for all ages.

At Cataloochee's sister snow-sports area, **Tube World** (US-19, next to Cataloochee Ski Area, 800/768-0285, www.cataloochee.com, $25, must be over 42 inches tall, late Nov.-mid-Mar.), you can zip down the mountain on inner tubes, and there's a "Wee Bowl" area for children (call ahead, $5).

Accommodations

The main drag through Maggie Valley (Soco Rd./US-19) is lined with motels, including some of the familiar national chains. Among the pleasant independent motels are the **Valley Inn** (236 Soco Rd., 800/948-6880, www.thevalleyinn.com, in-season rates vary, from $39 off-season) and **Jonathan Creek Inn and Villas** (4324 Soco Rd., 800/577-7812, www.jonathancreekinn.com, from $60), which has creek-side rooms with screened porches.

There is one fantastic campground in the area, the ★ **Balsam Mountain Campground** (Heintooga Spur Rd., MP 458.2, 828,269-2945, www.nps.gov/grsm, $20, tent and RV sites available), which is the highest campground in Great Smoky Mountains National Park at 5,310 feet. This primitive campground has 43 sites for tents and RVs, with a dedicated tent-only section. It's a beautiful, isolated campground that's often overlooked as it's slightly off the beaten path; that, in addition to the fact that it's a primitive campground (read: no showers), means that for most of the year you won't have many neighbors here. Plus, if you're driving a vehicle you feel comfortable driving on forest roads, the Balsam Mountain Road (sometimes called Round Bottom Road) continues on from the campground, making a nice trip through the forest down to Cherokee (it takes about two hours).

Food

★ **Joey's Pancake House** (4309 Soco Rd., 828/926-0212, www.joeyspancake.com, 7am-noon Fri.-Wed., about $8) has been flipping flapjacks for travelers and locals alike since 1966. The pancakes, waffles, and country ham are so good that lines form on the weekends—get here early.

J. Arthurs Restaurant (2843 Soco Rd., 828/926-1817, www.jarthurs.com, lunch noon-2:30pm Fri.-Sun., early bird dinner 4:30pm-6pm daily, dinner from 4:30pm daily, $15-25) is a popular spot locally for steaks, which are the house specialty;

they've been serving them up for more than 25 years. The restaurant also has a variety of seafood and pasta dishes, but there are few vegetarian options.

The **Mountaineer Restaurant** (6490 Soco Rd., 828/926-1730, breakfast, lunch, and dinner daily, $6-20) is a typical mountain café serving barbecue, steaks, catfish, trout, and country-cooking specialties.

A Maggie Valley dining institution that's been around since 1952 is **Maggie Valley Restaurant** (2804 Soco Rd., 828/926-0425, www.maggievalleyrestaurant.net, 7am-9pm daily May-Oct., breakfast $1-10, lunch and dinner $5-12). Expect comfort-food classics—meatloaf, meatloaf sandwiches, something called a chuck wagon, pork chops, biscuit sandwiches, grits, bottomless coffee, and even buttermilk—along with one of the best pieces of fresh fried trout you'll find in these mountains.

Soco Gap (MP 455.7)

When you reach the 4,570-foot Soco Gap, you're on the edge of the Qualla Boundary and Cherokee country. The overlook here is less of an overlook and more of a parking area until the National Parks Service clears a few trees. Don't worry about views, though. As you round some of the big sweeping turns on the descent toward Cherokee and the end of the Blue Ridge Parkway, you'll have plenty more views to take in.

Big Witch Gap Overlook (MP 461.9)

Like Devil's Courthouse, this spot is intriguing with the potential to see the namesake Big Witch, the Anglicized name of a famous Cherokee medicine man who lived in these parts for more than 90 years. Here, at the Big Witch Gap Overlook, you have an excellent view of the Great Smoky Mountains. If you're here at the right time of day or year, you'll see why they call them the Great Smoky Mountains as fog and mist rise like tendrils of smoke from what seems like every cove and hollow in these hills.

Southern End (MP 469.1)

Congratulations, you made it to the end of (or, if you're reading this book backwards, Welcome to) the Blue Ridge Parkway. At Milepost 469.1, you'll intersect US-441 just a mile or so from Cherokee to the south and east, and Great Smoky Mountains National Park to the north and west. This is the time to pull off, get out of the car and snap a selfie in front of the Blue Ridge Parkway sign at the southern end of the route. After that, it's on to Cherokee for a meal, a massage, and some blackjack.

US-441 South: Cherokee

The town of Cherokee is a study in juxtapositions: the cultural traditions of the Cherokee people, the region's natural beauty, a 24-hour casino, and community-wide preparation for the future. Cherokee is the seat of government of the Eastern Band of the Cherokee, who have lived in these mountains for centuries. Today, their traditional arts and crafts, government, and cultural heritage are very much alive. The Qualla ("KWAlah") Boundary is not a reservation but is a large tract of land owned and governed by the Cherokee people. Institutions like the Museum of the Cherokee Indian and the Qualla Arts and Crafts Mutual provide a solid base for the Eastern Band's cultural life. As you drive around, take a look at the road signs. Below each English road name is that same name in Cherokee, a beautiful script created by Sequoyah, a 19th-century Cherokee

Cherokee

OCONALUFTEE
INDIAN VILLAGE ★

QUALLA ARTS AND
CRAFTS MUTUAL ★

MUSEUM OF THE ★
CHEROKEE INDIAN

Fair
Grounds

LAMBERT BRANCH RD
TSALI BLVD
WASHINGTON DR
JOSEPH
ACQUONI RD
1361
441
BIA HWY 1390
BIA HWY 316
Oconaluftee River
441 19
TSALAGI RD

0   200 yds
0   200 m

To Harrah's Cherokee
Casino and Hotel
19

© AVALON TRAVEL

silversmith. This language was once nearly extinct, and few Cherokee people speak it fluently, but it is now being taught to the community's youth, and there is a Cherokee language immersion school on the Qualla Boundary.

The main street in Cherokee is a classic cheesy tourist district where you'll find "Indian" souvenirs—factory-made moccasins, plastic tomahawks, peace pipes, and faux bearskins. In a retro way, this part of Cherokee, with its predictable trinket shops and fudgeries, is charming; check out the garish 1950s motel signs with comic-book Indians outlined in neon. Aside from its proximity to the Great Smoky Mountains National Park

(which is just two miles from Cherokee along heavily-traveled Newfound Gap Road), the biggest draw in town is Harrah's Cherokee Casino, one of the largest casino hotels in the state. Take all that you see—the casino, the tacky tourist shops, and the stereotyping signs—with a grain of salt, as they don't represent the true nature of the Cherokee people and their long history.

Getting There

Cherokee is located on a particularly pretty winding section of US-19 between Maggie Valley and Bryson City, 2.5 miles south of the southern terminus of the Blue Ridge Parkway. From the Blue Ridge Parkway, a six-minute drive south along US-441 will take you right to the cultural center of Cherokee.

Sights
Harrah's Cherokee Casino

The Eastern Band of the Cherokee operates **Harrah's Cherokee Casino and Hotel** (777 Casino Dr., 828/497-7777, www. harrahscherokee.com, 24 hours daily). This full-bore Vegas-style casino has more than 3,800 digital games and slot machines along with around 150 table games, such as baccarat, blackjack, roulette, and a poker-only room. Inside the casino complex is a 3,000-seat concert venue where acts like Alicia Keys and the Black Crows have performed, a huge buffet, and a grab-and-go food court next to the casino floor. Unlike in the rest of the state, smoking is allowed on the casino floor, though certain areas have been designated as nonsmoking. If you're a nonsmoker, it may take some patience.

Inside the hotel portion of the casino are a restaurant, a Starbucks, and the **Mandara Spa,** which offers salon and spa services like massages and facials.

Museum of the Cherokee Indian

The **Museum of the Cherokee Indian** (589 Tsali Blvd., 828/497-3481, www. cherokeemuseum.org, 9am-7pm

Mon.-Fri., 9am-5pm Sat.-Sun. late May-early Sept., 9am-5pm daily early Sept.-late May, $10, $6 ages 6-12, free under age 6) was founded in 1948 and was originally housed in a log cabin. Today, it is a well-regarded modern museum and locus of community culture. The Museum of the Cherokee Indian traces their history from the Paleo-Indian people of the Pleistocene, when the ancestral Cherokees were hunter-gatherers, through the ancient days of Cherokee civilization, and into contact with European settlers. In the exhibits that trace the history of the Cherokee people, you may notice the disconcertingly realistic mannequins. Local community members volunteered to be models for these mannequins, allowing casts to be made of their faces and bodies so that the figures would not reflect an outsider's notion of what Native Americans look like.

A great deal of this exhibit focuses on the 18th and 19th centuries, when a series of tragedies befell the Cherokee as a result of the invasion of their homeland. It was also a time of great cultural advancement, including Sequoyah's development of the script to write the Cherokee language. The forced relocation of Native Americans called the Trail of Tears began near here, along the North Carolina-Georgia border, in the early 19th century. A small contingent of Cherokees remained in the Smokies at the time of the Trail of Tears, successfully eluding, and then negotiating with, the U.S. military, who were trying to force most of the Native Americans in the Southeast to move to Oklahoma. Those who stayed out in the woods, along with a few others who were able to return from Oklahoma, are the ancestors of today's Eastern Band, and their history is truly remarkable.

A favorite part of the museum are the stories, legends, and myths described on placards throughout the museum. There's the story of a boy who became a bear and convinced his entire clan to become bears also. There's one about Spearfinger, a frightening creature that some say still lives in these woods today. And there are tales about Selu, the corn mother, and Kanati, the lucky hunter. Cherokee member and contemporary writer Marilou Awiakta has written widely about Selu, tying the past and present together with taut lines of thought that challenge our views on culture and technology.

★ Qualla Arts and Crafts Mutual

Across the street from the museum is the **Qualla Arts and Crafts Mutual** (645 Tsali Blvd., 828/497-3103, http://quallaartsandcrafts.com, 8am-5pm Mon.-Sat., 9am-5pm Sun.), a community arts co-op where local artists sell their work. The gallery's high standards and the community's thousands of years of artistry make for a collection of very special pottery, baskets, masks, and other traditional art. As hard as it is to survive as an artist in a place like New York City, artists in rural areas such as this have an exponentially more difficult time supporting themselves through the sale of their art while maintaining the integrity of their vision and creativity. The Qualla co-op does a great service to this community in providing a year-round market for the work of traditional Cherokee artists, whose stewardship of and innovation in the arts are so important. The double-woven baskets are especially beautiful, as are the carvings of the masks representing each of the seven clans of the Cherokee people (Bird, Deer, Longhair, Blue, Wolf, Paint, and Wild Potato). You'll notice the water spider, credited in Cherokee legend for capturing the first fire, makes a frequent appearance on clay tusti bowls, in which the water spider is said to have held that first flame.

★ Oconaluftee Indian Village

Oconaluftee Indian Village (778 Drama Rd., 828/497-3481, http://cherokeehistorical.org, gates open and tours begin

Qualla Boundary: The Story of the Cherokee

The Cherokee believe that the mountains of western North Carolina have been part of their homeland dating back to at least the last Ice Age (some 11,000 years ago). By the time Spanish soldiers encountered the Cherokee Tribe in the 1540s, the tribe controlled around 140,000 square miles across the southern United States, living in log cabins in towns and villages throughout their territory. They farmed corn, squash, and beans (known as "The Three Sisters"); hunted elk, deer, and bear; and prospered in peace times and warred with other tribes periodically.

During the first two centuries of earnest European contact, the Cherokee were peaceful and hospitable with the colonists they encountered. Through the course of those 200 years, strings of broken treaties and concessions by the Cherokee had shrunk their once-vast empire dramatically. When President Andrew Jackson insisted that all Indians in the southeast be moved west of the Mississippi, the real trouble began.

As Jackson's forced march and relocation of the Cherokee and other tribes, known as the **Trail of Tears,** pressed on, a small group of Cherokee avoided relocation by becoming North Carolina citizens and a band of resistance fighters stayed behind near modern-day Cherokee, hiding in the hills, hollows, and caves high in the mountains. These holdouts would become the core of the **Eastern Band of Cherokee Indians.** Unable to own any land, the Cherokee turned to an adopted tribe member to purchase and hold land in his name. He did so, and in 1870, the Cherokee formed a corporation and took control of their land, which they called the Qualla Boundary.

Today, the Eastern Band of the Cherokee Indians has nearly 15,000 members (their counterparts in Oklahoma number 10 times as many), many of whom live within the 82-square-mile Qualla Boundary. Tribe members are fiercely proud of their heritage, traditions, stories, and language. An afternoon spent at the **Museum of the Cherokee Indian,** the **Qualla Arts and Crafts Mutual,** the **Oconaluftee Indian Village,** and an evening showing of *Unto These Hills* will give you a more complete understanding of their history.

at 10am Mon.-Sat. May-mid-Mar., tours run every 15 minutes until 4pm when the box office closes, village closes after final tour, usually around 5pm, $19 adults, $11 children, free 5 and under) is a recreated Cherokee Indian Village tucked into the hills above the town. Here, you'll see how the tribe lived in the 18th century. Tour guides in period costumes lead groups on walking lectures with stops at stations where you can see Cherokee cultural, artistic, and daily-life activities performed as authentically as possible. From cooking demos to flint knapping (for arrowheads and spear points) to wood carving and clay work, you'll get a look at how the Cherokee lived centuries ago. The highlight of the tour is the ritual dance demonstration showing half a dozen dances and explaining their cultural significance.

Entertainment

Of the several outdoor dramas for which North Carolina is known, among the longest running is Cherokee's *Unto These Hills* (Mountainside Theater, 688 Drama Rd., adjacent to Oconaluftee Indian Village, 866/554-4557, www.cherokeesmokies.com, 8pm Mon.-Sat. June-Aug., $18-22 adults, $8-12 ages 6-12, free under age 6). For more than 60 summers, Cherokee actors have told the story of their nation's history, from ancient times through the Trail of Tears. Every seat in the house is a good seat at the Mountainside Theater, and the play is certainly enlightening. Be warned: If you're gun-shy or easily startled, there is some cannon fire and gunfire in the play.

Hear stories, learn dances, and interact with Cherokee storytellers at the **Cherokee Bonfire** (Oconaluftee Islands

Park, Tsalagi Rd. and Tsali Blvd., where US-19 and US-441 intersect, 800/438-1601, http://visitcherokee.com, 7pm and 9pm Thurs.-Sat., free, including marshmallows). Bring your bathing suit and some water shoes to the bonfire; afterward, you may want to go for a wade or a quick dip in the Oconaluftee River, which is wide, rocky, and fun.

Recreation
Amusement Parks
Cherokee Fun Park (1897 Tsali Blvd., 828/497-5877, www.cherokeefunparknc.com, 10am-10pm Sun.-Thurs., 10am-11pm Fri.-Sat., single rider $8, doubles $12) has a great go-kart track. You can't miss it as you're driving to or from the Great Smoky Mountains National Park; there's an insane three-level corkscrew turn on one track and a pro track inside where you can drive faster-than-usual carts. And there's mini golf ($8).

Fishing
Cherokee has more than 30 miles of streams, rivers, and creeks ideal for fishing. Add to that the fact that the Eastern Band owns and operates a fish hatchery that releases around 250,000 trout into these waters every year and you have the perfect mix for fantastic fishing. Unlike the rest of North Carolina, you don't need a North Carolina fishing license; you need a **Tribal Fishing Permit** (1 day $10, 2 days $17, 3 days $27, 5 days $47), sold at a number of outlets in Cherokee. You'll find brook, brown, golden, and rainbow trout, and it's fly-rod only, so you have to have your cast down pat if you want to bring in a big one. There are both catch-and-release and catch-and-keep waters in the Qualla Boundary, but if you want to fish outside the boundary, where several streams and the Oconaluftee River have great fishing, you need a North Carolina or Tennessee fishing permit. Tennessee permits are only valid inside the Great Smoky Mountains National Park boundaries in North Carolina.

Golf
The **Sequoyah National Golf Club** (79 Cahons Rd., Whittier, 828/497-3000, www.sequoyahnational.com, 18 holes, par 72, greens fees from $40), five miles south of Cherokee in Whittier, is a stunning mountain golf course. Making the most of the contours and elevation, the course offers tee boxes with breathtaking views of the fairway and the Smoky Mountains. The course record is 62, an impressive feat on a normal course, but here it's something else. Holes like number 12, a par 5 that plays uphill the whole way, present the usual par-5 difficulties combined with steep elevation gain, and number 15, a par 4 that entices golfers to play overly aggressively and drop a ball short of the fairway and into the woods, test a golfer's club knowledge and course IQ. This is a tough course for first-timers because so many of the holes have blind approaches, doglegs, or both, but it's enjoyable enough.

Water Sports
For fun on the water, try **Smoky Mountain Tubing** (1847 Tsali Blvd., 828/497-4545, http://cherokeetubeandraft.com, 10am-6pm daily, weather permitting, $10). They do only one thing: rent tubes on which you'll drift down the river and splash your friends. Smoky Mountain Tubing has mountains of tubes, so rent one and float down the Oconaluftee River for two or three hours. They have a fleet of shuttle buses to pick you up a few miles downstream.

Accommodations
Cherokee has many motels, including a **Holiday Inn** (376 Painttown Rd., 828/497-3113, www.ihg.com, from $80) and an **Econo Lodge** (20 River Rd./US-19, 828/497-4575, www.econolodge.com, from $80, pets allowed).

The casino at ★ **Harrah's Cherokee Casino and Hotel** (777 Casino Dr., 828/497-7777, www.harrahscherokee.com, from $109) is separate from the two towers housing more than 1,100 hotel rooms and suites, with sky bridges joining the hotel to the casino. In the hotel you'll find a country-buffet restaurant and a Starbucks. If you want to relax, the **Mandara Spa** is an 18,000-square-foot oasis in the heart of the hotel that offers all sorts of luxurious treatments for individuals and couples. From basic massages (from $129) to body treatments like the Balinese Body Polish ($125), the Juniper Berry and Algae Detox ($165), and the Elemis Aroma Spa Seaweed Massage ($165) to rejuvenating spa experience packages (from $260), you can create the relaxing experience you need. They also provide an array of salon services, including blowouts, beard trims, facials, and manis and pedis.

There's something about visiting a place and living where the residents live, and ★ **Panther Creek Cabins** (Wrights Creek Rd., 828/497-2461, www.panthercreekresort.com, cabins $100-175) gives you that chance with your choice of eight cabins, ranging from private two-person affairs to larger lodges that could easily sleep you and seven others in four beds. These quaint cabins are quiet, just outside of downtown Cherokee, and comfortable.

Food
Harrah's Cherokee Casino
The arrival and expansion of Harrah's Cherokee Casino (777 Casino Dr., 828/497-7777, www.harrahscherokee.com) brought with it a bevy of restaurants. **Ruth's Chris Steak House** (dinner 5pm-10pm Mon.-Thurs., 5pm-11pm Fri.-Sat., lounge 4pm-11pm Mon.-Thurs., 4pm-midnight Fri.-Sat., lounge and dinner 4pm-9pm Sun., around $40) is here, and like its other locations, serves a variety of steaks and chops, a handful of seafood dishes, and more than 200 wines.

Brio Tuscan Grille (828/497-8233, 11:30am-10pm Sun.-Thurs., 11:30am-11pm Fri.-Sat., $14-30) is a fine Italian restaurant specializing in dishes from northern Italy. This isn't a spaghetti-and-meatballs kind of place; it's more refined, with dishes like lasagna Bolognese al forno, lobster and shrimp ravioli with crab insalata, Tuscan grilled pork chops, and bistecca alla Fiorentina. The ambience is nice, the wine list is nicer, and the food is great.

Downstairs in Harrah's, just off the casino floor, is an airport-style food court that includes the **Winning Streaks Deli** (11am-11pm daily, $10), a deli serving hot and cold sandwiches and panini made with Boars Head meats and cheeses; grab-and-go sandwiches are available 24 hours daily. There is also **Pizzeria Uno Express** (11am-11pm Sun.-Thurs., 11am-2am Fri.-Sat., around $10), serving thin-crust pizza, calzones, and pasta dishes; **Johnny Rockets** (24 hours daily, around $10), serving burgers, sandwiches, fries, milkshakes, and breakfast; and a **Dunkin' Donuts Express** (24 hours daily, around $5) that has doughnuts and coffee. The food court also has a variety of snacks and drinks available 24 hours daily.

Outside Cherokee

Just outside of the town of Cherokee is **Granny's Kitchen** (1098 Painttown Rd., 828/497-5010, www.grannyskitchencherokee.com, breakfast 7am-11am Tues.-Sun. June-Oct., 7am-11am Fri.-Sun. Apr.-May and Nov., lunch and dinner 11am-8pm Sun.-Thurs. Apr.-Nov., breakfast $8, lunch $8.50, dinner $12), a country-buffet restaurant where you can get some of the best fried chicken in North Carolina. You won't find Granny here; Granny is actually a man who likes to joke, "no one wants to eat at grandpa's, so I became granny."

Information and Services

The **Cherokee Welcome Center** (498 Tsali Blvd., 800/438-1601, www.visitcherokee-enc.com, 8am-8pm daily) can help you with tickets, directions, and things to do and see.

There's one radio station in Cherokee, and that's **WNCC** (101.3), a country station, though you can pick up distant stations with a wider selection.

◆ US-19 South: Bryson City

To look at the mountains here, you'd think that the defining feature in this part of North Carolina would be the surrounding peaks, but that is only half right. This is a land dominated by water. Smoke-thick fog crowds valleys in the pre-dawn hours. The peaks stand ringed in clouds. Moss, ferns, and dense forests crowd the edge of rivers and streams. All of it—the mountains, the mist, the ferns, the fog—makes it feel like you've stepped into a fairy tale when you're in the **Nantahala Gorge.** According to Cherokee stories, a formidable witch called Spearfinger lived here, as did a monstrous snake and even an inchworm so large it could span the gorge.

vista near the southern end of the Blue Ridge Parkway

Fly-Fishing the Foothills

As you travel west of Asheville, deeper into the foothills of the Smoky Mountains, you're entering fly-fishing country. The streams here are crystal clear, cool all year, and teeming with trout. Jackson County is the home of the first and only fly-fishing trail in the nation. The **Western North Carolina Fly Fishing Trail** (www.flyfishingtrail.com) includes 15 spots on some of the best trout streams in the Smokies, where you can catch rainbow, brook, and brown trout, even the occasional golden trout. Though the many mountain communities that are near the trail's streams are a short drive from the Parkway, they're still convenient if you feel the need to fish. Complimentary **maps** are available at www.flyfishingtrail.com, mountainlovers.com, and greatsmokiesfishing.com.

For an "urban" fishing experience, try the **Tuckasegee River** as it passes through Dillsboro, 17 miles to the east of Bryson City. You can park and fish at a number of places between Dillsboro Park and the Best Western River Escape Inn, and you run a good chance of catching a large rainbow or brown trout.

The **Lower Tuckasegee River**, running from Bakers Creek Bridge to Whittier along US-19/US-74, is around 10 miles of excellent fishing for rainbow and brown trout as well as smallmouth bass. Located about 15 miles east of Bryson City, you'll find some excellent fishing on streams beside the stretch of highway between Whittier and Dillsboro.

Fly Fishing Trail co-founder Alex Bell, who knows the waters of western North Carolina intimately, operates **AB's Fly Fishing Guide Service** (828/226-3833, www.abfish.org, half-day wading trips $150 for 1 person, $225 for 2 people, $300 for 3 people, full-day with lunch, $225 for 1 person, $300 for 2 people, and $375 for 3 people; float trips half day $275 one or two people, full day with lunch $350 one or two people). AB's supplies tackle and waders if you need them, as well as extensive lessons in proper casting, water reading, and fly selection, but you're responsible for securing your own North Carolina fishing license and trout stamp.

Spearfinger and her cohorts haven't been seen in years and the Nantahala River runs through the narrow gorge, attracting white-water enthusiasts to the rapids.

To reach Bryson City from Cherokee or the Blue Ridge Parkway, take US-19 south. Bryson City is 20 minutes from Cherokee.

★ Great Smoky Mountains Railroad

The **Great Smoky Mountains Railroad** (Bryson City Depot, 226 Everett St., 800/872-4681, www.gsmr.com, from $50 adults, from $29 children) is one of the best and most fun ways to see the Smokies. On historic trains, the GSMR carries sightseers on excursions, from two to several hours long, through some of the most beautiful scenery in the region. The half-day trips between Dillsboro and Bryson City (with a layover at each end for shopping and dining) follow the banks of the Tuckasegee River, while 4.5-hour round-trips from Bryson City follow the Little Tennessee and Nantahala Rivers deep into the Nantahala Gorge. Many other excursions are offered, including gourmet dining and wine- and beer-tasting trips, Thomas the Tank Engine and Little Engine That Could themed trips for kids, and runs to and from river rafting outfitters.

Recreation
★ Fly-Fishing the Tuckasegee River

The Smoky Mountains, especially the eastern grade of the Smokies, are laced with streams perfect for fly-fishing. Anglers from all over come here to float, wade, camp, fish, hone their fly-tying craft, and learn the finer points of fly-fishing. The Tuckasegee River flows right through downtown Bryson City, and many of its feeder streams and creeks are ideal spots to throw a line.

Fontana Guide Service (3336 Balltown Rd., Bryson City, 828/736-2318, www.fontanaguides.com, $225/half-day, $375/full day, $50 per additional angler) has a number of options depending on season, interest, and skill level, including options to fish in the national park. In addition to fly-fishing excursions, they also offer kayak fishing, bass and lake fishing, as well as night fishing in select spots.

Fly Fishing the Smokies (Bryson City, 828/488-7665, www.flyfishingthesmokies.net) has a number of guides and options for a day or more of fishing. Wade the streams with them for a half-day (1 person $150, 2 people $175) or full-day (1 person $200, 2 people $250) outing, try a float trip (half-day $225 per boat, full-day $300 per boat), or go backcountry camping and fly-fishing in the Great Smoky Mountains National Park. They also go bass fishing on nearby Fontana Lake (half-day $225, full-day $300).

Another top fishing guide in the Bryson City area is **Steve Claxton's Smoky Mountain Adventures** (Bryson City, 828/736-7501, http://steveclaxton.com), who specializes in leaving civilization behind in favor of camping, catching wild mountain trout, and getting a true taste of the wilderness. They offer three-day, two-night camping trips for 5-7 people (around $400 pp) and four-day, three-night trips ($450-500 pp). They also offer daylong fishing trips (1 person $225, 2 people $250, 3 people $300).

Thirty miles west of Bryson City in Robbinsville, **Nantahala Fly Fishing Co.** (Robbinsville, 828/479-8850, www.flyfishnorthcarolina.com, guided trips and private lessons half-day $150 pp, $75 per additional person, full-day $225 pp, $75 per additional person) provides guided

top to bottom: the Tuckasegee River; Nantahala Outdoor Center; biscuits and gravy trips for fly-rod fishing, but if you've never held one of these odd fishing rods in your hand, they also provide a fly-fishing school ($250 for 2 days) and private instruction. Best of all, they have a "No Fish, No Pay" guarantee.

Water Sports

The stunningly beautiful Nantahala River Gorge, just outside Bryson City in the Nantahala National Forest, supports scores of river guide companies, many clustered along US-19 West. "Nantahala" is said to mean "Land of the Noonday Sun," and there are indeed parts of this gorge where the sheer rock walls above the river are so steep that sunlight only hits the water at the noon hour. Eight miles of the Nantahala River flow through the gorge, over Class II and III rapids.

The nearby Ocoee River is also a favorite of rafters, and the Cheoah River, on the occasions of controlled releases, has some of the South's most famous and difficult Class III and IV runs. Because some of these rapids can be quite dangerous, be sure to call ahead and speak to a guide if you have any doubts as to your readiness. If rafting with children, check the company's weight and age restrictions beforehand.

Endless River Adventures (14157 US-19 W., near Bryson City, 800/224-7238, www.endlessriveradventures.com) gives white-water and flat-water kayaking instruction, rentals, and guided trips on the Nantahala, Ocoee, and Cheoah Rivers. They'll be able to suggest a run suited to your skill level.

Carolina Outfitters (715 US-19, Topton, 800/468-7238, www.carolinaoutfitters.com) has several package outings that combine river trips with horseback riding, bicycling, panning for gems, and riding on the Great Smoky Mountains Railroad.

Wildwater Rafting (10345 US-19 W., 12 miles west of Bryson City, 828/488-2384,

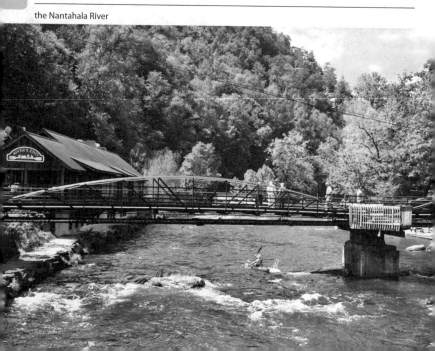

the Nantahala River

www.wildwaterrafting.com) offers river guide services.

The **Nantahala Outdoor Center** (13077 W. US-19, Bryson City, 800/232-7238, www.noc.com, 9am-5pm daily, adventures from $33) offers white-water rafting, stand-up paddleboarding (on the flat-water sections of the river), and other recreation options. Half-day, full-day, and overnight trips are a possibility with Nantahala Outdoor Center.

Other Recreation

Wildwater Rafting leads **Wildwater Jeep Tours** (10345 US-19 W., 12 miles west of Bryson City, 828/488-2384, www.wildwaterrafting.com, $46-99 adults, $36-74 children), half- and full-day **jeep excursions** through back roads and wilderness, and to waterfalls and old mountain settlements.

You can explore the mountains around Bryson City with the **Nantahala Outdoor Center** (13077 W. US-19, Bryson City, 800/232-7238, www.noc.com, 9am-5pm daily, adventures from $33). The NOC offers a variety of adventure options in addition to white-water rafting and stand-up paddleboarding, including **hiking, mountain biking,** and **ziplining.** Half-day, full-day, and overnight trips are a possibility with NOC, as is the intensity of your experience; choose from easier or more challenging mountain bike trails, hikes that are kid-friendly or aimed at the serious outdoorsperson, or excursions, like the Rapid Transit, that combine a relaxing morning train ride with an afternoon rafting trip.

Great Smoky Mountains

The Smokies draw more than 10 million visitors annually. It's easy to see why: these mountains are laced with hiking trails, rivers, and waterfalls and populated with diverse wildlife—from rare salamanders to huge elk.

Knoxville

TENNESSEE

36 mi / 60 km
1 hr

Pigeon Forge

HEN WALLOW FALLS TRAIL ★

CATALOOC

RICH MOUNTAIN ★

CADES COVE ★

Cherokee National Forest

Great Smoky Mountains National Park

ANDREWS ★ BALD
2 mi / 3.5 km
6 min

NORTH CAROLINA

Cherokee

Nantahala National Forest

© AVALON TRAVEL

Highlights

★ **Newfound Gap Road:**
Bisecting the Great Smoky
Mountains National Park, the
33-mile drive offers plenty
of long-distance views, short
hikes, and streamside driving
(page 282).

★ **Andrews Bald:** Hike to
one of the prettiest high-
altitude meadows in the
Smokies (page 285).

★ **Cataloochee:** Camping
in this secluded valley with
Milky Way views is bliss—and
driving through isn't half bad
either (page 290).

★ **Hen Wallow Falls Trail:**
An easy out-and-back day

hike leads to a beautiful
waterfall (page 293).

★ **Cades Cove:** Cades Cove
offers plenty of wildlife viewing and the largest collection
of intact historic structures in
the park (page 301).

★ **Rich Mountain:** Hike
up, up, up in the hills for gorgeous views of Cades Cove
(page 305).

★ **Dollywood:** Ride roller
coasters and get a taste of
southern Appalachian music,
history, and culture at this
theme park owned by a
country music legend
(page 315).

★ **East Tennessee History
Center:** Learn about the
history and culture of the
Tennessee foothills at this
downtown Knoxville land-
mark (page 323).

★ **Knoxville Museum of
Art:** This Tennessee marble
building is filled with impressive contemporary pieces,
including works by artists
native to the city and region
(page 323).

★ **Tennessee Theatre:**
The official state theater of
Tennessee is an architectural
marvel (page 324).

At the southern terminus of the Blue Ridge Parkway you'll find the most visited national park: Great Smoky Mountains National Park (GSMNP). The diversity of forest flora here remains unrivaled on the East Coast.

The 521,085-acre GSMNP straddles the North Carolina/Tennessee state line, and is just about equally split between the states. The slightly larger North Carolina side of the park is wilder and less developed than the Tennessee side, and in both places you can find spots so remote they have stood undisturbed by humans for untold lengths of time. You'll also find places like Cades Cove, a wide, secluded valley that welcomed some of the first pioneers to push west into Tennessee.

As you drive Newfound Gap Road from Cherokee, N.C., you'll climb high into the Smokies before descending into Tennessee and the touristy town of Gatlinburg, which is as quirky and cheeky as it is lovely. Dollywood, Dolly Parton's theme park, is here, and her hometown of Sevierville is just a few miles away.

Knoxville, the nearest proper city, is a half-hour away. Knoxville has been named to a number of lists—Best Outdoor Towns to Live In and Southern Cities on the Rise, to name a couple—and it lives up to the hype. In 1982, the World's Fair visited and the city's been on the upswing ever since. The food scene, kept busy by the population of young professionals and students from the University of Tennessee, is vibrant and growing, and the cultural offerings—museums, festivals, public art, and events—are rich. Here you'll find two lauded music venues, the Tennessee Theatre and the Bijou Theatre, and a field of local and touring musicians to rival Nashville.

Planning Your Time

Many visitors to Great Smoky Mountains National Park (GSMNP) only devote a day to the park. They drive Newfound Gap Road, take a short hike along the way, and circle Cades Cove before moving on. To do justice to the park and towns in the foothills of Eastern Tennessee, give the area at least five days. Spend one day in the Cataloochee Valley. Spend another day savoring the sights of Newfound Gap Road, including Clingmans Dome and Cades Cove. Visit Dollywood and

Best Accommodations

★ **LeConte Lodge, GSMNP:** The only non-camping option in GSMNP is a hike-in affair (page 286).

★ **Cataloochee Campground, Waynesville:** This secluded campsite inside GSMNP is a prime spot to view elk (page 290).

★ **Mountain Laurel Chalets, Gatlinburg:** Bunk down in a private and cozy cabin that's great for groups and families (page 311).

★ **The Lodge at Buckberry Creek, Gatlinburg:** This romantic lodge is nestled amongst hiking trails and a stream (page 312).

★ **Dollywood's DreamMore Resort, Pigeon Forge:** Family-friendly amenities and the perfect touch of Dolly's country charm meet at this new resort (page 320).

★ **The Oliver Hotel, Knoxville:** Enjoy exceptional service and ultimate comfort (page 328).

kitschy Gatlinburg and Pigeon Forge in a day, then spend two days in Knoxville.

Lodging is limited to camping within the park, unless you want to hike to the rustic LeConte Lodge, so your best bet for hotels, inns, cabins, and B&Bs is to look in Gatlinburg, Pigeon Forge, or Knoxville.

Seasons matter when visiting GSMNP and the Tennessee foothills towns. Fall is prime time, and the hiking trails can be crowded. If you seek another kind of fall color—the distinct orange of the University of Tennessee—you'll find Knoxville crowded and crazy on game day; you'll score tickets if you're lucky. In spring, the weather is mild and pleasant during the day and cool in the evenings. In summer, the park sees an uptick of visitors as those to the south flee to the cooler mountains and as vacationing families head to the park. Your best bet for missing the crowds is to be just ahead of them, and visit in early- to mid-spring, in September and the first part of October, or in winter. Knoxville, however, is great to visit in any season.

Driving Considerations

In fall, Newfound Gap Road and Cades Cove can become clogged with traffic. In winter, the Blue Ridge Parkway closes due to ice and snow, and Newfound Gap Road can be a nerve-wracking drive in the worst weather.

Getting There

Starting Points

This segment of your drive begins at the **southern terminus of the Blue Ridge Parkway,** just outside of Cherokee, N.C., and ends in **Knoxville, Tenn., 70 miles** to the northwest through Great Smoky Mountains National Park along US-441 and TN-71. It's easy to make the trip from one end to the other in an afternoon, though it may take a little longer in peak seasons.

Car

From Asheville, take **I-40** west 116 miles (two hours) to Knoxville; this route puts you an hour from Gatlinburg and the entrance to GSMNP. From Charlotte, where you'll find a major airport, take **US-74** west to I-40 west into Knoxville, a four-hour drive. Alternately, take the same route, but leave I-40 for US-19 into Cherokee, then take US-441/TN-71 through GSMNP and into Knoxville.

From the south, **I-75** offers a direct route into Knoxville from Chattanooga, Tenn. (one hour and 45 minutes), and Atlanta, Ga. (three hours). Likewise

Best Restaurants

★ **Big Daddy's Pizzeria, Gatlinburg:** Big Daddy's pies, wood-fired in a brick oven, include classic combos as well as creative twists (page 313).

★ **The Restaurant at Buckberry Creek, Gatlinburg:** Gatlinburg's best fine-dining restaurant focuses on seasonal ingredients. Their dessert is excellent (page 313).

★ **Poynor's Pommes Frites, Pigeon Forge:** Top your Belgian fries with bacon, cheese, or jalapenos (page 320).

★ **Mel's Diner, Pigeon Forge:** Open til midnight, Mel's serves up classic diner fare (page 321).

★ **Sweet P's Barbecue & Soul House, Knoxville:** Savor some excellent barbecue and equally excellent sides (page 329).

★ **Dead End BBQ, Knoxville:** Fill up on barbecue, but save a little room for the ultra-rich banana pudding (page 330).

I-40 is a direct route from Nashville to Knoxville (two hours and 45 minutes). From the north, Knoxville is accessible via I-81.

Fueling Up

There are no gas stations along the southern end of the Blue Ridge Parkway or along Newfound Gap Road. You'll need to fuel up and buy snacks in Cherokee, N.C., or in Gatlinburg or Pigeon Forge, Tenn., where you'll have your choice of filling stations.

Air

McGhee Tyson Airport (2055 Alcoa Hwy., Alcoa, Tenn., 865/342-3000, www. tys.org), the closest major travel hub to Knoxville and the southern end of the Blue Ridge Parkway, is about 12 miles south of Knoxville and is an easy drive into the city along the Alcoa Highway. **Charlotte Douglas International Airport** (5501 R C Josh Birmingham Pkwy., Charlotte, N.C., 704/359-4013, www. charlotteairport.com) is a four-hour drive to the southeast of Knoxville. **Asheville Regional Airport** (61 Terminal Dr., Asheville, N.C., 828/684-2226, www. flyavl.com) is about two hours east of Knoxville.

Bus

There is bus service to the **Knoxville Greyhound station** (100 E. Magnolia Ave., 865/525-9483, www.greyhound. com). **Knoxville Area Transit** (301 E. Church Ave., 865/215-7800, www.katbus. com, $1.50), or **KAT**, is a bus line running several routes throughout the city.

Great Smoky Mountains National Park

Great Smoky Mountains National Park (GSMNP, 865/436-1200, www.nps.gov/ grsm) was the first—and the largest—of three National Park Service units established in the southern Appalachians. The park was founded in 1934, followed in 1935 by the Blue Ridge Parkway and in 1936 by Shenandoah National Park. These sister facilities include some 600 miles of contiguous road and close to 800,000 acres of land, all of it acquired from private landholders, and all of it standing today as a testament to the wild, rugged beauty of the Appalachian Mountains and the people who helped tame these places.

GSMNP itself is the most visited National Park, with around 10 million visitors each year. In the 521,085-acre park, you'll find 800 miles of hiking trails, including 70 miles of the Appalachian Trail; 16 mountains over 6,000 feet; 2,100 miles of mountain streams and rivers; and an astoundingly diverse set of flora and fauna.

More than 17,000 species have been documented here, including more than 100 species of native trees, 1,500 flowering plant species, 200 species of birds, 66 types of mammals, 67 native species of fish, 39 varieties of reptiles, and 43 species of amphibians. And that's not even counting the mushrooms, mollusks, and millipedes. Plus, researchers believe an additional 30,000-80,000 may exist. No other area of a similar size in a similar climate can boast a higher number of species. A number of factors are believed to have contributed to this astounding number, including the wide range in elevation (from 875 to 6,643 feet), which provides quite a variance in temperature, as well as the fantastic growing conditions created by summer's high humidity and abundant rainfall (apart from the Pacific Northwest, these are the rainiest mountains in the country). Plus, as some of the oldest mountains in the world—it is believed that the Smokies were formed some 200-300 million years ago—they've seen a number of dramatic climactic changes. During the last ice age (10,000 years ago), the glacial intrusion

One Day In GSMNP

Morning

Enjoy breakfast at the **Pancake Pantry** (628 Parkway, 865/436-4724, 7am-4pm daily June-Oct., 7am-3pm daily Nov.-May, $6-10) in Gatlinburg, the first pancake house in Tennessee. Head out of town toward GSMNP and stop off at the **Sugarlands Visitor Center** (1420 Old TN-73 Scenic, Gatlinburg, 865/436-1200, www.nps.gov/grsm, daily except Christmas Day) to pick up maps, then continue on down Little River Road to **Cades Cove.** Easily the most popular auto tour in the park, Cades Cove has amazing scenery but even more amazing wildlife watching. Get there at the right time of day (early morning or near dusk) and you'll see herds of deer grazing the fields and black bears playing, eating, and napping in the remnants of former apple orchards.

If you're in an SUV, truck, or some sort of high-clearance, off-road-appropriate vehicle, leave Cades Cove via **Rich** **Mountain Road,** a beautiful, eight-mile road that takes you up and over the mountains to Townsend (not far to the west of Gatlinburg). The views of Cades Cove are unparalleled, so have your camera ready.

Afternoon

Leave the park for lunch in Gatlinburg, then hit the **Roaring Fork Motor Nature Trail,** from which you can hike to four falls with relative ease. For a 2.6-mile round-trip hike, try **Grotto Falls Trail,** which leads through a lovely forest before you reach the 25-foot Grotto Falls. You can hike behind the falls, and if you're lucky, you may see pack llamas hauling supplies to the LeConte Lodge. As you're leaving the Motor Nature Trail, stop at the **Thousand Drips Falls,** sometimes called Place of a Thousand Drips. It's literally just a few steps off the road and is an excellent cascade as it falls down the mossy rock face.

---

into the United States didn't reach the Smokies, making them a refuge for species of plants and animals displaced from their Northern homes.

Visiting the Park
Getting There and Around

Knoxville, Tenn., is 36 miles to the northwest of Great Smoky Mountains National Park along US-441 and TN-71.

The 33-mile **Newfound Gap Road** (US-441) bisects the park from north to south. It's the most heavily traveled route in the park and provides a good introduction for first-time visitors.

Entrances

There are three main entrances to Great Smoky Mountains National Park. Each main entrance is easily accessed from a nearby gateway town:

- From **Gatlinburg, TN,** follow US-441 south two miles into the park.

- From **Townsend, TN,** take TN-73 three miles east into the park.

- From **Cherokee, NC,** drive two miles north along US-441 into the park.

In addition to the main entrances, there are 17 other points to enter the park via automobile. The majority of these are gravel roads of varying states of maintenance and requiring varying degrees of driving confidence and skill, but if you're up for an adventure, you can find some beautiful corners of the park along these routes.

Permits and Regulations

GSMNP is unusual among the National Parks System in that it has **no entrance fee,** so if you see a Friends of the Smokies donation box and you're so inclined (or so moved by what you see around you), toss a few bucks their way.

There are very few permits required

for recreational activities within GSMNP. If you're an angler and you want to try your hand at fishing in the more than 2,100 miles of streams and rivers, you'll need to get a **fishing license** from either Tennessee or North Carolina, and then, depending on where you're fishing, you may need an additional permit from Gatlinburg or Cherokee. Permits are available for North Carolina at www.ncwildlife.org, and for Tennessee at www1.tn.wildlifelicense.com. To fish in Gatlinburg, pick up a license at the **Gatlinburg Welcome Center** (1011 Banner Rd., 865/277-8957, www.gatlinburg.com, 8:30am-7pm daily), and keep in mind that there's no fishing on Thursdays, that's when the town stocks their streams. In Cherokee, you can pick up an Eastern Band Sport Fishing License, also called a Tribal Fishing Permit, online at www.ebcis.sovsportsnet.net; at the **Cherokee Welcome Center** (498 Tsali Blvd., 800/438-1601, www.visitcherokeenc.com, 8am-5pm Mon.-Thurs., 8am-6pm Fri.-Sun.); or at other businesses in Cherokee. You can also arrange for a fishing guide to lead you to the best spots; most guides provide licenses to their clients, so that option is hassle free. For complete regulations on accessible streams, permitted tackle, daily limits, and the like, visit www.nps.gov/grsm or the websites of Cherokee and Gatlinburg.

Hikers are not required to get permits or register with rangers, except when staying overnight in the backcountry. Those on multi-day hikes or interested in backcountry **camping** can reserve (www.smokiespermits.nps.gov) tent sites and shelter space up to 30 days in advance of the trip. More information and trip planning assistance are available through the **Backcountry Office** (865/436-1297, daily 8am-5pm, permits $4/person/night). Hikers, campers, anglers, and equestrian enthusiasts are asked to follow Leave-no-Trace practices.

No dogs or other **pets** (other than

service animals) are permitted on park trails, except the Gatlinburg Trail and Oconaluftee River Trail, though they are allowed in frontcountry campsites and picnic areas, so long as they remain on leash.

And, of course, don't feed, touch, or tease wildlife, and don't approach within 50 yards (150 feet) of elk or bears.

Visitors Centers

Begin your exploration of GSMNP with a stop at one of the park's four visitors centers. You'll find rangers who know the trail and road conditions as well as what's blooming where. You can also grab detailed maps and trail guides.

If you're entering GSMNP from the North Carolina side, **Oconaluftee Visitor Center** (1194 Newfound Gap Rd., Cherokee, N.C., 828/497-1904, www.nps.gov/grsm, 8am-4:30pm daily Dec.-Feb., except Christmas Day, 8am-5pm daily Mar., 9am-6pm daily Apr.-May, 8am-7:30pm daily June-Aug., 8am.-6:30pm daily Sept.-Oct., 8am-5pm daily Nov.), just two miles north of Cherokee on US-441/Newfound Gap Road, is the best place to begin your tour.

Along Newfound Gap Road, you'll find the turnoff to Clingmans Dome and the **Clingmans Dome Visitor Contact Station** (Clingmans Dome Rd., off Newfound Gap Rd., 25 miles from Cherokee and 23 miles from Gatlinburg, 865/436-1200, www.nps.gov/grsm, 10am-6pm daily Apr.-Oct., 9:30am-5pm daily Nov.). Clingmans Dome is the highest peak in GSMNP and features a fantastic viewing platform. At the visitor contact station, you'll find information on the park, a bookstore, and restrooms.

The busiest information center in the park is also the first stop for visitors entering the park from the west. **Sugarlands Visitor Center and Park Headquarters** (1420 Old TN-73 Scenic, Gatlinburg, 865/436-1200, www.nps.gov/grsm, 8am-4:30pm daily Dec.-Feb., except Christmas Day, 8am-5pm daily Mar., 9am-6pm

Smoky Mountain Blooms and Foliage

You'll find the most abundant display of spring wildflower blooms in mid- to late April. Keep in mind that the dates for wildflower blooms and fall color displays are only guidelines. A number of factors contribute to the ideal timing of blooms and changing leaves. Check with park officials for the best times and places to experience the best each season has to offer. Fall offers colors, too: At the highest elevations, **leaves begin to change** during the first two weeks of October, creeping down the mountains and ending in late October or early November.

- **Catawba rhododendron:** Grows at elevations above 3,500 feet; blooms in June.
- **Flame azalea:** This wild shrub blooms at lower elevations in April and May, at higher elevations through June and early July.
- **Mountain laurel:** Blooms from early May through June.
- **Rosebay rhododendron:** Blooms in lower elevations in June and July.

daily Apr.-May, 8am-7:30pm daily June-Aug., 8am.-6:30pm daily Sept.-Oct., 8am-5pm daily Nov.) is located just inside the park, only two miles from Gatlinburg. Here you'll find the usual visitors center information as well as a 20-minute film introducing you to the park.

In Cades Cove, about halfway around the ever-popular Loop Road, is the **Cades Cove Visitor Center** (Cades Cove Loop Rd., 865/436-1200, www.nps.gov/grsm, 9am-4:30pm daily Dec.-Jan., except Christmas Day, 9am-5:30pm daily Feb. and Nov., 9am-6:30pm daily Mar. and Sept.-Oct., 9am-7pm daily Apr. and Aug., 9am-7:30pm daily May-June). Indoor and outdoor exhibits illustrate Southern mountain life and culture, and there are a number of historic structures to photograph and explore.

Seasons

The seasons have a major impact on visitation to GSMNP. Crowds arrive for the blooming of wildflowers in spring, and every autumn, GSMNP grows thick with visitors and even thicker with a blaze of red, yellow, and burgundy leaves on each mountainside. During fall, spots like Newfound Gap Road and Cades Cove can become absolutely lousy with cars (expect bumper-to-bumper as you loop Cades Cove), and the hiking trails crowded

with picture-takers. If fall color is on your agenda, consider spending more time exploring the back roads, long hikes, and seldom-seen corners of the park in the extreme north and south ends.

Winter can be an excellent time to visit the park, especially if there's been a dusting of snow. With fewer crowds and maintained roads like Cades Cove Loop and Newfound Gap Road, the mountains, trails, streams, and historic structures here can be a lonely, lovely sight.

Accommodations

As big as GSMNP may be, there are few places to stay within the boundaries, and all but one option are either campsites or backcountry shelters. The lone exception is **LeConte Lodge** (865/429-5704, www.lecontelodge.com, Mar.-Nov., adults $132, children ages 4-12 $85, includes lodging, breakfast, and dinner), a collection of cabins and small lodges and a central dining room/lodge. It's only accessible by hiking in, so you have to be dedicated to stay there.

Other lodging in the park includes **frontcountry camping** in 10 developed campgrounds featuring restrooms with cold running water and flush toilets. These sites are at Abrams Creek, Balsam Mountain, Big Creek, Cades Cove, Cataloochee, Cosby, Deep Creek,

Elkmont, Look Rock, and Smokemont. Only Cades Cove, Cataloochee, Cosby, Elkmont and Smokemont take reservations (877/444-6777, www.recreation.gov, $14-20); all others are first-come, first-served.

Backcountry camping includes more than a dozen shelters and around 100 campsites. They're sprinkled throughout the park at convenient intervals. To reserve a backcountry site, visit www.smokiespermits.nps.gov; you can call the GSMNP **Backcountry Office** (865/436-1297) for more information on your chosen campsite or for trail or campsite closings or warnings.

There are also seven **tent-only group campgrounds** (877/444-6777, www.recreation.gov, $26-65) at Big Creek, Cades Cove, Cataloochee, Cosby, Deep Creek, Elkmont, and Smokemont. Additionally, there are five **horse camps** (877/444-6777, www.recreation.gov, $20-25) at Anthony Creek, Big Creek, Cataloochee, Round Bottom, and Tow String.

Just outside the park, **Fontana Village** (300 Woods Roads, Fontana Dam, N.C., 800/849-2258, www.fontanavillage.com, rooms and suites $109-219, tent and RV sites $15-40, cabins $109-279) offers a place to lay your head in your choice of accommodations: tent or RV camping, one- to three-bedroom cabins, and lodge rooms. There are 100 lodge rooms, 110 cabins, and 20 campsites. At the lodge you'll find complimentary wireless Internet in the public areas; other amenities include an outdoor pool and lazy river, as well as a fitness center and small day spa.

Food and Supplies
Groceries and camping supplies are quite limited in GSMNP. Food is virtually nonexistent, so bring snacks. The **Sugarlands** and **Oconaluftee Visitors Centers** have a small selection of vending machine beverages and a few convenience items (batteries, memory cards), but little else. At the **Cades Cove**

Campground Store (10035 Campground Dr., Townsend, Tenn., 865/448-9034, www.explorecadescove.com, 9am-5pm daily Mar.-May, 9am-9pm daily June-Aug. 15, 9am-5pm daily Aug. 16-Nov.), you can grab breakfast, a sandwich or wrap, pizza, and other snack bar items as well as a very limited selection of groceries and camping supplies. **Elkmont Campground Concessions** (434 Elkmont Rd., Gatlinburg, Tenn., 865/430-5560, www.elkmontcampgroundconcessions.net, 4pm-8pm daily Mar. 8-May, 9am-9pm daily June-Aug. 15, 4pm-8pm daily Aug. 16-Oct., 4pm-6pm daily Nov.) has a handful of snack foods and beverages as well as firewood, ice, and a few camping items. That's it for food, so stock up in Gatlinburg, Cherokee, or whichever town you visit outside the park.

At **Fontana Village** (300 Woods Roads, Fontana Dam, N.C.), just outside GSMNP, there are two restaurants, a snack bar, ice cream shop, and general store. **Mountainview Restaurant** (828/498-2211, 7:30am-2:30pm and 5:30pm-8pm daily, breakfast $4-9, dinner $15-32) serves steaks, chicken, and a nice selection of seafood that includes several preparations of trout. Reservations are recommended during weekends and in peak season. **Wildwood Grill** (828/498-2211, daily 11:30am-9pm Apr.-Oct., $6-20) serves pizza, burgers, and an array of fried appetizers. In the summer, concerts on the deck give visitors a little listening enjoyment to go with dinner.

Information and Services
The official website of **Great Smoky Mountains National Park** (www.nps.gov/grsm) has a good deal of the information you'll need to plan a trip. At the visitors centers in Sugarlands, Oconaluftee, Cades Cove, and Clingmans Dome you'll find additional information from helpful rangers and fellow travelers.

The nearest hospitals from GSMNP are **LeConte Medical Center** (742 Middle Creek Rd., 865/446-7000, www.

lecontemedicalcenter.com) in Sevierville, Tenn., about 25 minutes from the west park entrance; **Blount Memorial Hospital** (907 E. Lamar Alexander Pkwy., 865/983-7211, www.blountmemorial.org) in Maryville, Tenn., about an hour away from the west park entrance; and **Swain County Hospital** (45 Plateau St., 828/488-2155, www.westcarehealth.org) in Bryson City, N.C., a little less than 30 minutes from the eastern park entrance in Cherokee.

★ Newfound Gap Road

Easily the most heavily traveled route in the Smokies, Newfound Gap Road (US-441) connects Cherokee with Gatlinburg and sees thousands of visitors a day. Newfound Gap Road is the perfect introduction to GSMNP for park newbies. Contour hugging curves, overlooks with million-dollar views, easy hikes right off the roadway, and a 3,000-foot elevation change all give you an introduction to these mountains and this spectacular park. During peak times in the summer and fall, it's not uncommon to encounter a traffic jam or two along this 33-mile scenic route, especially when bears are taking their time crossing the road.

Newfound Gap Road earned its name in 1872 when Swiss geographer Arnold Henry Guyot determined that a newly found gap was the lowest pass through the Great Smoky Mountains, so, naturally they named it Newfound Gap. Lower in elevation and easier to access than the former passage at Indian Gap, 1.5 miles away, Newfound Gap soon gave its name to the entire route.

Oconaluftee Visitor Center and Mountain Farm Museum

As you begin your trip along Newfound Gap Road through the park from the North Carolina side, your first stop will probably be the "Welcome to Great Smoky Mountains National Park" sign, but the **Oconaluftee Visitor Center and Mountain Farm Museum** (1194 Newfound

trail alongside the Oconaluftee River

Gap Rd., Cherokee, N.C., 828/497-1904, www.nps.gov/grsm, 8am-4:30pm daily Dec.-Feb., except Christmas Day, 8am-5pm daily Mar., 9am-6pm daily Apr.-May, 8am-7:30pm daily June-Aug., 8am-6:30pm daily Sept.-Oct., 8am-5pm daily Nov.), just two miles north of Cherokee on US-441/Newfound Gap Road, will likely be the second stop you make. You can pick up a park map, grab the schedule of ranger-led programs, and see exhibits on the people who called these hills home long before the park was in existence. The visitor center and adjacent comfort station are LEED Gold certified.

Next to the visitor center is **Mountain Farm Museum** (sunrise-sunset daily year-round, free), which showcases some of the finest farm buildings in the park. Most date to the early 1900s and among them are a barn, apple house, and the Davis House, a log home built from chestnut wood and constructed before the American chestnut blight decimated

the species. This collection of structures is original to the area and dates back to the turn of the 20th century. Though the barn is the only structure original to this site, the other buildings were moved here from inside and adjacent to the park and arranged much like the typical farm of the era would have been arranged. If you visit during peak times, you'll see living-history interpreters in costume, demonstrating the day-to-day chores that would've occurred on this farm: preparing meals; sewing, maintaining, and harvesting the garden; taking care of the hogs; and the like.

The **Smokemont Campground** (877/444-6777, www.recreation.gov, $17-20) is just off Newfound Gap Road, 3.2 miles from the Oconaluftee Visitor Center. There are 142 total sites available between tent campsites and RV sites. As it's located on the banks of the Oconaluftee River, it can get quite buggy, so be prepared.

Oconaluftee River Trail

Distance: 3 miles round-trip
Duration: 45 minutes
Elevation gain: 70 feet
Difficulty: easy
Trailhead: Oconaluftee Visitor Center, or just outside of Cherokee on US-441

This trail by the Oconaluftee River runs from the visitor center to the outskirts of Cherokee. It's great for walking or jogging and is one of two paths in GSMNP where you can walk your **dog** or ride your **bike.** Flat save for a bridge or two and a few gentle rises, the Oconaluftee River Trail is a lovely walk. In the spring, the banks of the Oconaluftee are blanketed with wildflowers, and throughout the year, you may see a herd of elk crossing the river at any number of places. Bring bug spray as it can get a bit buggy right by the river on a still day.

Deep Creek Valley Overlook

The Deep Creek Valley Overlook, 14 miles from the Oconaluftee Visitor

Center (and 16 miles from Sugarlands Visitor Center if you're coming from the other direction), is one of the most popular overlooks in the park, and for good reason. From here, you'll have a long view of the mountains, which roll away from you for as far as you can see.

Oconaluftee River Valley Overlook

Halfway through Newfound Gap Road is the Oconaluftee River Valley Overlook, a spot where you can spy the deep cut of the valley formed by the Oconaluftee River. This spot is ideal for a picnic, so if you're hungry and you've brought your blanket and something to eat, spread out and relax for a few minutes.

Newfound Gap

One of the most visited overlooks is at Newfound Gap. This is the highest elevation on Newfound Gap Road, at 5,048 feet, and though the views here are fantastic, the first thing you'll probably notice is the Rockefeller Memorial, a simple stone terrace that straddles the Tennessee/North Carolina state line and commemorates a $5 million gift made by the Rockefeller Foundation to acquire land for the park. In 1940, President Franklin D. Roosevelt dedicated the park from this site. Plan to spend a little time here, especially early in the morning or near sunset. At sunset, you can see the Smokies' namesake haze settling in the folds and wrinkles of the mountains, and in the early morning, the mountains emerge from a blue haze in a subtle display of color that's been the subject of many a postcard and computer desktop background.

Appalachian Trail to Mount LeConte via The Boulevard

Distance: 15.6 miles one-way

top to bottom: a typical cabin in the Great Smoky Mountains; a bridge near the Alum Cave Bluff trailhead; road sign warning of curves ahead

Duration: 7-8.5 hours

Elevation gain: 3,000 feet

Difficulty: strenuous

Trailhead: Appalachian Trail trailhead at the Newfound Gap Road Overlook

Directions: From the Sugarlands Visitor Center on Newfound Gap Road, drive 13 miles southeast along Newfound Gap Road to the Newfound Gap Overlook. This is a tough hike. The trail largely follows the crest of the mountains, and thusly rises and falls several times, and with some significant elevation gains and losses.

From the start, the trail climbs. For two miles you'll be on a steady incline, but there are views aplenty to give you a little boost. At 1.7 miles, just before you come to the junction with Sweat Heifer Creek Trail, you'll have a good look at Mount LeConte to the north. At 2.8 miles, The Boulevard forks off to the left.

Continue along The Boulevard, ignoring the sign for the Jump-Off Trail (you can hike the one-mile trail on the return trip if you want). Soon you'll drop down to an elevation around 5,500 feet, where you'll find the trail bounces back and forth between 5,500 and 6,000 feet until you begin to properly climb Mount LeConte and make your way to the Lodge there and the 6,593-foot peak.

Charlies Bunion Hike

Distance: 8.1 miles round-trip

Duration: 7-8.5 hours

Elevation gain: 1,700 feet

Difficulty: strenuous

Trailhead: Appalachian Trail trailhead at the Newfound Gap Road Overlook

Directions: From the Sugarlands Visitor Center on Newfound Gap Road, drive 13 miles southeast along Newfound Gap Road to the Newfound Gap Overlook. Originally named Fodderstack, Charlies Bunion earned its new name when two men, Charlie Conner and Horace Kephart, were hiking here. They stopped to rest at Fodderstack and, according to legend, Conner removed his boots and socks, revealing a bunion that Kephart felt resembled the rocks around them. Impressed, Kephart promised Charlie that he'd get the name of this place changed on official maps in honor of the bunion. Not sure if it's true, but it's a good story either way.

This trail follows the first leg of the Appalachian Trail and Boulevard to Mount LeConte. From the start, the trail climbs. For two miles you'll be on a steady incline, but there are views aplenty to give you a little boost. At 1.7 miles, just before you come to the junction with Sweat Heifer Creek Trail, you'll have a good look at Mount LeConte to the north. At 2.8 miles, The Boulevard forks off to the left; continue straight to reach Charlies Bunion.

The Icewater Spring Shelter, aptly named for the cold spring that flows out of the mountain here (treat the water before you drink it), is just 0.25 miles from the junction and is a good spot to rest. Continue on a little less than a mile to a short spur trail on your left that leads out to the rock outcrop known as Charlies Bunion.

Clingmans Dome

If you know where you're looking, you'll see Clingmans Dome, the highest peak in the park and Tennessee at 6,643 feet. To access the peak and the hikes here requires a seven-mile side trip down a spur road. From the parking area, it's a short, steep half-mile hike to the summit observation tower. The 360-degree view is worth the effort, and on the clearest days, you can see as far as Mount Mitchell, just outside of Asheville, N.C. These sort of blue-sky days are somewhat rare, so don't be surprised if you get to the top and find yourself socked in, surrounded by fog or mist. If this is the case, give it a few minutes, the weather can change in an instant.

★ Andrews Bald

Distance: 3.5 miles round-trip

Duration: 3 hours

Elevation gain: 1,200 feet

Difficulty: moderate

Trailhead: Clingmans Dome parking area at the end of Clingmans Dome Road

The highest grassy bald in GSMNP, Andrews Bald is a beautiful sight at the end of a nearly two-mile hike from Clingmans Dome. Balds are simply meadows found higher up on the mountain than you'd expect, and this one is absolutely lousy with flame azalea and rhododendron blooms in the summer.

Before recent trail renovations, the Andrews Bald hike had some of the most rugged sections of rocky trails in the park, but thanks to the Trails Forever program, work crews fixed drainage issues, rebuilt parts of the trail, and even built a few stairways from native rocks and trees. Now the hike is easier and safer and leads to a spectacular view of the Smoky Mountains. A bonus: the hike is just long enough to discourage some potential hikers, but it's still short enough to be doable by everyone in your party.

The first section of the trail passes through a spruce-fir forest, which was once beautiful, but of late has been ravaged by a tiny bug; what spruce and fir that still stand here are largely young trees. Keep climbing through the forest until the trees open upon the bald proper. Fantastic panoramic views await.

Mount LeConte

Just below the 6,593-foot peak of Mount LeConte, you'll find the only true lodging in GSMNP, the ★ **LeConte Lodge** (865/429-5704, www.lecontelodge.com, Mar.-Nov., adults $132, children ages 4-12 $85, includes lodging, breakfast, and dinner). Like the summit, the Lodge is accessible only via the network of hiking trails that crisscross the park. And if the accessibility limitation isn't rustic enough for you, this collection of cabins has no running water or electricity. What the Lodge does have is views for days and the seclusion of the Smoky Mountains

backcountry. Oh, and a hearty breakfast and dinner come with each room.

LeConte Lodge has no hot showers, but in every cabin there is a bucket for a sponge bath (which can be surprisingly refreshing after a hot day on the trail), which you can fill with warm water from the kitchen, though you need to supply your own washcloth and towel. There are a few flush toilets in a separate building and the only lights, aside from headlamps and flashlights, are kerosene lanterns, but for the most part, it's rustic, harkening back to the Lodge's 1934 arrival on the slopes of Mount LeConte. Your room does come with two meals: dinner and breakfast. Both are served at the same time every day, 6pm for dinner and 8am for breakfast, and at mealtime, plates are loaded with food hearty enough to fuel you for another day on the trail.

The Lodge doesn't lack for charm, but it does for comfort, so if you're the five-star hotel, breakfast-in-bed type, this may not be the place for you. Catering to hikers who are happier to have a dry place to sleep and a bed that's more comfy than their sleeping bag, it's short on the luxury amenities, and rooms are, in truth, bunk beds in small, drafty cabins. But if you're a hiker or if you just love to have a completely different experience when you travel, this is a one-of-a-kind accommodation. Make reservations well in advance as the Lodge books pretty quickly, up to a year in advance, especially during peak weekends and all throughout the fall color bonanza.

The **Roaring Fork Motor Nature Trail** at the foot of Mount LeConte has a trio of hiking trails that lead to LeConte Lodge. **Bull Head Trail** is a 6.8-mile trip from the trailhead to the Lodge, as is **Rainbow Falls Trail.** (Bull Head and Rainbow Falls Trails share a trailhead at the designated parking area on the Motor Nature Trail.) **Trillium Gap Trail,** which happens to be the trail used by the Lodge's pack llamas, passes by the beautiful Grotto Falls on this 6.7-mile hike (you'll find the trailhead at the Grotto Falls parking area on the Motor Nature Trail). Each of these three trails will take around four hours to reach the Lodge from the trailhead.

Three other trails lead to Mount LeConte from various places in the park. **Alum Cave Trail** (5 miles one-way), which comes in from Newfound Gap Road, is the shortest and easiest to access, but it's the steepest. **The Boulevard Trail** connects the Appalachian Trail to LeConte Lodge (13.2 miles from Newfound Gap Overlook). The Boulevard Trail is relatively easy with little elevation change, but there's the issue of exposure. This trail is rocky and has a few dizzying drops right off the trail. This, combined with the fact that it comes in from the Appalachian Trail, deters most day or overnight hikers from using it. **Brushy Mountain Trail** (11.8 miles round-trip) leads from the Porters Creek Trailhead off Greenbrier Road. Brushy Mountain has a significant elevation change, but it's relatively easy.

Alum Cave Bluff to Mount LeConte Hike

Distance: 5 miles one-way
Duration: 3-3.5 hours
Elevation gain: 2,560 feet
Difficulty: moderate with strenuous sections
Trailhead: Alum Cave Trailhead
Directions: From the Sugarlands Visitor Center on Newfound Gap Road, drive 8.7 miles southeast along Newfound Gap Road to the Alum Cave Trailhead.

This is one of the most popular hikes in the park, so if you plan on hiking to Mount LeConte and back in a day or spending the night at the Lodge, it's in your best interest to arrive early so you can get a parking space.

The trail starts off fairly gently as it climbs up to Arch Rock. Alum Cave Creek runs alongside the trail for a while, and here you'll have the chance to snap pictures of several cascades and beautiful rhododendron thickets (which bloom in late June and July). You'll reach Arch Rock, which is less arch and more natural tunnel, around 1.5 miles in.

Here the trail begins to climb more steeply. A set of stone steps leads out of Arch Rock and the forest changes from hemlock and hardwood to spruce and fir trees. In another half-mile, you'll reach Inspiration Point, a place where the view opens onto one of the mid-elevation balds.

When you reach Alum Cave Bluffs, you're halfway to Mount LeConte. The rock formations aren't caves, but rather deep overhangs that create an impressive shelter from the rain. The Smokies receive more than 85 inches of rain a year, yet the majority of the soil under the bluffs remain dry and dusty, totally arid in one of the wettest forests in the nation.

Most hikers turn around at Alum Cave Bluffs, but if you're pushing on to Mount LeConte, you'll find the path steepens and grows more challenging as you gain elevation. Soon, the trail will narrow to rock ledges where steel cables have been bolted into the mountain for you to use as a handhold. The drop may be precipitous, but the views on these parts are fantastic.

Soon, the trail intersects with Rainbow Falls Trail, leading you to the summit of Mount LeConte in short order.

Chimney Tops

Chimney Tops takes its name from the twin knobs that rise from a ridge like chimneys. These rocky summits are rare in the Smokies, but that's not the draw; what brings people up this steep, challenging trail is the 360-degree view.

Chimney Tops Hike

Distance: 4 miles out and back
Duration: 3.5 hours
Elevation gain: 1,400 feet
Difficulty: strenuous
Trailhead: Chimney Tops trailhead on Newfound Gap Road

This popular hike leads to an outstanding view from the pinnacles, but the trail has been largely closed for several years. In 2014, it was reopened for weekend hiking as trail improvements and repairs were nearing completion. The Trails Forever team repaired drainage issues, installed rock steps and staircases, built elevated turnpikes, and took other measures to mitigate the impact of the vast amount of rain that falls here and the number of hikers who take to this trail.

The trail is incredibly steep, gaining nearly 1,000 feet in the last mile. To reach the pinnacles, the actual Chimney Tops, requires a very steep scramble over bare rock, which can be dangerous, and it's easier to climb up it than come back down.

Many people pay a visit to the first few hundred yards of this trail as it's right off Newfound Gap Road, and the cascades, pools, and boulders found along Walker Camp Prong are picturesque and good for wading and sunning yourself. As you climb, you'll cross Road Prong, another stream, twice. Just after the second crossing, the trail splits, with one part following Road Prong and the other heading to Chimney Tops. Stay right and head to the chimneys.

After a brief ascent, the trail steepens quite significantly. Take a breather here before tackling this long, straight climb. The trail continues and narrows as you walk the ridgeline. Soon, you'll be at the foot of the Chimney Tops and you'll see a sign from the National Park Service warning you to proceed at your own risk. Heed this sign, as the last bit of "trail" to the summit is a scramble that doesn't require any specialized equipment but is quite risky if you're inexperienced in such terrain.

Campbell Overlook

The Campbell Overlook is only three miles from the Sugarlands Visitor Center, and it's home to one of the best views of Mount LeConte you'll find along the road. LeConte is an interesting mountain. At 6,593 feet, it's the third highest peak in the Smokies, but it's the tallest mountain east of the Mississippi in that

Hiking trails draw visitors to the Great Smoky Mountains National Park year-round.

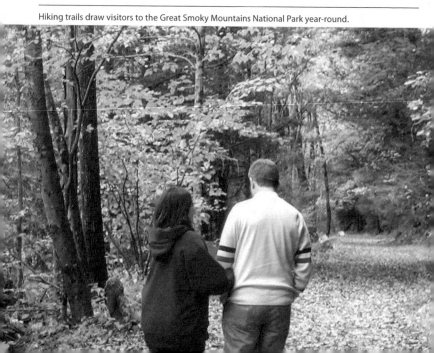

it rises more than a mile from the foot of the mountain to the summit.

Sugarlands Visitor Center

The **Sugarlands Visitor Center** (1420 Old TN-73 Scenic, Gatlinburg, 865/436-1200, www.nps.gov/grsm, 8am-4:30pm daily Dec.-Feb., except Christmas Day, 8am-5pm daily Mar., 9am-6pm daily Apr.-May, 8am-7:30pm daily June-Aug., 8am.-6:30pm daily Sept.-Oct., 8am-5pm daily Nov.) is the most visited in the park due to its proximity to Gatlinburg. There's the usual visitor center stuff—maps, guidebooks, a few gift items, some snacks—but it's also the origination point for the 1.9-mile Gatlinburg Trail.

Gatlinburg Trail

Distance: 3.8 miles out and back
Duration: 2 hours
Elevation gain: 20 feet
Difficulty: easy
Trailhead: Sugarlands Visitor Center

This is one of only two trails in the

park to allow **pets** and **bicycles** (the other is the Oconaluftee River Trail in Cherokee). More of a walk than a hike, the Gatlinburg Trail follows the West Prong Little Pigeon River and Newfound Gap Road for most of the trip. It's pretty and not especially challenging, but the optional walk to Cataract Falls—a few hundred yards up Cove Mountain Trail, which splits off the Gatlinburg Trail near the trailhead—can provide some photo opportunities and a pretty, easy to see waterfall.

Eastern Smokies

The eastern side of GSMNP was settled before the western side, so you'll find plenty of coves and hollows with historic structures or the ruins of cabins, barns, and other buildings in the fields and woods and along creek banks and floodplains. There are also several herds of elk here, introduced several years ago as a way to revive the species that once roamed these hills.

Balsam Mountain Road

Since most of the crowds who visit GSMNP use Newfound Gap Road exclusively, it's nice to find a route that's less traveled and possibly more beautiful. One such route is Balsam Mountain Road, a lovely drive where you may be lucky to see 10 other cars.

Accessible only from the Blue Ridge Parkway at Milepost 458 near Soco Gap, the road traverses 14 miles of ridgeline on a narrow, but well-maintained, gravel road. To reach Balsam Mountain Road, turn off the Parkway at Milepost 458 and follow Heintooga Ridge Road to the Heintooga Overlook and Picnic Area; here the road changes names to Balsam Mountain Road, and turns to gravel.

As soon as it turns into Balsam Mountain Road, it becomes one-way, so you're committed to follow it to its end. This will take about 1.5 hours (if you don't stop to hike or take in the scenery), primarily because the gravel road forces you to slow down. It's narrow but well maintained, so you can drive most cars along the route. If you're in doubt of the road's condition or are concerned about your vehicle's clearance, check the GSMNP website (www.nps.gov/grsm) for road closures and advisories.

Balsam Mountain Road is an excellent place to see spring wildflowers, summer rhododendron, and fall leaves. At these times, traffic may pick up, but the idea of a gravel road discourages enough visitors to keep this road the one less traveled.

When you've driven about 13 miles along Balsam Mountain Road, it become two-way again. Here, it begins to follow Straight Fork, which will lead you right onto Straight Fork Road, which cuts through the Cherokee Indian Reservation to US-441.

★ Cataloochee

Nestled in the folds of the mountains and encircled by 6,000-foot peaks, the Cataloochee Valley was settled in the early 1830s. This isolated valley on the northeastern edge of GSMNP was home to two communities—Big and Little Cataloochee— and more than 1,200 people in 1910. By the 1940s, all but a few were gone, leaving the valley, and its new status as one of the more beautiful spots in the new national park, for hills and hollows nearby. Today, the few historic structures that stand in Cataloochee Valley are all that remains of the communities that lived here, save a few memories and stories written down.

Cataloochee Valley is not far from I-40, but it can be a little difficult to find as the signage directing you here is poor at best. On I-40, take Exit 20 onto US-276. Take an immediate right onto Cove Creek Road. The condition of the road—it's alternately gravel and paved—and the narrow, winding route will make you doubt you made the right turn, but you did. Zigzag up this road

for about 12 miles and suddenly it will open up into the wide, grassy expanse that is Cataloochee Valley. Before you begin your descent into the valley, stop at the overlook just past the intersection with Big Creek Road. From here, you can marvel at the valley sweeping away before you and the mountains rising up all around.

The valley is open to vehicle traffic from 8am to sunset, so keep that in mind if you're visiting without plans to camp. Though less visited than other areas, like Cades Cove on the western side of the park, Cataloochee sees its fair share of visitors. Most arrive in the evenings shortly before sunset to see the elk grazing in the fields. If you don't plan on camping and you'd rather avoid the crowds, as small as they may be, visit in mid-day and take a hike and see if you can find the elk in the woods; it's where they go to escape the heat.

The ★ **Cataloochee Campground** (877/444-6777, www.recreation.gov, Mar.-Oct., $20, reservations required) has 27 tent and RV sites. There is a horse camp with seven sites not far up the valley; down the valley there's a group campground with three sites and room for much larger parties. This highly recommended campsite is one of the most secluded you'll find in the frontcountry.

Sights

There are four prominent structures still standing in Cataloochee Valley: two homes, a school, and a church. A few other structures and ruins, cemeteries, fences, and walls remain throughout the valley as well. The most prominent building is the **Palmer Chapel and Cemetery.** The chapel was built in 1898, but it's been some time since there's been a regular service here. Now it stands empty: its doors open to the forest, the view from its windows nothing but trees. Throughout the year there are some great opportunities to capture the chapel in all sorts

The Return of Native Elk

Elk are native to the mountains of North Carolina and Tennessee, though over-hunting decimated them across the region. In North Carolina, the last elk was believed to have been killed in the late 1700s; in Tennessee, the mid-1800s. In 2001, the National Park Service reintroduced elk into the park by bringing 25 elk to GSMNP from Land Between the Lakes National Recreation Area in Kentucky. The next year they brought in another 27 animals. Today, they believe somewhere between 150 and 200 elk live in the park.

The majority of the elk can be seen in the **Cataloochee Valley,** though a small herd does live near the **Oconaluftee Visitor Center** and **Smokemont Campground** and can be seen wading across the river and grazing in the fields and forest there.

Adult males, called bulls, weigh 600-700 pounds, while females, cows, are smaller, at around 500 pounds. Some bulls have antlers five feet across. They're territorial, and bulls do sometimes see humans as a threat and may charge. It's best to watch the elk from a safe distance. According to park guidelines, approaching within 50 yards (150 feet), or any distance that disturbs or displaces the elk, is illegal in the park.

At certain times of year, you may see calves walking close by their mothers. Never approach or touch a calf. If an elk calf is feels threatened and its mother is not nearby, its natural defense is to lie down and get still. It may look orphaned, but mom's within earshot, so back away slowly.

Elk are most active in the early morning and evening, much like deer. Also like deer, their diet is primarily grass, bark, leaves, and acorns. There are no natural predators of elk in the Smokies today, though sick, injured, and young elk are sometimes targets of opportunity for black bears, coyotes, or even the boldest of bobcats.

---

of lighting, weather, and seasonal conditions. Today, the chapel sees sporadic use, the most regular being the annual reunion of the descendants of some of the oldest Cataloochee families. Descendants of the Barnes, Bennett, Caldwell, Noland, and Palmer families gather here to eat, hold a short church service, and maintain the cemetery.

Across the road is the **Beech Grove School,** the last of three schools to serve the children of the valley. It's empty too, save a few artifacts. Beech Grove School operated on a very different school schedule than we're familiar with. The only regular school sessions were held from November to January, sometimes February and rarely into March.

Just up the road is the **Caldwell House.** We know from records that the owner, Hiram Caldwell, was prosperous, but you could tell that by looking at the 1906 home and thinking of the other historic homes in the park, which are, by and large, log cabins. The Caldwell House is frame-built (similar to houses now) with paneling on the interior walls.

The final structure is the **Palmer House,** located off Big Creek Road, not far from the Cataloochee Ranger Station. Once, this was a log home, two, actually, connected by a covered walkway called a dog trot, but as the owners came into money in the early 1900s, they began making improvements and remodeling the home. They covered the exterior and interior with weatherboarding and began using fancy wallpaper in some rooms (scraps of the wallpaper are there today). When the son inherited the property, he began to remodel, adding rooms on to the home and operating it as a boarding house. Renters were primarily anglers, there to fish in the three miles of stocked trout stream the family owned.

Boogerman Trail

Distance: 7.4-mile loop
Duration: 3.5-4 hours
Elevation gain: 1,050 feet
Difficulty: moderate
Trailhead: just past Cataloochee Campground

This trail isn't named for some fearsome and mythical creature from the woods; it's named for Robert "Boogerman" Palmer, the former owner of much of the land along this hike. Palmer is rumored to have earned his nickname in school, where he told his teacher that he wanted to be "the Boogerman" when he grew up. This trail is anything but fearsome, and in summer, you'll likely see a few other hikers; if it's solitude you're seeking, hit the trail during the shoulder seasons.

Start the hike by crossing Palmer Creek. Follow Caldwell Fork upstream for nearly a mile and you'll come to Boogerman Trail. Turn left onto the trail and begin a gentle climb. When you reach a lower ridgeline, the path levels out, then descends through a grove of pine trees before ascending again. Soon, the trail makes a steep ascent to another level ridge. This section of the hike features some of the largest trees, mostly poplars, that you'll see.

As you continue on this short ridgeline section, you'll encounter some signs of human settlement, the first of which is a stone wall. Continue your descent and cross the stream you're following a few times, passing more rock walls along the way. If the wildflowers aren't too high, you may spot a large, strange piece of metal just off the trail. It's the remnant of some sort of homesteading equipment, perhaps a sluice gate for a water flume, or maybe a piece from a sawmill. Whatever it is, it's alien here.

When you pass the decayed remains of a cabin, you're close to the junction with Caldwell Fork Trail. At Caldwell Fork Trail, turn right and cross Snake Branch (the stream you've been following) and soon thereafter, Caldwell Fork. You'll cross Caldwell Fork several more times before reaching the junction with Boogerman Trail and the path back to the trailhead.

Big Creek

Big Creek is the site of another beautiful and seldom-visited frontcountry **campground** and one of the best hikes for inexperienced backpackers and day hikers. The Big Creek Trail is more of an easy, creek-side walk than a hike, but it's long enough to make you feel accomplished when you're done. In addition to the long out-and-back that is Big Creek Trail, there are options for extending the hike into longer overnighters.

Big Creek Trail

Distance: 10.6 miles round-trip
Duration: 5-6 hours
Elevation gain: 600 feet
Difficulty: easy
Trailhead: Big Creek Picnic Area off I-40 at the Waterville exit (exit 457)

Big Creek Trail follows an old motor road built by the Civilian Conservation Corps (CCC) in the 1930s, so it's smooth and wide, with a very gentle grade for its entire length. The difficult part of this trail is the distance, so be sure to bring plenty of water and something to eat.

Roughly a mile in, you'll see Rock House, an impressive rock cliff just off the trail that has sheltered more than a few loggers, CCC workers, hunters, and hikers from a rainstorm. Just beyond Rock House is Midnight hole. Here, Big Creek flows through a narrow chute in the rock and drops six or seven feet into a deep, dark pool before flowing on.

Two miles in, you'll see Mouse Creek Falls, a 35-foot cascade that drops right into Big Creek. It's a fantastic spot to sit, relax, take some pictures, and enjoy the woods. It's also a great spot to turn around if you have younger or older hikers with you who may not be up for the whole 10-mile trip.

Push on past Mouse Creek Falls and you'll come upon Brakeshoe Spring. In another 2.5 miles you'll reach Walnut Bottoms and Campsite 37. This is one of the best campsites in the park if you're going to make this hike an overnighter. Once you're here, it's time to retrace your steps back to the trailhead.

Cosby

For the first half of the 20th century, Cosby was known as the moonshine capital of the world. The national prohibition on liquor turned many locals to making their own. When scientists and workers began to come to Oak Ridge to work on secret military projects like the Manhattan Project, they weren't accustomed to Tennessee's dry county laws, and the demand for moonshine skyrocketed. Today there isn't much by way of moonshine production in town, and most of the visitors come here for the national park.

Cosby's present reputation is as a friendly town with one of the lesser-used park entrances. That's good for you, because when autumn leaves begin to change and the crowds pack Gatlinburg and clog the easy-to-access trails along Newfound Gap Road, you can head to Cosby. In town you'll find a few restaurants and a handful of cabin rentals, but the park is the real treasure.

Cosby Campground (471 Cosby Campground Road A, Cosby, Tenn., 423/487-2683, www.recreation.gov, Apr.-Oct., $14) has 157 sites for tents and RVs. Despite being home to the park's third largest campground, Cosby is known as the quietest of the park's gateways. There are a number of trails that originate from the campground.

★ Hen Wallow Falls Trail

Distance: 4.4 miles out and back
Duration: 3.5 hours
Elevation gain: 900 feet
Difficulty: moderate
Trailhead: Gabes Mountain Trailhead, across the road from the Cosby Campground picnic area

From the outset, Gabes Mountain Trail is a steady climb on a trail that's, at times, rugged, but doable. Follow this trail until you see a sign for the side trail leading to the waterfall (2.1 miles into the hike). The 0.1-mile side trail is a little steep, but not problematically so.

Hen Wallow Falls tumbles 90 feet into a small pool below, where there are plenty of salamanders to see. The falls themselves are only 2 feet wide at the top, but fan out to 20 feet at the bottom; during dry months, the falls are still pretty, but less wow-inducing.

To get back to the trailhead, just retrace your steps.

Mount Cammerer Trail

Distance: 11.2 miles out and back
Duration: 7-7.5 hours
Elevation gain: 2,740 feet
Difficulty: strenuous
Trailhead: Low Gap Trailhead, just beyond the Cosby Campground amphitheater area

Park in the group parking area and walk along the road to where it curves into the B-Section of the campground. Just before campsite 92 you'll see a trailhead, follow it a short distance until it crosses Cosby Creek, then turn right on Low Gap Trail. From here, the trail climbs a little less than three miles up the mountain via a series of winding switchbacks until you reach the Appalachian Trail.

Turn left to join the Appalachian Trail for 2.1 miles. The first mile of this is more level, so it gives you a chance to catch your breath or make up some time. You'll know when you reach the junction with the Mount Cammerer Trail because the Appalachian Trail descends to the right; you want to stay straight. The summit is 0.6 miles from where you leave the Appalachian Trail.

At the summit, you'll find a stone fire tower built in the 1930s and restored by volunteers throughout the years. The view from the deck here is awesome, one of the best in the park.

Roaring Fork Motor Nature Trail

One of the most beautiful drives in GSMNP is the Roaring Fork Motor Nature Trail. This one-way loop passes through rhododendron thickets and dense hardwood forests as it follows the old roadbed of the Roaring Fork Community. To get here, turn onto Historic Nature Trail-Airport Road at traffic light #8 in Gatlinburg and follow the signs. Before you reach the trail, you'll drive a short distance on Cherokee Orchard Road, which runs through what was an 800-acre commercial orchard in the 1920s and '30s; shortly after the orchard, you'll be at the head of the trail and have the chance to purchase an inexpensive tour booklet from a roadside exhibit.

The roadbed here was built by hand in the 1850s, which explains both its narrowness and serpentine route. Around 25 families lived here, and though it may look quaint and primitive to our eyes, a few of the homes had running water, thanks to the system of troughs—some of which are still standing—that carried water right to the houses.

As the road climbs through the forest, roll down your windows and take in a few deep breaths of that fresh, cool mountain air. There is a pair of **overlooks,** though they're overgrown and in poor repair. When you stop, take in the silence. You'll soon find that you're surrounded by the sounds of nature: wind, birds calling, streams rumbling and echoing through the forest.

Be sure to stop at the cabins still standing here. **Ogle Place,** a two-room cabin surrounded by rhododendrons; **Ephraim Bales Cabin,** which is smack in the middle of a boulder field; and **Alfred Regan Cabin,** which has an amazing trough system still in place, are all worth spending a few minutes exploring and photographing.

There are three waterfalls within hiking distance of the Motor Nature Trail: **Rainbow Falls** (the most popular of the hikes); **Grotto Falls;** and **Baskins Falls.** If you're not up for a hike, **Thousand Drips Falls** (sometimes called the Place of a Thousand Drips) is just off the road. In wet times, it's a great cascade plummeting down the mountain, and during drier times, it's much more tame, but still serene.

Rainbow Falls Trail

Distance: 5.4 miles round-trip
Duration: 3.5-4 hours
Elevation gain: 1,700 feet
Difficulty: Strenuous
Trailhead: Roaring Fork Motor Nature Trail, 3.3 miles from Gatlinburg traffic light #8, at the Rainbow Falls and Bull Head Trail parking area

This trail is strenuous due to how steep and rocky it is and how slick it can become in places where the trail nears the water and as you get closer to the falls.

As you leave the parking area, you'll cross Trillium Gap Trail and begin to climb alongside LeConte Creek. Follow the trail as it goes through a couple of switchbacks, then crosses the creek on a log bridge. Here you'll enter a stretch where some impressive trees stand. Shortly, you'll cross LeConte Creek again. At this crossing, you can see Rainbow Falls above you. Continue up the trail to a spot just below the falls.

Here, LeConte Creek plunges 80 feet to the rocks below. During that plunge, the water becomes more of a heavy mist, giving us the name, Rainbow Falls. Though you can get some good photography from the trail, there are other interesting shots to be had from different angles around the falls. Be aware that if you scramble around the falls, the rocks are slick and you could slip and hurt yourself, and with a 2.7-mile hike back to the car, who wants to do that? If you decide to explore the area around the falls, use caution and stay safe.

You may notice that the Rainbow Falls Trail continues on past the waterfall itself. It is possible to take this trail to the summit of Mount LeConte, but that is a strenuous, steep, full-day hike of close to 14 miles.

Grotto Falls Trail

Distance: 2.6 miles round-trip
Duration: 2-2.5 hours
Elevation gain: 585 feet
Difficulty: moderate
Trailhead: Roaring Fork Motor Nature Trail, about 2 miles into the trail, Grotto Falls parking area on the left

From the parking area, you'll follow a short, unnamed spur before joining Trillium Gap Trail, which leads to Grotto Falls before continuing on to the top of Mount LeConte. As you hike, you'll notice the path is hard packed, that's because this trail is the resupply route for LeConte Lodge and it sees quite a bit of traffic as llama trains carry supplies up to the Lodge; if you're lucky, you'll see one.

The forest was once comprised largely of hemlock trees, but thanks to a nasty little bug—the hemlock woolly adelgid—many of these trees are dead or dying. Even though some of the trees are being ravaged, the forest is still thick, and opens dramatically where the stream plunges 25 feet to form Grotto Falls.

The most intriguing part of Grotto Falls is the grotto. Here, Trillium Gap Trail passes behind the falls, thanks to a hefty rock overhang. It makes for some interesting photographic opportunities and, because of this, is one of the most popular waterfall hikes on this side of the park.

Baskins Falls Trail

Distance: 3.2 miles
Duration: 3 hours
Elevation gain: 950 feet
Difficulty: strenuous
Trailhead: Roaring Fork Motor Nature Trail, on the left near the Jim Bales Place

This 30-foot waterfall is like a little secret here in the popular Roaring Fork Motor

top to bottom: Thousand Drips Falls; stream in GSMNP; bull elk in Cataloochee

Nature Trail. Seldom visited, it's like a forgotten hike, meaning you can have the falls to yourself.

As soon as you start the hike, you'll pass a cemetery before making a climb up to a ridgeline. A steep descent from the ridge will take you to Baskins Creek. Cross the creek (be careful, especially in high water) and make the steep climb over another ridge. From here you can see what's left of an old chimney standing in the woods. Just beyond a tiny, wildflower-filled meadow is the side path leading to the base of the falls. On the right side of this trail is an old home site, followed by a steep descent down to the falls.

Many hikers will turn around here and return to their car, but it is possible to continue along this trail another 1.5 miles and arrive near the entrance to the Motor Nature Trail. If you do this, know that you have a three-mile walk along the road back to your car.

Greenbrier

Greenbrier Cove, like many other coves in the park, was once home to a mountain community. It's a typical story: settled in the early 1800s, families farmed, trapped, and hunted the land until the arrival of the national park. One interesting note though, Dolly Parton's ancestors, Benjamin C. and Margaret Parton, moved here in the 1850s and their descendants left when the park came.

Greenbrier is stunning, especially in spring. The cove is known as a wildflower hot spot, but don't underestimate the beauty of this place in any season.

Ramsey Cascades Trail

Distance: 8 miles out and back
Duration: 5.5 hours
Elevation gain: 2,375 feet
Difficulty: strenuous
Trailhead: Ramsey Cascades Trailhead at the Greenbrier park entrance, six miles east of Gatlinburg off US-321

Ramsey Cascades is the tallest waterfall in GSMNP, spilling 100 feet in a series of steps before collecting in a pool at the base. As if that wasn't reason enough for the hike, this section of the park is known as a wildflower paradise, so springtime hikes are highly recommended.

The first portion of this trail follows a continuation of the gravel road you took to the parking area. You'll soon cross Little Laurel Branch and almost immediately after, the Middle Prong of Little Pigeon River via a long footbridge. If you've timed your hike with the bloom, the next half mile will be a riot of color.

The hiking here is easy until you reach the 1.5-mile mark where the Jeep trail you're on ends. To the left (north) is the Greenbrier Pinnacle Trail, a trail that's not maintained by the park; Ramsey Cascades Trail continues on through a thicket of rhododendron.

Now you find yourself on a trail where roots and rocks are more the norm, so watch your footing. Continue along this trail; it will turn steep, you'll cross the Ramsey Prong and a side stream, and you'll know you've arrived when you hear the waterfall. The final approach is rocky and slick, with a lot of scrambling, so use caution. When you've taken in all of the Ramsey Cascades you can take, simply reverse course to the trailhead.

Brushy Mountain to Mount LeConte Hike

Distance: 11.8 miles out and back
Duration: 6-7 hours
Elevation gain: 3,000 feet
Difficulty: moderate
Trailhead: Porters Creek Trailhead on Greenbrier Road, six miles east of Gatlinburg off US-321
Directions: At traffic light #3 in Gatlinburg (junction of US-441 and US-321), travel east on US-321. Drive six miles, turn right on Greenbrier Road (which becomes a gravel road soon). At the fork in the road 3.1 miles in, continue straight 1 mile to the Porters Creek Trailhead.

The first mile or so of the trail follows an old gravel road, the Porters Creek Trail. In spring, the trillium are profuse here. You'll pass a cemetery and several stone walls, then cross a footbridge at a fork in the road. Turn left at the fork, then meet another fork 100 yards or so down the trail; turn right onto Brushy Mountain Trail.

The trail continues on 4.5 miles, climbing some 2,500 feet as it does. At 5.5 miles, you'll meet Trillium Gap Trail. Turn left along Trilium Gap Trail and you'll reach Mount LeConte. Turn right and you can reach the summit of Brushy Mountain in 0.6 miles.

Western Smokies

The western Smokies are a bit wilder than the eastern Smokies. As pioneers moved in from the east, they first settled the coves and hollows there, then found passes through the Smokies and settled there. The mountains, are tall and steep, and the valleys deep, and where there are coves and meadows, they're broad, rich-soiled places that, before the Park, were home to several small communities.

Deep Creek

Just south of Cherokee and just north of Bryson City, Deep Creek is a spot more popular with locals than tourists, but it's worth a stop. Deep Creek is relatively placid, aside from a couple of waterfalls a ways upstream. If you're not into wading or tubing, don't worry, this is a lovely place to picnic and hike or even camp away from the crowds in some of the more popular spots in the park.

At the end of Deep Creek Road you'll find the trailheads leading to the waterfalls. You'll also find the **Deep Creek Campground** (877/444-6777, www.rec-reation.gov, $17). There are nearly 100 campsites here, many of which fill up with locals. If you want to camp here, arrive early or reserve well in advance.

Nearby, there's also the **Deep Creek Tube Center and Campground** (1090 W. Deep Creek Rd., Bryson City, 828/488-6055, Apr.-Oct. 31, reservations office: 9am-8pm daily), a charming collection

of tent and RV campsites and cabins for rent. As the name implies, they rent tubes for use on Deep Creek. Rentals ($5 for all-day use of your tube) are cheap, so you can play in the water as long as you like.

There are two nice waterfalls to see here. **Juney Whank Falls** (yes, that's its name) is less than a half mile from the Deep Creek Campground, and cuts an impressive figure as it drops a total of 90 feet in two stages. **Indian Creek Falls** is a stunning set of falls and cascades some 60 feet high located a mile from the campground.

Juney Whank Falls Trail

Distance: 0.6-mile loop
Duration: 30 minutes
Elevation gain: 120 feet
Difficulty: moderate
Trailhead: parking area at the end of Deep Creek Road across from the campground

Juney Whank Falls supposedly got its name from Junaluska "Juney" Whank, a Cherokee Indian said to have been buried near the falls. The path here is pretty straightforward: it's short, at times steep, and at the end, a little slick. You'll walk across a log bridge to get a look at the tall, skinny falls, which actually descend in two stages. The first stage drops 40 feet to a stone outcropping, then flows beneath the log bridge to fall and cascade another 50 feet below.

Indian Creek Falls Trail

Distance: 2 miles round-trip
Duration: 1 hour
Elevation gain: 160 feet
Difficulty: easy to moderate
Trailhead: parking area at the end of Deep Creek Road across from the campground

This easier, but longer, hike takes you past a smaller waterfall, Tom's Branch Falls, on your way to Indian Creek Falls. For about a mile, you'll follow a gently graded roadbed, and soon you'll arrive at the falls. Really, Indian Creek Falls is more of a steep, long, slick cascade of water than an actual waterfall, but it's quite serene.

Road to Nowhere

An odd place to visit is the so-called Road to Nowhere. Just south of the Deep Creek entrance outside Bryson City is a short stretch of highway leading north into GSMNP. Lonely, even spooky, the road is all that remains of a parkway planned to trace a path through the Smokies along Fontana Lake. Though construction was started on the parkway, it was abandoned. Today, the road stops quite abruptly about six miles inside the park, at a man-made stone tunnel. Though hard feelings over the failed parkway have softened, many families still hold a grudge against government officials who vowed to build a road along the lake to provide access to old family cemeteries there.

Cars are prohibited from using the tunnel at the end of the Road to Nowhere, but visitors on foot are welcome to stroll right through. After you pass through the tunnel, there's a marathon-length hike—seriously, it's 26 miles—weaving along the northern bank of Fontana Lake.

Fontana Lake Area

At the southern edge of GSMNP lies Fontana Lake, a 10,230-acre reservoir created in the 1940s as part of the Tennessee Valley Authority's (TVA) efforts to supply electricity to the various communities and government and industrial facilities in the region. The 480-foot tall, 2,365-foot wide Fontana Dam, complete with three hydroelectric generators, was completed in 1944, providing much needed electricity to the factories churning out materials for World War II, including Oak Ridge, Tenn., where research leading to the atomic bomb was conducted.

To build Fontana Dam, the Tennessee Valley Authority (TVA) purchased more than 1,000 tracts of land and relocated around 600 families in five communities.

Those folks left behind homes, schools, churches, and barns, all of which were covered by the lake. This displacement of so many families and elimination of these small communities was part of the tradeoff that resulted in the modernization of the region, with cheap, readily-available electric power, and the great number of jobs required to complete the project. The dam also provides much-needed flood control to a region that receives between 55 and 82 inches of rainfall each year. Today, the TVA can regulate the depth of the lake by releasing water as they anticipate flood events, and the water level of Fontana Lake can vary by as much as 50 feet.

Fontana Dam is the highest concrete dam east of the Mississippi, and it provides great recreational opportunities. The Appalachian Trail crosses the dam itself, and thousands of boaters and anglers take to the lake each year. There are more than 238 miles of shoreline along Fontana Lake, and over 10,000 acres of water surface. If you have your own boat, you can launch it from the **Fontana Marina** (40 Fontana Dam Rd., 828/498-2129, www.fontanavillage.com), or you can rent a kayak, canoe, or paddleboard (from $20/hour to $100/day); as well as a pontoon or fishing pontoon boat (from $50/hour to $330/day). Fishing guide services and seasonal tours of the lake are also available.

The exhibits at the **Fontana Dam Visitor Center** (Fontana Dam Rd., off NC-28 near the state line, www.tva.com/sites/fontana.htm, daily 9am-6pm May-Oct., free) tell the story of the region and the construction of the dam. There's also a small gift shop, and a viewing platform overlooking the dam. Hikers take note: They also sell backcountry camping permits and have showers in the back.

Twentymile

One of the most remote sections of the park, Twentymile is on the southern end, just past Fontana Lake and Dam, alongside the smaller Cheoah Lake. Despite the name, Twentymile Trail only goes 5 miles into GSMNP, but you can make it into a 20-mile journey by joining up with other trails, or you can keep it to a manageable day hike of around 8 miles by doing a smaller loop. Though this part of the park is out of the way, Twentymile is a popular hike, so expect to see some fellow hikers, especially on weekends and through the week on beautiful days in summer and autumn. There is a trio of **backcountry campsites** (reservations: www.smokiespermits.nps.gov) at Twentymile Trail: campsites 13, 92, and 93.

Twentymile Loop Trail
Distance: 7.6-mile loop
Duration: 3.5-4 hours
Elevation gain: 1,200 feet
Difficulty: easy
Trailhead: Twentymile Ranger Station
Directions: Twentymile Ranger Station is six miles west from Fontana Dam on NC-28. Turn at the sign for Twentymile.

This hike is very easy, following a roadbed and a well maintained trail along Twentymile Trail, Twentymile Loop Trail, and Wolf Ridge Trail. There are a number of stream crossings along this route, and though there are log bridges spanning Moore Springs Branch and Twentymile Creek, floods may wash them away, and if you're there before repair crews get around to fixing the bridges, you may have to wade across.

From the trailhead, go a half mile to where Wolf Ridge Trail branches off to the left. Follow Wolf Ridge Trail for 1.1 miles to Twentymile Loop Trail. Along Wolf Ridge, you'll cross Moore Springs Branch five times as you climb. Along the way, there are abundant wildflowers, including bloodroot, fire pink, and trilliums, and the opportunity to see bears, deer, and other wildlife.

After following Wolf Ridge just over a mile, you'll see Twentymile Loop Trail branching off to the right. Cross Moore

Springs Branch, and follow the trail 2.9 miles along an easy grade before descending to a crossing of Twentymile Creek and the junction with Twentymile Trail.

Turn right on Twentymile Trail to descend back along the creek and to the trailhead. From here, you're just over three miles back to your car.

Gregory Bald via Twentymile Trail
Distance: 15.7-mile loop
Duration: 9 hours—strenuous day hike or overnighter
Elevation gain: 3,650 feet
Difficulty: strenuous
Trailhead: Twentymile Ranger Station
Directions: Twentymile Ranger Station is six miles west from Fontana Dam on NC-28. Turn at the sign for Twentymile.

This hike makes Twentymile live up to its name, even though it's a mere 15.7 miles. It's doable in a day, but it's a long, hard day, so camping for a night in the backcountry is recommended.

From the trailhead, follow Twentymile Trail for a half mile until it intersects with Wolf Ridge Trail. Turn here and follow Wolf Ridge Trail 6.3 miles to Gregory Bald Trail. The grade of Wolf Ridge Trail is somewhat steep, but more than that, it's a relentless uphill climb all the way to where you crest the ridge before reaching Parson Bald. As you approach the ridge and Parson Bald, you'll find copious amounts of blueberry bushes, and, if they're in season, a fair number of bears enjoying blueberries. The same holds true at Parson Bald, just over the ridge. If you're on the trail in August, when the blueberries tend to ripen, be cautious.

When you reach Parson Bald, it's a short, easy walk to Sheep Pen Gap, where you'll find **Campsite 13** (reservations and information: 865/436-1297, www.smokiespermits.nps.gov) and the end of Wolf Ridge Trail. Turn right on Gregory Bald Trail and climb just under a half mile to Gregory Bald. Here, there are azaleas in great abundance and during mid-summer, the bald is a riot of blooms. But even if you come when there's not a bloom to be found, the views make the hike worth it.

From here, keep heading east to Rich Gap, where you'll come upon a four-way trail junction. You're following Long Hungry Ridge Trail to the right, heading south. This trail is pretty flat for the first mile, then it begins to descend, and the descent becomes increasingly noticeable as you move down the trail. You'll find Campsite 92 3.4 miles from Rich Gap. Once you've reached the campsite, you've left the steepest part of the hike behind you.

Continue down Long Hungry Ridge Trail to the place where it meets Twentymile Trail, following Twentymile Creek 2.6 miles back to the junction with Wolf Ridge Trail. At this point, you're only a half mile from the trailhead.

Elkmont

At the Elkmont Campground, only eight miles from Gatlinburg, drifts of male fireflies rise up from the grass to flash their mating signal, but they don't do so as individuals, they blink in coordinated ways that still baffle researchers. For a two-week window every summer (often early to mid-July, but it depends on a variety of factors), their nightly light snow delights crowds. It starts slowly, with only a few of these insects showing off, then more join in, and more until they reach a crescendo. Slowly, they begin to synchronize until, at the peak, whole fields may flash all at once, giving you a sudden and startling blink of light and just as sudden darkness. Or they may flash in waves moving around the fields and hillsides. Or large groups may appear to flash their lights at one another and wait in the darkness for a response. Whatever the reason, the synchronous fireflies are amazing little creatures. Nineteen species of fireflies live in GSMNP, but these are the only fireflies in the park to synchronize their flashing.

fall color near the Roaring Fork Motor Nature Trail

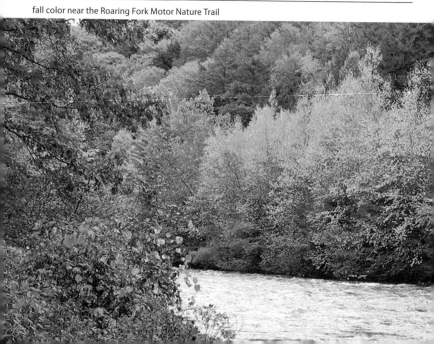

The synchronous fireflies may have been one of the reasons the Wonderland Park Hotel was built here in Elkmont. In 1908, the little logging town of Elkmont was born, and in 1912, the Wonderland Park Hotel was built. Cottages dotted the hillsides and bottoms. Once the park was established, cottage owners were granted lifetime leases on their property, and family members continued to renew the leases at 20-year intervals until the early 1990s. The Wonderland Park Hotel and the cottages were slated for demolition, but the Elkmont Historic District is now listed in the National Register of Historic Places. The hotel collapsed in the early 2000s, and the Park Service has visions of restoring a few of the remaining cottages, but work in earnest has yet to begin.

The **Elkmont Campground** (434 Elkmont Rd., Gatlinburg, 865/430-5560, www.recreation.gov, $17-23) has 220 campsites, 55 of them along the Little River, with front-row seats to the firefly light show, provided you're here at the right time. This is the largest of the campgrounds in GSMNP, and one of the most visited. In addition to the firefly show and the attraction of Little River, this site also serves as a good base for exploring the area.

Laurel Falls Trail

Distance: 2.5 miles round-trip
Duration: 1.5-2 hours
Elevation gain: 400 feet
Difficulty: easy to moderate
Trailhead: parking area 3.9 miles west of Sugarlands Visitor Center on Little River Road

As the shortest and possibly easiest waterfall hike in Great Smoky Mountains National Park, Laurel Falls is the most popular of such hikes. The trail is paved and the grade is gentle (after you get past a short steeper section at the start of the trail), and the falls are a little over 1.3 miles from the trailhead.

Prepare to be dazzled when you reach the falls. Laurel Falls drops 75 feet in a wide, picture-perfect cascade. It's a gorgeous spot to photograph, but be aware, you have to be there early in the day to get a shot of the falls without people in it.

Foothills Parkway

It's not in the park, but the Foothills Parkway is a great scenic drive that gives you high-elevation views without so much of the traffic you'll find on more popular routes in the park proper. You get to the Foothills Parkway on US-321, 5.5 miles from Townsend. The 17-mile stretch of road has plenty of places to pull off to picnic or take in the view. There's one short hike here at Look Rock, a 0.5-mile stroll to an observation tower.

★ Cades Cove

Easily the most popular auto tour loop in the Great Smoky Mountains National Park, Cades Cove receives around two million visitors a year. They come for the scenery—a long, wide, grassy-bottomed valley surrounded by undulating

Black Bears

Biologists estimate there are more than 1,500 black bears living in Great Smoky Mountains National Park, and if you know where and when to look, your chances of seeing one in the wild are quite good.

Though I've seen bears in a number of spots throughout the park, one of the most reliable places to see them is **Cades Cove.** Here, in the early morning and as dusk settles, the bears are more active, prowling the forest's edge and even eating apples that have fallen from the trees.

As awesome as it is to see a bear, they can present a problem to park visitors, and we can present a problem to them. With the great number of visitors to GSMNP, many bears have grown accustomed to seeing people and have therefore lost their natural fear of humans, automobiles, and horses. As they grow more used to people, we decide to give them "treats" and lure them closer to our cars and our campsites with food. Bears that are too accustomed to people, especially bears that have been fed a few times, can grow bold, even borderline aggressive, searching campsites and open cars for food or even approaching open car windows or picnic tables.

Fortunately, serious incidents with black bears are rare, but they do happen. In 2000, a mother bear and her cub attacked and killed a camper near the Elkmont Campground. Every year, campsites and trails are closed due to bear activity and the potential for interaction between bears and visitors.

Park staff and volunteers do their best to educate visitors on proper human-bear interaction. Throughout the park you'll see signs and placards advising you on how to properly store and dispose of food and reminding you not to approach bears. Remember that bears are wild animals and unpredictable, and keep these tips in mind:

- **Do not approach** within 50 yards or any distance that disturbs a bear, and do not allow a bear to approach you. For a good view, invest in a pair of binoculars.

- **Never feed bears.** It only gets them used to humans and causes them to think of us as a source of food.

- **Store food** in appropriate containers and in the proper places when camping. If you're not sure of the proper procedure, ask a ranger.

- **Dispose of garbage** in bear-proof receptacles.

- **Report** nuisance bear behavior or visitors breaking these rules to park officials.

In the unlikely event that **a bear approaches you,** stand tall, wave your arms, and make as much noise as possible. If you need to, throw sticks or rocks at the bear. In most cases, this will intimidate the bear and deter it from coming any closer. If the bear charges, don't run—they can sprint 30 miles per hour, so you don't stand a chance. Instead, keep making noise and back away slowly, never turning your back to the bear. Often, bears will make bluff charges, so this is likely what you're seeing. If a black bear actually makes contact, fight back with anything and everything available to you; with a loud enough and fierce enough fight, the bear may see you as too much to deal with and leave you alone.

mountains—to see the handful of preserved homesteads and historic structures, and because it's one of the park's best, and most reliable, spots to see wildlife.

The Cades Cove Loop is approximately 11 miles long, but in summer and especially in fall when the leaves are at their best, expect to spend two hours or more on this one-way road through the valley floor—and that's if you don't stop to photograph the wildlife or explore historic structures. If you're the curious type or find the light is perfect for taking pictures, you can easily double the amount of time you spend here. When you do stop, be sure to pull off the road and leave enough room for traffic to pass. One source of traffic jams in Cades Cove is visitors who stop in the middle of the road to ooh and ahh at the wildlife and scenery.

The popularity of this drive is very well deserved. In the hours around dawn and dusk, wildlife is especially active. Vast herds of white-tail deer are the most common sight (I once tallied 50 in a field before I quit counting), but black bears are also frequently spotted. The bears like to cozy up to the apple trees that dot the cove, and you'll occasionally spot them and their cubs napping or eating in the branches.

You may notice that the fields look especially manicured. They are, to an extent. Far from being mown and maintained like a golf course, the fields in Cades Cove are allowed to run wild, but only so wild. The National Park Service maintains the fields and fences, mowing, repairing, and reseeding as necessary to keep the valley looking much like it did when settlers lived here.

To take this lovely-in-any-season drive, follow Little River Road west from the Sugarlands Visitor Center for 17.2 miles, there it will turn into Laurel Creek Road and lead you into Cades Cove in another 7.4 miles. You can also access Cades Cove by entering the park at Townsend on TN-73, then turning right on Laurel Creek Road, following it for 16 miles to the entrance to the cove. Cades Cove is closed to vehicle traffic every Saturday and Wednesday morning from May until late September. On those days, the loop is open exclusively to bicycle and foot traffic until 10am. The rest of the year, the road is open to motor vehicles from sunrise to sunset daily, so long as the weather allows it.

The **Cades Cove Campground** (10042 Campground Drive, Townsend, Tenn., 877/444-6777, www.recreation.gov, $17-20) is a popular spot where you'll definitely want to reserve a campsite. This campground is open year-round, and though the occupancy is a little lower in the dead of winter, you'll still find a few intrepid visitors taking refuge from the cold in one of the 159 campsites here. Hikers, take note, there are several backcountry campsites off the trails in Cades Cove, making it a good base for overnight trips.

Sights

According to some historians, long before European settlers pushed west through the Smokies, the Cherokee Indians had hunting camps and possibly even a small settlement established in Cades Cove. In fact, the name Cades Cove is believed to have come from a Chief Kade, a little-known Cherokee leader. By the early 1820s, the first Europeans were here, building cabins and barns and carving a homestead out of the forest. More settlers arrived having heard of the rich, fertile bottomland in Cades Cove, and by 1850, nearly 700 people called the valley home. As the collection of cabins and homesteads grew into a community, community buildings, like churches and schools, were built. Families lived here even after the National Park Service began purchasing land. The last school closed in Cades Cove in 1944 and the post office in 1947.

Today, a number of historic structures remain standing along the valley floor. Among them is the most photographed structure in the park, the **Methodist Church.** From time to time, a wedding is held here, though it's more common for visitors to leave handwritten prayers on scraps of paper large and small at the altar.

The **Cable Mill Area** is the busiest section of the loop, even if the Methodist Church is the most photographed. At the Cable Mill, you can see an actual mill in operation, and even buy cornmeal or flour ground on site. In addition to the mill and Methodist church, there are two other churches, a few barns and log houses, and a number of smaller structures.

Halfway around the park, you'll find

the **Cades Cove Visitor Center** (Cades Cove Loop Rd., Townsend, Tenn., 865/448-2472, 9am-4:30pm daily Dec.-Jan., except Christmas Day, 9am-5:30pm daily Feb. and Nov., 9am-6:30pm daily Mar. and Sept.-Oct., 9am-7pm daily Apr. and Aug., 9am-7:30pm daily May-June), which has a good bookstore and gift shop, and, most importantly, the only public restroom you'll find on the tour.

Abrams Falls Trail

Distance: 5 miles out and back
Duration: 3 hours
Elevation gain: 350 feet
Difficulty: moderate
Trailhead: Turn right onto a gravel road 4.9 miles from the start of the Cades Cove Loop; at 0.4 miles in is a parking area and the trailhead.

From the parking area, several trails lead off into the woods, but it's obvious which route to take, you're looking for the most well-worn trail you see. And if you're in doubt, follow the group in front of you, most hikers use this parking area to trek to Abrams Falls. Only a few steps from the trailhead is a kiosk, which will set you on the right path.

The trail is pretty straightforward: it follows Abrams Creek all the way to the waterfall. The only real elevation gains come when you thrice leave the creek to climb up and around a ridge, crossing a feeder stream in the process. Your first stream is Arbutus Branch, then Stony Branch, then Wilson Branch, which is very close to the falls.

After you cross Wilson Branch on a log bridge, you'll follow the trail downstream, cross Wilson Branch once again, and arrive at the falls.

Abrams Falls is pretty, and in wet weather can be downright thunderous. Slick, mossy rocks make up the wall where the 20-foot waterfall, which has the largest volume of water of any waterfall in the park, tumbles into the pool below. Tempted as you may be to take a dip after a sweaty hike, don't do it; the currents are strong and a few folks have drowned here.

Rocky Top and Thunderhead Mountains Trail

Distance: 13.9 miles out and back
Duration: 7-8 hours
Elevation gain: 3,665 feet
Difficulty: strenuous
Trailhead: at the Cades Cove picnic area at the Anthony Creek Trailhead

Hiking to the famed Rocky Top is borderline brutal as you gain more than 3,500 feet in elevation, and on the first few miles of that, you share the trail with horses, so it can get quite muddy and slippery, slowing your pace. However, it's worth it as the hike is exceptional. Time your hike for mid-June to see the rhododendron and mountain laurel in full bloom.

Shortly after starting the Anthony Creek Trail, you'll reach Crib Trail Junction, then Anthony Creek Horse Camp. Follow Anthony Creek Trail 3.5 miles to the Bote Mountain Trail, where hikers will turn right.

Climbing Bote Mountain Trail, you'll enter a long series of rhododendron "tunnels" and at 5.1 miles in, you'll reach Spence Field and the Appalachian Trail. Turn left and you'll get some stunning views of North Carolina and equally stunning views of hillsides and meadows covered in mountain laurel. Continue east along the Appalachian Trail to reach Rocky Top and Thunderhead Mountain.

Thunderhead Mountain is made up of three distinct summits. The first summit is Rocky Top, 1.2 miles from the Bote Mountain/Appalachian Trail junction and arguably the best view in the park. Next, is the middle peak, sometimes called Rocky Top Two, just 0.3 miles beyond Rocky Top. Finally, another 0.3 miles on, is the unremarkable summit of Thunderhead. Many hikers turn around at Rocky Top, never summiting out on Thunderhead.

Parsons Branch

Another great drive, this one in the park, is **Parsons Branch Road**. Take a right turn just beyond the Cades Cove Visitor Center parking area and you'll find yourself on a 10-mile long, one-way, gravel road leading to US-129 and Deals Gap on the extreme southwestern edge of the park. At times pothole riddled and crossing 18 or so small streams along the way, the road is a slow one, taking around an hour to complete the drive. If you're careful, the drive is doable in a sedan, but you may feel more comfortable in a vehicle with a little more clearance.

The road passes Henry Whitehead Place, an odd looking pair of conjoined cabins. The story here is a good one. Henry Whitehead, a widower with three daughters, remarried Matilda Shields Gregory after she and her small child had been abandoned by her husband. During the crisis, the community rallied and built her the small cabin, which is in back of the main structure that Whitehead built after they married.

You'll cross the same stream several times before climbing to the crest of the drive. Here you'll find two trailheads: Hannah Mountain and Gregory Bald Trails. This is the halfway mark of the road and it is, as they say, all downhill from here.

★ Rich Mountain

Rich Mountain Road is a photographer's dream. Running north from Cades Cove over Rich Mountain to Tuckaleechee Cove and Townsend, this one-way, gravel road provides stunning views of Cades Cove. For eight miles the road makes its way through a hardwood forest that's largely oak. Don't try this in the family sedan or your economy rental. Try a truck or SUV instead as the road does become steep once it passes outside park boundaries.

If you're stuck with the rental or you aren't confident in your off-road driving abilities, you can always enjoy similar views on the 8.5-mile Rich Mountain Loop hike. And the hike is a great way to

see Cades Cove without the high-season gridlock.

Rich Mountain Loop
Distance: 8.5-mile loop
Duration: 4-4.5 hours
Elevation gain: 1,740 feet
Difficulty: moderate
Trailhead: Park at the entrance gate to Cades Cove; the trail begins in the opposite parking lot.

On the first part of this hike, you'll be passing by one of the meadows that makes Cades Cove such a fabulous place to see. For 1.4 miles you'll walk through the woods and the edge of the meadow until you reach the John Oliver Cabin, but 0.5 miles in, you'll pass Crooked Arm Ridge Trail, where you'll come out at the end of this hike.

The trail continues behind the cabin and soon meets up with Martha's Branch and begins to climb. As you climb, you'll cross the branch a number of times. At mile 3, you'll find a place where you have a tight view of Cades Cove; don't sweat it, better views are coming.

Continue on 0.3 miles to Indian Grave Gap Trail and turn right. In 0.8 miles is Campsite 5 (for backpackers) and the junction with Rich Mountain Trail. The saddle here has nice views.

Avoid the junction and follow Indian Grave Gap Trail 0.3 miles to a side trail. This path is only about 100 yards long and takes you to the highest point on Rich Mountain, Cerulean Knob, and the foundation of the former fire tower here. Views are okay, but not fantastic. Get back to the main trail and continue east where you'll find a much better view than on the top.

When you reach a power-line clearance, you're almost at Scott Mountain Trail and Campsite 4. From the junction of these trails, continue straight ahead on Crooked Arm Ridge Trail (it's what Indian Grave Gap Trail turns into). This trail is steep and rutted and littered with the evidence of horses, so watch your step, that horse evidence can be slippery.

This trail leads back to Rich Mountain Loop Trail 0.5 miles from the parking area.

Gatlinburg

On a typical Saturday night, when 40,000 people pack the restaurants and sidewalks of Gatlinburg, you would never know only about 4,000 people live here. As the unofficial capital of the Smokies and gateway to the national park, it benefits greatly from those 10 million visitors drawn here for the views, the wildlife, the hikes, and the kitsch. Because if there's anything Gatlinburg has in abundance, it's kitsch.

Gatlinburg is unabashedly a tourist town, and owning up to that fact makes it all the more charming. On Parkway, the cheekily-named main drag, there are T-shirt shops, candy stores and fudgeries, taffy pullers, more than one Ripley's attraction, novelties both racy (in that family-friendly, double-entendre way) and tame, knife shops, mini golf, ice cream parlors, restaurants, and more odd little art, craft, and gift shops than you can count. Don't let that deter you from staying (and even enjoying yourself) here. The Ripley's Aquarium is quite nice, and at Great Smoky Arts and Crafts Community and the Arrowcraft Shop, you'll find modern interpretations of traditional mountain arts that were handmade nearby.

Getting There and Around
Car
If you've followed the Blue Ridge Parkway to this point, you'll be coming into Gatlinburg along US-441 through GSMNP; on this route, one minute you're in the park, the next revolution of the wheels you're in Gatlinburg.

For those arriving from the north or west, I-40 is the most convenient road into town. Exit the interstate at Exit 407 and hop on US-66 south, a road that feeds into US-441 and will lead you into Gatlinburg. This is the easiest and most heavily traveled route into town from I-40. You can avoid the peak-season crowds by taking Exit 435 near Knoxville (an hour away) and follow US-321 south into Gatlinburg.

Coming in from the east on I-40, the best bet is to take Exit 443 and drive along the beautiful Foothills Parkway to US-321 south and cruise right into town.

Parking
Finding parking in Gatlinburg can be quite tough. There are a number of public and private parking lots and garages where you can park your car if you're not staying at a hotel nearby. Parking rates vary, depending on public or private ownership, so for affordability, it's often best to stick to the public parking garages at **Ripley's Aquarium of the Smokies** (88 River Rd., $1.75 first hour, $1 each hour after, or $6/day) and the **McMahan Parking Garage** (520 Parkway, at traffic light #3, $1.75 first hour, $1 each hour after, or $6/day).

Air
The **McGhee-Tyson Airport** outside of Knoxville is 42 miles from Gatlinburg. Head south to Maryville on US-129. Once you're in Maryville, take US-321 north to Pigeon Forge, then turn right and take US-441 into Gatlinburg.

Public Transportation
Gatlinburg has a great trolley system that can get you to and from every attraction in Gatlinburg and nearby Pigeon Forge, including Dollywood. The **Gatlinburg Trolley** (88 River Rd., Suite 101, 865/436-3897, www.gatlinburgtrolley.org, 10am-10pm daily Mar.-Apr., 8am-midnight daily May-Oct., 10am-6pm Sun.-Thurs and 10am-10pm Fri. and Sat. Nov.-Feb., extended hours on select holiday and event dates) has more than 100 stops in Gatlinburg alone. It's cheap, with most rides only $0.50, but your best bet is

to pick up an All Day Trolley Pass ($2) from the **Gatlinburg Welcome Center** (1011 Banner Rd., 865/277-8957, www.gatlinburg.com, 8:30am-7pm daily), the **Parkway Visitor Center** (520 Parkway, 10am-6pm daily) at traffic light #3, or the **Aquarium Welcome Center** (88 River Rd., 9am-9pm daily).

Sights

All of downtown Gatlinburg is a sight to behold. The mountains rise all around you, that namesake Smoky mist rising from them, and the street glitters and twinkles like a sort of vacationland Milky Way. One of the best ways to take it all in is from the **Space Needle** (115 Historic Nature Trail, 865/436-4629, www.gatlinburgspaceneedle.com, 9am-midnight Sun.-Thurs., 9am-1am Fri.-Sat., adults $8.50, seniors $5, children 5-12 $4, free under 4). I know what you're thinking, "But the Space Needle is in Seattle." Yeah, it is; this is the other one. From the observation deck 407 feet above Gatlinburg, you have truly stellar views. For the best views, get to the top shortly before sundown and watch as the mountains darken and the strip of downtown comes alive with lights. At the foot of the tower, there's a two-level 25,000-square-foot arcade with games galore, laser tag, a gift shop, snack bar, and restrooms.

The **Gatlinburg Sky Lift** (765 Parkway, 865/436-4307, www.gatlinburgskylift.com, 9am-9pm daily Apr.-May, 9am-11pm daily June-Aug., 9am-10pm daily Sept.-Oct., as posted Nov.-Mar., adults $15, children 3-11 $11.25) is a ski lift that carries you 1,800 feet up the side of a mountain to a gift shop and snack bar. You have pretty views of Gatlinburg on the way up and back down, and even better views from the top, and, nighttime tends to be the best time to ride the Sky Lift. The Sky lift was built in the early 1950s and was the first chair lift in the region, seeing more than 100,000 visitors by its third season in operation. You'll find the lift in the heart of downtown; it's impossible to miss.

Moonshine is a high-octane corn liquor made in the hills, hollows, and coves all throughout and around GSMNP, especially in Gatlinburg. Today, moonshine is brewed legally and there are a few distilleries right in Gatlinburg, the best of which is **Sugarlands Distilling Company** (805 Parkway, 865/325-1355, www.sugarlandsdistilling.com, 10am-10pm Mon.-Thurs., 10am-midnight Fri. and Sat., noon-7pm Sun., tours free). Sugarlands distillery puts their whole distilling process on display. Watch from screened windows open to the distilling floor or show up for a free tour. There's a gift shop where you can buy all sorts of logo-emblazoned clothing and drinking gear and, of course, moonshine. Before you buy a quart or two (or a case, it's that good and it makes a fun gift), stop by the Sippin' Posts where, with valid ID, you can sample all of the moonshine flavors Sugarlands sells. Sugarlands also has a great performance space called The Back Porch where all sorts of musicians and storytellers come to play songs and spin yarns.

At the other end of downtown from Sugarlands is **Doc Collier Moonshine** (519 Parkway, 800/398-5132, www.doccollier.co, 10am-11pm Mon.-Sat., 11am-7pm Sun.). Using the recipe of famed (he was famous locally anyway) Doc Collier, his ancestors continue the tradition of making some of the finest 'shine in Tennessee and selling it to the thirsty public at their Gatlinburg storefront. According to the family, Doc's moonshine was in such high demand, he needed a better way to distribute it, so he bought a mercantile, selling provisions to some customers and jars of white lightning to those in the know. In the store, you can see some great photos and even pieces of Doc's equipment while you sample some moonshine before grabbing a bottle and going on your way.

Ripley's Aquarium of the Smokies (traffic light #5, 88 River Rd., 865/430-8808, www.ripleyaquariums.com/

Wedding Fever

To say that Gatlinburg is a popular place to get married is a gross understatement. This tiny town is second in the nation only to Las Vegas in the number of weddings held each year. On average, around 20,000 couples tie the knot here (that's 55 ceremonies a day) and the number of witnesses and guests they bring push that number north of 600,000 people in town for weddings. Guess that explains why Gatlinburg is called the "wedding capital of the South."

What makes Gatlinburg such a hot spot for weddings, even celebrity weddings (Billy Ray Cyrus, Patty Loveless, and a few other names of note were married here)? It could be that Tennessee makes it easy.

No blood tests or waiting periods are required before getting married. It could be the abundance of wedding venues both natural and man-made. It could be the fact that there are plenty of romantic spots where one can retreat with their betrothed.

If being here has you in the mood for marriage, it's easy to find a place. In Gatlinburg alone there are more than a dozen chapels and more officiants than you can count. You can find all the information you'll ever need for planning a Smoky Mountain Wedding at the website of the **Smoky Mountain Wedding Association** (www.somkymountain-weddingassociation.com).

gatlinburg/, 9am-8pm Mon.-Thurs., 9am-10pm Fri.-Sun. Jan.-Feb.; 9am-9pm Mon.-Thurs., 9am-10pm Fri.-Sun. Mar.-Memorial Day; 9am-10pm Mon.-Thurs., 9am-11pm Fri.-Sun. Memorial Day-Labor Day; 9am-9pm Mon.-Thurs., 9am-10pm Fri.-Sun. Labor Day-New Year's Day; adults $26, children 6-11 $15.99, children 2-5 $7.99) is one of countless Ripley's attractions in Gatlinburg and Pigeon Forge. The other attractions are skippable unless you have kids in tow, but the aquarium is another story. Ripley's Aquarium is the largest aquarium in the state, with more than 1.4 million gallons of water. Exhibits include the Touch a Ray Bay, where you can touch a stingray; the Penguin Playhouse, where tunnels lead you through their exhibit, putting you eye to eye with penguins as they do their thing; and Shark Lagoon, where a 340-foot-long glide path takes you under the lagoon where sand tiger and nurse sharks swim with sea turtles and moray eels. On site, there are two restaurants and a monstrous gift shop.

Gatlinburg has a surprising artistic side. The artists and craftspeople here take their work very seriously. Many of them are carrying on mountain traditions, while others are finding new modes and mediums to express the inspiration they draw from the landscape here. Artists go to the **Arrowmont School of Arts and Crafts** (556 Parkway, 865/436-5860, www.arrowmont.org, 8:30am-5pm Mon.-Fri., 8:30am-4pm Sat, workshops $325-1,100) to hone their techniques. Founded in 1912 as a philanthropic project by the Pi Beta Phi women's fraternity, the Phi Beta Phi Settlement School sought to deliver basic education and health services to the children of the area. The schoolchildren brought the school staff homemade gifts—baskets, weavings, woodcarvings—made by their parents. Recognizing the talent here, the school brought in a weaving teacher and began some vocational education. Then in 1926, the school opened the Arrowcraft Shop, a market selling crafts and wares made by the people of the region. As this gained popularity, the idea of summer craft workshops came about. In 1945, 50 students attended the first of many summer workshops. Today the school holds weekend, one- and two-week workshops for adults every spring, summer, and fall. Classes include traditional and contemporary takes on weaving and fiber arts, pottery, metal and jewelry, painting, and drawing. Three galleries in the school include rotating and permanent exhibitions and are open year-round.

Entertainment
Nightlife
One spot to grab a drink other than moonshine is **Smoky Mountain Brewery** (1004 Parkway, 865-436-4200, www.smoky-mtn-brewery.com, 11:30am-1am daily, food $5-25, drinks $3-12), a microbrewery with close to a dozen handcrafted beers brewed here or at one of the three nearby sister breweries. Mainstay beers include a light beer, red ale, pilsner, porter, and pale ale; they also brew seasonal and specialty beers, like the creamy Winter Warmer Ale and the Brown Trout Stout. Stop in and grab a hot pretzel (or some wings or a pizza) and a sampler flight of beers.

Performing Arts
There are a number of stage shows going on nightly throughout Gatlinburg. The **Iris Theatre** (115 Historic Nature Trail, 888/482-3330, www.iristheater.com, show times vary, tickets adults $25, military and seniors $18, children 5-12 $8) is the home stage to several performers. **Head Case starring Mentalist Bill Gladwell** (7pm Tues. and Fri.-Sat.) uses his mastery of suggestion, skills as a hypnotist, and untold mental powers to create a thought-provoking, family-friendly show where he'll demonstrate everything from mindreading to psychokinesis. **A Brit of Magic!** (check schedule and buy tickets well in advance, they sell out) is a comedy and magic show with Keith Fields, a Briton living here in the Smokies. **Comedy Hypnosis with Guy Michaels** (usually 7pm Wed. and 9pm Thurs.-Sat.) is just that, family-friendly hypnosis where the hypnotist Guy Michaels gets willing audience members to become the stars of the show.

Then there's the **Sweet Fanny Adams Theatre** (461 Parkway, 877/388-5784, www.sweetfannyadams.com, box office open 10am-10pm on show days, shows vary, tickets adults $25, seniors, military, and AAA $23, children under 12 $9), home to a musical comedy review and "outrageous humor and hilarious fun" since 1977. Shows vary by the theater season, but typically include an improv showcase, a vaudeville-type revue, a holiday show, and other original musical comedies.

Festivals and Events
Throughout the year there are several events that draw attention to the things that make Gatlinburg the place it is. The **Spring Wildflower Pilgrimage** (865/974-0280, www.springwildflowerpilgrimage.org/faq, adults $25-75, students $15, children under 12 free), usually during mid-April, is a five-day event with around 150 guided walks and presentations that celebrate the spring blooms, a photography contest, and more. From the end of September to early November, celebrate **Oktoberfest at Ober Gatlinburg** (865/436-5423, www.obergatlinburg.com) with a beer hall, sing-alongs, yodeling, and authentic German food. **Gatlinburg Winter Magic** (800/588-1817) is a 120-day celebration of all things winter and holiday. From early November through February, the city is a riot of millions of LED bulbs strung up in trees and lining elaborate displays. There's a chili cook-off, carolers, a Christmas Parade, and more.

Shopping
Gatlinburg's touristy side has a big personality, and there are plenty of shops selling T-shirts and the expected souvenirs, but for something that truly speaks to the heritage of this place, you'll need to do a little looking around.

Great Smoky Arts and Crafts Community
Your first stop should be the **Great Smoky Arts and Crafts Community** (turn right at traffic light #3 and go three miles to Glades Rd., www.gatlinburgcrafts.com). Founded in 1937, it is among the largest

(if not the largest) group of independent artisans in the United States. There are more than 100 shops, studios, and galleries along this eight-mile loop consisting of Glades Road, Buckhorn Road, and US-321. Look for the logo denoting membership in the community so you know that what you're seeing and buying are from genuine local and regional artisans. One thing that sets this apart is the fact that you can interact with the artists in their studios and galleries. You can watch them work, ask questions, maybe even lend a hand (if asked). With 100 stops here, you can easily spend a day if you want to take a peek into each and every gallery, shop, and studio.

The shop artisans range from candlemakers to watercolor artists to photographers to leatherworkers to the creators of traditional mountain crafts. **Ogle's Broom Shop** (670 Glades Rd., 865/430-4402, 10am-5pm Mon.-Sat.) is one such traditional crafts shop, with third-generation broom-makers. The shop was opened by the grandfather of current owner David Ogle. He carries on the tradition today, making brooms from broom straw and hand-carving canes and walking sticks.

Otto Preske, Artist in Wood (535 Buckhorn Rd., 865/436-5339, www.ottopreskeartistinwood.com) is a superb woodcarver. He carves and turns Christmas ornaments, hiking staffs, fireplace mantels, religious carvings, and highly-detailed figures and relief carvings. The work is stunning, and to watch him carve is simply amazing.

Throughout the community there are several basket weavers, but nothing like what you'll find at **Licklog Hollow Baskets** (1360 E. Parkway, 865/436-3823). Not only do they have the strangest name, the work here is superb. Whether you're buying for form or function, you'll find a basket that fits your style and probably your budget.

One of my favorite stops is at **Woodland Tiles** (252 Buckhorn Rd.,

865/640-0989, www.woodlandtilesbyvmarie.com). Here they make tiles and functional pottery pieces inspired by the leaves on the trees surrounding Gatlinburg. Custom glazes capture the jewel green of summer and the blazing colors of fall, and the sizes and shapes are spot on as the tiles mirror the leaves that inspired them.

The Village

In downtown Gatlinburg you'll find **The Village** (634 Parkway, 865/436-3995, www.thevillageshops.com, 10am-5pm daily Jan.-Feb., 10am-6pm daily Mar., 10am-8pm Sun.-Fri. and 10am-10pm Sat. Apr.-May and Nov., 10am-10pm June-Oct., hours vary Dec.), a collection of 27 shops centered around a courtyard in a Bavarian-style structure. Among the shops here are **The Sock Shop** (865/325-6000, www.sockshoptn.com), where you'll find comfy, crazy, cool, and quirky socks. They also sell wool socks, dress socks, and more, as long as it goes on your feet. **The Day Hiker** (865/430-0970, www.thedayhiker.com) provides the basic gear you need to take day and short overnight hikes in GSMNP. **The Silver Tree** (865/430-3573) is a silver lover's paradise with plenty of silver jewelry and accessories to peruse. Last but not least is **The Donut Friar** (865/436-7306, www.the-donut-friar.com, from 5am daily), an amazing bakery making donuts, cinnamon bread, and other pastries. They sell coffee to go with your morning donut.

Other Shops

For a unique shop/museum (there is only one other place in the world like this and it's in Spain), stop in at **The Salt and Pepper Shaker Museum** (561 Brookside Village Way, 865/430-5515, www.thesaltandpeppershakermuseum.com, 10am-4pm daily, on call during winter, $3). The name tells you what you'll find here, but it doesn't prepare you for the more than 20,000 salt and pepper shakers from around the world and the growing collection of pepper mills. The collection began on a lark, growing from one pepper mill into this massive assembly of the most banal of kitchen accessories. It's weird, so it's worth the cost of admission, especially when you can apply your admission fee to any gift shop purchase, and who doesn't want a salt and pepper set shaped like outhouses?

Recreation

There is no end to the outdoor recreation opportunities near Gatlinburg. At **Nantahala Outdoor Center Gatlinburg** (1138 Parkway, 865/277-8209, www.noc.com, 10am-9pm daily), you'll find a huge retail store selling everything you'd ever need to gear up for an outdoor adventure. NOC is the region's leader in outdoor guide services, providing white-water rafting, float trips, and kayaking on several rivers across the region, guided hikes and fly-fishing trips, and more. Their trips vary by season, so check the website or ask someone at the store about current trips and activities.

Rafting in the Smokies (813 E. Parkway, 800/776-7238, www.raftingthesmokies.com, Tues.-Thurs. and Sat. Memorial Day-Labor Day, $42, but they often run specials) is another white-water rafting outfitter in the area. Trips depend on the weather and water levels, so it's a good idea to call ahead or check online for current trips and reservations. Once you've gotten it nailed down, check in at the rafting outpost in Hartford and I-40 Exit 447.

Zip Gatlinburg (125 Historic Nature Trail, 865/430-9475 or 877/430-9442, www.zipgatlinburg.com, zip line $59, ropes course $50) has a 9-element zip course and a 27-element ropes course on the hillside overlooking town. Between the zips, the swinging platforms, and a pair of sky bridges, you'll get your fill of high-flying thrills.

Ober Gatlinburg

Ober Gatlinburg (1001 Parkway, 865/436-5423, www.obergatlinburg.com, hours vary by activity, but generally 9:30am-9pm daily in spring, summer, and fall, 10am-7pm in winter, $4-12 or activity pass $22-33 adults, $19-28 children 5-11), the mountaintop resort that looks out over Gatlinburg, is a ski resort in the winter and a mountain playground the rest of the year. There are eight ski and snowboard trails and Ober Gatlinburg is equipped with plenty of snowmaking equipment to make up for what Mother Nature doesn't supply. Warm weather activities include the awesome Alpine Slide, a sort of luge that follows one of the ski slopes down the hill; a pair of raft-based water slides; a maze; and year-round indoor ice skating. There's also a Wildlife Encounter where you can see many of the native species found in the area. If you're hungry, there are several places to grab a bite ranging from a slice of pizza to a steak.

The resort is a little dated and leans toward the cheesy end of the spectrum, and many people skip it if it's not ski season. Others think it's worth the little bit of time and money to ride the tram to the top of the hill and ride the Alpine Slide one more time.

Accommodations

Something about being in Gatlinburg makes me want to stay in a cabin. Fortunately there are plenty of options whether you're traveling solo, as a pair, or with even the largest of groups.

★ **Mountain Laurel Chalets** (440 Ski Mountain Rd., 800/315-4965, www.mtnlaurelchalets.com, $89-750/night for a huge 24-person lodge) has several lodges and large houses sleeping anywhere from 10-24 people if you're traveling with your extended family, or smaller cabins that sleep a couple or small group on a getaway. The cabins are spread out over a huge property, so they're private in addition to being cozy. Some of the cabins, the last ones in line for a refresh, are dated, but others are quite nice inside, so check cabin descriptions online if this matters to you.

Located between Gatlinburg and Pigeon Forge, **Autumn Ridge** (505 Gatlin At Crest, 865/436-4111, www.autumn-ridgerentals.com, Jan.-Mar. $105, Apr.-Dec. $115, Oct. and holidays $125) has five cabins, each with a two-night minimum and a view you'll come back for. King-size beds are the norm here, as are whirlpool tubs or hot tubs and wood-burning fireplaces (firewood provided). This is a romantic spot and a popular one for honeymoons, so make your reservation sooner rather than later.

Laurel Springs Lodge Bed and Breakfast (204 Hill St., 888/430-9211, www.laurelspringslodge.com, $130-160) is lovely, comfortable, and highly regarded. There are five rooms, all well decorated and comfortable, and a gourmet breakfast is served every morning. Downtown is a short walk away, but even though you're close, you're away from the buzz of Gatlinburg's main drag and can relax when you come back to your room.

The Foxtrot Bed and Breakfast (1520 Garrett Lane, 865/436-3033, www.thefoxtrot.com, $190-230) is a little different than most B&Bs in that an actual chef prepares breakfast. That's just one thing that sets it apart. The Foxtrot is high on the hill, well above the noise, traffic, and bustle of downtown Gatlinburg, making it a true retreat. There are several packages you can add to your room, like spa packages, honeymoon and anniversary packages, cooking schools, and more.

One of the finest places to stay in Gatlinburg is ★ **The Lodge at Buckberry Creek** (961 Campbell Lead Rd., 865/430-8030, www.buckberrylodge.com, $180-460). Though it calls itself "The Great Camp of The Smokies," the rooms here are anything but camp-like. Sure, the walls are wood paneled and elements of the decor say rustic, but the finishes speak to luxury. Situated on 26 acres, The Lodge is surrounded by hiking trails, a trout stream, and romantic pavilions along the banks of Buckberry Creek. With the best fine-dining restaurant in Gatlinburg at The Lodge, this is the kind of place you could come for the weekend and never leave the property.

Throughout Gatlinburg there are a number of chain hotels with prices ranging from budget to mid-range. Three of the more reliable hotels are The Park Vista, Hampton Inn Gatlinburg, and Hilton Garden Inn. **The Park Vista** (705 Cherokee Orchard Rd., 865/436-9211, www.parkvista.com, $135-190), a Doubletree by Hilton hotel, has excellent views from each room's private balcony. The rooms are spacious and comfortable, and the hotel is adjacent to the Roaring Fork Motor Nature Trail. The **Hampton Inn Gatlinburg** (967 Parkway, 865/436-4878, www.hamptoninn3.hilton.com, $150-190) has private balconies and is within walking distance to most of Gatlinburg's attractions. Finally, the **Hilton Garden Inn** (635 River Rd., 865/436-0048, www.hiltongardeninn3.hilton.com, $140-190) is also walkable to downtown and has free parking.

Food

Dining in Gatlinburg, especially for foodies, can be tricky. In a town where, literally, millions of people pass through, you get a lot of restaurants that have stopped caring about repeat customers and seek only to provide a heaping plate of food and mediocre service at premium prices, knowing their diners will be in for one, maybe two meals during their visit. And there are plenty of major chains ready to take your dining dollars. That said, it is possible to find a good, even great, meal here.

The **Smoky Mountain Trout House** (410 Parkway, 865/436-5416, www.gatlinburgtrouthouse.com, from 5pm nightly, around $20) has a mesmerizing aquarium window teeming with rainbow trout. The menu is trout heavy: rainbow trout grilled, broiled, pan fried, seasoned with dill or parmesan; trout almandine; and smoked trout. There are a few items—prime rib, a rib eye steak, country ham, chicken, catfish, and shrimp—that aren't trout on the menu. The food tastes better than the dining room would have you believe, and this is a pretty good meal, especially if you like trout.

Another longtime Gatlinburg eatery, **The Peddler** (820 River Rd., 865/436-5794, www.peddlergatlinburg.com, from 5pm Sun.-Fri., from 4:30pm Sat., $23-37), is still a solid choice for a steak. The dining room overlooks the river, making it a nice spot to eat. The menu is steak heavy, but they also have shrimp, chicken, and trout, and every entrée comes with a pretty robust salad bar.

Bennett's Pit Barbecue (714 River Rd., 865/436-2400, www.bennetts-bbq. com, breakfast from 8am daily, lunch from 11am daily, dinner from 3pm daily, breakfast buffet $9.79, lunch $9-15, dinner $10-36) serves hickory-smoked barbecue in many forms: pork ribs, pulled pork, chicken, beef brisket, hot smoked sausage, and burnt ends (a brisket treat that's not to be missed). The platters of food are, as they are in most barbecue joints, obscenely big, so don't feel bad if you can't finish your meal.

For the last several years, **Alamo Steakhouse and Saloon** (705 E. Parkway, 865/436-9998, www.alamosteakhouse. com, lunch 11am-3pm daily, dinner from 3pm daily, $14-31) has been named Best Steak, so sit down and order yourself a steak, they have plenty to choose from. If you're not in the mood for steak, there are a number of pork, chicken, and seafood dishes. The service is generally very good, but, like all restaurants in a busy vacation town, can get bogged down in the high season.

★ **Big Daddy's Pizzeria** (714 River Rd., 865/436-5455, www.bigdaddyspizzeria.net, from 11am daily, $9-23) has locations in Gatlinburg, Pigeon Forge, and Sevierville. Their claim to fame is a wood-fired brick oven and a creative flair in the creation of their pies. Get the tried and true pepperoni and cheese, or go wild with the Smoky Mounty Cheese Steak (with shaved prime rib, caramelized onions, gorgonzola cheese, and potato slices), The Herbivore (a veggie-packed delight), or one of their other signature pizzas. They also have sandwiches prepared on house-made focaccia, fresh salads, and meatballs.

Across the street from the aquarium is **No Way Jose's Cantina** (555 Parkway, 865/436-5673, www.nowayjosescantina. com, 11:30am-10pm daily, $5-15). Grab a riverside seat and order a basket of chips and killer homemade salsa before you even glance at the menu. The rest of the menu is pretty standard Tex-Mex faire, but the difference is how fresh this tastes in comparison.

Gatlinburg has pancake houses in spades. The oldest pancake house in town opened in 1960 and it also happens to be the first of its kind in Tennessee. **Pancake Pantry** (628 Parkway, 865/436-4724, 7am-4pm daily June-Oct., 7am-3pm daily Nov.-May, $6-10) still puts out a great spread of flapjacks. There are 24 varieties of pancakes and crepes, as well as a half dozen waffles, omelets, and French toast. Breakfast is served all day, but if you feel like a burger or sandwich for lunch, they have a few of those too.

Wild Plum (555 Buckhorn Rd., 865/436-3808, www.wildplumtearoom.com, 11am-3pm Mon.-Sat., $10-16) is a lunch-only restaurant inspired by Austrian teahouses. They serve the southern classic, Tomato Pie, but the real stars of the menu are the Chef Specials. The specials vary daily, but in the past have included lobster pie, a salmon burger, smoke salmon sandwiches, and yellow fin tuna.

Hands down the best fine-dining experience in Gatlinburg, ★ **The Restaurant at Buckberry Creek** (961 Campbell Lead Rd., 865/430-8030, www.buckberrylodge.com, breakfast from 8am daily, dinner 5:30pm-9pm Thurs.-Sat Jan. and

Feb., Tues.-Sat Mar.-Sept. and Nov.-Dec., daily in Oct., $20-45) serves a small, ever-changing menu. During tomato season, expect to see fried green tomatoes as a first bite and tomatoes on and in most of the salads and entrées; wild mushrooms and ramps may appear in spring, and other ingredients as they ripen throughout the season. Entrées commonly include pan-seared duck, beef tenderloin, and tuna, sea bass, or another flavorful fish. Don't skip dessert: The crème brûlée and the fresh sorbet are quite nice.

Information and Services

There are three visitor centers in Gatlinburg, the **Gatlinburg Welcome Center** (1011 Banner Rd., 865/277-8957, www.gatlinburg.com, 8:30am-7pm daily), the **Parkway Visitor Center** (520 Parkway, 10am-6pm daily) at traffic light #3, and the **Aquarium Welcome Center** (88 River Rd., 9am-9pm daily).

On the radio, **WWST** (93.7 FM) plays the Top 40. **WSEV** (105.5 FM) is an adult contemporary station.

LeConte Medical Center (742 Middle Creek Rd., Sevierville, 865/446-7000, www.lecontemedicalcenter.com) is the nearest hospital, just over 20 minutes away. The **Gatlinburg Police** (1230 E. Parkway, 865/436-5181) are available if the need arises.

Pigeon Forge and Sevierville

The most dominating presence in Pigeon Forge and Sevierville is Dolly Parton. Her namesake amusement park is in Pigeon Forge and she was born and raised in Sevierville, where a statue of Dolly stands in front of the courthouse. You'll see her face, hear her music, and maybe even meet one of her many cousins everywhere across these two towns.

These towns have grown a lot since Dolly was born, thanks largely to the popularity of the National Park. More growth came in the 1970s when the amusement park that would become Dollywood opened its doors, and again in 1982 when nearby Knoxville hosted the World's Fair. But to keep more than 10 million annual visitors coming back year after year, Pigeon Forge and Sevierville had to become destinations unto themselves, and, for the most part, they've succeeded. Pigeon Forge has become one of the biggest "tourist traps" (which I say not with disdain, but astonishment as the place is a wonderland of vacation delights) on the East Coast. Want to ride go karts and go bungee jumping at 9pm on a Wednesday? No problem. Midnight mini golf? Got it. Roller coasters, neon signs, and fudge shops? Pigeon Forge has got you covered. But don't be fooled by all the neon, hotels, and attractions around, like Gatlinburg, Pigeon Forge is small; less than 7,000 people live here full time.

In the midst of this swirl of touristy flotsam is a surprising center for engaging with the community's culture: Dollywood. This amusement park has been around in some form or another since the 1960s, though in the early days it was kitsch over culture. As the park matured and expanded, so did its attention to the culture of mountain living. Today the park is home to some great bluegrass and country shows and a good deal of shops and exhibits where Appalachian crafters showcase their skills and their wares.

Getting There and Around

The most traveled route to Pigeon Forge and Sevierville is I-40, carrying visitors in from the east and west. Exit 407 puts you on US-66 southeast, which leads into Sevierville and then feeds into US-441, taking you to Pigeon Forge. Most travellers will be going north on US-441, following the road from Great

Smoky Mountains National Park and Gatlinburg.

It's surprising to see a well-organized public transit system in a town the size of Pigeon Forge, but the **Fun Time Trolley** (186 Old Mill Ave., 865/453-6444, www.pigeonforgetrolley.org, 8am-midnight daily Mar.-Oct., 10am-10pm daily Nov.-Dec., $0.50-0.75 or an all-day pass for $2.50) has more than 100 regular stops in Pigeon Forge, Sevierville, and Gatlinburg. Routes run on a regular schedule, as traffic allows, and stops include all of the high points in the area. Passes are available at Fun Time Trolley.

Sights
★ Dollywood

At **Dollywood** (2700 Dollywood Parks Blvd., Pigeon Forge, 800/365-5996, www.dollywood.com, Apr.-Dec., $46-58, parking $10), you might just catch a glimpse of Dolly Parton walking through the park or performing for the crowds at the park's opening. Even if you don't see her, the park has plenty of rides, cultural stops, shows, and nature experiences to keep you busy.

Dollywood started in 1961, when Rebel Railroad, a small attraction with a steam train, general store, blacksmith shop, and saloon, opened. By 1977, the park had grown and changed hands more than once. Renamed Silver Dollar City, the park eventually caught the attention of Dolly Parton. She became a partner and lent the park her name. Since then it's become Tennessee's most-visited tourist attraction (outside GSMNP) and is consistently named among the top theme parks in the world.

Dollywood has a great look: one part Appalachian village, one part small southern town. There are tree-lined streets and paths, and several streams follow their courses through the park. You don't see the rides until you're right up on them because they're tucked away in the woods.

One of the best-known spots in the park is **Showstreet,** where stages and theaters are always busy with musicians, square dances, and storytellers. There's also a bevy of master craftspeople practicing their Appalachian arts for all to see: blacksmiths, basket-makers, candle-makers, and woodworkers. On Showstreet, you may see some of Dolly's relatives playing and singing in shows throughout the year. Seasonal shows include a half-dozen Christmas concerts, Harvest Celebration Southern Gospel, and more.

Also on Showstreet is a carriage, sled, and wagon shop called **Valley Carriage Works.** The Carriage Works takes orders from clients from around the world and builds beautiful, fully functional, historically accurate carriages. At the Museum of the Cherokee Indian in Cherokee, N.C., you can see a replica Cherokee wagon that they built to commemorate the 165th anniversary of the Trail of Tears.

It's easy to find a souvenir in the park, whether you want a Dollywood keepsake or a handcrafted gift from one of the shops in Craftsman's Valley. There you'll find handcrafted goods like leather belts, blown glass, and baskets.

Given that the park allows nature to be such a prominent feature in its design, it's no surprise to learn that Dollywood has partnered with the American Eagle Foundation and is authorized by U.S. Fish and Wildlife Services and the Tennessee Wildlife Resources Agency to possess eagles and other birds for education, exhibition, rehabilitation, and breeding. The 30,000-square-foot **aviary** is home to the nation's largest group of non-releasable bald eagles (many of these birds have been injured and wouldn't survive if released into nature). Daily shows put visitors in close proximity to these incredible birds.

Dollywood has more than 40 rides and attractions that range from kid-friendly to thrilling. My favorites were the Blazing Fury, an indoor roller coaster where you're trying to outrun an out-of-control fire; Thunderhead, a great wooden coaster; and Daredevil Falls, an updated version of the log flume ride.

Plenty of snack stands and restaurants are located throughout the park. I remember loving the berries and cream and having my first plate of whole-hog barbecue here. The memories are good, but those meals weren't cheap. But, it's an amusement park and you'll be there all day, so what are you going to do?

Dollywood's Splash Country

Waterparks abound in Pigeon Forge and Sevierville, but the best is **Dollywood's Splash Country** (2700 Dollywood Parks Blvd., Pigeon Forge, 800/365-5996, www.dollywood.com, May-Sept., $42-47, parking $10). This water park has 29 waterslides, a lazy river, three water play areas for kids, a 7,500-square-foot leisure pool, and 25,000-square-foot wave pool. There are also concessions and a gift shop, stroller rentals, and lockers to rent.

Dolly Parton Statue

Local artist Jim Gray sculpted a **statue** (125 Court Ave.) that shows Dolly with a wide smile and her guitar, as if she's ready to write a song at any moment. Stop by downtown Sevierville to take a picture with the statue, located on the courthouse lawn.

Tennessee Museum of Aviation

Head to the Gatlinburg Pigeon Forge Airport in Sevierville to brush up on your aviation history at the **Tennessee Museum of Aviation** (135 Air Museum Way, Sevierville, 866/286-8738, www.tnairmuseum.com, 10am-6pm Mon.-Sat., 1pm-6pm Sun., adults $12.75, seniors $9.75, children 6-12 $6.75). Housed in a 35,000-square-foot hangar are a number of exhibits and a dozen historic aircraft, including two airworthy P-47 Thunderbolts (that sometimes take to the air), a MiG-21, and F-86 Saberjet. But the best treat is when you visit the museum

Wild Eagle roller coaster in Dollywood

and one of the historic WWII aircraft is taking flight.

Titanic Pigeon Forge

One somewhat odd attraction is the *Titanic* **Pigeon Forge** (2134 Parkway, Pigeon Forge, 800/381-7670, www.titanicpigeonforge.com, from 9am daily, closed Jan. 12-15 and Christmas Day, adults $24.25, children 5-12 $11.25). This massive museum includes three decks and 20 galleries in its 30,000 square feet. The galleries feature artifacts salvaged from the sunken luxury ship. There's a reproduction of the Marconi wireless room, a first-class suite and third-class cabin, as well as a full-scale reproduction of the grand staircase. Touring the ship takes about two hours.

WonderWorks

WonderWorks (100 Music Rd., Pigeon Forge, 865/868-1800, www.wonderworksonline.com, 9am-10pm daily, adults from $24, senior and children 4-12 $15) is

another weird one. From the outside, the building appears to be upside down, and inside there are more than 100 interactive exhibits, some, like the Tesla Coil and the Earthquake Café, are strange and seem dangerous, while others challenge you to use your imagination to solve challenges or test your willpower. While it's definitely geared toward kids in the tween range, adults will find plenty to marvel at.

Entertainment

If you want to wet your whistle in Pigeon Forge, your options are exclusively bars in restaurants. The two best bars happen to be in Smoky Mountain Brewery and Mellow Mushroom at the Island in Pigeon Forge. **Smoky Mountain Brewery** (2530 Parkway, Suite 15, Pigeon Forge, 865/868-1400, www.smoky-mtn-brewery.com, 11:30am-1am daily, food $5-25, drinks $3-12) brews every drop of their draft beer in house or at one of their three sister restaurants, and they serve up some good grub if you want something to munch on or are hungry enough for a full meal. **Mellow Mushroom** (131 Island Dr., #3101, Pigeon Forge, www.mellowmushroom.com, 11am-midnight daily, $9-20) specializes in the best national and regional craft beer and some very tasty pizza, subs, and salads. **Iron Boar Saloon** (104 Waldens Main St., Pigeon Forge, 865/429-7774, www.ironboarsaloon.com, 11am-late daily, around $10) has a bottom-shelf beer selection, but it's the only biker bar in town. Come here for the crowd and to hang out with other bikers and bike lovers. Plus, they have good tacos.

Dolly Parton's Dixie Stampede (3849 Parkway, Pigeon Forge, 865/453-9473, www.dixiestampede.com, daily, call for show times, $25-55) is one part dinner, one part show. The dinner's a four-course country feast and the show's jam packed with horseback stunts, comedy, pyrotechnics, and some genuinely surreal sights to take in while you're eating in what is essentially a small arena.

The Smoky Mountain Opry (2046 Parkway, Pigeon Forge, 865/428-7469, www.smokymtnopry.com, daily, show times vary, adults $40, children $10) is a variety show filled with singers and dancers, jugglers and aerial acrobats, magicians, comedians, and musicians; they even have a white lion for some reason. They also have a Christmas show that draws quite the crowd.

Shopping

There's no shortage of touristy shopping around here, but you can find specialty shops, galleries, and decent shopping if you know where to look.

Pigeon Forge earned part of its name from a forge set up in 1820 by Isaac Love. (The other part of its name came from the incredible number of passenger pigeons the early settlers found living along the banks of the Little Pigeon River.) A decade later Love's son established a mill, which is now a National Historic Site that you can visit: the **Old Mill Square** (175 Old Mill Ave., Pigeon Forge, 865/428-0771, www.old-mill.com, hours vary by store) is a collection of shops and restaurants in a cute restored and re-created historic area. **The Old Mill General Store** (865/453-4628, 8:30am-9pm Mon.-Sat, 9am-8pm Sun., hours vary off-season) has all sorts of country provisions, including fresh-ground grains milled next door at the Old Mill. **The Old Mill Farmhouse Kitchen** (865/428-2044, 9:30am-8pm Sun.-Thurs., 9am-9pm Fri.-Sat., hours vary off-season) also sells a variety of provisions and ingredients that you need to cook your own country meal at home. They also have a nice pottery shop and gift baskets.

You can get your fill of candy at **The Old Mill Candy Kitchen** (865/453-7516, 9am-8:30pm Mon.-Thurs., 9am-9pm Fri.-Sat., 9am-8pm Sun., hours vary off-season), and kids will love visiting **The Old Mill Toy Bin** (865/774-2258, 9:30am-8pm Sun.-Thurs., 9am-9pm Fri.-Sat., hours vary off-season), where they'll find all sorts of wooden toys and old-fashioned playthings.

The **Incredible Christmas Place** (2470 Parkway, Pigeon Forge, 865/453-0145, 9am-9pm daily Memorial Day-July 4, 9am-10pm daily July 4-Dec., call for hours Jan.-May) is just that, an incredible store that's all Christmas all the time. Get bows, ornaments, decorations, trees, lights, and any number of collectibles from Boyds Bears, Department 56, and Snowbuddies.

At **The Apple Barn Cider Mill and General Store** (230 Apple Valley Rd., Sevierville, 865/453-9319, www.applebarncidermill.com, 9am-7pm Mon.-Thurs., 9am-9pm Fri.-Sat., 9am-5:30pm Sun.), you can buy fresh cider, a bushel of just-picked apples, a pie hot from the oven, and more. At this great stop, you'll be on a working orchard with more than 4,000 trees, and you can watch the cider presses at work while you munch on an apple donut.

Tanger Outlets (1645 Parkway, Sevierville, 865/453-1053, www.tangeroutlet.com, 9am-9pm Mon.-Sat., 10am-7pm Sun.) in Sevierville has dozens of shops including brand name outlets like Coach, Levi's, Michael Kors, Polo Ralph Lauren, Samsonite, Vera Bradley, and Banana Republic.

If you're looking for a home decor souvenir, look no further than **Aunt Debbie's Country Store** (1753 Wears Valley Rd., Sevierville, 865/366-7359, www.auntdebbiescountrystore.com, 8am-5pm Mon.-Sat.). Barnwood signs, cedar swings, primitive decor, and rustic elements that would bring a touch of the Smokies into your home are on display here. There's a lot to see, so when you stop by, be sure you budget a bit of time to this store.

Recreation

There is plenty to get into when you're in Pigeon Forge and Sevierville. Of course you can hike in the National Park, but you can also white-water raft, ride a crazy alpine coaster, or even try skydiving, but with a twist.

You can try indoor skydiving at **Flyaway Indoor Skydiving** (3106 Parkway, Pigeon Forge, 877/293-0639, www.flyawayindoorskydiving.com, 10am-8pm daily, $34 first flight, $22 additional flight). Indoor skydiving is done in a vertical wind tunnel—think a silo with some giant fans in the base—with an experienced skydiving instructor. After a brief ground school where you'll familiarize yourself with the proper body positions, basics of maneuvering yourself, and hand signals used to communicate with your instructor, you'll get dressed and be ready to fly. In the wind tunnel, it's disorienting the first time you leave your feet and assume the skydiving position because you're floating a few feet off the net where you were just standing. Relax, follow your instructor's directions, and enjoy the experience. If you're lucky, before or after your session, you'll get to see some experienced indoor skydivers perform amazing acrobatic tricks that look like something out of *The Matrix* as they whirl around the tunnel with precise control.

One of the newest, and most interesting, outdoor activities is the **Smoky Mountain Alpine Coaster** (867 Wears Valley Rd., Pigeon Forge, 865/365-5000, www.smokymountainalpinecoaster.com, 9am-9pm daily weather permitting, adults $15, children 7-12 $12, children 3-6, $5). This odd little quasi-rollercoaster puts you in a track-mounted sled complete with an automatic speed control and manual brakes and sends you down a one-mile track, spiraling through tight turns and down a few steep(ish) drops.

Get a view of the Smokies that few others see with **Scenic Helicopter Tours** (tickets at 1965 Parkway, Sevierville, heliport at 1949 Winfield Dunn Parkway, Sevierville, 865/453-0014, www.scenichelicoptertours.com, flight times vary, $27-1,230). Choose from a dozen tours flying over different parts of the region. Short tours like the 8-mile flight along the French Broad River are fun and affordable, while the huge, 100-mile Smoky Mountains Spectacular will set you back more than a thousand bucks, but it's worth it as this tour circles much of the national park.

Smoky Mountain Ziplines (509 Mill Creek Rd., Pigeon Forge, www.smokymountainziplines.com, daily, times vary, call for availability, $70-125) has a 9-line and 14-line canopy tour as well as two super zip lines that are 800 feet long and 100 feet high. This is fun and family friendly. Note that for kids to zip solo, they must be at least 8 years old and 60 pounds; children 5-7 or under 60 pounds may be able to ride tandem with the guide.

Though most of the golf you've seen has been of the mini variety, the **Gatlinburg Golf Course** (520 Dollywood Lane, Pigeon Forge, 800/231-4128, www.golf.gatlinburg.com, daily, call for hours and tee times, $30-60) offers you a full sized round on a beautiful course. Designed by William Langford and renovated twice by Bob Cupp & Associates, this 18-hole course has some dramatic holes. The signature 12th hole, nicknamed "Sky Hi," is 194 yards long and has a 200 foot drop from the tee to the green, making it a puzzling hole for many golfers and a fun one for all. The pro shop here has everything you'll need to play a round, including a full-service restaurant so you can grab a bite and a beer after your round.

The Island In Pigeon Forge (131 Island Dr., 865/286-0119, www.islandpigeonforge.com, 10am-11pm Mon.-Thurs., 10am-midnight Fri.-Sat., 10am-10pm Sun.) is a tourist extravaganza. You'll find a half dozen restaurants and as many snack shops, 20 or so stores selling everything from jerky to puzzles to gems, and rides galore. Rides and entertainment options include the 200-foot tall Great

Smoky Mountain Wheel, a mirror maze, and a huge arcade.

Accommodations

There are several chain hotels in Pigeon Forge and Sevierville, and for the most part they're all the same. However, the **Clarion Inn** (124 Waldens Main St., Pigeon Forge, 865/868-5300, $105-150) is convenient to anything you'll want to do in Pigeon Forge, and it has a pool, lazy river, and slide for the kids. Plus, they have a pretty good breakfast.

Whispering Pines Condominiums (205 Ogle Dr., Pigeon Forge, 800/429-4361, www.whisperingpinescondos.com, $150-300) has a great location if you want a front-row seat on the action of Pigeon Forge, or you can opt for mountain views and unwind a little. The condos here are large, so they're ideal for families or small groups traveling together, especially if you don't want to break the bank.

The Inn at Christmas Place (119 Christmas Tree Lane, Pigeon Forge, 888/465-9644, www.innatchristmasplace.com, $150-310) is an outstanding place to stay. Given that the place is permanently festooned with Christmas decorations (they are somewhat subdued from January to October) and they play Christmas music on a constant loop, I was surprised at how great this property is. Impeccable landscaping; a beautiful, turreted building; a robust breakfast; an indoor and outdoor pool, complete with a 95-foot waterslide; and a game room are only a few of the reasons this inn is such a find.

RiverStone Resort and Spa (212 Dollywood Lane, Pigeon Forge, 877/703-3220, www.riverstoneresort.com, $130-420) has condos and cabins that are luxurious through and through. Add to that an on-site full-service spa, and you have a truly relaxing place to stay. A playground and a lazy river keep the youngest guests occupied outdoors. There is a game room indoors. This is a great

hotel for golfers as it's adjacent to the Gatlinburg Golf Course.

★ **Dollywood's DreamMore Resort** (2525 DreamMore Way, Pigeon Forge, 800/365-5996, www.dreammoreresort.com, starting at $179) opens in summer 2015. Inspired by Dolly's own family-filled front porch, DreamMore promises that same family focus in its 307 rooms, indoor and outdoor pools, storytelling stations, restaurant, and Smoky Mountain views. It's the first hotel on Dollywood property, and as such, staying here has its privileges, like a complimentary shuttle to the park.

Food

At Old Mill there's a quaint collection of shops and a pair of restaurants. **The Old Mill Restaurant** (160 Old Mill Ave., Pigeon Forge, 865/429-3463, www.old-mill.com, 8am-9pm daily, off-season hours vary, breakfast around $9, lunch $9-11, dinner $13-23, kids $6-7 at each meal) is family-friendly and has a small selection for kids. The Pigeon River flows by right outside the dining room, and this is a bigger draw than the food, which is traditional country fare, though breakfast is pretty good.

The Pottery House Café and Grill (175 Old Mill Ave., Pigeon Forge, 865/453-6002, www.old-mill.com, lunch 11am-4pm daily, dinner 4pm-8pm Sun.-Thurs., 4pm-9pm Fri.-Sat., lunch $8.50-12, dinner $8-19) is known for its delicious quiche and outstanding dessert. They serve everything from steaks to fried chicken livers (served with Buffalo sauce and blue cheese dressing) and sandwiches. Rather than trout, which is served by many area eateries, they serve catfish here, which is just as good. If you like what you get for dessert, it's likely you can get a whole cake or pie to take home with you.

★ **Poynor's Pommes Frites** (131 The Island Dr., Suite 3107, Pigeon Forge, 865/774-7744, 11am-10pm daily, $5-10) may not look like much from the outside, but the food is great. The specialty is the pommes frites (French fries). Done in a Belgian style (fried, cooled, then fried again), they're crispy on the outside and fluffy inside, and served plain, with your choice of sauce, or even topped with cheese, bacon, onions, and jalapenos. You can't make a meal of French fries, so Poynor's serves a short menu of German bratwurst served on a German hard roll.

★ **Mel's Diner** (119 Wears Valley Rd., Pigeon Forge, 865/429-2184, www.melsdinerpf.com, 7am-midnight daily, breakfast $3-10, lunch and dinner $6-10) serves up classic diner food with a side of 1950s flair. With tasty, relatively inexpensive dishes served at breakfast, lunch, and dinner (and even rare late-night dining), you can't go wrong here. The breakfast plates are quite hearty, and the burgers and sandwiches piled high with toppings, but save room for dessert and order a whopping six-scoop banana split or a more reasonable shake or malt.

If you're prepared for a feast, head to **Huck Finn's Catfish** (3330 Parkway, Pigeon Forge, 865/429-3353, www.huckfinnsrestaurant.com, from 11:30am daily, lunch $8, dinner $12-19). Their all-you-can-eat catfish and chicken dinners are their claim to fame. They serve a limited lunch menu of catfish and chicken done up several ways and "all 'u'can eat vittles"; vittles include hush puppies, mashed potatoes, fries, cole slaw, pickles, and baked beans. If you like your meal, buy a T-shirt to commemorate it, because if you buy a shirt, your next meal is free.

All throughout the Smokies, pancake houses rule the breakfast world. Though it looks nothing like a log cabin, one of the best in Pigeon Forge is **Log Cabin Pancake House** (4235 Parkway, Pigeon Forge, 865/453-5748, www.logcabinpancakehouse.com, 7am-2pm daily). The silver dollar pancakes are good, and there are 20 pancake choices, plus waffles, and the expected breakfast dishes. They have a lunch buffet if you're starving when it's time for your midday meal, otherwise, it's hard to beat their patty melt.

The wings at **Blue Moose Burgers and Wings** (2430 Teaster Lane #108, Pigeon Forge, 865/286-0364, wwwbluemooseburgersandwings.com, 11am-midnight daily) are the best in town. There are around two dozen wing sauces, plus the rest of the menu, which includes wraps, sandwiches, burgers, salads, and a couple of platters. Unfortunately, their beer selection is bottom shelf.

Mama's Farmhouse (208 Pickel St., Pigeon Forge, 865/908-4646, www.mamasfarmhouse.com, 11am-9pm Sun.-Thurs., 11am-10pm Fri.-Sat., closed an hour earlier in winter, $6-19) is the place for a family-style Southern meal. Every meal is all you can eat, and once you put in your drink order, the food will arrive, and there's a whole lot of it. For dinner, you'll get three meats—fried chicken with meatloaf, turkey and stuffing, ham, country fried steak, or turkey pot pie—and your choice of five sides, plus soup or salad, biscuits, and dessert. Try the peach butter on your biscuits; you can thank me later.

Information and Services

The **Pigeon Forge Welcome Center** (1950 Parkway, 800/251-9100, www.mypigeonforge.com, 8:30am-5pm Mon.-Sat., 1pm-5pm Sun.) is located at traffic light #0 on Parkway. Here, and at the **Pigeon Forge Information Center** (3107 Parkway, 8:30am-5pm. Mon.-Fri.), you can find all the information on the area and volunteers ready to help you plan your time here.

The folks at the **Sevierville Chamber of Commerce Visitors Center** (3099 Winfield Dunn Parkway, 888/738-4378, www.visitsevierville.com, 8:30am-5:30pm Mon.-Sat., 9am-6pm Sun.) are ready to help with trip planning or simply pointing you in the right direction and helping you enjoy your vacation.

If you need a hospital, **LeConte Medical Center** (742 Middle Creek Rd., Sevierville, 865/446-7000, www.lecontemedicalcenter.com) is your best bet.

There are three police departments

here: the **Sevier County Sheriff's Office** (106 W. Bruce St., 865/453-4668), the **Pigeon Forge Police Department** (225 Pine Mountain Rd., 865/453-9063), and the **Sevier County Police Department** (300 Gary Wade Blvd., 865/453-5506).

Knoxville

Perhaps best known among college football fans, Knoxville is the biggest city in East Tennessee and a major travel hub granting access to Great Smoky Mountains National Park and, beyond that, the Blue Ridge Parkway. Unlike Nashville and Memphis, which have national reputations as music towns, Knoxville's comes from the University of Tennessee Volunteers athletics, but that's a bit unfair as the city is home to the historic Tennessee Theatre and the Bijou Theatre, and has a very lively music scene of its own.

In the last decade or so, downtown Knoxville has undergone a significant revitalization. Knoxville's downtown had suffered as businesses and residents left in favor of suburbs, office parks, and strip malls. Then, in 1982, the World's Fair came along and reignited Knoxville's hometown pride. Throughout the preparation for the Fair, for the six months it was here, and for the year afterwards, the city rode this wave of positive energy. When that wave lifted many residents and business owners saw what Knoxville could become. Historic restoration projects, downtown revitalization initiatives, and awareness campaigns began to roll out, and slowly, Knoxville began to turn. By the early 2000s, downtown Knoxville resonated with business owners. Restaurants and shops began to open in spruced-up buildings from yesteryear. Bars followed, and boutiques began to flourish. Soon, downtown had turned into what it is today—a fun cultural center for the city and a place to visit rather than flee.

Getting There and Around
Car
Driving to Knoxville is easy. If you've followed the Blue Ridge Parkway through Great Smoky Mountains National Park, just stay on US-441, which runs right into downtown. Coming from the east or west via I-40, take Exit 388 for Gay Street.

From Asheville, take I-40 West 116 miles (two hours) to Knoxville. From Charlotte, where you'll find a major airport, take US-74 West to I-40 West into Knoxville, a four-hour drive. Alternately, take the same route, but leave I-40 for US-19 into Cherokee, then take US-441/TN 71 through GSMNP and into Knoxville.

From the south, I-75 offers a direct route into Knoxville from Chattanooga, Tenn. (one hour and 45 minutes), and Atlanta, Ga. (three hours). Likewise I-40 is a direct route from Nashville to Knoxville (two hours and 45 minutes). From the north, Knoxville is accessible via I-81.

Air
McGhee Tyson Airport (2055 Alcoa Highway, Alcoa, 865/342-3000, www.flyknoxville.com) is located 20 minutes south of Knoxville in Alcoa, Tenn. You can get there on US-129. From I-40, take Exit 386-B to US-129 south; it's 12 miles to the airport. Airlines serving McGhee Tyson include **Allegiant** (702/505-8888, www.allegiantair.com), **American Airlines American Eagle** (800/433-7300, www.aa.com), **Delta** (800/221-1212, www.delta.com), **Frontier** (800/432-1359, www.flyfrontier.com), **United** (800/525-0208, www.ual.com), and **US Airways** (800/428-4322, www.usairways.com).

If you need taxi service between the airport and Knoxville, **A&B Ground Transportation** (865/389-0312), **Discount Taxi** (865/755-5143), **Odyssey Airport Taxi** (865/577-6767), and **Knoxville Taxi** (865/691-1900) are just a few of the car services you can call.

Public Transportation

Once you're in town, there is plenty to walk to. **Knoxville Trolley Lines** (301 Church Ave., 865/637-3000, free), operated by Knoxville Area Transit, also run throughout downtown. Check online or call for current schedules and routes.

Sights
★ East Tennessee History Center

In the heart of downtown, there's a great little museum telling the story of more than 200 years of East Tennessee's history. The **East Tennessee History Center** (601 S. Gay St., 865/215-8830, www. easttnhistory.org, 9am-4pm Mon.-Fri., 10am-4pm Sat., 1pm-5pm Sun., adults $5, seniors $4, children 16 and under free, free admission on Sun.) has exhibits on the Cherokee, the local involvement in skirmishes and battles from the Civil War, notable slaves and former slaves from the region, the origins of country music, and many displays and scenes showing Knoxville throughout the years. There are also displays on logging and mining, two vocations important to the region, as well as Oak Ridge National Laboratory, where important work in WWII's Manhattan Project went on.

The museum itself is great, but also take note of the wonderful neoclassical Italianate architecture of the building as you walk in. It's Knoxville's old Customs House, built in 1874. Since then, it has served several purposes—a court house, post office, TVA offices. Like many building around town, it's built from Tennessee marble.

★ Knoxville Museum of Art

The **Knoxville Museum of Art** (1050

Worlds Fair Park Dr., 865/525-6101, www.knoxart.org, 10am-5pm Tues.-Sat., 1pm-5pm Sun., free, donations accepted) is a three-story showcase of art and artists of East Tennessee. A huge exhibition, *Cycle of Life: Within the Power of Dreams and the Wonder of Infinity,* from renowned glass artist Richard Jolley, hangs on the walls and ceiling of the ground floor, and a colorful, impressive element of it—a nebula of colored glass orbs—can be seen as you walk through the museum doors. On the top level, two galleries show historic and contemporary works created by artists from or inspired by East Tennessee. The main level has another pair of galleries with rotating exhibits where they display national, international, and regional works, single-artist shows, and themed collections, like the assembly of more than a dozen pieces of amazing blown and cast glass sculptures.

★ Tennessee Theatre

The **Tennessee Theatre** (604 S. Gay St., 865/684-1200, www.tennesseetheatre.com, box office 10am-5pm Mon.-Fri., show times and ticket prices vary) is magnificent. In October 1928, this fabulous space opened its doors to rave reviews. The exterior features that classic marquee we just don't make today, but the inside puts any contemporary movie theater or music hall to shame. The Spanish-Moorish style interior was painstakingly restored to its original grandeur in 2003 with a price tag north of $25 million, all funded through public and private donations. Today, when you walk into the lobby, huge chandeliers twinkle high above. You follow the lines of the ceiling and the patterns on the wall to the marble floor. Twin staircases lead to the balcony upstairs, and once in the theater, there's more ornate wood and plaster work. On stage, there's a gorgeous Wurlitzer organ from the same era as the theater. The best part is the theater actually has someone who knows how to play it, and play it well.

Shows here vary from national and international musicians to plays and stage shows to a handful of films.

Sunsphere

When the World's Fair came in 1982, the city was transformed. The most dramatic transformation is one that has permanently transformed the skyline and become an easily-recognizable symbol of the city. The **Sunsphere** (810 Clinch Ave., Fl. 5, 865/251-6861, www.worldsfairpark.org, 9am-10pm daily Apr.-Oct., 11am-6pm daily Nov.-Mar., free) is a 266-foot-tall tower topped by a huge golden ball. Inside the ball are private offices, a lounge, and a great observation deck that gives you a 360-degree view of Knoxville. It's a shame that the Sunsphere sat mostly unused from the end of the Fair until 1999, when it was opened briefly, then closed just as suddenly. In 2005, Knoxville's mayor announced that the Sunsphere and the adjacent Tennessee Amphitheater (6am-midnight, show times vary), another World's Fair attraction, would be renovated and returned to public use. This is a great structure that symbolizes many things for this city, so it's good to see it in use again.

Knoxville Zoo

The **Knoxville Zoo** (3500 Knoxville Zoo Dr., 865/637-5331, www.knoxvillezoo.org, 9:30am-6pm daily, closed Christmas Day, adults $20, seniors and children 2-12 $17, parking free) has more than 900 animals from all over the world including the expected zoo animals and some surprises. There are a number of red pandas here (the zoo is a breeding facility for them), a giraffe you can feed, and Budgie Landing, an enclosed aviary in Clayton Family Kids Cove that's filled with what seems like a million budgies (a type of small parrot) flying around.

Women's Basketball Hall of Fame

Given the basketball prowess of the University of Tennessee Lady Vols

Tennessee's Unsung Music Town

Knoxville gets short shrift when folks talk about Tennessee music. Ever eclipsed by Nashville and overlooked by bluegrass and mountain string band lovers for spots like Gatlinburg and Pigeon Forge, Knoxville is forgotten. But no more. The music scene in this hip Southern town is lively and growing livelier by the minute. Bands like The Black Lillies, with their mountain-influenced indie rock, and The Black Cadillacs, who take a more bluesy spin, have made a name for themselves nationally in recent years, playing at Bonnaroo and the Grand Ole Opry.

All across town you'll find buskers playing on the street, bands tucked into restaurants and bars, and free concerts on the Market Square during the summer. Jam sessions pop up and band members flow freely from one impromptu band to another until they find the perfect fit. Two historic venues—The **Tennessee Theatre** (the state's official theater, and a stunning place to see a band) and the **Bijou Theatre**—host concerts with clockwork regularity.

Music festivals, like **Big Ears Festival** (www.bigearsfestival.com), **Smoky Mountain Music Fest** (www.smm-festival.com), and **Rhythm N Blooms Fest** (www.rhythmnbloomsfest.com), celebrate the sounds of the city and bring in visiting bands and music fans from all over.

Make it a point while you're in town to take in one of the daily free shows at **WDVX-FM,** where their noontime Blue Plate Special concert series brings in local and regional acts to play for a live radio broadcast in front of a studio audience.

and famed former coach Pat Summitt, Knoxville is a fitting place for the **Women's Basketball Hall of Fame** (700 Hall of Fame Dr., 865/633-9000, www.wbhof.com, 11am-5pm Tues.-Fri., 10am-5pm Sat. Labor Day-Apr., 10am-5pm Mon.-Sat. May-Labor Day, adults $8, seniors and children 6-15 $6). This facility, the only one to be devoted entirely to women's basketball achievements at all levels, opened in 1999 and celebrates the rich history of women's basketball. The exhibits here are more than just a plaque and write-up on Hall of Fame members, there are interactive areas like the basketball court where you can practice passing and dribbling skills or shoot a few balls at baskets both contemporary and from the earliest days of the game. Other exhibits include displays honoring current NCAA national champions and a set of mannequins dressed in uniforms from over the years. There's also a gift shop where you can pick up basketballs autographed by Hall of Fame members. Oh, and the building is hard to miss as one end has the world's largest basketball, which appears to be dropping into a net.

Circle G Ranch

The **Circle G Ranch** (831 Thorngrove Pike, Strawberry Plains, 865/932-0070, www.ridecamels.com, 10am-5pm daily, adults $9, children 2-13 $7) is a drive-through zoo with more than 500 animals including camels, zebra, ostrich, and emu, to name a few. It's weird and it's fun, but it's even better if you take a guided tour with Matt, one of the owners of the ranch. His knowledge of these animals and anecdotes about working with them makes the drive very entertaining indeed. No matter how you choose to tour, buy a few buckets of food, the animals know it's coming and they'll beat a path to your car, making for some entertaining photos.

Tours

Haunted Knoxville Ghost Tours (301 S. Gay St., 865/377-9677, www.hauntedknoxville.net, adults $25, children 9-12 $20, tour dates and times vary, reserve online) is more than just a person walking around telling some "scary" stories filled with local color, these guides offer one of the leading historical and investigation-based ghost tours. They've dug up some juicy, and creepy, stories that reveal a hidden side of this friendly city. And they continue to carry our investigations, bringing with them on every tour a host of tools used to gather information on the paranormal.

Entertainment
Nightlife

Hops & Hollers (937 N. Central St., 865/312-5733, www.hopsandhollers.com, noon-midnight Mon.-Sat., noon-10pm Sun.) is a fun little craft beer bar with 100 bottles and cans and 32 on draft. The bartenders know their brews and can make reliable recommendations (when in doubt, ask for a tasting pour). Musicians play here on a regular basis and food trucks stop by just about every night of the week.

Casual Pint (421 Union St., 865/951-2160, www.thecasualpint.com, 3pm-11pm Mon.-Thurs., 3pm-2am Fri., 11am-2am. Sat., noon-11pm Sun.) brews several beers in-house and always has a deep lineup on draft. Grab a sampler flight or the pint of your choice, or fill up a growler to take your brew home with you.

Club XYZ (1215 N. Central St., 865/637-4999, www.clubxyz-knoxville.com, 5:30pm-3am Mon.-Fri., 9pm-3am Sat., 7pm-3am Sun.) is one of the best gay bars in Knoxville. They have drag shows, karaoke nights, dance parties, and great happy hour specials.

Icon Ultra Lounge (810 Clinch Ave., on the 5th Fl. of the Sunsphere, 865/249-7321, www.knoxvilleicon.com, 4pm-midnight Tues.-Thurs., 4pm-2am Fri.-Sat.) has some fantastic views, good drinks, and a dinner and late-night menu. It's a great place to visit for a drink or two before heading out for further adventures, or for stopping by for a nightcap and something to munch on before heading back to your hotel.

Performing Arts

Along with the Tennessee Theatre, the **Bijou Theatre** (803 S. Gay St., 865-522-0832, www.knoxbijou.com, ticket prices vary) is one of Knoxville's most important venues for live musical performances.

Side Splitters Comedy Club (9246 Parkwest Blvd., 865/934-5233, www.sidesplitterscomedy.com, 6pm-2am Thurs.-Sat., showtimes and ticket prices vary) brings in some big names in standup comedy (Dom Irrera, Dan Cummins, Mitch Fatel, Pauley Shore, and Alonzo Bodden have played there). In addition to national and regional touring comedians, they have an open mic night every other Thursday night. **Knox Comedy Live** (www.knoxcomedy.com) isn't a comedy club, but rather a group of comedians living in the region who are helping to spread the word about smaller comedy shows and open mic opportunities. Check their website for upcoming shows.

Festivals and Events

Knoxville has several great events throughout the year, and two good ones are **Boomsday** (865/342-9105, www.boomsday.org), the largest Labor Day fireworks show in the United States, and the **International Biscuit Festival** (865/238-5219, www.biscuitfest.com), an annual spring gathering of foodies, food writers, and biscuit enthusiasts. The Biscuit Festival is a strange one, but entertaining, and Boomsday can get insanely crowded. Both events are worth seeing at least once.

Shopping

Market Square (865/215-4248, www.knoxvillemarketsquare.com) provides a center square (actually, a rectangle) around which people can gather. Just one block off Gay Street, this excellent little shopping and dining district is always busy. Summer concerts, buskers, and a small fountain for the kids to play draw folks here, and the variety of people walking by and stores to peruse makes it easy to kill time while waiting for your table to be ready. There are a half dozen restaurants on the Square, and close to a dozen shops, including the **Mast General Store** (865/546-1336, www.maststoreknoxville, 10am-6pm Mon.-Wed., 10am-9pm Thurs.-Sat., noon-6pm Sun.), where you can buy everything from camping gear to home goods to penny candy; **Earth to Old City** (865/522-8270, www.earthtooldcity.com, 10am-9pm Mon.-Sat., noon-6pm Sun.) carries all sorts of odd and funky home decor (some of it may be more at home in a dorm room than your house); and twin shops **Bliss** (865/329-8868, www.shopinbliss.com, 10am-9pm Mon.-Thurs., 10am-10pm Fri.-Sat., 11am-7pm Sun.) and **Bliss Home** (865/673-6711, 10am-9pm Mon.-Sat., 11pm-7pm Sun.), selling home goods and lifestyle accessories. The **Market Square Farmer's Market** (11am-2pm Wed. and 9am-2pm Sat. May-Nov.) shows up in late spring,

the Sunsphere looking over Worlds Fair Park in Knoxville

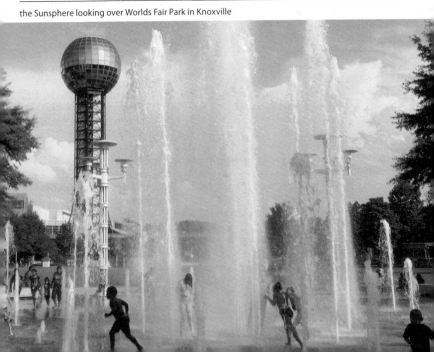

bringing with it dozens of farmers and craftspeople selling their wares, edible or not.

Nothing Too Fancy (435 Union Ave., 865/951-2916, www.nothingtoofancy. com, 10am-9pm Mon.-Fri., 9am-9pm Sat., 11am-6pm Sun.) has some very cool T-shirts and other silk-screened goods designed by local artists. Reflecting the culture, in-jokes, and vibe of Knoxville in their work, the shirts are fun, even for those not in the know.

Reruns Boutique (521 Union Ave., 865/525-9525, www.rerunsboutique.com, 11am-7pm Tues.-Sat., 1pm-5pm Sun.) is an upscale consignment shop featuring almost exclusively women's clothing. Prices are reasonable and the fashion is high, so if you're looking for something special, check here.

Recreation

Definitely the star of Knoxville's recreational scene is **Ijams Nature Center** (2915 Island Home Ave., 865/577-4717, www.ijams.org, 9am-5pm Mon.-Sat., 1pm-5pm Sun.). This 300-acre urban wilderness is laced with hiking and single-track mountain biking trails, former quarries to explore on foot or even paddle around, and it's dog friendly. This vast, wild space is a strange thing so close to the city, but people love it. At any time of any day there are walkers, hikers, trail runners, bikers, families, couples, and singles on the trails here. From Ijams Nature Center, you can connect with a larger nearly-contiguous loop some 40 miles long. Grab a map when you come in or download one and plan your route ahead of time, or you could just bring some water and your camera and just wander.

World's Fair Park (www.worlds-fairpark.org) is the best city park in Knoxville. This 10-acre park has walking paths, a small lake, open grassy spaces, soccer fields, fountains, and a gorgeous stream running right down the middle. It's the home of the Sunsphere and Tennessee Amphitheatre, and at the north end of the park, past a fantastically large fountain, is a 4,200-square-foot playground. The playground and fountain get pretty crowded with kids, but there are other places you can go if you're traveling without a few of your own.

Accommodations

★ **The Oliver Hotel** (407 Union Ave., 865/521-0050, www.theoliverhotel.com, $160-265) is an outstanding boutique hotel. The service is impeccable and the rooms amazing—everything is done to a luxurious, but not ostentatious, level. When you first find it, you'll likely walk right past it as it blends in with the rest of the block almost seamlessly. Built originally in 1876 as a bakery, it was converted into a hotel for the World's Fair. There are 24 guest rooms with wet bars, coffee service, and fabulous bedding.

Maplehurst Inn (800 West Hill Ave., 865/851-8383, www.malehurstinn.com, $125-175) is dated, but worth considering because of the friendly service and a pretty good breakfast. Your hosts make you feel at home and you can tell they care about your experience. Plus, it's a mansion in a truly lovely part of town.

Maple Grove Inn (880 Westland Dr., 865/951-2315, www.maplegroveinn.com, $150-300) has seven lovely rooms in one of the oldest residences in Knoxville. A popular spot for weddings, this full-service bed-and-breakfast sits on 15 acres of gardens, giving you the opportunity to truly check out of day-to-day life and relax in the moment.

Hilton Knoxville (501 W. Church Ave., 865/523-2300, www.hilton.com, $142-200) is only two blocks off Gay Street and has fantastic rooms. With on-site dining, a Starbucks right in the lobby, and parking next door, it's the best of the name-brand hotels you'll find.

There are a number of other chain hotels in town, including the **Hampton Inn**

Knoxville North (5411 Pratt Rd., 855/271-3622, www.hamptoninn3.hilton.com, $120-170) and the Country Inn & Suites Knoxville at Cedar Bluff (9137 Cross Park Dr., 800/596-2375, www.countryinns.com, $120-185).

Food

Knoxville Food Tours (865/201-7270, www.knoxvillefoodtours.com, $59) shows off some of the best spots to drink and dine in downtown Knoxville. Tour dates are Friday and Saturday afternoons and evenings, but custom tours are available any day. The walk's not far—generally under a mile—and you get to find a place to have dinner, all while under the tutelage of a local foodie.

The tiny shop Just Ripe (513 Union Ave., 865/851-9327, www.justripeknoxville.com, 8am-7pm Mon.-Sat., $1.50-10) sells coffee, a few baked goods, a pair of burritos, grab-and-go healthy lunch items, and these incredible biscuits and biscuit sandwiches. They're just the right mix of dense and fluffy, and with a little bacon or smoky tomato jam (or both) they are out of this world.

When a former rock musician opens a restaurant, you expect it to have a lot of personality, and ★ Sweet P's Barbecue & Soul House (3725 Maryville Pike, 865/247-7748, www.sweetpbbq.com, 11am-8pm Tues.-Thurs., 11am-9pm Fri.-Sat., noon-7pm Sun., $4-22) delivers. Owner and Pitmaster Chris Ford ate in every barbecue joint he could find while on tour with his band and began developing recipes long before he had the idea for a restaurant. Then, when the time came for Sweet P's, he was ready. This is some fine barbecue: the ribs, the brisket, and the sides. The potato salad is good and the mac and cheese done just right, but the cole slaw is out of this world.

top to bottom: the historic Tennessee Theatre; Ijams Nature Center; musicians on Market Square

★ **Dead End BBQ** (3621 Sutherland Ave., 865/212-5655, www.deadendbbq.com, 11am-9pm Sun.-Thurs., 11am-10pm Fri.-Sat., $8-23) was started by a group of guys who would get together and make barbecue. Turns out they were onto something good. After their neighbors and wives praised them enough, they decided to enter a barbecue competition. They did well, very well, and entered another and not long after, they accumulated a wall of first and second place trophies. Naturally, this little obsession turned into a restaurant, and a damn good one at that. Everything they do here is top notch, so unless the brisket or ribs or some other dish catch your eye, get the sampler plate. They have one dish you don't see very often—beef brisket burnt ends. Far from being burnt, these succulent little morsels are trimmings off the brisket, and they go down easy. The sauce here is fantastic, and the sides outstanding. Save room for dessert, their banana pudding is so rich and thick that it's more like cheesecake.

Pete's Coffee Shop (540 Union Ave., 865/523-2860, www.petescoffeeshop.com, 6:30am-2:30pm Mon.-Fri., 7am-2pm Sat., $2-8) is a diner that's dirt cheap and super tasty. Their French toast is exceptional, as are their pancakes, and for lunch, Pete's Supreme (ham and melted Swiss on a hoagie) is excellent as is the patty melt.

At **The Tomato Head** (12 Market Square, 865/637-4067, www.thetomatohead.com, 11am-9:30pm Mon.-Thurs., 11am-10:30pm Fri., 10am-10:30pm Sat., 10am-9pm Sun., brunch 10am-3pm Sat.-Sun., $3-28), sit outside, weather permitting, and watch the crowds on Market Square while you eat your pizza. The menu here features pizzas, sandwiches, burritos, and salads, but stick to the pizza, not because the other stuff is bad, but because the pizza is so good. You can build your own or get one already put together. Odd combos like fresh spinach and black bean, lamb sausage and sundried tomato, and smoked salmon and pesto actually go down quite easily.

Stock & Barrel (35 Market Square, 865/766-2075, www.thestockandbarrel.com, 11am-late daily, $7-16) has an unparalleled bourbon selection, a list of burgers that are as tasty as they are creative, and a line out the door. Even if you make a reservation, you'll wait for a seat, but it's worth it because once you get in, you won't want to leave. Get a flight of bourbon and whatever burger pushes your buttons, and enjoy.

Nama Sushi Bar (506 S. Gay St., 865/633-8539, www.namasushibar.com, 11am-midnight Mon.-Thurs., 11am-2am Fri.-Sat., noon-midnight Sun., $4-24) is the best option for sushi in Knoxville. Their fish is always fresh and they serve both traditional rolls and rolls that are a little more inventive. The moon special roll and the orange crush go pretty far afield from your basic roll to make a delicious bite of food. This place gets crowded, especially on weekends or when Knoxville is hopping, so get there early or make a reservation.

The Crown & Goose (123 S. Central St., 865/524-2100, www.thecrownandgoose.com, 11am-11pm Mon.-Wed., 11am-midnight Thurs., 11am-1am Fri.-Sat., 11am-3pm Sun., $8-26) is a gastropub serving a fusion of traditional British and contemporary European dishes and techniques. Nothing here pushes the boundaries too far, but they do use some great ingredients in their interpretations of fish and chips, shepherd's pie, and in their small plates.

Information and Services
The **Knoxville Visitors Center** (301 S. Gay St., 800/727-8045, www.visitknoxville.com, 8:30am-5pm Mon.-Fri., 9am-5pm Sat., noon-4pm Sun.) is what visitor centers should be. They have the

expected rack of maps and helpful volunteers on hand to answer questions, but what sets them apart is the gift shop filled with locally made art and foodstuffs, a kid's corner, coffee, and radio station. This is the only visitor center I know of where you can watch a free concert every day at lunch or listen to it as a live radio broadcast.

The local public radio station, **WDVX-FM** (301 S. Gay St., 865/544-1029, www.wdvx.com) at 89.9 FM, is also the host of the Blue Plate Special concert series held on the stage in the Knoxville Visitors Center during lunch hour on weekdays. Listen to classic rock at **WIMZ** (103.5 FM). **WUTK** (90.3 FM) is a college station from the University of Tennessee. Tune in to public radio from UT at **WUOT** (91.9).

If you need medical care, there are more than a half dozen clinics and hospitals in Knoxville. The **University of Tennessee Medical Center** (1924 Alcoa Highway, 865/305-9000, www.utmedicalcenter.org) is a 581-bed teaching hospital, and **Fort Sanders Regional Medical Center** (1901 Clinch Ave., 865/541-1111, www.fsregional.com) is conveniently located downtown.

Essentials

Getting There

Air

While most visitors drive to the Blue Ridge Parkway, Shenandoah National Park and Skyline Drive, or Great Smoky Mountains National Park, it's convenient to fly into a nearby city, rent a car, and hit the road at any point along the route.

Washington DC

Three airports serve the Washington area. **Dulles International Airport** (1 Saarinen Circle, Dulles, Va., 703/572-2700, www.metwashairports.com) accommodates domestic and international travelers. Around three-dozen airlines serve Dulles, and if you're flying internationally, this airport is much closer to downtown than your other options.

Reagan National Airport (2401 Smith Blvd., Arlington, Va., 703/417-8000, www.metwashairports.com) sees primarily domestic flights, though a few international flights come in. Airlines here include Air Canada, Delta, Frontier, Jet Blue, Southwest, United, and Virgin America.

In Baltimore, Md., 35 miles to the northeast, the **Baltimore Washington International Airport** (410/859-7111, www.bwiairport.com) sees a handful of international flights but mostly domestic airlines very similar to those serving Reagan National Airport. Depending on your departure city, Baltimore may be a cheaper flight into the region, but know that even though it's only 35 miles distant, the traffic around Washington is notorious and it could be a costly cab ride or frustrating commute in your rental car if this is where you land.

Virginia

Charlottesville is served by **Charlottesville Albemarle Airport** (100 Bowen Loop, Charlottesville, 434/973-8342, www.gocho.com). Airlines here include Delta, American Airlines, United Airlines, and US Airways.

The largest airport in southwest Virginia is the **Roanoke-Blacksburg Regional Airport** (5202 Aviation Dr., NW, Roanoke, 540/362-1999, www.flyroa.com). Airlines serving this airport include Allegiant Air, American Airlines, Delta Airlines, United Airlines, and US Airways.

The **Richmond International Airport** (1 Richard E. Byrd Terminal Dr., Richmond, 804/226-3000, www.flyrichmond.com) is only about 90 minutes east of Rockfish Gap and Milepost 0 of the Blue Ridge Parkway, and may be a viable option.

North Carolina

Asheville Regional Airport (61 Terminal Dr., 828/684-2226, www.flyavl.com) is located south of the city in Fletcher. The next-closest airport in North Carolina is the **Charlotte-Douglas International Airport** (5501 Josh Birmingham Pkwy., 704/359-4910, www.charmeck.org), two hours away. Charlotte-Douglas is the tenth-largest hub in the United States, with nonstop flights to and from more than 125 destinations worldwide.

The **Piedmont Triad International Airport** (1000 A. Ted Johnson Pkwy., 336/665-5600, www.flyfrompti.com), in Greensboro, is less than 90 minutes from the Blue Ridge Parkway and is served by Allegiant, American Airlines American Eagle, Delta Airlines, Frontier Airlines, United, and US Airways.

Farther to the east, the **Raleigh-Durham International Airport** (RDU, 2400 John Brantley Blvd., Morrisville, 919/840-2123, www.rdu.com) sits between the cities of Durham and Raleigh. Eight airlines serve RDU, providing close to 400 nonstop flights to around 40 destinations daily. AirTran Airways, Southwest, Air Canada, American Airlines, Delta, Frontier Airlines, Jet Blue Airways, United, and US Airways stop at RDU coming from domestic and international destinations. RDU is close to two hours from the Blue Ridge Parkway, but the volume of air traffic and the ease of reaching the Parkway make this a good choice when price shopping flights.

South Carolina

The **Greenville-Spartanburg International Airport** (2000 GSP Dr., Greer, S.C., 864/848-6254, www.gspairport.com) is an 80 minutes south of Asheville. Airlines serving Greenville-Spartanburg include Allegiant, American Airlines, Delta, Southwest, and United.

Tennessee

The **McGhee Tyson Airport** (2055 Alcoa Hwy., Alcoa, Tenn., 865/342-3000, www.tys.org) in Alcoa, Tenn., is about two hours from Cherokee, and about 20 minutes south of Knoxville. Airlines serving McGhee Tyson include Allegiant, American Airlines American Eagle, Delta, Frontier, United, and US Airways.

Bus

You can take a **Greyhound bus** (800/231-2222, www.greyhound.com) to every major city and most of the larger towns on or near the Blue Ridge Parkway. The most useful routes are those that take you to Washington DC's **Union Station** (WAS, 50 Massachusetts Ave. NE, 202/289-5141, 24 hours); the **Charlottesville Greyhound station** (310 W. Main St., 434/295-5131, 4am-10am, 11:30am-6:30pm, and 8am-10pm daily); the **Roanoke Greyhound station** (26 Salem Ave. SW, 540/343-5436, midnight-2am and 9am-5pm daily); or the **Knoxville Greyhound station** (100 E. Magnolia Ave. (865/525-9483), because they put you in a position where it's easy to get started on the Parkway. At Washington DC's Union Station, a number of buses arrive daily from cities from across the country. Both the Charlottesville and Roanoke stations are downtown, where it's easy to get to your accommodations or to a rental car agency. The **Asheville Greyhound station** (2 Tunnel Rd., 828/253-8451) is another option, though the route does take a bit longer to get into town due to Asheville's location.

Train

Amtrak (800/872-7245, www.amtrak. com) service is limited to parts of Virginia and Washington DC, but where it is available, it's dependable. Amtrak pulls into Washington DC's **Union Station** (50 Massachusetts Ave. NE, 202/906-3000, 24 hours) with trains coming from and going to destinations all over the eastern seaboard. Amtrak services include the Acela Express, Northeast Regional, Silver Service/Palmetto, Cardinal/Hoosier State, Crescent, Vermonter, Capitol Limited, and Carolinian/Piedmont. Amtrak also serves **Charlottesville** (CVS, 810 W Main St., 434/296-4559,

The Smokies are stunning, even in winter.

6am-9:30pm daily), where the Cardinal/ Hoosier State, Crescent, and Northeast Regional Lines pass through daily.

Near Roanoke, **Lynchburg** (LYH, 825 Kemper St., Lynchburg, 800/872-7245, 5am-12:45pm and 4pm-11:45pm daily) is served by Amtrak's Crescent and Northeast Regional Lines. In 2014, Virginia and Norfolk Southern Railroad signed an agreement to improve tracks and build a station in Roanoke, extending Amtrak passenger service from Lynchburg to Roanoke. As of the writing of this book, Amtrak and Norfolk Southern estimated that service will begin no later than fall of 2017.

Major Highways

Two major interstates—**I-64** and **I-77**—intersect the Blue Ridge Parkway at the northern and southern ends, and **I-81** provides easy access as it runs diagonally up the western border of Virginia, parallel to the Parkway.

I-66 connects Washington DC with the beginning of Skyline Drive in northern Virginia. **I-64** passes by Shenandoah National Park and is the de facto dividing line between Skyline Drive and the Parkway, providing easy access to both at Rockfish Gap just outside Waynesboro. To the south, **I-77** crosses the Parkway at Fancy Gap, Va. **I-40** skirts the Parkway at several points in North Carolina and Great Smoky Mountains National Park in Tennessee. A number of smaller roads, from U.S. Highways to State Routes, offer access to the Parkway and parks at various points along the way. Cities like Charlottesville, Waynesboro, and Roanoke, Va., are just a few miles off the Parkway or Skyline Drive. In North Carolina, the Parkway goes right by Asheville and ends in Cherokee. In Tennessee, Knoxville (touched by both **I-40** and **I-75**) is the nearest city to Great Smoky Mountains National Park, though the towns of Gatlinburg and Pigeon Forge are nestled close to the park's borders.

Road Rules

Along the Blue Ridge Parkway, **mileposts** mark the way. Starting at the southern end of Shenandoah National Park with Milepost 0 at Rockfish Gap all the way through Milepost 469 in Cherokee, North Carolina, you'll pass stone markers along the side of the road. Overlooks, hikes, historic sites, and spots to stop and explore are referenced both by name and milepost. Skyline Drive through Shenandoah National Park is marked by mileposts as well.

Car Rental

Rental cars are available at every airport listed in this guide, and if you take a train to your departure point, you'll find rental agencies in or near the station. Since many bus and train stations share a facility or are near one another, the same is true if you bus in. The major rental players—Hertz, National, and Enterprise, among others—will be readily available with their standard fleet of cars, but if you are looking for a specific vehicle (like a 4x4 or convertible), check availability with the agencies and reserve your vehicle. Most of these vehicles will be available for one-way rental, allowing you to rent a car at one end and drive it to another, returning it there before boarding a plane, or hopping a bus or train back home. Before you embark on a long, one-way trip with a rental vehicle, be sure you can return it at the other end. Check with your car rental agency about additional fees for one-way rentals, as some charge hefty fees for this type of rental.

Driving Rules and Highway Safety

Foreign visitors who wish to drive should obtain an **International Driving Permit,** which is available from the nation that issued your driver's license. Drivers licensing rules vary from state to state. It's a good idea to familiarize yourself with

Bridges and Tunnels

The **viaducts, 168 bridges,** and **26 tunnels** are some of the most distinctive architectural elements you'll find along the Blue Ridge Parkway. The bridges make extensive use of native stone as a decorative and functional element (the stonework was used as the form for the concrete frames on each bridge). The same goes for the tunnels: their faces are both decorative and structural and make the same use of native materials.

While the bridges are regular features for the length of the Parkway, the tunnels and the most striking of the viaducts (the Linn Cove Viaduct at Milepost 304.4) are a North Carolina thing. In North Carolina, the mountains grow sharper and steeper and at times it's easier to go through rather than around them. That's why of the 26 tunnels, only 1, the Bluff Mountain Tunnel at Milepost 53.1, is found in Virginia; the other 25 are found within a 130-mile stretch of the southern section in North Carolina.

For those traveling in cars or on motorcycles, the tunnels are little more than another pretty aspect of the roadway. But if you're hauling a **trailer** or driving an **RV**, you'll be more concerned with the tunnels' height and length. Visit http://www.nps.gov/blri/planyourvisit/tunnel-heights.htm for a list of the 26 tunnels, complete with mileposts, length, and height restrictions.

driving rules in the states that you'll be visiting (you can do this at www.usa.gov). Throughout the United States, drivers drive on the right side of the road, and distance and speed is measured in miles. Speedometers display both miles and kilometers; road signs display only miles.

On Skyline Drive, the **speed limit** is 35 miles per hour; it's 45 miles per hour along most of the Blue Ridge Parkway, though it does slow in areas; in the Great Smoky Mountains National Park, the speed limit is 45 miles per hour as well. Please observe the posted speed limit. Maintaining the speed limit allows you time to stop or avoid wildlife, debris, or other hazards on the road surface as well as pedestrians or other vehicles. Since long sections of all three segments of this route are unprotected—read: no guardrails to break up the view—obeying the speed limit has the added benefit of keeping you and your passengers safe from leaving the roadway on an unexpected downhill trip. Mind the posted speed limit on highways and interstates as well, especially in Virginia, where speeding violations can result in jail time.

One reason for the low speed limits along this scenic drive is to keep **wildlife** free from harm. You'll see a number of woodland creatures on your drive, and as your route cuts through the forests where they live, you'll see many animals on or near the roadway. Be extra vigilant at dawn and dusk, when wildlife is most active. If you must stop in the road to allow an animal to cross, use your hazard flashers to alert other drivers, and try not to stop in blind curves or just over the crest of a hill where you'll be difficult to see.

Weather Considerations

From Skyline Drive through to Gatlinburg, Tenn., the weather can slow and stop traffic or even shut down sections of the route under the most severe conditions. Generally, though, the weather is quite pleasant and **winter** is the only time when there are widespread closures of Skyline Drive or the Blue Ridge Parkway. In both cases, the route is high and exposed, making it vulnerable to ice and snow; that, combined with the expense of the equipment necessary for proper snow and ice removal make wintertime closures an inevitability. Newfound Gap Road through Great Smoky Mountains National Park is a public highway and is maintained throughout the year. It may still close

Mind the Gaps

You'll encounter more **gaps** in the Blue Ridge Parkway than I can count, and if you're not from the mountains, this may be an unfamiliar term. Gaps, sometimes called passes, are simply low spots in the mountain chain. If you needed to get across the mountain, you'd look for these low spots for your crossing, as opposed to going up and over the high, steep, rocky places. Rockfish Gap, at Blue Ridge Parkway Milepost 0, is one such low spot. At only 1,909 feet high, it offered wildlife, then Native Americans, then colonists and settlers, and now endless interstate traffic an easy place to pass through these mountains.

if heavy snowfall is expected or is more than road crews can cope with, but closure is rare. More often you'll be delayed as crews clear the road. Road conditions are available by contacting the **National Park Service** (828/298-0398, www.nps. gov/maps/blri/road-closures).

Spring generally brings a good amount of rain to the Blue Ridge Mountains. During the earliest months, and even toward the first part of April in the highest elevations, you can experience road closures if a spring snowstorm visits the high passes. The rest of the season, it may rain, but it doesn't impede traffic.

In **summer,** there is a chance of thunderstorms, and on rare occasions hail, along the route. Most likely, you'll encounter a rain shower or fog. The fog can be quite dense, so slowing down or even pulling off at a socked-in overlook is advisable.

In **autumn,** there are occasional rainstorms, and in the latest part of the season, the rare high-altitude snowstorm that dusts the tops of the mountains white. Traffic is generally not a consideration on the Blue Ridge Parkway or elsewhere along the route, but autumn sees the highest number of visitors to Skyline Drive, the Blue Ridge Parkway, and GSMNP, and leaf lookers often slow down well below the speed limit, causing some **congestion on the roadway.** Autumn color seekers also fill overlooks and line the sides of the road to snap pictures and take in the views, slowing traffic in these busy areas as drivers watch for pedestrians.

Road Etiquette

If this is your first visit to the South, you can start fitting in by simply waving. Many drivers along the Blue Ridge Parkway and Skyline Drive and in the Smokies will raise a finger or two from the steering wheel or proffer a little salute to passing drivers, as if to say, "Beautiful, ain't it?" and "Sure is" with the return wave. So give a little wave, nod, or two-fingered salute at your fellow travelers.

Standard etiquette applies—only use your bright headlights if there's no oncoming traffic, for example—but there are a few things to remember. You're on this road trip to relax, so loosen up, slow down, and lose yourself to the rambling speed of these mountaintop byways. There's no need for tailgating, horn honking, or agitation, and if you encounter this type of frustrated, rush-everywhere traveler, pull off at the next overlook while they move on down the road.

Parking

All along Skyline Drive, the Blue Ridge Parkway, and Great Smoky Mountains National Park, parking is limited to designated parking areas at overlooks and trailheads, though parking is permitted along the road shoulder, provided all four wheels are off the road surface and your vehicle doesn't impede traffic.

Fuel

Fuel is not readily available on the Blue Ridge Parkway, a slightly inconvenient byproduct of efforts to protect the Parkway from unintentional spills or leaks. The Blue Ridge Parkway Association (www.blueridgeparkway.org) provides an index of fuel availability by milepost, which is listed at the beginning of each applicable chapter in this guidebook. At major highway intersections and any place you meet a town or city, you'll find fuel close at hand.

In Shenandoah National Park, there's only one gas station located at the Big Meadows Wayside (Milepost 51.2), but you will find fuel at Front Royal, at the north end of the park, and in Waynesboro and all along the I-64 corridor on the south end of the park.

You won't find any fuel inside Great Smoky Mountains National Park, but you will find it in Cherokee and the other towns on the North Carolina side. Gas stations are plentiful on the Tennessee side once you leave the national park.

Maps
One of the best resources for exploring a new region is a good map. DeLorme's atlas and gazetteers are indispensible. The detail provided is enough to plan short day hikes or longer expeditions, and they point out everything from trailheads and boat launches to campgrounds, hunting and fishing spots, and back roads of all types. Look for the *North Carolina Atlas & Gazetteer* (Yarmouth, ME: DeLorme, 2012), the *Tennessee Atlas & Gazetteer* (Yarmouth, ME: DeLorme, 2014), and the *Virginia Atlas & Gazetteer* (Yarmouth, ME: DeLorme, 2009).

Motorcycles
Motorcyclists love the Blue Ridge Parkway for its views, mild temperature, and fun twists and turns. Helmets are required and all other road regulations should be followed. During autumn, motorcyclists should exercise a little extra caution as wet leaves on the roadway can be quite slick. Many bike enthusiasts consider a trip through Great Smoky Mountains National Park a must, and the curves along Newfound Gap in particular provide thrills.

Bicycles
Of the three roads along this trip, the Blue Ridge Parkway is, hands down, the most popular for cyclists. This 469-mile ride through picturesque peaks provides challenges and thrills to cyclists in spring, summer, and fall. Elevations range from 600 feet to more than 6,000, so there's the challenge of long climbs and the reward of lazy downhills. The Parkway was originally intended for automobile traffic, so there are no bike lanes along the route. It's best to adopt a defensive mindset and assume that most drivers have no experience around cyclists. Always wear your helmet, be sure lights and reflectors are in good condition, and ride in single file.

The route is spread out, and there is almost nothing by way of bicycle-specific facilities, so prepare for the worst, bringing your tool kit, spare tubes, and anything else you'll need to perform a quick repair. The facilities that exist—campgrounds, visitor centers, and the like—do have potable water, though it isn't advisable to drink from streams without purification first.

Keep in mind that mountain bikes aren't permitted on Blue Ridge Parkway trails, but they are permitted in national forests, of which the Parkway abuts a number. Check for specific trails within each national forest.

Public Transportation
There's no public transportation that runs along Skyline Drive, the Blue Ridge Parkway, or through Great Smoky Mountains National Park. Only in cities along the way will you find any sort of public transportation infrastructure in place.

Travel Tips

Visas and Officialdom

Visitors from other countries must present a valid **passport** and **visa** issued by a U.S. consular official unless they are citizens of a country eligible for the Visa Waiver Program (such as Canada) in order to enter the United States. For more information on traveling to the United States from a foreign country, visit www.usa.gov.

Access for Travelers with Disabilities

The overwhelming majority of hikes in Shenandoah National Park, the Blue Ridge Parkway, and Great Smoky Mountains National Park are not accessible for travelers with disabilities, particularly those that impede mobility. Luckily, a huge number of attractions, accommodations, and restaurants are accessible.

Traveling with Children

There's no shortage of kid-friendly activities along Skyline Drive, the Blue Ridge Parkway, or in Great Smoky Mountains National Park. Along the route, there are kid-friendly hikes, Junior Ranger programs, animals galore, and visitor centers and gift shops where you can pick up a little something to keep the youngest traveler occupied while in transit. In the cities, you'll find children's museums, parks, zoos, and playgrounds.

Senior Travelers

Aside from stubble-faced and bearded bikers cruising the Parkway, one of the most common sights is the gray-haired couple tooling about in their Subaru, RV, or truck towing an RV. Many attractions, accommodations, and dining options have senior discounts, so flash that AARP card and save a few bucks. Overall, the route from Front Royal to the Smoky Mountains is a safe and leisurely one for seniors.

Gay and Lesbian Travelers

While the Blue Ridge Mountains doesn't have the same kind of atmosphere as San Francisco or Key West, LGBTQ travelers may be pleasantly surprised at how tolerant the region is, despite being rural and, in areas, part of the Bible belt. Washington DC and Knoxville, our travel bookends, have open and active gay cultures, and in larger cities along the way, including Charlottesville and Roanoke, Va., and Asheville, N.C., the culture is open and accepting. This isn't to say you won't encounter any problems, but generally, you'll find that locals hardly bat an eye.

Environmental Concerns

The parklands and forests along the route are preserved so future generations can enjoy nature in as pristine a state as possible. That's why there's no gas available on the Blue Ridge Parkway. It also explains the constant reminders to adhere to **Leave No Trace** (www.LNT.org) principles. Leave no Trace principles are remarkably similar to the Boy Scouts of America teachings: Plan ahead and prepare, travel and camp on durable surfaces, dispose of waste properly, leave what you find, minimize campfire impacts, respect wildlife, be considerate of other visitors. These easy rules can improve the outdoor experience for everyone.

If you pack something in, pack it out, and consider carrying a **trash bag** on trails to pick up after less responsible hikers. If each of us would make this a habit, we could clean up a lot of litter that clutters up our view and is detrimental to the environment.

Dogs are allowed on some trails throughout our route, though they must be on leash or under physical control at all times. If you have Fido out on the trail or let him use the grassy facilities at an overlook or wayside, be sure to pick up what he's putting down.

You'll pass several ponds and lakes as

you travel from Virginia to Tennessee, but unless there's a designated **swimming** area, going for a dip isn't cool. There are exceptions, but those exceptions are noted near the potential swimming hole. When in doubt, ask before you dive in.

You'll spot lots of **wildlife** on your trip. Common animals include white-tailed deer, raccoon, opossum, turtles, bobcat, and even black bear. Coyote are becoming a more frequent sight along the way, and in certain areas of the Smoky Mountains, you can even see the occasional elk. Many times, a herd of deer will be in a pasture off the Parkway. If you see deer (or any other animal), and you want to get a photograph, keep a safe distance from the animal and don't offer them any food as it makes them grow accustomed to people and can have negative impacts on their health.

Health and Safety

For the most part, you trip should be unremarkable as far as health and safety are concerned, provided you're attentive to your situation and surroundings, but there are a few things you should know. Those going on long hikes would also be wise to familiarize themselves with the **10 essentials** (www.rei.com/learn/expert-advice/ten-essentials.html).

Emergencies

For emergencies anywhere in the United States, dial **911** on your phone for immediate assistance. In Virginia, dialing **#77** will connect you with the state police. In North Carolina, dialing *77 connects you to state police and *67 puts you in contact with the highway patrol. In Tennessee, dial *847 for police assistance. If you have to call, try to note your mile marker as a reference point for any assistance that's headed your way.

Wilderness Safety

Hikers should beware of **ticks,** some of which can transmit Lyme disease. An insect repellant and some thorough body checks (use a partner for more fun) should keep you tick free after a jaunt through the woods. If you do get a bite or if you notice a red circular rash that's similar to a bull's eye, consult a physician as Lyme disease can be life-threatening in the worst cases.

You'll encounter woodland animals including bees, wasps, yellow jackets, and hornets, so if you're allergic, be sure to have an **epi-pen** on hand. A number of **snakes,** including rattlesnakes and copperheads, live in these woods. Be alert and keep an ear open for that warning rattle, and if you unexpectedly smell cucumbers in the woods, you may be near a copperhead; in either case, back away slowly and detour around. **Spiders** can be a concern in places, namely woodpiles and some of these backcountry shelters. Most are harmless, though the brown recluse is seen from time to time, but more commonly you'll see a black widow spider, easily identifiable by the red hourglass on the female's abdomen.

Along the trails and roadsides you'll likely encounter **poison ivy, poison oak,** and **poison sumac,** all of which deliver an itchy blister when you come in contact with the oils they secrete. These oils are active for several months, so if you walk through a field of poison ivy, be sure to wash your pants, socks, and boots well lest you inadvertently get poison ivy a month later. You may also come upon **stinging nettles,** which leave itchy welts akin to mosquito bites; these are harmless and generally go away quickly.

Information and Services

Money

If you're traveling to the United States from a foreign country, you'll need to exchange your currency at the airport or at a bank or currency exchange in your destination city as every attraction, restaurant, and lodging on the route accepts U.S. dollars only. **Credit cards** are widely accepted, but for moments when you need cash, there are plenty of **ATMs** along the route. Though ATMs are limited in Shenandoah National Park and along the Blue Ridge Parkway, you will find them at some visitor centers.

Communications
Internet Access

Nearly every hotel, B&B, inn, or lodge will have Wi-Fi, often for free. You won't find Wi-Fi at the lodgings in Shenandoah National Park, or at most of the campgrounds along the Blue Ridge Parkway. With the exception of campgrounds, in most places where Wi-Fi is not available, you'll find a computer or business center you can use at your lodging. When you have cell service, you will likely have a 3G or 4G connection, affording you Internet access on your phone.

Cell Phones

Around all of the cities and most of the towns, cell reception should be fine and free Wi-Fi abundant. From Washington DC to Front Royal, Va., you'll have excellent coverage. As you enter Shenandoah National Park, expect a quick drop-off in signal quality, but the signal should strengthen at a few overlooks. Around Waynesboro and Charlottesville, the signal returns, just in time to get on the Blue Ridge Parkway and enter a cell-signal wilderness (surrounded by actual wilderness).

Cyclists loves the challenge presented by the Parkway.

Accommodations
Hotel and Motel Chains

The great thing about chain hotels is this: they're everywhere and you always know what you're getting. They make it easy to travel on a budget and also to travel without reservations, as they typically have a large number of rooms and, when full, can refer you to a sister-hotel in the area. I prefer inns, cottages, and B&Bs, but those may require advance reservations. Chain hotels come in a variety of budgets and amenity levels. All along the route you'll find chain hotels and motels including Marriott, Holiday Inn, Hilton (in larger cities), Hampton Inn, Sleep Inn, and La Quinta.

Camping

Along the Blue Ridge Parkway and in both Shenandoah and Great Smoky Mountains National Parks, no unauthorized backcountry camping is allowed. Reserve a spot at a backcountry shelter or campground, or get a spot at a frontcountry campground. In National Forests, like the Jefferson, Washington, and Pisgah National Forests, you can camp in the backcountry so long as you do so responsibly. This means no campfires. Due to the hazard of fire, campfires are generally only permitted in frontcountry campsites. If you are frontcountry camping, be aware that you can't bring in your own fire wood, you'll need to purchase or gather it on site. This is to prevent the spread of insect infestations, parasites, and disease that may harm local plants.

Reservations

For much of the year, you should be able to travel without reservations, though even in the off season, you may not be able to get into your first choice of campgrounds, lodges, hotels, or B&Bs. During peak seasons, namely October and late summer, you'll need reservations as visitors increase exponentially to see the autumn color show or squeeze in one more summer getaway. For some of the most popular campgrounds and lodging along the route, you will want to book months in advance.

Suggested Reading

Travel

Fussell, Fred, and Steve Kruger. *Blue Ridge Music Trails of North Carolina: A Guide to Music Sites, Artists, and Traditions of the Mountains and Foothills.* Chapel Hill, NC: UNC Press, 2013. A guide to destinations—festivals, restaurants, oprys, church singings—in North Carolina, where authentic bluegrass, old-time, and sacred music rings through the hills and hollers. An accompanying CD gives you a chance to hear some tunes rather than just read about them.

Simmons, Nye. *Best of the Blue Ridge Parkway: The Ultimate Guide to the Parkway's Best Attractions.* Johnson City, TN: Mountain Trail Press, 2008. Beautiful photography of some of the most iconic and picturesque spots along the Parkway accompanied by write-ups of some of the highlights.

History and Culture

Hall, Karen J. *Building the Blue Ridge Parkway.* Charleston, SC: Arcadia Publishing, 2007. Narrative and archival photos combine to tell the story of the early days of the Blue Ridge Parkway including construction, folkways, and cultural tidbits.

Pegram, Tim. *The Blue Ridge Parkway by Foot: A Park Ranger's Memoir.* Jefferson, NC: McFarland & Company, 2007. A fascinating story of a former park ranger who decided to hike the Parkway—not the trails along the Parkway, but along the roadside, experiencing the 469-mile drive on foot.

Hiking

Adams, Kevin. *Hiking Great Smoky Mountains National Park.* Guilford, CT: Globe Pequot Press, 2013. An excellent hiking-only guide to trails and on-foot sights in Great Smoky Mountains National Park from FalconGuides.

Gildart, Bert, and Jane Gildart. *Hiking Shenandoah National Park.* Guilford, CT: Globe Pequot Press, 2011. Another FalconGuides look at trails and hikes in Shenandoah National Park.

Johnson, Randy. *Hiking the Blue Ridge Parkway: The Ultimate Travel Guide to America's Most Popular Scenic Roadway.* Guilford, CT: Globe Pequot Press, 2010. A thorough trail guide to the Blue Ridge Parkway from FalconGuides.

Internet Resources

General Tourism Information

Washington DC
Destination DC
www.washington.org
The official tourism site of Washington DC has itineraries, travel tips, calendars, and planning tools.

Arlington Convention and Visitors Service
www.stayarlington.com
Arlington, Va., is just across the Potomac River from DC, and is an excellent place to stay. You'll find details on lodging and activities in Arlington, but also information on a trip into Washington DC.

Virginia
Virginia Tourism Corporation
www.virginia.org
Trip ideas, lists and maps of festivals and fairs, itineraries, and other fantastic trip-planning tools are here.

North Carolina
North Carolina Division of Tourism
www.visitnc.com
This comprehensive guide contains trip itineraries in each region, including a dedicated section on the Blue Ridge Parkway. The site is rich with photos and videos, and their index of accommodations, attractions, and more is comprehensive.

Tennessee
Tennessee Department of Tourist Development
www.tnvacation.com
The official site of Tennessee's state tourism office is user friendly, allowing you to narrow your focus on one region with just a couple of clicks. Resources for the Smokies and East Tennessee include interactive maps that provide a great overview of the region's offerings from natural sights to man-made attractions.

National Park Information
Blue Ridge Parkway
Blue Ridge Parkway
www.nps.gov/blri
Details the history of the park, and provides real-time road maps that show detours, delays, and closures; downloadable maps that make hiking and planning a trip section-by-section easy; and write-ups on the flora, fauna, and geographical features of the Parkway.

Virtual Blue Ridge
www.virtualblueridge.com
Information on the Blue Ridge Parkway including wildflower and fall color reports, road conditions and closures, and weather along the route. You'll also find a store with maps, books, and mementos.

Blue Ridge National Heritage Area
www.blueridgeheritage.com
Created in 2003 to recognize the unique character, culture, landscape, and beauty of the Blue Ridge, this organization promotes the history, folkways, arts and crafts, and exploration of the region.

Blue Ridge Parkway Association
www.blueridgeparkway.org
A nonprofit association of businesses and individuals promoting tourism along the Blue Ridge Parkway, from Virginia to Tennessee. Their website includes interactive maps; indexes to activities, sights, restaurants, hikes, and more along the Parkway; highlights of the route; real-time road reports; regional breakdowns; and other resources to help you plan a trip.

Great Smoky Mountains National Park
Great Smoky Mountains National Park
www.nps.gov/grsm
An extensive history of the park; details on the flora, fauna, and natural features in the park; and downloadable maps and contact information for rangers and park offices.

Friends of the Smokies
www.friendsofthesmokies.org
Friends of the Smokies works to raise funds for park initiatives, trail maintenance and improvement, and a variety of other needs. They accept donations of time and money, so if you had a good time in the Smokies, consider lending them a hand or a few bucks.

Great Smoky Mountains Association
www.smokiesinformation.org
A nonprofit partner of Great Smoky Mountains National Park, the group operates retail stores in and benefiting the park; provides guidebooks, maps, logo-emblazoned clothing and gear, and other gifts; and helps with expenses associated in promoting the park.

Washington DC
National Mall and Memorial Parks
www.nps.gov/nama
Excellent historical, educational, and kids' resources for Washington DC's National Mall along with maps of the Mall, contact information, and tips.

Shenandoah National Park
Shenandoah National Park
www.nps.gov/shen
Information on trails and park activities as well as Skyline Drive, the flora and fauna, the history, and the landscape. Skyline Drive details include maps of the road and trails, contact information for various waysides and lodges, and links to secure in-park lodging.

Outdoor Recreation
Appalachian Trail Conservancy
www.appalachiantrail.org
The Appalachian Trail Conservancy provides support to the Appalachian Trail, which parallels and even crosses the Blue Ridge Parkway in many places.

North Carolina State Parks
www.ncparks.gov

Since a number of state parks brush against the Blue Ridge Parkway in Virginia, many travelers use their campgrounds and facilities as resources and waypoints along their journey. Learn more about the facilities and amenities of Parkway-adjacent parks at the website of the North Carolina State Parks system.

North Carolina Wildlife
Resources Commission
www.ncwildlife.org

Information on hunting, fishing, and boating in North Carolina, including easy-to-understand hunting and fishing regulations and online license procurement.

Tennessee Wildlife Resources Agency
www.state.tn.us/twra

Need-to-know information regarding hunting and fishing regulations and licenses.

Virginia Department of Game
and Inland Fisheries
www.dgif.virginia.gov

The Virginia Department of Game and Inland Fisheries manages the state's wildlife to ensure that everyone—hunters, anglers, hikers, and nature-lovers—can enjoy the state's outdoor offerings. They handle licensing and permits, so if you want to hunt or fish, they're the folks to see.

Virginia Outdoors
www.virginiaoutdoors.com

A comprehensive list of activities, outfitters, and resources for planning an outdoor getaway in any season.

Virginia State Parks
www.dcr.virginia.gov/state-parks

Information on parks, programs, lodging, and activities. This site can be a little difficult to navigate, but your patience is rewarded as just about any question you have can be answered with a little looking.

INDEX

INDEX

LIST OF MAPS

PHOTO CREDITS

MOON BLUE RIDGE PARKWAY ROAD TRIP

Avalon Travel
a member of the Perseus Books Group
1700 Fourth Street
Berkeley, CA 94710, USA
www.moon.com

Editor: Nikki Ioakimedes
Copy Editor: Naomi Adler Dancis
Graphics and Production Coordinator:
  Lucie Ericksen
Cover Design: Erin Seaward-Hiatt
Moon Logo: Tim McGrath
Map Editor: Albert Angulo
Cartographer: Stephanie Poulain, Brian Shotwell,
  Albert Angulo
Indexer: Greg Jewett

ISBN-13: 978-1-63121-031-0
ISSN: 2377-7362

Printing History
1st Edition — May 2015
5 4 3 2

Some photos and illustrations are used by permission and are the property of the original copyright owners.

Front cover photo: Chimney Rock at Chimney Rock State Park © Sean Pavone / Alamy

Printed in Canada by Friesens

All recommendations, including those for sights, activities, hotels, restaurants, and shops, are based on each author's individual judgment. We do not accept payment for inclusion in our travel guides, and our authors don't accept free goods or services in exchange for positive coverage.

Although every effort was made to ensure that the information was correct at the time of going to press, the author and publisher do not assume and hereby disclaim any liability to any party for any loss or damage caused by errors, omissions, or any potential travel disruption due to labor or financial difficulty, whether such errors or omissions result from negligence, accident, or any other cause.